Applied Cryptography

Protocols, Algorithms,
and Source Code
in C

Applied Cryptography

Protocols, Algorithms,
and Source Code
in C

Bruce Schneier

John Wiley & Sons, Inc.

NEW YORK • CHICHESTER • BRISBANE • TORONTO • SINGAPORE

Associate Publisher: Katherine Schowalter
Editor: Paul Farrell
Managing Editor: Beth Austin
Editorial Production & Design: Editorial Services of New England, Inc.

This publication is designed to provide accurate and authoritative information in regard to the subject matter covered. It is sold with the understanding that the publisher is not engaged in rendering professional services. If legal, accounting, medical, psychological, or any other expert assistance is required, the services of a competent professional person should be sought. ADAPTED FROM A DECLARATIONS OF PRINCIPLES OF A JOINT COMMITTEE OF THE AMERICAN BAR ASSOCIATION AND PUBLISHERS.

In no event will the publisher or author be liable for any consequential, incidental, or indirect damages (including damages for loss of business profits, business interruption, loss of business information, and the like) arising from the use or inability to use the protocols and algorithms in this book, even if the publisher or author has been advised of the possibility of such damages.

Some of the protocols and algorithms in this book are protected by patents and copyrights. It is the responsibility of the reader to obtain all necessary patent and copyright licenses before implementing in software any protocol or algorithm in this book. This book does not contain an exhaustive list of all applicable patents and copyrights.

Some of the protocols and algorithms in this book are regulated under the United States Department of State International Traffic in Arms Regulations. It is the responsibility of the reader to obtain all necessary export licenses before implementing in software for export any protocol or algorithm in this book.

This text is printed on acid-free paper.

Trademarks
Designations used by companies to distinguish their products are often claimed as trademarks. In all instances where John Wiley & Sons, Inc. is aware of a claim, the product names appear in initial capital or all capital letters. Readers, however, should contact the appropriate companies for more complete information regarding trademarks and registration.

Library of Congress Cataloging-in-Publication Data
Schneier, Bruce
    Applied cryptography : protocols, algorithms, and source code in C
  / Bruce Schneier.
    p. cm.
    Includes bibliographical references and index.
    ISBN 0-471-59756-2 (paper)
    1. Computer security. 2. Telecommunication—security measures. 3. Cryptography. 4. Title

QA76.9.A25S35 1993
005.8'2—dc20   93-2139
                                                          CIP

Printed in the United States of America
10 9 8 7 6 5 4 3 2

Contents

PART **FIVE**
SOURCE CODE

Foreword

The literature of cryptography has a curious history. Secrecy, of course, has always played a central role, but until the First World War, important developments appeared in print in a more or less timely fashion and the field moved forward in much the same way as other specialized disciplines. As late as 1918, one of the most influential cryptanalytic papers of the 20th century, William F. Friedman's monograph *The Index of Coincidence and Its Applications in Cryptography,* appeared as a research report of the private Riverbank Laboratories [355]. And this, despite the fact that the work had been done as part of the war effort. In the same year Edward H. Hebern of Oakland, California filed the first patent for a rotor machine [418a], the device destined to be a mainstay of military cryptography for nearly fifty years.

After the First World War, however, things began to change. U.S. Army and Navy organizations, working entirely in secret, began to make fundamental advances in cryptography. During the thirties and forties a few basic papers did appear in the open literature and several treatises on the subject were published, but the latter were farther and farther behind the state of the art. By the end of the war the transition was complete. With one notable exception, the public literature had died. That exception was Claude Shannon's paper "The Communication Theory of Secrecy Systems," which appeared in the *Bell System Technical Journal* in 1949 [804]. It was similar to Friedman's 1918 paper, in that it grew out of wartime work of Shannon's. After the Second World War ended it was declassified, possibly by mistake.

From 1949 until 1967 the cryptographic literature was barren. In that year a different sort of contribution appeared: David Kahn's history, *The Codebreakers* [462]. It didn't contain any new technical ideas, but it did contain a remarkably complete history of what had gone before, including mention of some things that the government still considered secret. The significance of *The Codebreakers* lay not just in its remarkable scope, but also in the fact that it enjoyed good sales and made tens of thousands of people, who had never given the matter a moment's thought, aware of cryptography. A trickle of new cryptographic papers began to be written.

At about the same time, Horst Feistel, who had earlier worked on identification friend or foe devices for the Air Force, took his lifelong passion for cryptography to the IBM Watson Laboratory in Yorktown Heights, New York. There, he began development of what was to become the U.S. Data Encryption Standard, and by the early 1970s several technical reports on this subject by Feistel and his colleagues had been made public by IBM [339,837,839].

This was the situation when I entered the field in late 1972. The cryptographic literature wasn't abundant, but what there was included some very shiny nuggets.

Cryptology presents a difficulty not found in normal academic disciplines: the need for the proper integration of cryptography and cryptanalysis. This arises out of the fact that in the absence of real communications requirements, it is easy to propose a system that appears unbreakable. Many academic designs are so complex that the would-be cryptanalyst doesn't know where to start; exposing flaws in these designs is much harder than designing them in the first place. The result is that the competitive process, which is one strong motivation in academic research, cannot take hold.

When Martin Hellman and I proposed public key cryptography in 1975 [299], one of the indirect aspects of our contribution was to introduce a problem that does not even appear easy to solve. Now an aspiring cryptosystem designer could produce something that would be recognized as clever — something that did more than just turn meaningful text into nonsense. The result has been a spectacular increase in the number of people working in cryptography, the number of meetings held, and the number of books and papers published.

In my acceptance speech for the Donald E. Fink award — given for the best expository paper to appear in an IEEE journal — which I received jointly with Hellman in 1980, I told the audience that in writing "Privacy and Authentication" I had an experience that I suspected was rare even among the prominent scholars who populate the IEEE awards ceremony; I had written the paper I had wanted to study, but could not find, when I first became seriously interested in cryptography. Had I been able to go to the Stanford bookstore and pick up a modern cryptography text, I would probably have learned about the field years earlier. But the only things available in the fall of 1972 were a few classic papers and some obscure technical reports.

The contemporary researcher has no such problem. The problem now is choosing where to start among the thousands of papers and dozens of books. The contemporary researcher, yes, but what about the contemporary programmer or engineer who merely wants to use cryptography? Where does that person turn? Until now, it has been necessary to spend long hours hunting out and then studying the research literature before being able to design the sort of cryptographic utilities glibly described in popular articles.

This is the gap that Bruce Schneier's *Applied Cryptography: Protocols, Algorithms, and Source Code in C* has come to fill. Beginning with the objectives of communication security and elementary examples of programs used to achieve these objectives, Schneier gives us a panoramic view of the fruits of fifteen years of public research. The table of contents tells it all; from the mundane objective of having a secure conversation the very first time you call someone to the possibilities of digital money and cryptographically secure elections, this is where you'll find it.

Not satisfied that the book was about the real world merely because it went all the way down to the code, Schneier has included an account of the world in which cryptography is developed and applied, and discusses entities ranging from the International Association for Cryptologic Research to the National Security Agency.

When public interest in cryptography was just emerging in the late seventies and early eighties, the National Security Agency (NSA), America's official cryptographic organ, made several attempts to quash it. The first was a letter from a long-time NSA employee allegedly, avowedly, and apparently acting on his own. The letter was sent to the IEEE and warned that the publication of cryptographic material was a violation of the International Traffic in Arms Regulations (ITAR). This viewpoint turned out not even to be supported by the regulations themselves —which contained an explicit exemption for published material— but gave both the public practice of cryptography and the 1977 Information Theory Workshop lots of unexpected publicity.

A more serious attempt occurred in 1980, when NSA funded the American Council on Education to examine the issue with a view to persuading Congress to give it legal control of publications in the field of cryptography. The results fell far short of NSA's ambitions and resulted in a program of voluntary review of cryptographic papers; researchers were requested to ask the NSA's opinion on whether disclosure of results would adversely affect the national interest before publication.

As the eighties progressed, pressure focused more on the practice than the study of cryptography. Existing laws gave the NSA the power, through the Department of State, to regulate the export of cryptographic equipment. As business became more and more international and the American fraction of the world market declined, the pressure to have a single product in both domestic and offshore markets increased. Such single products were subject to export control and thus the NSA acquired substantial influence not only over what was exported, but of what was sold in the United States.

As this is written, a new challenge confronts the public practice of cryptography. The government proposes to replace the widely published and available Data Encryption Standard with a secret algorithm implemented in tamper-resistant chips. These chips will incorporate a codified mechanism of government monitoring. The negative aspects of this proposal range from a potentially disastrous impact on personal privacy to the high cost of having to add hardware to products that had previously encrypted in software. It has attracted widespread negative comment, especially from independent cryptographers. Some people, however, see more future in programming than politicking and have redoubled their efforts to provide the world with strong cryptography that is accessible to public scrutiny.

A sharp step back from the notion that export control law could supersede the First Amendment seemed to have been taken in 1980 when the Federal Register announcement of a revision to ITAR included the statement: ". . . provision has been added to make it clear that the regulation of the export of technical data does not purport to interfere with the First Amendment rights of individuals." But the fact that tension between the First Amendment and the export control laws has not gone away should be evident from statements at a recent conference held by RSA Data Security. NSA's representative from the export control office expressed the opinion that people who published cryptographic programs were "in a gray area" with respect to the law. If that is so, it is a gray area on which this book can be expected to shed some light.

The shift in the NSA's strategy, from attempting to control cryptographic research to tightening its grip on the development and deployment of cryptographic products, is presumably due to its realization that all the great cryptographic papers in the world do not protect a single bit of traffic. Sitting on the shelf, this volume might be able to do no better than the books and papers that preceded it, but sitting next to a workstation, where a programmer is writing cryptographic code, it just might.

Whitfield Diffie
Mountain View, CA

Preface

There are two kinds of cryptography in this world: cryptography that will stop your kid sister from reading your files, and cryptography that will stop major governments from reading your files. This book is about the latter.

If I take a letter, lock it in a safe, and hide the safe somewhere in New York . . . and then tell you to read the letter, that's not security. That's obscurity. On the other hand, if I take a letter and lock it in a safe, and then give you the safe along with the design specifications of the safe and a hundred identical safes with combinations so that you and the world's best safecrackers can study the locking mechanism . . . and you still can't open the safe and read the letter, that's security.

For many years, this sort of cryptography was the exclusive domain of the military. The United States' National Security Agency, and its counterparts in the Soviet Union, England, France, Israel, and elsewhere, have spent billions of dollars in the very serious game of securing their own communications while trying to break everyone else's. The private individual, with far less expertise and budget, has been powerless to protect his own privacy against these governments.

During the last twenty years, there has been an explosion of public academic research in cryptography. For the first time, state-of-the-art computer cryptography is being practiced outside the secured walls of the military agencies. It is now possible for you and me to employ security practices that can protect against the most powerful of adversaries—security that may even protect against the military agencies.

Does the average person really need this kind of security? I say yes. He may be planning a political campaign, discussing his taxes, or having an illicit affair. He may be designing a new product, discussing a marketing strategy, or planning a hostile business takeover. He may be living in a country that does not respect the rights of privacy of its citizens. He may be doing something that he feels shouldn't be illegal, but is. Whatever his reasons, his data and communications are personal, private, and nobody's business but his own.

This book is being published in a tumultuous time. The Clinton Administration has just proposed the Clipper chip, which ensures the government the ability to conduct electronic surveillance. Clipper is based on the Orwellian assumption that the government has the right to listen to private communications. It promotes the power of the government over the power of the individual. This is not simply a little government proposal in some obscure area; it is a preemptive and unilateral attempt to usurp powers that previously belonged to the people.

Clipper does not protect privacy; it forces individuals to unconditionally trust that the government will respect their privacy. It assumes that the government is the good guy and private citizens are all bad guys. The same law enforcement authorities that illegally tapped Martin Luther King, Jr.'s phones can easily tap a phone protected with Clipper. During the past five years, local police authorities have been either charged criminally or sued civilly in numerous jurisdictions — including Maryland, Connecticut, Vermont, Georgia, Missouri, and Nevada —for conducting illegal wiretaps. It's a poor idea to deploy technologies that could someday facilitate a police state.

At the time I am writing, it is too early to tell what will happen to the Clipper chip. At one extreme, it could become a minor anecdote about a failed attempt by the government to invade peoples' privacy—people reading this five years from now will wonder what I am talking about. At the other, it could be the first in a series of initiatives designed to outlaw private encryption—five years from now most of the techniques described in this book will be illegal. The truth will probably lie somewhere in the middle.

Encryption is too important to be left to the government.

HOW TO READ THIS BOOK

I wrote *Applied Cryptography* to be a comprehensive reference work for modern cryptography. The first chapter introduces cryptography, defines many terms, and briefly discusses pre-computer cryptography.

Part 1 (Chapters 2 through 6) discuss cryptographic protocols. This is what you can do with cryptography. The protocols range from the simple (sending encrypted messages from one person to another) to the complex (flipping a coin over the telephone) to the esoteric (secure and anonymous digital money). Some of these protocols are obvious; others are almost amazing. If you are interested, read through all of the things cryptography can do that seem impossible. If these protocols start getting tedious, skip to the next section.

Part II discusses cryptographic techniques. Both chapters in this section are important for even the most basic uses of cryptography. Chapter 7 is about keys: how long should a key be in order to be secure, how do you generate keys, how do you store keys, how do you dispose of keys, etc. Key management is the hardest part of cryptography, and often the Achilles heel of an otherwise secure system. Chapter 8 discusses different ways of using cryptographic algorithms, and how to choose algorithms for communication, data storage, etc.

In Part III, the book finally turns to algorithms. Chapter 9 is a mathematical background. This chapter is only required if you are interested in public-key algorithms. If you just want to implement DES (or something similar), you can skip this chapter. Chapter 10 discusses DES. Chapter 11 discusses other symmetric algorithms. If you want something more secure than DES, skip to the section on IDEA. If you want to read about a bunch of algorithms, some of which may be more secure than DES, read the whole chapter. Chapters 12 and 13 discuss public-key algorithms; if you just want the basics, read the introduction to Chapter 12, the section on Diffie-Hellman, the section on RSA, and the section in Chapter 13 on DSS. Chapter 14 is about one-way hash functions: MD5 and SHA are the most common, although I discuss many more. Chapter 15 is about random number generation and stream ciphers. There is a bias in cryptographic research in the world; most of the work on stream ciphers is done in Europe, while in the United States stream cipher research takes a back seat to block cipher research. To some degree, this book perpetuates the bias. And finally, Chapter 16 discusses algorithms specifically designed to implement some of the protocols in Part I. The math can get complicated here; wear your seat belt.

Part IV has two chapters. Chapter 17 discusses some real-world implementations of these algorithms and protocols, and chapter 18 touches on some of the political issues surrounding cryptography. These are by no means intended to be comprehensive.

Finally, Part V gives source code listings for some of the algorithms in Part IV. I wanted to include much more code than I was able to, but space limitations got in the way. There is an associated source code disk that includes these listings, as well as all the listings that I didn't have space for. If you are at all interested in implementing or playing with the cryptographic algorithms in this book, get the disk.

This book is not intended to be a mathematical text. Although I have not deliberately given any false information, I do play fast and loose with theory. For those who are interested in formalism, there are copious pointers to references in the academic literature.

If there was a criticism of this book, it is that its encyclopedic nature takes away from its readability. This is true, but I wanted to provide a single reference for those who might come across an algorithm in the academic literature or in a product. There is a lot being done in the field; this is the first time so much of it has been gathered under one roof. For those who are more interested in a tutorial, I apologize. Even so, there are many things that space forced me to leave out. I tried to cover topics that I felt were important, topics that I felt were practical, and topics that I felt were interesting. If I couldn't cover a topic in depth, I gave references to articles and papers that did. If there are aspects of cryptography that you wish were covered in more depth, I apologize.

I have done my best to hunt down and eradicate all errors in this book, but many have assured me that it is an impossible task. Any errors I find after publication will be corrected on the source code disk. Any new information discovered after publication will also be on the disk. If someone finds an error, please tell me. The first person to find each error in the book will get a free copy of the source code disk.

ACKNOWLEDGMENTS

The list of people who had a hand in this book seems unending, but all are worthy of mention. I would like to thank Don Alvarez, Ross Anderson, Karl Barrus, Steve Bellovin, Dan Bernstein, Eli Biham, Joan Boyar, Karen Cooper, Whitfield Diffie, Joan Feigenbaum, Phil Karn, Neal Koblitz, Xuija Lai, Tom Leranth, Mark Markowitz, Ralph Merkle, Bill Patton, Peter Pearson, Mark Riordan, and Marc Schwartz for reading and editing all or parts of the manuscript; Lawrie Brown, Leisa Condie, Peter Gutmann, Alan Insley, Xuija Lai, Peter Pearson, Ken Pizzini, Richard Outerbridge, RSA Data Security Inc., Michael Wood, and Phil Zimmermann for providing source code; the readers of sci.crypt for commenting on ideas and answering questions, Paul MacNerland for creating the figures; Randy Seuss for providing Internet access; Jeff Duntemann and Jon Erickson for helping me find a publisher; Paul Farrell for editing this book; assorted random Insleys for the impetus, encouragement, support, conversations, friendship, and dinners; and AT&T Bell Labs for firing me and making this all possible. These people helped to create a far better book than I could have done alone.

Bruce Schneier
Oak Park, Ill.

CHAPTER
1

Foundations

1.1 TERMINOLOGY

Sender and Receiver

Suppose someone, whom we shall call the **sender,** wants to send a **message** to someone else, whom we shall call the **receiver.** Moreover, the sender wants to make sure an intermediary cannot affect the message in any way: specifically, the receiver cannot intercept and read the message, intercept and modify the message, or fabricate a realistic-looking substitute message.

Messages and Encryption

A message is called either **plaintext** or **cleartext.** The process of disguising a message in such a way as to hide its substance is called **encryption.** An encrypted message is called **ciphertext.** The process of turning ciphertext back into plaintext is called **decryption.** This is shown in Figure 1.1.

The art and science of keeping messages secure is called **cryptography,** and it is practiced by **cryptographers.** **Cryptanalysts** are practitioners of **cryptanalysis,** the art and science of breaking ciphertext, i.e., seeing through the disguise. The branch of mathematics embodying both cryptography and cryptanalysis is called **cryptology,** and its practitioners are called **cryptologists.** These days almost all cryptologists are also theoretical mathematicians—they have to be.

Figure 1.1
Encryption and decryption.

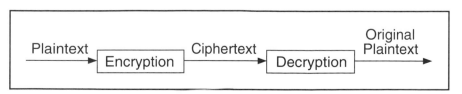

Plaintext is denoted by P. It can be a stream of bits, a text file, a stream of digitized voice, or a digital video image. As far as a computer is concerned, P is simply binary data. (Outside the historical chapter, this book concerns itself with binary data.) The plaintext can be intended for either transmission or storage. In any case, P is the message to be encrypted.

Ciphertext is denoted by C. It is also binary data, sometimes the same size as P, sometimes larger. (By combining compression and encryption, C may be smaller than P. However, encryption alone usually does not accomplish this.) The encryption function E operates on P to produce C. Or, in mathematical notation:

$$E(P) = C$$

In the reverse process, the decryption function D operates on C to produce P:

$$D(C) = P$$

Since the whole point of encrypting and then decrypting a message is to recover the original plaintext, the following identity must hold true:

$$D(E(P)) = P$$

Algorithms and Ciphers

A **cryptographic algorithm,** also called a **cipher,** is the mathematical function used for encryption and decryption. To encrypt a plaintext message, apply an **encryption algorithm** to the plaintext. To decrypt a ciphertext message, apply a **decryption algorithm** to the ciphertext.

If the security of an algorithm is based on keeping the nature of the algorithm secret, it is called **restricted.** Restricted algorithms have historical interest, but by today's data security standards they provide woefully inadequate security. A large or changing group of users cannot use them, because users will eventually reveal the secret. When they do, the whole security of the system fails. More important, most restricted cryptosystems are trivial to break by experienced cryptanalysts. Despite this, restricted algorithms are enormously popular for low-security applications. Zenith's video-scrambling technique is an example of a restricted algorithm.

For real security, all modern encryption algorithms use a **key,** denoted by k. This key can take on one of many values (a large number is best). The range of possible values of the key is called the **keyspace.**

The value of the key affects the encryption and decryption functions, so the encryption and decryption functions now become:

$$E_k(P) = C$$
$$D_k(C) = P$$

And if the encryption key and the decryption key are the same, then:

$$D_k(E_k(P)) = P$$

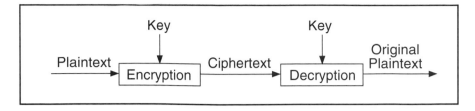

Figure 1.2
Encryption and decryption
with key.

This is shown in Figure 1.2.

There are algorithms where the encryption key and the decryption key come in pairs (see Figure 1.3). That is, the encryption key, k_1, is different from the corresponding decryption key, k_2. In this case:

$$E_{k_1}(P) = C$$
$$D_{k_2}(C) = P$$
$$D_{k_2}(E_{k_1}(P)) = P$$

Symmetric Algorithms and Public-Key Algorithms

There are two general forms of key-based algorithms: symmetric and public-key. **Symmetric algorithms** are algorithms where the encryption key can be calculated from the decryption key and vice versa. In many such systems, the encryption key and the decryption key are the same. These algorithms, also called **secret-key algorithms, single-key algorithms,** or **one-key algorithms,** require the sender and receiver to agree on a key before they pass messages back and forth. This key must be kept secret. The security of a symmetric algorithm rests in the key; divulging the key means that anybody could encrypt and decrypt messages in this cryptosystem.

Encryption and decryption with a symmetric algorithm are denoted by:

$$E_k(P) = C$$
$$D_k(C) = P$$

Symmetric algorithms can be divided into two categories. Some operate on the plaintext a single bit at a time; these are called **stream algorithms** or **stream ciphers.** Others operate on the plaintext in groups of bits. The groups of bits are called **blocks,** and the algorithms are called **block algorithms** or **block ciphers.** For algorithms that are implemented on computer, a typical block size is 64 bits—large enough to preclude analysis and small enough to be workable. In both block and stream algorithms, the same key is used for both encryption and

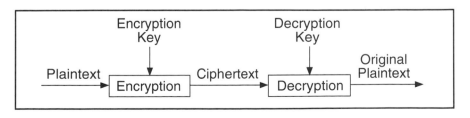

Figure 1.3
Encryption and decryption
with two keys.

decryption. (Before computers, algorithms generally operated on plaintext one character at a time. You can either think of this as a stream algorithm operating on a stream of characters or as a block algorithm operating on 8-bit blocks.)

Public-key algorithms are different. They are designed so that the key used for encryption is different from the key used for decryption. Furthermore, the decryption key cannot be (at least in any reasonable amount of time) calculated from the encryption key. They are called public-key systems because the encryption key can be made public: a complete stranger can use the encryption key to encrypt a message, but only someone with the corresponding decryption key can decrypt the message. In these systems, the **encryption key** is often called the **public key,** and the **decryption key** is often called the **private key.** In instances when both keys must be kept secret, sometimes the terms "encryption key" and "decryption key" will be used. The private key is sometimes also called the **secret key,** but to avoid confusion with symmetric algorithms, that moniker won't be used here.

Encryption using public key k is denoted by:

$$E_k(P) = C$$

Even though the public key and private key are different, decryption with the corresponding private key is denoted by:

$$D_k(C) = P$$

Sometimes, messages will be encrypted with the private key and decrypted with the public key; this is used in digital signatures (see Section 2.6). Despite the possible confusion, these operations will be denoted by, respectively:

$$E_k(P) = C$$
$$D_k(C) = P$$

In this book, "algorithm" will refer specifically to the mathematical transformations for encryption and decryption. "Cryptosystem" will refer to the algorithm, plus the way in which it is implemented. "Cipher" will often be used to refer to a family of algorithms, e.g., "block cipher."

Cryptanalysis

The primary purpose of cryptography is to keep the plaintext (or the key, or both) secret from **eavesdroppers** (also called **adversaries, attackers, interceptors, interlopers, intruders, opponents,** or simply **the enemy**). Cryptanalysis is the science of recovering the plaintext of a message without the key. Successful cryptanalysis may recover the plaintext or the key. It also may find weaknesses in a cryptosystem that eventually lead to the above results.

An attempted cryptanalysis is called an **attack.** A successful attack is called a **method.** An attack assumes that the cryptanalyst has the details of the cryptographic algorithm. While this is not always the case in real-life cryptanalysis, it is the conventional assumption for academic cryptanalysis. It is a good assumption to make; if your security depends on the secrecy of the algorithm, then there is only minimal security.

There are six general types of cryptanalytic attacks, listed in order of power. Each of them assumes that the cryptanalyst has complete knowledge of the encryption algorithm used:

1. **Ciphertext-only attack.** In this attack, the cryptanalyst has the ciphertext of several messages, all of which have been encrypted using the same encryption algorithm. The cryptanalyst's job is to recover the plaintext of as many messages as possible, or better yet deduce the key (or keys) used to encrypt the messages in order to decrypt other messages encrypted with the same keys.

    Given: $C_1 = E_k(P_1)$, $C_2 = E_k(P_2)$, ... $C_i = E_k(P_i)$
    Deduce: Either P_1, P_2, ... P_i; k; or an algorithm to infer P_{i+1} from $C_{i+1} = E_K(P_{i+1})$

2. **Known-plaintext attack.** The cryptanalyst not only has access to the ciphertext of several messages but also to the plaintext of those messages. The job is to deduce the key (or keys) used to encrypt the messages or an algorithm to decrypt any new messages encrypted with the same key.

    Given: P_1, $C_1 = E_k(P_1)$, P_2, $C_2 = E_k(P_2)$, ... P_i, $C_i = E_k(P_i)$
    Deduce: Either k, or an algorithm to infer P_{i+1} from $C_{i+1} = E_k(P_{i+1})$

3. **Chosen-plaintext attack.** Cryptanalysts not only have access to the ciphertext and associated plaintext for several messages, but they also choose the encrypted plaintext. This is more powerful than a known-plaintext attack, because cryptanalysts can choose specific plaintext blocks to encrypt, ones that might yield more information about the key. The job is to deduce the key (or keys) used to encrypt the messages or an algorithm to decrypt any new messages encrypted with the same key.

    Given: P_1, $C_1 = E_k(P_1)$, P_2, $C_2 = E_k(P_2)$, ... P_i, $C_i = E_k(P_i)$, where the cryptanalysts choose P_1, P_2, ... P_i
    Deduce: Either k, or an algorithm to infer P_{i+1} from $C_{i+1} = E_k(P_{i+1})$

4. **Adaptive-chosen-plaintext attack.** This is a special case of a chosen-plaintext attack. Not only can cryptanalysts choose the plaintext that is encrypted, but they can modify the choice based on the results of previous encryption. In a chosen-plaintext attack, cryptanalysts might just be able to choose one large block of plaintext to be encrypted; in an adaptive-chosen-plaintext attack they can choose a smaller block of plaintext and then choose another based on the results of the first, etc.

5. **Chosen-ciphertext attack.** Cryptanalysts can choose different ciphertexts to be decrypted and have access to the decrypted plaintext. In an instance

when cryptanalysts have a tamperproof box that does automatic decryption, the job is to deduce the key.

Given: C_1, $P_1 = D_k(C_1)$, C_2, $P_2 = D_k(C_2)$, . . . C_i, $P_i = D_k(C_i)$
Deduce: k

This attack is primarily applicable to public-key cryptosystems and will be discussed in Section 12.4. A chosen-ciphertext attack also works against symmetric algorithm, but due to the symmetry of these cryptosystems it is equivalent in complexity to a chosen-plaintext attack.

6. **Chosen-key attack.** This is not an attack when you're given the key. It's strange and obscure, not very practical, and is discussed in Section 10.1.

Known-plaintext attacks and chosen-plaintext attacks are more common than you might think. It is not unheard of for a cryptanalyst to get a plaintext message that has been encrypted or to bribe someone to encrypt a chosen message. You may not even have to bribe someone; if you give a message to an ambassador, you will probably find that it gets encrypted and sent back to the United States for consideration. Many messages have standard beginnings and endings that might be known to the cryptanalyst. Encrypted source code is especially vulnerable because of the regular appearance of keywords: `#define`, `struct`, `else`, `return`. Encrypted executable code has the same kinds of problems, called protocols, loop structures, etc. David Kahn's books [462,463,464] have some historical examples of these kinds of attacks.

One of the fundamental axioms of cryptography is that the enemy is in full possession of the details of the algorithm and lacks only the specific key used in the encryption. (Of course, one would assume that the CIA does not make a habit of telling Mossad about its cryptographic algorithms, but Mossad probably finds out anyway.) While this is not always true in real-world cryptanalysis, it is always true in academic cryptanalysis; and it's a good assumption to make in real-world cryptanalysis. If others can't break an algorithm even with knowledge of how it works, then they certainly won't be able to break it without that knowledge.

Cryptanalysts don't always have access to the algorithm—for example, when the United States broke the Japanese diplomatic code, PURPLE, during World War II [462]—but they often do. If the algorithm is being used in a commercial security program, it is simply a matter of time and money to disassemble the program and recover the algorithm. If the algorithm is being used in a military communications system, it is simply a matter of time and money to buy (or steal) the equipment and reverse-engineer the algorithm. There have been many historical instances when cryptanalysts did not know the encryption algorithms; sometimes they broke the algorithm anyway, and sometimes they did not. In any case, it is unrealistic to rely on it.

Those who claim to have an unbreakable cipher simply because they can't break it are either geniuses or fools. Unfortunately, there are more of the latter in the world. Beware of people who extol the virtues of their algorithms, but refuse to make them public; trusting their algorithms is like trusting snake oil.

On the other hand, a good algorithm can be made public without worry. You can send it to your adversaries, publish it in a magazine, or shout it from the rooftops. It doesn't matter; even the designer of the algorithm can't decrypt messages without the key.

Good cryptographers rely on peer review to separate the good algorithms from the bad.

Security of Cryptosystems

Different cryptosystems have different levels of security, depending on how hard they are to break. As we will see, all algorithms but one are theoretically **breakable,** given enough time and computing resources. If the time and money required to break an algorithm is more than the value of the encrypted data, then it is probably safe. Computers are becoming increasingly faster and cheaper. At the same time, the value of the data decreases over time. It is important that those two lines never cross.

Some algorithms are only breakable with the benefit of more time than the universe has been in existence and a computer larger than all the matter in the universe. These algorithms are theoretically breakable, but not breakable in practice. An algorithm that is not breakable in practice is **secure.**

An algorithm is **unconditionally secure** if, no matter how much ciphertext a cryptanalyst has, there is not enough information to recover the plaintext. In point of fact, only a one-time pad (see Section 1.2.4) is unbreakable given infinite resources. Cryptography is more concerned with cryptosystems that are computationally unfeasible to break. An algorithm is considered **computationally secure,** or **strong,** if it cannot be broken with available (current or future) resources. Exactly what constitutes "available resources" is open to interpretation.

The amount of computing time and power required to recover the encryption key is called the **work factor,** and is expressed as an order of magnitude. If an algorithm has a work factor of 2^{128}, then 2^{128} operations are required to break the algorithm. These operations can be very complex and time-consuming, but details of the operations are left to the implementation. Still, if you assume that you have enough computing speed to perform a million of them every second, and you set a million parallel processors against the task, it will still take over 10^{19} years to recover the key. (For comparison's sake, the age of the universe is estimated at 10^{10} years.) I would consider an algorithm that takes a billion times the age of the universe to break to be computationally secure.

While the work factor required to break a given algorithm is constant (that is, until some cryptanalyst finds a better cryptanalytic attack), computing power is anything but. During the last half-century we have seen phenomenal advances in computing power, and there is no reason to think that it will change anytime soon. Many cryptanalytic attacks are perfect for parallel machines: the task can be broken down into billions of tiny pieces and none of the processors needs to interact with another. Pronouncing that an algorithm is secure simply because it is unfeasible to break, given current technology, is dicey at best. Good cryptosystems are designed to be unfeasible to break with the computing power that is expected to evolve many years in the future.

Historical Terms

There are other cryptographic terms. A cryptosystem is also called a **code** or a **cipher.** Encrypting is also called **encoding** or **enciphering,** and decrypting is also called **decoding** or **deciphering.**

Historically, q code refers to a cryptosystem that deals with linguistic units: words, phrases, sentences, etc. For example, the word "MULBERRY" might be the ciphertext for the entire phrase "TURN LEFT 90 DEGREES"; the word "LOLLIPOP" might be the ciphertext for "TURN RIGHT 90 DEGREES"; and the words "BENT EAR" might be the ciphertext for "HOWITZER." Codes of this type are not discussed in this book; they are discussed in [462,463].

The word "cipher" has historically been used to refer to cryptosystems in which individual letters are swapped and substituted or otherwise scrambled to hide the plaintext. This is what this book is about.

Ciphers were useful because they were general-purpose. If there was no entry in a codebook for "ANTEATERS," then you couldn't say it. On the other hand, any message can be encrypted with the cipher.

1.2   CLASSICAL CRYPTOGRAPHY

Before computers, cryptography consisted of character-based cryptosystems. Different cryptographic algorithms either substituted characters for one another or transposed characters with one another. The better cryptosystems did both—many times each.

Things are more complex these days, but the philosophy has remained the same. The primary change is that algorithms work on bits instead of characters. This is actually just a change in the alphabet size, from 26 elements to two elements and nothing more. Most good cryptographic algorithms still combine elements of substitution and transposition (there are exceptions).

1.2.1 Substitution Ciphers and Transposition Ciphers

Substitution Ciphers

A **substitution cipher** is one in which each character in the plaintext is substituted for another character in the ciphertext. This substitution serves to obscure the plaintext from everyone but the recipient, who inverts the substitution on the ciphertext to recover the plaintext.

In classical cryptography, there are four basic types of substitution ciphers:

- A **simple substitution cipher** is one in which a character of the plaintext is replaced with a corresponding character of ciphertext. The cryptograms in newspapers are simple substitution ciphers.

- A **homophonic substitution cipher** is like a simple substitution cryptosystem, except a single character of plaintext can map to one of several characters of ciphertext. For example, "A" could correspond to either 5, 13, 25, or 56, "B" could correspond to either 7, 19, 31, or 42, etc.

- A **polyalphabetic substitution cipher** is made up of multiple simple substitution ciphers. For example, there might be five different simple substitution ciphers used; the particular one used changes with the position of each character of the plaintext.

- A **polygram substitution cipher** is one in which blocks of characters are encrypted in groups. For example, "ABA" could correspond to "RTQ," "ABB" could correspond to "SLL," etc.

The famous **Caesar Cipher,** in which each plaintext character is replaced by the character three to the right mod 26 (A is replaced by D, B is replaced by E, . . . , W is replaced by Z, . . . , X is replaced by A, Y is replaced by B, and Z is replaced by C) is a simple substitution cipher.

ROT13 is a simple encryption program commonly found on UNIX systems. In this cipher, A is replaced by N, B is replaced by O, etc. Every letter is rotated thirteen places. This is a simple substitution cipher.

```
#include   <stdio.h>
main()    /* streamlined version of copy input to output */
{
  int c;
  while ((c =getchar()) !=EOF)
    {
      if( c>= 'a' && c<= 'm'  )
        c=c+13;
    else if( c >= 'n'  && c <= 'z'  )
      c=c-13;
    else if( c >= 'A'  && c <= 'M'  )
      c=c+13;
    else if( c >= 'N'  && c <= 'Z'  )
      c=c-13;
    putchar(c);
  }
}
```

Encrypting a file twice with ROT13 restores the original file.

$$P = \text{ROT13}(\text{ROT13}(P))$$

ROT13 is not intended for security; it is often used in electronic mail messages to hide potentially offensive text, to avoid giving away the solution to a puzzle, etc.

These ciphers can be easily broken because the cipher does not hide the underlying frequencies of the different letters of the plaintext. All it takes is about 25 English characters before a good cryptanalyst can reconstruct the plaintext [806]. A general algorithm for solving these sorts of ciphers can be found in [689].

Homophonic substitution ciphers were used as early as 1401 by the Duchy of Mantua [462]. They are much more complicated to break than simple substitution ciphers but still do not obscure all of the statistical properties of the plaintext language. With a known-plaintext attack, the ciphers are trivial to break. A ciphertext attack is harder, but only takes a few seconds on a computer. Details are in [710].

Polyalphabetic substitution ciphers were invented by Leon Battista in 1568 [462]. They were used by the Union army during the American Civil War. Despite the fact that they can be broken easily [475,355,360,462] (especially with the help of computers), many commercial computer security products use ciphers of this form [744]. (Details on how to break this encryption scheme as it was found in the WordPerfect word-processing program versions can be found in [80,84].) The Vigenère cipher and the Beaufort cipher are examples of polyalphabetic substitution ciphers.

Polyalphabetic substitution ciphers have multiple one-letter keys, each of which is used to encrypt one letter of the plaintext. The first key encrypts the first letter of the plaintext, the second key encrypts the second letter of the plaintext, and so on. After all the keys are used, the keys are recycled. If there were 20 one-letter keys, then every twentieth letter would be encrypted with the same key. This is called the **period** of the cipher. In classical cryptography, ciphers with longer periods were significantly harder to break than ciphers with short periods. With computers, there are techniques that can easily break substitution ciphers with very long periods.

A **running-key cipher,** in which one text is used to encrypt another text, is another example of this sort of cipher. Even though this cipher has a period the length of the text, it can also be broken easily [354,462].

Polygram substitution ciphers are ciphers in which groups of letters are encrypted together. The Playfair cipher, invented in 1854, was used by the British during World War I [462]. It encrypts pairs of letters together. Its cryptanalysis is discussed in [360,832,500]. The Hill cipher is another example of a polygram substitution cipher [436].

Transposition Ciphers

A **transposition** cipher is one in which the characters in the plaintext remain the same, but their order is shuffled around. In a simple columnar transposition cipher, the plaintext is written horizontally onto a piece of graph paper of fixed width, and the ciphertext is read off vertically (see Figure 1.4). Decryption is a matter of writing the ciphertext vertically onto a piece of graph paper of identical width and then reading the plaintext off horizontally. Cryptanalysis of these ciphers is discussed in [360,832].

The German ADFGVX cipher, used during World War I, is a transposition cipher (plus a simple substitution). It was a very complex algorithm for its day but was broken by Georges Painvin, a French cryptanalyst [462].

Although many modern cryptosystems use transposition, it is troublesome because it requires a lot of memory and sometimes requires messages to be a multiple of a certain length. Substitution is far more common.

Plaintext: COMPUTER GRAPHICS MAY BE SLOW BUT AT LEAST IT'S EXPENSIVE.

```
COMPUTERGR
APHICSMAYB
ESLOWBUTAT
LEASTITSEX
PENSIVE
```

Ciphertext: CAELP OPSEE MHLAN PIOSS UCWTI TSBIU EMUTE RATSG YAERB TX

Figure 1.4
Columnar transposition cipher.

Rotor Machines

In the 1920s, various mechanical encryption devices were invented to automate the process of encryption. They were based on the concept of a **rotor,** a mechanical wheel that was wired to perform a general cryptographic substitution. For example, a rotor might be wired to substitute "F" for "A," "U" for "B," "L" for "C," etc. These devices used multiple rotors to implement a version of the Vigenère cipher with a very long period and were called **rotor machines.**

A rotor machine has a keyboard and a series of rotors. Each rotor has 26 positions and performs a simple substitution. The rotations of the rotors are a Caesar Cipher. It is the combination of all these rotors that makes the machine secure. Because the rotors all move, and at different rates, the period for an n-rotor machine is 26^n.

The best-known rotor device is the Enigma. The Enigma was used by the Germans during World War II. The basic idea was invented by Arthur Scherbius and Arvid Gerhard Damm in Europe. It was patented in the United States by Arthur Scherbius [772]. The Germans beefed up the basic design considerably for wartime use.

There was a plugboard that slightly permuted the plaintext. There was a reflecting rotor that forced each rotor to operate on each plaintext letter twice. As complicated as the Enigma was, it was broken during World War II. A team of Polish cryptographers broke a simplified Enigma; a British team, including Alan Turing, broke the actual Enigma. For explanations of how rotor ciphers work and how they were broken, see [462,45,301,258,500,740,873]. Two fascinating accounts of how the Enigma was broken are [438,464].

Further Reading

This is not a book about classical cryptography, so I will not dwell further on these subjects. Two excellent precomputer cryptology books are [360,832]. Dorothy Denning discusses many of these ciphers in [268], and [500] has some fairly complex mathematical analyses of the same ciphers. An article that presents a good overview of the subject is [356]. David Kahn's historical cryptography books are also excellent [462,463,464].

1.2.2 Computer Algorithms

There are many cryptographic algorithms. These are three of the most common:

- **DES** (Data Encryption Standard) is currently the most popular computer encryption algorithm. DES is a U.S.-government standard encryption algorithm and has been endorsed by the U.S. military for encrypting "Unclassified but Sensitive" information. It is a symmetric algorithm; the same key is used for encryption and decryption.

- **RSA** (named for its creators—Rivest, Shamir, and Adleman) is the most popular public-key algorithm. It can be used for both encryption and digital signatures.

- **DSA** (Digital Signature Algorithm, used as part of the Digital Signature Standard) is another public-key algorithm. It cannot be used for encryption, but only for digital signatures.

1.2.3 Simple XOR

It's an embarrassment to put this algorithm in a book like this because it's nothing more than a Vigenère cipher. It is included because it is so prevalent in commercial software packages, at least those in the MS-DOS and Macintosh worlds [847]. Unfortunately, if a software security program proclaims that it has a "proprietary" encryption algorithm—one that is significantly faster than DES—the odds are that it is some variant of this.

```
/* Usage:  crypto key input_file output_file  */

void main (int argc, char *argv[])
{
  FILE *fi, *fo;
  int *cp;
  int c;

  if (cp = argv[1])  {
    if ((fi = fopen(argv[2], "rb")) != NULL)  {
      if ((fo = fopen(argv[3], "wb")) != NULL)  {
        while ((c = getc(fi)) != EOF)  {
          if (!*cp) cp = argv[1];
          c ^= *(cp++);
          putc(c,fo);
        }
        fclose(fo);
      }
      fclose(fi);
    }
  }
}
```

This is a symmetric algorithm; the same key is used for both encryption and decryption. The plaintext is being XORed with a keyword to generate the ciphertext. Since XORing the same value twice restores the original, encryption and decryption use exactly the same program:

$$P \text{ XOR } K = C$$
$$C \text{ XOR } K = P$$
$$(P \text{ XOR } K) \text{ XOR } K = P$$

There's no real security here. This kind of encryption is trivial to break, even without computers [360,832]. It will only take a few minutes with a computer.

Assume the plaintext is English. Furthermore, assume the key length is an arbitrary small number of bytes (although in the source code example, it is always eight bytes). Here's how to break it:

1. Discover the length of the key by a procedure known as **counting coincidences** [355]. Trying each byte displacement of the key against itself, count those bytes that are equal. If the two ciphertext portions have used the same key, something over 6% of the bytes will be equal. If they have used a different key, then less than 0.4% will be equal (assuming a random key encrypting normal ASCII text; other plaintext will have different numbers). The smallest displacement that indicates an equal key length is the length of the repeated key.

2. Shift the key by that length and XOR it with itself. This removes the key and leaves you with text XORed with itself. Since English has about one bit of real information per byte (see Section 9.1), there is plenty of redundancy for choosing a unique decryption.

Despite this, the list of software vendors that tout this sort of algorithm as being "almost as secure as DES" is staggering [774]. It might keep your kid sister from reading your files, but it won't stop a cryptographer for more than a few minutes.

1.2.4 One-time Pads

Believe it or not, there is a perfect encryption scheme. It's called a **one-time pad** and was invented in 1917 by Major Joseph Mauborgne and AT&T's Gilbert Vernam [462]. In its classical form, a one-time pad is nothing more than a large nonrepeating set of truly random key letters, written on sheets of paper and glued together in a pad. The sender uses each key letter on the pad to encrypt exactly one plaintext character. The receiver has an identical pad and uses each key on the pad, in turn, to decrypt each letter of the ciphertext.

Each key is used exactly once, for only one message. The sender encrypts the message and then destroys the pad's pages. The receiver does the same thing after decrypting the message. New message—new page and new key letters.

Assuming an adversary can't get access to the pages of the one-time pad used to encrypt the message, this scheme is perfectly secure. A given ciphertext message is equally likely to be any possible plaintext message of equal size. For example, if the message is:

ONETIMEPAD

and the key sequence from the pad is

TBFRGFARFM

then the ciphertext is

IPKLPSFHGQ

Since every key sequence is equally likely (remember, the keys are generated in a random manner), an adversary has no information with which to cryptanalyze the ciphertext. The key sequence could just as likely be:

POYYAEAAZX

which would decrypt to:

SALMONEGGS

or

BXFGBMTMXM

which would decrypt to:

GREENFLUID

This point bears repeating: since every plaintext message is equally possible, there is no way for the cryptanalyst to determine which plaintext message is the correct one. A random key sequence XORed with a nonrandom plaintext message produces a completely random ciphertext message, and no amount of computing power can change that.

The caveat, and this is a big one, is that the key letters have to be generated randomly. Any attacks against this scheme will be against the method used to generate the key sequence. If you use a cryptographically weak algorithm to generate your key sequence, there might be trouble. If you use a real random source—this is much harder than it might first appear—it is safe.

Using a pseudo-random number generator doesn't count; often they have nonrandom properties. Many of the stream ciphers described later in this book try to approximate this system with a pseudo-random sequence, but most fail. The sequences they generate only seem random, but careful analysis yields nonrandomness, which a cryptanalyst can exploit. However, it is possible to generate real random numbers, even with a microcomputer. Some techniques for how to do this will be covered in Section 15.3.

The idea of a one-time pad can easily be extended to the encryption of binary data. Instead of a one-time pad consisting of letters, use a one-time pad of bits. Everything else remains the same, and the security is just as perfect.

This all sounds good, but there are a few problems. The length of the key sequence is equal to the length of the message. This might be suitable for a few short messages, but this will never work for a 1.44 Mbps communications channel. However, you can store 650 megabytes worth of random bits on a CD-ROM. This would make a perfect one-time pad for certain low-bandwidth applications, although then you have to deal with the problem of storing the CD-ROM when it is not in use and then destroying it once it has been completely used.

Even if you solve the key distribution and storage problem, you have to make sure the sender and receiver are perfectly synchronized. If the receiver is off by a bit, the message won't make any sense. On the other hand, if some bits are garbled during transmission, only those bits will be decrypted incorrectly.

One-time pads still have their applications in today's world, primarily for ultrasecure low-bandwidth channels. The hotline between the United States and the former Soviet Union was (is it still active?) rumored to be encrypted with a one-time pad. Many Soviet spy messages to agents were encrypted using one-time pads. These messages are still secure today and will remain that way forever. It doesn't matter how long the supercomputers work on the problem; it doesn't matter how many people may still be working on the problem half a century later with unimaginable machines and techniques. Even after the aliens from Andromeda land with their massive spaceships and undreamed-of computing power, they will not be able to read the Soviet spy messages encrypted with one-time pads (as long as the one-time pads used to generate the messages have been destroyed).

1.3   LARGE NUMBERS

Throughout this book use some large numbers to describe various cryptographic algorithms. It's easy to lose sight of these numbers and what they actually mean. Table 1.1 gives physical analogues for the kinds of numbers used in cryptography.

These numbers are order-of-magnitude estimates, and have been culled from a variety of sources. Many of the astrophysics numbers are explained in Freeman

TABLE 1.1

Large Numbers

Odds of being killed in an automobile accident (in the U.S. per year)	1 in 5600 (2^{-12})
Odds of being killed in an automobile accident (in the U.S. per lifetime)	1 in 75 (2^{-6})
Odds of drowning (in the U.S. per year)	1 in 59,000 (2^{-16})
Time Until the Next Ice Age	14,000 (2^{14}) years
Time Until the Sun Goes Nova	10^9 (2^{30}) years
Age of the Planet	10^9 (2^{30}) years
Age of the Universe	10^{10} (2^{34}) years

If the Universe Is Closed:

Total Lifetime of Universe	10^{11} (2^{37}) years
	10^{18} (2^{61}) seconds

If the Universe Is Open:

Time Until Low-Mass Stars Cool Off	10^{14} (2^{47}) years
Time Until Planets Detach from Stars	10^{15} (2^{50}) years
Time Until Stars Detach from Galaxies	10^{19} (2^{64}) years
Time Until Orbits Decay by Gravitational Radiation	10^{20} (2^{67}) years
Time Until Black Holes Decay by the Hawking Process	10^{64} (2^{213}) years
Time Until All Matter Is Liquid at Zero Temperature	10^{65} (2^{216}) years
Time Until All Matter Decays to Iron	$10^{10^{26}}$ years
Time Until All Matter Collapses to Black Holes	$10^{10^{76}}$ years

Number of Atoms in the Planet	10^{51} (2^{170})
Number of Atoms in the Sun	10^{57} (2^{190})
Number of Atoms in the Galaxy	10^{67} (2^{223})
Number of Atoms in the Universe (Dark Matter Excluded)	10^{77} (2^{265})

Volume of the Universe	10^{84} (2^{280}) cm^3

Dyson's paper, "Time Without End: Physics and Biology in an Open Universe," in *Reviews of Modern Physics,* v. 52, n. 3, July 1979, pp. 447–460. Automobile accident deaths are calculated from the Department of Transportation's statistic of 178 road accidents per million people and an average lifespan of 75.4 years.

PART
ONE

Cryptographic
Protocols

Protocol Building Blocks

2.1 INTRODUCTION TO PROTOCOLS

The whole point of cryptography is to solve problems. (Actually, that's the whole point of computers—something many people tend to forget.) The types of problems that cryptography solves revolve around secrecy, distrustful and dishonest people, and privacy. You can learn all about algorithms and techniques, but these are merely interesting unless they solve problems. This is why we are going to look at protocols first.

A **protocol** is a series of steps, involving two or more parties, designed to accomplish a task. This is an important definition. A "series of steps" means that the protocol has a sequence, from start to finish. Every step must be executed in turn, and no step can be taken before the previous step is finished. "Involving two or more parties" means that at least two people are required to complete the protocol; one person alone does not make a protocol. Certainly one person can perform a series of steps to accomplish a task (e.g., baking a cake), but this is not a protocol. Finally, "designed to accomplish a task" means that the protocol must do something. Something that looks like a protocol but does not accomplish a task is not a protocol—it's a waste of time.

Protocols have other characteristics:

1. Everyone involved in the protocol must know the protocol and all of the steps to follow in advance.

2. Everyone involved in the protocol must agree to follow it.

3. The protocol must be unambiguous; each step must be well defined and there must be no chance of a misunderstanding.

4. The protocol must be complete; there must be a specified action for every possible situation.

The protocols in this book are organized as a series of steps. Execution of the protocol proceeds linearly through the steps, unless there are instructions to branch to another step. Each step involves at least one of two things: computations by one or more parties, or messages from one party to another.

Cryptographic Protocols

A **cryptographic protocol** is a protocol that uses cryptography. The parties involved can be friends and trust one another implicitly, or they can be adversaries and not trust one another at all. Of course, a cryptographic protocol involves some cryptographic algorithm, but generally the goal of the protocol is something beyond simple secrecy. The parties participating in the protocol might want to share parts of their secrets to compute a value, jointly generate a random sequence, convince one another of their identity, or simultaneously sign a contract. Cryptographic protocols that accomplish such goals have radically changed our ideas of what mutually distrustful parties can accomplish over a network.

The Purpose of Protocols

In daily life, there are informal protocols for almost everything: ordering goods over the telephone, playing poker, voting in an election. No one thinks much about these protocols; they have evolved over time, everyone knows how to use them, and they work.

More and more, people are communicating over computer networks instead of communicating face-to-face. Computers need formal protocols to do the same things that people do without thinking. If you moved from one state to another (or even from one country to another) and found a voting booth that looked completely different from the ones you were used to, you could easily adapt. Computers are not nearly so flexible.

Many face-to-face protocols rely on people's presence to ensure fairness and security. Would you send a stranger a pile of cash to buy groceries for you? Would you play poker with someone if you couldn't see him or her shuffle and deal? Would you mail the government your secret ballot without some assurance of anonymity?

It is naive to assume that the people on a computer network are going to be honest. It is naive to assume that the managers of a computer network are going to be honest. It is even naive to assume that the designers of a computer network were honest. Most will be honest, but it is the dishonest few we need to guard against. By formalizing protocols, we can examine ways in which dishonest parties can try to cheat and develop protocols that foil these cheaters.

In addition to formalizing behavior, protocols are useful because they abstract the process of accomplishing a task from the mechanism by which the task is accomplished. A communications protocol between two computers is the same whether the computers are IBM PCs, VAX computers, or facsimile machines. This abstraction allows us to examine the protocol for good features without getting bogged down in the implementation details. When we are convinced we have a good protocol, we can implement it in everything from computers to telephones to intelligent muffin toasters.

The Company

To help demonstrate the protocols, I have enlisted the aid of several people (see Table 2.1). Alice and Bob are the first two. They will perform all general two-person protocols. As a rule, Alice will initiate all protocols. Bob will play the second part. If the protocol requires a third or fourth person, Carol and Dave will perform those roles. Other actors will play specialized supporting roles; they will be introduced later.

Arbitrated Protocols

An **arbitrator** is a disinterested third party trusted to complete a protocol (see Figure 2.1a). Disinterested means that the arbitrator has no particular reason to complete the protocol and no particular allegiance to any of the people involved in the protocol. Trusted means that all people involved in the protocol accept that

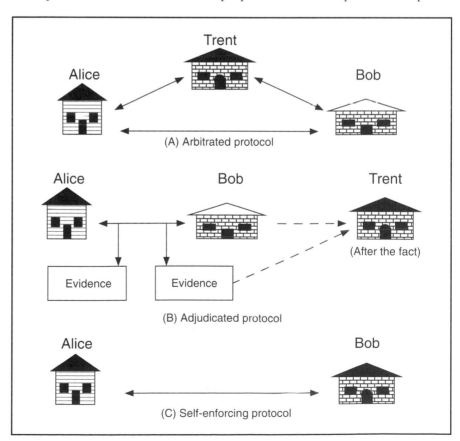

Figure 2.1
Types of protocols.

TABLE 2.1
Dramatis Personae

Alice	Participant in all the protocols.
Bob	Participant in the two-, three-, and four-party protocols.
Carol	Participant in the three- and four-party protocols.
Dave	Participant in the four-party protocols.
Eve	Eavesdropper.
Mallet	Malicious active attacker.
Trent	Trusted arbitrator.
Walter	Warden; he'll be guarding Alice and Bob in some protocols.
Peggy	Prover.
Victor	Verifier.

what is said is true, what is done is correct, and that his or her part of the protocol will be complete. Arbitrators can help complete protocols between two mutually distrustful parties.

In the real world, lawyers are often used as arbitrators. For example, Alice is selling a car to Bob, a stranger. Bob wants to pay by check, but Alice has no way of knowing if the check is good or not. Alice wants the check to clear before she turns the title over to Bob. Bob, who doesn't trust Alice any more than she trusts him, doesn't want to hand over a check without receiving a title.

Enter a lawyer trusted by both. With the help of the lawyer, Alice and Bob can agree on the following protocol to ensure that neither cheats the other:

(1) Alice gives the title and the keys to the lawyer.

(2) Bob gives the check to Alice.

(3) Alice deposits the check.

(4) After waiting a specified time period for the check to clear, the lawyer gives the title to Bob.

(5) If the check does not clear within the specified time period, Alice shows proof of this to the lawyer and the lawyer returns the title and the keys to Alice.

In this protocol, Alice trusts the lawyer not to give Bob the title and the keys unless the check has cleared and to give them back to her if the check does not clear. Bob trusts the lawyer to hold the title and the keys until the check clears before giving them to him. The lawyer doesn't care if the check clears or not. He will do what he is supposed to do in either case.

In the example, the lawyer is playing the part of an escrow agent. Escrow agents often arbitrate financial transactions. Lawyers act as arbitrators for wills and sometimes for contract negotiations. The various stock exchanges act as arbitrators between buyers and sellers.

Bankers also arbitrate protocols. Bob can use a certified check to buy a car from Alice:

(1) Bob writes a check and gives it to the bank.

(2) After putting enough of Bob's money on hold to cover the check, the bank certifies the check and gives it back to Bob.

(3) Alice gives the title and the keys to Bob.

(4) Bob gives the certified check to Alice.

(5) Alice deposits the check.

This protocol works because Alice trusts the banker's certification. Alice trusts the bank to hold her money and not to use it to finance shaky real estate operations in mosquito-infested countries.

A notary public is another arbitrator. When Bob receives a notarized document from Alice, he is convinced that Alice signed the document voluntarily and with her own hand. The notary can, if necessary, stand up in court and attest to that fact.

The concept of an arbitrator is as old as society. There have always been people—rulers, priests, and so on—who have the authority to act fairly. Arbitrators have a certain social role and position in our society; betraying the public trust would jeopardize that. Lawyers who play games with escrow accounts face almost-certain disbarment, for example. This rosy picture doesn't always exist in the real world, but it's the ideal.

This ideal can translate to the computer world, but there are several problems with translating arbitrators into computers:

- It is easier to find and trust a neutral third party if you know who the party is, can see his face, or have a feeling that he is a real person. Two parties suspicious of each other are also likely to be suspicious of some faceless arbitrator somewhere else on the network.

- The computer network must bear the cost of maintaining an arbitrator. We all know what lawyers charge; who wants to bear that kind of network overhead?

- There is a delay inherent in any arbitrated protocol. The arbitrator must deal with every transaction.

- Arbitrators are potential bottlenecks in large-scale implementations of any protocol. Increasing the number of arbitrators in the implementation can mitigate this problem, but then the cost increases.

- Since everyone on the network must trust the arbitrator, he represents a vulnerable point for anyone trying to subvert the network.

Even so, arbitrators still have a role to play. In protocols using a trusted arbitrator, the part will be played by Trent.

Adjudicated Protocols

Because of the high cost of hiring arbitrators, arbitrated protocols can be subdivided into two lower-level subprotocols. One is a nonarbitrated subprotocol, executed every time people want to complete the protocol. The other is an arbitrated subprotocol, executed only in exceptional circumstances—when there is a dispute. This special type of arbitrator is called an **adjudicator** (see Figure 2.1b).

An adjudicator is also a disinterested and trusted third party. Unlike an arbitrator, he is not directly involved in every protocol. The adjudicator is called in only to determine whether a transaction was performed fairly.

Judges are professional adjudicators. Unlike a notary public, a judge is brought in only if there is a dispute. Alice and Bob can enter into a contract without a judge. A judge never sees the contract unless one of them hauls the other into court.

This contract-signing protocol can be formalized in this way:

Nonarbitrated subprotocol (executed every time):

(1) Alice and Bob negotiate the terms of the contract.

(2) Alice signs the contract.

(3) Bob signs the contract.

Adjudicated subprotocol (executed only in case of a dispute):

(1) Alice and Bob appear before a judge.

(2) Alice presents her evidence.

(3) Bob presents his evidence.

(4) The judge rules on the evidence.

The key difference between an adjudicator and an arbitrator (as I use the terms in this book) is that the adjudicator is not always necessary. If there is a dispute, a judge is called in to adjudicate. If there is no dispute, using a judge is unnecessary.

There are adjudicated computer protocols. These protocols rely on the involved parties to be honest; but if someone cheats, there is a body of data collected so that a disinterested third party could determine if someone cheated. In a good, adjudicated protocol, the adjudicator could also determine the cheater's identity. In real life, adjudicators are seldom called. The inevitability of detection discourages cheating, and people remain honest.

Self-Enforcing Protocols

A **self-enforcing protocol** is the best type of protocol. The protocol itself guarantees fairness (see Figure 2.1c). No arbitrator is required to complete the protocol. No adjudicator is required to resolve disputes. The protocol is constructed so that there cannot be any disputes. If one of the parties tries to cheat, the other party immediately detects the cheating and the protocol stops. Whatever the cheating party hoped would happen by cheating doesn't happen.

In the best of all possible worlds, every protocol would be self-enforcing. Unfortunately, there is not a self-enforcing protocol for every situation. I'll do my best, though.

Attacks Against Protocols

Attacks against protocols can be directed against the cryptographic algorithms used in the protocol, the cryptographic techniques used to implement the algorithm (e.g., key generation), or the protocol iself. This section of the book discusses only the protocols. For the time being we will assume that the cryptographic algorithms and techniques are secure, and look only at attacks against the protocols themselves.

There are various ways people can try to attack a protocol. Someone not involved in the protocol can eavesdrop on some or all of the protocol. This is called a **passive attack,** because the attacker does not affect the protocol. All he can do is observe the protocol and attempt to gain information. This kind of attack corresponds to a ciphertext-only attack, as discussed in Section 1.1. In these protocols, the part of the eavesdropper will be played by Eve.

Alternatively, an attacker could try to alter the protocol to his own advantage. He could introduce new messages in the protocol, delete existing messages, substitute one message for another, destroy a communications channel, or alter stored information in a computer. These are called **active attacks,** because they require active intervention.

Passive attackers are concerned solely with obtaining information about the parties involved in the protocol. They do this by collecting the messages passing among various parties and attempting to cryptanalyze them. Active attacks, on the other hand, can have much more diverse objectives. The attacker could be interested in obtaining information, degrading system performance, corrupting existing information, or gaining unauthorized access to resources.

Active attacks are much more serious, especially in protocols in which the different parties don't necessarily trust one another. The attacker does not have to be a complete outsider. He could be a legitimate system user. There could even be many active attackers, all working together, each of them a legitimate system user. The part of the malicious active attacker will be played by Mallet.

It is also possible that the attacker could be one of the parties involved in the protocol. He may lie during the protocol or not follow the protocol at all. This type of attacker is called a **cheater. Passive cheaters** follow the protocol but try to obtain more information than the protocol intends them to. **Active cheaters** disrupt the protocol in progress in an attempt to cheat.

It is very difficult to maintain a system's security if most of the parties involved are active cheaters, but sometimes it is possible for legitimate parties to detect that active cheating is going on. Certainly, protocols should be secure against passive cheating.

2.2   COMMUNICATIONS USING SYMMETRIC CRYPTOGRAPHY

How do two parties communicate securely? They encrypt their communications, of course. The complete protocol is more complicated than that. Let's look at what must happen for Alice to send an encrypted message to Bob.

(1) Alice and Bob agree on a cryptosystem.

(2) Alice and Bob agree on a key.

(3) Alice takes her plaintext message and encrypts it using the encryption algorithm and the key. This creates a ciphertext message.

(4) Alice sends the ciphertext message to Bob.

(5) Bob decrypts the ciphertext message with the same algorithm and key and reads it.

What can Eve, an eavesdropper sitting between Alice and Bob, learn from listening in on this protocol? If all she hears is the transmission in step (4), she must try to cryptanalyze the ciphertext. This passive attack is a ciphertext-only attack; there are an array of algorithms that are resistant (as far as we know) to whatever computing power Eve could bring to bear on the problem.

Eve isn't stupid, though. She knows that if she can listen in on steps (1) and (2), she's succeeded. She would know the algorithm and the key; she would know just as much as Bob. When the message comes across the communications channel in step (4), all she has to do is decrypt it herself.

This is why key management is such an important matter in cryptography. A good cryptosystem is one in which all the security is inherent in the key and none is inherent in the algorithm. With a symmetric algorithm, Alice and Bob can perform step (1) in public, but they must perform step (2) in secret. The key must remain secret before, during, and after the protocol; otherwise the message will no longer be secure. (Public-key cryptography solves this problem another way and will be discussed in Section 2.5.)

Mallet, an active attacker, could do a few other things. He could attempt to break the communications path in step (4), ensuring that Alice could not talk to Bob at all. Mallet could also intercept Alice's messages and substitute ones of his own. If he also knew the key (by intercepting the communication in step (2), or by breaking the cryptosystem), he could encrypt his own message and send it to Bob in place of the intercepted message. Bob would have no way of knowing that the message had not come from Alice. If Mallet didn't know the key, he could only create a replacement message that would decrypt to gibberish. Bob, thinking the message came from Alice, might conclude that either the network or Alice had some serious problems.

What about Alice? What can she do to disrupt the protocol? She can give a copy of the key to Eve. Now Eve can read whatever Bob says. Bob, who has no idea that Eve has the key, thinks he is talking securely to Alice. He has no idea Eve is reprinting his words in the *New York Times*. Although serious, this is not a problem with the protocol. There is nothing to stop Alice from giving Eve a copy of the plaintext at any point during the protocol. Of course, Bob could also do anything that Alice could. This protocol assumes that Alice and Bob trust each other.

In summary, symmetric cryptosystems have the following problems:

- If the key is compromised (stolen, guessed, extorted, bribed, etc.), then the adversary who had the key can decrypt all message traffic encrypted with that key. He or she can also pretend to be one of the parties and produce false messages to fool the other party. It is very important to change keys frequently to minimize this problem.

- Keys must be distributed in secret. They are more valuable than any of the messages they encrypt, since knowledge of the key means knowledge of all the messages. For encryption systems that span the world, this can be a daunting task. Often couriers hand-carry keys to their destinations.

- Assuming a separate key is used for each pair of users in a network, the total number of keys increases rapidly as the number of users increases. For example, 10 users need 45 different keys to talk with one another; 11 users need 55 different keys. This problem can be minimized by keeping the number of users small, but that is not always possible.

2.3   ONE-WAY FUNCTIONS

The notion of **one-way functions** is central to public-key cryptography. While not a protocol in itself, one-way functions are a fundamental building block for most of the protocols described in this book.

A one-way function is a function that is relatively easy to compute but significantly harder to undo or reverse. That is, given x it is easy to compute $f(x)$, but given $f(x)$ it is hard to compute x. In this context, "hard" means, in effect, that it would take millions of years to compute the function even if all the computers in the world were assigned to the problem.

Taking a watch apart is a good example of a one-way function. It is easy to smash a watch into hundreds of tiny pieces. However, it's not easy to put all of those tiny pieces back together into a functional watch.

This sounds accurate, but in fact it isn't demonstratively true. If we are being strictly mathematical, there is no proof that one-way functions exist, nor is there any real evidence that they can be constructed [138,322,366,393]. Even so, there are many functions that look and smell one-way: we can compute them efficiently and, as of now, know of no easy way to reverse them. For example, x^2 is easy to compute, but $\sqrt{x}$ is much harder. For the rest of this section, I'm going to pretend that there are one-way functions. I'll talk more about this in Section 9.2.

So, what good are one-way functions? I can't use them for encryption as is. A message encrypted with the one-way function isn't useful; no one could decrypt it. (Exercise: Write a message on a plate, smash the plate into tiny bits, and then give the bits to a friend. Ask the friend to read the message. Observe how impressed your friend is with the one-way function.) For encryption, we need something called a **trap-door one-way function.** (There are cryptographic applications for one-way functions; see Section 3.2.)

A **trap-door one-way function** is a special type of one-way function with a secret trap door. It is easy to compute in one direction and hard to compute in the other direction. But, if you know the secret, you can easily compute the function in the other direction. That is, it is easy to compute $f(x)$ given x, and hard to compute x given $f(x)$. However, there is some secret information, y, such that given $f(x)$ and y it is easy to compute x. In our watch example, the secret information might be a set of assembly instructions for the watch.

A mailbox is a good example of a trap-door one-way function. Anyone can easily put mail into the box; just open the slot and drop it in. Putting mail in a mailbox is a public activity. Opening the mailbox is not a public activity. It's hard; you would need welding torches or other tools. However, if you have the secret (the key or the combination), it's easy to open the mailbox. Public-key cryptography is a lot like that.

2.4   ONE-WAY HASH FUNCTIONS

A **one-way hash function** has many names: **compression function, contraction function, message digest, fingerprint, cryptographic checksum, data integrity check (DIC), manipulation detection code (MDC), message authentication code (MAC),** and **data authentication code (DAC).** Whatever you call it, it is central to modern cryptography. One-way hash functions are another building block for many protocols.

Hash functions have been used in computer science for a long time. A hash function is a function, mathematical or otherwise, that takes an input string and converts it to a fixed-size (often smaller) output string. A simple hash function would be a function that takes an input string and returns a byte consisting of the XOR of all the input bytes. The whole point here is to fingerprint the input string: to produce a value that can indicate whether a candidate string is likely to be the same as the input string. Because hash functions are typically many to one, we cannot use them to determine with certainty that the two strings are equal, but we can use them to get a reasonable assurance of equality.

A one-way hash function is a hash function that is also a one-way function: it is easy to compute a hash value from an input string, but it is hard to generate a string that hashes to a particular value. The hash function in the previous paragraph is not one-way: given a particular byte value, it is trivial to generate a string of bytes whose XOR is that value. You can't do that with a one-way hash function.

A particular one-way hash function may return values on the order of 128 bits long, so that there are 2^{128} possible hashes. The number of trials required to find a random string with the same hash value as a given string is 2^{128}, and the number of trials required to find two random strings having the same (random) hash value is 2^{64}.

There are two primary types of one-way hash functions: those with a key and those without a key. One-way hash functions without a key can be calculated by anyone; the hash is solely a function of the input string. One-way hash functions with a key are a function of both the input string and the key; only someone with the key can calculate the hash value. (It's the same as calculating the one-way hash and then encrypting it.)

Algorithms specifically designed to be one-way hash functions have been developed (see Chapter 14). These are **pseudo-random** functions; any hash value is equally likely. The output is not dependent on the input in any discernible way. A single change in any input bit changes, on the average, half the output bits. Given a hash value, it is computationally unfeasible to find an input string that hashes to that value.

Think of it as a way of fingerprinting files. If you want to verify that someone has a particular file (that you also have), but you don't want her to send it to you, then ask her for the hash value. If she sends you the correct hash value, then it is almost certain that she has that file. Normally, you would use a one-way hash function without a key, so that anyone can verify the hash. If you only want the recipient to be able to verify the hash, then use a one-way hash function with a key.

2.5   COMMUNICATIONS USING PUBLIC-KEY CRYPTOGRAPHY

Think of a symmetric algorithm as a safe. The key is the combination. Someone with the combination can open the safe, put a document inside, and close it again. Someone else with the combination can open the safe and take the document out. Anyone without the combination is forced to learn safecracking.

In 1976, Whitfield Diffie and Martin Hellman changed that paradigm of cryptography forever [299]. They described **public-key cryptography.** Instead of one key, there are two different keys: one public and the other private. Moreover, it is computationally unfeasible to deduce the private key from the public key. Anyone with the public key (which, presumably, is public) can encrypt a message but not decrypt it. Only the person with the private key can decrypt the message. It is as if someone cut a mail slot into the cryptographic safe. Anyone can slip messages into the slot, but only someone with the private key can open the safe and read the messages.

Mathematically, the process is based on the trap-door one-way functions discussed above. Encryption is the easy direction. Instructions for encryption are the public key; anyone can encrypt a message. Decryption is the hard direction. It's made hard enough that people with Cray computers and thousands (even millions) of years couldn't decrypt the message without the secret. The secret, or trap door, is the private key. With that secret, decryption is as easy as encryption.

This is how Alice can send a message to Bob using public-key cryptography:

(1) Alice and Bob agree on a public-key cryptosystem.

(2) Bob sends Alice his public key.

(3) Alice encrypts her message using Bob's public key and sends it to Bob.

(4) Bob then decrypts Alice's message using his private key.

Notice how public-key cryptography solves the primary problem with symmetric cryptosystems: by distributing the key. With a conventional cryptosystem, Alice and Bob have to agree on the same key. Alice could choose one at random, but she still has to get it to Bob. She could hand it to him sometime beforehand, but that requires foresight. She could send it to him by registered mail, but that takes time. With public-key cryptography, there is no problem. With no prior arrangements, Alice can send a secure message to Bob. Eve, listening in on the entire exchange, has Bob's public key and a message encrypted in that key, but cannot recover either Bob's private key or the message.

More commonly, a network of users agrees on a public-key cryptosystem. Every user has his or her own public key and private key, and the public keys are all published in a database somewhere. Now the protocol is even easier:

(1) Alice gets Bob's public key from the database.

(2) Alice encrypts her message using Bob's public key and sends it to Bob.

(3) Bob then decrypts Alice's message using his private key.

In the first protocol, Bob had to send Alice his public key before she could send him a message. The second protocol is more like traditional mail. Bob is not involved in the protocol until he wants to read his message.

Attacks Against Public-Key Cryptography

In all these public-key digital signature protocols, I glossed over how Alice gets Bob's public key. Section 3.1 discusses this in detail, but it is worth mentioning here.

The obvious way to exchange a public key is from a secure database somewhere. The database has to be public, so that anyone can get anyone else's public key. The database also has to be protected from access by anyone except Trent; otherwise Mallet could substitute a key of his choosing for Alice's. After he did that, Bob couldn't read his messages, but Mallet could.

Even if the public keys are stored in a secure database, Mallet could still substitute one for another during transmission. To prevent this, Trent can sign each of the public keys with his own private key. Trent, when used in this manner, is often known as a **Key Certification Authority** or **Key Distribution Center (KDC).** In practical implementations, the KDC signs a compound message consisting of the user's name, the public key, and any other important information about the user. This signed compound message is stored in the KDC's database. When Alice gets Bob's key, she verifies the KDC's signature to assure herself of the key's validity.

In the final analysis, this is not making things impossible for Mallet, only more difficult. Alice still has the KDC's public key stored somewhere. Mallet has to substitute that key for his own public key, corrupt the database, and substitute the valid keys with his own keys, all signed with his private key as if he were the KDC, and then he's in business. But even paper-based signatures can be forged if Mallet goes to enough trouble. As mentioned earlier, this will be discussed in minute detail in Section 3.1.

Hybrid Cryptosystems

Public-key algorithms are significantly slower than symmetric algorithms; symmetric algorithms are generally at least 1000 times faster than public-key algorithms. In most practical implementations public-key cryptography is used to secure and distribute session keys, and those session keys are used with symmetric algorithms to secure message traffic [499]. This is sometimes called a **hybrid cryptosystem** (see Section 3.1).

2.6 DIGITAL SIGNATURES

Handwritten signatures on documents have long been used as proof of authorship of, or at least agreement with, the contents of the document. What is it about a signature that is so compelling?

1. The signature is unforgeable. The signature is proof that the signer deliberately signed the document.

2. The signature is authentic. The signature convinces the document's recipient that the signer deliberately signed the document.

3. The signature is not reusable. The signature is part of the document, and an unscrupulous person cannot move the signature to a different document.

4. The signed document is unalterable. After the document is signed, it cannot be altered.

5. The signature cannot be repudiated. The signature and the document are physical things. The signer cannot later claim that he or she didn't sign it.

In reality, none of these statements about signatures is completely true. Signatures can be forged; signatures can be lifted from one piece of paper and moved to another. Documents can be altered after signing. However, we are willing to live with these problems because of the difficulty to cheat and the risk of detection.

We would like to do this sort of thing on computers, but there are problems. First, bit streams are easy to copy. Even if a person's signature were difficult to forge (a graphical image of a written signature, for example), it is easy to move a valid signature from one document to another document. The mere presence of such a signature means nothing. Second, documents are easy to modify after they are signed, without leaving any evidence of modification.

Signing Documents with Symmetric Cryptosystems and an Arbitrator

Alice wants to sign a digital message and send it to Bob. With the help of Trent and a symmetric cryptosystem, she can.

Trent is a powerful, trusted arbitrator. He can communicate with both Alice and Bob (and everyone else who may want to sign a digital document). He shares a secret key, K_A, with Alice, and a different secret key, K_B, with Bob. These keys have been established long before the protocol begins and can be reused multiple times for multiple signings.

(1) Alice encrypts her message to Bob with K_A and sends it to Trent.

(2) Trent decrypts the message with K_A.

(3) Trent takes the decrypted message, a statement that he has received this message from Alice, and a copy of Alice's encrypted message. He encrypts the whole bundle with K_B.

(4) Trent sends the encrypted bundle to Bob.

(5) Bob decrypts the bundle with K_B. He can now read both the message and Trent's certification that Alice sent it.

How does Trent know that the message is from Alice, and not from some imposter? He infers it from the message's encryption. Since only he and Alice share their secret key, only Alice could encrypt a message using it.

Is this as good as a paper signature? Let's look at the characteristics we want:

1. This signature is unforgeable. Only Alice (and Trent—but everyone trusts him) knows K_A, so only Alice could have sent Trent a message encrypted with K_A. If someone tried to impersonate Alice, Trent would have immediately realized this in step (2) and would not send the message to Bob.

2. This signature is authentic. Trent is a trusted arbitrator, and Trent knows that the message came from Alice. Trent's certification is proof enough.

3. This signature is not reusable. If Bob tried to take Trent's certification and attach it to another message, Alice would cry foul. An arbitrator (it could be Trent, or it could be a completely different arbitrator with access to the same information) would ask Bob to produce both the message and Alice's encrypted message. The arbitrator would then encrypt the message with K_A and notice that it did not match the encrypted message that Bob gave him. Bob, of course, could not produce an encrypted message that does match because he does not know K_A.

4. The signed document is unalterable. Were Bob to try to alter the document after receipt, Trent could prove foul play in exactly the same manner described above.

5. The signature cannot be repudiated. Even if Alice later claims that she never sent the message, Trent's certification says otherwise. Remember, Trent is trusted by everyone; what he says is true.

If Bob wants to show Carol a document signed by Alice, he can't reveal his secret key to her. He has to go through Trent again:

(1) Bob takes the message and the statement that the message came from Alice, encrypts them with K_B, and sends them back to Trent.

(2) Trent decrypts the bundle with K_B.

(3) Trent re-encrypts the bundle with the secret key he shares with Carol, K_C, and sends it to Carol.

(4) Carol decrypts the bundle with K_C. She can now read both the message and Trent's certification that Alice sent it.

These protocols work, but they're time-consuming for Trent. He has to spend his days decrypting and encrypting messages, acting as the intermediary between every pair of people who want to send signed documents to one another. He is going to be a bottleneck in any communications system, even if he's a mindless software program.

Harder still is creating and maintaining someone like Trent, someone that everyone on the network trusts. Trent has to be infallible; even if he makes one mistake in a million signatures, no one is going to trust him. Trent has to be completely secure. If his database of secret keys ever gets out, or if someone manages to modify his code, everyone's signatures would be completely useless. False documents purported to be signed years ago could appear. Chaos would result. This might work in theory, but it doesn't work very well in practice.

Signing Documents with Public-Key Cryptography

There are public-key algorithms that can be used for digital signatures. In some algorithms—RSA (see Section 12.4) is an example—either the public key or the private key can be used for encryption. Encrypt a document using your private key and you have a secure digital signature. In other cases—DSA (see Section 13.5) is an example—there is a separate algorithm for digital signatures that cannot be used for encryption. This idea was first invented by Diffie and Hellman [299] and further expanded and elaborated on in other texts [723,749,570,724].

The basic protocol is simple:

(1) Alice uses a digital signature algorithm with her private key to sign the message.

(2) Alice sends the document to Bob.

(3) Bob uses the digital signature algorithm with Alice's public key to verify the signature.

This protocol is far better than the previous one. Trent is not necessary; Alice and Bob can do it by themselves. Bob does not even need Trent to resolve disputes: if he cannot perform step (3), then he knows the signature is not valid.

This protocol also satisfies the characteristics we're looking for:

1. The signature is unforgeable; only Alice knows her private key.

2. The signature is authentic; when Bob verifies the message with Alice's public key, he knows that she signed it.

3. The signature is not reusable; the signature is a function of the document and cannot be transferred to any other document.

4. The signed document is unalterable; if there is any alteration to the document, it can no longer be verified with Alice's public key.

5. The signature cannot be repudiated. Bob doesn't need Alice's help to verify her signature.

Signing Documents and Timestamps

Actually, Bob can cheat Alice in certain circumstances. He can reuse the signature and the document together. This isn't exciting if Alice signed a contract (what's another copy of the same contract, more or less?), but it can be very exciting if Alice signed a digital check.

Let's say Alice sends Bob a signed digital check for $100. Bob takes the check to the bank, which verifies the signature and moves the money from one account to the other. Bob, who is an unscrupulous character, saves a copy of the digital check. The following week, he again takes it to the bank (or maybe to a different bank). The bank verifies the signature and moves the money from one account to the other. If Alice never balances her checkbook, Bob can keep this up forever.

Consequently, digital signatures often include timestamps. The date and time of the signature are attached to the message and signed along with the rest of the message. The bank stores this timestamp in a database. Now, when Bob tries to cash Alice's check a second time, the bank checks the timestamp against its database. Since the bank already cashed a check from Alice with the same timestamp, the bank calls the police. Bob then spends fifteen years in Leavenworth Prison reading up on cryptographic protocols.

Signing Documents with Public-Key Cryptography and One-Way Hash Functions

In practical implementations, public-key algorithms are often too inefficient to encrypt long documents. To save time, digital signature protocols are often implemented with one-way hash functions [246,247]. Instead of signing a document, Alice signs the hash of the document. In this protocol, both the one-way hash function and the digital signature algorithm are agreed upon beforehand.

(1) Alice produces a one-way hash of a document.

(2) Alice signs the hash with her private key, thereby signing the document.

(3) Alice sends the document and the signed hash to Bob.

(4) Bob produces a one-way hash of the document that Alice sent. He then verifies the signed hash with Alice's public key and compares it with the hash he generated. If they match, the signature is valid.

Speed increases drastically, and, since the chances of two different documents having the same 160-bit hash are only one in 2^{160}, anyone can safely equate a signature of the hash with a signature of the document. If a non-one-way hash function were used, it would be an easy matter to create multiple documents that hashed to the same value, so that anyone signing a particular document would be duped into signing a multitude of documents. This protocol cannot work without one-way hash functions.

This protocol has other benefits. First, the signature has to be kept separate from the document. Second, the recipient's storage requirements for the document and signature are much smaller.

An archival system can use this type of protocol to verify the existence of documents without storing their contents. The central database could just store the hashes of files. It doesn't have to see the files at all; users submit their hashes to the database, and the database timestamps the submissions and stores them. If there is any disagreement in the future about who created a document and when, the database could resolve it by finding the hash in its files. This has vast implications concerning privacy: Alice could copyright a document but still keep the document secret. Only if she wished to prove her copyright would she have to make the document public. (See Section 3.8.)

Algorithms and Terminology

There are many digital signature algorithms. All of them are public-key algorithms: there is some secret information that only allows someone who knows the information to sign documents, and there is some public information that allows everyone to verify documents. Sometimes the signing process is called **encrypting with a private key,** and the verification process is called **decrypting with a public key.** This is misleading and is only true for one algorithm. Additionally, there are often implementation differences. For example, one-way hash functions and timestamps sometimes add extra steps to the process of signing and verifying. Many algorithms can be used for digital signatures, but not for encryption.

In general, I will refer to the signing and verifying processes without any details of the algorithms involved. Signing a message with private key K is:

$$S_K(M)$$

and verifying a message with the corresponding public key is:

$$V_K(M)$$

The bit string attached to the document when signed (in the above example, the one-way hash of the document encrypted with the private key) will be called the **digital signature,** or just the **signature.** The entire protocol, by which the receiver of a message is convinced of the identity of the sender and the integrity of the message, is called **authentication.** Further details on these protocols are in Section 3.2.

Multiple Signatures

How could Alice and Bob sign the same digital document? Without one-way hash functions, there are two options. In the first option, Alice and Bob sign separate copies of the document itself. The resultant message would be twice the size of the original document—this is not optimal. In the second option, Alice would sign the document first and then Bob would sign Alice's signature. This works, except it is impossible to verify Alice's signature without also verifying Bob's.

If a one-way hash of the document is signed instead of the document itself, multiple signatures are easy:

(1) Alice signs the document.

(2) Bob signs the document.

(3) Bob sends his signature to Alice.

(4) Alice or Bob sends the document, her signature, and his signature to Carol.

(5) Carol verifies both Alice's signature and Bob's signature.

Alice and Bob can do steps (1) and (2) either in parallel or in series. In step (5), Carol can verify one signature without having to verify the other.

Cheating with Digital Signatures

Alice can cheat with digital signatures, and there's nothing that can be done about it. She wishes to sign a document and then later claim that she did not. First, she signs the document normally. Then, she anonymously publishes her private key, conveniently loses it in some public place, or just pretends to do either of the above. Now, anyone who finds the key can pretend to be Alice and sign documents. Alice then claims that her signature has been compromised and that others are using it, pretending to be her. She disavows signing the document and any others that she signed using that private key. Timestamps can limit the effects of this kind of cheating, but Alice can always claim that her key was compromised earlier. If Alice times things well, she can sign a document and then successfully claim that she didn't. This is why one hears so much about private keys buried in tamper-resistant modules—so that Alice can't get at hers and abuse it.

Although there is nothing that can be done about this possible abuse, one can take steps to guarantee that old signatures are not invalidated by actions taken in disputing new ones. (For example, Alice could "lose" her key to prevent her from paying Bob for the junker he sold her yesterday and in the process invalidate her year-old mortgage.) The solution is for the receiver of a signed document to have it timestamped by an arbitrator. This timestamp proves that the document was signed at a given time. Now, when Alice either pretends to lose or actually loses her key, only documents signed after she reports the loss are considered invalid. This is similar to the rules about reporting a stolen credit card.

Applications of Digital Signatures

One of the earliest proposed applications of digital signatures was to facilitate the verification of nuclear test ban treaties [817]. The United States and the former Soviet Union can put seismometers on each other's soil to monitor each other's nuclear tests. The problem is that the monitoring nation must assure itself that the host nation is not tampering with the data from the monitoring nation's seismometers. Simultaneously, the host nation wants to assure itself that the monitor is sending only the specific information needed for monitoring. Conventional authentication techniques can solve the first problem, but only digital signatures can solve both problems. The host nation can read, but not alter, data from the seismometer; and the monitoring nation knows that the data has not been tampered with.

2.7   DIGITAL SIGNATURES WITH ENCRYPTION

By combining digital signatures with public-key cryptography, we can develop a protocol that combines the security of encryption with the authenticity of digital signatures. For example, think of a signed letter in an envelope: the digital signature provides proof of authorship, and encryption provides privacy.

(1) Alice signs the message with her private key.

$$S_A(M)$$

(2) Alice encrypts the signed message with Bob's public key and sends it to Bob.

$$E_B(S_A(M))$$

(3) Bob decrypts the message with his private key.

$$D_B(E_B(S_A(M))) = S_A(M)$$

(4) Bob verifies with Alice's public key and recovers the message.

$$V_A(S_A(M)) = M$$

Of course, timestamps should be used with this protocol to prevent reuse of messages. Timestamps can also protect against other potential pitfalls, such as the one described in the next section.

Resending the Message as a Receipt

Consider an implementation of this protocol, with the additional feature of confirmation messages. Whenever someone receives a message, he or she sends it back to the sender as a confirmation of receipt.

(1) Alice signs a message with her private key, encrypts it with Bob's public key, and sends it to Bob.

$$E_B(S_A(M))$$

(2) Bob decrypts the message with his private key and verifies the signature with Alice's public key, thereby verifying that Alice signed the message and recovering the message.

$$V_A(D_B(E_B(S_A(M)))) = M$$

(3) Bob signs the message with his private key, encrypts it with Alice's public key, and sends it back to Alice.

$$E_A(S_B(M))$$

(4) Alice decrypts the message with her private key, and verifies the signature with Bob's public key. If the resultant message is the same one she sent to Bob, she knows that Bob received the message accurately.

If the same algorithm is used for both encryption and digital signatures there is a possible attack [305]. In these cases, the digital signature operation is the inverse of the encryption operation: $V_X = E_X$ and that $S_X = D_X$.

Assume that Mallet is a legitimate system user with his own public and private key. Now, let's watch as he reads Bob's mail. First, he records Alice's message to Bob in step (1). Then, at some later time, he sends that message to Bob, claiming that it came from him (Mallet). Bob thinks that it is a legitimate message from Mallet, so he decrypts the message with his private key and then tries to verify Mallet's signature by decrypting it with Mallet's public key. The resultant message, which is pure gibberish, is:

$$E_M(D_B(E_B(D_A(M)))) = E_M(D_A(M))$$

Even so, Bob goes on with the protocol and sends Mallet a receipt:

$$E_M(D_B(E_M(D_A(M))))$$

Now, all Mallet has to do is decrypt the message with his private key, encrypt it with Bob's public key, decrypt it again with his private key, and encrypt it with Alice's public key. Voilà! Mallet has M.

It is not unreasonable to imagine that Bob may automatically send Mallet a receipt. This protocol may be embedded in his communications software, for example, and send a receipt automatically upon receipt. It is this willingness to acknowledge the receipt of gibberish that creates the insecurity. If Bob checked the message for comprehensibility before sending a receipt, he could avoid this security problem.

There are enhancements to this attack that allow Mallet to send Bob a different message from the one he eavesdropped on. It is important never to sign arbitrary messages from other people or to decrypt arbitrary messages and give the results to other people.

Foiling the Resend Attack

The above attack works because the encrypting operation is the same as the signature-verifying operation, and the decryption operation is the same as the signature operation. If the protocol used even a slightly different operation for encryption and digital signatures, this would be avoided. Digital signatures with one-way hash functions solve the problem (see Section 2.6); so does using different keys for each operation; so do timestamps, which make the incoming message and the outgoing message different.

In general, then, this protocol is perfectly secure:

(1) Alice signs a message.

(2) Alice encrypts the message and signature with Bob's public key (using a different encryption algorithm than she used for the signature) and sends it to Bob.

(3) Bob decrypts the message with his private key.

(4) Bob verifies Alice's signature.

It is possible to modify the protocol so that Alice encrypts the message before signing it. While this might be suitable for some circumstances, when an intermediate party would need to verify the signature without being able to read the message, in general it is better to encrypt everything. Why give Eve any information at all?

2.8   RANDOM AND PSEUDO-RANDOM SEQUENCE GENERATION

Why even bother with random number generation in a book on cryptography? There's already a random number generator built into most every compiler, a mere function call away. Unfortunately, those random number generators are almost definitely not cryptographically secure, and probably not even very random. Most of them are embarrassingly bad.

Random sequence generators are not random because they don't have to be. Most simple applications, like computer games, need so few random numbers that they hardly notice. However, cryptography is extremely sensitive to the properties of random number generators. Use a poor random sequence generator and you start getting weird correlations and strange results [686,691]. If security depends on your random number generator, weird correlations and strange results are the last things you want.

The problem is that a random number generator doesn't produce a random sequence. It probably doesn't produce anything that looks even remotely like a random sequence. Of course, it is impossible to produce something truly random on a computer. Knuth quotes John von Neumann as saying: "Anyone who considers arithmetical methods of producing random digits is, of course, in a state of sin" [488]. Computers are deterministic beasts: stuff goes in one end, completely predictable operations occur inside, and different stuff comes out the other end. Put the same stuff in on two separate occasions and the same stuff comes out both times. Put the same stuff into two identical computers, and the same stuff comes out of both of them. There are only a finite number of states in which a computer can exist (a large finite number, but a finite number nonetheless), and the stuff that comes out will always be a deterministic function of the stuff that went in and the computer's current state. That means that any random sequence generator on a computer (at least, on a Turing machine) is, by definition, periodic. Anything that is periodic is, by definition, predictable. And if something is predictable, it can't be random. A true random sequence generator requires some random input; a computer can't provide that.

2.8.1 Pseudo-Random Sequences

The best a computer can produce is a **pseudo-random** sequence generator. What's that? Many people have taken a stab at defining this formally, but I'll hand-wave here. The sequence's period should be long enough so that a finite sequence of reasonable length, i.e., one that is actually used, is not periodic. That is, if you need a billion random bits, don't choose a sequence generator that repeats after only sixteen thousand bits. These relatively short, non-periodic subsequences should be as indistinguishable as possible from random sequences. For example, they should have about the same number of ones and zeros; about half the runs (sequences of the same bit) should be runs of zeros and the other half should be runs of ones; half the runs should be of length one, one quarter of length two, one eighth of length three, etc. These properties can be empirically measured and then compared to statistical expectations using a chi-square test.

For our purposes, a sequence generator is pseudo-random if it has this property:

1. **It looks random.** This means that it passes all the statistical tests of randomness that we can find. (Start with the ones in [488].)

A lot of effort has gone into producing good pseudo-random sequences on computers. Discussions of generators abound in the academic literature, along with various tests of randomness. All of these generators are periodic (there's no escaping that); but with potential periods of 2^{256} bits and higher, they can be used for the biggest applications.

The problem is still those weird correlations and strange results. Every deterministic generator is going to produce them if you use them in a certain way. And that's what a cryptanalyst will use to attack the system.

2.8.2 Cryptographically Secure Pseudo-Random Sequences

Cryptographic applications demand much more of a pseudo-random sequence generator than do most other applications. Cryptographic randomness doesn't mean just statistical randomness, although that's part of it. For a sequence to be **cryptographically random,** it must have this additional second property:

2. **It is unpredictable.** It must be computationally unfeasible to predict what the next random bit will be, given complete knowledge of the algorithm or hardware generating the sequence and all of the previous bits in the stream.

Like any cryptographic algorithm, cryptographically secure pseudo-random sequence generators are subject to attack. Just as it is possible to break an encryption algorithm, it is possible to break a cryptographically secure pseudo-random sequence generator.

2.8.3 Real Random Sequences

Now we're meandering into the domain of philosophers. Is there such a thing as randomness? What is a random sequence? How do you know if a sequence is random? Is "101110100" more random than "101010101"? Quantum mechanics tells us that there is honest-to-goodness randomness in the real world. But is that randomness preserved when brought to the macroscopic world of computer chips and finite-state machines?

Philosophy aside, from our point of view a sequence generator is **real-world random** if it has this additional third property:

3. **It cannot be reliably reproduced.** If you run the sequence generator twice with the exact same input (at least as exact as humanly possible), you will get two different random sequences.

Additionally, real random sequences cannot be compressed. Cryptographically secure pseudo-random sequences cannot, in practice, be compressed.

The output of a generator with these properties will be good enough for a one-time pad, key generation, and any other cryptographic properties for which one might want it.

CHAPTER
3

Basic
Protocols

3.1 KEY EXCHANGE

A common cryptographic technique is to encrypt each individual conversation between two people with a separate key. This is called a **session key,** because it is used for only one particular communications session. How this common session key gets into the hands of the conversants can be a complicated matter.

Key Exchange with Symmetric Cryptography

(1) Alice calls a Key Distribution Center (KDC) and requests a session key to communicate with Bob.

(2) The KDC generates a random session key. It encrypts two copies of it: one in Alice's key and the other in Bob's key. The KDC also encrypts information about Alice's identity with Bob's key. The KDC sends both copies to Alice.

(3) Alice decrypts her copy of the session key.

(4) Alice sends Bob his copy of the session key and the identity information.

(5) Bob decrypts his copy of the session key and the identity information. He uses the identity information to determine who Alice is. (Presumably Alice knows who Bob is; she called him and only he can decrypt the key.)

(6) Both Alice and Bob use this session key to communicate securely.

This protocol works, but it relies on the absolute security of the KDC. If Mallet corrupts the KDC, the whole network is compromised. He has all of the secret keys that the KDC shares with each of the users; he can read all past communications traffic and all future communications traffic. All he has to do is to tap the communications lines and listen to the encrypted message traffic.

Key Exchange with Public-Key Cryptography

The hybrid cryptosystem was discussed in Section 2.5.

(1) Bob sends Alice his public key.

(2) Alice generates a random session key, k, encrypts it using Bob's public key, and sends it to Bob.

$$E_B(k)$$

(3) Bob decrypts Alice's message using his private key to recover the session key.

(4) Both of them encrypt their communications using the same session key.

Key Exchange with Public-Key Cryptography Using a Public-Key Database

In some practical implementations, both Alice's and Bob's signed public keys will be available on a database. This makes the key exchange protocol even easier, and Alice can send a message to Bob even if she has never met him:

(1) Alice gets Bob's public key from a central database.

(2) Alice generates a random session key, encrypts it using Bob's public key, and sends it to Bob.

(3) Bob then decrypts Alice's message using his private key.

(4) Both of them encrypt their communications using the same session key.

Man-in-the-Middle Attack

While Eve cannot do better than try to break the public-key algorithm or attempt a ciphertext-only attack on the ciphertext, Mallet can decrypt messages between Alice and Bob. Mallet is a lot more powerful than Eve. Not only can he listen to messages between Alice and Bob, he can also modify messages, delete messages, and generate totally new ones. Mallet can imitate Bob when talking to Alice and imitate Alice when talking to Bob. Here's how the attack works:

(1) Alice sends Bob her public key. Mallet intercepts this key and sends Bob his own public key.

(2) Bob sends Alice his public key. Mallet intercepts this key and sends Alice his own public key.

(3) When Alice sends a message to Bob, encrypted in "Bob's" public key, Mallet intercepts it. Since the message is really encrypted with his own

public key, he decrypts it with his private key, re-encrypts it with Bob's public key, and sends it on to Bob.

(4) When Bob sends a message to Alice, encrypted in "Alice's" public key, Mallet intercepts it. Since the message is really encrypted with his own public key, he decrypts it with his private key, re-encrypts it with Alice's public key, and sends it on to Alice.

Even if Alice and Bob's public keys are stored on a database, this attack will work. Mallet can intercept Alice's database inquiry, and substitute his own public key for Alice's. He can do the same to Bob. He can break into the database surreptitiously and substitute his key for Alice's and Bob's. The next day he simply waits for Alice and Bob to talk with each other. Then he intercepts and modifies the messages, and he has succeeded.

This **man-in-the-middle attack** works because Alice and Bob have no way to verify that they are talking to each other. Assuming Mallet is quick and doesn't cause any noticeable network delays, the two of them have no idea that someone sitting between them is reading all of their supposedly secret communications.

The easiest way to protect against this is for Alice and Bob to confirm that they are using the same key. If they can communicate via voice (or another way that allows them to unambiguously identify each other), they can each read a one-way hash of their key to the other. Of course, this isn't always possible.

Interlock Protocol

The **interlock protocol,** invented by Ron Rivest and Adi Shamir [748], has a good chance of foiling the man-in-the-middle attack. Here's how it works:

(1) Alice sends Bob her public key.

(2) Bob sends Alice his public key.

(3) Alice encrypts her message using Bob's public key. She sends half of the encrypted message to Bob.

(4) Bob encrypts his message using Alice's public key. He sends half of the encrypted message to Alice.

(5) Alice sends the other half of her encrypted message to Bob.

(6) Bob puts the two halves of Alice's message together and decrypts it with his private key. Bob sends the other half of his encrypted message to Alice.

(7) Alice puts the two halves of Bob's message together and decrypts it with her private key.

The important point is that half of the message is useless without the other half; it can't be decrypted. Bob cannot read any part of Alice's message until step (6); Alice cannot read any part of Bob's message until step (7). There are a number of ways to do this:

- If the encryption algorithm is a block algorithm, half of each block (for example, every other bit) could be sent in each half message.

- Decryption of the message could be dependent on an initialization vector (see Section 8.1.3), which would be sent with the second half of the message.

- The first half of the message could be a one-way hash function of the encrypted message (see Section 2.4), and the encrypted message itself could be the second half.

To see how this causes a problem for Mallet, let's review his attempt to subvert the protocol. He can still substitute his own public keys for Alice's and Bob's in steps (1) and (2). But now, when he intercepts half of Alice's message in step (3), he cannot decrypt it with his private key and re-encrypt it with Bob's public key. He has to invent a totally new message and send half of it to Bob. When he intercepts half of Bob's message to Alice in step (4), he has the same problem. He cannot decrypt it with his private key and re-encrypt it with Alice's public key. He has to invent a totally new message and send half of it to Alice. By the time he intercepts the second halves of the real messages in steps (5) and (6), it is too late for him to change the new messages he invented. The conversation between Alice and Bob will necessarily be completely different.

Mallet could possibly get away with this scheme. If he knows Alice and Bob well enough to mimic both sides of a conversation between them, they might never realize that they are being duped. But surely this is much harder than sitting between the two of them, intercepting and reading their messages.

Key Exchange with Digital Signatures

Implementing digital signatures during a session-key exchange protocol circumvents this man-in-the-middle attack as well. A KDC signs both Alice's and Bob's public keys. The signed keys include a signed certification of ownership. When Alice and Bob receive the keys, they each verify the KDC's signature. Now they know that the public key belongs to that other person. The key exchange protocol can then proceed.

Mallet has serious problems. He cannot impersonate either Alice or Bob because he doesn't know either of their private keys. He cannot substitute his public key for either of theirs because it isn't signed by the KDC. All he can do is listen to the encrypted traffic go back and forth or disrupt the lines of communication and prevent Alice and Bob from talking.

This protocol also uses a KDC, but the risk of compromising the KDC is much less. If Mallet breaks into the KDC, all he gets is the KDC's private key. This key enables him only to sign new keys; it does not let him decrypt any session keys or read any message traffic. To be able to read the traffic, Mallet has to be able to impersonate a user on the network and trick legitimate users into encrypting messages with his phony public key.

Mallet can launch that kind of attack. With the KDC's private key, he can create phony signed keys to fool both Alice and Bob. Then, he can either exchange them in the database for real signed keys, or he can intercept users' database requests and reply with his phony keys. This enables him to launch a man-in-the-middle attack and read people's communications.

This attack will work, but remember that Mallet has to be a powerful attacker. Intercepting and modifying messages is a lot more difficult than passively sitting on a symmetric network and reading messages as they go by. Active wiretaps are much harder to put in place and much easier to detect. On a broadcast channel, such as a radio network, it is almost impossible to replace one message with another.

Key and Message Transmission

There is no reason for Alice and Bob to complete the key-exchange protocol before exchanging messages. In this protocol, Alice sends Bob the message, M, without any previous key-exchange protocol:

(1) Alice generates a random session key, K, and encrypts M using K.

$$E_K(M)$$

(2) Alice gets Bob's public key from the database.

(3) Alice encrypts K with Bob's public key.

$$E_B(K)$$

(4) Alice sends both the encrypted message and encrypted session key to Bob.

$$E_K(M), E_B(K)$$

(For added security against man-in-the-middle attacks, Alice can sign the transmission.)

(1) Bob decrypts Alice's session key, K, using his private key.

(2) Bob decrypts Alice's message using the session key.

This is how public-key cryptography is most often used in a communications system. It can be combined with digital signatures, timestamps, and any other security protocols.

Key and Message Broadcast

There is no reason Alice can't send the encrypted message to several people. In this example, Alice will send the encrypted message to Bob, Carol, and Dave:

(1) Alice generates a random session key, K, and encrypts M using K.

$$E_K(M)$$

(2) Alice gets Bob's, Carol's, and Dave's public keys from the database.

(3) Alice encrypts K with Bob's public key, encrypts K with Carol's public key, and then encrypts K with Dave's public key.

$$E_B(K),\ E_C(K),\ E_D(K)$$

(4) Alice broadcasts the encrypted message and all the encrypted keys to anybody who cares to receive it.

(5) Only Bob, Carol, and Dave can decrypt the K key using his or her private key.

(6) Only Bob, Carol, and Dave can decrypt Alice's message using K.

This protocol can be implemented on a store-and-forward network. A central server can forward Alice's message to Bob, Carol, and Dave along with their particular encrypted key. The server doesn't have to be secure or trusted, since it will not be able to decrypt any of the messages.

3.2   AUTHENTICATION

When Alice logs into a computer (or an automatic teller, or a telephone banking system, for example), how does the computer know who she is? How does the computer know she is not someone else trying to falsify her identity? Traditionally, passwords solve this problem. Alice enters her password, and the computer confirms that it is correct. Both Alice and the computer know this secret piece of knowledge, and the computer requests it from Alice every time she tries to log in.

What several cryptographers realized is that the computer does not need to know the passwords; the computer just has to be able to differentiate valid passwords from invalid passwords. This is easy with one-way functions [320,621,715,879]. Instead of storing passwords, the computer stores one-way functions of the passwords.

(1) Alice sends the computer her password.

(2) The computer performs a one-way function on the password.

(3) The host compares the result of the one-way function to the value stored in the computer.

Since the computer no longer stores a table of everybody's valid password, the threat of someone breaking into the computer and stealing the password list is mitigated. The list of passwords operated on by the one-way function is useless, because the one-way function cannot be reversed to recover the passwords.

Dictionary Attacks and Salt

Even a file of passwords encrypted with a one-way function is vulnerable. In his spare time, Mallet compiles a list of the 100,000 most common passwords. He operates on all 100,000 of them with the one-way function and stores the results.

If each password is about eight bytes, the resulting file will be no more than 800K; it will fit on a single floppy disk. Now, Mallet steals the encrypted password file. He compares the encrypted password with his file of encrypted possible passwords and sees what matches.

This is a **dictionary attack,** and it's surprisingly successful (see Section 7.2.1). **Salt** is a way to make it more difficult.

Salt is a random string that is concatenated with the password before being operated on by the one-way function. Then, both the salt value and the result of the one-way function are stored in the database. If the number of possible salt values is large enough, this practically eliminates a dictionary attack against commonly used passwords. This is a simple attempt at an **Initialization Vector** (see Section 8.1.3).

A lot of salt is needed. Most UNIX systems use only twelve bits of salt. Even with that, Daniel Klein developed a password-guessing program that cracks 21% of the passwords on a given system in about a week [482]. David Feldmeier and Philip Karn compiled a list of about 732,000 common passwords concatenated with each of 4096 possible salt values. They estimate that 30% of passwords on a given system can be broken with this list [346].

Salt isn't a panacea; increasing the number of salt bits won't solve everything. Salt only protects against general dictionary attacks on a password file, not against a concerted attack on a single password. It obscures people who have the same password on multiple machines, but doesn't make poorly chosen passwords any better.

User Identification with Public-Key Cryptography

Even with salt, the above protocol has serious security problems. First, when Alice types her password into the system, anyone who has access to her data path can read it. She might be accessing her computer through a convoluted transmission path that passes through four industrial competitors, three foreign countries, or two forward-thinking universities, and a partridge in a pear tree. Any one of those points can have an Eve listening to Alice's log-in sequence. Second, anyone with access to the processor memory of the computer system can see the password before the system encrypts it.

Public-key cryptography can solve this problem. The host computer keeps a file of every user's public key; all users keep their own private key. Here is a naive attempt at a protocol. When logging in, the protocol proceeds as follows:

(1) The host sends Alice a random string.

(2) Alice encrypts the string with her private key and sends it back to the host, along with her identity.

(3) The host looks up Alice's public key in its database and decrypts the message using that public key.

(4) If the decrypted string matches what the host sent Alice in the first place, the host allows Alice access to the system.

No one else has access to Alice's private key, so no one else can impersonate the user. More important, Alice never sends her private key over the transmission line to the host. Eve, listening in on the interaction, cannot get any information that would enable her to deduce the private key and impersonate Alice.

The private key is both long and non-mnemonic, and will probably be processed automatically by the user's hardware or communications software. This requires an intelligent terminal that Alice trusts, but neither the host nor the communications path needs to be secure.

In general, it is foolish to encrypt random strings sent by another party; attacks similar to the one discussed in Section 12.4 can be mounted.

In general, secure proof-of-identity protocols take the following form:

(1) Alice performs a computation based on some random numbers and her secret key and sends the result to the host.

(2) The host sends Alice a different random number.

(3) Alice makes a computation based on the random numbers (both the ones she generated and the one she received from the host) and her secret key and sends the result to the host.

(4) The host does a computation on the various numbers received from Alice and her public key to verify that she knows her private key.

(5) If she does, her identity is verified.

If Alice does not trust the host any more than the host does not trust Alice, then Alice will then require the host to prove its identity.

Step (1) might seem unnecessary and confusing, but it is required to prevent attacks against the protocol. Section 12.7 and Section 13.1 mathematically describe several algorithms and protocols. See also [527].

Mutual Authentication Using the Interlock Protocol

Alice and Bob are two users who want to authenticate each other. Each of them has a password: Alice has P_A and Bob has P_B. Here's a protocol that will not work:

(1) Alice and Bob trade public keys.

(2) Alice encrypts P_A with Bob's public key and sends it to him.

(3) Bob encrypts P_B with Alice's public key and sends it to her.

(4) Alice decrypts P_B and verifies that it is correct.

(5) Bob decrypts P_A and verifies that it is correct.

The problem is that Mallet can launch a successful man-in-the-middle attack (see Section 3.1):

(1) Alice and Bob trade public keys. Mallet intercepts both messages. He substitutes his public key for Bob's and sends it to Alice, then he substitutes his public key for Alice's and sends it to Bob.

(2) Alice encrypts P_A with "Bob's" public key and sends it to him. Mallet intercepts the message, decrypts P_A with his private key, re-encrypts it with Bob's public key and sends it on to him.

(3) Bob encrypts P_B with Alice's public key and sends it to her. Mallet intercepts the message, decrypts P_B with his private key, re-encrypts it with Alice's public key, and sends it on to her.

(4) Alice decrypts P_B and verifies that it is correct.

(5) Bob decrypts P_A and verifies that it is correct.

From what Alice and Bob see, nothing is different. However, Mallet knows both P_A and P_B.

Davies and Price describe how the interlock protocol can defeat this attack [249]:

(1) Alice and Bob trade public keys.

(2) Alice encrypts P_A with Bob's public key and sends half of it to him.

(3) Bob encrypts P_B with Alice's public key and sends half of it to her.

(4) Alice sends the other half of encrypted P_A to Bob.

(5) Bob combines the two halves, decrypts P_A, and verifies that it is correct.

(6) Bob sends the other half of encrypted P_B to Alice.

(7) Alice combines the two halves, decrypts P_B, and verifies that it is correct.

Steve Bellovin and Michael Merritt discuss ways to attack this protocol [60]. If Alice is a user and Bob is a host, Mallet can pretend to be Bob, complete steps (1) through (5) of the protocol with Alice, and then drop the connection. True artistry demands Mallet do this by simulating line noise or network failure, but the final result is that Mallet has Alice's password. He can then connect with Bob and complete the protocol. Voilà. Mallet now has Bob's password.

The protocol can be modified so that Bob gives his password before Alice, under the assumption that the user's password is much more sensitive than the host's password. This falls to a more complicated attack, also described in [60].

SKID

SKID2 and SKID3 are secret-key identification protocols developed for RACE's RIPE project [727] (see Section 18.8). They use a keyed one-way hash function (a MAC) to provide security, and both assume that both Alice and Bob share a secret key, K.

SKID2 allows Bob to prove his identity to Alice. Here's the protocol:

(1) Alice chooses a random number, RA. (The RIPE document specifies a 64-bit number.) She sends it to Bob.

(2) Bob chooses a random number, RB. (The RIPE document specifies a 64-bit number.) He sends Alice:

$RB,HK(RA,RB,\text{Bob})$

HK is the MAC. (The RIPE document suggests the RIPE-MAC function—see Section 14.14.) Bob is Bob's name.

(3) Alice computes $HK(RA,RB,\text{Bob})$ and compares it with what she received from Bob. If the results are identical, then Alice knows that she is communicating with Bob.

SKID3 provides mutual authentication between Alice and Bob. Steps (1) through (3) are identical to SKID2, and then the protocol proceeds with:

(4) Alice sends Bob:

$HK(RB,\text{Alice})$

Alice is Alice's name.

(5) Bob computes $HK(RB,\text{Alice})$, and compares it with what he received from Bob. If the results are identical, then Bob knows that he is communicating with Alice.

3.3   AUTHENTICATION AND KEY EXCHANGE

These protocols solve a general computer problem: Alice and Bob are sitting on other ends of the network. They want to talk securely. How can Alice and Bob exchange a secret key and at the same time each be sure they are talking to the other and not to Mallet?

Wide-Mouth Frog

The Wide-Mouth Frog protocol [180] is probably the simplest symmetric key-management protocol that uses a trusted server. Both Alice and Bob share a secret key with Trent. These keys are themselves distributed secretly and authentically over some external channel, which we shall assume to be secure. The keys are just used for key distribution and not to encrypt any actual messages between users. Just by using two messages, a session key is transferred from Alice to Bob:

(1) Alice concatenates a timestamp, T_A, Bob's name, B, and a random session key, K, and encrypts the whole message with the key she shares with Trent. She sends this to Trent, along with her identifier, A.

$A,E_A(T_A,B,K)$

(2) Trent concatenates a timestamp, T_B, Alice's name, and the random session key and encrypts the whole message with the key he shares with Bob. Trent sends it to Bob:

$$E_B(T_B,A,K)$$

The biggest assumption made in this protocol is that Alice is competent enough to generate good session keys. Remember that random numbers aren't easy to generate; it might be more than Alice can be trusted to do properly.

Yahalom

This protocol is by Yahalom [180]. Like the previous protocol, both Alice and Bob share a secret key with Trent.

(1) Alice concatenates her name and a random number, R_A, and sends it to Bob.

$$A,R_A$$

(2) Bob concatenates Alice's name, Alice's random number, another random number, R_B, and encrypts it with the key he shares with Trent. He sends this to Trent, along with his name.

$$B,E_B(A,R_A,R_B)$$

(3) Trent generates two messages. The first consists of Bob's name, a random session key for Alice and Bob, K, Alice's random number, and Bob's random number, all encrypted with the key he shares with Alice. The second consists of Alice's name and the random session key, encrypted with the key he shares with Bob. He sends both messages to Alice.

$$E_A(B,K,R_A,R_B),E_B(A,K)$$

(4) Alice decrypts the message encrypted with her key, extracts K, and confirms that R_A has the same value as it did in step (1). Alice sends Bob two messages. The first is the message received from Trent, encrypted with Bob's key. The second is R_B, encrypted with the session key.

$$E_B(A,K),E_K(R_B)$$

(5) Bob decrypts the message encrypted with his key, extracts K, and confirms that R_B has the same value as it did in step (2).

At the end, Alice and Bob are each convinced that they are talking to the other and not to a third party. The novelty here is that Bob is the first one to contact Trent, who only sends one message to Alice.

Needham and Schroeder

This protocol, invented by Needham and Schroeder [645], also uses symmetric cryptography and Trent.

(1) Alice sends a message to Trent consisting of her name, A, Bob's name, B, and some random value R_A.

$$(A,B,R_A)$$

(2) Trent generates a random session key, K. He encrypts a message consisting of K and Alice's name with the secret key he shares with Bob. Then he encrypts Alice's random value, Bob's name, the key, and the encrypted message with the secret key he shares with Alice. Finally, he sends her the encrypted message:

$$E_A(R_A,B,K,E_B(K,A))$$

(3) Alice decrypts the message and extracts K. She confirms that R_A is the same value that she sent Trent in step (1). Then she sends Bob the message that Trent encrypted in his key.

$$E_B(K,A)$$

(4) Bob decrypts the message and extracts K. He then generates another random value, R_B. He encrypts the message with K and sends it to Alice.

$$E_K(R_B)$$

(5) Alice decrypts the message with K. She generates R_B-1 and encrypts it with K. Then she sends the message back to Bob.

$$E_K(R_B-1)$$

(6) Bob decrypts the message with K and verifies that it is R_B-1.

All of this fussing around with R_A and R_B and R_B-1 is to guarantee that there are no replay attacks. The presence of R_A in step (3) assures Alice that Trent's message is legitimate and not a replay of an old response from a previous execution of the protocol. When Alice successfully decrypts R_B and sends Bob R_B-1 in step (5), Bob is ensured that Alice's messages are not replays from earlier executions of the protocol.

The biggest security problem with this protocol is that old session keys are valuable. If Mallet gets access to an old K, he can launch a successful attack [272]. All he has to do is record Alice's messages to Bob in step (3). Then, once he has K, he can pretend to be Alice:

(1) Mallet sends Bob the following message:

$$E_B(K,A)$$

(2) Bob extracts K, generates R_B, and sends "Alice":

$$E_K(R_B)$$

(3) Mallet intercepts the message, decrypts it with K, and sends Bob:

$$E_K(R_B-1)$$

(4) Bob verifies that "Alice's" message is R_B-1.

Now, Mallet has Bob convinced that he is Alice.

A stronger protocol, using timestamps, can defeat this attack [272]. This protocol requires a secure and accurate system clock, not a trivial problem in itself. This modified protocol is the basis for the Kerberos authentication protocols (see Section 17.4).

There are even more drastic consequences if K_A is ever compromised. Mallet can use it to obtain session keys to talk with Bob (or anyone else he wishes to talk to). Even worse, Mallet can continue to do this even after Alice changes her key [47].

Needham and Schroeder attempted to correct these problems in a modified version of their protocol [646]. Their new protocol is essentially the same as the Otway-Rees protocol, published in the same issue of the same journal.

Otway-Rees

Otway and Rees's protocol also uses symmetric cryptography [684]. As usual, Trent shares a separate key with everyone on the network.

(1) Alice generates a message consisting of an index number, I, her name, A, Bob's name, B, and a random number, R_A, all encrypted in the key she shares with Trent. She sends this message to Bob along with the index number, her name, and his name:

$$I,A,B,E_A(R_A,I,A,B)$$

(2) Bob generates a message consisting of a new random number, R_B, the index number, Alice's name, and Bob's name, all encrypted in the key he shares with Trent. He sends it to Trent, along with Alice's encrypted message, the index number, her name, and his name:

$$I,A,B,E_A(R_A,I,A,B),E_B(R_B,I,A,B)$$

(3) Trent generates a random session key, K. Then he creates two messages. One is Alice's random number and the session key, encrypted in the key he shares with Alice. The other is Bob's random number and the session key, encrypted in the key he shares with Bob. He sends these two messages, along with the index number, to Bob:

$$I,E_A(R_A,K),E_B(R_B,K)$$

(4) Bob sends Alice the message encrypted in her key, along with the index number:

$$I,E_A(R_A,K)$$

Assuming that all the random numbers match, and the index number hasn't changed along the way, Alice and Bob are now convinced of each other's identity, and they have a secret key with which to communicate.

Kerberos

Kerberos has been implemented and is discussed in detail in Section 17.4. The basic Kerberos Version 5 protocol is as follows: Alice and Bob each share keys with Trent. Alice wants to generate a session key for a conversation with Bob.

(1) Alice sends a message to Trent with her identity, A, and Bob's identity, B.

A,B

(2) Trent generates a message with a timestamp, T, a lifetime, L, a random session key, K, and Alice's identity. He encrypts this in the key he shares with Bob. Then he takes the timestamp, the lifetime, the session key, and Bob's identity, and encrypts this in the key he shares with Alice:

$E_A(T,L,K,B),E_B(T,L,K,A)$

(3) Alice generates a message with her identity and the timestamp, encrypts it in K, and sends it to Bob. Alice also sends Bob the message encrypted in Bob's key from Trent.

$E_K(A,T),E_B(T,L,K,A)$

(4) Bob sends a message consisting of the timestamp plus one, encrypts it in K, and sends it to Alice.

$E_K(T+1)$

This protocol works, but it assumes that everyone's clocks are synchronized with Trent's clock. In practice, the effect is obtained by synchronizing clocks to within a few minutes of a secure time server and detecting replays within the time interval.

SPX

The SPX protocols, developed at Digital Equipment Corporation, also provide for mutual authentication and key exchange [851,850]. Unlike the other protocols, SPX uses both public-key and symmetric cryptography. Alice and Bob each has a private key. Trent has signed copies of their public keys.

(1) Alice sends a message to Trent, consisting of Bob's identity, B.

B

(2) Trent sends Alice Bob's public key, K_B, signed in Trent's private key, T.

$S_T(K_B)$

(3) Alice verifies Trent's signature to confirm that the key she received is actually Bob's public key. She generates a random secret key, K, and a random public-key/private-key key pair: K_P. She encrypts the time, T_A, with K. Then she signs a key lifetime, L, her identification, A, and K_P with

her private key, K_A. Finally, she encrypts K with Bob's public key, and signs it with K_P. She sends all of this to Bob.

$$E_K(T_A),\ S_{K_A}(L,A,K_P), S_{K_P}(K_B(K))$$

(4) Bob sends a message to Trent (this may be a different Trent), consisting of Alice's identity.

$$A$$

(5) Trent sends Bob Alice's public key, signed in Trent's private key.

$$S_T(K_A)$$

(6) Bob verifies Trent's signature to confirm that the key he received is actually Alice's public key. He then verifies Alice's signature and recovers K_P. He verifies the signature and uses his private key to recover K. Then he decrypts T_A to make sure this is a current message.

(7) If mutual authentication is required, Bob encrypts a new timestamp, T_B, with K, and sends it to Alice.

$$E_K(T_B)$$

(8) Alice decrypts T_B with K to make sure that the message is current.

DEC has a working implementation of the SPX protocols. Additional information can be found in [18].

Other Protocols

There are many other protocols in the literature. The CCITT X.509 protocols are discussed in Section 17.6. KryptoKnight is discussed in Section 17.5. Another protocol, Encrypted Key Exchange, is discussed in Section 16.2.

3.4 MULTIPLE-KEY PUBLIC-KEY CRYPTOGRAPHY

In public-key cryptography, there are two keys. A message encrypted with one key can be decrypted with the other. Usually one key is private and the other is public. However, let's assume that Alice has one key and Bob has the other. Now Alice can encrypt a message so that only Bob can decrypt it, and Bob can encrypt a message so that only Alice can read it.

This concept was generalized by Colin Boyd [134]. Imagine a variant of public-key cryptography with three keys: K_A, K_B, and K_C. Alice has the first, Bob the second, and Carol the third. In addition, Dave has both K_A and K_B. Ellen has both K_B and K_C. Frank has both K_C and K_A. Any number of keys can be used to encrypt a message. The remaining keys are required to decrypt that message.

Alice can encrypt a message with K_A so that Ellen, with K_B and K_C, can decrypt it, as can Bob and Carol in collusion. Bob can encrypt a message so that Frank can read it, and Carol can encrypt a message so that Dave can read it. Dave can encrypt a message with K_A so that Ellen can read it, with K_B so that Frank can read it, or with both K_A and K_B so that Carol can read it. Similarly, Ellen can encrypt a message so that either Alice, Dave, or Frank can read it. No other pairs can communicate. This is summarized in Table 3.1:

TABLE **3.1**
Three-Key Message Encryption

ENCRYPTED WITH KEYS:	MUST BE DECRYPTED WITH KEYS:
K_A	K_B and K_C
K_B	K_A and K_C
K_C	K_A and K_B
K_A and K_B	K_C
K_A and K_C	K_B
K_B and K_C	K_A

This can be extended to n keys. If a certain subset of the keys is used to encrypt the message, then the other keys are required to decrypt the message.

Broadcasting a Message

Imagine that you have three operatives out in the field: Alice, Bob, and Carol. You want to be able to send messages to subsets of them but don't know which subsets in advance. You can either encrypt the message separately for each person or give out keys for every possible combination. The first option requires a lot more communications traffic; the second requires a lot more keys.

Multiple-key cryptography is much easier. You give Alice K_A and K_B, Bob K_B and K_C, and Carol K_C and K_A. Now you can talk to any subset you want. If you want to send a message so that only Alice can read it, encrypt it with K_C. When Alice receives the message, she decrypts it with K_A and then K_B. If you want to send a message so that only Bob can read it, encrypt it with K_A; so that only Carol can read it, with K_B. If you want to send a message so that both Alice and Bob can read it, encrypt it with K_A and K_C, and so on.

This might not seem exciting, but with 100 operatives one can appreciate the ease of this scheme. If you want to send messages to subsets of those operatives, you have three choices: you can share a key with each operative (100 keys total) and send individual messages. You can distribute $2^{100}-1$ keys to account for every possible subset. Or, you can use this scheme; it works with only one encrypted message and 100 different keys.

There are other techniques for message broadcasting. These are discussed in Section 16.4.

3.5   SECRET SPLITTING

Imagine that you've invented a new, extra gooey, extra sweet, cream filling. Perhaps you've made a burger sauce that is even more tasteless than your competitors'. This is important; you have to keep it secret. You could tell only your most trusted employees the exact mixture of ingredients, but what if one of them defects to the competition? There goes the secret, and before long every grease palace on the block will be making burgers with sauce as tasteless as yours.

This calls for **secret splitting.** There are ways to take a message and divide it up into pieces [338]. Each piece by itself means nothing, but put them together and the message appears. If each employee has a piece of the recipe, then only together can they make the sauce. If any employee resigns with one piece of the recipe, the information is useless by itself.

The simplest sharing problem splits a message between two people. Here's a protocol in which Trent can split a message between Alice and Bob:

(1) Trent generates a random bit string, R, the same length as the message, M.

(2) Trent XORs M with R to generate P.

M XOR $R = P$

(3) Trent gives P to Alice and R to Bob.

To reconstruct the message, Alice and Bob have only one step to do:

(4) Alice and Bob XOR their pieces together to reconstruct the message:

P XOR $R = M$

This technique, if done properly, is absolutely secure. Each piece, by itself, is absolutely worthless. Only together can Alice and Bob reconstruct the message.

Essentially, Trent is encrypting the message with a one-time pad and giving the ciphertext to one person and the pad to the other person. Section 1.2.4 discusses one-time pads; they have perfect security. No amount of computing power can determine the message from one of the pieces.

It is easy to extend this scheme to more people. To split a message among more than two people, XOR more random bit strings into the mixture. In this example, Trent divides up a message into four pieces:

(1) Trent generates three random bit strings, R, S, and T, the same length as the message, M.

(2) Trent XORs M with the three pieces to generate P:

M XOR R XOR S XOR $T = P$

(3) Trent gives P to Alice, R to Bob, S to Carol, and T to Dave.

And here are Alice, Bob, and Carol reconstructing the message:

(4) Alice, Bob, and Carol get together and compute:

$$P \text{ XOR } R \text{ XOR } S \text{ XOR } T = M$$

This is an adjudicated protocol. Trent has absolute power and can do whatever he wants. He can hand out gibberish and claim that they are valid pieces of the secret; no one will know it until they try to reconstruct the secret. He can hand out a piece to Alice, Bob, Carol, and Dave, and later tell everyone that only Alice, Carol, and Dave are needed to reconstruct the secret, and then he can fire Bob. But since this is Trent's secret to divide up, this isn't a problem.

However, there is a problem with this protocol: if any of the pieces gets lost, so does the message. So if Carol, who has a piece of the sauce recipe, goes to work for the competition and takes her piece with her, the rest of them are out of luck. She can't reproduce the recipe, but neither can Alice, Bob, or Dave. All Alice, Bob, and Dave, combined, know is the length of the message—nothing more. Her piece is as critical to the message as every other piece combined. The next section shows how to fix this problem.

3.6   SECRET SHARING

You're setting up a launch program for a nuclear missile. You want to make sure that no single raving lunatic can initiate a launch. You want to make sure that no two raving lunatics can initiate a launch. You want at least three out of five officers to be raving lunatics before you allow a launch.

This is an easy problem to solve. Make a mechanical launch controller. Give each of the five officers a key and require that at least three officers stick their keys in the proper slots before you'll allow them to blow up whomever we're blowing up this week. (If you're really worried, make the slots far apart and require the officers to insert the keys simultaneously—you wouldn't want an officer who steals two keys to be able to vaporize an entire city.)

We can get even more complicated. Maybe the general and two colonels can launch the missile, but if the general is busy playing golf then five colonels have to get together. Make the launch controller so that it requires five keys. Give the general three keys and the colonels one each. The general together with any two colonels can launch the missile. So can the five colonels, but a general and one colonel cannot; neither can four colonels.

A more complicated sharing scheme, called a **threshold scheme,** can do all of this and more. At its simplest level, you can take any message (e.g., a secret recipe, launch codes, or even a laundry list) and divide it into n pieces, called **shadows,** such that any m of them can be used to reconstruct the message. More precisely, this is called an **(m,n)-threshold scheme.**

With a (3,4)-threshold scheme, Trent can divide his secret sauce recipe among Alice, Bob, Carol, and Dave, such that any three of them can put their shadows together and reconstruct the message. If Carol is on vacation, Alice, Bob, and Dave can do it. If Bob gets run over by a bus, Alice, Carol, and Dave can do it. However, if Bob gets run over by a bus while Carol is on vacation, Alice and Dave can't reconstruct the message.

Threshold schemes are far more versatile than that. Any sharing scenario can be modeled using this scheme. You can divide a message among the people in your building so that you need seven people from the first floor and five people from the second floor, unless there is someone from the third floor, in which case you only need that person and three people from the first floor and two people from the second floor, unless there is someone from the fourth floor, in which case you need that person and one person from the third floor, or that person and two people from the first floor and one person from the second floor, and so on.

This idea was invented independently by Adi Shamir [788] and G. R. Blakley [117]. There are several different algorithms, discussed in Section 16.5.

Secret Sharing with Cheaters

There are many ways to cheat with a threshold scheme. Here are just a few of them:

Scenario 1: Colonels Alice, Bob, and Carol are in a bunker deep below somewhere. One day, they get a coded message from the president: "Launch those missiles. We're going to eradicate the last vestiges of neural network research in the country." Alice, Bob, and Carol reveal their shadows, but Carol enters a random number. She's actually a pacifist and doesn't want the missiles launched. Since Carol doesn't enter the correct shadow, the secret they recover is the wrong secret. The missiles stay in their silos. Even worse, no one knows why. Alice and Bob, even if they work together, cannot prove that Carol's shadow is invalid.

Scenario 2: Colonels Alice and Bob are sitting in the bunker with Mallet. Mallet has disguised himself as a colonel, and none of the others is the wiser. The same message comes in from the president, and everyone reveals their shadows. "Ha, Ha!" shouts Mallet. "I faked that message from the president. Now I know both of your shadows." He races up the staircase and escapes before anyone can catch him.

Scenario 3: Colonels Alice, Bob, and Carol are sitting in the bunker with Mallet, who is again disguised. The same message comes in from the president, and everyone reveals their shadows. Mallet reveals his shadow only after he has heard the other three. Since the other three reconstruct the secret, he quickly creates a valid shadow and reveals that. Now, not only does he know the secret, but no one realizes that he isn't part of the scheme.

Some protocols that handle these sorts of cheaters are discussed in Section 16.5.

Secret Sharing Without Trent

A bank wants its vault to open only if three out of five officers enter their keys. This sounds like a basic (3,5)-threshold scheme, except there is a catch. No one is to know the entire secret. There is no Trent to divide the secret up into five pieces. There are protocols by which the five officers can create a secret and each get a piece, such that none of the officers knows the secret until they all reconstruct it. See [443] for further details about this protocol.

3.7   CRYPTOGRAPHIC PROTECTION OF DATABASES

The membership database of a professional organization is a valuable commodity. On the one hand, you want to distribute the database to all members. You want them to communicate with one another, exchange ideas, and invite each other over for tea. On the other hand, if you distribute copies of the membership database to everyone, copies are bound to fall into the hands of insurance salesmen and other annoying purveyors of junk mail.

Cryptography can ameliorate this problem. We can encrypt the database in such a way that it is easy to extract the address of a single person but hard to extract a mailing list of all the members.

The scheme, from [337,336], is straightforward. Choose a one-way hash function and a symmetric encryption algorithm. Each record of the database consists of two fields. The index field is the last name of the member, operated on by the one-way hash function. The data field is the full name and address of the member, encrypted using the last name as the key.

Searching for a member with a specific last name is easy. First, hash the last name and look for the hashed value in the index field of the database. If there is a match, then there is a person in the database with the last name. If there are several matches, then there are several people in the database with the last name. Finally, for each matching entry, decrypt the full name and address using the last name as the key.

In [337] the authors use this system to protect a natural-language dictionary of 6000 Spanish verbs. They report minimal performance degradation due to the encryption. Additional complications in [336] handle searching on multiple indexes, but the idea is the same. The primary problem with this system is that it's impossible to search for people when you don't know how to spell their name. You can try variant spellings until you find the correct one, but it isn't practical to scan through everyone whose name begins with "Sch" when looking for "Schneier."

This protection isn't perfect. It is possible for a particularly persistent salesperson to reconstruct the membership database by trying every possible last name. If he or she has a telephone database, that can be used. This might take a few weeks of dedicated computer crunching, but it can be done. Still, it makes the job harder.

Another approach, in [120], allows statistics to be compiled on encrypted data.

3.8   TIMESTAMPING SERVICES

There are many situations in which people need to certify that a document existed on a certain date. Think about a copyright or patent dispute: the party that can produce the earliest copy of the disputed work wins the case. There are many ways to do this with paper documents. Notaries can sign documents; lawyers can safeguard copies. If a dispute arises, the notary or the lawyer provides testimony that the letter existed on a certain date. (Of course, it is easy to send an unsealed empty envelope to yourself and then fill it with a letter at a later date.)

In the digital world, this is far more complicated. There is no way to examine a digital document for signs of tampering. They can be copied and modified endlessly without anyone being the wiser. It's trivial to change the date stamp on a computer file. No one can look at a digital document and say: "Yes, this document was created before December 10th, 1942."

Stuart Haber and W. Scott Stornetta at Bellcore thought about the problem [411,412,48]. They wanted a digital timestamping protocol that has the following three properties:

- The data itself must be timestamped, without any regard to the physical medium on which it resides.

- It must be impossible to change even one bit of the document without that change being apparent.

- It must be impossible to timestamp a document with a date and time different from the actual one.

Arbitrated Solution

This protocol uses Trent, who has a trusted timestamping service. Of course, Alice wishes to timestamp a document.

(1) Alice transmits a copy of the document to Trent.

(2) Trent records the date and time he received the document and retains a copy of the document for safekeeping.

Now, if anyone called into question Alice's claim of when the document was created, she just has to call up Trent. He will produce his copy of the document and verify that he received the document on the date stamped.

This protocol works, but has some obvious problems. First, there is no privacy. Alice has to give a copy of the document to Trent. Anyone listening in on the communications channel could read it. She could encrypt it, but still the document has to sit in Trent's databanks. Who knows how secure that databank is?

Second, the databank itself would have to be huge, since the storage requirements would be so great. And the bandwidth requirements to send large documents to Trent would be enormous.

The third problem has to do with the potential errors. An error in transmission, or a magnetic failure somewhere in Trent's central computers, could completely invalidate Alice's claim of a timestamp.

Fourth, there might not be someone as honest as Trent to run the timestamping service. Maybe Alice is using Bob's Time Stamp and Taco Stand. There is nothing to stop Alice and Bob from colluding and timestamping a document with any time that they want.

Improved Arbitrated Solution

One-way hash functions and digital signatures can clear up most of the problems easily:

(1) Alice produces a one-way hash of the document.

(2) Alice transmits the hash to Trent.

(3) Trent appends the date and time he received the hash onto the hash and then digitally signs the result.

(4) Trent sends the signed hash and timestamp back to Alice.

This solves every problem but the last. Alice no longer has to worry about revealing the contents of her document; the hash is sufficient. Trent no longer has to store copies of the document (or even of the hash), so the massive storage requirements and security problems are solved (remember, one-way hash functions don't have a key). Alice can immediately examine the signed timestamp she receives in step (4), so she will immediately catch any transmission errors. The only problem remaining is that Alice and Trent can still collude to produce any timestamp they want.

Linking Protocol

One way to solve this problem is to link Alice's timestamp with the previously received timestamps. Since the order that Trent receives the different timestamp requests can't be known in advance, Alice's timestamp must have occurred after the previous one. And since the request that came after is linked with Alice's timestamp, then hers must have occurred before. Alice's request is thus sandwiched in time.

If A identifies Alice, the hash value that Alice wants timestamped is H_n, and the previous timestamp is T_{n-1}, then the protocol is:

(1) Alice sends Trent H_n and A.

(2) Trent sends back to Alice:

$$T_n = S_K(n, A, H_n, T_n; ID_{n-1}, H_{n-1}, T_{n-1}, H(ID_{n-1}, T_{n-1}, H_{n-1}))$$

(3) Alice's name identifies her as the originator of the request. The parameter n indicates the sequence of the request: this is the nth timestamp Trent has issued. The parameter T_n is the time. The additional information is the identification, original hash, time, and hashed timestamp of the previous document Trent stamped.

(4) After Trent stamps the next document, he sends Alice the identification of the originator of that document: ID_{n+1}.

If someone challenges Alice's timestamp, she just contacts the originators of the previous and following documents: ID_{n-1} and ID_{n+1}. If their documents are called into question, they can get in touch with ID_{n-2} and ID_{n+2}, and so on. Every person can show that their document was timestamped after the one that came before and before the one that came after.

This protocol makes it very difficult for Alice and Trent to collude and produce a document stamped with a different time than the actual one. Trent cannot forward-date a document, since that would require knowing in advance what document request came before it. Even if he could fake that, he would have to know what document request came before *that,* and so on. He cannot back-date a document, because the timestamp must be embedded in the timestamps of the document issued immediately after, and that document has already been issued. The only possible way to break this scheme is to invent a fictitious chain of documents both before and after Alice's document, long enough to exhaust anyone challenging the timestamp.

Distributed Protocol

People die; timestamps get lost. Many things could happen between the timestamping and the challenge to make it impossible for Alice to get a copy of ID_{n-1}'s timestamp. This problem could be alleviated by embedding the previous ten people's timestamps into Alice's, and then sending Alice the IDs of the next ten people. Alice has a greater chance of finding people who still have their timestamp.

Along a similar line, the following protocol does away with Trent altogether.

(1) Using H_n as input, Alice generates a string of random values using a cryptographically secure pseudo-random number generator:

$$V_1, V_2, V_3 \ldots V_k$$

(2) Alice interprets each of these values as the ID of another person. She sends H_n to each of these people.

(3) Each of these people attaches the date and time to the hash, signs the result, and sends it back to Alice.

(4) Alice collects and stores all the signatures as the timestamp.

The cryptographically secure pseudo-random number generator in step (1) prevents Alice from deliberately choosing corrupt IDs as verifiers. Even if she makes trivial changes in her document in an attempt to construct a set of corrupt IDs, her chances of getting away with this are negligible. The hash function randomizes the IDs; Alice cannot force them.

This protocol works because the only way for Alice to fake a timestamp would be to convince all of the k people to cooperate. Since she chose them at random in step (1), the odds against this are very high. The more corrupt the society is, the higher a number k should be.

Additionally, there should be some mechanism for dealing with people who can't promptly return the timestamp. Some subset of k is all that would be required for a valid timestamp. The details depend on the implementation.

Further Work

Further improvements to timestamping protocols are presented in [48]. Based on an idea by Ralph Merkle [588], the authors use binary trees to increase the number of timestamps that depend on a given timestamp, reducing even further the possibility that someone could create a chain of fictitious timestamps. They also recommend publishing a hash of the day's timestamps in a public place, such as the newspaper. This serves a function similar to sending the hash to random people in the distributed protocol. In fact, Bellcore has been doing that in every Sunday's *New York Times* since 1992.

CHAPTER
4

Intermediate Protocols

4.1 SUBLIMINAL CHANNEL

Alice and Bob have been arrested and are going to jail. He's going to the male prison, and she's going to the female prison. Their only means of communication will be via messages. Walter, the warden, is willing to let Alice and Bob exchange messages, but he won't allow them to be encrypted. Walter expects that they are going to coordinate an escape plan, so he wants to be able to read everything.

Walter also hopes that he can deceive either Alice or Bob. He wants one of them to accept a fraudulent message as a genuine message from the other. Alice and Bob are willing to go along with this risk of deception, otherwise they cannot communicate at all, and they have to coordinate their plans. To do this they have to deceive the warden and find a way of communicating secretly. They have to set up a **subliminal channel,** a covert communications channel between them, in full view of Walter, even though the messages themselves contain no secret information. Through the exchange of perfectly innocuous, signed messages they will pass secret information back and forth and fool Walter, even though Walter is watching all the communications.

An easy subliminal channel might be the number of words in a sentence. An odd number of words in a sentence might correspond to "1," while an even number of words might correspond to "0." So, while you read this seemingly innocuous paragraph, I have sent my operatives in the field the message "101." The problem with that algorithm is there is no key; the security is dependent on the secrecy of the algorithm. Better security is certainly possible.

Peter Wayner's **mimic functions** obfuscate messages. These functions hide the identity of a message by modifying it so that its statistical profile resembles that of something else: the classifieds section of the *New York Times,* a play by

Shakespeare, or a newsgroup on the Internet [871,872]. There are no keys involved; this is a restricted algorithm.

Gustavus Simmons invented the concept of a subliminal channel in a conventional digital signature algorithm [821]. Since the subliminal messages are hidden in what looks like normal digital signatures, this is a form of obfuscation. Walter sees signed innocuous messages pass back and forth, but he completely misses the information being sent over the subliminal channel. In fact, the subliminal-channel signature algorithm is indistinguishable from a normal signature algorithm, at least to Walter. Walter not only cannot read the subliminal message, but he also has no idea that one is even present. (Of course, any warden who gives his prisoners computers and high-speed modems deserves what he gets.)

In general the protocol looks like this:

(1) Alice generates an innocuous message, at random.

(2) Using a secret key shared with Bob, Alice signs the innocuous message in such a way as to hide her subliminal message in the signature. (This is the meat of the subliminal channel protocol; see Section 16.6.)

(3) Alice sends this signed message to Bob via Walter.

(4) Walter reads the innocuous message and checks the signature. Finding nothing amiss, he passes the signed message to Bob.

(5) Bob checks the signature on the innocuous message, confirming that the message came from Alice.

(6) Bob ignores the innocuous message and, using the secret key he shares with Alice, extracts the subliminal message.

What about cheating? Walter doesn't trust anyone and no one trusts him. He can always prevent communication, but he has no way of introducing phony messages. Since he can't generate any valid signatures, Bob will detect his attempt in step (3). And since he does not know the shared key, he can't read the subliminal messages. Even more important, he has no idea that the subliminal messages are there. Signed messages using a digital signature algorithm look no different from signed messages with subliminal messages embedded in the signature.

Cheating between Alice and Bob is more problematic. In some implementations of a subliminal channel, the secret information Bob needs to read the subliminal message is the same information Alice needs to sign the innocuous message. If this is the case, Bob can impersonate Alice. He can sign messages purporting to come from her, and there is nothing Alice can do about it. If she is to send him subliminal messages, she has to trust him not to abuse her private key.

Other subliminal channel implementations don't have this problem. A secret key shared by Alice and Bob allows Alice to send Bob subliminal messages, but it is not the same as Alice's private key and does not allow Bob to sign messages. Alice does not have to trust Bob not to abuse her private key.

Applications of Subliminal Channel

The most obvious application of the subliminal channel is in a spy network. If everyone is sending and receiving signed messages, spies will not be noticed sending subliminal messages in signed documents. Of course, the enemy's spies can do the same thing.

Using a subliminal channel, Alice could safely sign a document under threat. She would, when signing the document, embed the subliminal message, saying, "I am being coerced." Other applications are more subtle. A company can sign documents and embed subliminal messages, allowing them to be tracked throughout the document's lifespan. The government can "mark" digital currency. A malicious signature program can leak the private key. The possibilities are endless.

Subliminal-Free Signatures

Alice and Bob are sending signed messages to each other, negotiating the terms of a contract. They use a digital signature protocol. However, this contract negotiation has been set up as a cover for Alice's and Bob's spying activities. When they use the digital signature algorithm, they don't care about the messages they are signing. They are using a subliminal channel in the signatures to send secret information to each other. The counterespionage service, however, doesn't know that the contract negotiations and the use of signed messages are just cover-ups.

The use of subliminal channels has led people to create **subliminal-free signature schemes.** These are digital signature schemes that cannot be modified to contain a subliminal channel. See [283,284].

4.2   UNDENIABLE DIGITAL SIGNATURES

The Alice Software Company distributes DEW (Do-Everything-Word™). To ensure that their software is virus-free, they include a digital signature. However, they want only legitimate buyers of the software, not pirates, to be able to verify the signature. At the same time, if copies of DEW are found containing a virus, there should be no way for the Alice Software Company to deny a valid signature.

Conventional digital signatures can be copied exactly. Sometimes this property is useful, as in the dissemination of public announcements. Other times they could be a problem. Imagine a digitally signed personal or business letter. If many copies of that document were floating around, each of which could be verified by anyone, this could lead to embarrassment or blackmail. The best solution is a digital signature that can be proven to be valid, but one that the recipient cannot show to a third party without the signer's consent.

Undeniable signatures, invented by David Chaum [207], are suited to these tasks. Like a normal digital signature, an undeniable signature depends on the signed document and the signer's private key. But unlike normal digital signatures, an undeniable signature cannot be verified without the signer's consent.

The mathematics behind this protocol can be found in Section 16.7, but the basic idea is simple:

(1) Alice presents Bob with a signature.

(2) Bob generates a random number and sends it to Alice.

(3) Alice does a calculation, using the random number and her private key, and sends Bob the result. Alice could only do this calculation if the signature is valid.

(4) Bob confirms this.

Bob can't turn around and convince Carol that Alice's signature is valid, because Carol doesn't know that Bob's numbers are random. He could have easily worked the protocol backwards on paper, without any help from Alice, and then shown Carol the result. Carol cannot be convinced that Alice's signature is valid unless she does the protocol with Alice herself. This might not make much sense now, but it will once the mathematics are shown.

This solution isn't perfect. Yvo Desmedt and Moti Yung show that it is possible, in some applications, for Bob to convince Carol that Alice's signature is valid [292].

For instance, Bob buys a legal copy of DEW. He can validate the signature on the software package whenever he wants. Then, Bob convinces Carol that he's a salesman from the Alice Software Company. He sells her a pirated copy of DEW. When Carol tries to validate the signature with Bob, he simultaneously validates the signature with Alice. When Carol sends him the random number, he then sends it to Alice. When Alice replies, he sends it to Carol. Carol is convinced that she is a legitimate buyer of the software, even though she isn't. This attack is an instance of the chess grandmaster problem and is discussed in detail in Section 5.4.

4.3   FAIL-STOP DIGITAL SIGNATURES

Let's say Eve is a very powerful adversary. She has vast computer networks, rooms full of Cray computers: orders of magnitude more computing power than Alice. All of these computers function day and night, trying to break Alice's private key. Then, finally—success. Eve can now impersonate Alice, forging her signature on documents at will.

Fail-stop digital signatures, introduced by Birgit Pfitzmann and Michael Waidner [693], prevent this kind of cheating. If Eve forges signatures in this manner, then Alice can prove they are forgeries. If Alice signs a document and then disavows the signature, claiming forgery, a court can verify that it is not a forgery.

The basic idea behind fail-stop signatures is that for every possible public key, there are many possible private keys that would work with it. Each of these private keys yields many different possible signatures. However, Alice has only one private key and can compute just one signature. Alice doesn't know any of the other private keys.

Eve is trying to break Alice's private key. (In this case, Eve could be Alice, trying to compute a second private key for herself.) She collects signed messages and, using her array of Cray computers, tries to recover her private key. Even if she manages to recover a valid private key, because there are many possible private keys, it is likely that she has discovered a different one. The probability of Eve's recovering the proper private key can be made so small as to be negligible.

Now, when Eve forges a signed document using the private key she generated, it will be a different signature than if Alice signs the document herself. When Alice is hauled off to court, she can produce two different signatures for the same message and public key (corresponding to her private key and to the private key Eve created) to prove forgery. On the other hand, if Alice cannot produce the two different signatures, there is no forgery and Alice is still bound by her signature.

This signature scheme protects against Eve's breaking Alice's signature scheme by sheer computational power; it does nothing against Mallet's much more likely attack of breaking into Alice's house and stealing her private key, or Alice's attack of signing a document and then conveniently losing her private key. Additional theory and applications of fail-stop signatures can be found in [692,694,434,435].

4.4   GROUP SIGNATURES

David Chaum introduces this problem in [200]:

> A company has several computers, each connected to the local network. Each department of that company has its own printer (also connected to the network) and only persons of that department are allowed to use their department's printer. Before printing, therefore, the printer must be convinced that the user is working in that department. At the same time, the company wants privacy; the user's name may not be revealed. If, however, someone discovers at the end of the day that a printer has been used too often, the director must be able to discover who misused that printer, and send that person a bill.

The solution to this problem is called a **group signature.** Group signatures have the following properties:

- Only members of the group can sign messages.
- The receiver of the signature can verify that it is a valid signature from the group but cannot determine which member of the group made the signature.
- In the case of a dispute, the signature can be "opened" to reveal the identity of the signer.

Group Signatures with a Trusted Arbitrator

This protocol uses a trusted arbitrator:

(1) Trent generates a large pile of public-key/private-key key pairs and gives every member of the group a different list of unique private keys. No key on any of the lists is identical.

(2) Trent publishes the master list of all public keys for the group, in random order. Trent keeps a secret record of which keys belong to whom.

(3) When group members want to sign a document, they choose a key at random from their personal list.

(4) When they want to verify that a signature belongs to the group, they look in the public database for the corresponding public key and verify the signature.

(5) In the event of a dispute, Trent knows which public key corresponds to which group member.

The problem with this protocol is that it requires that Trent is trustworthy. He knows everyone's private keys and can fake signatures. Also, all members must have a list of keys long enough to preclude attempts to analyze which keys they use.

Chaum's paper lists a number of other protocols, some in which Trent is unable to fake signatures and others in which Trent is not even required.

4.5   COMPUTING WITH ENCRYPTED DATA

Alice wants to know the solution to some function $f(x)$, for some particular value of x. Unfortunately, her computer is broken. Bob is willing to compute $f(x)$ for her, but Alice isn't so keen on letting Bob know her x. How can Alice let Bob compute $f(x)$ for her, without telling him x?

This is the general problem of **computing with encrypted data,** also called **hiding information from an oracle.** (Bob is the oracle; he answers questions.) There are ways to do this for certain functions; they are discussed in Section 16.8.

4.6   BIT COMMITMENT

The Amazing Alice, magician extraordinaire, will now perform a mystifying feat of mental prowess. She will guess the card Bob will choose before he chooses it! Watch as Alice writes her prediction on a piece of paper. Marvel as Alice puts that piece of paper in an envelope and seals it shut. Thrill as Alice hands that sealed envelope to a random member of the audience. "Pick a card, Bob, any card." He looks at it and shows it to Alice and the audience. It's the seven of diamonds. Alice now takes the envelope back from the audience. She rips it open. The prediction, written before Bob chose his card, says "seven of diamonds"! Applause.

The magic solution is that Alice switched envelopes at the end of the trick. However, cryptographic protocols can provide a method immune from any sleight of hand. Why is this useful? Here's a more mundane story:

Stockbroker Alice wants to convince investor Bob that her method of picking winning stocks is sound.

Bob: "Pick five stocks for me. If they are all winners, I'll give you my business."

Alice: "If I pick five stocks for you, you could invest in them yourself, without paying me. Why don't I show you the stocks I picked last month?"

Bob: "How do I know you didn't change last month's picks after you knew their outcome? If you tell me your picks now, I'll know that you can't change them. I won't invest in those stocks until after I've purchased your method. Trust me."

Alice: "I'd rather show you my picks from last month. I didn't change them. Trust me."

Here is the problem: Alice wants to commit to a prediction but does not want to reveal that prediction to Bob until sometime later. Bob, on the other hand, wants to make sure that Alice cannot change her mind after she has committed to her prediction.

Bit Commitment Using Symmetric Cryptography

This bit-commitment protocol uses conventional cryptography:

(1) Bob generates a random bit string, R, and sends it to Alice.

$$R$$

(2) Alice creates a message consisting of the bit she wishes to commit to, b (it can actually be several bits), and Bob's random string. She encrypts it with some random key, K, and sends the result back to Bob.

$$E_K(R,b)$$

That is the commitment portion of the protocol. Bob cannot decrypt the message, so he does not know what the bit is.

When it comes time for Alice to reveal her bit, the protocol continues:

(1) Alice sends Bob the key.

(2) Bob decrypts the message to reveal the bit. He checks his random string to verify the bit's validity.

If the message did not contain Bob's random string, Alice could secretly decrypt the message she handed Bob with a variety of keys until she found one that gave her a bit other than the one she committed to. Since the bit has only two possible values, she is certain to find one after only a few tries. Bob's random string prevents her from using this attack; she has to find a new message that not only has her bit inverted, but also has Bob's random string exactly reproduced. If the encryption algorithm is good, the chance of her finding this is miniscule. Alice cannot change her bit after she commits to it.

Bit Commitment Using One-Way Functions

This protocol uses one-way functions:

(1) Alice generates two random bit strings, R_1 and R_2.

$$R_1, R_2$$

(2) Alice creates a message consisting of her random strings and the bit she wishes to commit to (it can actually be several bits).

$$(R_1, R_2, b)$$

(3) Alice hashes the message and sends the result to Bob, as well as one of the random strings.

$$H(R_1, R_2, b), R_1$$

This transmission from Alice is evidence of commitment. Alice used a one-way function in step (3), so Bob can't invert the function and figure out the bit.

When it comes time for Alice to reveal her bit, the protocol continues:

(4) Alice sends Bob the original message.

$$(R_1, R_2, b)$$

(5) Bob hashes the message and compares it and R_1 with the hash and R_1 he received in step (3). If they match, the bit is valid.

The benefit of this protocol over the previous one is that, after the protocol is established, it requires only one-way communication: Bob does not have to talk to Alice. Alice sends Bob one message to commit to a bit and another message to reveal the bit.

Bob's random string isn't required because the result of Alice's commitment is a message operated on by a one-way hash function. Alice cannot cheat and find another message (R_1, R_2, b'), such that $f(R_{1'}, R_{2'}, b') = f(R_1, R_2, b')$. If Alice didn't send Bob R_1, then she could change the value of R_2 and then the value of the bit. The fact that Bob already knows R_1 prevents her from doing so.

Bit Commitment Using Pseudo-Random Sequence Generators

This protocol uses a pseudo-random sequence generator [631]:

(1) Bob generates a random bit string and sends it to Alice.

$$R_B$$

(2) Alice generates a random seed for a pseudo-random bit generator. Then, for every bit in Bob's random bit string, she sends Bob either:
(a) the output of the generator, if Bob's bit is zero, or
(b) the XOR of output of the generator and her bit, if Bob's bit is 1.

When it comes time for Alice to reveal her bit, the protocol continues:

(3) Alice sends Bob her random seed.

(4) Bob completes step (2) to confirm that Alice was acting fairly.

If Bob's random bit string is long enough, and the pseudo-random bit generator is unpredictable, then there is no practical way Alice can cheat.

Blobs

These strings that Alice sends to Bob to commit to a bit are sometimes called **blobs.** A blob is a sequence of bits, although there is no reason in the protocols why it has to be. As Gilles Brassard said, "They could be made out of fairy dust if this were useful" [144]. Blobs have these properties:

- Alice can commit to blobs. By committing to a blob, she is committing to a bit.

- Alice can open any blob she has committed to. When she opens a blob, she can convince Bob of the value of the bit she committed to when she committed to the blob. Thus, she cannot open any blob as both a zero and a 1.

- Bob cannot learn anything about how Alice is able to open any unopened blob she has committed to. This is true even after Alice has opened other blobs.

- Blobs do not carry any information other than the bit Alice committed to. The blobs themselves, as well as the process by which Alice commits to and opens them, are uncorrelated to anything else that Alice might wish to keep secret from Bob.

All of the above protocols satisfy these four properties.

4.7   FAIR COIN FLIPS

It's story time, with Joe Kilian [479]:

> Alice and Bob wanted to flip a fair coin, but had no physical coin to flip. Alice offered a simple way of flipping a fair coin mentally. "First, you think up a random bit, then I'll think up a random bit. We'll then exclusive-or the two bits together," she suggested.
>
> "But what if one of us doesn't flip a coin at random?" Bob asked.
>
> "It doesn't matter. As long as one of the bits is truly random, the exclusive-or of the bits should be truly random," Alice replied, and after a moment's reflection, Bob agreed.
>
> A short while later, Alice and Bob happened upon a book on artificial intelligence. A good citizen, Alice said, "One of us must pick up this book

and find a suitable waste receptacle." Bob agreed and suggested they use their coin-flipping protocol to determine who would have to throw the book away.

"If the final bit is a zero, then you will pick the book up, and if it is a one, then I will," said Alice. "What is your bit?"

Bob replied, "one."

"Why, so is mine," said Alice, slyly. "I guess this isn't your lucky day."

Needless to say, this coin flipping protocol had a serious bug. While it is true that a truly random bit, x, exclusive-ored with any independently distributed bit, y, will yield a truly random bit, Alice's protocol did not ensure that the two bits were distributed independently. In fact, it is not hard to verify that no mental protocol can allow two infinitely powerful parties to flip a fair coin. Alice and Bob were in trouble until they received a letter from an obscure graduate student in cryptography. The information in the letter was too theoretical to be of any earthly use to anyone, but the envelope the letter came in was extremely handy.

The next time Alice and Bob wished to flip a coin, they played a modified version of the original protocol. First, Bob decided on a bit, but instead of announcing it immediately, he wrote it down on a piece of paper and placed the paper in the envelope. Next, Alice announced her bit. Finally, Alice and Bob took Bob's bit out of the envelope and computed the random bit. This bit was indeed truly random whenever at least one of them played honestly. Alice and Bob had a working protocol, the cryptographer's dream of social relevance was fulfilled, and they all lived happily ever after.

Those envelopes sound a lot like bit commitment blobs. When Manuel Blum introduced the problem of flipping a fair coin over modem [122], he solved it using a bit commitment protocol:

(1) Alice commits to a random bit, using any of the bit commitment schemes listed above.

(2) Bob tries to guess the bit.

(3) Alice reveals the bit to Bob. Bob wins the flip if he correctly guessed the bit.

In general, we need a protocol with these properties:

- Alice must flip the coin before Bob guesses.

- Alice must not be able to re-flip the coin after hearing Bob's guess.

- Bob must not be able to know how the coin landed before making his guess.

There are any number of ways in which we can do this.

Coin Flipping Using One-Way Functions

If Alice and Bob can agree on a one-way function, this protocol is simple:

(1) Alice chooses a random number, x. She computes $y = f(x)$, where $f(x)$ is the one-way function.

(2) Alice sends y to Bob.

(3) Bob guesses whether x is even or odd and sends his guess to Alice.

(4) If Bob's guess is correct, the result of the coin flip is heads. If Bob's guess is incorrect, the result of the coin flip is tails. Alice announces the result of the coin flip and sends x to Bob.

(5) Bob confirms that $y = f(x)$.

The security of this protocol rests in the choice of $f(x)$. If Alice can find x and x', such that x is even and x' is odd, and $y=f(x)=f(x')$, then she can cheat Bob every time. Additionally, $f(x)$ must produce even and odd numbers with equal probability. If not, Bob can cheat Alice at least some of the time. For example, if $f(x)$ produces even numbers 75% of the time, Bob can continuously guess even in step (3) and win 75% of the coin flips.

Coin Flipping Using Public-Key Cryptography

There is another protocol that works with either public-key cryptography or symmetric cryptography. The only requirement is that the algorithm commute. That is:

$$D_{K_1}(E_{K_2}(E_{K_1}(M))) = E_{K_2}(M)$$

In general, this property is not true for symmetric algorithms, but it is true for some public-key algorithms (the RSA public-key algorithm, for example). This is the protocol:

(1) Alice and Bob both generate a public/private key pair (or, in theory, a commutative secret key).

(2) Alice generates two messages, one indicating heads and the other indicating tails. These messages should contain some unique random string, so that she can verify their authenticity later in the protocol. Alice encrypts both messages with her key and sends them to Bob.

$$E_A(M_1), E_A(M_2)$$

(3) Bob, who cannot read either message, chooses one at random. (He can flip a coin, engage a malicious computer to a vain attempt to decide which one to choose, or consult the *I Ching*—it doesn't matter.) He encrypts it with his key and sends it back to Alice.

$$E_B(E_A(M))$$

(4) Alice, who cannot read the message sent back to her, decrypts it with her key and then sends it back to Bob.

$$D_A(E_B(E_A(M))) = E_B(M_1) \text{ or } D_A(E_B(E_A(M_2))) = E_B(M_2)$$

(5) Bob decrypts the message with his key to reveal the result of the coin flip. He sends the decrypted message to Alice.

$$D_B(E_B(M_1)) = M_1 \text{ or } D_B(E_B(M_2)) = M_2$$

(6) Alice reads the result of the coin flip and verifies that the random string is correct.

(7) Both Alice and Bob reveal their keys so that both can verify that the other did not cheat.

This protocol is self-enforcing. Either party can immediately detect cheating by the other, and no trusted third party is required to participate in either the actual protocol or any adjudication after the protocol has been completed. To see how this works, let's try to cheat.

If Alice wanted to cheat and force heads, she has three potential ways of affecting the outcome. First, she could encrypt two "heads" messages in step (2). Bob would discover this when Alice revealed her key (or keys) at step (7). Second, she could incorrectly decrypt the message in step (4). However, she could not figure out how to decrypt the message to force another message, only gibberish. Bob would discover this in step (5). Third, she could lie about the validity of the message in step (6). Bob would also discover this in step (7), when Alice could not prove that the message was not valid. Of course, Alice could refuse to participate in the protocol at any step, at which point Alice's attempted deception would be obvious to Bob.

If Bob wanted to cheat and force "tails," his options are just as poor. He could incorrectly encrypt a message at step (3), but Alice would discover this when she looked at the final message at step (6). He could improperly perform step (5), but this would also result in gibberish, which Alice would discover at step (6). He could claim that he could not properly perform step (5) because of some cheating on the part of Alice, but this form of cheating would be discovered at step (7). Finally, he could send a "tails" message to Alice at step (5), regardless of the message he decrypted, but Alice would immediately be able to check the message for authenticity at step (6).

Flipping Coins into a Well

It is interesting to note that in all these protocols, neither party learns the result of the coin flip at the same time. There is some point in the protocol where one of the parties (Alice in the first protocol, Bob in the second protocol, and Alice in the third protocol) knows the result of the coin flip but cannot change it. That party can, however, delay disclosing the result to the other party. This is known as **flipping coins into a well.** Imagine a well. Alice is next to the well, and Bob is far away. Bob throws the coin and it lands in the well. Alice can now look into the well and see the result, but she cannot reach down to change it. Bob cannot see the result until Alice lets him come close enough to look.

Key Generation Using Coin Flipping

A real application for this protocol is key generation. Coin flipping protocols allow Alice and Bob to generate a random key such that neither can influence what the key will be. And assuming that Alice and Bob encrypt all of their exchanges, this key generation will be secure from eavesdropping as well.

4.8   MENTAL POKER

A protocol similar to Fair Coin Flip Protocol #3 allows Alice and Bob to play poker with each other over electronic mail. Instead of Alice making and encrypting two messages, one for heads and one for tails, she makes 52 messages, $M_1, M_2, \ldots,$ M_{52}, one for each card in the deck. Bob chooses five messages at random, encrypts them with his public key, and then sends them back to Alice. Alice decrypts the messages and sends them back to Bob, who decrypts them to determine his hand. He then sends five more messages to Alice, who decrypts them to determine her hand. During the game, additional cards can be dealt to either player by repeating the procedure. At the end of the game, Alice and Bob both reveal their cards and key pairs so that either can be assured that the other did not cheat.

Mental Poker with Three Players

Poker is more fun with more players. The basic mental-poker protocol can easily be extended to three or more players. Again, the cryptographic algorithm must be commutative.

(1) Alice, Bob, and Carol all generate a secret key, or a public/private key pair.

(2) Alice generates 52 messages, one for each card in the deck. These messages should contain some unique random string, so that she can verify their authenticity later in the protocol. Alice encrypts all the messages with her key and sends them to Bob.

$$E_A(M_n)$$

(3) Bob, who cannot read any of the messages, chooses five at random. He encrypts them with his key and sends them back to Alice.

$$E_B(E_A(M_n))$$

(4) Bob sends the other 47 messages to Carol.

$$E_A(M_n)$$

(5) Carol, who cannot read any of the messages, chooses five at random. She encrypts them with her key and sends them to Alice.

$$E_C(E_A(M_n))$$

(6) Alice, who cannot read any of the messages sent back to her, decrypts them with her key and then sends them back to Bob or Carol (depending on where they came from).

$$D_A(E_B(E_A(M_n))) = E_B(M_n)$$
$$D_A(E_C(E_A(M_n))) = E_C(M_n)$$

(7) Bob and Carol decrypt the messages with their keys to reveal their hands.

$$D_B(E_B(M_n)) = M_n$$
$$D_C(E_C(M_n)) = M_n$$

(8) Carol chooses five more messages at random from the remaining 42. She sends them to Alice.

$$E_A(M_n)$$

(9) Alice decrypts the messages to reveal her hand.

$$D_A(E_A(M_n)) = M_n$$

(10) Alice, Bob, and Carol all reveal their hands and all of their keys so that everyone can make sure that no one has cheated.

Additional cards can be dealt in the same manner. If either Bob or Carol wants a card, they take the encrypted deck and go through the protocol with Alice. If Alice wants a card, whoever currently has the deck sends her a random card.

Ideally, step (10) would not be necessary. People shouldn't be required to reveal their hands at the end of the protocol; only those players who haven't folded should be required to reveal their hands. Since step (10) is part of the protocol designed only to catch cheaters, perhaps there are things to do.

In poker, one is only interested in whether or not the winner cheated. Everyone else can cheat as much as they want, as long as they still lose. So, let's look at cases in which different players win.

If Alice wins, she reveals her hand and her keys. Bob can use Alice's private key to confirm that Alice performed step (2) correctly—that each of the 52 messages corresponded to a different card. Carol can confirm that Alice is not lying about her hand by encrypting the cards with Alice's key and verifying that they are the same as the encrypted messages she sent to her in step (8).

If either Bob or Carol wins, they reveal their hand and keys. Alice can confirm that the cards are legitimate by checking her random strings. She can also confirm that the cards are the ones dealt by encrypting the cards with the winner's key and verifying that they are the same as the encrypted messages she received in step (3) or (5).

If someone has evidence that someone is cheating, the players will have to reveal all of their information in order to catch the culprit. But at that point the game has ceased to be friendly; revealing folded hands becomes less important.

This protocol isn't secure against collusion among malicious players. Alice and another player can effectively gang up on the third and together swindle that player out of everything without raising any suspicion. Therefore, it is important to check all the keys and random strings every time the players reveal their hands. And if you're sitting around the virtual table with two people who never reveal their hands whenever one of them is the dealer (Alice, in the above protocol), stop playing.

Attacks Against Poker Protocols

Cryptographers have shown that a small amount of information is leaked by these poker protocols if the RSA public-key algorithm is used [263,352]. Specifically, if the binary representation of the card is a quadratic residue (see Section 9.3), then the encryption of the card is also a quadratic residue. This property can be used to "mark" some cards—all the aces, for example. This does not reveal much about the hands, but in a game such as poker even a tiny bit of information can be an advantage in the long run.

Shafi Goldwasser and Silvio Micali [377] developed a two-player mental-poker protocol that fixes this problem, although its complexity makes it far more theoretical than practical. No one has developed a general n-player poker protocol that eliminates the problem of information leakage.

Other research on poker protocols can be found in [352,898,228]. A complicated protocol that allows players to not reveal their hands can be found in [229]. Don Coppersmith discusses two ways to cheat at mental poker using the RSA algorithm [224].

Anonymous Key Distribution

While it is unlikely that anyone is going to use this protocol to play poker over a modem link, Charles Pfleeger discusses a situation in which this type of protocol would come in handy [696].

Consider the problem of key distribution. If we assume that people cannot generate their own keys (they have to be of a certain form, or have to be signed by some organization, or something similar), then we have to set up some central key server to generate and distribute keys. The problem is that we have to figure out some way of distributing keys such that no one, including the server, can figure out who got what key.

This protocol solves the problem:

(1) Alice generates a public/private key pair. For this protocol, she keeps both keys secret.

(2) The KDC generates a continuous stream of keys.

(3) The KDC encrypts the keys, one by one, with its own private key.

(4) The KDC transmits the encrypted keys, one by one, onto the network.

(5) Alice chooses a key at random.

(6) Alice encrypts the chosen key with her public key.

(7) Alice waits a while (long enough so the server has no idea which key she has chosen) and sends the double-encrypted key back to the KDC.

(8) The KDC decrypts the double-encrypted key with its private key, leaving a key encrypted with Alice's public key.

(9) The server sends the encrypted key back to Alice.

(10) Alice decrypts the key with her private key.

Eve, sitting in the middle of this protocol, has no idea what key Alice chose. She sees a continuous stream of keys go by in step (4). When Alice sends the key back to the server in step (7), it is encrypted with her public key, which is also secret. Eve has no way of correlating it with the stream of keys. When the server sends the key back to Alice in step (9), it is also encrypted with Alice's public key. Only when Alice decrypts the key in step (10) is the key revealed.

If you use RSA, there is information leakage with this protocol, at a rate of one bit per message. It's the quadratic residues again. If you're going to distribute keys in this manner, make sure this leakage isn't enough to matter. Of course, if Alice can't trust the KDC, then leakage is inevitable. A malicious KDC could presumably keep records of every key it generates. Then, it could search them all to determine which is Alice's.

This protocol also assumes that Alice is going to act fairly. There are things she can do, using RSA, to get more information than she might otherwise. This is not a problem in our scenario. The next protocol addresses this problem.

CHAPTER
5

Advanced
Protocols

5.1 FAIR CRYPTOSYSTEMS

This excerpt is from Silvio Micali's introduction to the topic [600]:

> Court-authorized line tapping currently is society's most effective method for preventing crimes and securing criminals to justice. Thus, there is a legitimate concern that widespread use of public-key cryptography may be a big boost for criminal and terrorist organizations. Indeed, many bills propose that a proper governmental agency, under circumstances allowed by law, should be able to obtain the clear text of any communication over a public network. At the present time, this requirement would translate into coercing citizens to either (1) *using weak cryptosystems*—i.e., cryptosystems that the proper authorities (but also everybody else!) could crack with a moderate effort—or (2) *surrendering, a priori, their secret key* to the authority. It is not surprising that such alternatives have legitimately alarmed many concerned citizens, generating as reaction the feeling that privacy should come before national security and law enforcement.

The challenge here is to develop a cryptosystem that both protects individual privacy but at the same time allows for court-authorized wiretaps.

Micali goes on to develop **fair cryptosystems.** These are cryptosystems in which the private key is broken up into pieces and distributed to different authorities. Like a secret sharing scheme, the authorities can get together and reconstruct the private key. However, the pieces have the additional property that they can be individually verified to be correct, without reconstructing the private key.

This means that Alice can create her own private key and give a piece of each to n trustees. None of these trustees can recover Alice's private key. However, all the trustees can verify that their piece is a valid piece of the private key; Alice cannot send each of the trustees a random bit string and hope to get away with it. If the courts authorize a wiretap, the relevant law enforcement authorities can serve a court order on the five trustees to surrender their piece. With all five pieces, the authorities reconstruct the private key and can wiretap Alice's communications lines. On the other hand, Mallet has to corrupt all n trustees in order to be able to reconstruct Alice's key and violate her privacy.

Here's how the protocol works:

(1) Alice creates her private-key/public-key key pair. She splits the private key into several public pieces and private pieces.

(2) Alice sends a public piece and corresponding private piece to each of the trustees. This message must be encrypted. She also sends the public key to the KDC.

(3) The trustees perform a calculation to confirm that the public piece and private piece are correct. Each trustee stores the private piece somewhere secure and sends the public piece to the KDC.

(4) The KDC performs another calculation on the public pieces and the public key. Assuming that everything is correct, it signs the public key and either sends it back to Alice or posts it in a database somewhere.

If the courts (or another party) orders a wiretap, then each of the trustees surrenders his or her piece to the KDC, and the KDC can reconstruct the private key. Neither the KDC nor any individual trustee can reconstruct the private key; all the trustees are required to reconstruct the key.

Any public-key cryptography algorithm can be made fair in this manner. Some particular algorithms are discussed in Section 16.10. Micali's paper [600] discusses ways to combine this with a threshold scheme, so that a subset of the trustees (for example, three out of five) is required to reconstruct the private key. He also shows how to combine this with oblivious transfer (see Section 6.1) so that the trustees do not know whose private key is being reconstructed.

5.2   ALL-OR-NOTHING DISCLOSURE OF SECRETS

Imagine that Alice is a former agent of the former Soviet Union, now unemployed. In order to make money, Alice sells secrets. Anyone who is willing to pay the price can buy a secret. She even has a catalog. All the secrets are listed by number, with tantalizing titles: "Where is Jimmy Hoffa?" "Who is secretly controlling the Trilateral Commission?" "Why does Boris Yeltsin always look like he swallowed a live frog?" etc.

Alice won't give away two secrets for the price of one or even partial information about any of the secrets. Bob, a potential buyer, doesn't want to pay for random secrets. He also doesn't want to tell Alice which secrets he wants. It's none of Alice's business, and besides, Alice could then add "what secrets Bob is interested in" to her catalog.

This is called **all-or-nothing disclosure of secrets (ANDOS)** because, as soon as Bob has gained any information whatsoever about one of Alice's secrets, he has wasted his chance to learn anything about any of the other secrets.

A poker protocol won't work in this case, because at the end of the protocol Alice and Bob have to reveal their hands to each other. There are also tricks Bob can do to learn more than one secret.

There are several ANDOS protocols in the cryptographic literature. Some of them will be discussed in Section 16.11.

5.3   ZERO-KNOWLEDGE PROOFS OF KNOWLEDGE

Alice: "I know the password to the Federal Reserve System computer, the ingredients in McDonald's secret sauce, and the contents of Volume Four of Knuth."

Bob: "No, you don't."

Alice: "Yes, I do."

Bob: "Do not!"

Alice: "Do too!"

Bob: "Prove it!"

Alice: "All right. I'll tell you." (She whispers the password.)

Bob: "That's interesting. Now I know it, too. I'm going to tell the *Washington Post*."

Alice: "Oops."

Unfortunately, the normal way for Alice to prove something to Bob is for Alice to tell him. But then he knows it, too. Now, Bob can tell anyone else he wants to, and Alice can do nothing about it.

In the literature, different players are often used in these protocols. Peggy is usually cast as the prover, and Victor is the verifier. Their names appear in the upcoming examples.

Using one-way functions, Peggy could perform a **minimum-disclosure proof.** This is a protocol that proves to Victor that Peggy does have a piece of information, but it does not give Victor any way of determining what the information is. If Victor does not learn anything at all other than that Peggy knows a proof, then the protocol is a **zero-knowledge proof.**

Yes, there is a difference there. In a minimum-disclosure proof, the following properties hold:

- The prover cannot cheat the verifier. If the prover does not know the proof, her chances of convincing the verifier that she knows the proof are negligible.

- The verifier cannot cheat the prover. He doesn't get the slightest hint of the proof, apart from the fact that the prover knows the proof. In particular, the verifier cannot demonstrate the proof to anyone else without proving it himself from scratch.

In a zero-knowledge proof, there is an additional condition:

- The verifier learns nothing from the prover that he could not learn by himself without the prover.

This concept was introduced in [374,379]. Similar theories, based on different mathematical assumptions, were developed independently in [146,151,194]. There is considerable mathematical difference between proofs that are only minimum-disclosure and those that are zero-knowledge. (That subject is beyond the scope of this book, but more sophisticated readers are welcome to peruse the References section at the end.)

This proof takes the form of an interactive protocol. Victor asks Peggy a series of questions. If Peggy knows the information, she can answer all the questions correctly. If she does not, she has a 50% chance of answering correctly. After ten or so questions, Victor will be convinced that Peggy knows the information. Furthermore, none of the questions or answers give Victor any information about Peggy's information—only about her knowledge of it.

Basic Zero-Knowledge Protocol

Jean-Jacques Quisquater and Louis Guillou [722] explain zero-knowledge with a story about a cave. The cave, illustrated in Figure 5.1, has a secret. Someone who knows the magic words can open the secret door between C and D. To everyone else, both passages lead to dead ends.

Peggy knows the secret of the cave. She wants to prove her knowledge to Victor, but she doesn't want to reveal the magic words. Here's how she convinces him:

(1) Victor stands at point A.

(2) Peggy walks all the way into the cave, either to point C or point D.

(3) After Peggy has disappeared into the cave, Victor walks to point B.

(4) Victor shouts to Peggy, asking her either to:

    (a) come out of the left passage or
    (b) come out of the right passage.

(5) Peggy complies, using the magic words to open the secret door if she has to.

(6) Peggy and Victor repeat steps (1) through (5) n times.

The technique is called **cut and choose,** because of its similarity to the classic protocol for dividing anything fairly:

(1) Alice cuts the thing in half.

(2) Bob chooses one of the halves for himself.

(3) Alice takes the remaining half.

It is in Alice's best interest to divide fairly in step (1), because Bob is able to choose whichever half he wants in step (2). Michael Rabin was the first person to use the cut-and-choose technique in cryptography [723]. The concepts of **interactive protocol** and zero-knowledge were formalized later [379,380].

The cut-and-choose protocol works because there is no way Peggy can repeatedly guess which side Victor will ask her to come out of. If Peggy didn't know the secret, she could come out the way she came in but not the other way. She has a 50% chance of guessing which side Victor will ask in each round of the protocol, so she has a 50% chance of fooling him. The chance of her fooling him in two rounds is 25%, and the chance of her fooling him all n times is one in 2^n. After 16 rounds, Peggy has a one in 65,536 chance of fooling Victor every time. Victor can safely assume that if all 16 of Peggy's proofs are valid, then she must know the secret words to open the door between points C and D.

The cave analogy isn't perfect. Peggy can simply walk in one side and out the other; there's no need for any cut-and-choose protocol. However, the mathematical proof requires it.

Assume that Peggy knows a piece of information and furthermore that the information is the solution to a hard problem. The basic protocol consists of several rounds.

(1) Peggy uses her information and some random number to transform the hard problem into another hard problem, one that is isomorphic to the original function. She then uses her information and the random number to solve the new hard problem.

Figure 5.1
The zero-knowledge cave.

(2) Peggy commits to the solution of the new hard problem, using some bit commitment scheme.

(3) Peggy reveals to Victor the new hard problem. Victor cannot use this new problem to get any information about the original problem or its solution.

(4) Victor asks Peggy either to:

   (a) prove to him that the old and new problems are isomorphic, or
   (b) open the solution she committed to in step (2) and prove that it is a solution to the new problem.

(5) Peggy complies.

(6) Peggy and Victor repeat steps (1) through (5) n times.

The mathematics behind this type of proof is complicated. The problems and the random transformation must be chosen carefully, so that Bob does not get any information about the solution to the original problem, even after many iterations of the protocol. Not all "hard problems" can be used for zero-knowledge proofs, but a lot of them can.

Hamiltonian Cycles

An example might go a long way to explain this concept. This one comes from graph theory and was first presented by Manuel Blum [123]. A network of lines connecting points is called a graph. Perhaps Alice knows a circular, continuous path along the lines that pass through each point exactly once. This is called a **Hamiltonian cycle.**

For an extremely large graph, finding this path can take years of computer time; it is one of those one-way functions discussed earlier. This is the piece of information that Peggy has, and this is what she wants to convince Victor that she knows.

Peggy knows the Hamiltonian cycle of a graph, G. This is how the protocol works:

(1) Peggy randomly permutes G. She moves the points around and changes their labels to make a new graph, H. Since G and H are topologically isomorphic (i.e., the same graph), if she knows the Hamiltonian cycle of G then she can easily find the Hamiltonian cycle of H. If she didn't create H herself, determining the isomorphism between two graphs would be another hard problem; it can also take years of computer time.

(2) Peggy gives Victor a copy of H.

(3) Victor asks Peggy either to:

   (a) prove to him that G and H are isomorphic, or
   (b) show him a Hamiltonian cycle for H.

(4) Peggy complies. She either:

    (a) proves that G and H are isomorphic, without showing a Hamiltonian cycle for either G or H, or

    (b) shows a Hamiltonian cycle for H, without proving that G and H are topologically isomorphic.

(5) Peggy and Victor repeat steps (1) through (4) n times.

If Peggy is honest, she can provide either proof in step (3) to Victor. However, if she does not know a Hamiltonian cycle for G, she cannot create graph H, which can meet both challenges. The best she can do is to create a graph that is either isomorphic to G, or one that has the same number of points and lines and a valid Hamiltonian cycle. While she has a 50% chance of guessing which proof Victor will ask her to perform in step (3), Victor can repeat the protocol enough times to convince himself that Peggy knows a Hamiltonian cycle for G.

This protocol is a zero-knowledge proof because Victor never gets any information to help him determine a Hamiltonian cycle for the original graph. In each round, Peggy could show him one of two things. She could show him that the two graphs are isomorphic. This doesn't help Victor, because finding the Hamiltonian cycle for the new graph is just as difficult as finding the Hamiltonian cycle for the old graph. On the other hand, she could show him the Hamiltonian cycle for the new graph. This doesn't help him either, because finding the isomorphism between the old and new graphs is no easier than finding the Hamiltonian cycle of either graph. Since Peggy permutes the original graph differently in each round, Victor gets no information, no matter how many times they go through the protocol.

Graph Isomorphism

Another example comes from [374]. Assume that Peggy knows that two graphs, G_1 and G_2, are isomorphic. The following protocol will convince Victor of Peggy's knowledge:

(1) Peggy randomly permutes the vertices of G_1 to produce some other graph, H, that is isomorphic to G_1. Because Peggy knows the isomorphism between G_1 and H, she also knows the isomorphism between H and G_2. For anyone else, finding an isomorphism between G_1 and H or between H and G_2 is just as hard as finding an isomorphism between G_1 and G_2.

(2) Peggy sends H to Victor.

(3) Victor asks Peggy either to:

    (a) prove that G_1 and H are isomorphic, or
    (b) prove that G_2 and H are isomorphic.

(4) Peggy complies. She either:

    (a) proves that G_1 and H are isomorphic, without proving that G_2 and H are isomorphic, or

 (b) proves that G_2 and H are isomorphic, without proving that G_1 and H are isomorphic.

(5) Peggy and Victor repeat steps (1) through (4) n times.

 If Peggy does not know an isomorphism between G_1 and G_2, she cannot create graph H, which is isomorphic to both. She can create a graph that is either isomorphic to G_1 or one that is isomorphic to G_2. Like the previous example, she has only a 50% chance of guessing which proof Victor will ask her to perform in step (3).

 This protocol doesn't give Victor any useful information to aid him in figuring out an isomorphism between G_1 and G_2. Because Peggy generates a new graph H for each round of the protocol, there is no information Victor can get even after many rounds. He won't be able to figure out an isomorphism between G_1 and G_2 from Peggy's answers.

Parallel Zero-Knowledge Proofs

The basic zero-knowledge protocol involves n exchanges between Peggy and Victor. There's no reason why they can't do them all in parallel:

(1) Peggy uses her information and some random numbers to transform the hard problem into n different isomorphic problems. She then uses her information and the random number to solve the n new hard problems.

(2) Peggy commits to the solution of the n new hard problems.

(3) Peggy reveals to Victor the n new hard problems. Victor cannot use this new problem to get any information about the original problem or its solution.

(4) For each of the n new hard problems, Victor asks Peggy either to:

 (a) prove to him that the old and new problems are isomorphic, or
 (b) open the solution she committed to in step (2) and prove that it is a solution to the new problem.

(5) Peggy complies for each of the n new hard problems.

This protocol is just as secure, but with fewer (albeit longer) messages passing between Peggy and Victor.

Convincing a Third Party

Victor wants to convince Carol that Peggy knows the information. He keeps a transcript of the protocol and then shows that transcript to Carol. Should Carol be convinced?

 No, because two people who do not know the information can collude to fool Carol. They can agree previously on which questions Victor will ask in which round. With that knowledge, Mallet, who does not know the secret, can *pretend* to know. He can always answer one of the two questions; by colluding with Victor he is sure that Victor always asks the one he can. A transcript of the protocol between Victor and Mallet, in which the two of them agree on the questions in advance, looks just like the protocol between Victor and an honest Peggy. There is no way for Carol to tell the difference.

Noninteractive Zero-Knowledge Proofs

Carol can't be convinced because the protocol is interactive, and she is not involved in the interaction. To convince Carol, and anyone else who may be interested, we need a noninteractive protocol.

Protocols have been invented for noninteractive zero-knowledge proofs [280,125,281,124]. These protocols do not require any interaction; Peggy could publish them and thereby prove to anyone who takes the time to check that the proof is valid.

The basic protocol is similar to the parallel zero-knowledge proof, but a one-way function takes the place of Victor:

(1) Peggy uses her information and some random numbers to transform the hard problem into n different isomorphic problems. She then uses her information and the random number to solve the n new hard problems.

(2) Peggy commits to the solution of the n new hard problems.

(3) Peggy uses all of these commitments as an input to a one-way hash function. (After all, the commitments are nothing more than bit strings.) She then saves the first n bits of the output of this one-way hash function.

(4) Peggy takes the n bits generated in step (3). Depending on whether the nth bit is 0 or 1, she takes the nth new hard problem and either:

    (a) proves that the old and new problems are isomorphic, or
    (b) opens the solution she committed to in step (2) and proves that it is a solution to the new problem.

(5) Peggy publishes all the commitments from step (2) as well as the solutions in step (4).

(6) Victor, or Carol, or whoever is interested, verifies that steps (1) through (5) were executed properly.

This is amazing: Peggy publishes some data that contains no information about her secret, yet it can be used to convince anyone of the secret's existence.

The reason this works is that the one-way function acts as an unbiased random bit generator. For Peggy to cheat, she has to be able to predict the output of the one-way hash function. (Remember, if she doesn't know the solution to the hard problem, she can do either (a) or (b) of step (3), but not both.) If she somehow knew what the one-way hash function would ask her to do, then she could cheat. However, there is no way for Peggy to force the one-way function to produce certain bits, or to guess which bits it will produce. The one-way function is, in effect, Victor's surrogate in the protocol—randomly choosing one of two proofs in step (3).

In a noninteractive protocol, there have to be many more iterations of the challenge/reply sequence. Peggy is picking the hard problems using random numbers; Victor doesn't control them. She can pick different problems, hence different commitment vectors, till the hash function produces something she likes. In an interactive protocol, 20 iterations—a probability of one in 2^{20} that Peggy can be cheating—are fine. However, that's not enough for noninteractive zero-knowledge proofs; Peggy can do steps (1) through (3) repeatedly until she gets 20 bits she likes. Noninteractive protocols need 64 iterations, or even 128 iterations, to be valid.

Generalities

Blum proved that any mathematical theorem can be converted into a graph such that the proof of that theorem is equivalent to a Hamiltonian cycle. In this way, any mathematical proof can be converted into a zero-knowledge proof. Using this technique, researchers can prove to the world that they know the solution to a particular theorem without revealing what that solution is. Blum could, in effect, have published his results without revealing them.

Over the years there has been extensive work done, both theoretical and applied, on minimum-disclosure and zero-knowledge proofs. Mike Burmester and Yvo Desmedt invented **broadcast interactive proofs,** where one prover can broadcast a zero-knowledge interactive proof to a large group of verifiers [179]. A bevy of cryptographers proved that *everything* that can be proved with an interactive proof can also be proved with a zero-knowledge interactive proof [82]. For additional mathematical details, variations, protocols, and applications, consult [362,374,146,194,375,61,147,853,392,145,373,308,132,55,133,480,52,529,285], and the proceedings from almost any CRYPTO conference, EUROCRYPT conference, Foundations of Computer Science (FOCS) conference, or Symposium on the Theory of Computing (STOC) conference. There is *a lot* written on this subject.

5.4   ZERO-KNOWLEDGE PROOFS OF IDENTITY

In the real world, we use physical tokens as proofs of identity: passports, drivers' licenses, credit cards, etc. The card contains something that links it to a person: a picture, usually, but it could almost as easily be a thumbprint, a retina scan, or a dental x-ray. Wouldn't it be nice to do the same thing digitally?

Using zero-knowledge proofs as proofs of identity was first proposed by Uriel Feige, Amos Fiat, and Adi Shamir [348,349]. Alice's private key becomes a function of her "identity." Using a zero-knowledge proof, she proves that she knows her private key and therefore proves her identity.

This idea is quite powerful. It allows people to prove their identity without any physical token. However, it's not perfect.

The Chess Grandmaster Problem

Here's how Alice, who doesn't even know the rules to chess, can defeat a grandmaster. She challenges both Gary Kasparov and Anatoly Karpov to a game, at the same time and place, but in separate rooms. She plays white against Kasparov and black against Karpov. Neither grandmaster knows about the other.

Karpov, as white, makes his first move. Alice records the move and walks into the room with Kasparov. Playing white, she makes the same move against Kasparov. Kasparov makes his first move as black. Alice records the move, walks into the room with Karpov, and makes the same move. This continues until she wins one game and loses the other (or ends both in a draw).

In reality, Kasparov is playing Karpov, and Alice is simply acting as the middleperson, mimicking the moves of one grandmaster on the other's board. However, if neither Karpov nor Kasparov knows about the other's presence, each is going to be quite impressed with Alice's play.

This kind of fraud can be used against zero-knowledge proofs of identity [288,66].

The Mafia Fraud: When discussing his zero-knowledge identification protocol, Adi Shamir said [797]: "I could go to a Mafia-owned store a million successive times and they will still not be able to misrepresent themselves as me."

Here's how the Mafia can. Alice is eating at Bob's Diner, a Mafia-owned restaurant. Carol is shopping at Dave's Emporium, an expensive jewelry store. Bob and Carol are both members of the Mafia and are communicating by a secret radio link. Alice and Dave are unaware of the fraud.

At the end of Alice's meal, when she is ready to pay and prove her identity to Bob, Bob signals Carol that the fraud is ready to begin. Carol buys some expensive diamonds and gets ready to prove her identity to Dave. Now, as Alice proves her identity to Bob, Bob radios Carol and Carol performs the same protocol with Dave. When Dave asks a question in the protocol, Carol radios the question back to Bob, and Bob asks it of Alice. When Alice answers, Bob radios the correct answer to Carol. Actually, Alice is just proving her identity to Dave, and Bob and Carol are simply sitting in the middle of the protocol passing messages back and forth. When the protocol finishes, Alice has proved herself to Dave and has purchased some expensive diamonds (which Carol disappears with).

The Terrorist Fraud: If Alice is willing to collaborate with Carol, they can also defraud Dave. In this protocol, Carol is a well-known terrorist. Alice is helping her enter the country. Dave is the immigration officer. Alice and Carol are connected by a secret radio link.

When Dave asks Carol questions as part of the zero-knowledge protocol, Carol radios them back to Alice, who answers them herself. Carol recites these answers to Dave. In reality, Alice is proving her identity to Dave, with Carol acting as a communications path. When the protocol finishes, Dave thinks that Carol is Alice and lets her into the country. Three days later, Carol commits a terrorist act.

Both the Mafia and terrorist frauds are possible because the conspirators can communicate via a secret radio. One way to prevent this would be to require all identifications to take place inside Faraday cages, which block all electromagnetic radiation. In the terrorist example, this would assure immigration officer Dave that Carol was not receiving her answers from Alice. In the Mafia example, Bob could simply build a faulty Faraday cage in his restaurant, but jeweler Dave would have a working one; Bob and Carol would not be able to communicate.

Thomas Beth and Yvo Desmedt proposed another solution, one using accurate clocks [92]. If each step in the protocol must take place at a given time interval, then there will be no time available for the conspirators to communicate. Using the chess grandmaster story, if every move must be made as a clock strikes one minute, then Alice will have no time to run from room to room, or Bob and Carol to pass questions and answers to one another.

Shifting Identities Problem

There are other abuses to the protocol, also discussed in [288,66]:

The Multiple Identity Fraud: In some implementations, there is no check when an individual registers a public key. Hence, Alice can have several private keys and, therefore, several identities. This can be a great help if she wants to commit tax fraud. Alice can also commit a crime and disappear. First, she creates and publishes several identities. One of them she doesn't use. Then, she uses that identity once and commits a crime so that the person who identified her is the witness. Then, she immediately stops using that identity. The witness knows the identity of the person who committed the crime, but Alice never uses that identity again—she's untraceable.

To prevent this, there has to be some mechanism by which each person has only one identity. In [66] the authors suggest the "terrifying" idea of tamperproof babies who are unable to be cloned and contain a unique number as part of their genetic code. They also suggested having each baby apply for an identity at birth. (Actually, the parents would have to do this as the baby would be otherwise occupied.) This could easily be abused; parents could apply for multiple identities at the child's birth. In the end, the uniqueness of an individual is based on trust.

Renting Passports: Alice wants to travel to Argentina, but the government won't give her a visa. Carol offers to rent her identity to Alice. (Bob offered first, but there were some obvious problems.) Carol sells Alice her private key, and Alice goes off to Argentina pretending to be Carol.

Carol has not only been paid for her identity, but now she has a perfect alibi. She commits her crime while Alice is in Argentina. "Carol" has proved her identity in Argentina; how could she commit a crime back home?

Of course, Alice is free to commit crimes as well. She does so either before she leaves or after she returns, near Carol's home. First she identifies herself as Carol (she has Carol's private key, so she can easily do that), then she commits a crime and runs away. The police will come looking for Carol. Carol will claim she rented her identity to Alice, but who would believe such a nonsensical story?

The problem is that Alice isn't really proving her identity, she is proving that she knows a piece of secret information. It is the link between that information and the person that is being abused. The tamperproof-baby solution would protect against this type of fraud, as would a police state where all citizens would have to prove their identity very frequently (at the end of each day, at each street corner, etc.).

5.5 BLIND SIGNATURES

An essential in all digital signature protocols is that the document's signers always know what they are signing. This is all right, except when we want the reverse.

There are times when we want people to sign a document without their ever seeing its contents. It's not a terribly useful protocol by itself, but we will use it later when we implement voting and digital cash protocols. There are ways that signers can *almost* know what they are signing.

Completely Blind Signatures

Bob is a notary public. Alice wants him to sign a document but does not want him to have any idea what he is signing. Bob doesn't care what the document says; he is just certifying that it was notarized at a certain time. He is willing to go along with this.

(1) Alice takes the document and multiplies it by a random value. This random value is called a **blinding factor.**

(2) Alice sends the blinded document to Bob.

(3) Bob signs the blinded document.

(4) Alice divides out the blinding factor, leaving the original document signed by Bob.

This protocol only works if the signature function and the multiplication function are commutative. If they are not, there are other ways to modify the document other than by using multiplication. Some relevant math algorithms appear in Section 16.13. For now, assume that the operation is multiplication and all the math works.

Can Bob cheat? Can he collect any information about the document that he is signing? If the blinding factor is truly random, he cannot. The blinded document Bob signs in step (2) looks nothing like the document Alice began with. The blinded document with Bob's signature on it in step (3) looks nothing like the signed document at the end of step (4). Even if Bob got his hands on the document, with his signature, after completing the protocol, he cannot prove (to himself or to anyone else) that he signed it in that particular protocol. He knows that his signature is valid. He knows that he (or someone else with his private key) signed the document; he can, like anyone else, verify the signature. However, there is no way for him to correlate any information he received during the signing protocol with the signed document. If he signed a million documents using this protocol, he would still have no way of knowing in which instance he signed which document.

The properties of completely blind signatures are:

- Bob's signature on the document is valid. The signature is proof that Bob signed the document. It will convince Bob that he signed the document if it is ever shown to him. It also has all of the other properties of digital signatures discussed previously.

- Bob cannot correlate the signed document with the act of signing the document. Even if he keeps records of every blind signature he makes, when presented with a signed document, he cannot determine when he signed it.

Eve, who is in the middle, watching this protocol, has even less information than Bob.

Blind Signatures

With the completely blind signature protocol, Alice can have Bob sign anything: "Bob owes Alice a million dollars," "Bob owes Alice his first-born child," "Bob owes Alice a bag of jelly beans." The possibilities are endless. Needless to say, this protocol isn't particularly useful.

However, there is a way that Bob can know what he is signing, while still maintaining the useful properties of a blind signature. The heart of this protocol is the cut-and-choose technique. Consider an example. Many people enter this country every day, and the customs department wants to make sure they are not smuggling cocaine. The officials can search everyone, but instead they use a probabilistic solution. They will search one-tenth of the people coming in. One person in ten has his belongings inspected; the other nine get through untouched. Chronic smugglers will get away with their misdeeds most of the time, but they have a 10% chance of getting caught. And if the court system is effective, the penalty for getting caught once will more than wipe out the gains from the other nine times.

If the customs department wants to increase the odds of catching smugglers, they have to search more people. If they want to decrease the odds, they have to search fewer people. By manipulating the probabilities, they control how successful the protocol is to catch smugglers.

The blind signature protocol works in a similar manner. Bob will be given a large pile of different blinded documents. He will examine all but one and then sign the last.

The next scenario involves a group of counterintelligence agents. Their identity is secret; not even the counterintelligence agency knows who they are. The agency's director wants to give each of the agents a signed document stating: "The bearer of this signed document, (insert agent's cover name here), has full diplomatic immunity." All of the agents have their own list of cover names, so the agency can't just hand out signed documents. The agents do not want to send their cover name to the agency; the enemy might have corrupted the agency's computer. On the other hand, the agency doesn't want blindly to sign any document the agent gives it. A clever agent might substitute a message such as: "Agent (name) has retired and collects a million-dollar-a-year pension. Signed: Mr. President." In this case, a blind signature could be useful.

Assume that all the agents have ten possible cover names, which they have chosen themselves and are known by no one else. Also assume that the agents don't care under which cover name they are going to get diplomatic immunity. Also assume that the agency's computer is called Agency's Large Intelligent Computing Engine, or ALICE.

(1) Agent prepares ten documents, each using a different cover name, giving that agent diplomatic immunity.

(2) Agent blinds each of these documents with a different blinding factor.

(3) Agent sends the ten blinded documents to ALICE.

(4) ALICE chooses nine documents at random and asks Agent for the blinding factors for each of those documents.

(5) Agent sends ALICE the appropriate blinding factors.

(6) ALICE removes the blinding factors from the nine documents and makes sure they are correct.

(7) ALICE signs the tenth document and sends it to Agent.

(8) Agent removes the blinding factor and reads the new cover name: Bob.

"Damn," says Bob. "I was hoping for 'The Crimson Streak.'"

This protocol is secure against Bob cheating. For him to cheat, he would have to predict accurately which document ALICE would not examine. The odds of his doing this are 10%; not very good. (It *is* possible to increase the number of documents that Bob sends to ALICE. In fact, it is possible to make the odds of Bob's getting away with deception as small as necessary.) ALICE knows this as well and feels confident signing the tenth document; the one that she is not able to examine. With this one document, the protocol is the same as the previous blinded signature protocol and maintains all of its properties of anonymity.

There is another way that Bob can cheat. He can generate two different documents, one that ALICE is willing to sign and one that ALICE is not. Then he can find two different blinding factors that transform each document into the same blinded document. That way, if ALICE asks to examine the document, Bob gives her the blinding factor that transforms it into the benign document. If ALICE doesn't ask to see the document and signs it, he uses the blinding factor that transforms it into the malevolent document. While this is theoretically possible, the mathematics of the particular algorithms involved make the odds of Bob's being able to find such a pair negligibly small. This issue is discussed further in Section 16.13.

Envelopes

David Chaum refers to the blinded document as being in an **envelope.** The process of blinding the document is putting the document in an envelope, and the process of removing the blinding factor is opening the envelope. When the document is in an envelope, nobody can read it. The document is signed by having a piece of carbon paper in the envelope—when signers sign the envelope, their signatures go through the carbon paper and sign the document as well.

CHAPTER
6

Esoteric
Protocols

6.1 OBLIVIOUS TRANSFER

Cryptographer Bob is desperately trying to factor a 500-bit number. He knows it's the product of five 100-bit numbers, but nothing more. (This is a serious problem for Bob. If he can't recover the key, he'll have to work overtime and he'll miss his weekly mental poker game with Alice.)

The scenario is illustrated here, using Alice and Bob as characters:

> "I happen to know one factor of the number," Alice says, "and I'll sell it to you for one hundred dollars. That's a dollar a bit." To show she's serious, she uses a bit commitment scheme and commits to each bit individually.

> Bob is interested, but he has only $50. Alice is unwilling to lower her price, and offers to sell Bob half the bits for half the price. "It'll save you a considerable amount of work," she says.

> "But how do I know that your number is actually a factor of n? If you show me the number and let me verify that it is a factor, then I will agree to your terms," Bob says.

> Alice doesn't go along with this plan, so they were at an impasse. Alice could not convince Bob that her number was a factor of n without revealing it, and Bob was unwilling to buy 50 bits of a number that could very well be useless.

This story, borrowed from Joe Kilian [479], introduces the concept of oblivious transfer. Alice transmits a group of messages to Bob. Bob receives a subset of those messages, but Alice has no idea which ones he receives. This doesn't completely solve the above problem, however. After Bob has received a random half of the bits, Alice then has to convince him that those bits constitute a factor of n using a zero-knowledge proof.

In the following protocol, Alice will send Bob one of two messages. Bob will receive one, and Alice will not know which.

(1) Alice generates two public-key key pairs, or four keys in all. She sends both public keys to Bob.

(2) Bob chooses a key in a symmetric algorithm (DES, for example). He picks one of Alice's public keys at random and encrypts his DES key with it. He sends the encrypted key to Alice without telling her which of her public keys he used to encrypt it.

(3) Alice decrypts Bob's key with both of her private keys. In one of the cases, she uses the correct key and successfully decrypts Bob's DES key. In the other case, she uses the wrong key and only manages to generate a meaningless pile of bits that nonetheless looks like a random DES key. Since she does not know the correct plaintext, she has no idea which is which.

(4) Alice encrypts one message with each of the DES keys she generated in the previous step (one real and one meaningless) and sends both of them to Bob.

(5) Bob attempts to decrypt both of Alice's messages, but only successfully decrypts one of them. At this point the oblivious transfer is complete. Bob has received one of the two messages (the one encrypted in his DES key), and Alice has no way of knowing which.

(6) After the protocol is complete and both possible results of the transfer are known, Alice must give Bob her private keys so that he can verify that she did not cheat. After all, she could have encrypted the same message with both keys in step (4).

The protocol is secure against an attack by Alice because she has no way of knowing which of the two DES keys is the real one. It is secure against an attack by Bob because, before the protocol is complete, there is no way he can get Alice's private keys to determine the DES key with the other encrypted message. This may still seem like nothing more than a more complicated way to flip coins over a modem, but it has extensive implications when used in more complicated protocols.

Of course, there is nothing stopping Alice from sending Bob two completely useless messages: "Nyah, nyah" and "You sucker." This protocol ensures that Alice sends Bob one of two messages; it does nothing to ensure that Bob wants to receive either of them.

There are other oblivious transfer protocols in the literature. Some of them are noninteractive, meaning that Alice can publish her two messages and Bob can learn only one of them. He can do this on his own; he doesn't have to communicate with Alice [56]. Many of the other protocols in this chapter make use of the oblivious transfer protocol.

6.2 SIMULTANEOUS CONTRACT SIGNING

Contract Signing with an Arbitrator

Alice and Bob want to enter into a contract. They've agreed on the wording, but neither wishes to sign unless the other signs as well. Face to face, this is easy: both sign together. Over a distance, they could use an arbitrator.

(1) Alice signs a copy of the contract and sends it to Trent.

(2) Bob signs a copy of the contract and sends it to Trent.

(3) Trent sends a message to both Alice and Bob indicating that the other has signed the contract.

(4) Alice signs two copies of the contract and sends them to Bob.

(5) Bob signs both copies of the contract, keeps one for himself, and sends the other to Alice.

(6) Alice and Bob both inform Trent that they each have a copy of the contract signed by both of them.

(7) Trent tears up his two copies of the contract with only one signature each.

This protocol works because Trent prevents either of the parties from cheating. If Bob were to refuse to sign the contract in step (5), Alice could appeal to Trent for a copy of the contract already signed by Bob. If Alice were to refuse to sign in step (4), Bob could do the same. When Trent indicates that he received both contracts in step (3), both Alice and Bob know that the other is bound by the contract. If Trent does not receive both contracts, he tears up the one he received and neither party is bound.

Simultaneous Contract Signing Without an Arbitrator (Face-to-Face)

If Alice and Bob were sitting face-to-face, they could sign the contract this way [696]:

(1) Alice signs the first letter of her name and passes the contract to Bob.

(2) Bob signs the first letter of his name and passes the contract to Alice.

(3) Alice signs the second letter of her name and passes the contract to Bob.

(4) Bob signs the second letter of his name and passes the contract to Alice.

(5) This continues until both Alice and Bob have signed their entire names.

If you ignore the obvious problem with this protocol (Alice has a longer name than Bob), it will work. After signing only one letter, Alice knows that no judge will bind her to the terms of the contract. But the letter is an act of good faith, and Bob responds with a similar act of good faith.

After each party has signed several letters, a judge could probably be convinced that both parties signed the contract. The details are murky, though. Surely they are not bound after only the first letter; just as surely they are bound after they sign their entire names. At what point in the protocol do they become bound? After signing one-half of their names? Two-thirds of their names? Three-quarters?

Since neither Alice nor Bob is certain of the exact point at which they are bound, they have at least some fear that they are bound at each point. There is no point when Bob can say: "You signed four letters and I only signed three. You are bound, but I am not." There is no reason for Bob not to continue with the protocol. The longer they continue, the greater the probability that a judge will rule that they are bound. Again, there is no reason not to continue with the protocol. After all, they both wanted to sign the contract; they just didn't want to sign before the other one.

Simultaneous Contract Signing Without an Arbitrator (Not Face-to-Face)

This protocol, courtesy of Michael Ben-Or, Oded Goldreich, Silvio Micali, and Ron Rivest [83], uses the same sort of uncertainty. Alice and Bob alternate taking baby steps toward a signed contract until both have signed.

In the protocol, Alice and Bob exchange a series of signed messages of the form: I agree that with probability p, I am bound by this contract.

The recipient of this message can take it to a judge and, with probability p, the judge will find the contract on the signatory.

(1) Alice and Bob agree on a date by which signing the protocol is to be completed.

(2) Alice and Bob decide on a probability difference that they are willing to live with. For example, Alice might decide that she is not willing to be bound with a greater probability than 2% over Bob's probability. Call Alice's difference A; call Bob's difference B.

(3) Alice sends Bob a signed message with $p = A$.

(4) Bob sends Alice a signed message with $p = A+B$.

(5) Let p' be the probability of the message Alice received in the previous step from Bob. Alice sends Bob a signed message with $p = p'+A$ or 1, whichever is smaller.

(6) Let p' be the probability of the message Bob received in the previous step from Alice. Bob sends Alice a signed message with $p = p'+B$ or 1, whichever is smaller.

(7) Alice and Bob continue alternating steps (5) and (6) until both have received messages with $p = 1$, or until the date agreed to in step (1) has passed.

As the protocol proceeds, both Alice and Bob agree to be bound to the contract with a greater and greater probability. For example, Alice's first message might state that she is bound with 2% probability. Bob might respond that he is bound with 3% probability. Alice's next message might state that she is bound with 4% probability, and so on, until both are bound with 100% probability.

If both Alice and Bob complete the protocol, all is well. If the protocol completion date passes, either party can take the contract to the judge, along with the other party's last signed message. The judge simply chooses a random value between 0 and 1. If the value is less than the probability the other party signed, then both parties are bound. If the value is greater than the probability, then both parties aren't bound. (The judge then saves the value, in case there will be a ruling on another matter regarding the same contract.) This is what is meant by being bound to the contract with probability p.

That's the basic protocol, but there can be more complications. If Alice starts signing messages with smaller and smaller increases in probability, Bob can respond in kind. The judge can make a ruling in the absence of one of the parties. The judge's ruling either binds both parties or neither party; there is no situation where one party is bound and the other one is not. As long as one party is willing to have a slightly higher probability of being bound than the other (no matter how small), the protocol will terminate.

Simultaneous Contract Signing Without an Arbitrator (Using Cryptography)

The cryptographic protocol uses the same baby-step approach [321]. DES is used in the protocol description, although any symmetric algorithm will do.

(1) Alice and Bob both randomly select 200 DES keys, grouped in pairs. There is nothing special about the pairs; they are just grouped that way for the protocol.

(2) Alice and Bob both generate 100 pairs of messages, L_n and R_n: "This is the left half of my nth signature" and "This is the right half of my nth signature," for example. The identifier, n, runs from 1 to 100. The messages will probably also include a digital signature of the contract, as defined previously, and a timestamp. The contract is considered signed if the other party can produce both halves, L_n and R_n, of a single signature pair.

(3) Alice and Bob both encrypt their message pairs in each of the DES key pairs, the left message with the left key in the pair and the right message with the right key in the pair.

(4) Alice and Bob send each other their pile of 200 encrypted messages, making sure the other knows which messages are which halves of which pairs.

(5) Alice and Bob send each other every key pair, using the oblivious transfer protocol for each pair. That is, Alice sends Bob either the key used to encrypt the left message, or the key used to encrypt the right message, independently, for each of the 100 pairs. Bob does the same. They can either alternate sending halves, or one can send 100 and then the other—it doesn't matter. Now both Alice and Bob have one key in each key pair, but neither knows which halves the other one has.

(6) Alice and Bob both decrypt the message halves they can, using the keys they received. They make sure that the decrypted messages are valid.

(7) Alice and Bob send each other the first bits of all 200 DES keys.

(8) Alice and Bob repeat step (7) for the second bits of all 200 DES keys, the third bits, and so on, until all the bits of all the DES keys have been transferred.

(9) Alice and Bob decrypt the remaining halves of the message pairs and the contract is signed.

Why do Alice and Bob have to go through all this work? Let's assume Alice wants to cheat and see what happens. In steps (4) and (5), Alice could disrupt the protocol by sending Bob nonsense bit strings. Bob would catch this in step (6), when he tried to decrypt whatever half he received. Bob could then stop safely, since Alice could not decrypt any of Bob's message pairs. If Alice were very clever, she could only disrupt half the protocol. She could send the left half of each pair correctly but send a gibberish string for the right half. Bob has only a 50% chance of receiving the right half, so half the time Alice could cheat. However, this only works if there is one key pair. If there were only two pairs, this sort of deception would succeed 25% of the time. That is why there are 100 key pairs in this protocol. Alice has to guess correctly the outcome of 100 oblivious transfer protocols. Since she only has a 1 in 2^{100} chance of doing this, Bob can safely assume that if he didn't catch her deception in step (6), then there was none.

Alice could also send Bob random bits in step (8). Perhaps Bob won't know that she is sending him random bits until he receives the whole key and tries to decrypt the message halves. But again, Bob has probability on his side. He has already received half of the keys, and Alice does not know which half. Alice is sure to send him a nonsense bit to a key he has already received, and he will know immediately that Alice is trying to deceive him.

Maybe Alice will just go along with step (8) until she has enough bits of the keys to break the DES messages and then stop transmitting bits. DES has a 56-bit-long key. If she receives 40 of the 56 bits, she only has to try 2^{16} (65,536) keys in order to read the message—a task certainly within the realm of a computer's capability. But Bob will have exactly the same number of bits of her keys (or one less bit at the most), so he can do the same thing. Alice has no real choice but to continue the protocol.

The basic point is that Alice has to play fairly, because the odds of fooling Bob are just too small. At the end of the protocol, both parties have 100 signed message pairs, any one of which is sufficient for a valid signature.

There are three weaknesses with protocols of this type [83]. First, there is a problem if one of the parties has significantly more computing power than the other. If, for example, Alice can break the algorithm faster than Bob can, then she can stop sending bits early in step (8) and figure out Bob's keys herself. Bob, who cannot do the same in a reasonable amount of time, will not be happy.

Second, there is a problem if one of the parties stops the protocol early. If Alice abruptly stops the protocol, both face the same computational effort, but Bob does not have any real legal recourse. If, for example, the contract specifies that he do something in a week, and Alice terminated the protocol at a point when Bob would have to spend a year's worth of computing power before she is really committed, then there could be a problem. The real difficulty here is that there is no near-term deadline by which the process cleanly terminates with either both parties bound or neither party bound.

Third, there are problems with some of the underlying mathematical assumptions. Successful cryptanalysis of the algorithms used could give one party an advantage over the other.

6.3 DIGITAL CERTIFIED MAIL

The same simultaneous oblivious transfer protocol used for contract signing can also be used for computer certified mail, but with some modifications. Suppose Alice wants to send a message to Bob, but she does not want him to read it without a signed receipt. Surly postal workers take care of this process in real life, but the same thing can be done with cryptography. Whitfield Diffie first discussed this problem in [293].

At first glance, the simultaneous contract signing protocol can do this. Alice simply encrypts her message with a DES key. Her half of the protocol can be something like: "This is the left half of the DES key: 32F5." Bob's half can be something like: "This is the left half of my receipt." Everything else stays the same.

To see why this won't work, remember that the protocol hinges on the fact that the oblivious transfer in step (5) keeps both parties honest. Both of them know that they sent the other party a valid half, but neither knows which. They don't cheat in step (8) because the odds of getting away with it are miniscule. If Alice is sending Bob not a receipt but half of a DES key, there is no way for Bob to check the validity of the DES key in step (6). Alice can still check the validity of Bob's receipt, so Bob is still forced to be honest. Alice can freely send Bob some garbage DES key, and he won't know the difference until she has a valid receipt. Tough luck, Bob.

Getting around this problem requires some adjustment of the protocol:

(1) Alice encrypts her message using a random DES key and sends it to Bob.

(2) Alice generates 100 pairs of DES keys. The first key of each pair is generated at random; the second key of each pair is the exclusive OR of the first key and the message encryption key.

(3) Alice encrypts a dummy message with each of her 200 keys.

(4) Alice sends the whole pile of encrypted messages to Bob, making sure he knows which messages are which halves of which pairs.

(5) Bob generates 100 pairs of random DES keys.

(6) Bob generates a pair of messages that indicates a valid receipt. "This is the left half of my receipt" and "this is the right half of my receipt" are good candidates, with the addition of some kind of validation. He makes 100 receipt pairs, each numbered. As with the previous protocol, the receipt is considered valid if Alice can produce both halves of a receipt (with the same number) and all of her encryption keys.

(7) Bob encrypts each of his message pairs with DES key pairs, the nth message pair with the nth key pair, the left message with the left key in the pair, and the right message with the right key in the pair.

(8) Bob sends his pile of message pairs to Alice, making sure that Alice knows which messages are which halves of which pairs.

(9) Alice and Bob send each other every key pair using the oblivious transfer protocol. That is, Alice sends Bob either the key used to encrypt the left message or the key used to encrypt the right message, for each of the 100 pairs. Bob does the same. They can either alternate sending halves or one can send 100 and then the other—it doesn't matter. Now both Alice and Bob have one key in each key pair, but neither knows which halves the other has.

(10) Alice and Bob both decrypt the halves they can and make sure that the decrypted messages are valid.

(11) Alice and Bob each send each other the first bits of all 200 DES keys. (If they are worried about Eve's being able to read the mail message, then they should encrypt their transmissions to each other.)

(12) Alice and Bob repeat step (11) for the second bits of all 200 DES keys, the third bits, and so on until all the bits of all the DES keys have been transferred.

(13) Alice and Bob decrypt the remaining halves of the message pairs. Alice has a valid receipt from Bob, and Bob can exclusive-OR any key pair to get the original message encryption key.

Steps (5) through (8) for Bob, and steps (9) through (12) for both Alice and Bob, are the same as the contract signing protocol. The twist is all of Alice's dummy messages. They give Bob some way of checking the validity of her oblivious transfer in step (10), which forces her to stay honest during steps (11) through (13). And as with the simultaneous contract signing protocol, both a left and a right half of one of Alice's message pairs are required to complete the protocol.

6.4   SIMULTANEOUS EXCHANGE OF SECRETS

The previous two protocols are implementations of this more general protocol, one that lets Alice and Bob exchange secrets simultaneously [321].

Alice knows secret A; Bob knows secret B. Alice is willing to tell Bob A, if Bob tells her B. Bob is willing to tell Alice B, if Alice tells him A. This protocol can be observed in a schoolyard—clearly it does not work:

(1) Alice: "I'll tell if you tell me first."

(2) Bob: "I'll tell if you tell me first."

(3) Alice: "No, you first."

(4) Bob: "Oh, all right." (Bob whispers.)

(5) Alice: "Ha! I won't tell you."

(6) Bob: "That's not fair."

Cryptography can make it fair. Rather than repeat the whole protocol, the following is a sketch of the modifications to the Digital Certified Mail protocol.

Alice performs steps (1) through (5) using A as the message. Bob goes through similar steps using B as his message. Alice and Bob perform the oblivious transfer in step (10), decrypt the halves they can in step (11), and go through the iterations in steps (12) and (13). If they are concerned about Eve, they should encrypt their messages. Finally, both Alice and Bob decrypt the remaining halves of the message pairs, and XOR any key pair to get the original message encryption key.

This protocol allows Alice and Bob to exchange secrets simultaneously, but it says nothing about the quality of the secrets exchanged. Alice could promise Bob the solution to the Minotaur's labyrinth, but actually send him a map of Boston's subway system. Bob will get the secret Alice sends him, whatever it is.

6.5   SECURE ELECTIONS

Computerized voting will never be used for general elections unless there is a protocol that both prevents cheating and maintains individual privacy. The ideal protocol has, at the very least, these five characteristics:

1. Only authorized voters can vote.

2. No one can vote more than once.

3. No one can determine for whom anyone voted.

4. No one can change anyone else's vote without being discovered.

5. All voters can make sure that their vote has been taken into account in the final tabulation.
    Additionally, some voting schemes may have the following requirement:

6. Everyone knows who voted and who didn't.

Before launching into the complicated voting protocols that have these characteristics, let's look at some simplistic protocols that don't.

Simplistic Voting Protocol #1

(1) All voters encrypt their vote with the public key of a Central Tabulating Facility (CTF).

(2) All voters send their vote to the CTF.

(3) The CTF decrypts the votes, tabulates them, and makes the results public.

This protocol has problems at every point. The CTF has no idea where the votes are coming from, so it doesn't know if the votes are coming from eligible voters or not. They have no idea if eligible voters are voting more than once. On the plus side, no one can change anyone else's vote, but no one would try to modify someone else's vote when it is far easier to vote an infinite number of times for the result of your choice.

Simplistic Voting Protocol #2

(1) All voters sign their vote with their private key.

(2) All voters encrypt their signed vote with the CTF's public key.

(3) All voters send their vote to a CTF.

(4) The CTF decrypts the votes, checks the signatures, tabulates the votes, and makes the results public.

This protocol satisfies properties one and two: only authorized voters can vote, and no one can vote more than once. The CTF has to keep a record of votes received in step (3) to do that. The votes are signed with the voters' private keys, so the CTF knows who voted, who didn't, and how often each voter voted. If a vote comes in that isn't signed by an eligible voter, or if a vote comes in signed by a voter who has already voted, the facility ignores it. People cannot change anyone else's vote either, even if they intercept it in step (2), because of the digital signature.

The problem with this protocol is that because the signature is attached to the vote, the CTF knows who voted for whom. Encrypting the votes with the CTF's public key prevents anyone from eavesdropping on the protocol and figuring out who voted for whom; but this isn't good enough. It's analogous to having an election judge staring over your shoulder in a voting booth.

Voting with Blind Signatures

What we need to do is somehow to dissociate the vote from the voter, while still maintaining authentication. The blind signature protocol does just that.

(1) All voters generate a set of messages, each set containing a valid vote for each possible outcome (for example, if the vote is a "yes" or "no" question, each set contains two votes, one for "yes" and the other for "no"). Each message also contains a randomly generated serial number, large enough to avoid duplicates with other voters.

(2) All voters individually blind all of the messages (see Section 5.5) and send the results to the CTF.

(3) The CTF checks its database to make sure voters have not submitted blinded votes for their signature previously. Then it individually signs each

message in the set. It then sends them back to the voters and stores the names of the voters in its database.

(4) The voters unblind the messages, leaving a set of votes signed by the CTF. (These votes are signed but unencrypted, so the voters can easily see which vote is "yes" and which is "no.")

(5) The voters choose one of the votes (ah, Democracy) and encrypt it with the CTF's public key.

(6) The voters send their vote in.

(7) The CTF decrypts the votes, checks the signatures, checks its database for a duplicate serial number, saves the serial number, and tabulates the votes. It publishes the results of the election, along with every serial number and its associated vote.

There is no reason to use the full blind signature protocol. The CTF doesn't have to check nine out of ten message sets to verify that Alice's votes are properly formed before signing them. It is in Alice's best interest to make sure her votes are created correctly, otherwise they can't be counted.

A malicious voter, call him Mallet, cannot cheat this system. The blind signature protocol ensures that his votes are unique. If he tries to send in the same vote twice, the CTF will notice the duplicate serial number in step (7) and throw out the second vote. If he tries to get multiple-signed votes in step (2), the CTF will discover this in step (3). Mallet cannot generate his own votes because he doesn't know the facility's private key. He can't intercept and change other people's votes for the same reason.

A malicious CTF cannot figure out how individuals voted. Because the blind signature protocol prevents the facility from seeing the serial numbers on the votes before they are cast, the CTF cannot link the blinded vote it signed with the vote eventually cast. Publishing a list of serial numbers and their associated votes allows voters to confirm that their vote was tabulated correctly.

There are still problems. If the CTF can record who sent in which vote, then it can figure out who voted for whom. However, if it receives votes in a locked ballot box and then tabulates them later, it cannot. Also, while the CTF may not be able to link votes to individuals, it can generate a large number of signed, valid votes.

Voting with Two Central Facilities

One solution is to divide the power of the CTF between two parties. Neither party would have enough power to cheat on its own.

The following protocol uses a Central Legitimization Agency (CLA) to certify voters and a separate CTF to count votes [763].

(1) All voters send a message to the CLA asking for a validation number.

(2) The CLA sends the voters back a random validation number, *L*. The CLA maintains a list of validation numbers. The CLA also keeps a list of the validation numbers' recipients, in case they try to vote again.

(3) The CLA sends the list of validation numbers to the CTF.

(4) All voters choose an individual random identification number, *I*. They create a message with their identification number, the validation number they received from the CLA, and their vote, *v*. They send this message to the CTF.

$$M = (L, I, v)$$

(5) The CTF checks the validation number against the list it received from the CLA in step (3). If the number, *L*, is there, the CTF crosses it off (to prevent anyone from voting twice). The CTF adds the identification number to the list of people who voted for a particular candidate and adds one to the tally.

(6) After all votes have been received, the CTF publishes the outcome, as well as the lists of identification numbers and whom their owners voted for.

One benefit of this system is that all voters can look at the lists of identification numbers and find their own. This gives them proof that their vote was counted. Of course, all messages passing among the varying parties in the protocol should be encrypted and signed, to prevent someone from impersonating someone else or from intercepting transmissions.

The CTF cannot modify votes because all voters will look for their identification string. If voters don't find their identification string, or find their identification string in another tally than the one they voted for, they will immediately know there was foul play. The CTF cannot stuff the ballot box because it is being watched by the CLA. The CLA knows how many voters have been certified and their certification numbers. Any modifications to either of those will immediately be detected. Mallet, who is not an eligible voter, can try to cheat by guessing a valid validation number. The probability of success of this attack can be minimized by making the number of possible validation numbers much larger than the number of actual validation numbers: a million actual 100-digit numbers, for example. Of course, the validation numbers must be generated randomly.

Despite this, the CLA is still a trusted authority in some respects. It can certify ineligible voters. It can certify eligible voters multiple times. This risk could be minimized by having the CLA publish a list of certified voters (but not their certification numbers). If the number of voters on this list is less than the number of votes tabulated, then something is awry. If more voters were certified than votes tabulated, it probably means that some certified people didn't bother voting. (Many people are registered to vote but choose not to cast ballots.) This protocol is also vulnerable to collusion between the CLA and the CTF. If the two of them got together, they could correlate databases and figure out who voted for whom.

Voting with a Single Central Facility

A more complex protocol can be used to overcome the danger of collusion between the CLA and the CTF [763]. This protocol is identical to the previous one, with two modifications:

- The CLA and the CTF are one organization, and

- ANDOS (see Section 5.2) is used to distribute anonymous validation numbers in step (2).

Since the anonymous key distribution protocol prevents the CTF from knowing which voter got which validation number, there is no way for the CTF to correlate validation numbers with votes received. The CTF still has to be trusted not to give validation numbers to ineligible voters, though.

Improved Voting with a Single Central Facility

This protocol, by Hannu Nurmi, Arto Salomaa, and Lila Santean [659], also uses ANDOS. It is an excellent protocol and satisfies all five requirements of a good voting protocol. It doesn't satisfy the sixth requirement, but has two additional properties to those listed at the beginning of the section:

(7)   Voters can change their mind (i.e., retract their vote and vote again) within a given period of time.
(8)   If voters find out that their vote is miscounted, they can identify and correct the problem without jeopardizing the secrecy of their ballot.

Here's the protocol:

(1) The CTF publishes a list of all legitimate voters.

(2) Within a specified deadline, everybody intending to vote reports his intentions to the CTF.

(3) The CTF publishes a list of voters participating in the election.

(4) All voters receive an identification number, i, using an ANDOS protocol.

(5) All voters generate a public/private key pair: e and d. If v is the vote, they generate the following message and send it to the CTF:

$$i, E_e(i, v)$$

(6) The CTF acknowledges receipt of the vote by publishing:

$$E_e(i, v)$$

(7) All voters send the CTF:

$$i, d$$

(8) The CTF uses d to decrypt the votes. At the end of the election, it publishes the results of the election and, for each different vote, the list of all $E_e(i,v)$ values that contained that vote.

(9) If voters observe that their vote is not properly counted, they protest by sending the CTF:

$$i, E_e(i,v), d$$

(10) If voters want to change their vote (this is possible in some elections) from v to v', they send the CTF:

$$i, E_e(i,v), v'$$

Steps (1) through (3) are preliminary to the actual voting. Their purpose is to find out and publicize the total number of actual voters. Although some of them probably will not participate, it reduces the ability of the CTF to add fraudulent votes.

In step (4), it is possible for two voters to get the same identification number. This possibility can be minimized by having far more possible identification numbers than actual voters. If two voters submit votes with the same identification tag, the CTF generates a new identification number, i', chooses one of the two votes, and publishes:

$$i', E_e(i,v)$$

The owner of that vote recognizes it and sends in a second vote, by repeating step (5), with the new identification number.

Step (6) gives all voters the capability to check that the CTF received their vote accurately. And if their vote is miscounted, they can prove their case in step (9). Assuming all voters' votes are correct in step (6), the message they send in step (9) constitutes proof that their vote was miscounted.

The primary problem with the protocol is that the CTF can allocate the votes of people who respond in step (2) but who do not actually vote. Another problem is the complexity of the ANDOS protocol. The authors recommend dividing a large population of voters into smaller populations, such as election districts. They also point out another problem, one common among all computer voting protocols: "The incentives for selling and buying of votes become considerably stronger as the buyer can be sure that the seller also delivers the goods, i.e., votes as promised."

Voting Without a Central Tabulating Facility

This protocol would involve dispensing with the CTF entirely. Designed by Michael Merritt [262,595,263], it is so unwieldy that it cannot be implemented practically for more than a handful of people, but it is useful to learn from nevertheless.

Alice, Bob, Carol, and Dave are voting yes or no (0 or 1) on a particular issue. Assume each voter has a public and private key. Also assume that everyone knows everyone else's public keys.

(1) All voters choose a vote and do the following:

    (a) Attach a random string to their vote.

    (b) Encrypt the result of step (a) with Dave's public key.

    (c) Encrypt the result of step (b) with Carol's public key.

    (d) Encrypt the result of step (c) with Bob's public key.

    (e) Encrypt the result of step (d) with Alice's public key.

    (f) Attach a new random string to the result of step (e) and encrypt the whole thing with Dave's public key. They record the value of the random string.

    (g) Attach a new random string to the result of step (f) and encrypt it with Carol's public key. They record the value of the random string.

    (h) Attach a new random string to the result of step (f) and encrypt it with Bob's public key. They record the value of the random string.

    (i) Attach a new random string to the result of step (h) and encrypt it with Alice's public key. They record the value of the random string.

If E is the encryption function, R is a random string, and V is the vote, the vote looks like:

$$E_A(R_5, E_B(R_4, E_C(R_3, E_D(R_2, E_A(E_B(E_C(E_D(V, R_1))))))))$$

All voters save the intermediate results at each point in the calculation. These results will be used later in the protocol to confirm that their vote is among those being counted.

(2) All voters send their vote to Alice.

(3) Alice decrypts all of the votes with her private key, checks to see that her vote is among the set of votes (by looking for her random string among the votes), and then removes all of the random strings at that level.

(4) Alice scrambles the order of all the votes and sends the result to Bob.

Each vote now looks like this:

$$E_B(R_4, E_C(R_3, E_D(R_2, E_A(E_B(E_C(E_D(V, R_1)))))))$$

(5) Bob decrypts all of the votes with his private key, checks to see that his vote is among the set of votes, removes all the random strings at that level, scrambles all the votes, and then sends the result to Carol.

Each vote now looks like this:

$$E_C(R_3, E_D(R_2, E_A(E_B(E_C(E_D(V, R_1))))))$$

(6) Carol decrypts all of the votes with her private key, checks to see that her vote is among the set of votes, removes all the random strings at that level, scrambles all the votes, and then sends the result to Dave.

Each vote now looks like this:

$$E_D(R_2,E_A(E_B(E_C(E_D(V,R_1)))))$$

(7) Dave decrypts all of the votes with his private key, checks to see that his vote is among the set of votes, removes all the random strings at that level, scrambles all the votes, and sends them to Alice.

Each vote now looks like this:

$$E_A(E_B(E_C(E_D(V,R_1))))$$

(8) Alice decrypts all the votes with her private key, checks to see that her vote is among the set of votes, signs all the votes, and then sends the result to Bob, Carol, and Dave.

Each vote now looks like this:

$$S_A(E_B(E_C(E_D(V,R_1))))$$

(9) Bob verifies and deletes Alice's signatures. He decrypts all the votes with his private key, checks to see that his vote is among the set of votes, signs all the votes, and then sends the result to Alice, Carol, and Dave.

Each vote now looks like this:

$$S_B(E_C(E_D(V,R_1)))$$

(10) Carol verifies and deletes Bob's signatures. She decrypts all the votes with her private key, checks to see that her vote is among the set of votes, signs all the votes, and then sends the result to Alice, Bob, and Dave.

Each vote now looks like this:

$$S_C(E_D(V,R_1))$$

(11) Dave verifies and deletes Carol's signatures. He decrypts all the votes with his private key, checks to see that his vote is among the set of votes, signs all the votes, and then sends the result to Alice, Bob, and Carol.

Each vote now looks like this:

$$S_D(V,R_1)$$

(12) All verify and delete Dave's signature. They check to make sure that their vote is among the set of votes (by looking for their random string among the votes).

(13) Everyone removes the random strings from each vote and tallies the votes.

Not only does this protocol work, it is self-adjudicating. Alice, Bob, Carol, and Dave will immediately know if someone tries to cheat. No CTF or CLA is required. To see how this works, let's try to cheat.

If someone tries to stuff the ballot, Alice will detect the attempt in step (3) when she receives more votes than people. If Alice tries to stuff the ballot, Bob will notice in step (4).

A more devious way of cheating is to substitute one vote for another. Since the votes are encrypted with various public keys, anyone can create as many valid votes as needed. There are two rounds to the decryption protocol: round 1 consists of steps (3) through (7), and round 2 consists of steps (8) through (11). Vote substitution is detected differently in the different rounds.

If someone substitutes one vote for another in round 2, the actions are discovered immediately. At every step the votes are signed and sent to all the voters. If one (or more) of the voters noticed that her vote is no longer in the set of votes, she immediately stops the protocol. Because the votes are signed at every step, and because everyone can backtrack through the second round of the protocol, it is easy to detect who substituted the votes.

Substituting one vote for another during round 1 of the protocol is more subtle. Alice can't do it in step (3), because Bob, Carol, or Dave will detect it in step (5), (6), or (7). Bob could try in step (5). If he replaces Carol's or Dave's vote (remember, he doesn't know which vote corresponds to which voter), Carol or Dave will notice in step (6) or (7). They wouldn't know who tampered with their vote (although it would have had to be someone who had already handled the votes), but they would know that their vote was tampered with. If Bob is lucky and picks Alice's vote to replace, she won't notice until the second round. Then, she will notice her vote missing in step (8). Still, she would not know who tampered with her vote. In the first round, the votes are shuffled from one step to the other and unsigned; it is impossible for anyone to backtrack through the protocol to determine who tampered with the votes.

A more subtle form of cheating is to try to figure out who voted for whom. Because of the scrambling in the first round, it is impossible for someone to backtrack through the protocol and link votes with voters. The removal of the random strings in the second round is also crucial to preserving anonymity. If they are not removed, the scrambling of the votes could be reversed by re-encrypting the emerging votes with the scrambler's public key. As the protocol stands, the confidentiality of the votes is secure.

Even more strongly, because of the initial random string, R_1, even identical votes are encrypted differently at every step of the protocol. No one knows the outcome of the vote until step (11).

What are the problems with this protocol? First, the protocol has an enormous amount of computation. The example described had only four voters, and *it* was complicated. This would never work in a real election, with tens of thousands of voters. Second, Dave learns the results of the election before anyone else does. While he still can't affect the outcome, this gives him some power that the others do not have. On the other hand, this is also true with centralized voting schemes.

Other Voting Schemes

Many complex secure election protocols have been proposed. One protocol [216,215,64,63] hides the actual value of the votes. The protocol guarantees the accuracy of the voting and preserves the confidentiality of votes from other voters. However, it only protects the privacy of voters to the extent that different "parts" of the government (or whoever is administering the voting) do not conspire against the voter. (This idea of breaking a central authority into different parts, who are only trusted when together, comes from [191].)

Another protocol, by David Chaum [197], ensures that voters who attempt to disrupt an election can be traced. However, the election must then be repeated, without the interfering voter; this approach is not practical for large-scale elections.

Another, more complex, voting protocol that solves some of these problems can be found in [449,450]. There is even a voting protocol that uses multiple-key ciphers [135]. Yet another voting protocol, which claims to be practical for large-scale elections, is in [359]. All of these protocols are beyond the scope of this book.

6.6 SECURE MULTIPARTY COMPUTATION

Secure multiparty computation is a protocol in which a group of people can get together and compute a function of each of their inputs in a special way. Everyone in the group knows the value of the function, but no one learns anything about the inputs of any of the other members. Here are some examples:

Protocol #1

How can a group of people calculate their average salary without anyone learning the salary of anyone else?

(1) Alice adds a secret random number to her salary, encrypts the result with Bob's public key, and sends it to Bob.

(2) Bob decrypts Alice's result with his private key. He adds his salary to what he received from Alice, encrypts the result with Carol's public key, and sends it to Carol.

(3) Carol decrypts Bob's result with her private key. She adds her salary to what she received from Bob, encrypts the result with Dave's public key, and sends it to Dave.

(4) Dave decrypts Carol's result with his private key. He adds his salary to what he received from Carol, encrypts the result with Alice's public key, and sends it to Alice.

(5) Alice decrypts Dave's result with her private key. She subtracts the random number from step (1) to recover the sum of everyone's salaries.

(6) Alice divides the result by the number of people (four, in this case), and announces the result.

This protocol assumes that everyone is honest. If the participants lie about their salary, the average will be wrong. A more serious problem is that Alice can misrepresent the result to everyone. She can subtract any number she likes from the result, and no one would be the wiser. Alice could be prevented from doing this by requiring her to commit to her random number using any of the bit commitment schemes from Section 4.6, but when she revealed her random number at the end of the protocol Bob could learn her salary.

Protocol #2

Alice and Bob are at a restaurant together, having an argument over who is older. They don't want to tell the other their age, but both are interested in knowing who is older. They could each whisper their age into the ear of a trusted neutral party (the waiter, for example), who could compare the numbers in his head and announce the result to both Alice and Bob.

There arc two problems with the above protocol. One, your average waiter doesn't have the computational ability to handle situations more complex than determining which of two numbers is greater. And two, if Alice and Bob were really concerned about the secrecy of their information, they would be forced to drown the waiter in a bowl of vichyssoise lest he tell the wine steward.

The next solution uses public-key cryptography. There is a protocol by which Alice, who knows a value a, and Bob, who knows a value b, can together determine if $f(a,b)$, so that Alice gets no information about b and Bob gets no information about a. And, both Alice and Bob are convinced of the validity of the computation. Since the cryptographic algorithm used is an essential part of the protocol, details can be found in Section 16.15.

Of course, this protocol doesn't protect against active cheaters. There's nothing to stop Alice (or Bob, for that matter) from lying about their ages. If Bob were a computer program that blindly executed the protocol, Alice could learn his age (is the age of a computer program the length of time since it was written, or the length of time since it started running?) by repeated applications of the protocol. Alice might execute the protocol, giving her age as 60. After learning that she is older, she could execute the protocol again with her age as 30. After learning that Bob is older, she could execute the protocol again with her age as 45, and so on, until Alice discovers Bob's age to any degree of accuracy she wishes.

Assuming that the participants don't actively cheat, it is easy to extend this protocol to multiple participants. Any number of people can find out the order of their ages by a sequence of honest applications of the protocol; and no participant can learn the age of another participant.

Protocol #3

Alice likes to do kinky things with teddy bears. Bob has erotic fantasies about marble tables. Both are pretty embarrassed about their particular fetish, but would love to find a mate who shared in their . . . um . . . lifestyle.

At the Secure Multiparty Computation Dating Service™, we've designed a protocol for people like them. We've numbered an astonishing list of fetishes, from "aardvarks" to "zoot suits." Discreetly separated by a modem link, Alice and Bob can participate in a secure multiparty protocol. Together, they can determine whether or not they share the same fetish. If they do, they might look forward to a happy relationship. If they don't, they can part company, secure in the knowledge that their particular personal information remains confidential. No one, not even the Secure Multiparty Computation Dating Service™, will ever know.

This is similar to Protocol #2. Alice knows a, Bob knows b, and together they will determine whether $a = b$, such that Bob does not learn anything about a and Alice does not learn anything about b. Details are in Section 16.15.

Protocol #4

This is another problem for secure multiparty computation, found in [763]. There is a council that meets regularly to cast secret ballots on certain issues. (All right, they secretly rule the world—don't tell anyone I told you.) All council members can vote yes or no. In addition, two parties have the option of casting "super votes": S-yes and S-no. They do not have to cast super votes; they can cast regular votes if they prefer. If no one casts any super votes, then the majority of votes decides the issue. In the case of a single or two equivalent super votes, all regular votes are ignored. In the case of two contradicting super votes, the majority of ordinary votes decides. We want a protocol that securely performs this style of voting.

Two examples should illustrate the voting process. Assume there are five regular voters, N_1 through N_5, and two super voters: S_1 and S_2. Here's the vote on issue #1:

S_1	S_2	N_1	N_2	N_3	N_4	N_5
S-yes	no	no	no	no	yes	yes

In this instance the only vote that matters is S_1's, and the result is yes.

Here is the vote on issue #2:

S_1	S_2	N_1	N_2	N_3	N_4	N_5
S-yes	S-no	no	no	no	yes	yes

Here the two super votes cancel, and the majority of regular no votes decide the issue.

If it isn't important to hide the knowledge of whether the super vote or the regular vote was the deciding vote, this is an easy application of a secure voting protocol. If it is important to hide that knowledge, a more complicated secure multiparty computation protocol is required.

This kind of voting could occur in real life. It could be part of a corporation's organizational structure, where certain people have more power than others. Or it could be part of the United Nations' procedures, where certain nations have more power than others.

Secure Circuit Evaluation

Alice has her input, a. Bob has his input, b. Together they wish to compute some general function, $f(a,b)$, such that Alice learns nothing about Bob's input and Bob learns nothing about Alice's input. The general problem of secure multiparty computation is also called **secure circuit evaluation.** Here, Alice and Bob can create an arbitrary Boolean circuit. This circuit accepts inputs from Alice and from Bob and produces an output. Secure circuit evaluation is a protocol that accomplishes three things:

1. Alice can enter her input without Bob's being able to learn it.

2. Bob can enter his input without Alice's being able to learn it.

3. Both Alice and Bob can calculate the output, with both parties being sure the output is correct and that neither party has tampered with it.

Details on secure circuit evaluation can be found in [479].

6.7 DIGITAL CASH

Cash is a problem. It's annoying to carry, it could spread germs, and people can steal it from you. The existence of credit and debit cards has greatly reduced the amount of physical cash flowing through our society, but the complete elimination of cash is virtually impossible. It'll never happen; drug dealers and politicians would never stand for it. Credit cards come with an audit trail; you can't hide to whom you gave money. As long as this problem remains, people will need a way to exchange money without a trace.

Happily, there is a complicated protocol that allows for authentic but untraceable messages. Lobbyist Alice can transfer digital "cash" to Senator Bob so that newspaper reporter Eve does not know the identity of Alice. Bob can then deposit that electronic money into his bank account, even though the bank has no idea who Alice is. But if Alice tries to bribe two different Congresspersons with the same piece of digital cash, which is easy to try with a bit copy program, she will be detected by the bank. And if Bob tries to deposit the same piece of digital cash into two different accounts, he will be detected—but Alice will remain anonymous.

Let's break down this complex series of steps into individual parts. For more formal details, read [193,206,198,202,418].

Protocol #1

The first few protocols are physical analogies of cryptographic protocols. This first protocol is a simplified physical protocol for anonymous money orders:

(1) Alice prepares 100 anonymous money orders for $1000.

(2) Alice puts one each, and a piece of carbon paper, into 100 different envelopes. She gives them all to the bank.

(3) The bank opens 99 envelopes and confirms that each is a money order for
$1000.

(4) The bank signs the one remaining unopened envelope. The signature goes
through the carbon paper to the money order. The bank hands the
unopened envelope back to Alice and deducts $1000 from her account.

(5) Alice opens the envelope and spends the money order with a merchant.

(6) The merchant checks for the bank's signature to make sure the money
order is legitimate.

(7) The merchant takes the money order to the bank.

(8) The bank verifies its signature and credits $1000 to the merchant's account.

This protocol works. The bank never sees the money order it signed, so when
the merchant brings it to the bank, the bank has no idea that it was Alice's. The
bank is convinced that it is valid, though, because of the signature. The bank is
confident that the unopened money order is for $1000 (and not for $100,000 or
$100,000,000) because of the cut-and-choose protocol (see Section 5.3). It verifies
the other 99 envelopes, so Alice has only a 1% chance of cheating the bank. Of
course, the bank will make the penalty for cheating great enough so that it isn't
worth that chance. If the bank refuses to sign the last check (if Alice is caught
cheating) without penalizing Alice, she might continue to try until she gets lucky.
(Prison terms are a better deterrent.)

Protocol #2

The previous protocol prevents Alice from writing a money order for more than
she claims to, but it doesn't prevent Alice from photocopying the money order and
spending it twice. For that, we need a complication:

(1) Alice prepares 100 anonymous money orders for $1000 each. On each
money order she includes a different random uniqueness string, one long
enough to make the chance of another person also using it negligible.

(2) Alice puts one each, and a piece of carbon paper, into 100 different
envelopes. She gives them all to the bank.

(3) The bank opens 99 envelopes and confirms that each is a money order for
$1000 and that all the random uniqueness strings are different.

(4) The bank signs the one remaining unopened envelope. The signature goes
through the carbon paper to the money order. The bank hands the
unopened envelope back to Alice and deducts $1000 from her account.

(5) Alice opens the envelope and spends the money order with a merchant.

(6) The merchant checks for the bank's signature to make sure the money order is legitimate.

(7) The merchant takes the money order to the bank.

(8) The bank verifies its signature and checks its database to make sure a money order with the same uniqueness string has not been previously deposited. If it hasn't, the bank credits $1000 to the merchant's account. The bank records the random string in a database.

(9) If it has been previously deposited, the bank doesn't accept the money order.

Now, if Alice tries to spend a photocopy of the money order, or if the merchant tries to deposit a photocopy of the money order, the bank will know about it.

Protocol #3

The previous protocol protects the bank from cheating, but it doesn't identify the cheater. The bank doesn't know if the person who bought the money order (the bank has no idea it's Alice) tried to cheat the merchant or if the merchant tried to cheat the bank. This protocol corrects that:

(1) Alice prepares 100 anonymous money orders for $1000 each. On each of the money orders she includes a different random uniqueness string, one long enough to make the chance of another person also using it negligible.

(2) Alice puts one each, and a piece of carbon paper, into 100 different envelopes. She gives them all to the bank.

(3) The bank opens 99 envelopes and confirms that each is a money order for $1000 and that all the random strings are different.

(4) The bank signs the one remaining unopened envelope. The signature goes through the carbon paper to the money order. The bank hands the unopened envelope back to Alice and deducts $1000 from her account.

(5) Alice opens the envelope and spends the money order with a merchant.

(6) The merchant checks for the bank's signature to make sure the money order is legitimate.

(7) The merchant asks Alice to write a random identity string on the money order.

(8) Alice complies.

(9) The merchant takes the money order to the bank.

(10) The bank verifies the signature and checks its database to make sure a money order with the same uniqueness string has not been previously deposited. If it hasn't, the bank credits $1000 to the merchant's account.

The bank records the uniqueness string and the identity string in a database.

(11) If the uniqueness string is in the database, the bank refuses to accept the money order. Then, it compares the identity string on the money order with the one stored in the database. If it is the same, the bank knows that the merchant photocopied the money order. If it is different, the bank knows that the person who bought the money order photocopied it.

This protocol assumes that the merchant cannot change the identity string once Alice writes it on the money order. The money order might have a series of little squares, which the merchant would require Alice to fill in with either X's or O's. The money order might be made out of paper that tears if erased.

Since the interaction between the merchant and the bank takes place after Alice spends the money, the merchant is stuck with the bad money order. Practical implementations of this protocol might require Alice to wait by the cash register during the merchant-bank interaction, much the same way as credit-card purchases are handled today.

Alice could try to frame the merchant. She could spend a copy of the money order a second time, giving the same identity string in step (7). Unless the merchant keeps a database of money orders it already received, the merchant will be fooled. The next protocol eliminates that problem.

Protocol #4

If it turns out that the person who bought the money order tried to cheat the merchant, it would behoove the bank to know who that person was. To do that requires moving away from a physical analogy and into the world of cryptography.

The technique of secret splitting can be used to hide Alice's name in the digital money order.

(1) Alice prepares 100 anonymous money orders for $1000 each. Each of the money orders looks like this:

> Amount: $1000
> Uniqueness String: X
> Identity Strings: $I_1 = (I_{1_L}, I_{1_R})$
> $I_2 = (I_{2_L}, I_{2_R})$
>   .
>   .
>   .
>
> $I_{100} = (I_{100_L}, I_{100_R})$

Each of the money orders contains a different random uniqueness string, X, one long enough to make the chance of two being identical negligible.

On each money order, there are also 100 pairs of identity bit strings, I_n. (That's 100 different pairs on *each* check.) Each of these pairs is generated as follows: Alice creates a string that gives her name, address, and any other piece of identifying information that the bank wants to see.

Then, she splits it into two pieces using the secret splitting protocol (see Section 3.5). Then, she commits to each piece using a bit commitment protocol.

For example, I_{37} consists of two parts: I_{37_L} and I_{37_R}. Each part is a bit-committed packet that Alice can be asked to open and whose proper opening can be instantly verified. The combination of any pair, : I_{37_L} and I_{37_R}, but not I_{37L} and I_{38R}, reveals Alice's identity.

(2) Alice blinds all 100 money orders, using a blind signature protocol. She gives them all to the bank.

(3) The bank asks Alice to unblind 99 of the money orders and confirms that they are all well formed. The bank checks the amount, the uniqueness string, and asks Alice to reveal all of the identity strings.

(4) If the bank is satisfied that Alice did not make any attempts to cheat, it signs the one remaining blinded money order. The bank hands the blinded money order back to Alice and deducts $1000 from her account.

(5) Alice unblinds the money order and spends it with a merchant.

(6) The merchant verifies the bank's signature to make sure the money order is legitimate.

(7) The merchant asks Alice to randomly reveal either the left half or the right half of each identity string on the money order. In effect, the merchant gives Alice a random 100-bit **selector string,** $b_1, b_2, \ldots, b_{100}.$ Alice opens either the left or right half of I_i, depending on whether b_i is a 0 or a 1.

(8) Alice complies.

(9) The merchant takes the money order to the bank.

(10) The bank verifies the signature and checks its database to make sure a money order with the same uniqueness string has not been previously deposited. If it hasn't, the bank credits $1000 to the merchant's account. The bank records the uniqueness string and all of the identity information in a database.

(11) If the uniqueness string is in the database, the bank refuses to accept the money order. Then, it compares the identity string on the money order with the one stored in the database. If it is the same, the bank knows that the merchant copied the money order. If it is different, the bank knows that the person who bought the money order photocopied it. Since the second merchant who accepted the money order handed Alice a different identity string than did the first merchant, the bank finds a bit position where one merchant had Alice open the left half and the other merchant had Alice open the right half. The bank XORs the two halves together to reveal Alice's identity.

This is quite an amazing protocol, so let's look at it from various angles.

Can Alice cheat? Her digital money order is nothing more than a string of bits, so she can copy it. Spending it the first time won't be a problem; she'll just complete the protocol and everything will go smoothly. The merchant will give her a random 100-bit selector string in step (7), and Alice will open either the left half or right half of each I_i in step (8). In step (10), the bank will record all of this data, as well as the money order's uniqueness string.

When she tries to use the same digital money order a second time, the merchant (either the same merchant or a different merchant) will give her a different random identity string in step (7). Alice must comply in step (8); not doing so will immediately alert the merchant that something is suspicious. Now, when the merchant brings the money order to the bank in step (10), the bank would immediately notice that a money order with the same uniqueness string was already deposited. The bank then compares the opened halves of the identity strings. The odds that the two random selector strings are the same is 1 in 2^{100}; it isn't likely to happen before the next ice age. Now, the bank finds a pair with one half that was opened the first time and the other half opened the second time. It XORs the two halves together, and out pops Alice's name. The bank knows who tried to spend the money order twice.

This protocol doesn't require Alice to stand around while the merchant and bank go through their section of the protocol. Only if Alice cheats will the bank know her identity. Alice can't stop her identity from being revealed. She can't change either the uniqueness string or any of the identity strings, because then the bank's signature will no longer be valid. The merchant will immediately notice that in step (6).

Alice could try to sneak a bad money order past the bank, one on which the identity strings don't reveal her name; or better yet, one whose identity strings would reveal someone else's name. The odds of her getting this ruse past the bank in step (3) are 1 in 100. These aren't impossible odds, but if you make the penalty bad enough, Alice won't try it. Or, you could increase the number of redundant money orders that Alice makes in step (2).

Can the merchant cheat? His chances are even worse. He can't deposit the money order twice; the bank will notice the repeated use of the selector string. He can't fake blaming Alice; only she can open any of the identity strings.

Even collusion between Alice and the merchant can't cheat the bank. As long as the bank signs the money order with the uniqueness string, the bank is assured of having only to make good on the money order once.

What about the bank? Is there some way for it to figure out that the money order it deposited was the one it signed for Alice? Alice is protected by the blind signature protocol in steps (2) through (5). There is no way for the bank to make the connection, even if it keeps complete records of every transaction. Even more strongly, there is no way for the bank and the merchant to get together to figure out who Alice is. Alice can walk in the store and, completely anonymously, make her purchase.

This protocol lies somewhere between an arbitrated protocol and a self-enforcing protocol. Both Alice and the merchant trust the bank to make good on the money orders, but Alice does not have to trust the bank with her identity.

Other Digital Cash Protocols

In [674], Tatsuaki Okamoto and Kazuo Ohta list six properties of an ideal digital cash system:

1. **Independence.** The security of the digital cash is not dependent on any physical location. The cash can be transferred through computer networks.

2. **Security.** The digital cash cannot be copied and reused.

3. **Privacy (Untraceability).** The privacy of users is protected; no one can trace the relationship between users and their purchases.

4. **Off-Line Payment.** When a user pays for a purchase with electronic cash, the protocol between the user and the merchant is executed off-line. That is, the shop does not need to be linked to a host to process the user's payment.

5. **Transferability.** The digital cash can be transferred to other users.

6. **Divisibility.** A piece of digital cash in a given amount can be subdivided into smaller pieces of cash in smaller amounts. (Of course, everything has to total up properly in the end.)

The protocols discussed here satisfy properties 1, 2, 3, and 4, but not 5 and 6. There are on-line digital cash systems that satisfy all properties except 4 [193,235,695]. The first off-line digital cash system that satisfies properties 1, 2, 3, and 4, similar to the one discussed here, was proposed in [206]. T. Okamoto and K. Ohta proposed a system that satisfies properties 1 through 5 [673]; they also proposed a system that satisfies properties 1 through 6 as well, but the data requirements for the purchase on one article was approximately 200 megabytes.

The digital cash scheme proposed in [674], by the same authors, satisfies properties 1 through 6, without the enormous data requirements. The total data transfer for a payment is about 20 kilobytes, and the protocol can be completed in several seconds. The authors consider this the first ideal untraceable electronic cash system.

Digital Cash and the Perfect Crime

Digital cash has its dark side, too. Sometimes people don't want so much privacy. Watch Alice commit the perfect crime [867]:

(1) Alice kidnaps a baby.

(2) Alice prepares 10,000 anonymous money orders for $1000 (or as many as she wants for whatever denomination she wants).

(3) Alice blinds all 10,000 money orders, using a blind signature protocol. She sends them to the authorities with the threat to kill the baby unless the following instructions are met:

    (a) Have a bank sign all 10,000 money orders.

   (b) Publish the results in a newspaper.

(4) The authorities comply.

(5) Alice buys a newspaper, unblinds the money orders, and starts spending
     them. There is no way for the authorities to trace the money orders to her.

(6) Alice frees the baby.

   Note that this situation is much worse than any random one involving physical
tokens—cash, for example. Since there is no need for physical contact, the police
have less opportunity to apprehend the kidnapper.

Practical Digital Cash

A Dutch company, DigiCash, has implemented digital cash protocols in working
products. Anyone interested should contact:

   DigiCash BV
   Kruislaan 419
   1098 VA Amsterdam
   NETHERLANDS

6.8   ANONYMOUS MESSAGE BROADCAST

You can't go out to dinner with a bunch of cryptographers without raising a ruckus.
In [196], David Chaum introduced the Dining Cryptographers Problem:

> Three cryptographers are sitting down to dinner at their favorite three-star
> restaurant. Their waiter informs them that arrangements have been made with
> the maître d'hôtel for the bill to be paid anonymously. One of the
> cryptographers might be paying for the dinner, or it might have been the NSA.
> The three cryptographers respect each other's right to make an anonymous
> payment, but they wonder if the NSA is paying.

   How do the cryptographers, named Alice, Bob, and Carol, determine if one of
them is paying for dinner, while at the same time preserving the anonymity of the
payer?
   Chaum goes on to solve the problem:

> Each cryptographer flips an unbiased coin behind his menu, between him and
> the cryptographer to his right, so that only the two of them can see the
> outcome. Each cryptographer then states aloud whether the two coins he can
> see—the one he flipped and the one his left-hand neighbor flipped—fell on
> the same side or on different sides. If one of the cryptographers is the payer,
> he states the opposite of what he sees. An odd number of differences uttered
> at the table indicates that a cryptographer is paying; an even number of

differences indicates that NSA is paying (assuming that the dinner was paid for only once). Yet, if a cryptographer is paying, neither of the other two learns anything from the utterances about which cryptographer it is.

To see that this works, imagine Alice trying to figure out which other cryptographer paid for dinner (assuming that neither she nor the NSA paid). If she sees two different coins, then either both of the other cryptographers, Bob and Carol, said, "same" or both said, "different." (Remember, an odd number of cryptographers saying "different" indicates that one of them paid.) If both said, "different," then the payer is the cryptographer closest to the coin that is the same as the hidden coin (the one that Bob and Carol flipped). If both said, "same," then the payer is the cryptographer closest to the coin that is different from the hidden coin. However, if Alice sees two coins that are the same, then either Bob said, "same" and Carol said, "different," or Bob said, "different" and Carol said, "same." If the hidden coin is the same as the two coins she sees, then the cryptographer who said, "different" is the payer. If the hidden coin is different from the two coins she sees, then the cryptographer who said, "same" is the payer. In all of these cases, Alice needs to know the result of the coin that Bob and Carol flipped to determine which of them paid.

This protocol can be generalized to any number of cryptographers; they all sit in a ring and flip coins among them. Even two cryptographers can perform the protocol; of course they know who paid, but someone watching the protocol could tell only if a cryptographer paid or the NSA paid; they could not tell which cryptographer paid.

The applications of this protocol go far beyond sitting in a restaurant. This is an example of **unconditional sender and recipient untraceability.** A group of users on a network can use this protocol to send anonymous messages.

(1) The users arrange themselves into a logical circle.

(2) At regular intervals adjacent pairs of users flip coins between them, using some fair coin flip protocol. They make sure all their messages are encrypted so no one else can figure out the result of their coin flips.

(3) At regular intervals every user announces either "same" or "different."

If the users wish to broadcast a message individually, they simply start inverting the statement in those rounds corresponding to a 1 in the binary representation of the message. For example, if the message were "1001," they would invert their statement, tell the truth, tell the truth, and then invert their statement. Assuming the result of the flips were "odd," "even," "even," "even," they would say "even," "even," "even," "odd."

If the users notice that the overall outcome of the protocol doesn't match the message they are trying to send, they know that someone else is trying to send a message as well. They then stop sending the message and wait a random number of rounds before trying again. The exact parameters have to be worked out based on the amount of message traffic on this network, but the idea should be clear.

To make things even more interesting, these messages can be encrypted in one of the other user's public keys. Then, when everyone receives the message (a real implementation of this should add some kind of standard message-beginning and message-ending strings), only the intended recipient can decrypt and read the message. No one else knows who sent it. No one else knows who could read it. Traffic analysis, which traces and compiles patterns of people's communications even though the messages themselves may be encrypted, is useless.

An alternative to flipping coins between adjacent parties would be for them to keep a common file of random bits. Maybe they could keep them on a CD-ROM, or one member of the pair could generate a pile of them and send them to the other party (encrypted, of course). Alternatively, they could agree on a cryptographically secure pseudo-random number generator between them, and they could each generate the same string of pseudo-random bits for the protocol.

Multiparty Unconditionally Secure Protocols

This is just a simple case of the general theorems stating that any function of n inputs can be computed by a set of n players in a way that will let all learn the value of the function, but any set of less than n-2 players will not get any additional information that does not follow from their own inputs and the value of the output information. For details, see [81,201,726].

PART
TWO

Cryptographic Techniques

Keys

7.1 KEY LENGTH

The security of a symmetric cryptosystem is a function of two things: the strength of the algorithm and the length of the key. The latter is easier to demonstrate.

Assume that the strength of the algorithm is perfect. This is extremely difficult to achieve in practice, but easy enough for this example. By perfect, I mean that there is no better way to break the cryptosystem other than to try every possible key; this is called a brute-force attack. If the key is 8 bits long, there are 2^8=256 possible keys. Therefore, it will take 256 attempts to find the correct key, with an expected number of attempts of 128. If the key is 56 bits long, then there are 2^{56} possible keys. Assuming a supercomputer can try a million keys a second, it will take 2000 years to find the correct key. If the key is 64 bits long, then it will take the same supercomputer almost 600,000 years to find the correct key among the 2^{64} possible keys. If the key is 128 bits long, it will take 10^{25} years. The universe is only 10^{10} years old, so 10^{25} years is probably long enough. With a 2048-bit key, a million million-attempts-per-second computers working in parallel will spend 10^{597} years finding the key. By that time the universe may have collapsed or expanded into nothingness.

Before you rush to invent a cryptosystem with an 8-Kbyte key, remember that there is another half to this strength equation: the algorithm must be so secure that there is no better way to break it than with a brute-force attack. This is not as easy as it might seem. Cryptography is a subtle art. Cryptosystems that look perfect are often extremely poor. Strong cryptosystems, with a couple of minor changes, can become weak. Two strong cryptosystems, if used together poorly, can counteract each other and produce an output that is easy to break. The warning to the amateur cryptographer is to have a healthy, almost paranoid, suspicion of any new algorithm. It is best to trust algorithms because professional cryptographers have scrutinized them for years without cracking them, not because the algorithm's designer makes grandiose claims about its security.

This brings up another important point: the security of a cryptosystem should rest in the key, not in the details of the algorithm. If the strength of your new cryptosystem relies on the fact that the attacker does not know the algorithm's insides, you're sunk. If you believe that keeping the algorithm's insides secret improves the security of your cryptosystem more than letting the academic community analyze it, you're wrong. And it is naive to think that someone won't disassemble your source code or reverse-engineer your algorithm. (The National Security Agency keeps their algorithms secret from outsiders, but they have the best cryptographers in the world working within their walls. Additionally, they discuss their algorithms with one another, relying on peer review to uncover any weaknesses in their work.)

Assume that some cryptanalysts have access to all the details of your algorithm. Assume they have access to as much ciphertext as they want and can mount an intensive ciphertext-only attack. Assume that they can mount a plaintext attack with as much data as needed. Even assume they can mount a chosen-plaintext attack. If your cryptosystem can remain secure even in the face of all that knowledge, then you've got the security you need.

That warning aside, there is still plenty of room in cryptography to maneuver. In reality, there are many situations in which the kind of security discussed here isn't really necessary. Most adversaries don't have the knowledge and computing resources of a major government, and even the ones who do probably aren't that interested in breaking your cryptosystem. If you're plotting to overthrow a major government, stick with the tried and true algorithms in Section 3. The rest of you, have fun.

Time and Cost Estimates for Brute-Force Attack

If you assume that a brute-force attack is the most efficient attack possible against an algorithm—a big assumption—then the key must be long enough to make the attack unfeasible. How long is that?

Two parameters determine the speed of a brute-force attack: the number of keys to be tested and the speed of each test. Most symmetric algorithms accept any fixed-length bit pattern as the key. DES has a 56-bit key; there are 2^{56} possible DES keys. (The key is actually 64 bits, but 8 of those bits are parity bits.) Some algorithms discussed in this book have a 64-bit key; there are 2^{64} possible keys for those algorithms. Others have a 128-bit key.

The speed at which each possible key can be tested is also a factor, but a less important one. For the purposes of this analysis, I will assume that each different algorithm can be tested in the same amount of time. The reality may be that one algorithm may be tested two, three, or even ten times faster than another. But since we are looking for key lengths that are millions of times more difficult to crack than would be feasible, small differences due to test speed are irrelevant.

Most of the debate in the cryptologic community about the efficiency of brute-force attacks has centered on the DES algorithm. In 1977, Whitfield Diffie and Martin Hellman [300] postulated the existence of a special-purpose DES cracking machine. This machine consisted of a million chips, each capable of testing a million keys per second. Such a machine could test 2^{56} keys in 20 hours. If built to attack an algorithm with a 64-bit key, it could test all 2^{64} keys in 214 days.

A brute-force attack is tailor-made for parallel processors. Each processor can test a subset of the keyspace. The processors do not have to communicate among themselves; the only communication required at all is a single message signifying success. There are no shared memory requirements. It is easy to design a machine with a million parallel processors, each working independent of the others.

Special-purpose chips capable of testing a million keys per second are not farfetched. Chips capable of testing four million keys per second are feasible using today's technology [367]:

> We estimate that such chips [capable of 32,000,000 encryption operations per second] will be feasible within five years, based upon the history of semiconductor fabrication over the past twenty years. Today, using state-of-the-art techniques, it should be possible to develop a chip from scratch capable of checking 4,000,000 keys per second. If we limit ourselves to proven technology, chips that checked two million keys per second are possible. Within ten years we should be able to design chips capable of checking 256,000,000 keys per second.

With an array of four thousand chips, each capable of checking 265 million keys per second, all possible 56-bit keys can be tested within 24 hours. An array of 800,000 chips can test all possible 64-bit keys in the same period. If your data needs to be secure for more than ten years, these key lengths are inadequate.

Table 7.1 gives the number of parallel processors required for a brute-force attack against a given key length and within a specified period, assuming different speeds of the individual processors.

These numbers tell only part of the story. If a cracking machine will definitely recover a key in a year, there is an 8% chance it will recover the key in a month. If the key is only changed once a month, then there is an 8% chance that an adversary will recover the key while it is still being used. If that key is being used to authenticate a financial transfer system, this is a serious problem. Even if an adversary learns a valid key ten minutes before it is changed, he can make some very profitable transactions.

Table 7.2 gives the probability of finding an arbitrary key in a given period, assuming an adversary has a brute-force machine. For example, an adversary who has a machine capable of finding a key in a month has a 0.14% chance of finding the key within an hour. This means that if you change your key every hour, then in any given month, the adversary has a 63% chance of finding one of the keys before it is changed. This 63% is independent of the frequency of the key change.

TABLE 7.1

Number of Processors Required for a Brute-Force Attack Against Different Algorithms Within a Given Time Period

(NUMBER OF ENCRYPTIONS PER SECOND)	NUMBER OF PROCESSORS REQUIRED TO BREAK A 56-BIT KEY IN:			
	1 YEAR	1 MONTH	1 WEEK	1 DAY
1 million	2,300	28,000	120,000	830,000
2 million	1,100	14,000	60,000	420,000
4 million	570	7,000	30,000	210,000
32 million	71	870	3,700	26,000
256 million	9	100	470	3,300

(NUMBER OF ENCRYPTIONS PER SECOND)	NUMBER OF PROCESSORS REQUIRED TO BREAK A 64-BIT KEY IN:			
	1 YEAR	1 MONTH	1 WEEK	1 DAY
1 million	590,000	7,100,000	3.1×10^7	2.1×10^8
2 million	290,000	3,600,000	1.5×10^7	1.1×10^8
4 million	150,000	1,800,000	7,600,000	5.3×10^7
32 million	18,000	220,000	950,000	6,700,000
256 million	2,300	28,000	120,000	830,000

(NUMBER OF (ENCRYPTIONS PER SECOND)	NUMBER OF PROCESSORS REQUIRED TO BREAK A 128-BIT KEY IN:			
	1 YEAR	1 MONTH	1 WEEK	1 DAY
1 million	1.1×10^{25}	1.3×10^{26}	5.6×10^{26}	3.9×10^{27}
2 million	5.4×10^{24}	6.6×10^{25}	2.8×10^{26}	2.0×10^{27}
4 million	2.7×10^{24}	3.3×10^{25}	1.4×10^{26}	9.9×10^{26}
32 million	3.4×10^{23}	4.1×10^{24}	1.8×10^{25}	1.2×10^{26}
256 million	4.2×10^{22}	5.1×10^{23}	2.2×10^{24}	1.5×10^{25}

Changing keys frequently limits the amount of damage an adversary can do with a single recovered key, but in many applications this is still an unacceptable risk.

The other variable governing the feasibility of a brute-force cracking machine is the cost. The analysis used here, which appears in [367], was created using the following assumptions:

TABLE **7.2**

Probability of Recovering a Key Within a Given Time (Assuming the Capability to Launch a Brute-Force Attack)

(BRUTE-FORCE ATTACK SPEED)	1 HOUR	1 DAY	1 WEEK	1 MONTH	1 YEAR
1 Day	0.0417	1.0000	1.0000	1.0000	1.0000
1 Week	0.0060	0.1429	1.0000	1.0000	1.0000
1 Month	0.0014	0.0329	1.2308	1.0000	1.0000
1 Year	0.0001	0.0027	0.0192	0.0833	1.0000

In arriving at an estimate of the cost of breaking [the algorithm] we have to make a number of rather broad simplifications. Based on the technology assessment . . . we assume that the cost of a given technology will decrease roughly as quickly as it is outdated. In other words, a chip costing $100.00 today will cost (in today's dollars) $7.83 five years from now. Exotic chips available in ten years through custom fabrication will still be too expensive to be practical, but today's exotic technologies will be dirt cheap. To be conservative, a cost of $25.00 per processor was assumed for the cheapest available technology, rising by a factor of ten for each "generation" of technology (roughly, five years newer and ten times faster), and decreasing by a factor of 10 (before inflation) every five years. The base figure of $25.00 includes the cost of designing boards, control software and manufacturing. The cost reported is the average of the cheapest solution and the second cheapest solution in order to discount economies of scale. . . . The results represent a guess with an error of perhaps 50%.

Table 7.3 gives different cost estimates based on the year the machine could be built, the key length, and the time required to recover the key. (The original tables also included estimates for inflation, which I omitted.) The 1990 estimates look at the average cost of a machine using chips capable of one million encryptions per second and a machine using chips capable of two million encryptions per second; chips capable of four million encryptions per second, while possible, are assumed to be too expensive to consider using. The 1995 estimates average two-million-encryptions-per-second machines and four-million-encryptions-per-second machines. The year 2000 estimates average four-million-encryptions-per-second machines and 32-million-encryptions-per-second machines.

For 56- and 64-bit keys, these numbers are within the realm of the military budgets of many industrialized nations. Breaking a 128-bit key is still far beyond the realm of possibility.

If attackers want to break a key badly enough, all they have to do is spend the requisite amount of money. Consequently, it seems prudent to try to estimate the minimum "value" of a key: how much value can be trusted to a single key before it makes economic sense to try to break? To give an extreme example, if a plaintext message worth $1.39 is encrypted with an algorithm, then it wouldn't make much

TABLE 7.3
Cost of a Brute-Force Cracking Machine

	MACHINE CAPABLE OF BREAKING A 56-BIT ALGORITHM WITHIN:			
YEAR	1 YEAR	1 MONTH	1 WEEK	1 DAY
1990	$130,000	$1.6M	$6.7M	$47M
1995	$64,000	$780,000	$3.3M	$23M
2000	$16,000	$190,000	$830,000	$5.8M
2005	$2000	$24,000	$100,000	$730,000

	MACHINE CAPABLE OF BREAKING A 64-BIT ALGORITHM WITHIN:			
YEAR	1 YEAR	1 MONTH	1 WEEK	1 DAY
1990	$33M	$400M	$1.7B	$12B
1995	$16M	$200M	$850M	$6.0B
2000	$4.1M	$50M	$210M	$1.5B
2005	$510,000	$6.2M	$27M	$190M

	MACHINE CAPABLE OF BREAKING A 128-BIT ALGORITHM WITHIN:			
YEAR	1 YEAR	1 MONTH	1 WEEK	1 DAY
1990	$6.0\times10^{26}	$7.3\times1027	$3.2\times10^{28}	$2.2\times10^{29}
1995	$3.0\times10^{26}	$3.7\times10^{27}	$1.6\times10^{28}	$1.1\times10^{29}
2000	$7.5\times10^{25}	$9.2\times10^{26}	$3.9\times10^{27}	$2.8\times10^{28}
2005	$9.4\times10^{24}	$1.2\times10^{26}	$4.9\times10^{26}	$3.4\times10^{27}

financial sense to set a $40-million cracker to the task of recovering the key. On the other hand, if the plaintext message is worth $100 million, then decrypting that single message would justify the cost of building the cracker alone, even today.

The question of when a key is worth attacking is also addressed in [367]. The authors assumed that attackers require a 25% annual return on their investment over a five-year period to cover the cost of financing construction of the machine and operating expenses. (25% is an arbitrary figure, but sufficient for estimating purposes.) Anything above that is profit; anything below that is loss.

Table 7.4 gives the attacker's cost per period: the cost required to recover a single key. If, over the course of five years, each key recovered is worth the cost to recover it, then the attacker breaks even. If each key is worth more, then the attacker makes a profit. This assumes that the cracking machine is running continuously—24 hours a day, 365 days a year. It does not assume that every key recovered is worth the minimum amount, only that on the average, every key is worth the minimum amount. A single high-value key can make the entire five-year operation profitable.

TABLE **7.4**
Cost-per-Period of Breaking a 56-bit Key, Assuming Compounding-per-Period of 25% per Annum

"BREAK-EVEN" COST-PER-PERIOD TO BREAK A 56-BIT KEY IN:			
YEAR	1 YEAR	1 MONTH	1 WEEK	1 DAY
1990	$47,000	$46,000	$45,000	$45,000
1995	$24,000	$23,000	$22,000	$22,000
2000	$5,900	$5,700	$5,600	$5,600
2005	$740	$710	$700	$700

"BREAK-EVEN" COST-PER-PERIOD TO BREAK A 64-BIT KEY IN:			
YEAR	1 YEAR	1 MONTH	1 WEEK	1 DAY
1990	$12M	$12M	$12M	$11M
1995	$6.1M	$6.0M	$5.8M	$5.7M
2000	$1.5M	$1.5M	$1.4M	$1.4M
2005	$190,000	$180,000	$180,000	$190,000

"BREAK-EVEN" COST-PER-PERIOD TO BREAK A 128-BIT KEY IN:			
YEAR	1 YEAR	1 MONTH	1 WEEK	1 DAY
1990	$2.2\times10^{26}	$2.2\times10^{26}	$2.1\times10^{26}	$2.1\times10^{26}
1995	$1.1\times10^{26}	$1.1\times10^{26}	$1.1\times10^{26}	$1.1\times10^{26}
2000	$2.8\times10^{25}	$2.7\times10^{25}	$2.7\times10^{25}	$2.6\times10^{25}
2005	$3.5\times10^{24}	$3.4\times10^{24}	$3.3\times10^{24}	$3.3\times10^{24}

Software Crackers

Without special-purpose hardware and massively parallel machines, brute-force attacks are significantly harder. Software is so slow that economic brute-force attacks will be unfeasible for years to come, even for a 56-bit key. A Motorola 68040 microprocessor can perform an estimated 23,200 DES encryptions per second. If history is to be a guide, the speed increase has been sixteenfold over the past ten years. At this rate, within five years microprocessors will be able to run DES software at a rate of 64,000 encryptions per second. Within ten years that rate will increase to 256,000 encryptions per second. This is still a thousand times slower than today's best hardware implementations.

The real threat of a software-based, brute-force attack is not that it is certain, but that it is "free." There is no cost involved in setting up a microcomputer when it is idle to test possible keys. If it finds the correct key—great. If it doesn't, then nothing is lost. There is no cost involved in setting up an entire microcomputer network to do that. A recent experiment with DES used the collective idle time of 40 workstations to test 2^{34} keys in a single day [367]. At this speed, it will take four million days to test all keys, but if enough people try attacks like this, then someone somewhere will get lucky.

> The crux of the software threat is sheer bad luck. Imagine a university computer network of 512 workstations, networked together. On some campuses this would be a medium-sized network. They could even be spread around the world, coordinating their activity through electronic mail. Assume each workstation is capable of running [the algorithm] at a rate of 15,000 encryptions per second.... Allowing for the overhead of testing and changing keys, this comes down to ... 8,192 tests per second per machine. To exhaust [a 56-bit] keyspace with this setup would take 545 years (assuming the network was dedicated to the task twenty-four hours per day). Notice, however, that the same calculations give our hypothetical student hackers one chance in 200,000 of cracking a key in one day. Over a long weekend their odds increase to one chance in sixty-six thousand. The faster their hardware, or the more machines involved, the better their chance becomes. These are not good odds for earning a living from horse racing, but they're not the stuff of good press releases either. They are much better odds than the Government gives on its lotteries, for instance. "One-in-a-million"? "Couldn't happen again in a thousand years"? It is no longer possible to say such things honestly. Is this an acceptable ongoing risk? [367]

Using an algorithm with a 64-bit key instead of a 56-bit key makes this attack 256 times more difficult. With a 40-bit key, the picture is far more bleak. A network of 400 computers, each capable of performing 32,000 encryptions per second, can complete a brute-force attack against a 40-bit key in a single day. (In 1992, the RC2 and RC4 algorithms were approved for export with a 40-bit key—see Section 11.8.)

Using a 128-bit key makes this attack ridiculous even to contemplate. Industry estimates suggest that by 1996 there will be 200 million computers in use worldwide. This estimate includes everything from giant Cray mainframes to subnotebooks. If every one of those computers worked together on this brute-force attack, and each computer performed a million encryptions per second every second, it would still take a million times the age of the universe to recover the key.

Viruses

Probably the main difficulty with getting millions of computers to work on a brute-force attack is convincing the individual computer owners to let their computers participate. You could ask politely, but that's time-consuming. Even worse, they might say no. You could break into their machines at night, but that's even more time-consuming. Even worse, you might get arrested. Computer viruses could spread the cracking program more efficiently over as many computers as possible.

This is a particularly insidious idea, first presented in [875]. The attacker writes and lets loose a computer virus. This virus doesn't reformat the hard drive or delete files; all it does is work on a brute-force cryptanalysis problem whenever the computer is idle. Various studies have shown that microcomputers are idle between 70% and 90% of the time, so the virus shouldn't have any trouble finding time to work on its task. If it is otherwise benign, it might even escape notice while it does its work.

Eventually, one machine will stumble on the correct key. At this point there are two ways of proceeding. First, the virus could spawn a different virus. It wouldn't do anything but reproduce and delete any copies of the cracking virus it finds but would contain the information about the correct key. This new virus would simply propagate through the computer world until it lands on the computer of the person who wrote the original virus.

A second, sneakier approach would be to display this message on the screen:

```
There is a serious bug in this computer.
Please call 1-800-123-4567 and read the
following 64-bit number to the operator:

xxxx xxxx xxxx xxxx

There is a $100 reward for the first
person to report this bug.
```

How efficient is this attack? Assume the typical infected computer can try a thousand keys per second. This is far less than the computer's maximum potential, because we have to assume it will be doing other things occasionally. Also assume that the typical virus infects ten million machines. This virus can break a 56-bit key in 83 days and a 64-bit key in 58 years. You might have to bribe the antiviral software makers, but that's your problem. Any increase in computer speeds or the virus infection rate would, of course, make this attack more efficient.

The Chinese Lottery

The Chinese Lottery is an eclectic, but possible, suggestion for a massively parallel DES cracker [718]. Imagine that a brute-force, million-test-per-second cracking chip was built into every radio and television sold. Each chip is programmed to test a different set of keys automatically upon receiving a plaintext/ciphertext pair over the airwaves. Then, every time the Chinese government wants to break a key, it broadcasts the data. All the radios and televisions in the country start chugging away. Eventually, the correct key will appear on someone's display, somewhere in the country. The Chinese pays a lottery prize to that person; this makes sure that the result is reported properly and also helps the sale of radios and televisions with the cracking chips.

If every man, woman, and child in China owns a radio or television, then the correct key to a 56-bit algorithm will appear in 64 seconds. If only one in ten Chinese owns a radio or television—closer to reality—the correct key will appear in eleven minutes. The correct key for a 64-bit algorithm will appear in 4.5 hours—45 hours if only one in ten owned a radio or television.

Some modifications are required to make this attack practical. First, it would be easier to have each chip try random keys instead of a unique set of keys. This would make the attack about 37% slower—not much in light of the numbers we're working with. Also, the Chinese Communist party would have to mandate that every person listen to or watch a certain show at a certain time, just to make sure that all of the radios and televisions are operating when the plaintext/ciphertext pair is broadcast. Finally, everyone would have to be instructed to call a Central-Party-Whatever-It's-Called if their "Found the Key" light ever goes off, and then to read the string of numbers that appears on their screen. The Party could even make it a lottery; the person who finds the key wins a prize.

Table 7.5 shows the effectiveness of the Chinese Lottery for different countries and different key lengths. China is clearly in the best position to launch such an attack, but they would have to outfit every man, woman, and child with their own television or radio. The United States has fewer people but a lot more equipment per capita. The state of Wyoming could break a 56-bit key all by itself in less than a day.

Biotechnology

If biochips are possible, then it would be foolish not to use them as a distributed brute-force cryptanalysis tool. Consider a hypothetical animal, unfortunately called a "DESosaur" [718]. It consists of biological cells capable of testing possible keys. The plaintext/ciphertext pair is broadcast to the cells via some optical channel (these cells are transparent, you see). Solutions are carried to the DESosaur's speech organ via special cells that propagate through the animal's circulatory system.

The typical dinosaur has about 10^{14} cells (excluding bacteria). If each of them can perform a million encryptions per second (granted, this is a big if), breaking a 56-bit key would take seven ten-thousandths of a second. Breaking a 64-bit key would take less than two-tenths of a second. Breaking a 128-bit key would still take 10^{11} years, though.

Another biological approach is to use genetically engineered cryptanalytic algae that are capable of performing brute-force attacks against cryptographic

TABLE 7.5
Brute-Force Cracking Estimates for Chinese Lottery

| | | | TIME TO BREAK | |
| | | # OF TELEVISIONS | 56-BIT | 64-BIT |
LOCATION	POP. (APPROX.)	& RADIOS	ALGORITHM	ALGORITHM
China	1,130,065,000	265,000,000	272 secs.	19 hrs.
U.S.	248,709,873	687,000,000	104 secs.	7.4 hrs.
Iraq	18,782,000	4,800,000	4.2 hrs.	44 days
Israel	4,371,000	2,620,000	7.6 hrs.	81 days
Wyoming	453,588	1,256,000	16 hrs.	170 days
Morehead, NC	6,046	16,700	50 days	35 yrs.

(Data on population and number of radios and televisions per capita taken from the *1992 World Almanac.*)

algorithms [718]. These organisms would make it possible to construct a distributed machine with more processors, because they could cover a larger area. The plaintext/ciphertext pair could be broadcast by satellite. If an organism found the result, it could induce the nearby cells to change color to communicate the solution back to the satellite.

Assume the typical algae cell is the size of a cube 10 microns on a side (this is probably a large estimate), then 10^{15} of them can fill a cubic meter. Pump them into the ocean and cover 200 square miles (518 square kilometers) of water to a meter deep (you figure out how to do it—I'm just the idea man), and you'd have 10^{23} (over a hundred billion gallons) of them floating in the ocean. (The *Exxon Valdez* spilled 10 million gallons of oil.) If each of them can try a million keys per second, they will recover the key for a 128-bit algorithm in just over 100 years. (The resulting algae bloom is your problem.) Breakthroughs in either algae processing speed, algae diameter, or even the size puddle one could spread across the ocean, would reduce these numbers significantly.

Don't even ask me about nanotechnology.

How Long Should a Key Be?

The answer depends on your application. How long does your data need to be secure? How much is your data worth? You can even specify the security requirement in this manner. For example:

> The key length must be such that there is a probability of no more than 1 in 2^{32} that an attacker with \$100 million to spend could break the system, even assuming a growth rate of 30% per annum over the period.

Table 7.6, taken partially from [93], gives the estimated secrecy requirements for different kinds of information.

Future computing power is harder to estimate, but here is a reasonable rule of thumb: The efficiency of computing equipment divided by price increases by a factor of ten every five years [93]. Thus, in 50 years the fastest computers will be 10^{10} times faster than today! And these numbers only relate to general-purpose computers; who knows what kind of specialized cryptosystem-breaking equipment will be developed in the next 50 years?

Assuming that a cryptographic algorithm will be in use for 30 years, you can get some idea how secure it must be. An algorithm designed today probably will not see general use until 2000, and will still be used in 2030 to encrypt messages that must remain secret until 2080 or later.

7.2   KEY MANAGEMENT

Alice and Bob have a secure communications system. They play mental poker, simultaneously sign contracts, even securely evaluate circuits together. Their protocols are all secure. Their cryptographic algorithms are top-notch.

TABLE **7.6**
Security Requirements for Different Information

TYPE OF TRAFFIC	LIFETIME	MIN. KEY LENGTH
Tactical military information	minutes/hours	56 bits
Product announcements, mergers, interest rates	days/weeks	56–64 bits
Trade secrets (e.g., recipe for Coca-Cola)	decades	64 bits
H-bomb secrets	> 40 years	128 bits
Identities of spies	> 50 years	128 bits
Personal affairs	> 50 years	128 bits
Diplomatic embarrassments	> 65 years	at least 128 bits
U.S. census data	100 years	at least 128 bits

Unfortunately, they buy their keys from Eve's "Keys-R-Us," whose slogan is "You can trust us: security is the middle name of our ex-mother-in-law's travel agent."

Eve doesn't have to break the algorithms. She doesn't have to rely on subtle flaws in the protocols. She can read all of Alice's and Bob's message traffic without lifting a cryptanalytic finger.

In the real world, key management is the hardest security problem. Designing secure cryptographic algorithms and protocols isn't easy, but making sure the keys stay secret is even harder. Cryptanalysts often attack both symmetric and public-key cryptosystems through their key management. Why bother going through all the trouble trying to break the cryptographic algorithm if the key can easily be recovered as a result of sloppy key management procedures? At the very least, Alice and Bob must protect the keys to the same degree as the data itself. The world's most secure algorithm won't help much if the users habitually choose their spouse's names for keys, or write their keys on little pieces of paper in their wallets. Further information on key management can be found in [269,53,714,685,452,214].

7.2.1 Generating Keys

The security of an algorithm rests in the key. If you're using a cryptographically weak process to generate your keys, then your whole system is weak. Eve doesn't have to attempt to cryptanalyze your cryptographic algorithm when she can cryptanalyze your key generation algorithm.

For example, the DiskLock program for Macintosh (version 2.1), sold at most software stores, claims the security of DES encryption. It encrypts files using DES. Its implementation of the DES algorithm is correct. However, DiskLock stores the DES key with the encrypted file. If you know where to look for the key in the encrypted file, all you have to do to read a file encrypted with DiskLock's DES is to recover the key from the encrypted file and then decrypt the file. It doesn't matter that this program uses DES encryption—the implementation is completely insecure.

Reduced Keyspaces

DES has a 56-bit key. Implemented properly, any 56-bit string can be the key; there are 2^{56} (10^{16}) possible keys. One DES software encryption program only allows keys made up of lowercase letters and digits, allowing only 10^{12} possible keys. The poor key generation procedures in this program have made its DES ten thousand times easier to break than a proper implementation.

Table 7.7 gives the number of possible keys with various constraints on the input strings. Table 7.8 gives the time required for an exhaustive search through all of those keys, given a million attempts per second. Remember, the differences in the orders of magnitude mean that there is very little time differential between an exhaustive search for 8-byte keys and an exhaustive search of 4-, 5-, 6-, 7-, and 8-byte keys.

All of the specialized brute-force hardware and parallel implementations will work here. Testing a million keys per second (either with one machine or with multiple machines in parallel), it is feasible to crack lowercase-letter and lowercase-letter-and-number keys up to 8 bytes long, alphanumeric-character keys up to 7 bytes long, printable character and ASCII-character keys up to 6 bytes long, and 8-bit-ASCII-character keys up to 5 bytes long.

And remember, computers are continuously getting faster and cheaper. In other words, don't expect your keys to stand up against brute-force attacks for ten years.

Poor Key Choices

When people choose their own keys, they generally choose poor ones. They're far more likely to choose "Barney" than "*9($hH\A-$". This is not always due to poor security practices; "Barney" is easier to remember than "*9($hH\A-$". Any smart brute-force attack isn't going to try all possible keys in numerical order. It's going to try the easiest keys first: English words, names, trivial extensions to English words, etc. This is called a **dictionary attack,** because the attacker uses a dictionary of common keys. Daniel Klein was able to crack 25% of the passwords on the average computer using this system [482]:

1. Try using the user's name, initials, account name, and other relevant person information as a possible password. All in all, up to 130 different

TABLE 7.7
Number of Possible Keys of Various Keyspaces

	4-BYTES	5-BYTES	6-BYTES	7-BYTES	8-BYTES
Lowercase letters (26):	460,000	1.2×10^7	3.1×10^8	8.0×10^9	2.1×10^{11}
Lowercase letters and digits (36):	1,700,000	6.0×10^7	2.2×10^9	7.8×10^{10}	2.8×10^{12}
Alphanumeric characters (62):	1.5×10^7	9.2×10^8	5.7×10^{10}	3.5×10^{12}	2.2×10^{14}
Printable characters (95):	8.1×10^7	7.7×10^9	7.4×10^{11}	7.0×10^{13}	6.6×10^{15}
ASCII characters (128):	2.7×10^8	3.4×10^{10}	4.4×10^{12}	5.6×10^{14}	7.2×10^{16}
8-bit ASCII characters (256):	4.3×10^9	1.1×10^{12}	2.8×10^{14}	7.2×10^{16}	1.8×10^{19}

TABLE **7.8**

Exhaustive Search of Various Keyspaces (assume one million attempts per second)

	4-BYTES	5-BYTES	6-BYTES	7-BYTES	8-BYTES
Lowercase letters (26):	0.5 sec.	12 secs.	5 mins.	2.2 hrs.	2.4 days
Lowercase letters and digits (36):	1.7 sec.	1 min.	36 mins.	22 hrs.	33 days
Alphanumeric characters (62):	15.0 sec.	15 mins.	16 hrs.	41 days	6.9 yrs.
Printable characters (95):	1.4 mins.	2.1 hrs.	8.5 days	2.2 yrs.	210 yrs.
ASCII characters (128):	4.5 mins.	9.5 hrs.	51 days	18 yrs.	2,300 yrs.
8-bit ASCII characters (256):	1.2 hrs.	13 days	8.9 yrs.	2,300 yrs.	580,000 yrs.

passwords were tried based on this information. For an account name **klone** with a user named "Daniel V. Klein," some of the passwords that would be tried were: klone, klone0, klone1, klone123, dvk, dvkdvk, dklein, DKlein, leinad, nielk, dvklein, danielk, DvkkvD, DANIEL-KLEIN, (klone), KleinD, etc.

2. Try using words from various databases. These included lists of men's and women's names (some 16,000 in all); places (including permutations so that "spain," "spanish," and "spaniard" would all be considered); names of famous people; cartoons and cartoon characters; titles, characters, and locations from films and science fiction stories; mythical creatures (garnered from Bulfinch's mythology and dictionaries of mythical beasts); sports (including team names, nicknames, and specialized terms); numbers (both as numerals—"2001," and written out—"twelve"); strings of letters and numbers ("a," "aa," "aaa," "aaaa," etc.); Chinese syllables (from the Pinyin Romanization of Chinese, an international standard system of writing Chinese on an English keyboard); the King James Bible; biological terms; common and vulgar phrases (such as "fuckyou," "ibmsux," and "deadhead"); keyboard patterns (such as "qwerty," "asdf," and "zxcvbn"); abbreviations (such as "roygbiv"—the colors in the rainbow, and "ooottafagvah"—a mnemonic for remembering the 12 cranial nerves); machine names (acquired from */etc/hosts*); characters, plays, and locations from Shakespeare; common Yiddish words; the names of asteroids; and a collection of words from various technical papers I had previously published. All told, more than 60,000 separate words were considered per user (with any inter- and intra-dictionary duplicates being discarded).

3. Try various permutations on the words from step 2. This included making the first letter upper case or a control character, making the entire word upper case, reversing the word (with and without the aforementioned capitalization), changing the letter 'o' to the digit '0' (so that the word "scholar" would also be checked as "sch0lar"), changing the letter 'l' to

the digit '1' (so that the word "scholar" would also be checked as "scho1ar"), and performing similar manipulation to change the letter 'z' into the digit '2', and the letter 's' into the digit '5'. Another test was to make the word into a plural (irrespective of whether the word was actually a noun), with enough intelligence built in so that "dress" became "dresses," "house" became "houses," and "daisy" became "daisies." We did not consider pluralization rules exclusively, though, so that "datum" forgivably became "datums" (not "data"), while "sphynx" became "sphynxs" (and not "sphynges"). Similarly, the suffixes "-ed," "-er," and "-ing" were added to transform words like "phase" into "phased," "phaser," and "phasing." These 14 to 17 additional tests added another 1,000,000 words to the list of possible passwords that were tested for each user.

4. Try various capitalization permutations on the words from step 2 that were not considered in step 3. This included all single letter capitalization permutations (so that "michael" would also be checked as "mIchael," "miChael," "micHael," "michAel," etc.), double letter capitalization permutations ("MIchael," "MiChael," "MicHael," . . . , "mIChael," "mIcHael," etc.), triple letter permutations, etc. The single letter permutations added roughly another 400,000 words to be checked per user, while the double letter permutations added another 1,500,000 words. Three letter permutations would have added at least another 3,000,000 words per user had there been enough time to complete the tests. Tests of 4, 5, and 6 letter permutations were deemed to be impracticable without much more computational horsepower to carry them out.

5. Try foreign language words on foreign users. The specific test that was performed was to try Chinese language passwords on users with Chinese names. The Pinyin Romanization of Chinese syllables was used, combining syllables together into one, two, and three syllable words. Because no tests were done to determine whether the words actually made sense, an exhaustive search was initiated. Since there are 298 Chinese syllables in the Pinyin system, there are 158,404 two syllable words, and slightly more than 16,000,000 three syllable words. A similar mode of attack could as easily be used with English, using rules for building pronounceable nonsense words.

6. Try word pairs. The magnitude of an exhaustive test of this nature is staggering. To simplify the test, only words of 3 or 4 characters in length from */usr/dict/words* were used. Even so, the number of word pairs is $O(10^7)$ (multiplied by 4096 possible salt values), and as of this writing, the test is only 10% complete.

A dictionary attack is much more powerful when it is used against a file of keys and not a single key. A single user may be smart enough to choose good keys. If a thousand people each choose their own key as a password to a computer system, the odds are excellent that at least one person will choose a key in the attacker's dictionary.

Generating Good Keys

Good keys are random bit strings. If the key is 64 bits long, every possible 64-bit key must be equally likely. Generate the key bits from either a reliably random source (see Section 15.3), or a cryptographically secure pseudo-random bit generator (see Section 15.2). If these automatic processes are unavailable, flip a coin or roll a die.

Some cryptographic algorithms have weak keys: specific keys that are less secure than the other keys. I advise testing for these weak keys and generating a new one if you discover one. DES has only 16 weak keys, so the odds of generating any of these keys are incredibly small. It has been argued that a potential enemy has no idea that a weak key is being used and therefore gains no advantage from their accidental use. However, testing for the few weak keys is so easy that it seems imprudent not to do so.

Generating keys for public-key cryptography systems is much harder, because the keys must have certain mathematical properties (they may have to be prime, be a quadratic residue, etc.). Techniques for generating large random prime numbers are discussed in Section 9.5. The important thing to remember from a key management point of view is that the random seeds for those generators must be just that: random.

Generating a random key isn't always possible. Sometimes you need to remember your key (see how long it takes you to remember 25E8 56F2 E8BA C820). If you have to generate an easy-to-remember key, make it obscure. The ideal would be something easy to remember, but difficult to guess. Here are some suggestions:

- Word pairs separated by a punctuation character, for example "turtle*moose" or "zorch!splat"

- Strings of letters that are the initials to a longer phrase, for example "Mein Luftkissenfahrzeug ist voller Aale!" generates the key "MLivA!"

A better solution is a technique called **key crunching,** which converts easy-to-remember text strings into random keys. Use a one-way hash function to transform an arbitrary-length text string into a pseudo-random bit string.

For example, the easy-to-remember text string:

My name is Ozymandias, king of kings. Look on my works, ye mighty, and despair.

might crunch into this 64-bit key:

E6C1 4398 5AE9 0A9B

The text string is often referred to as a **pass phrase.** If the phrase is long enough, the resulting key will be random. Exactly what "long enough" means is open to interpretation. For a 64-bit key, a pass phrase of about 10 to 15 normal English words should be sufficient. As a rule of thumb, figure that you need one letter of phrase for each bit of the key—64 letters for a 64-bit key. That's assuming only lowercase letters and spaces, without capitalization or punctuation. To increase the randomness of the key, the entire printable ASCII character set (upper- and lowercase characters, numbers, punctuation, and spaces) should be allowed in the pass phrase.

This technique can even be used to generate private keys for public-key cryptography systems: the text string could be crunched into a random seed, and that seed could be fed into a deterministic system that generates public/private key pairs.

X9.17 Key Generation

The ANSI X9.17 standard specifies a method of key generation. This does not generate easy-to-remember keys; it is more suitable for generating session keys within a system. The cryptographic algorithm used to generate keys is DES, but it could just as easily be any algorithm.

Let $E_k(X)$ be DES encryption of X with key k. The key k is a key reserved for secret key generation. V_0 is a secret 64-bit seed. T is a timestamp. To generate the random key R_i, calculate:

$$R_i = E_k(E_k(T_i) \text{ XOR } V_i)$$

To generate V_{i+1}, calculate:

$$V_{i+1} = E_k(E_k(T_i) \text{ XOR } R_i)$$

To turn R_i into a DES key, simply adjust every eighth bit for parity. If you need a 64-bit key, use it as is. If you need a 128-bit key, generate a pair of keys and concatenate them together.

7.2.2 Transferring Keys

Alice and Bob are going to use a conventional cryptographic algorithm to communicate securely; they need the same key. Alice generates a key using a random-key generator. Now she has to give it to Bob—securely. If Alice can meet Bob somewhere (a back alley, a windowless room, or the dark side of the moon), she can give him a copy of the key. Otherwise, they have a problem.

Alice could send Bob the key over their communications channel—the one they are going to encrypt. This is foolish; if the channel warrants encryption, sending the encryption key in the clear over the same channel guarantees that anyone eavesdropping on the channel can decrypt all communications.

Public-key cryptography solves the problem nicely (see Section 3.1), but those techniques are not always available. Some systems use alternate channels known to be secure. Alice could send Bob the key with a trusted messenger. She could send it by certified mail or through an overnight delivery service. Alternatively, she could set up another communications channel with Bob and hope no one is eavesdropping on that one.

A better solution would be to split the key into several different parts and send each of those parts over a different channel. One part could be sent over the telephone, one by mail, one by overnight delivery service, one by carrier pigeon, etc. (see Figure 7.1). Since an adversary can collect all but one of the parts and still have no idea what the key is, this method will work in all but extreme cases. Section 3.5 discusses schemes for splitting a key into several parts.

However, if a system uses a new encryption key every day, it could quickly become cumbersome. One solution is for Alice to send Bob a month's worth of keys simultaneously. This key list is very valuable, and Alice and Bob must both securely store the list after receipt. Compromise the list, and the entire month of communications is at risk.

Some systems solve the problem by creating a **master key,** or a **key-encryption key.** Alice sends Bob the key-encryption key securely, either by a face-to-face meeting or the key splitting technique discussed above. Once Alice and Bob both have the key-encryption key, Alice can send Bob daily keys over the same communications channel. Alice encrypts each daily key with the key-encryption key. Since the amount of traffic being encrypted with the key-encryption key is low, it does not have to be changed as often. However, since compromise of the key-encryption key could compromise every message encrypted with every key that was encrypted with the key-encryption key, it must be stored securely.

Key Distribution in Large Networks

Key-encryption keys shared by pairs of users works well in small networks, but can quickly get cumbersome if the networks become large. Since every pair of

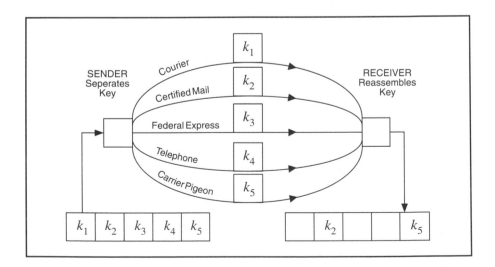

Figure 7.1
Key distribution in pieces.

users must exchange keys, the total number of key exchanges required in an n-person network is $n(n-1)/2$.

In a six-person network, fifteen key exchanges are required. In a 1000-person network, nearly 500,000 key exchanges are required. In these cases, creating a central key server (or servers) makes the operation much more efficient.

Alternatively, any of the conventional cryptography or public-key-cryptography protocols in Section 3.1 provides for secure key distribution.

7.2.3 Verifying Keys

When Bob receives his key, how does he know it was from Alice and not from someone pretending to be Alice? If Alice and Bob met face-to-face, it's easy. If Alice sends her key via a trusted courier, then Bob has to trust the courier. If the key is encrypted with a key-encryption key, then Bob has to trust the fact that only Alice has that key. If Alice uses a digital signature protocol to sign the key, Bob has to trust the public-key database when he verifies that signature. If a Key Distribution Center (KDC) signs Alice's public keys, Bob has to trust that his copy of the KDC's public key has not been tampered with.

In the end, someone who controls the entire network around Bob can make him think whatever he likes. Mallet could send an encrypted and signed message purporting to be from Alice. When Bob tried to access the public-key database to verify Alice's signature, Mallet could substitute his own public key. Mallet could invent his own false KDC and exchange the real KDC's public key for his own creation. Bob wouldn't be the wiser.

Some people have used this argument to claim that public-key cryptography is useless. Since the only way for Alice and Bob to ensure that their keys have not been tampered with is to meet face-to-face, public-key cryptography doesn't enhance security at all.

This view is naive. In theory, it is true. The reality is far more complicated. Public-key cryptography, used with digital signatures and trusted KDCs, makes it much more complicated to substitute one key for another. Bob can never be absolutely certain that Mallet isn't controlling his entire reality, but Bob can be confident that doing so requires more resources than most real-world Mallets have access to.

Bob could verify Alice's key over the telephone, where he can hear her voice. It's a public key; he can recite it over the telephone. If the key is too long, Alice and Bob can use a one-way hash function to verify the key. There are many possibilities.

Sometimes, it may not even be important to verify exactly whom a public key belongs to. It may be necessary to verify that it belongs to the same person to whom it belonged last year. If someone sends a signed withdrawal message to a bank, the bank does not have to be concerned who withdraws the money, only whether it is the same person who deposited the money in the first place.

Error Detection

Sometimes keys can get garbled in transmission. Since a garbled key can mean megabytes of undecryptable ciphertext, pains must be taken to minimize this problem. All keys should be transmitted with some kind of error detection and correction bits. At the minimum, a checksum should be appended to the key. This way errors in transmission can be easily detected, and if required the key can be re-sent.

One of the most widely used methods is to encrypt a constant (either all 0's, or all 1's) with the key, and to send the first two to four bytes of the ciphertext along with the key. At the receiving end, do the same thing. If the encrypted constants match, then the key has been transmitted without error. The chance of an undetected error ranges from one in 2^{16} to one in 2^{24}.

7.2.4 Using Keys

Software encryption is scary. Gone are the days of microcomputers under the control of single programs. Now there's Macintosh System 7, Windows NT, and UNIX. There is no telling when the operating system will suspend the encryption application in progress, write everything to disk, and take care of some pressing task. When the operating system finally gets back to encrypting whatever is being encrypted, everything will look just fine. No one will ever realize that the operating system wrote the encryption application to disk, and that it wrote the key along with it. The key will sit on the disk, unencrypted, until the computer writes over that area of memory again. It could be minutes or it could be months. It could even be never; the key could still be sitting there when an adversary goes over the hard drive with a fine-tooth comb.

In a preemptive, multitasking environment, you can set your encryption operation to a high enough priority so it will not be interrupted. This would mitigate the risk. Even so, the whole thing is dicey at best.

Hardware implementations are easier. Many encryption devices are designed to erase the key if tampered with. For example, the IBM PS/2 encryption card has an epoxy unit containing the DES chip, battery, and memory. Of course, you have to trust the hardware manufacturer to implement the feature properly. Software implementations should try to do that as well, but nothing works perfectly.

7.2.5 Storing Keys

The easiest key storage problem is that of single users encrypting files for later use. Since they are the only persons involved, they are the only persons responsible for the key. Some systems take the easy approach: the key is stored in the user's brain and never on the system. The user is responsible for remembering the key and entering it every time a file is to be encrypted or decrypted.

An example of this system is IPS [501]. Users can either directly enter the 64-bit key, or users can enter the key as a long character string. The system then generates a 64-bit key from the character string using a key-crunching technique.

Another solution is to store the key in a ROM key or a magnetic stripe card [343,267]. Users could then enter their key into the system by inserting the key or card into a special reader attached to the encryption box or to the computer terminal.

This technique could be made even more secure by splitting the key into two halves, storing one half in the terminal and the other half in a ROM key. This way, losing the ROM key does not compromise the key—change it and everything is back to normal. The same with the loss of the terminal. This way, compromise of either the ROM key or the system does not compromise the key. An adversary must have both parts to reconstruct the actual key.

Hard-to-remember keys can be stored in encrypted form, using something similar to a key-encryption key. For example, an RSA private key could be encrypted with a DES key and stored on disk. To recover the RSA key, the user has to type in the DES key to a program that will decrypt it.

If the keys are generated deterministically (with a cryptographically secure pseudo-random number generator), it might be easier to regenerate the keys every time they are required from an easy-to-remember password.

7.2.6 Backup Keys

Alice is the chief financial officer at Secrets, Inc. Like any good corporate officer, she follows the company's security guidelines and encrypts all her data. Unfortunately, she ignores the company's street-crossing guidelines and gets hit by a truck. What does the company's president, Bob, do?

Unless Alice left Bob a copy of her key, he's in deep trouble. The whole point of encryption is to make files unrecoverable without the key. Unless Alice was a moron and used lousy encryption software, her files are lost.

There are several ways Bob can avoid this. The simplest is to require all of his employees to write down their keys and give them to the company's security officer, who will lock them in a safe somewhere (or encrypt them all with a master key). Now, when Alice is bowled over on the interstate, Bob can ask his security officer for her key. Bob should make sure to have the combination to the safe himself as well, otherwise if the security officer is run over, Bob will be back where he started from.

The problem with this system is that Bob has to trust his security officer not to misuse everyone's keys. Even more significantly, all the employees have to trust the security officer not to misuse their keys. A far better solution is to use a secret-sharing protocol (see Section 3.6).

When Alice generates a key, she also divides up that key into some number of pieces. She then sends each piece to a different company officer—encrypted, of course—according to the company's security guidelines. None of those pieces alone is the key, but someone can gather all the pieces together and reconstruct the key. Now Alice is protected against any one malicious person, and Bob is protected against losing all of Alice's data after her run-in with the truck. Or, she could just store the different pieces on her own hard disk, encrypted with each of the officer's different public keys. That way, no one has to get involved with the key management until it becomes necessary.

7.2.7 Compromised Keys

All of the protocols, techniques, and algorithms in this book are secure only if the key (the private key in the case of a public-key system) remains secret. If the key is lost, stolen, printed in the newspaper, or otherwise compromised, then all security is lost.

There's not much to do if the key is lost. Ideally, users know when their key is compromised. If a KDC is managing the keys, users should notify it that the key has been compromised. If there is no KDC, then they should notify all correspondents who might receive messages from them. Someone should make public the fact that any message received after the key was lost is suspect, and that no one should send messages to the user with the key (or associated public key). The system should use some sort of timestamp, and then users can figure out which messages are legitimate and which are suspect.

If users don't know exactly when their key was compromised, things become even more difficult. They may want to back out of a contract because the person who stole the key signed it instead of them. If you always allow this, then you give anyone the ability to back out of a contract by claiming that the key was compromised before it was signed. It has to be a matter for an adjudicator to decide.

The compromise of a private key is generally more serious than the compromise of a secret key, because private keys are more permanent. Secret keys are changed regularly; public/private key pairs are not. If Bob gets access to Alice's private key, he can impersonate her on the network: reading encrypted mail, signing correspondence, entering into contracts, etc.

It is vital that news of a private key's compromise propagate quickly through the network. Any databases of public keys must immediately be notified that a particular private key has been compromised, lest some unsuspecting person encrypt a message in that compromised key.

These procedures and tips aren't terribly optimal, but it's the best solution possible. The moral of the story is to protect keys, and protect private keys in the system above all else.

7.2.8 Lifetime of Keys

No encryption key should be used for an indefinite period. There are several reasons for this:

> The longer a key is used, the greater the chance that it is compromised. People write keys down; people lose them. Accidents happen. If you use the same key for a year, there's a far greater chance of compromise than if you use it for a day.

> The longer a key is used, the greater the loss if the key is compromised. If a key is used only to encrypt a single budgetary document on a file server, then the loss of the key means only the compromise of that document. If the same key is used to encrypt all the budgetary information on the file server, then its loss is much more devastating.

> The longer a key is used, the greater the temptation for someone to spend the effort necessary to break it—even if that effort is a brute-force attack. Breaking a key shared between two military units for a day would enable someone to read and fabricate messages between those units for that day.

Breaking a key shared by the entire military command structure for a year would enable that same person to read and fabricate messages throughout the world throughout the year. Which key do you think a nameless government agency, in our budget-conscious post–cold war world, would choose to attack?

It is generally easier to do cryptanalysis with more ciphertext encrypted with the same key.

For any cryptographic application, there must be a policy that determines the permitted lifetime of a key. Different keys may have different lifetimes. Communication session keys should have relatively short lifetimes, depending on the value of the data and the amount of data encrypted during a given period. The key for a gigabit-per-second communications link might have to be changed more often than the key for a 9600-baud modem link. Assuming there is an efficient method of transferring new keys using key-encryption keys, session keys should be changed at least daily.

On the other hand, key-encryption keys don't have to be replaced as frequently. They are used only occasionally (roughly once per day) for key exchange. There is little ciphertext for a cryptanalyst to work with. However, the potential loss if a key-encryption key is compromised is extreme: all communications encrypted with every key encrypted with the key-encryption key. In some applications, key-encryption keys are replaced just once a month or once a year.

Encryption keys used to encrypt data files for storage cannot be changed often. The files may sit encrypted on disk for months or years before someone needs them again. Decrypting them and re-encrypting them with a new key every day doesn't enhance security in any way; it just gives a cryptanalyst more to work with. One solution might be to encrypt each file with a unique file key, and then encrypt all the file keys with a key-encryption key. The key-encryption key should then be either memorized or stored in a secure location, perhaps in a safe somewhere. Of course, losing this key would mean losing all the individual file keys.

Private keys for public-key cryptography applications have varying lifetimes, depending on the application. Private keys used for digital signatures and proofs of identity may have to last years (even a lifetime). Private keys used for coin flipping protocols can be discarded immediately after the protocol is completed. Even if the security of a key is expected to last a lifetime, it may be prudent to change the key every couple of years. The private keys in many public-key cryptography networks are good only for two years; after that the user must get a new private key. The old key would still have to remain secret, in case the person needed to verify a signature from that period. But the new key would be used to sign new documents, reducing the number of signed documents a cryptanalyst would have for an attack.

7.2.9 Destroying Keys

Given that keys must be replaced regularly, old keys must be destroyed. Old keys are valuable, even if they are never to be used again. With them, an adversary can read old messages encrypted with that key [35].

Keys must be destroyed securely. If the key is written on paper, the paper should be shredded or burned. Be careful to use a high-quality shredder; there are many poor-quality shredders on the market. The algorithms in this book are secure against brute-force attacks costing millions of dollars and taking millions of years. If an adversary can recover your key by potentially taking a bag of shredded documents from your trash and paying 100 unemployed workers ten cents per hour for a year to piece the shredded pages together, then that would be $26,000 well spent.

If the key is in a hardware EEPROM, the key should be overwritten multiple times. If the key is in a hardware EPROM or PROM, the chip should be smashed into tiny bits and scattered to the four winds. If the key is stored on a computer disk, the actual bits of the storage should be overwritten multiple times (see Section 8.9).

A potential problem is that, in a computer, keys can be easily copied and stored in multiple locations. Any computer that does its own memory management, constantly swapping programs in and out of memory, exacerbates the problem. There is no way to ensure that successful key erasure has taken place in the computer, especially if the computer's operating system controls the erasure process. The more paranoid among you should consider writing a special erasure program that scans all disks looking for copies of the key's bit pattern on unused blocks, and then erase those blocks. Also remember to erase the contents of a "swap" file, if necessary.

7.3 PUBLIC-KEY KEY MANAGEMENT

Public-key cryptography makes key management easier, but it has its own unique problems. Each person has only one public key, regardless of the number of people on the network. If Alice wants to send a message to Bob, she has to get Bob's public key. There are several ways she can go about this:

> She can get it from Bob.
> She can get it from a centralized database.
> She can get it from her own private database.

Section 2.5 discusses a number of possible attacks against public-key cryptography, based on Mallet's substituting his key for Bob's. The scenario is that Alice wants to send a message to Bob. She goes into the public-key database and gets Bob's public key. But Mallet, who is sneaky, substituted his own key for Bob's. (If Alice asks Bob directly, Mallet has to intercept Bob's transmission and substitute his key for Bob's.) Alice encrypts her message in Mallet's key and sends it to Bob. Mallet intercepts the message, decrypts it, and reads it. He re-encrypts it with Bob's real key and sends it on to Bob. Neither Alice nor Bob is the wiser.

Public-Key Certificates

A public-key certificate is someone's public key, signed by a trustworthy person. Certificates are used to thwart attempts to substitute one key for another. Bob's certificate, in the public-key database, contains a lot more than his public key. It contains information about Bob—his name, address, etc.—and it is signed by someone Alice trusts: Trent (usually known as a **certifying authority,** or CA). By signing both the key and the information about Bob, Trent certifies that the information about Bob is correct, and that the public key belongs to Bob. Alice checks the signature, and then she can use the public key, secure in the knowledge that it is Bob's and no one else's. Certificates play an important role in a number of public-key protocols: PEM [476] (see Section 17.7) and CCITT X.509 [188] (see Section 17.6).

Distributed Key Management

In some situations, centralized key management will not work. Perhaps there is no certifying authority whom both Alice and Bob trust. Perhaps Alice and Bob trust only their friends. Perhaps Alice and Bob trust no one.

Distributed key management, used in the public-domain program Pretty Good Privacy [908] (see Section 17.9), solves this problem with **introducers.** Introducers are other users of the system who sign their friends' public keys. For example, when Bob generates his public key, he gives copies to his friends Carol and Dave. They know Bob, so they each sign Bob's key and give Bob a copy of the signature. Now, when Bob presents his key to a stranger, Alice, he presents it with the signatures of these two introducers. If Alice also knows and trusts Carol, she has reason to believe that Bob's key is valid. If she knows and trusts Carol and Dave a little, she has reason to believe that Bob's key is valid. If she doesn't know either Carol or Dave, she has no reason to trust Bob's key.

Over time, Bob will collect many more introducers. If Alice and Bob travel in similar circles, the odds are good that Alice will know one of Bob's introducers.

To prevent against Mallet's substituting one key for another, introducers must be sure that Bob's key belongs to Bob before they sign it. Perhaps introducers should require the key to be given face-to-face or verified over the telephone.

The benefit of this mechanism is that there is no KDC that everyone has to trust. The down side is that when Alice receives Bob's public key, there is no guarantee that she will know any of the introducers and therefore no guarantee that she will trust the validity of the key.

CHAPTER
8

Using Algorithms

8.1 BLOCK CIPHER MODES

Block algorithms operate on blocks of plaintext and ciphertext—usually 64 bits. It's not sufficient to place a block algorithm in a program and walk away. You can use the block algorithm in one of several ways, depending on your specific needs.

8.1.1 Electronic Codebook Mode

The most obvious way to use a block cipher is to encrypt each block of plaintext into a block of ciphertext. This is called **electronic codebook (ECB)** mode, because one block of plaintext always encrypts to the same block of ciphertext. The typical block size is 64-bits, so the codebook will have 2^{64} entries—much too large to precompute. And remember, there is a different codebook for each key.

This is the easiest mode to work with. The benefit is that each plaintext block is encrypted independently. You don't have to encrypt a file linearly; you can encrypt the ten blocks in the middle first, then the blocks at the end, and finally the blocks in the beginning. This is important for encrypted files that have to be accessed randomly, for example, a database. If a database is encrypted with ECB mode, then any record can be decrypted independently of any other record. Records can be added into and deleted from the middle of that database (assuming that a record consists of a discrete number of encryption blocks).

The problem with ECB mode is that if cryptanalysts have the plaintext and ciphertext for several messages, they can start to compile a codebook without knowing the key. In most real-world situations, fragments of messages tend to repeat. One message may have bit sequences in common with another. Computer-generated messages, like electronic mail, may have a regular structure. Messages may have parameters that take only a few values or long strings of 0's or spaces. Other computer-generated messages may always have important data in the same place.

If cryptanalysts learn that the plaintext block "5e081bc5" encrypts to the ciphertext block "7ea593a4", they can immediately decrypt that ciphertext block whenever it appears in another message. If the application encrypts messages with a lot of redundancies, and these redundancies tend to show up in the same places in the message, this can be a very powerful attack.

This vulnerability is greatest at the beginning and end of messages, where well-defined headers and footers contain information about the sender, receiver, date, etc. This problem is sometimes called **stereotyped beginnings** and **stereotyped endings,** and it will be solved in the modes discussed below.

8.1.2 Block Replay

Another, potentially more serious, problem with ECB is that an adversary could modify encrypted messages without knowing the key (or even details of the algorithm) in such a way as to fool the intended recipient. This problem was first discussed in [183].

To illustrate the problem, consider an interbank money transfer system. Banks routinely transfer money between accounts in different banks. To make life easier for the different computer systems, a bank network agrees on a standard message format for money transfer that looks like this:

Sending Bank Name	12 bytes
Receiving Bank Name	12 bytes
Depositor's Name	48 bytes
Depositor's Account	16 bytes
Amount of Deposit	8 bytes

Of course the messages are encrypted, using some block algorithm in ECB mode.

Mallet, who is listening on the communications line between two banks, Bank 1 and Bank 2, can use this information to get rich. First, he sets up his computer to record all of the encrypted messages from Bank 1 to Bank 2. Then, he transfers $100 from Bank 1 to his account in Bank 2. Later, he does it again. Using his computer, he correlates the recorded messages looking for a pair of identical messages. These messages are the ones authorizing the $100 transfers to his account. If there is more than one pair of identical messages (surely there are other people transferring money back and forth between the two banks), he does another money transfer and records those results. Eventually he can isolate the message that authorized his money transaction.

Now he can insert that message into the communications link at will. Every time he sends the message to Bank 2, another $100 will be credited to his account. When the two banks reconcile their transfers (probably at the end of the day), they will notice the phantom transfer authorizations; but if Mallet was clever he would have already withdrawn the money and headed for South America. And he probably did his scam with dollar amounts far larger than $100, and with lots of different banks.

At first glance, the banks could easily prevent this by adding a timestamp to their messages.

Date/Timestamp:	1 block
Sending Bank Name	1.5 blocks
Receiving Bank Name	1.5 blocks
Depositor's Name	6 blocks
Depositor's Account	2 blocks
Amount of Deposit	1 block

Two identical messages would be easy to spot using this system. Still, using a technique called **block replay,** Mallet can still get rich. Assuming the block size of the cryptographic algorithm is 64 bits (standard for DES and many others), the record will be encrypted in 13 blocks, as shown in Figure 8.1. By looking at this figure, Mallet can pick out the eight ciphertext blocks that correspond to Alice's name and account number: blocks 5 through 10. A diabolical laugh is appropriate at this point, because Mallet is now ready.

He intercepts random messages from Bank 1 to Bank 2 and replaces blocks 5 through 10 in the message with the bytes that correspond to his name and account number. Then he sends them on to Bank 2. He doesn't have to know who the original depositor was; he doesn't even have to know what the amount was (although he could correlate the messages he doctored with the various deposits into his account and determine the encrypted blocks corresponding to some dollar amount). He simply changes the name and account numbers to his own and watches his account balance grow.

This will take longer than a day for the banks to catch. When they reconcile their transfers at the end of the day, everything will match. It probably won't be until the legitimate depositors notice that the money didn't end up in their account, or when someone flagged unusual activity in Mallet's account, that the banks will figure out the scam. Mallet isn't stupid, and by then he will have closed his account, changed his name, and bought a villa in Argentina.

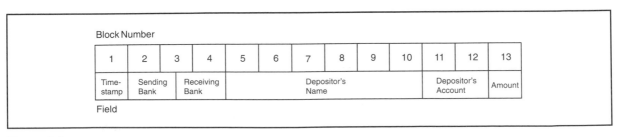

Figure 8.1
Encryption blocks.

Banks can minimize the problem by changing their keys frequently, but this only means that Mallet is going to have to work more quickly. This is a fundamental problem with block ciphers in ECB mode: because they treat each block of plaintext independently, they are prone to block replay attacks. The solution is a technique called **chaining.**

8.1.3 Cipher Block Chaining Mode

Chaining uses a **feedback** mechanism, because the results of the encryption of previous blocks are fed back into the encryption of the current block. In other words, the previous block is used to modify the encryption of the next block. Each ciphertext block is dependent not just on the plaintext block that generated it but on all the previous plaintext blocks.

In **cipher block chaining (CBC)** mode, the plaintext is XORed with the previous ciphertext block before it is encrypted. Figure 8.2 shows block chaining in action. After a plaintext block is encrypted, the resulting ciphertext is also stored in a feedback register. Before the next plaintext block is encrypted, it is XORed with the feedback register to become the next input to the encrypting routine. The resultant ciphertext is again stored in the feedback register, to be XORed with the next plaintext block, and so on until the end of the message. The encryption of each block depends on all the previous blocks.

Decryption is just as straightforward. A ciphertext block is decrypted normally, and also saved in a feedback register. After the next block is decrypted, it is XORed

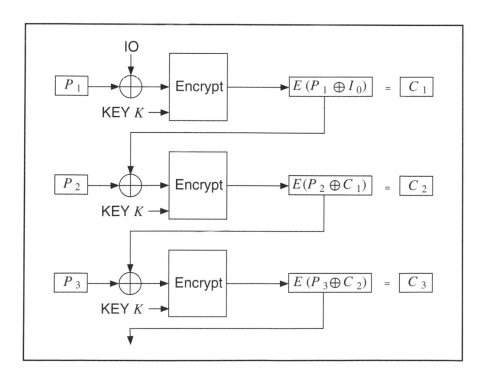

Figure 8.2
Cipher block chaining mode.

with the results of the feedback register. Then the next ciphertext block is stored in the feedback register, and so on, until the end of the message.

Mathematically, this looks like:

$$C_i = E_K(P_i \text{ XOR } C_{i-1})$$
$$P_i = C_{i-1} \text{ XOR } D_K(C_i)$$

Initialization Vector

CBC forces identical plaintext blocks to encrypt to different ciphertext blocks only if some of the previous plaintext blocks are different. Two identical messages will still encrypt to the same ciphertext. Even worse, two messages that begin the same will encrypt in the same way up to the first difference. Some messages have a common header: a letterhead, or a "From" line, for instance. While block replay would still be impossible, this identical beginning might give a cryptanalyst some useful information.

The way to prevent this is to encrypt random data as the first block. This block of random data is called the **initialization vector (IV), initializing variable,** or **initial chaining value.** The IV has no meaning; it's just there to make each message unique. It doesn't have to be kept secret. When receivers decrypt this block, they just use it to fill the feedback register and otherwise ignore it.

The IV should be a random number. It can be a serial number, which increments after each message and does not repeat during the lifetime of the key. For data encrypted for storage, it can be a function of the index used to look up the data.

With the addition of IVs, even an identical plaintext block will encrypt to a different ciphertext message. Thus, it will be impossible for an eavesdropper to learn any information about the plaintext from the ciphertext.

The IV does not have to be kept secret and can be transmitted with the ciphertext. However, it should be changed with every message.

Padding

Most messages don't divide neatly into 64-bit (or whatever size) encryption blocks; there is usually a short block at the end. There are two ways to deal with this.

The easiest is to pad the block with some regular pattern—zeros, ones, alternating 1's and 0's—to make it a complete block. If your application needs to be able to delete the padding after decryption, add the number of padding bytes as the last byte of the message. For example, assume the block size is 64 bits, and the last block consists of 3 bytes (24 bits). Forty bits (five bytes) of padding are required to make the last block 64 bits; add 4 bytes of zeros and a final byte with the number 5. After decryption, the program knows to delete the last 5 bytes of the last decryption block. You can also use an end-of-file character to denote the final plaintext byte.

You can't always do this; there are applications where the ciphertext has to be exactly the same size as the plaintext. Maybe a plaintext file has to be encrypted and then replaced in the exact same memory location. In this case, you have to encrypt the last short block differently. Assume the last block has j bits. After encrypting the last full block, encrypt the same ciphertext again, select the left-most *j* bits of the encrypted ciphertext, and XOR that with the short block to generate the ciphertext. Figure 8.3 illustrates this.

The weakness with this method is that while Mallet cannot recover the last plaintext block, he can change it systematically by changing individual bits in the ciphertext. If the last few bits of the ciphertext contain essential information, this is a weakness. If the last bits simply contain a checksum or other housekeeping information, it isn't a problem.

Error Propagation

CBC can be characterized as **feedback** of the ciphertext at the encryption end and **feedforward** of the ciphertext at the decryption end. This has implications having to do with errors. A single error in a plaintext block will affect that ciphertext block and all subsequent ciphertext blocks. This isn't significant because decryption will reverse that effect, and the recovered plaintext will have the same single error.

Ciphertext errors are more common. They can easily result from a noisy communications path or a malfunction in the storage medium. In CBC mode, a single-bit error in the ciphertext affects one block and one bit of the recovered plaintext. The block containing the error is completely garbled. The subsequent block has a 1-bit error in the same bit position as the error.

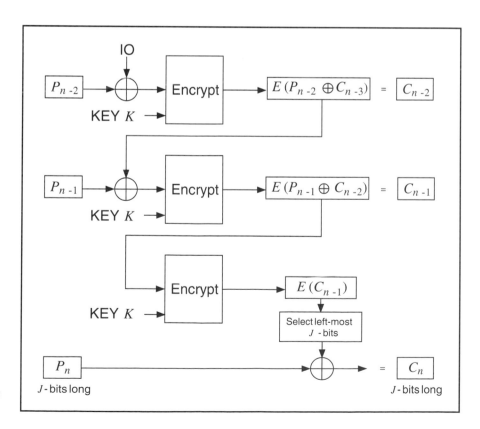

Figure 8.3

A method for encrypting the last block.

Blocks after the second are not affected by the error, so CBC is **self-recovering.** Two blocks are affected by an error, but the system recovers and continues to work correctly for all subsequent blocks.

While CBC recovers quickly from bit errors, it doesn't recover at all from synchronization errors. If a bit is added or lost from the ciphertext stream, then all subsequent blocks are shifted one bit out of position, and decryption will generate garbage indefinitely. Any cryptosystem that uses CBC must ensure that the block structure remains intact, either by **framing** or by storing data in multiple-block-sized chunks.

This property of taking a small ciphertext error and converting it into a large plaintext error is called **error extension.** It is a major annoyance. To help prevent it, error detection and recovery facilities on the communication line should be applied after encryption and before decryption, not before encryption and after decryption (see Figure 8.4). If there is noise in the communications path, decryption will only make that noise worse.

8.1.4 Cipher Feedback Mode

With CBC, encryption cannot begin until a complete block of data is received. This is a problem in some network applications. For example, in a secure network environment, a terminal must transmit each character to the host as it is entered. When data has to be processed in byte-sized chunks, CBC mode is inadequate.

In **cipher feedback (CFB)** mode, data is encrypted in units smaller than the block size. This example will encrypt one ASCII character at a time (this is called **8-bit CFB**), but there is nothing sacred about the number eight. You can encrypt data 1 bit at a time, using 1-bit CFB.

Figure 8.5 shows 8-bit CFB working with a 64-bit algorithm. A block algorithm in CFB mode operates on a queue the size of the input block (64 bits in the figure). Initially, the queue is filled with an initial chaining value, as in CBC mode. The queue is encrypted, and the left-most 8 bits of the result are XORed with the first 8-bit character of the plaintext to become the first 8-bit character of the ciphertext.

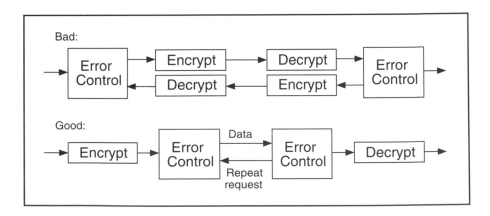

Figure 8.4
Error control with
encryption.

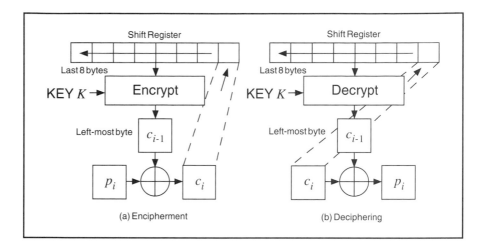

Figure 8.5
8-bit cipher feedback mode.

This character can be transmitted. The same 8 bits are also moved to the right-most 8 bit positions of the queue, and all the other bits move 8 to the left. The 8 left-most bits are discarded. Then the next character is encrypted in the same manner. Decryption is the reverse of this process. On both the encryption and the decryption side, the block algorithm is used in its encryption mode.

Like CBC, CFB links the plaintext characters together, so that the ciphertext depends on all the preceding plaintext.

Initialization Vector

To initialize the CFB process, the shift register must be filled with an IV. A different IV should be used for every message during the lifetime of the key. However, there is no security benefit in keeping the IV secret; the IV can be transmitted in the clear.

Error Propagation

With CFB, an error in the plaintext affects all subsequent ciphertext, as with CBC. Again, like CBC, this error is reversed at decryption.

An error in the ciphertext is more interesting. The first effect of a single-bit error in the ciphertext is to cause a single error in the plaintext. After that the error enters the shift register, where it causes ciphertext to be garbled until it falls off the other end of the register. In 8-bit CFB, 9 bytes of ciphertext are garbled by the single-bit error. After that, the system recovers, and all subsequent ciphertext is decrypted correctly.

One subtle problem with this kind of error propagation is that if Mallet knows the plaintext of a transmission, he can toggle bits in a given block and make that block decrypt to whatever he wants. The *next* block will decrypt to garbage but, depending on the application, the damage may already be done. It is quite easy to make this serious mistake.

CFB is self-recovering with respect to synchronization errors as well. The error enters the shift register, where it garbles 8 bytes of data until it falls off the other end.

8.1.5 Output Feedback Mode

Output feedback (OFB) mode is similar to cipher feedback mode, except that part of the previous output block is moved into the right-most positions of the queue (see Figure 8.6). Decryption is the reverse of this process. On both the encryption and the decryption sides, the block algorithm is used in its encryption mode. This method is sometimes called **internal feedback,** because the feedback mechanism is independent of both the plaintext and the ciphertext streams [183].

Initialization Vector

The OFB shift register must also be initially loaded with an IV. A different IV should be used for every message during the lifetime of the key. These IV values can be transmitted in the clear.

Error Propagation

The benefit of OFB is that there is no error extension. A single-bit error in the ciphertext causes a single-bit error in the recovered plaintext. This can be useful in some digitized analog transmissions, like digitized voice or video, where the occasional single-bit error can be tolerated but error extension cannot.

On the other hand, a loss of synchronization is fatal. If the shift registers on the encryption end and the decryption end are not identical, then the recovered plaintext will be gibberish. Any system that uses OFB must have a mechanism for detecting a synchronization loss and a mechanism to fill both shift registers with a new (or the same) IV to regain synchronization.

Security Problems with OFB

An analysis of OFB by Gait [361] demonstrates that OFB should be used only when the feedback size is the same as the block size. For example, you should only use a 64-bit algorithm in 64-bit OFB. Even though the U.S. government authorizes other feedback possibilities for DES [637], these should be avoided.

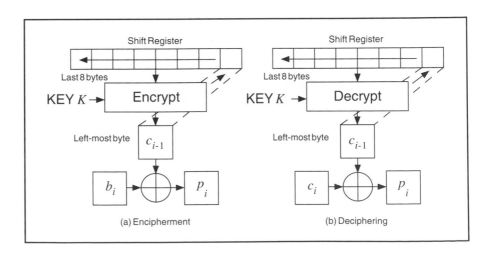

Figure 8.6
Output feedback mode.

8.1.6 Counter Mode

A mode similar to OFB, proposed by [478,301,422], uses sequence numbers. Instead of using the output of the encryption algorithm to fill the register, the input to the register is a counter. After each encryption block, the counter increments by some constant, typically 1. The synchronization and error propagation characteristics of this mode are identical to those of OFB.

8.1.7 Other Modes

Block Chaining Mode

To use a block algorithm in **block chaining (BC)** mode, simply XOR the input to the block cipher with the XOR of all the previous ciphertext blocks. As with CBC, an initialization vector, I_0, starts the process.

Mathematically, this looks like:

$$C_i = E_K(P_i \text{ XOR } F_i); F_{i+1} = F_i \text{ XOR } C_i$$
$$P_i = F_i \text{ XOR } D_K(C_i); F_{i+1} = F_i \text{ XOR } C_i$$

Like CBC, BC's feedback process has the property of extending errors in the plaintext. The primary problem with BC is that because the decryption of a ciphertext block depends on all the previous ciphertext blocks, a single error in the ciphertext will result in the incorrect decryption of all subsequent ciphertext blocks.

Propagating Cipher Block Chaining Mode

Propagating cipher block chaining (PCBC) [597] mode is similar to CBC mode, except that both the previous plaintext block and the previous ciphertext block are XORed with the current plaintext block before encryption (or after decryption) (see Figure 8.7).

$$C_i = E_K(P_i \text{ XOR } C_{i-1} \text{ XOR } P_{i-1})$$
$$P_i = C_{i-1} \text{ XOR } P_{i-1} \text{ XOR } D_K(C_i)$$

PCBC is used in Kerberos version 4 (see Section 17.4) to perform both encryption and integrity checking in one pass. In PCBC mode, an error in the ciphertext will result in incorrect decryption of all blocks that follow. This means that checking a standard block at the end of a message will ensure the integrity of the entire message.

Unfortunately, there is a problem with this mode [496]. Swapping two ciphertext blocks will result in the incorrect decryption of the two corresponding plaintext blocks, but due to the nature of the XOR with the plaintext and the ciphertext, the errors will cancel. So if the integrity checker looks only at the last few blocks of the decrypted plaintext, it could be fooled into accepting a partially garbled message. This feedback scheme was proposed for Kerberos version 4, but was replaced in version 5 by CBC mode after the above flaw was discovered.

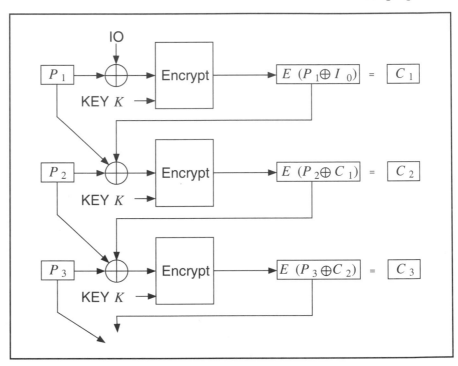

Figure 8.7
Propagating cipher block
chaining mode.

More Modes

There are other modes possible, although they are not extensively used. Some of them are described in [453]. **Plaintext block chaining (PBC)** is like CBC except the previous plaintext block is XORed with the plaintext block instead of with the ciphertext block. **Plaintext feedback (PFB)** is like CFB, except the plaintext fills the shift register instead of the ciphertext. Another method, found in [249], incorporates encryption in both the data path and the feedback path. There is also **cipher block chaining of plaintext difference (CBCPD)** and **output feedback with a non-linear function (OFBNLF).**

If cryptanalysts have a keysearch machine, then if they can guess one of the plaintext blocks, they can recover the key. Some of these stranger modes amount to light encryption before applying DES: e.g., XORing the text with a fixed secret string or permuting the text. Almost anything nonstandard will help frustrate this sort of cryptanalysis.

8.1.8 Choosing a Cipher Mode

If simplicity and speed are your main concerns, ECB is the easiest and fastest mode to use a block cipher. It is also the weakest. Besides being vulnerable to replay attacks, an algorithm in ECB mode is the easiest to cryptanalyze. I don't recommend ECB.

Use either CBC, CFB, or OFB. Which mode you choose depends on your specific requirements. CBC is generally best for encrypting files. It is trivially slower than ECB; the only difference is an extra block-size memory register and an XOR per block. The increase in security is significant; and while there are sometimes bit errors in stored data, there are almost never synchronization errors. If your application is software-based, this is almost always the best choice.

Both OFB and CFB are significantly slower than CBC; they encrypt fewer bits of plaintext per iteration of the block algorithm. If you can accept some error propagation in exchange for the ability to recover from a synchronization loss, use CFB. If you can't handle any error propagation, use OFB.

CFB is generally the mode of choice for encrypting streams of characters when each character has to be treated individually, as in a link between a terminal and a host. OFB is most often used in high-speed synchronous systems where error propagation is intolerable.

Stay away from the "weird" modes. One of the four basic modes—ECB, CBC, OFB, and CFB—is suitable for almost any application. These modes are not overly complex and probably do not reduce the security of the system. While it is possible that a complicated mode might increase the security of a system, most likely it just increases the complexity. None of the weird modes has any better error propagation or error recovery characteristics.

8.2 MULTIPLE ENCRYPTION

Multiple encryption happens when you encrypt the same plaintext block multiple times. Encrypting a plaintext block twice with the same algorithm and the same key does not affect the complexity of a brute-force search. To enhance security, you need multiple keys.

8.2.1 Double Encryption

A naive way of improving the security of a block algorithm is to encrypt a block twice with two different keys. First encrypt a block with the first key, and then encrypt it with the second key. Decryption is the reverse process.

$$C = E_{K_2}(E_{K_1} P)$$
$$P = D_{K_1}(D_{K_2} C)$$

If the block algorithm is not a group (this is a mathematical term; see Section 10.1), then there would not necessarily exist a K_3, such that:

$$C = E_{K_2}(E_{K_1} P) = E_{K_3}$$

In this case, the resultant doubly encrypted ciphertext block should be much harder to break using an exhaustive search. Instead of 2^n attempts (where n is the bit length of the key), it would require 2^{2n} attempts. If the algorithm is a 64-bit algorithm, the doubly encrypted ciphertext would require 2^{128} attempts to find the key—seemingly more than can be done in any lifetime.

This turns out not to be true. Merkle and Hellman [594] developed a time-memory tradeoff that, using a known plaintext attack, could break this double encryption scheme in 2^{n+1} attempts, not in 2^{2n} attempts. (They showed this for DES, but the result can be generalized to any block algorithm.) The attack is called a **meet-in-the-middle attack,** and it works by encrypting from one end, decrypting from the other, and matching the results in the middle.

The attack works as follows: The cryptanalyst knows P_1, C_1, P_2, and C_2, such that:

$$C_1 = E_{K_2}(E_{K_1}(P_1))$$
$$C_2 = E_{K_2}(E_{K_1}(P_2))$$

For each possible K (either K_1 or K_2), compute $E_K(P_1)$ and store the result in memory. After you have them all, compute $D_K(C_1)$ for each K and look for the same result in memory. If you find it, it is possible that the current key is K_2 and the key in memory is K_1. Try encrypting P_2 with K_1 and K_2; if you get C_2 you can be pretty sure (with a probability of success of 2^{2n-2b}, where b is the block size, that you have k. If not, keep looking. Expect to get about $(2^{2n}-2^b)$ false positives before you find the right one. The maximum number of encryption trials you will probably have to run is 2×2^n, or 2^{n+1}. If the probability of error is too large, you can use a third ciphertext block to get a probability of success of 2^{2n-3b}. There are still other optimizations.

This attack requires a lot of memory, 2^n blocks. For a 56-bit algorithm, this translates to 2^{56} 64-bit blocks, or 2^{59} bytes. This is still considerably more memory storage than one could comfortably comprehend, but it's enough to convince the most paranoid of cryptographers that double encryption is not worth anything.

If the block cipher is a group, then encrypting with K_1 followed by K_2 is the same as encrypting with a third key, K_3. This doesn't increase security at all. While it is very hard to prove that an encryption algorithm is not a group, cryptographers try hard to design their algorithms so they are not. DES, for example, is not a group (see Section 10.1).

8.2.2 Triple Encryption

A better idea, proposed by Tuchman in [857], is to encrypt a block three times with the two keys: first with the first key, then with the second key, and finally with the first key again. He suggested that the sender first encrypt with the first key, then decrypt with the second key, and finally encrypt with the first key. The receiver decrypts with the first key, then encrypts with the second key, and finally decrypts with the first key. This is sometimes called **encrypt-decrypt-encrypt (EDE)** mode.

$$C = E_{K_1}(D_{K_2}(E_{K_1}P))$$
$$P = D_{K_1}(E_{K_2}(D_{K_1}C))$$

If the block algorithm has an n-bit key, then this scheme has a $2n$-bit key. The curious encrypt-decrypt-encrypt scheme was designed by IBM to preserve compatibility with conventional implementations of the algorithm: setting the two keys equal to each other is identical to encrypting once with the key. There is no security inherent in the encrypt-decrypt-encrypt pattern, but this scheme has been adopted to improve the DES algorithm in the X9.17 and ISO 8732 standards [30,445].

This technique is not susceptible to the same meet-in-the-middle attack described earlier. But Merkle and Hellman developed another time-memory tradeoff that could break this technique in 2^{n-1} steps, using 2^n blocks of memory [594]. This is a chosen-plaintext attack, requiring an enormous amount of chosen plaintext to mount. Paul van Oorschot and Michael Wiener converted this to a known-plaintext attack, taking four orders of magnitude less time than a brute-force search for the two keys (2^{2n-4}) [859].

For the ultra-paranoid, I recommend triple encryption with three different keys. The key length is longer, but storing keys is usually not a problem.

$$C = E_{K_3}(D_{K_2}(E_{K_1}P))$$
$$P = D_{K_1}(E_{K_2}(D_{K_3}C))$$

The best time-memory tradeoff attack takes 2^{2n} steps and requires 2^n blocks of memory [594]. To be compatible with single encryption, set all three keys equal to one another.

Triple encryption, with three independent keys, is as secure as one might naively expect double encryption to be.

8.2.3 Triple Encryption with Padding

If the message is long enough (more than a few encryption blocks), then triple encryption can be further enhanced by padding. Pad the text with a string of random bits, half a block in length, between the first and second and between the second and third encryptions (see Figure 8.8):

$$C = E_{K_3}(\text{PAD}(D_{K_2}(\text{PAD}(E_{K_1}P))))$$

This padding not only disrupts patterns but also overlaps encrypted blocks like bricks.

8.2.4 Doubling the Block Length

Richard Outerbridge has proposed doubling the block length of an algorithm using multiple encryptions [185]. Before implementing any of these, look for the possibility of meet-in-the-middle attacks. The scheme illustrated in Figure 8.9 is susceptible to a meet-in-the-middle attack, similar to the one described above. Outerbridge's scheme, illustrated in Figure 8.10, is secure [186].

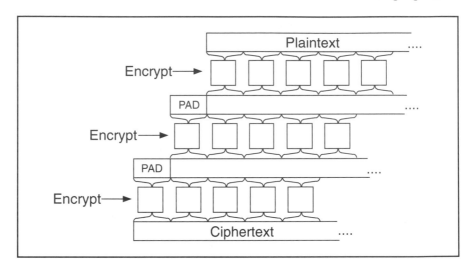

Figure 8.8
Triple encryption with padding.

8.2.5 Multiple Encryption with Multiple Algorithms

What about encrypting a block once with algorithm A and key K_A, and then again with algorithm B and key K_B? Aside from this being susceptible to the same meet-in-the-middle attacks, there is no guarantee that the two algorithms will work together to increase security. There may be subtle interactions between the two algorithms that actually *decrease* security. Even triple encryption with two or three different algorithms may not be as secure as you think. Cryptography is a tricky art.

8.3 STREAM CIPHERS

Stream ciphers are algorithms that convert plaintext to ciphertext 1 bit at a time. The simplest implementation of a stream cipher is shown in Figure 8.11. A

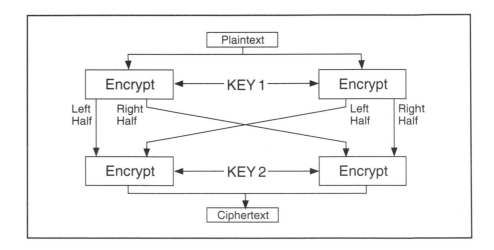

Figure 8.9
Doubling the block length susceptible to attack.

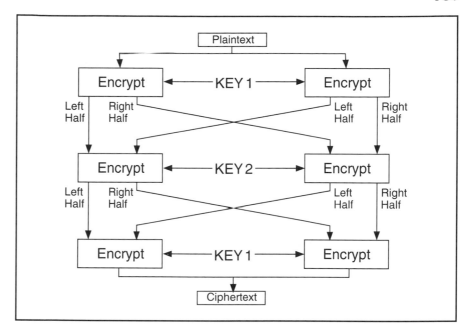

Figure 8.10
Correctly doubling the block length.

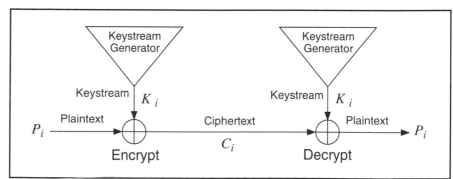

Figure 8.11
Stream cipher.

keystream generator that outputs a stream of bits: k_1, k_2, k_3 . . . k_i. This keystream is XORed with a stream of plaintext bits, $p_1, p_2, p_3, \ldots p_i$, to produce the stream of ciphertext bits.

$$c_i = p_i \text{ XOR } k_i$$

At the decryption end, the ciphertext bits are XORed with an identical keystream to recover the plaintext bits.

$$p_i = c_i \text{ XOR } k_i$$

Since

$$p_i \text{ XOR } k_i \text{ XOR } k_i = p_i$$

this works nicely.

The system's security depends entirely on the insides of the keystream generator. If the keystream generator outputs an endless stream of 0's, the ciphertext will equal the plaintext and the whole operation will be worthless. If the keystream generator spits out a repeating 16-bit pattern, the algorithm will be a simple XOR with negligible security. If the keystream generator spits out an endless stream of random (not pseudo-random, but real random) bits, you have a one-time pad and perfect security.

The reality of stream ciphers lies somewhere between the simple XOR and the one-time pad—ideally it is closer to the one-time pad. The keystream generator generates a bit stream that looks random, but is actually a deterministic stream that can be flawlessly reproduced at decryption time. The closer the keystream generator's output is to random, the harder time a cryptanalyst will have breaking it. As you might guess, creating a keystream generator that produces output that looks random is no easy matter.

There is more to stream ciphers than the output. If the keystream generator produces the same bit stream every time it is turned on, the resulting cryptosystem will be trivial to break. An example will show why.

If the plaintext message is:

10001101

then the keystream generator outputs the keystream

01100111

and the resulting ciphertext is

11101010

Eve has a copy of the ciphertext and also managed to acquire the plaintext. Now all she has to do is to XOR the plaintext and the ciphertext to get the keystream. Or, if she has two different ciphertexts encrypted with the same keystream, she can XOR them together and get two plaintext messages XORed with each other. This is easy to break, and then she can XOR one of the plaintexts with the ciphertext to get the keystream.

Now, whenever another ciphertext message comes along, she has the keystream bits necessary to decrypt it. In addition, she can decrypt and read any old ciphertext messages she has previously intercepted. When Eve gets a single plaintext/ciphertext pair, she can read everything.

This is why all stream ciphers include keys. Figure 8.12 shows how keys are added to the system. The output of the keystream generator is a function of the key. With one key, the keystream generator might produce the bit stream "01100111." With another key, it might produce "11001110." Now, if Eve gets a plaintext/ciphertext pair, she can only read messages encrypted with a single key. Change the key, and the adversary is back to square one.

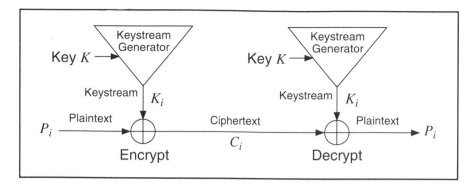

Figure 8.12
Stream cipher with keys.

Because it is necessary to change the key with each message, stream ciphers are not usually used to encrypt discrete messages. They are more useful in encrypting never-ending streams of communications traffic: a T-1 link between two computers, for example.

Since the keystream generator must generate the same output on both the encryption and decryption ends, it must be deterministic. Because it is implemented in a finite state machine (i.e., a computer), the sequence will eventually repeat. These keystream generators are called **periodic.** Except for one-time pads, all keystream generators are periodic.

It is an important design goal for the keystream generator to have a long period, one far longer than the number of bits the generator will output between key changes. A keystream generator encrypting a continuous T-1 link will encrypt 10^{11} bits per day. The keystream generator's period must be orders of magnitude larger than that, even if the key is changed daily. If the period is long enough, you might only have to change the key weekly or even monthly.

Prying the hood off a keystream generator, you can see that it consists of three basic parts (see Figure 8.13). The internal state describes the current state of the keystream generator. Two keystream generators, with the same key and the same internal state,

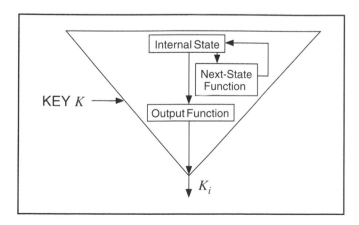

Figure 8.13
Inside a keystream generator.

will produce the same keystream. The output function takes the internal state and generates a keystream bit. The next-state function takes the internal state and generates a new internal state.

Designing a good keystream generator is no easy task. There has been much effort put into this task over the years. Section 15.2 will discuss the design of keystream generators in minute detail. For purposes of this section, I will assume that I already have a very secure keystream generator.

8.3.1 Synchronous Stream Ciphers

In a **synchronous stream cipher** the keystream is generated independent of the message stream, as shown in Figure 8.12. On the encryption side, a keystream generator spits out keystream bits, one after the other. On the decryption side, another keystream generator spits out the identical keystream bits, one after the other. This works well, as long as the two keystream generators are synchronized. If one of them skips a cycle or if a ciphertext bit gets lost during transmission, then every ciphertext character after the error will be decrypted incorrectly.

If this happens, the sender and receiver must resynchronize their keystream generators before they can proceed. Frustrating matters even further, they must do this in such a way as to ensure that no part of the keystream is repeated, so the obvious solution of resetting the keystream generator to an earlier state won't work.

On the plus side, synchronous ciphers do not propagate transmission errors. If a bit is garbled during transmission, which is far more likely than a bit being lost altogether, then only the garbled bit will be decrypted incorrectly. All preceding and subsequent bits will be unaffected. As we will see later, this is not the case with **self-synchronous stream ciphers.**

Synchronous stream ciphers also protect against any insertions and deletions in the ciphertext, because they will cause a loss of synchronization and be immediately detected. They do not, however, fully protect against bit toggling. Like block ciphers in CFB mode, Mallet can toggle individual bits in the stream. If he knows the plaintext, he can make those bits decrypt to whatever he wants. Subsequent bits will decrypt to garbage (until the system recovers), but in certain applications Mallet can still do considerable damage.

Synchronous stream ciphers can be further classified according to the mode they operate in: **output feedback mode** or **counter mode.**

Output Feedback Mode

A stream cipher is in output feedback mode if the key affects the next-state function (see Figure 8.14). The output function is not dependent on the key; very often it is something simple like a single bit of the internal state, or the XOR of multiple bits of the internal state. The cryptographic complexity is in the next-state function; this function is key-dependent. This method is also called internal feedback [183], because the feedback mechanism is internal to the key generation algorithm.

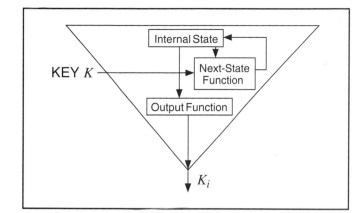

Figure 8.14
A keystream generator in output feedback mode.

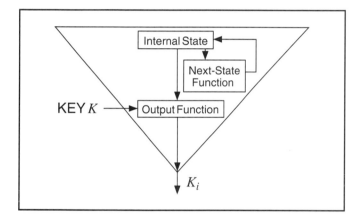

Figure 8.15
A keystream generator in counter mode.

There is a variant of this mode where the key, K, only determines the initial state of the keystream generator. After K sets the internal state of the generator, the generator runs undisturbed from then on.

Counter Mode

Stream ciphers in counter mode have simple next-state functions and complicated output functions dependent on the key. This technique, illustrated in Figure 8.15, was suggested in [301,422]. The next-state function can be something as simple as a counter, adding one to the previous state. In a counter-mode stream cipher, the cryptographic complexity is in the output function.

With a counter-mode stream cipher, it is possible to generate the ith key bit, k_i, without having to first generate all the previous key bits. Simply set the counter manually to the ith internal state and generate the bit. This method is useful for securing random-access data files; you can decrypt a specific block of data without having to decrypt the entire file.

Insertion Attack

Both the output feedback mode and the counter mode are vulnerable to an **insertion attack** [49]. Mallet has recorded a ciphertext stream but does not know the plaintext or the keystream used to encrypt the plaintext.

Original plaintext: $p_1 \; p_2 \; p_3 \; p_4 \ldots$
Original keystream: $k_1 \; k_2 \; k_3 \; k_4 \ldots$
Original ciphertext: $c_1 \; c_2 \; c_3 \; c_4 \ldots$

Mallet inserts a known single bit, p', into the plaintext after p_1 and then manages to get the modified plaintext encrypted with the same keystream. He records the resultant new ciphertext:

New plaintext: $p_1 \; p' \; p_2 \; p_3 \; p_4 \ldots$
Original keystream: $k_1 \; k_2 \; k_3 \; k_4 \; k_5 \ldots$
Updated ciphertext: $c_1 \; c'_2 \; c'_3 \; c'_4 \; c'_5 \ldots$

Assuming he knows the value of p', he can determine the entire plaintext after that bit from the original ciphertext and new ciphertext:

$k_2 = c'_2 \text{ XOR } p'$, and then $p_2 = c_2 \text{ XOR } k_2$
$k_3 = c'_3 \text{ XOR } p'$, and then $p_3 = c_3 \text{ XOR } k_3$
$k_4 = c'_4 \text{ XOR } p'$, and then $p_4 = c_4 \text{ XOR } k_4$

Mallet doesn't even have to know the exact position in which the bit was inserted; he can just compare the original and updated ciphertexts to see where they begin to differ. To protect against this attack, never use the same keystream to encrypt two different messages.

8.3.2 Self-Synchronous Stream Ciphers

In a **self-synchronous stream cipher,** each keystream bit is a function of a fixed number of previous ciphertext bits [767]. (The basic idea was patented in 1946 [398].) Commonly, these stream ciphers operate in **cipher-feedback mode.**

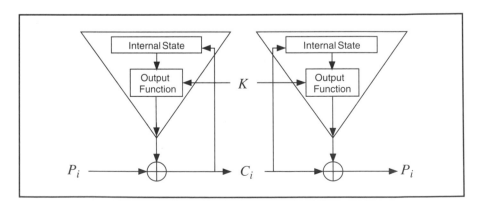

Figure 8.16
A keystream generator in cipher feedback mode.

Figure 8.16 shows a stream cipher in cipher-feedback mode. The internal state is a function of the previous n ciphertext bits. The cryptographic complexity is in the output function, which takes the internal state and generates a keystream bit.

Since the internal state is wholly dependent on the previous n ciphertext bits, the decryption keystream generator will automatically synchronize with the encryption keystream generator after receiving n ciphertext bits.

In smart implementations of this mode, each message begins with a random header n bits long. That header is encrypted, transmitted, and then decrypted. The decryption will be incorrect, but after those n bits both keystream generators will be synchronized.

The downside of a self-synchronous stream cipher is error propagation. For each ciphertext bit garbled in transmission, the decryption keystream generator will incorrectly produce n keystream bits. Therefore for each ciphertext error, there will be n corresponding plaintext errors, until the garbled bit works its way out of the internal state.

Self-synchronous stream ciphers are also vulnerable to a playback. Mallet records some ciphertext bits. Then, at a later time, he substitutes this recording into current traffic. After some initial garbage while the receiving end resynchronizes, the old ciphertext will decrypt as normal. The receiving end has no way of knowing that this is not current data, but old data being replayed. Unless date stamps are used, Mallet can convince a bank to credit his account again and again, by replaying the same message (assuming the key hasn't been changed, of course).

8.3.3 Using Block Ciphers as Stream Ciphers

Block algorithms can be used as keystream generators in any of the various modes. The block algorithm provides the cryptographic security for the cryptosystem.

Figure 8.17 shows a stream cipher in output feedback mode, with the block algorithm acting as the output function. The least significant bit of the internal state becomes the output of the keystream generator. Then the internal state of the keystream generator becomes the input to the block algorithm, which is used to modify the internal state. This modification can take one of two forms. The entire

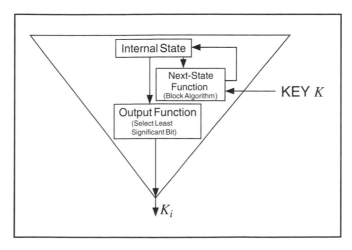

Figure 8.17

A keystream generator in output feedback mode using a block algorithm.

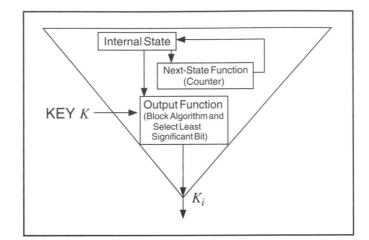

Figure 8.18
A keystream generator in counter mode using a block algorithm.

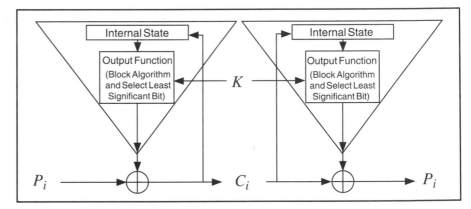

Figure 8.19
A keystream generator in cipher-feedback mode using a block algorithm.

output of the block algorithm can become the new internal state, or one bit of the output is used to modify the internal state in some simple way—sometimes the internal state is nothing more than the previous n bits from the next-state function.

Figure 8.18 shows a stream cipher in counter mode, with the block algorithm acting as the output function. The entire internal state is the input to the block algorithm, and the least significant bit of the block algorithm's output becomes the output of the keystream generator. The next-state function is a simple counter.

Figure 8.19 shows a stream cipher in cipher-feedback mode, with the block algorithm acting as the output function. The entire internal state is the input to the block algorithm, and the least significant bit of the block algorithm's output becomes the output of the keystream generator. The internal state is the previous n ciphertext bits.

8.4   STREAM CIPHERS VS. BLOCK CIPHERS

The difference between stream ciphers and block ciphers is more practical than theoretical. Stream ciphers only encrypt and decrypt data one bit at a time and are not really suitable for software implementation. Block ciphers are much easier to implement in software, because bit manipulations are time-consuming.

Cryptographically, block ciphers are more general, and their algorithms can be made stronger in principle. On the other hand, stream ciphers are easier to analyze mathematically. The essential difference between the two is in error propagation. With a block cipher, a single error will at the very least garble a block's worth of data. With various feedback modes, it could be even worse. Stream ciphers can be implemented so that a single bit of garbled ciphertext generates only a single bit of garbled plaintext. In some applications, it's important to have sufficient error propagation so that errors are noticed. In other applications, lack of error propagation is critical.

The other consideration is the type of data being encrypted. If you want to encrypt ASCII data from a computer terminal, then a 64-bit block algorithm won't work very well. You need an algorithm that can encrypt a single 7- or 8-bit ASCII character. On the other hand, data on a computer disk is written and read in blocks—this would be ideal for a block algorithm.

8.5   PUBLIC-KEY CRYPTOGRAPHY VS. SYMMETRIC CRYPTOGRAPHY

Which is better, public-key cryptography or symmetric cryptography? This debate has been going on since public-key cryptography was invented. Unfortunately, the debate assumes that a fair comparison can be made between the two. It doesn't make any sense to ask which is more secure. The security of any algorithm is dependent on the length of the key. Most symmetric algorithms have a specific key length. Public-key algorithms have variable key lengths. DES, with a fixed 56-bit key, is more secure than RSA with a 40-bit key. RSA with a 1000-bit key, is more secure than DES.

Needham and Schroeder [645] pointed out that the number and length of messages are far greater with public-key protocols than with symmetric protocols. Their conclusion was that the symmetric protocol was more efficient than the public-key protocol. While this is true, this analysis overlooks the significant security benefits of the public-key scheme.

Whitfield Diffie writes [295,297]:

> In viewing public-key cryptography as a new form of cryptosystem rather than a new form of key management, I set the stage for criticism on grounds of both security and performance. Opponents were quick to point out that the RSA system ran about one-thousandth as fast as DES and required keys about ten times as large. Although it had been obvious from the beginning that the use of public key systems could be limited to exchanging keys for conventional cryptography, it was not immediately clear that this was necessary. In this context, the proposal to built *hybrid* systems [499] was hailed as a discovery in its own right.

Public-key cryptography and symmetric cryptography work best together. The strength of public-key cryptography is in key distribution and protocols.

Public-key cryptography can do things that symmetric cryptography could never do. Symmetric cryptography, on the other hand, is orders of magnitude faster. Symmetric algorithms are ideal for encrypting files and communications channels. Public-key algorithms are ideal for encrypting and distributing keys, providing authentication, and performing any of the functions described in the previous chapters.

8.6 ENCRYPTING COMMUNICATIONS NETWORKS

In theory, encryption can take place at any layer in the OSI (Open Systems Interface) communications model. Depending on where encryption takes place, though, there are different problems that have to be accounted for.

Link-by-Link Encryption

The easiest place to add encryption is at the physical layer (see Figure 8.20). This is called **link-by-link encryption.** The interfaces to the physical layer are the most standardized, and it is easy to connect hardware encryption devices at this point. These devices encrypt all data passing through them, including data, routing information, protocol information, etc. They can be used for every type of digital communication link. On the other hand, any intelligent switching or storing nodes between the sender and the receiver needs to decrypt the data stream before it can be processed.

This type of encryption is very effective. Because everything is encrypted, cryptanalysts can get no information about the structure of the information. They have no idea who is talking to whom, how long the messages they are sending are, what times of day they communicate, etc. This is called **traffic-flow security:** the enemy is not only denied access to the information, but also access to the knowledge of where the information is flowing and how much is flowing there.

System security depends solely on the algorithm selected, not on any traffic management techniques. Key management is also simple; only the two endpoints of the line need a common key, and they can change their key independently from the rest of the network.

Imagine a synchronous communications line, encrypted using 1-bit CFB. After initialization, the line can run indefinitely, recovering automatically from bit or synchronization errors. The line encrypts messages whenever messages are sent from one end to the other; otherwise it just encrypts and decrypts random data.

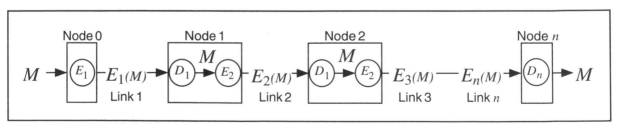

Figure 8.20
Link encryption.

Eve has no idea when messages are being sent and when they are not; she has no idea when messages begin and when they end. All she sees is an endless stream of random-looking bits.

If the communications line is asynchronous, the same 1-bit CFB mode can be used. The difference is that the adversary can get information about the rate of transmission. If this information must be concealed, some provision must be made for passing dummy messages during idle times.

The biggest problem with encryption at the physical layer is that each physical link in the network needs to be encrypted; leaving any link unencrypted jeopardizes the security of the entire network. If the network is large, the cost may quickly become prohibitive for this kind of encryption.

Additionally, every node in the network must be protected, since it processes unencrypted data. If all the users of the network trust one another, and all the nodes are in secure locations, this may be tolerable. But this is unlikely. Even in a single corporation, information might have to be kept secret within a department. If the network accidentally misroutes information, anyone can read it.

End-to-End Encryption

Another approach is to put encryption equipment between the network layer and the transport layer. The encryption device must understand the data according to the protocols up to layer three and encrypt only the transport data units, which are then recombined with the unencrypted routing information and sent to lower layers for transmission.

This approach avoids the problem with encryption at the physical layer. By providing **end-to-end encryption,** the data remains encrypted until it reaches its final destination (see Figure 8.21). The primary problem with end-to-end encryption is that the routing information for the data remains unencrypted; a good cryptanalyst can learn much from who is talking to whom, at what times and for how long, without ever knowing the contents of those conversations. Key management is also more difficult, since individual users must make sure they have keys in common with one another.

Building encryption equipment that works at this layer is difficult. Each particular communications system has its own protocol. Sometimes the interfaces among these levels are not well defined, making the task even more difficult.

If encryption takes place at a high layer of the communications architecture, like the applications layer or the presentation layer, then it can be independent of the type of communication network used. It is still end-to-end encryption, but the

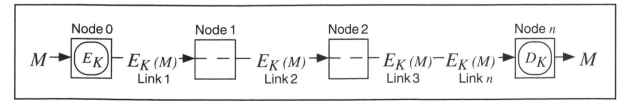

Figure 8.21
End-to-end encryption.

encryption implementation does not have to bother about line codes, synchronization between modems, physical interfaces, etc. In the early days of electromechanical cryptography, encryption and decryption took place entirely off-line; this is only one step removed from that.

Encryption at these layers interacts with the software at the layers. This software is different for different computer architectures, and so the encryption must be optimized for different computer systems. Encryption takes place in software itself or in specialized hardware. In the latter case, the computer will send the data to the specialized hardware for encryption before sending it to lower layers of the communication architecture for transmission. This process requires some intelligence and is not suitable for unintelligent terminals. Additionally, there may be compatibility problems with different types of computers.

Combining the Two

Combining end-to-end encryption with link-by-link encryption is the most effective way of securing a network. Encryption of each physical link makes any analysis of the routing information impossible, while end-to-end encryption reduces the threat of unencrypted data at the various nodes in the network. Key management for the two schemes can be completely separate: the network managers can take care of encryption at the physical level, while the individual users have responsibility for end-to-end encryption.

8.7   ENCRYPTING DATA FOR STORAGE

Encrypting data for storage and later retrieval is a different issue from encrypting data for communication, with a completely different set of problems [214]:

The time cryptanalysts have to break the algorithm is limited only by how long they think the data is valuable for.

The data may also exist in plaintext form, either on another disk, in another computer, or on paper. There is much more opportunity for cryptanalysts to perform a known-plaintext attack.

In database applications, pieces of data may be smaller than the block size of most algorithms. This will cause the ciphertext to be considerably larger than the plaintext.

The speed of I/O devices demands fast encryption and decryption. Hardware encryption will probably be required. In some applications, special high-speed algorithms may be required.

Safe, long-term storage for keys is required.

Key management is much more complicated, since different people need access to different files, different portions of the same file, etc.

If the encrypted files are not structured as records and fields, such as text files, retrieval is easier. The entire file is decrypted before use. If the encrypted files are database files, this solution is more problematic. Decrypting the entire database to access a single record is inefficient, but encrypting records independently might be susceptible to a block-replay kind of attack.

In addition, you have to make sure the unencrypted file is erased after encryption (see Section 8.9). For further details and insights, consult [242,350].

8.8   HARDWARE ENCRYPTION VS. SOFTWARE ENCRYPTION

Hardware

Until very recently, all encryption products were in the form of specialized hardware. These were encryption/decryption boxes that plugged into a communications line and encrypted all the data going across that line. Although software encryption is becoming more prevalent today, hardware is still the mode of choice for most commercial and military applications. There are several reasons why this is so.

The first is speed. As we will see in the next chapter, encryption algorithms contain many complicated operations on strings of bits. These are not the sorts of operations that are built into the run-of-the-mill computer. The two most common encryption algorithms, DES and RSA, contain steps that run inefficiently on microprocessors. While some cryptographers have kept this in mind and have tried to make their algorithms more suitable for software implementation, security is always the primary driving force behind any design. Specialized hardware will always win a speed race.

Additionally, encryption is often a computation-intensive task. Tying up the computer's microprocessor for this is inefficient. Moving encryption to another chip, even if that chip is just another processor, makes the whole system faster.

The second reason for the prevalence of hardware is security. There is no physical protection for an encryption algorithm written in software. Mallet can go in with various debugging tools and surreptitiously modify the algorithm without anyone ever realizing it. Hardware encryption devices can be securely encapsulated to prevent this. Tamper-proof boxes can prevent someone from modifying a hardware encryption device. Special-purpose VLSI chips can be coated with a chemical such that any attempt to access their interior will result in the destruction of the chips' logic. The U.S. government's Clipper and Capstone chips are designed to be tamper-proof. The chips can be designed so that it is impossible for Mallet to read the unencrypted key.

IBM developed a cryptographic system for encrypting data and communications on mainframe computers [312,571]. It includes a tamper-resistant module to hold the keys. This system is discussed in Section 17.1.

Electromagnetic radiation can sometimes reveal what is going on inside a piece of electronic equipment. Dedicated encryption boxes can be shielded, so that they leak no compromising information. General-purpose computers can be shielded as well, but it is far more complex a problem. The U.S. military calls this operation TEMPEST, a subject far beyond the scope of this book.

The final reason for the prevalence of hardware is the ease of installation. Most encryption applications don't involve general-purpose computers. People may wish to encrypt their telephone conversations, facsimile transmissions, or data links. It is much more efficient to put special-purpose encryption hardware in the telephones, facsimile machines, and modems than it is to put in a microprocessor or software.

Even when the encrypted data comes from a computer, it is easier to install a dedicated hardware encryption device than it is to modify the computer's system software. Encryption should be invisible; it should not hamper the user. The only way to do this in software is to write encryption deep into the operating system. This isn't easy. On the other hand, even computer neophytes can plug an encryption box between their computer and their modem.

There are three basic kinds of encryption hardware on the market today: self-contained encryption modules (that perform functions such as password verification and key management for banks), dedicated encryption boxes for communications links, and boards that plug into personal computers.

Some encryption boxes are designed for certain types of communications links. For example, T-1 encryption boxes are designed not to encrypt synchronization bits. Facsimile encryptors are optimized for that type of data. There are encryption boxes for synchronous communications lines, and different boxes for asynchronous communications lines. The trend is toward higher bit-rates and greater flexibility of use.

Even so, many of these devices have some hardware or software incompatibilities. Buyers should be aware of this and be well versed in their particular needs, lest they find themselves the owners of a piece of encryption equipment unable to perform the task at hand. Pay attention to restrictions in hardware type, operating system, applications software, network, etc.

PC boards usually encrypt everything written to the hard disk and can be configured optionally to encrypt everything sent to the floppy disk and serial port as well. These boards are not shielded against electromagnetic radiation or physical interference, since there would be no benefit in protecting the boards if the computer remained unaffected. Additionally, more companies are starting to put encryption hardware into their communications equipment. Secure telephones, facsimile machines, and modems are all available.

Internal key management for these devices is generally secure, although there are as many different schemes as there are equipment vendors. Some schemes are more suited for one situation than another, and buyers should know what kind of key management is incorporated into the encryption box and what they are expected to provide themselves.

Software

Any encryption algorithm can be implemented in software. The disadvantages are in speed, cost, and ease of use. The advantages are in flexibility and portability. The algorithms written in C at the end of this book can be implemented, with little modification, on any computer. They can be inexpensively copied and installed on many machines. They can be incorporated into larger applications, such as communications programs or word processors.

Software encryption programs are popular and are available for all major operating systems. These are meant to protect individual files; the user generally has to manually encrypt and decrypt specific files. It is important that the key management scheme be secure: the keys are not stored on disk anywhere (or even written to a place in memory from where the processor swaps out to disk). Keys and unencrypted files should be erased after encryption. Many programs are sloppy in this regard, and a user has to choose carefully.

8.9   FILE ERASURE

When you delete a file on a computer, the file isn't really deleted. The only thing deleted is an entry in the disk's index file, telling the machine that the file is there. Many software vendors have made a fortune selling file-recovery software that recovers files even after they have been deleted.

To erase a file so that these software packages cannot read it, you have to physically write over all of the file's bits on the disk. According to the National Computer Security Center [642]:

> Overwriting is a process by which unclassified data are written to storage locations that previously held sensitive data. . . . To purge the . . . storage media, the DoD requires overwriting with a pattern, then its complement, and finally with another pattern; e.g., overwrite first with 0011 0101, followed by 1100 1010, then 1001 0111. The number of times an overwrite must be accomplished depends on the storage media, sometimes on its sensitivity, and sometimes on different DoD component requirements. In any case, a purge is not complete until a final overwrite is made using unclassified data.

Most commercial programs that claim to implement the DoD standard overwrite three times: first with all 1's, then with all 0's, and finally with a repeating 1-0 pattern. Given my general level of paranoia, I recommend overwriting a deleted file seven times: the first time with all 1's, the second time with all 0's, and five times with a cryptographically secure pseudo-random sequence. Recent developments at the National Institute of Standards and Technology with electron-tunneling microscopes suggest even that might not be enough.

And there's yet another worry: virtual memory means your computer can be reading and writing memory to disk any time. Even if you don't save it, you never know when a sensitive document you are working on is shipped off to disk. It makes sense to occasionally overwrite all of the unused space on a disk, as well as to swap files and the unused parts of the last blocks of files.

8.10   CHOOSING AN ALGORITHM

When it comes to evaluating algorithms and choosing one for personal use, people have several alternatives:

- They can choose a published algorithm, based on the belief that a published algorithm has been scrutinized by many cryptographers. If none of them has broken the algorithm yet, it must be pretty good.

- They can trust the manufacturer, based on the belief that a well-known manufacturer has a reputation to uphold and is unlikely to risk that reputation by selling equipment with inferior algorithms.

- They can trust a private consultant, based on the belief that an impartial consultant is best-equipped to make a reliable evaluation of different algorithms on the market.

- They can trust the government, based on the belief that the government is trustworthy and wouldn't steer its citizens wrong.

- They can write their own algorithm, based on the belief that their cryptographic ability is second-to-none, and that they should trust nobody.

Certainly any of these alternatives has problems, but the first has the fewest. Putting your trust in a single manufacturer, consultant, or government is probably asking for trouble. Most people who call themselves security consultants (even those from big-name firms) usually don't know anything about encryption. Most security manufacturers are no better. The National Security Agency has some of the world's best cryptographers working for it, but it is hard to know if they're telling all they know. And unless you're a genius, writing your own algorithm and then using it without any peer review is just plain foolish.

All the algorithms in this book are public; they have appeared in the open literature and have been cryptanalyzed by experts in the field. I list all published results, both positive and negative. I don't have access to the cryptanalysis done by any of the myriad military security organizations in the world (which are probably better than the academic organizations—they've been doing it longer and are better funded), so it is possible that these algorithms have been broken. Even so, it is far more likely that they are more secure than an algorithm designed and implemented in secret by a security company.

Algorithms for Export

Algorithms for export must be approved by the U.S. government (actually, the NSA—see Section 18.1). It is widely believed that these export-approved algorithms can be broken by the NSA.

Although no one has admitted to this on the record, these are some of the things the NSA is privately rumored to suggest to companies wishing to export their cryptographic products:

- Leak a key bit once in a while, embedded in the ciphertext.

- "Dumb down" the effective key to something in the 30-bit range. For example, while the algorithm might accept a 100-bit key, only a third of those bits might actually be used.

- Encrypt a known header at the beginning of each encrypted message. This allows for a chosen-plaintext attack.

- Generate a few random bytes, encrypt them with the key, and then put both the plaintext and the ciphertext of those random bytes at the beginning of the encrypted message. This also allows for a known-plaintext attack.

NSA gets a copy of the source code, but the algorithm's details remain secret from everyone else. Certainly no one advertises any of these deliberate weaknesses.

PART
THREE

Cryptographic Algorithms

Mathematical
Background

9.1   INFORMATION THEORY

Modern information theory was first defined in 1948 by Claude Elmwood Shannon [803,804]. (His papers were recently reprinted by the IEEE Press [805].) For a good mathematical treatment of the topic, consult [363]. In this section, I will just sketch some important topics.

Entropy and Uncertainty

Information theory defines the **amount of information** in a message as the minimum number of bits needed to encode all possible meanings of that message. For example, the day-of-the-week field in a database contains no more than 3 bits of information, because the information can be encoded with 3 bits:

000 = Sunday

001 = Monday

010 = Tuesday

011 = Wednesday

100 = Thursday

101 = Friday

110 = Saturday

111 is unused

If this information were represented by corresponding ASCII character strings, it would take up more memory space but would not contain any more information. Similarly, the "sex" field of a database contains only 1 bit of information, even though it might be stored as one of two 6-byte ASCII strings: "MALE " or "FEMALE."

Formally, the amount of information in a message M is measured by the **entropy** of a message, denoted by $H(M)$. The entropy of a message indicating sex is 1 bit; the entropy of a message indicating the day of the week is slightly less than 3 bits. In general, the entropy of a message is $\log_2 n$, in which n is the number of possible meanings. This assumes that each meaning is equally likely.

The entropy of a message also measures its **uncertainty.** This is the number of plaintext bits needed to be recovered when the message is scrambled in ciphertext in order to learn the plaintext. For example, if the ciphertext block "QHP*5M" is either "MALE " or "FEMALE," then the uncertainty of the message is 1. A cryptanalyst has to learn only one well-chosen bit to recover the message.

Public-key cryptosystems are vulnerable to a ciphertext-only attack if the uncertainty of the plaintext is too small. For example, if $C = E(P)$, when P is one plaintext out of a set of n possible plaintexts, then cryptanalysts have only to encrypt all n possible plaintexts and compare the results with C (remember, the encryption key is public). They won't be able to recover the decryption key this way, but they will be able to determine M.

For example, if P were a dollar amount less than \$1 million, this attack would work; the cryptanalyst tries all million possible dollar amounts. (Probabilistic encryption solves the problem; see Section 16.16.) Symmetric cryptosystems are not vulnerable to this attack because cryptanalysts cannot perform trial encryptions with an unknown key.

Rate of a Language

For a given language, the **rate of the language** is

$$r = H(M)/N$$

in which N is the length of the messages. The rate of normal English takes various values between 1.0 bits/letter and 1.5 bits/letter, for large values of N. (For the purposes of this book, we will take Shannon's estimate of 1.2 [806].) The **absolute rate** of a language is the maximum number of bits that can be coded in each character, assuming each character sequence is equally likely. If there are L characters in a language, the absolute rate is:

$$R = \log_2 L$$

This is the maximum entropy of the individual characters.

For English, with 26 letters, the absolute rate is $\log_2 26 = 4.7$ bits/letter. It should come as no surprise to anyone that the actual rate of English is much less than the absolute rate; English is a highly redundant language.

The **redundancy** of a language, called D, is defined by:

$$D = R-r$$

Given that the rate of English is 1.2, the redundancy is 3.5 bits/letter. This means that each English character carries only 1.2 bits of information; all the rest is redundant. An ASCII message that is nothing more than printed English still has 1.2 bits of information per 8 bits of message. This means it has 3.5 bits of redundant information, giving it an overall redundancy of 0.56 bits of information per bit of ASCII text. The same message in EBCDIC (Extended Binary-Coded Decimal Interchange Code), at 5 bits per character, has a redundancy of 0.30 bits and an entropy of 0.70 bits per bit of EBCDIC text. Spacing, punctuation, numbers, and formatting will modify these results.

Security of a Cryptosystem

Shannon defined a precise mathematical model of what it means for a cryptosystem to be secure. The goal of cryptanalysts is to determine the key k, the plaintext p, or both. However, they may be satisfied with some probabilistic information about p: if it is digitized audio, if it is German text, if it is spreadsheet data, etc.

In most real-world cryptanalysis, cryptanalysts have some probabilistic information about p before starting. They probably know the language of encryption. This language has a certain redundancy associated with it. If it is a message to Bob, it probably begins with "Dear Bob." Certainly "Dear Bob" is more probable than "$e8T\&g[,m$." The purpose of cryptanalysis is, through analysis, to modify the probabilities associated with each possible plaintext. Eventually one plaintext will emerge from the pile of possible plaintexts as certain (or at least, very probable).

There is such a thing as a cryptosystem that achieves **perfect secrecy.** This is a cryptosystem in which the ciphertext yields no possible information about the plaintext (except possibly its length). Shannon theorized that it is only possible if the number of possible keys is at least as large as the number of possible messages. In other words, the key must be at least as long as the message itself, and no key can be reused. In still other words, this is a one-time pad.

Perfect secrecy aside, the ciphertext yields some information about the corresponding plaintext. This is unavoidable. A good cryptographic algorithm keeps this information to a minimum; a good cryptographer exploits this information to determine the plaintext.

Cryptanalysts use the natural redundancy of language to reduce the number of possible plaintexts. The more redundant the language, the easier it is to cryptanalyze. This is the reason that many real-world cryptographic implementations use a compression program to reduce the size of the text before encrypting it. Compression reduces the redundancy of a message.

The entropy of a cryptosystem is a measure of the size of the keyspace. It is approximated by the base two logarithm of the number of keys:

$$H(K) = \log_2 (\text{number of keys})$$

A cryptosystem with a 64-bit key has an entropy of 64; a cryptosystem with a 56-bit key has an entropy of 56. In general, the greater the entropy, the harder it is to break a cryptosystem.

Unicity Distance

For a message of length n, the number of different keys that will decipher a ciphertext message to some intelligible plaintext in the same language as the original plaintext is given by the following formula [419,50]:

$$2^{H(K) - nD} - 1$$

Shannon [804] defined the **unicity distance,** also called the **unicity point,** as an approximation of the amount of ciphertext such that the sum of the real information (entropy) in the corresponding plaintext plus the entropy of the encryption key equals the number of ciphertext bits used. He then went on to show that ciphertexts longer than this distance are reasonably certain to have only one meaningful decryption. Ciphertexts significantly shorter than this are likely to have multiple, equally valid decryptions and therefore gain security from the opponent's difficulty in choosing the correct one.

For most symmetric cryptosystems, the unicity distance is defined as the entropy of the cryptosystem divided by the redundancy of the language.

$$U = H(K)/D$$

Unicity distance, like all statistical or information-theoretic measures, does not make deterministic predictions but gives probabilistic results. Unicity distance points to the minimum amount of ciphertext for which it is likely that there is only a single intelligible plaintext decryption when a brute-force attack is attempted. Generally, the longer the unicity distance, the better the cryptosystem. For DES, with a 56-bit key, and an ASCII English message, the unicity distance is

$$56/6.8 = 8.2$$

about 8.2 ASCII characters, or 66 bits. (The unicity points for some classical cryptosystems are found in [257].)

Unicity distance is not a measure of how much ciphertext is required for cryptanalysis, but how much ciphertext is required for there to be only one reasonable solution for cryptanalysis. A cryptosystem may be computationally unfeasible to break even if it is theoretically possible to break it with a small amount of ciphertext. (The largely esoteric and completely impractical theory of **relativized cryptography** is relevant here [138,139,140,141,142,143].) The unicity distance is inversely proportional to the redundancy. As redundancy approaches zero, even a trivial cipher can be unbreakable.

Shannon defined a cryptosystem whose unicity distance is infinite as one that has **ideal secrecy.** Note that an ideal cryptosystem is not necessarily a perfect cryptosystem, although a perfect cryptosystem would necessarily be an ideal cryptosystem. If a cryptosystem has ideal secrecy, even successful cryptanalysis will leave some uncertainty about whether the recovered plaintext is the real plaintext.

Information Theory in Practice

While these concepts have great theoretical value, actual cryptanalysis seldom proceeds along these lines. Unicity distance guarantees insecurity if it's too small, but does guarantee security if it's high. Few practical algorithms are absolutely impervious to analysis; all manner of characteristics might serve as entering wedges to crack some encrypted messages. However, similar information-theoretic considerations are occasionally useful, for example, to determine a recommended key change interval for a particular algorithm. Cryptanalysts also employ a variety of statistical and information-theoretic tests to help guide the analysis in the most promising directions.

Unfortunately, most literature on the application of information statistics to cryptanalysis remains classified, including the seminal 1940 work of Alan Turing.

Confusion and Diffusion

The two basic techniques for obscuring the redundancies in a plaintext message are, according to Shannon, confusion and diffusion [804].

Confusion obscures the relationship between the plaintext and the ciphertext. This frustrates attempts to study the ciphertext looking for redundancies and statistical patterns. The easiest way to do this is through **substitution.** A simple substitution cipher, like the Caesar shift, is one in which every identical letter of plaintext is substituted for a single letter of ciphertext. Modern substitution ciphers are more complex; a long block of plaintext is substituted for a different block of ciphertext, and the mechanics of the substitution changes with each bit in the plaintext. This type of substitution is not necessarily enough; the German Enigma is a complex substitution algorithm that was broken before computers.

Diffusion dissipates the redundancy of the plaintext by spreading it out over the ciphertext. A cryptanalyst looking for those redundancies will have a harder time finding them. The simplest way to cause diffusion is through **transposition** (also called **permutation**). A simple transposition cipher, like columnar transposition, simply rearranges the letters of the plaintext. Modern ciphers do this type of permutation, but they also employ other forms of diffusion that can diffuse parts of the message throughout the entire message. Stream ciphers rely on confusion alone. Block algorithms use both confusion and diffusion. Diffusion alone is easily cracked.

9.2   COMPLEXITY THEORY

Complexity theory provides a methodology for analyzing the **computational complexity** of different cryptographic techniques and algorithms. It compares cryptographic algorithms and techniques and determines their security. Information theory tells us that all cryptographic algorithms (except one-time pads) can be broken. Complexity theory tells us if they can be broken before the heat death of the universe.

Complexity of Algorithms

A cipher's strength is determined by the computational power needed to break it. The computational complexity of an algorithm is measured by two variables: T (for **time complexity**) and S (for **space complexity,** or memory requirement). Both T and S are commonly expressed as functions of n, when n is the size of the input. Throughout this section, I refer to an algorithm used to break a cipher as a "cracking algorithm."

Generally, the computational complexity of an algorithm is expressed in what is called "big O" notation: the order of magnitude of the computational complexity. The order of magnitude of the complexity is just the term of the complexity function that grows the fastest as n gets larger; all constant and lower-order terms are ignored. For example, if the time complexity of a given algorithm is $4n^2 + 7n + 12$, then the computational complexity is on the order of n^2, expressed $O(n^2)$.

The advantage of measuring time complexity this way is that it is system-independent. You don't have to know the exact timings of various instructions or the number of bits used to represent different variables or even the speed of the processor. One computer might be 50% faster than another and a third might have a data path twice as wide, but the order-of-magnitude complexity of an algorithm remains the same. This isn't cheating; when you're dealing with algorithms as complex as the ones presented here, the other information is usually negligible compared to the order-of-magnitude time complexity.

What this notation allows you to see is how the time and space requirements are affected by the size of the input. For example, if $T=O(n)$, then doubling the size of the input doubles the running time of the algorithm. If $T=O(2^n)$, then adding 1 bit to the size of the input doubles the running time of the algorithm.

Generally, algorithms are classified according to their time or space complexities. An algorithm is constant if its complexity is independent of n: $O(1)$. An algorithm is **linear,** $O(n)$ if its complexity grows linearly with n. Algorithms can also be **quadratic, cubic,** etc. All these algorithms are **polynomial;** their complexity is $O(n^t)$, when t is a constant. Algorithms that have a polynomial time complexity class are called **polynomial time** algorithms.

Algorithms whose complexities are $O(t^{f(n)})$, in which t is a constant and $f(n)$ is some polynomial function of n, are called **exponential.** Those whose complexities are $O(t^{f(n)})$, where t is a constant and $f(n)$ is more than constant but less than linear, are called **superpolynomial.**

Ideally, cryptographers would like to be able to say that any cracking algorithm for their ciphers must be of exponential time complexity. In practice, the strongest statements that can be made, given the current state of the art of computational complexity theory, are of the form "all known cracking algorithms for this cipher are of superpolynomial time complexity." That is, for the ciphers that are used in practice, the cracking algorithms that we know are of superpolynomial time complexity, but it is not yet possible to prove that no polynomial-time cracking algorithm could ever be discovered. Advances in computational complexity may some day make it possible to design ciphers for which the existence of polynomial-timecracking algorithms can be ruled out with mathematical certainty.

As *n* grows, the time complexity of an algorithm can make an enormous difference in whether the algorithm is practical. Table 9.1 shows the running times for different algorithm classes in which *n* equals one million.

Assuming that the unit of "time" for our computer is a microsecond, the computer can complete a constant algorithm in a microsecond, a linear algorithm in a second, and a quadratic algorithm in 11.6 days. It would take 32,000 years to complete a cubic algorithm; not terribly practical, but if the universe still exists then, it would be possible for a computer to deliver a solution eventually. Solving the exponential algorithm is futile, no matter how well you extrapolate computing power, parallel processing, or contact with superintelligent aliens.

TABLE **9.1**
Running Times of Different Classes of Algorithms

CLASS	COMPLEXITY	# OF OPERATIONS FOR $n = 10^6$	TIME AT 10^6 O/S
Constant	$O(1)$	1	1 microsec.
Linear	$O(n)$	10^6	1 sec.
Quadratic	$O(n^2)$	10^{12}	11.6 days
Cubic	$O(n^3)$	10^{18}	32,000 yrs.
Exponential	$O(2^n)$	$10^{301,030}$	$10^{301,006}$ times the age of the universe

Look at the problem of a brute-force attack against a cryptosystem. The time complexity of this attack is proportional to the number of possible keys, which is an exponential function of the key length. If *n* is the length of the key, then the complexity of a brute-force attack is $O(2^n)$. Section 10.1 discusses the controversy surrounding a 56-bit key for DES instead of a 112-bit key. The complexity of a brute-force attack against a 56-bit key is 2^{56} (2285 years, assuming a million attempts per second); against a 112-bit key the complexity is 2^{112} (10^{20} years, with the same assumptions). The former is on the edge of possibility; the latter is absolutely not.

Complexity of Problems

Complexity theory also classifies problems according to the algorithms required to solve them. (An excellent introduction to this topic is [366]; see also [14, and 606].) The theory looks at the minimum time and space required to solve the hardest instance of the problem on a theoretical computer known as a **Turing machine.** A Turing machine is a finite-state machine with an infinite read-write memory tape. It turns out that a Turing machine is a realistic model of computation.

Problems that can be solved with polynomial-time algorithms are called **tractable,** because they can usually be solved in a reasonable amount of time for reasonable-sized inputs. (The exact definition of "reasonable" depends on the circumstance.) Problems that cannot be solved in polynomial time are called **intractable,** because calculating their solution quickly becomes unfeasible. Intractable problems are sometimes just called **hard.** They are. Problems that can be solved with algorithms that are exponential or superpolynomial are computationally intractable, even for relatively small values of n.

It gets worse. Alan Turing proved that some problems are **undecidable.** It is impossible to devise any algorithm to solve them, let alone a polynomial-time algorithm.

Problems can be divided into complexity classes, which depend on the complexity of their solutions. Figure 9.1 shows the more important complexity classes and their presumed relationships (unfortunately, not much about this material has been proved mathematically).

On the bottom, the class **P** consists of all problems that can be solved in polynomial time. The class **NP** consists of all problems that can be solved in polynomial time on a nondeterministic Turing machine. This is a variant of a normal Turing machine, which can make guesses. The machine guesses the solution to the problem and checks its guess in polynomial time.

NP's relevance to cryptography is as follows: many conventional classes of ciphers can be cracked in nondeterministic polynomial time. Given a ciphertext C, the cryptanalyst simply guesses a plaintext X and a key k, and in polynomial time runs the encipherment algorithm on inputs X and k and checks whether the result is equal to C. This is important theoretically, because it puts an upper bound on the complexity of cryptanalysis for ciphers in these classes. In practice, of course, it is a deterministic polynomial-time algorithm that the cryptanalyst seeks. Furthermore, this argument is not applicable to all classes of ciphers; in particular, it is not applicable to one-time pads—for any C, there are many X, k pairs that yield C when run through the encipherment algorithm, but most of these X's are nonsense, not legitimate plaintexts.

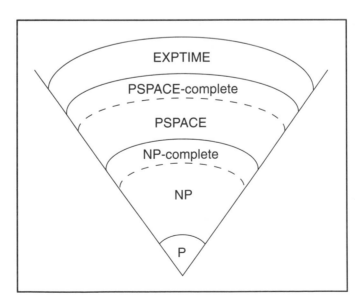

Figure 9.1
Complexity classes.

The class **NP** includes the class **P,** because any problem solvable in polynomial time on a deterministic Turing machine is also solvable in polynomial time on a nondeterministic Turing machine, because the guessing stage can simply be omitted.

If all **NP** problems are solvable in polynomial time on a deterministic machine, then **P = NP.** Although it seems obvious that some **NP** problems are much harder than others (a brute-force attack against a cipher vs. encrypting a random block of plaintext), it has never been proven that **P = NP.** However, everyone working in complexity theory suspects that they are unequal.

Stranger still, there are specific problems in **NP** that can be proven to be as difficult as any problem in the class. Cook [220] proved that the SATISFIABILITY problem (given a propositional Boolean formula, is there a way of assigning truth values to the variables that makes the formula true?) is **NP-complete.** This means that, if SATISFIABILITY is solvable in polynomial time, then **P = NP.** Conversely, if any problem in **NP** can be proven not to have a deterministic polynomial-time algorithm, the proof will show that SATISFIABILITY does not have a deterministic polynomial-time algorithm either. Thus SATISFIABILITY is the hardest problem in **NP.** Since Cook's seminal paper was published, a huge number of problems have been shown to be equivalent to SATISFIABILITY; hundreds are listed in [366], and examples are given below. By equivalent, I mean that these problems are also **NP-complete:** i.e., that they are also as hard as any problem in **NP.** If their solvability in deterministic polynomial time were resolved, the **P** vs. **NP** question would be solved. This question, does **P** equal **NP,** is the central unsolved question of computational complexity theory, and no one expects it to be solved anytime soon. If someone showed that **P = NP,** then most of this book would be irrelevant: as explained above, many classes of ciphers are trivially breakable in nondeterministic polynomial time, and if **P = NP,** they are breakable by feasible, deterministic algorithms.

Further out in the complexity hierarchy is **PSPACE.** Problems in **PSPACE** can be solved in polynomial space, but not necessarily polynomial time. **PSPACE** includes **NP,** but there are problems in **PSPACE** that are thought to be harder than **NP.** Of course, this isn't proven either. There is a class of problems, the so-called **PSPACE-complete** problems, with the property that, if any one of them is in **NP,** then **PSPACE = NP** and if any one of them is in **P,** then **PSPACE = P.**

And finally, there is the class of problems called **EXPTIME.** These problems are solvable in exponential time. The **EXPTIME-complete** problems can actually be proven not to be solvable in deterministic polynomial time. That is, it has been shown that **P** does not equal **EXPTIME.**

NP-Complete Problems

Michael Garey and David Johnson compiled a list of over 300 **NP-complete** problems [366]. Here are just a few of them:

> TRAVELING SALESMAN Problem. A traveling salesman has to visit n different cities, and he only has one tank of gas (i.e., there is a maximum distance he can travel). Is there a route that allows him to visit each city

exactly once on that single tank of gas? (This is a generalization of the HAMILTONIAN CIRCUIT problem—see Section 5.3.)

THREE-WAY MARRIAGE Problem. There is a roomful of n men, n women, and n members of the clergy (priests, rabbis, etc.). There is also a list of acceptable marriages, which consists of one man, one woman, and one clergyperson willing to officiate. Given this list of possible triples, is it possible to arrange n marriages such that everyone is either marrying one person or officiating in one marriage?

THREE-SATISFIABILITY. There is a list of n logical statements, each with three literals: if (x and y) then z, (x and w) or (not z), if ((not u and not x) or (z and (u or not x))) then ((not z and u) or x), etc. Is there a truth assignment for all the literals that satisfies all the statements? (This is a special case of the SATISFIABILITY problem mentioned above.)

9.3   NUMBER THEORY

This isn't a book on number theory, so I'm just going to touch on a few points that are applicable to cryptography. If you want a detailed mathematical text in number theory, consult one of these books: [802,38,656,7,543,410,441,237]. My two favorite books on finite fields are [549,581].

Modular Arithmetic

You all learned modular arithmetic in school; it was called "clock arithmetic." Remember these word problems: if Mildred says she'll be home by 10:00, and she's 13 hours late, what time does she get home and for how many years does her father ground her? That's arithmetic modulo 12.

$$(10 + 13) \bmod 12 = 11$$

Another way of writing this is:

$$10 + 13 \equiv 11 \ (\bmod \ 12)$$

Basically, $a \equiv b \ (\bmod \ n)$ if $a = b + kn$ for some integer k. If a and b are positive and a is less than n, you can think of a as the remainder of b when divided by n. In general, a and b leave the same remainder when divided by n. Sometimes, b is called the **residue** of a, modulo n. Sometimes a is called **congruent** to b, modulo n (the triple equals sign, $\equiv$, denotes congruence). These are just different ways of saying the same thing.

The set of integers from 0 to $n-1$ forms what is called a **complete set of residues** modulo n. This means that, for every integer a, its residue modulo n is some number from 0 to $n-1$.

The operation $a \bmod n$ denotes the residue of a, such that the residue is some integer from 0 to $n-1$. This operation is **modular reduction.** For example, 5 mod 3 = 2.

Notice that this definition of mod may be different from the definition used in some programming languages. For example, PASCAL's modulo operator sometimes returns a negative number. It returns a number between $-n-1$ and $n-1$. In C, the % operator returns the remainder from the division of the first expression by the second; this can be a negative number if either operand is negative. For all the algorithms in this book, make sure you add n to the result of the modulo operator if it returns a negative number.

Modular arithmetic is just like normal arithmetic: it's commutative, associative, and distributive. Also, reducing each intermediate result modulo n is the same as doing the whole calculation and then reducing the result modulo n.

$$(a + b) \bmod n = ((a \bmod n) + (b \bmod n)) \bmod n$$
$$(a - b) \bmod n = ((a \bmod n) - (b \bmod n)) \bmod n$$
$$(a \times b) \bmod n = ((a \bmod n) \times (b \bmod n)) \bmod n$$
$$(a \times (b + c)) \bmod n = (((a \times b) \bmod n) + ((a \times c) \bmod n)) \bmod n$$

Cryptography uses computation modulo n a lot, because problems like calculating discrete logarithms and square roots are hard. It's also easier to work with, because it restricts the range of all intermediate values and the result. For a k-bit modulus, n, the intermediate results of any addition, subtraction, or multiplication will not be more than $2k$-bits long. So we can perform exponentiation in modular arithmetic without generating huge intermediate results.

Calculating the power of a number modulo a number,

$$a^x \bmod n$$

is just a series of multiplications and divisions. There are speedups to make it go even faster. Because the operations are distributive, it is faster to do the exponentiation as a stream of successive multiplications, taking the modulus every time. It doesn't make much difference now, but it will when you're working with 200-bit numbers.

For example, if you want to calculate $a^8 \bmod n$, don't use the naive approach and perform seven multiplications and one huge modular reduction:

$$(a \times a \times a \times a \times a \times a \times a \times a) \bmod n$$

Instead, perform three smaller multiplications and three smaller modular reductions:

$$((a^2 \bmod n)^2 \bmod n)^2 \bmod n.$$

By the same token,

$$a^{16} \bmod n = (((a^2 \bmod n)^2 \bmod n)^2 \bmod n)^2 \bmod n.$$

Computing $a^x \bmod n$, where x is not a power of 2, is only slightly harder. Binary notating expresses n as a sum of powers of 2: 25 is 11001 in binary, so $25 = 2^4 + 2^3 + 2^0$. So

$$a^{25} \bmod n = (a \times a^{24}) \bmod n = (a \times a^8 \times a^{16}) \bmod n = (a \times ((a^2)^2)^2 \times$$
$$(((a^2)^2)^2)^2) \bmod n = ((((a^2 \times a)^2)^2)^2 \times a) \bmod n$$

With judicious storing of intermediate results, you only need six multiplications:

$$(((((((a^2 \bmod n) \times a) \bmod n)^2 \bmod n)^2 \bmod n)^2 \bmod n) \times a) \bmod n$$

In C, the algorithm looks like this:

```c
int modexp (int a, int x, int n)
{
    int r = 1;

    while (x > 0){
        if (x % 2 == 1)    /* is x odd? */
            r = (r * a) % n;
        a = (a*a) % n;
        x /= 2;
    }
    return r;
}
```

This technique reduces the operation to, on the average, 1.5×k operations, if k is the length of the number in bits. Finding the shortest possible sequence is a hard problem (it has been proven that the sequence must contain at least k-1 operations), but it is not too hard to get the number of operations down to 1.1×k or better, as k grows. See [488] for more details.

The opposite of exponentiation modulo n is calculating a **discrete logarithm.** I'll discuss this shortly.

Prime Numbers

A **prime** number is a number, greater than 1, whose only factors are 1 and itself: no other number evenly divides it. Two is a prime number. So are 73, 2521, 2365347734339, and $2^{756839}-1$. There are an infinite number of primes. Cryptography uses large primes (512 bits and even larger) often.

Evengelos Kranakis wrote an excellent book on number theory, prime numbers, and their applications to cryptography [508]. Paulo Ribenboim wrote two excellent references on prime numbers in general [734,735].

Greatest Common Divisor

Two numbers are **relatively prime** when they share no factors in common other than 1; in other words, if the **greatest common divisor** of a and n is equal to 1. This is written:

$$\gcd (a,n) = 1$$

The numbers 15 and 28 are relatively prime, 15 and 27 are not, and 13 and 500 are. A prime number is relatively prime to all other numbers except its multiples.

The easiest way to compute the greatest common divisor of two numbers is with **Euclid's algorithm.** Euclid described the algorithm in his book, *Elements,* written around 300 B.C. He didn't invent it. Historians believe the algorithm could be 200 years older. It is the oldest nontrivial algorithm that has survived to the present day, and it is still good today. Knuth describes the algorithm and some modern modifications [488].

In C:

```
/* returns GCD of x and y, assuming x and y are > 0 */

int gcd (int x, int y)
{
  int g;

  if (x < 0)
    x = -x;
  if (y < 0)
    y = -y;
  g = y;
  while (x > 0) {
    g = x;
    x = y % x;
    y = g;
  }
  return g;
}
```

This algorithm can be generalized to return the GCD of an array of m numbers:

```
/* returns the GCD of x1, x2...xm, assuming all x values are
greater than 0 */

int multiple_GCD (int m, int *x)
{
  size_t i;
  int g;

  if (m < 1)
    return 0;
  g = x[0]
  for (i=1; i<m; ++i) {
    g = gcd(g, x[i]);
    /* optimization, since for random x[i], g==1 60% of the time: */
    if (g == 1)
      return 1;
  }
  return g;
}
```

Inverses Modulo a Number

Remember inverses? The multiplicative inverse of 4 is 1/4, because $4 \times 1/4 = 1$. In the modulo world, the problem is more complicated:

$$4 \times x \equiv 1 \bmod 7$$

This equation is equivalent to finding an x and k such that

$$4x = 7k + 1$$

where both x and k are integers.

The general problem is finding an x such that

$$1 = (a \times x) \bmod n$$

This is also written as:

$$a^{-1} \equiv x \pmod n$$

The modular reduction problem is a lot more difficult to solve. Sometimes there is a solution; sometimes there isn't. For example, the inverse of 5, modulo 14, is 3; $5 \times 3 = 15 \equiv 1 \pmod{14}$. On the other hand, 2 has no inverse modulo 14.

In general, $a^{-1} \equiv x \pmod n$ has a unique solution if a and n are relatively prime. If a and n are not relatively prime, then $a^{-1} \equiv x \pmod n$ has no solution. If n is a prime number, then every number from 1 to $n-1$ is relatively prime to n and has exactly one inverse in that range.

So far, so good. Now, how do you go about finding the inverse of a modulo n? There are a couple of ways. Euclid's algorithm can also compute the inverse of a number modulo n. Sometimes this is called the **extended Euclidean algorithm.**

Here's the algorithm in C:

```
static void Update (int *un, int *vn, int q)
{
  int tn;

  tn = *un - *vn *q;
  *un= *vn;
  *vn = tn;
}

/* return == gcd(x, n) == u*u1 + v*u2 */

int extended_euclidian (int u, int v, int *u1_out, int *u2_out)
{
  int u1 = 1;
  int u3 = u;
  int v1 = 0;
  int v3 = v;
  int q;

  while (v3 > 0) {
    q = u3 / v3;
    Update(&u1, &v1, q);
```

```
        Update(&u3, &v3, q);
    }
    *u1_out = u1;
    *u2_out = (u3 - u1 * u) / v;
    return u3;
}
```

I'm not going to prove that it works or give the theory behind it. Details can be found in [488], or in any of the number theory texts listed above.

The algorithm is iterative and can be slow for large numbers. Even so, an algorithm whose complexity is O(ln n) is much quicker than algorithms to solve those hard problems I discussed earlier. Knuth showed that the average number of divisions performed by the algorithm is

$$.843 \times ln\ (n) + 1.47$$

Solving for Coefficients

Euclid's algorithm can be used to solve the following class of problems. Given an array of m variables $x_1, x_2, \ldots x_m$, find an array of m coefficients, $u_1, u_2 \ldots u_m$, such that:

$$u_1 \times x_1 + \ldots + u_m \times x_m = 1$$

Fermat's Little Theorem

If m is a prime, and a is not a multiple of m, then **Fermat's little theorem** says:

$$a^{m-1} \equiv 1\ (\text{mod}\ m).$$

Euler's Totient Function

There is another method for calculating the inverse modulo n, but it's not always possible to use it. The **reduced set of residues** mod n is the subset of the complete set of residues that is relatively prime to n. For example, the reduced set of residues mod 12 is $\{1,5,7,11\}$. If n is prime, then the reduced set of residues mod n is the set of all numbers from 1 to $n-1$. The number 0 is never part of the reduced set of residues.

The **Euler totient function,** also called the **Euler phi function** and written as $\phi(n)$, is the number of elements in the reduced set of residues modulo n. In other words, $\phi(n)$ is the number of positive integers less than n that are relatively prime to n. (Leonhard Euler, pronounced "Oiler," was a Swiss mathematician who lived from 1707–1783.)

If n is prime, then $\phi(n) = n-1$. If $n = p \times q$, where p and q are prime, then $\phi(n) = (p-1)(q-1)$. These numbers appear a lot in the public-key algorithms described later; this is where they all come from.

According to **Euler's generalization of Fermat's little theorem**, if $\gcd(a,n) = 1$, then

$$a^{\phi(n)} \bmod n = 1$$

Now it is easy to compute $a^{-1} \bmod n$:

$$x = a^{\phi(n)-1} \bmod n$$

For example, what is the inverse of 5, modulo 7? Since 7 is prime, $\phi(7) = 7-1 = 6$. So, the inverse of 5, modulo 7, is

$$5^{6-1} \bmod 7 = 5^5 \bmod 7 = 3$$

Both methods for calculating inverses can be extended to solve for x in the general problem (if $\gcd(a,n) = 1$):

$$(a \times x) \bmod n = b$$

Using Euler's generalization, solve:

$$x = (b \times \exp(a^{\phi(n)-1} \bmod n)) \bmod n$$

Using Euclid's algorithm, solve:

$$x = (b \times \mathrm{inv}(a,n)) \bmod n$$

If $\gcd(a,n) \neq 1$, all is not lost. In this general case, $(a \times x) \bmod n = b$, can have multiple solutions or no solution. In general, Euclid's algorithm is a faster method for calculating inverses, especially for numbers in the 500-bit range.

Chinese Remainder Theorem

If you know the prime factorization of n, then you can use something called the **Chinese remainder theorem** to solve a whole system of equations. The basic version of this theorem was discovered by the first-century Chinese mathematician, Sun Tse.

In general, if the prime factorization of $n = p_1 \times p_2 \times \ldots p_t$, then the system of equations

$$(x \bmod p_i) = a_i, \text{ where } i = 1, 2, \ldots, t$$

has a unique solution, x, where x is less than n. (Note that some primes can appear more than once and that, for example, p_1 might equal p_2.)

So, for an arbitrary $a < p$ and $b < q$ (where p and q are prime), then there exists a unique x, when x is less than $p \times q$, such that

$$x \equiv a \pmod{p}, \text{ and } x \equiv b \pmod{q}$$

To find this x, first use Euclid's algorithm to find u, such that:

$$u \times q \equiv 1 \pmod{p}$$

Then compute:

$$x = (((a - b) \times u) \bmod p) \times q + b$$

Here is the Chinese remainder theorem in C:

```
/* r is the number of elements in arrays m and u;
   m is the array of (pairwise relatively prime) moduli
   u is the array of coefficients
   return value is n such than n == u[k]%m[k] (k=0..r-1) and
                              n < m[0]*m[1]*...*m[r-1]
*/

/*  totient() is left as an exercise to the reader.  */

int chinese_remainder (size_t r, int *m, int *u)
{
  size_t i;
  int modulus;
  int n;

  modulus = 1;
  for (i=0; i<r; ++i)
    modulus *= m[i];

  n = 0;
  for (i=0; i<r; ++i) {
    n += u[i] * modexp(modulus / m[i], totient(m[i]),
m[i]);
    n %= modulus;
  }

  return n;
}
```

A corollary of the Chinese remainder theorem can be used to find the solution to a similar problem: if p and q are primes, and p is less than q, then there exists a unique x, when x is less than $p \times q$, such that

$$a \equiv x \ (\bmod\ p), \text{ and } b \equiv x \ (\bmod\ q)$$

If $a \geq b \bmod p$, then

$$x = (((a - (b \bmod p)) \times u) \bmod p) \times q + b$$

If $a < b \bmod p$, then

$$x = (((a + p - (b \bmod p)) \times u) \bmod p) \times q + b$$

Quadratic Residues

If p is prime and a is less than p, then a is a **quadratic residue** mod p if

$$x^2 \equiv a \pmod{p}, \text{ for some } x.$$

Not all values of a satisfy this property. For example, if $p = 7$, the quadratic residues are 1, 2, and 4:

$$1^2 = 1 \equiv 1 \pmod{7}$$
$$2^2 = 4 \equiv 4 \pmod{7}$$
$$3^2 = 9 \equiv 2 \pmod{7}$$
$$4^2 = 16 \equiv 2 \pmod{7}$$
$$5^2 = 25 \equiv 4 \pmod{7}$$
$$6^2 = 36 \equiv 1 \pmod{7}$$

Note that each quadratic residue appears twice on this list.

There are no values of x that satisfy any of these equations:

$$x^2 = 3 \pmod{7}$$
$$x^2 = 5 \pmod{7}$$
$$x^2 = 6 \pmod{7}$$

The **quadratic nonresidues** modulo 7 are 3, 5, and 6.

Although I will not do so here, it is easy to prove that there are exactly $(p-1)/2$ quadratic residues mod p and the same number of quadratic nonresidues mod p. Also, if a is a quadratic residue mod p, then a has exactly two square roots: one of them between 0 and $(p-1)/2$, and the other between $(p-1)/2$ and $(p-1)$. One of these square roots is also a quadratic residue mod p; this is called the **principle** square root.

If n is the product of two primes, p and q, there are exactly $(p-1)(q-1)/4$ quadratic residues mod n. A quadratic residue mod n is a perfect square modulo n. For example, there are six quadratic residues mod 35: 1, 4, 9, 11, 16, 29. Each quadratic residue has exactly four "square roots."

Legendre Symbol

The **Legendre symbol,** written $L(a,p)$, is defined when a is any integer and p is a prime greater than 2. It is equal to 0, 1, or -1:

$L(a,p) = 0$ if a divides p.

$L(a,p) = 1$ if a is a quadratic residue mod p.

$L(a,p) = -1$ if a is a nonresidue mod p.

An easy way to calculate $L(a,p)$ is:

$$L(a,p) = a^{(p-1)/2} \bmod p$$

Jacobi Symbol

The **Jacobi symbol,** written J(a,n), is a generalization of the Legendre symbol: it is defined for any pair of integers, a and n. The function shows up in primality testing. The Jacobi symbol is a function on the set of reduced residues of the divisors of n and can be calculated according to the following formula:

> If n is prime, then the Jacobi symbol J(a,n) = 1 if a is a quadratic residue modulo n.
>
> If n is prime, then the Jacobi symbol J(a,n) = −1 if a is a quadratic nonresidue modulo n.
>
> If n is composite, then the Jacobi symbol J(a,n) = J(h,p_1) × . . . × J(h,p_m), where $p_1 \ldots p_m$ is the prime factorization of n.

This algorithm computes the Jacobi symbol recursively:

> 1. J(1,k) = 1
> 2. J($a \times b,k$) = J(a,k) × J(b,k)
> 3. J(2,k) = 1 if (k^2−1)/8 is even, −1 otherwise.
> 4. J(b,a) = J((b mod a),a)
> 5. If GCD(a,b) = 1:
>   a. J(a,b) × J(b,a) = 1 if (a−1)(b−1)/4 is even
>   b. J(a,b) × J(b,a) = −1 if (a−1)(b−1)/4 is odd

Here is the algorithm in C:

```
/* factor2 (a, &b, &c) is left as an exercise to the reader. */

int jacobi (int a, int b)
{

  int a1, a2;

  if (a >= b)
    a%=b;
  if (a == 0)
    return 0;
  if (a == 1)
    return 1;
  if (a == 2)
    if (((b*b-1) / 8) % 2 == 0)
      return 1;
    else
      return -1;

  if (a & b & 1) /* both a and b are odd */
    if (((a-1)*(b-1)/4) % 2 == 0)
```

```
      return +jacobi (b, a);
    else
      return -jacobi (b, a);
  if (gcd(a, b) == 1
    if (((a-1)*(b-1)/4) % 2 == 0)
      return +jacobi (b, a);
    else
      return -jacobi(b, a);

  factor2(a, &a1, &a2);
  return jacobi(a1, b) * jacobi(a2, b);
}
```

If p is prime, there is a better way to compute the Jacobi symbol:

1. If $a = 1$, then $J(a/p) = 1$
2. If a is even, then $J(a,p) = J(a/2,p) \times (-1)^{(p^2-1)/8}$
3. If a is odd (and $\neq 1$), then $J(a,p) = J(p \bmod a,a) \times (-1)^{(a-1)\times(p-1)/4}$

Note that this is also an efficient way to determine whether a is a quadratic residue mod p (only when p is a prime, though). If $J(a,p) = 1$, then it is. If $J(a,p) = -1$, then it isn't.

Also note that if $J(a,n) = 1$ and n is composite, it is not necessarily true that a is quadratic residue modulo n. For example:

$$J(7,143) = J(7,11) \times J(7,13) = (-1)(-1) = 1$$

However, there is no integer x such that $x^2 \equiv 7 \bmod 143$.

For a to be a quadratic residue modulo n, it must be a quadratic residue modulo all the prime factors of n.

Blum Integers

If p and q are two primes, and both are congruent to 3 modulo 4, then $n = p \times q$ is called a **Blum integer.** If n is a Blum integer, each quadratic residue has exactly four square roots, one of which is also a square; this is the **principle** square root. For example, the principle square root of 139 mod 437 is 24. The other three square roots are 185, 252, and 413.

Blum integers are used in some public-key algorithms. Consult any number theory book for details, theory, and proofs.

Generators

If p is a prime, and g is less than p, then g is a **generator** mod p if:

for each n from 0 to $p-1$, there exists some a where $g^a \equiv n \pmod{p}$

Another way of saying this is that g is **primitive** with respect to p.

For example, if $p = 11$, 2 is a generator mod 11:

$$2^{10} = 1024 \equiv 1 \ (\text{mod } 11)$$
$$2^1 = 2 \equiv 2 \ (\text{mod } 11)$$
$$2^8 = 256 \equiv 3 \ (\text{mod } 11)$$
$$2^2 = 4 \equiv 4 \ (\text{mod } 11)$$
$$2^4 = 16 \equiv 5 \ (\text{mod } 11)$$
$$2^9 = 512 \equiv 6 \ (\text{mod } 11)$$
$$2^7 = 128 \equiv 7 \ (\text{mod } 11)$$
$$2^3 = 8 \equiv 8 \ (\text{mod } 11)$$
$$2^6 = 64 \equiv 9 \ (\text{mod } 11)$$
$$2^5 = 32 \equiv 10 \ (\text{mod } 11)$$

Every number from 1 to 10 can be expressed as $2^a \ (\text{mod } p)$.

For $p=11$, the generators are 2, 6, 7, and 8. The other numbers are not generators. For example, 3 is not a generator because there is no solution to:

$$3^a \equiv 2 \ (\text{mod } 11)$$

In general, finding a generator is not an easy problem. It is easy, however, if you know the factorization of $p-1$. Let $q_1, q_2, \ldots, q_n$ be the prime factors of $p-1$. To test if a number, g, is a generator mod p, calculate

$$g^{(p-1)/q} \ (\text{mod } p)$$

for all values of $q = q_1, q_2, \ldots, q_n$.

If that number equals 1 for some value of q, then g is not a generator. If that value does not equal q for any values of q, then g is a generator.

For example, let $p = 11$. The prime factors of $p-1 = 10$ are 2 and 5. To test if 2 is a generator:

$$2^{(11-1)/5} \ (\text{mod } 11) = 4$$
$$2^{(11-1)/2} \ (\text{mod } 11) = 10$$

Neither result is 1, so 2 is a generator.

To test if 3 is a generator:

$$3^{(11-1)/5} \ (\text{mod } 11) = 9$$
$$3^{(11-1)/2} \ (\text{mod } 11) = 1$$

Therefore, 3 is not a generator.

Computing in a Galois Field

Don't be alarmed; that's what we were just doing. If n is prime, then we have what mathematicians call a **finite field.** (Actually, if n is a power of a prime, it is also a finite field.) Therefore, we'll call it p instead of n. In fact, this type of finite field is so exciting that mathematicians gave it its own name: a **Galois field,** denoted as GF(p). (Évariste Galois was a French mathematician who lived in the early nineteenth century and did a lot of work in number theory before he was killed at age 21 in a duel.)

In a Galois field, addition, subtraction, multiplication, and division are all well defined. There is an additive identity, 0, and a multiplicative identity, 1. Every nonzero number has a unique inverse (this would not be true if p were not prime). The commutative, associative, and distributive laws are true.

Arithmetic in a Galois field is used a great deal in cryptography. All of the number theory works, it keeps numbers a finite size, and division doesn't have any rounding errors. Many cryptosystems are based on GF(p), where p is a large prime.

Computing in GF(2^n)

To make matters even more complicated, cryptographers also use arithmetic modulo **irreducible** polynomials of degree n whose coefficients are integers modulo q, where q is prime. These fields are called GF(q^n). All arithmetic is done modulo some $p(x)$, which is an irreducible polynomial of degree n.

The mathematical theory behind this is far beyond the scope of the book, although I will describe some cryptosystems that use it. If you want to work more with this, GF(2^3) has the following elements: 0, 1, x, $x+1$, x^2, x^2+1, x^2+x, x^2+x+1. There is an algorithm for computing inverses in GF(2^n) that is suitable for parallel implementation [238].

When talking about polynomials, the term "prime" is often replaced by the term **irreducible.** A polynomial is irreducible if it cannot be expressed as the product of two other polynomials (except for 1 and itself, of course). The polynomial x^2+1 is irreducible over the integers. The polynomial x^3+2x^2+x is not; it can be expressed as $x(x+1)(x+1)$.

Polynomials that are generators in a given field are called **primitive.** We'll see primitive polynomials again when we talk about pseudo-random sequence generators (see Section 15.1).

Computation in GF(2^n) can be quickly implemented in hardware with linear feedback shift registers. For that reason, computation over GF(2^n) is often quicker than computation over GF(p). Just as exponentiation is much more efficient in GF(2^n), so is calculating discrete logarithms [115,116,223,226]. If you want to learn more about this, read [85].

For a Galois field GF(2^n), cryptographers like to use the trinomial $p(x) = x^n+x+1$ as the modulus, because the long string of zeros between the x^n and x coefficients makes it easy to implement a fast modular multiplication [118]. The trinomial must be primitive, otherwise the math does not work. Values of n less than 1000 [906,905] for which $x^n + x + 1$ is primitive are:

1, 3, 4, 6, 9, 15, 22, 28, 30, 46, 60, 63, 127, 153, 172, 303, 471, 532, 865, 900

There exists a hardware implementation of $GF(2^{127})$ where $p(x) = x^{127}+x+1$ [896,897,628]. An article that discusses efficient hardware architectures for implementing exponentiation in $GF(2^n)$ is [91].

9.4 FACTORING

Factoring a number means finding its prime factors:

$$10 = 2 \times 5$$
$$60 = 2 \times 2 \times 3 \times 5$$
$$252601 = 41 \times 61 \times 101$$
$$2^{113} - 1 = 3391 \times 23279 \times 65993 \times 1868569 \times 1066818132868207$$

The factoring problem is one of the oldest in number theory. It's simple to verify if a number is prime: test all primes less than the number to see if any are factors of the number. Modern algorithms don't test *all* possible prime numbers, but they still do tests on the candidate number—one after the other. There have been some major advances in the state of the art, though.

Currently, the best factoring algorithms are:

Quadratic Sieve [707,890,709]. This is the fastest known algorithm for numbers less than 150 decimal digits long and has been used extensively [253]. A faster version of this algorithm is called the **Multiple Polynomial Quadratic Sieve** [816,187]. The fastest version of this algorithm is called the **Double Large Prime Variation of the Multiple Polynomial Quadratic Sieve.**

Number Field Sieve (NFS) [537,11,538]. This is the fastest-known factoring algorithm. It was impractical when originally proposed, but that has changed due to a series of improvements over the last few years. The multiple polynomial quadratic sieve is still faster for smaller numbers (the break-even point is between 110 and 135 decimal digits, depending on implementation). The NFS was used to factor the ninth Fermat number [539].

There are other factoring algorithms, but for the most part these have been supplanted by the above two:

Elliptic Curve Method (ECM) [541,616,617]. This method has been used to find 38-digit factors, but nothing larger. For larger factors, the other algorithms are faster.

Pollard's Monte Carlo Algorithm [704,152]. (This algorithm also appears in volume 2, page 370 of Knuth [488].)

Continued Fraction Algorithm. See [623] for a practical implementation and [702] about specialized VLSI hardware to speed the algorithm. (This algorithm also appears in volume 2, pages 381–82 of Knuth [488].)

Trial Division. This is the oldest factoring algorithm, and involves testing every prime number less than the square root of the candidate number.

See [154] for a good introduction to these different factoring algorithms, except for the number field sieve—it's too new. Other, older references are [304,881,708]. Information on parallel factoring can be found in [153].

If n is the number being factored, the fastest quadratic sieve variants take a number of operations equivalent to, more or less:

$$e^{(\ln n)^{\frac{1}{2}} (\ln (\ln n))^{\frac{1}{2}}}$$

For 664-bit (200-digit) numbers, this results in about 10^{23} operations. At a rate of a million operations per second (an operation is a complex iteration of the algorithm, not a simple microcomputer operation), this translates to 3.7 billion years.

The number field sieve is faster for numbers larger than about 120 digits, with an asymptotically heuristic time estimate of:

$$e^{(\ln n)^{\frac{1}{3}} (\ln (\ln n))^{\frac{2}{3}}}$$

The NFS is considerably faster for a number of certain special forms, like $2^{523}-1$.

In 1970, the big news was the factoring of a 41-digit hard number [623]. (A "hard" number is one that does not have any small factors and is not of a special form that allows it to be factored more easily.) Ten years later, factoring hard numbers twice that size took a few hours of work by a Cray computer [253].

At the time of this writing, 110-digit hard numbers are regularly being factored. This advance is due to improvements in both factoring theory and computing hardware.

Carl Pomerance has designed a modular factoring machine, using custom VLSI chips [709]. The size of number you can factor depends on how large a machine you can afford to build. Pomerance's demonstration model is a $25,000 implementation that can factor 100-digit numbers in two weeks. A $10 million machine could factor a 150-digit number in a year. Theoretically, there is no upper limit to this factoring model. To factor a 200-digit number in a year, the machine would cost $100 billion. As Diffie pointed out [295,297]: "This is a high price to be sure, but not beyond human grasp."

In addition to massively parallel machines, there have been significant developments in the successful implementation of factoring algorithms on computer networks [187,539]. In their factoring of a 116-digit number, Lenstra and Manasse used the spare time on an array of computers around the world for a few months: the equivalent of a 400-mips (million instructions per second) computer running for a year [540]. The machines communicated to one another via E-mail.

This kind of operation can only improve. The Lenstra-Manasse implementation is extendable to networks with many more machines. Since every tenfold increase in computing power allows one to factor numbers slightly over 10 decimal digits longer, it is not unreasonable to expect networks of workstations around some universities or large corporations to factor 130-digit numbers in a few weeks or months of spare time [169]. And these workstations are far more common than Pomerance's factoring machine. A. K. Lenstra estimates that factoring a 155-digit (512-bit) number with the NFS will take one year on fifty large machines. And he considers this estimate pessimistic.

Factorization is a fast-moving field. If no new methods are developed, then 2048-bit numbers (created by multiplying two 1024-bit primes) will always be safe from factorization. However, no one can predict the future. Before the number field sieve was discovered, many people conjectured that the quadratic sieve was asymptotically as fast as any factoring method could be. They were wrong.

Square Roots Modulo N

If n is the product of two primes, then the ability to calculate square roots mod n is computationally equivalent to the ability to factor n [724]. In other words, someone who knows the prime factors of n can easily compute the square roots of a number mod n, but for everyone else the computation has been proven to be as hard as computing the prime factors of n.

9.5   PRIME NUMBER GENERATION

One-way functions were discussed in Section 2.3. Multiplying two large primes is conjectured to be a one-way function; it's easy to multiply the numbers to get a product but hard to factor the product and recover the two large primes. There are ways to use this one-way function to make a trap-door one-way function.

Testing whether an integer is prime is another matter entirely, and it is one that is significantly easier than factoring. Overviews of recent developments in the field can be found in [706,128]. Other important papers are [842,227,6,12,379,391,511,51].

Public-key cryptography needs prime numbers. Any reasonably sized network needs lots of them. There are several ways to generate these primes.

First, I will resolve a few obvious questions:

1. If everyone needs a different prime number, won't we run out? No, Santa would never run out of prime numbers for all the good little boys and girls. In fact, there are over 10^{150} primes of length 512 bits or less. (For numbers of size N, the probability that a random number is prime is approximately one in $\log N$.) There are only 10^{84} atoms in the universe. If every atom in the universe needed a billion new primes every microsecond from the beginning of time until now, there would still be 10^{110} primes left over.

2. What if two people accidentally pick the same prime number? With over 10^{150} prime numbers to choose from, the odds of that happening are less than the odds of a computer spontaneously combusting. It's nothing to worry about.

If factoring a 200-digit number takes such a long time, how much easier can it be to find 200-digit prime numbers? Not much, if you find prime numbers by generating random candidates and then trying to factor them. However, there are several tests that can determine if a random number is prime with a confidence of over 50% (possibly more). If a number suspected to be prime fails the test, it is definitely not prime. If a number suspected to be prime passes this test, it is at most 50% likely not prime. If the number passes two of the tests, it is at most 25% likely not prime. If the number passes ten of these tests, the likelihood that it is not prime is at most $1/2^{10}$, or one in 1024.

If you set the number of tests at 100, this overall procedure will fail once in 2^{100} tries, or about 1 in 10^{30}. If for some reason you need more confidence that the number is prime, choose more random numbers to test against. On the other hand, if you consider that the odds of the number being composite are less than the odds of being killed in a car accident, you might not worry about it so much.

Solovay-Strassen

Solovay and Strassen developed a probabilistic primality testing algorithm [842]. This algorithm uses the Jacobi function.

To test if p is prime, here is the algorithm:

(1) Choose a random number a less than p.

(2) If the gcd(a,p) ≠ 1, then p fails the test and is composite.

(3) Calculate $j = a^{(p-1)/2} \bmod p$.

(4) Calculate the Jacobi symbol J(a,p).

(5) If j ≠ J(a,p), then p is definitely not prime.

(6) If j = J(a,p), then the likelihood that p is not prime is at most 50%.

Repeat this test n times, with n different random values for a. The odds of a composite number, p, passing all n tests is no more than one in 2^n.

In real-world implementations, the algorithm goes quickly. Generate a large random number p to test for primality. Check to make sure that it is not divisible by any small primes: 2, 3, 5, 7, 11, etc. Then generate another random number, r, and compute gcd(p,r) and $r^{(p-1)/2} \bmod p$. Perform the various tests. If p passes, generate another random r and go through the test again. Repeat until satisfied.

Rabin-Miller

This algorithm was developed by Rabin, based in part on Miller's ideas [603,725]. Actually, this is a simplified version of the algorithm recommended in NIST's (National Institute of Standards and Technology) DSS proposal [650,651]. (This algorithm also appears in volume 2 of Knuth, [488], page 379.)

First choose a random number, p, to test. Calculate b, where b is the number of times 2 divides $p-1$ (i.e., 2^b is the largest power of 2 that divides $p-1$). Then calculate m, such that $n = 1 + 2^b m$.

(1) Choose a random number, a, such that a is less than p.

(2) Set $j=0$ and set $z=a^m \bmod p$.

(3) If $z=1$, or if $z=p-1$, then p passes the test and may be prime.

(4) If $j > 0$ and $z=1$, then p is not prime.

(5) Set $j=j+1$. If $j < b$ and $z \neq p-1$, set $z=z^2 \bmod p$ and go back to step (4).

(6) If $j=b$ and $z \neq p-1$, then p is not prime.

This test converges faster than the previous one. It will produce a false prime no more than $1/4^n$ of the time, when n is the number of iterations. Do this test a dozen times (or however many times you like) on a number that is not divisible by any small primes, and the result is almost certainly a prime.

Lehmann

Another, simpler, test was developed independently by Lehmann [533]. Here is the algorithm with the number of iterations set at 100:

(1) Choose a random number, n, to test.

(2) Make sure that n is not divisible by any small primes. Testing 2, 3, 5, 7, and 11 will speed up the algorithm significantly.

(3) Choose 100 random numbers, $a_1, a_2, \ldots a_{100}$ between 1 and $n-1$.

(4) Calculate $a_i^{(n-1)/2} \pmod{n}$ for all $a_i = a_1 \ldots a_{100}$. Stop if you find an a_i for which the test fails.

(5) If $a_i(n-1)/2 = 1 \pmod{n}$ for all i, then n is probably composite.
If $a_i(n-1)/2 \neq 1$ or $-1 \pmod{n}$ for any i, then n is composite.
If $a_i(n-1)/2 = 1$ or $-1 \pmod{n}$ for all i (but does not $= 1$ for all i), then n is prime.

Strong Primes

Much of the RSA literature suggests that **strong primes** should be used for p and q. These are prime numbers with certain properties that make the product n difficult to factor by specific factoring methods. Among the properties suggested have been [391,749]:

The greatest common divisor of $p-1$ and $q-1$ should be small.

Both $p-1$ and $q-1$ should have large prime factors, respectively p' and q'.

Both $p'-1$ and $q'-1$ should have a large prime factor, respectively p'' and q''.

Both $(p-1)/2$ and $(q-1)/2$ should be prime [117].

Whether strong primes are necessary is a subject of debate. These properties were designed to thwart some factoring algorithms. However, the fastest factoring algorithms have equally as good a chance of factoring numbers that meet these criteria as they do of factoring numbers that do not [479].

However, this may change. New factoring algorithms may be discovered that work better on numbers with certain properties than on numbers without them. If so, strong primes may be required once again. Check your local theoretical mathematics journal for late-breaking news.

I recommend using strong primes even though they are not necessary to make factoring difficult. It can't hurt, although it makes it that much harder to generate primes.

9.6 DISCRETE LOGARITHMS IN A FINITE FIELD

Modular exponentiation is another one-way function used frequently in cryptography. Evaluating this expression is easy:

$$a^x \bmod n$$

The inverse problem of modular exponentiation is that of finding the **discrete logarithm** of a number. This is a hard problem.

Find x where $a^x = b \bmod n$

For example:

If $3^x \bmod 17 = 15$, then $x = 6$

Not all discrete logarithms have solutions (remember, the only valid solutions are integers). It's easy to see that there is no solution, x, to the equation:

$$3^x \bmod 13 = 7$$

It's even more difficult to solve these problems using 1024-bit numbers.

Calculating Discrete Logarithms in a Finite Group

There are three main groups whose discrete logarithms are of interest to cryptographers:

- The multiplicative group of prime fields: GF(p)
- The multiplicative group of finite fields of characteristic 2: GF(2^n)
- Elliptic curve groups over finite fields F: EC(F)

The security of many public-key algorithms is based on the problem of finding discrete logarithms, and so the problem has been extensively studied. A good comprehensive overview of the problem, and the best solutions at the time, can be found in [660,579]. The best current article on the topic is [526].

If p is the modulus and is prime, then the complexity of finding discrete logarithms in GF(p) is essentially the same as factoring an integer n of about the same size, when n is the product of two approximately equal-length primes [648,526]. This is:

$$e^{(\ln p)^{1/2} \ln (\ln p))^{1/2}}$$

The number field sieve is faster, with an asymptotically heuristic time estimate of:

$$e^{(\ln p)^{1/3} \ln (\ln p))^{2/3}}$$

It's still impractical, though.

The caveat to this is that if p is the modulus, then $p-1$ should have at least one large factor. Otherwise, it is much easier to calculate discrete logarithms in GF(p).

Pohlig and Hellman found a fast way of computing discrete logarithms in GF(p) if $p-1$ has only small prime factors [703]. For this reason, some fields are not used in cryptography. Another algorithm [9] computes discrete logarithms at a speed comparable to factoring; it was then expanded to fields of the form GF(p^n) [423]. This algorithm was criticized [433] for having some theoretical problems. More articles [874] show how difficult the problem really is.

Currently, there are three methods for calculating discrete logarithms in a prime field [224,526,388]: the linear sieve, the Guassian integer scheme, and the number field sieve.

The main amount of computing has to be done only once per field. Afterward, individual logarithms can be quickly calculated. This is a security disadvantage for systems based on these fields. It is important for different users to use different prime fields. Luckily, there are a lot of prime numbers, and therefore a lot of prime fields.

In the world of polynomial fields, GF(2^n) hasn't been ignored by researchers. A heuristic algorithm was proposed in [433]. Coppersmith's algorithm makes finding discrete logarithms in fields such as GF(2^{127}) reasonable and finding them in fields around GF(2^{400}) barely possible [223]. This was based on work in [115]. The precomputation stage of this algorithm is enormous, but otherwise it is nice and efficient. A practical implementation of a less efficient version of the same algorithm, after a seven-hour precomputation period, found discrete logs in GF(2^{127}) in several seconds each [629]. Another team had similar success with GF(2^{127}) [115]. This particular field, once used in some cryptosystems [87,896,897], is insecure. For surveys of some of these results, consult [660,579].

More recently, the precomputations for $GF(2^{227})$, $GF(2^{313})$, and $GF(2^{401})$ are complete, and significant progress has been made toward $GF(2^{503})$. These calculations are being executed on an nCube-2 massively parallel computer with 1024 processors [389,390]. Computing discrete logarithms in $GF(2^{593})$ is still out of reach, but in a few years it may not be. Like discrete logarithms in a prime field, the precomputation required to calculate discrete logarithms in a polynomial field has to be done only once. ElGamal [317] gives an algorithm for calculating discrete logs in the field $GF(p^2)$.

CHAPTER
10

Data Encryption Standard (DES)

10.1 DATA ENCRYPTION STANDARD (DES)

The Data Encryption Standard (DES) has been a worldwide standard for over 15 years. Although it is showing signs of old age, it has held up remarkably well against years of cryptanalysis and is still secure against all but possibly the most powerful of adversaries.

Development of the Standard

In the early 1970s, nonmilitary cryptography research was haphazard. Almost no research papers were published in the field. Most people knew that the military used special coding equipment to communicate, but few understood the science of cryptography. The National Security Agency (NSA) had considerable knowledge, but they did not even publicly admit their own existence.

Several small companies made and sold cryptographic equipment, primarily to overseas governments. They were all different; none of the devices could communicate with each other. And no one really knew if they were secure or not; there was no independent body to certify their security. Those buying cryptography didn't know what they were buying. As one government report said, "The intricacies of relating key variations and working principles to the real strength of the encryption/decryption equipment were, and are, virtually unknown to almost all buyers, and informed decisions as to the right type of on-line, off-line, key generation, etc., which will meet buyers' security needs, have been most difficult to make" [254].

In 1972, the National Bureau of Standards (NBS), now the National Institute of Standards and Technology (NIST), initiated a program to protect computer and communications data. As part of that program, they wanted to develop a single, standard cryptographic algorithm to protect digital data during both transmission and storage. A single algorithm could be tested and certified, and different cryptographic equipment could be interoperable. It would also be cheaper to implement and readily available.

In the May 15, 1973 *Federal Register,* the NBS issued a public request for proposals for a standard cryptographic algorithm. They specified a series of design criteria:

- The algorithm must provide a high level of security.

- The algorithm must be completely specified and easy to understand.

- The security of the algorithm must reside in the key; the security should not depend on the secrecy of the algorithm.

- The algorithm must be available to all users.

- The algorithm must be adaptable for use in diverse applications.

- The algorithm must be economically implementable in electronic devices.

- The algorithm must be efficient to use.

- The algorithm must be able to be validated.

- The algorithm must be exportable.

Public response indicated that there was considerable interest in a cryptographic standard, but that there was little public expertise in the field. Some mathematicians sent in crude outlines of algorithms. None of the submissions came close to meeting the requirements.

The NBS issued a second request in the August 27, 1974 *Federal Register.* Eventually they received a promising candidate: an algorithm based on one developed by IBM during the early 1970s, called LUCIFER [837,839,339]. The algorithm, although complicated, was straightforward. It used only simple logical operations on small groups of bits and could be implemented fairly efficiently in both hardware and software.

The NBS requested the NSA's help in evaluating the algorithm's security and to determine its suitability as a federal standard. IBM had already patented the algorithm [311], but they were willing to make their intellectual property available to others for manufacture, implementation, and use. The NBS worked out the terms of agreement with IBM and eventually received a nonexclusive, royalty-free license to make, use, and sell apparatus that implemented the algorithm.

Finally, in the March 17, 1975 *Federal Register,* the NBS published both the details of the algorithm and IBM's statement granting a nonexclusive, royalty-free license for the algorithm [327]. Another notice, in the August 1, 1975 *Federal Register,* requested comments from agencies and the general public.

And there were comments [429,300,622]. Many cryptographers were leery of the NSA's "invisible hand" in the development of the algorithm. They were afraid that the NSA had modified the algorithm to install a trap door. They complained that the NSA reduced the key size from Lucifer's original 112-bits to 56-bits (see Section 11.1). They complained about the inner workings of the algorithm. The reasoning behind much of this became clear in the early 1990s, but in the 1970s it seemed mysterious and worrisome.

In 1976, the NBS held two workshops to evaluate the proposed standard. The first workshop discussed the mathematics of the algorithm and the possibility of a trap door [633]. The second workshop discussed the possibility of increasing the algorithm's key length [137]. The algorithm's designers, evaluators, implementors, vendors, users, and critics were invited. From all reports, the workshops were lively.

Nevertheless, the Data Encryption Standard was adopted as a federal standard on November 23, 1976 [137] and authorized for use on all unclassified government communications. The official description of the standard, FIPS PUB 46, "Data Encryption Standard" [634], was published on January 15, 1977. FIPS PUB 81, "DES Modes of Operation," was published in 1980 [637]. FIPS PUB 74, "Guidelines for Implementing and Using the NBS Data Encryption Standard," was published in 1981 [636]. NBS also published FIPS PUB 112, specifying DES for password encryption [638], and FIPS PUB 113, specifying DES for computer data authentication [639].

Adoption of the Standard

The American National Standards Institute (ANSI) approved DES as a private-sector standard (ANSI X3.92) [25]. They called it the Data Encryption Algorithm (DEA). ANSI published a standard for DEA modes of operation (ANSI X3.106) [27], which mirrored the NBS document, and a standard for network encryption that uses DES (ANSI X3.105) [26].

Two other groups within ANSI, representing retail and wholesale banking, developed DES-based standards. Retail banking involves transactions among financial institutions and private individuals, and wholesale banking involves transactions among financial institutions and corporate customers.

ANSI's Financial Institution Retail Security Working Group developed a standard for the management and security of PINs (ANSI X9.8) [28] and another DES-based standard for the authentication of retail financial messages (ANSI X9.19) [31]. The group has a draft standard for secure key distribution (ANSI X9.24) [33].

ANSI's Financial Institution Wholesale Security Working Group developed its own set of standards for message authentication (ANSI X9.9) [29], key management (ANSI X9.17) [30], encryption (ANSI X9.23) [32], and secure personal and node authentication (ANSI X9.26) [34].

The American Bankers Association develops voluntary standards for the financial industry. They published a standard recommending the use of DES whenever encryption is required [1] and another for the management of cryptographic keys [2].

Before the Computer Security Act of 1987, the General Services Administration (GSA) had the responsibility for the development of federal telecommunications standards. Since the Computer Security Act, that responsibility transferred to NIST. The GSA published three standards that used DES: two for general security and interoperability requirements (Federal Standard 1026 [394] and Federal

Standard 1027 [395]), and one for Group 3 facsimile equipment (Federal Standard 1028) [396].

The Department of the Treasury wrote a policy directive requiring that all electronic-funds transfer messages be authenticated with DES [276,278]. They also wrote DES-based criteria that all authentication devices must meet [277].

The International Organization for Standardization (ISO) first voted to approve DES (renamed DEA-1) as an international standard, then decided not to play a role in the standardization of cryptography. However, the International Wholesale Financial Standards group of ISO used DES in an international authentication standard [444] and for key management [445].

Validation and Certification of DES Equipment

As part of the standard, the DES NIST validates hardware and firmware implementations of DES. This validation confirms that the implementation follows the standard. No software implementations have been validated; according to the standard the algorithm may not be implemented in software. Even so, there are at least two validated DES implementations in general-purpose microprocessors; sometimes it's hard to draw the line between hardware and software. As of May 7, 1991, 45 different implementations have been validated, and approximately three new implementations are validated each year [836].

Federal Standard 1027 contains additional requirements, beyond those in FIPS 46, FIPS 74, and FIPS 81. To satisfy the standard, the DES hardware must be placed in an enclosure with physical access controls, including locks and alarms, and the equipment must be designed in such a way that failures cannot compromise sensitive data. The NSA certifies that equipment meets the requirements of Federal Standard 1027. As of 1991, at least 32 products met the standard [836].

For authentication, NIST developed a program to certify that equipment conformed to ANSI X9.9 and FIPS 113. As of May 7, 1991, 29 products have been validated. The Department of the Treasury has an additional certification procedure. NIST is currently developing a program to validate that equipment conforms to ANSI X9.17 for wholesale key management.

1987

The terms of the standard stipulate that it be reviewed every five years. In the March 6, 1987 *Federal Register,* NBS published a request for comments on the second five-year review. NBS offered three alternatives for consideration [835,836]: reaffirm the standard for another three years, withdraw the standard, or revise the applicability of the standard.

NBS and NSA reviewed the standard. NSA was more involved this time. Because of an executive directive, signed by Ronald Reagan, called NSDD-145, NSA had veto power over the NBS in matters of cryptography. Initially, the NSA announced that it would not recertify the standard. The problem was not that DES had been broken, or even that it was suspected of having being broken. It was simply increasingly likely that it would soon be broken.

In its place, the NSA proposed the Commercial COMSEC Endorsement Program (CCEP), which would eventually provide a series of algorithms to replace DES [44]. These NSA-designed algorithms would not be made public (a protective coating on the VLSI chips would prevent reverse-engineering).

This announcement wasn't very well received. Many people pointed out that business (especially the financial industry) uses DES extensively, and that no adequate alternative is available. Withdrawal of the standard would leave many organizations with no protection for their data. After much debate, DES was reaffirmed as a U.S. government standard until 1992 [635]. According to the NBS, DES would not be certified again [835].

1992

Never say "not." In 1992, there was still no alternative for DES. The NBS, now called NIST, again solicited comments on DES in the *Federal Register* [331]:

> The purpose of this notice is to announce the review to assess the continued adequacy of the standard to protect computer data. Comments from industry and the public are invited on the following alternatives for FIPS 46-1. The costs (impacts) and benefits of these alternatives should be included in the comments:
>
> > —Reaffirm the standard for another five (5) years. The National Institute of Standards and Technology would continue to validate equipment that implements the standard. FIPS 46-1 would continue to be the only approved method for protecting unclassified computer data.
> > —Withdraw the standard. The National Institute of Standards and Technology would no longer continue to support the standard. Organizations could continue to utilize existing equipment that implements the standard. Other standards could be issued by NIST as a replacement for the DES.
> > —Revise the applicability and/or implementation statements for the standard. Such revisions could include changing the standard to allow the use of implementations of the DES in software as well as hardware; to allow the iterative use of the DES in specific applications; to allow the use of alternative algorithms that are approved and registered by NIST.

The comment period closed on December 10, 1992. Even though the Office of Technology Assessment quoted Dennis Branstead as saying that the useful lifetime of DES would end in the late 1990s [661], the algorithm was recertified. According to a statement by the acting director of NIST [472]:

> Last year, NIST formally solicited comments on the recertification of DES. After reviewing those comments, and the other technical inputs that I have received, I plan to recommend to the Secretary of Commerce that he recertify DES for another five years. I also plan to suggest to the Secretary that when we announce the recertification we state our intention to consider alternatives to it over the next five years. By putting that announcement on the table, we hope to give people an opportunity to comment on orderly technological

transitions. In the meantime, we need to consider the large installed base of systems that rely upon this proven standard.

Overview of the Algorithm

DES is a block cipher; it encrypts data in 64-bit blocks. A 64-bit block of plaintext goes in one end of the algorithm, and a 64-bit block of ciphertext comes out the other end. Both encryption and decryption use the same algorithm (except for differences in the key schedule).

The key length is 56 bits. (The key is usually expressed as a 64-bit number, but every eighth bit is used for parity checking and is ignored.) The key can be any 56-bit number and can be changed at any time. A handful of numbers are considered weak keys, but they can easily be avoided. All security rests within the key.

At its simplest level, the algorithm is nothing more than a combination of the two basic techniques of encryption: confusion and diffusion. The fundamental building block of DES is a single combination of these techniques (a substitution followed by a permutation) on the text, based on the key. This is known as a **round.** DES has 16 rounds; it applies the same combination of techniques on the plaintext block 16 times (see Figure 10.1).

The algorithm uses only standard arithmetic and logical operations on numbers of at most 64 bits, so it was easily implemented in late 1970s hardware technology. Initial software implementations were clumsy, but current implementations are somewhat better; and the repetitive nature of the algorithm makes it ideal for use on a special-purpose chip.

Outline of the Algorithm

DES operates on a 64-bit block of plaintext. After an initial permutation, the block is broken into a right half and a left half, each 32 bits long. Then there are 16 rounds of identical operations, called Function f, in which the data is combined with the key. After the sixteenth round, the right and left halves are joined, and a final permutation (the inverse of the initial permutation) finishes off the algorithm.

In each round, the key bits are shifted, and then 48 bits are selected from the 56 key bits. The right half of the data is expanded to 48 bits via an expansion permutation, combined with 48 bits of a shifted and permuted key via an exclusive-or, substituted for 32 new bits using a substitution algorithm, and permuted again. These four operations make up Function f. The output of Function f is then combined with the left half via another exclusive-or. The result of these operations becomes the new left half; the old left half becomes the new right half. These operations are repeated 16 times, making 16 rounds of DES (see Figure 10.2).

If B_i is the result of the ith iteration, L_i and R_i are the left and right halves of B_i, K_i is the 48-bit key for round i, and f is the function that does all the substituting and permuting and XORing with the key, then a round looks like:

$$L_i = R_{i-1}$$
$$R_i = L_{i-1} \text{ XOR } f(R_{i-1}, K_i)$$

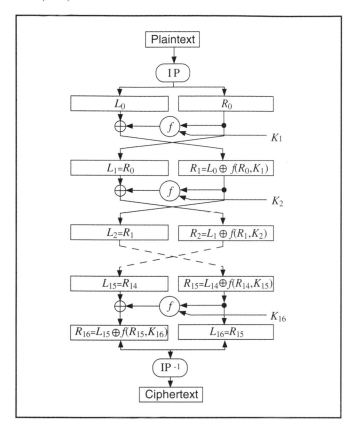

Figure 10.1
DES.

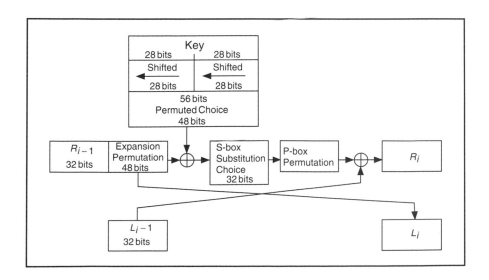

Figure 10.2
One round of DES.

The Initial Permutation

The initial permutation transposes the input block, as described in Table 10.1. This table, as well as the other tables in this chapter, should be read left to right, top to bottom. For example, the initial permutation transposes bit 1 to bit 58, bit 2 to bit 50, bit 3 to bit 42, etc.

TABLE 10.1
Initial Permutation

58	50	42	34	26	18	10	2	60	52	44	36	28	20	12	4
62	54	46	38	30	22	14	6	64	56	48	40	32	24	16	8
57	49	41	33	25	17	9	1	59	51	43	35	27	19	11	3
61	53	45	37	29	21	13	5	63	55	47	39	31	23	15	7

The initial permutation and the corresponding final permutation do not affect DES's security. Since this bit-wise permutation is difficult in software (although it is trivial in hardware), many software implementations of DES leave out both the initial and final permutations. While this new algorithm is no less secure than DES, it does not follow the DES standard and should not be called DES.

The Key Transformation

Initially, the 64-bit DES key is reduced to a 56-bit key by ignoring every eighth bit. This is described in Table 10.2. These bits can be used as parity check to ensure that there were no errors entering the key. After the 56-bit key is extracted, a different 48-bit key is generated for each round of DES. These keys, k_i, are determined in the following manner:

TABLE 10.2
Key Permutation

57	49	41	33	25	17	9	1	58	50	42	34	26	18
10	2	59	51	43	35	27	19	11	3	60	52	44	36
63	55	47	39	31	23	15	7	62	54	46	38	30	22
14	6	61	53	45	37	29	21	13	5	28	20	12	4

First, the 56-bit key is divided into two 28-bit halves. Then, the halves are shifted left by either one or two digits, depending on the round. The number of bits shifted is given in Table 10.3.

TABLE 10.3
Key Shifts Per Round

ROUND	1	2	3	4	5	6	7	8	9	10	11	12	13	14	15	16
# OF SHIFTS	1	1	2	2	2	2	2	2	1	2	2	2	2	2	2	1

After being shifted, 48 out of the 56 bits are selected. Because this operation permutes the order of the bits as well as selecting a subset of bits, it is called a **compression permutation,** or the **permuted choice.** This operation provides a subset of bits the same size as the output of the expansion permutation. Table 10.4 defines the compression permutation (also called the permuted choice). For example, the bit in position 33 of the shifted key moves to position 35 of the output, and the bit in position 18 of the shifted key is ignored.

TABLE 10.4
Compression Permutation

14	17	11	24	1	5	3	28	15	6	21	10
23	19	12	4	26	8	16	7	27	20	13	2
41	52	31	37	47	55	30	40	51	45	33	48
44	49	39	56	34	53	46	42	50	36	29	32

The Expansion Permutation

In this operation the right half of the data, R_i, is expanded from 32 bits to 48 bits. Because this operation changes the order of the bits as well as repeating certain bits, it is known as an **expansion permutation.** This operation has two purposes: it makes the result the same size as the key for the XOR operation, and it provides a longer result that can be compressed during the substitution operation.

Neither of those is its main cryptographic purpose, though. By allowing one bit to affect two substitutions, the dependency of the output bits on the input bits spreads faster. This is called **avalanche criteria.** Much of DES's design revolves around reaching as quickly as possible the condition of having every bit of the ciphertext depend on every bit of the plaintext and every bit of the key.

Figure 10.3 defines the expansion permutation. This is sometimes called the **E-box.** For each 4-bit input block, the first and fourth bits represent 2 bits of the output block, while the second and third bits represent one bit of the output block. The table shows which output positions that correspond to which input positions. For example, the bit in position 3 of the input block moves to position 4 of the output block, and the bit in position 21 of the input block moves to positions 30 and 32 of the output block. This is summarized in Table 10.5.

TABLE 10.5
Expansion Permutation

32	1	2	3	4	5	4	5	6	7	8	9
8	9	10	11	12	13	12	13	14	15	16	17
16	17	18	19	20	21	20	21	22	23	24	25
24	25	26	27	28	29	28	29	30	31	32	1

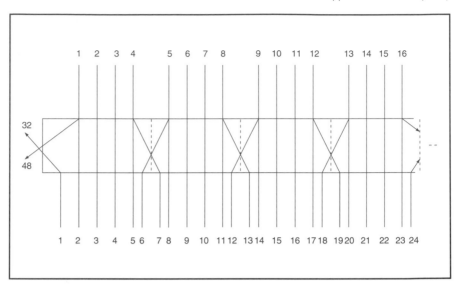

Figure 10.3
Expansion permutation.

Although the output block is larger than the input block, there is only one input block that can generate a specific output block.

The S-Box Substitution

After the compressed key is XORed with the expanded block, the 48-bit result moves to a substitution operation. The substitutions are performed by eight **substitution boxes,** or **S-boxes.** The 48 bits are divided into eight 6-bit blocks. Each separate block is operated on by a separate S-box: block 1 is operated on by S-box 1, block 2 is operated on by S-box 2, etc.

Each S-box is a table of 4 rows and 16 columns. Each entry in the box is a 4-bit number. The six input bits of the S-box specify under which row and column number to look for the output. Table 10.6 shows all eight S-boxes.

The input bits specify an entry in the S-box in a very particular manner. Consider an S-box input of 6 bits, labeled b1, b2, b3, b4, b5, and b6. Bits b1 and b6 are combined to form a 2-bit number, from 0 to 3, which corresponds to a row in the table. The middle 4 bits, b2 through b5, are combined to form a 4-bit number, from 0 to 16, which corresponds to a column in the table.

For example, assume that the input to the sixth S-box (that is, bits 31 through 36 of the XOR function) are 110010. The first and last bits combine to form 10, which corresponds to the third row of the sixth S-box. The middle 4 bits combine to form 1001, which corresponds to the ninth column of the same S-box. The entry under row 3, column 9 of S-box 6 is 14. The value 1110 is substituted for 110010.

This is the critical step in the algorithm. All the other operations are linear and easy to analyze. The S-boxes are nonlinear and, more than anything else, they give DES its security.

The result of this substitution phase are eight 4-bit blocks, which are recombined into a single 32-bit block. This block moves to the next step: the P-box permutation.

TABLE 10.6
S-Boxes

S-BOX 1:

14	4	13	1	2	15	11	8	3	10	6	12	5	9	0	7
0	15	7	4	14	2	13	1	10	6	12	11	9	5	3	8
4	1	14	8	13	6	2	11	15	12	9	7	3	10	5	0
15	12	8	2	4	9	1	7	5	11	3	14	10	0	6	13

S-BOX 2:

15	1	8	14	6	11	3	4	9	7	2	13	12	0	5	10
3	13	4	7	15	2	8	14	12	0	1	10	6	9	11	5
0	14	7	11	10	4	13	1	5	8	12	6	9	3	2	15
13	8	10	1	3	15	4	2	11	6	7	12	0	5	14	9

S-BOX 3:

10	0	9	14	6	3	15	5	1	13	12	7	11	4	2	8
13	7	0	9	3	4	6	10	2	8	5	14	12	11	15	1
13	6	4	9	8	15	3	0	11	1	2	12	5	10	14	7
1	10	13	0	6	9	8	7	4	15	14	3	11	5	2	12

S-BOX 4:

7	13	14	3	0	6	9	10	1	2	8	5	11	12	4	15
13	8	11	5	6	15	0	3	4	7	2	12	1	10	14	9
10	6	9	0	12	11	7	13	15	1	3	14	5	2	8	4
3	15	0	6	10	1	13	8	9	4	5	11	12	7	2	14

S-BOX 5:

2	12	4	1	7	10	11	6	8	5	3	15	13	0	14	9
14	11	2	12	4	7	13	1	5	0	15	10	3	9	8	6
4	2	1	11	10	13	7	8	15	9	12	5	6	3	0	14
11	8	12	7	1	14	2	13	6	15	0	9	10	4	5	3

S-BOX 6:

12	1	10	15	9	2	6	8	0	13	3	4	14	7	5	11
10	15	4	2	7	12	9	5	6	1	13	14	0	11	3	8
9	14	15	5	2	8	12	3	7	0	4	10	1	13	11	6
4	3	2	12	9	5	15	10	11	14	1	7	6	0	8	13

S-BOX 7:

4	11	2	14	15	0	8	13	3	12	9	7	5	10	6	1
13	0	11	7	4	9	1	10	14	3	5	12	2	15	8	6
1	4	11	13	12	3	7	14	10	15	6	8	0	5	9	2
6	11	13	8	1	4	10	7	9	5	0	15	14	2	3	12

S-BOX 8:

13	2	8	4	6	15	11	1	10	9	3	14	5	0	12	7
1	15	13	8	10	3	7	4	12	5	6	11	0	14	9	2
7	11	4	1	9	12	14	2	0	6	10	13	15	3	5	8
2	1	14	7	4	10	8	13	15	12	9	0	3	5	6	11

The P-Box Permutation

The 32-bit output of the S-box substitution are permuted according to a P-box. This permutation maps each input bit to an output position; no bits are used twice and no bits are ignored. This is called a **straight permutation,** or just a **permutation.** Table 10.7 shows the position to which each bit moves. For example, bit 4 moves to bit 21, while bit 23 moves to bit 4.

TABLE 10.7
P-Box Permutation

16	7	20	21	29	12	28	17	1	15	23	26	5	18	31	10
2	8	24	14	32	27	3	9	19	13	30	6	22	11	4	25

Finally, the result of the P-box permutation is XORed with the left half of the initial 64-bit block. Then the left and right halves are switched and another round begins.

The Final Permutation

The final permutation is the inverse of the initial permutation, and is described in Table 10.8. Note that the left and right halves are not exchanged after the last round of DES; instead the concatenated block $R_{16}L_{16}$ is used as the input to the final permutation. There's nothing going on here; exchanging the halves and shifting around the permutation would yield exactly the same result; this is so that the algorithm can be used to both encrypt and decrypt.

TABLE 10.8
Final Permutation

40	8	48	16	56	24	64	32	39	7	47	15	55	23	63	31
38	6	46	14	54	22	62	30	37	5	45	13	53	21	61	29
36	4	44	12	52	20	60	28	35	3	43	11	51	19	59	27
34	2	42	10	50	18	58	26	33	1	41	9	49	17	57	25

Decrypting DES

After all the substitutions, permutations, XORs, and shifting around, you might think that the decryption algorithm is completely different and just as confusing as the encryption algorithm. On the contrary, the various operations were chosen to produce a very useful property: the same algorithm works for both encryption and decryption.

With DES it is possible to use the same function to encrypt or decrypt a block. The only difference is that the keys must be used in the reverse order. That is, if the encryption keys for each round are k1, k2, k3, . . . k16, then the decryption keys are k16, k15, k14 . . . k1. The algorithm that generates the key used for each round is circular as well. The key shift is a right shift, and the number of positions shifted is taken from the bottom of the table up, instead of top down.

Modes of DES

FIPS PUB 81 specifies four modes of operation: Electronic Codebook, Cipher Block Chaining, Output Feedback, and Cipher Feedback [637]. The ANSI banking standards specify ECB and CBC for encryption, and CBC and n-bit CFB for authentication [27].

In the software world, certification is a nonissue. Because of its simplicity, Electronic Codebook is most often used in off-the-shelf commercial software products, although it is the most vulnerable to attack. Cipher Block Chaining is used occasionally, even though it is just slightly more complicated than Electronic Codebook and provides much more security.

Hardware and Software Implementations of DES

Much has been written on efficient hardware and software implementations of the algorithm [561,41,324,325,251,440,866,172]. An excellent article that gives practical advice for speeding up the algorithm in software is [111].

At this writing, the recordholder for the fastest DES chip is a prototype developed at Digital Equipment Corporation [309]. It supports ECB and CBC modes and is based on a GaAs gate array of 50K transistors. Data can be encrypted and decrypted at a rate of 1 GBit/second, which translates to 15.6 million blocks per second. This is impressive.

A software implementation of DES on an IBM 3090 mainframe can perform 32,000 DES encryptions per second. Microcomputers are slower, but impressive nonetheless. Table 10.9 [367,461] gives actual results and estimates for various Intel and Motorola microprocessors.

TABLE 10.9

DES Speeds on Different Microprocessors

PROCESSOR	SPEED (in Mhz)	BUS WIDTH (in bits)	DES BLOCKS (per second)
8088	4.7	8	370
68000	7.6	16	900
80286	6.0	16	1,100
68020	16.0	32	3,500
68030	16.0	32	3,900
80286	25.0	16	5,000
68030	50.0	32	9,600
68040	25.0	32	16,000
68040	40.0	32	23,200
80486	33.0	32	40,600†

†This software is written in C and assembler, and can be purchased from Utimaco-Belgium, Interleuvenlaan 62A, B-3001 Leuven, Belgium. Code size is approximately 64K. ANSI C implementation is about 20% slower.

Security of DES

People have long questioned the security of DES. There has been much speculation on the key length, number of iterations, and design of the S-boxes. The S-boxes were particularly mysterious—all those constants, without any apparent reason as to why they're that way. Some people feared that the NSA embedded a "trap door" into the algorithm, so they would have an easy means of decrypting messages.

The U.S. Senate Select Committee on Intelligence, with full top-secret clearances, investigated the matter in 1978. The findings of the committee are classified, but an unclassified summary of those findings exonerated the NSA from any improper involvement in the algorithm's design. "It was said to have convinced IBM that a shorter key was adequate, to have indirectly assisted in the development of the S-box structures and to have certified that the final DES algorithm was, to the best of their knowledge, free of any statistical or mathematical weaknesses" [249]. However, since the government never made the details of the investigation public, many people remained unconvinced.

Tuchman and Meyer, two of the IBM cryptographers who designed DES, said the NSA did not alter the design [481]:

> Their basic approach was to look for strong substitution, permutation, and key scheduling functions. . . . IBM has classified the notes containing the selection criteria at the request of the NSA. . . . "The NSA told us we had inadvertently reinvented some of the deep secrets it uses to make its own algorithms," explains Tuchman.

Later in the article, Tuchman is quoted: "We developed the DES algorithm entirely within IBM using IBMers. The NSA did not dictate a single wire!" Tuchman reaffirmed this when he spoke on the history of DES at the 1992 National Computer Security Conference.

NSA, when questioned regarding any imposed weakness in DES, said [218]:

> Regarding the Data Encryption Standard (DES), we believe that the public record from the Senate Committee for Intelligence's investigation in 1978 into NSA's role in the development of the DES is responsive to your question. That committee report indicated that NSA did not tamper with the design of the algorithm in any way and that the security afforded by the DES was more than adequate for at least a 5–10 year time span for the unclassified data for which it was intended. In short, NSA did not impose or attempt to impose any weakness on the DES.

Very recently some new cryptanalysis results have shed some light on this issue, but for many years they have been the subject of much speculation.

Weak Keys

Because of the way the initial key is modified to get a subkey for each round of the algorithm, certain initial keys are **weak keys** [429,243]. Remember that the initial value is split into two halves, and each half is shifted independently. If all the bits in each half are either 0 or 1, then the key used for any cycle of the algorithm is the same for all the cycles of the algorithm. This can occur if the key is entirely 1's, entirely 0's, or if one half of the key is entirely 1's and the other half is entirely 0's. Also, two of the weak keys have other properties that make them less secure [243].

The four weak keys are shown in hexadecimal notation in Table 10.10. (Remember that every eighth bit is a parity bit, and that the initial permutation scrambles the key order slightly.)

TABLE 10.10
DES Weak Keys

WEAK KEY VALUE	ACTUAL KEY
0101 0101 0101 0101	0000000 0000000
FEFE FEFE FEFE FEFE	FFFFFFF FFFFFFF
1F1F 1F1F 1F1F 1F1F	0000000 FFFFFFF
E0E0 E0E0 E0E0 E0E0	FFFFFFF 0000000

Additionally, there are pairs of keys that encrypt plaintext to the identical ciphertext. In other words, one key in the pair can decrypt messages encrypted with the other key in the pair. This is also due to the way in which DES generates subkeys; instead of generating 16 different subkeys, these keys generate only two different subkeys. Each of these subkeys is used eight times in the algorithm. These keys are called **semi-weak keys,** and are shown in hexadecimal notation in Table 10.11.

TABLE 10.11
DES Semi-Weak Keys

01FE	01FE	01FE	01FE
1FE0	1FE0	0EF1	0EF1
01E0	01E0	01F1	01F1
1FFE	1FFE	0EFE	0EFE
011F	011F	010E	010E
E0FE	E0FE	F1FE	F1FE
FE01	FE01	FE01	FE01
E01F	E01F	F10E	F10E
E001	E001	F101	F101
FE1F	FE1F	FE0E	FE0E
1F01	1F01	0E01	0E01
FEE0	FEE0	FEF1	FEF1

There are also keys that produce only four subkeys, each used four times in the algorithm. These keys are listed in Table 10.12.

Before condemning DES for having weak keys, consider that this list of 64 keys is miniscule compared to the total set of 72,057,594,037,927,936 possible keys. If you select keys randomly, the odds of picking one of these weak keys is negligible. If you were truly paranoid, you could always check for weak keys during key generation. Some people don't think it's worth the bother. Others say that it's so easy to check, there's no reason not to.

There is further analysis on weak and semi-weak keys in [620], and additional key patterns have been investigated for weaknesses. None have been found.

Complement Keys

Take the bit-wise complement of a key; that is, replace all the 0's with 1's and the 1's with 0's. Now, if the original key encrypts a block of plaintext, then the complement of the key will encrypt the complement of the plaintext block into the complement of the ciphertext block.

If x' is the complement of x, then the identity is as follows:

$$E_K(P) = C$$
$$E_{K'}(P') = C'$$

What this means is that a chosen-plaintext attack against DES only has to test half the possible keys: 2^{55} keys instead of 2^{56} [597]. Biham and Shamir showed [106] that there is a known-plaintext attack of the same complexity, with at least 2^{33} known-plaintexts.

It is questionable whether this is a weakness or not, since most messages don't have complement blocks of plaintext (in random plaintext, the odds against it are quite high) and users can be warned not to use complement keys.

Is DES a Group?

The number of different ways of mapping all possible 64-bit plaintext blocks onto all possible 64-bit ciphertext blocks is 2^{64}!. The DES algorithm, with its 56-bit key, gives us 2^{56} (10^{16}) of these mappings. Using multiple encryption, it seems possible to reach a larger portion of those possible mappings. However, this is only true if the DES operation is not a group.

To give an analogy, addition over the integers is a group. Adding two integers together always results in another integer. Multiplication and division over the integers are not a group. Multiplying two integers together always results in another integer, but dividing two integers sometimes results in a fraction.

If DES were a group, then cryptanalysis would be easier. Multiple encryption would be useless: there would always be a K_3 such that $E_{K_2}(E_{K_1}(P)) = E_{K_3}(P)$. In other words, encrypting a set of plaintext blocks with K_1 followed by K_2 would be identical to encrypting the blocks with K_3. Even worse, DES would be vulnerable to a meet-in-the-middle plaintext attack that runs in only 2^{28} steps, far fewer than the 2^{56} steps required for exhaustive search [470].

TABLE 10.12
DES Possibly Weak Keys

1F	1F	01	01	0E	0E	01	01	E0	01	01	E0	F1	01	01	F1
01	1F	1F	01	01	0E	0E	01	FE	1F	01	E0	FE	0E	01	F1
1F	01	01	1F	0E	01	01	0E	FE	01	1F	E0	FE	01	0E	F1
01	01	1F	1F	01	01	0E	0E	E0	1F	1F	E0	F1	0E	0E	F1
								FE	01	01	FE	FE	01	01	FE
E0	E0	01	01	F1	F1	01	01	E0	1F	01	FE	F1	0E	01	FE
FE	FE	01	01	FE	FE	01	01	E0	01	1F	FE	F1	01	0E	FE
FE	E0	1F	01	FE	F1	0E	01	FE	1F	1F	FE	FE	0E	0E	FE
E0	FE	1F	01	F1	FE	0E	01								
FE	E0	01	1F	FE	F1	01	0E	1F	FE	01	E0	0E	FE	01	F1
E0	FE	01	1F	F1	FE	01	0E	01	FE	1F	E0	01	FE	0E	F1
E0	E0	1F	1F	F1	F1	0E	0E	1F	E0	01	FE	0E	F1	01	FE
FE	FE	1F	1F	FE	FE	0E	0E	01	E0	1F	FE	01	F1	0E	FE
FE	1F	E0	01	FE	0E	F1	01	01	01	E0	E0	01	01	F1	F1
E0	1F	FE	01	F1	0E	FE	01	1F	1F	E0	E0	0E	0E	F1	F1
FE	01	E0	1F	FE	01	F1	0E	1F	01	FE	E0	0E	01	FE	F1
E0	01	FE	1F	F1	01	FE	0E	01	1F	FE	E0	01	0E	FE	F1
								1F	01	E0	FE	0E	01	F1	FE
01	E0	E0	01	01	F1	F1	01	01	1F	E0	FE	01	0E	F1	FE
1F	FE	E0	01	0E	FE	F0	01	01	01	FE	FE	01	01	FE	FE
1F	E0	FE	01	0E	F1	FE	01	1F	1F	FE	FE	0E	0E	FE	FE
01	FE	FE	01	01	FE	FE	01								
1F	E0	E0	1F	0E	F1	F1	0E	FE	FE	E0	E0	FE	FE	F1	F1
01	FE	E0	1F	01	FE	F1	0E	E0	FE	FE	E0	F1	FE	FE	F1
01	E0	FE	1F	01	F1	FE	0E	FE	E0	E0	FE	FE	F1	F1	FE
1F	FE	FE	1F	0E	FE	FE	0E	E0	E0	FE	FE	F1	F1	FE	FE

Various mathematicians have wrestled with this question [225,361,243, 245,431,459,470,471,620,472]. These experiments gathered "overwhelming evidence" that DES is not a group, but it wasn't until 1992 that cryptographers proved that DES is not a group [184].

Length of the Key

When IBM first designed Lucifer, it had a 128-bit key. By the time the DES became a standard, that was reduced to a 56-bit key. Many cryptographers argued for the longer key. Their arguments centered on the possibility of a brute-force attack (see Section 7.1).

In 1979, Diffie and Hellman argued that a special-purpose DES-cracking parallel computer could recover the key in a day and cost $20 million—in 1977 dollars. In 1981, Diffie increased this to a two-day search time and a cost of $50 million [294]. Diffie and Hellman argued then that this was out of reach for everybody except organizations like the NSA, but that by 1990 DES would be totally insecure [421].

Hellman [423] presented another argument against the small key size: by trading memory space for time it would be possible to speed up the searching process. He suggested the possibility of computing and storing 2^{56} possible results of encrypting a single plaintext block under every possible key. Then, to break an unknown key, all that would be required would be for the cryptanalyst to insert the plaintext block into the encryption stream, recover the resulting ciphertext, and look the key up. Hellman pegged the cost of this cracking machine at $5 million.

Arguments for and against the existence of a DES cracker lurking in some government basement somewhere have continued. Several people pointed out that the mean time between failures for the DES chips would never be low enough to ensure that the machine would work. This objection was shown to be superfluous in [718]. Others suggested ways to speed the process even further and to reduce the effects of chip failures.

Meanwhile, hardware implementations of DES slowly approached the million-encryptions-per-second requirement of Diffie and Hellman's special-purpose machine. In 1984 DES chips capable of performing 256,000 encryptions per second had been produced [324,325]. By 1987 chips performing 512,000 encryptions per second were being developed, and a version capable of checking over a million keys per second was feasible [440,866].

At this time, no one has admitted building a DES-cracker, although there is one good theoretical argument for its existence. At a recent conference, Martin Hellman had this to say about the possibility of a brute-force cracking machine [425]:

> Even though the cost of a machine to do brute force search of DES has fallen to less than $10M (including design costs), and replicas can be built for under $1M, I doubt that any commercial entity has built one or will do so in the near future. That much money would require high level collusion among a number of people, and since no company can officially support such spying, that would be hard to do. Also, once you've built the machine, you still have to tap into the communication channels of interest.

The situation is very different with NSA and its foreign equivalents, particularly the French Direction Generale de la Securite Exterieure (DGSE), which has openly boasted of using commercial intelligence to help French companies win bidding wars for large contracts. They are legally encouraged to spy, have large budgets, and routinely intercept vast amounts of data.

Whether they have built a brute force machine or something cleverer, I don't know. But I would be surprised if they did not have some kind of special purpose machine for breaking DES.

In the 1980s, the East German company Robotron fabricated hundreds of thousands of DES chips for the Soviet Union (they claimed it was for encryptor chips in IBM-PC XT clones). This implies one of two things: the Soviet Union used these chips to build a DES cracker, or the Soviet Union used DES to encrypt its own communications—which means the NSA built one.

It was not until 1990 that two Israeli mathematicians, Biham and Shamir, discovered **differential cryptanalysis,** a technique that put to rest the question of key length. Before we discuss that technique, let's turn to some other design criticisms of DES.

Number of Iterations

Why 16 rounds? Why not 32? Alan Konheim showed that after eight iterations, the ciphertext was essentially a random function of every plaintext bit and every key bit [500]. Why doesn't the algorithm stop after eight rounds?

Over the years, there have been successful attacks against variants of DES with a reduced number of rounds. DES with three or four rounds was easily broken in 1982 [242]. DES with six rounds fell some years later [203]. It was Biham and Shamir's differential cryptanalysis that explained this as well; DES with any number of rounds fewer than 16 could be broken with a known-plaintext attack more efficiently than by brute force.

Design of the S-Boxes

In addition to being accused of reducing the key length, NSA was also accused of modifying the contents of the S-boxes. When pressed for design justification for the S-boxes, the NSA indicated that elements of the algorithm's design were "sensitive" and would not be made public. Many cryptographers were concerned that the NSA designed the S-boxes to hide a trap door, making it possible for only them to cryptanalyze the algorithm.

Since then, considerable effort has gone into analyzing the design and operation of the S-boxes. In the mid-1970s, Lexar Corporation [544] and Bell Laboratories [622] examined the operation of the S-boxes. Neither analysis revealed any weaknesses, although the Bell Laboratories team said that the S-boxes may have hidden trap doors.

At the second workshop on DES, the National Security Agency revealed several design criteria behind the S-boxes [137]:

> No S-box is a linear affine function of its input. In other words, there is no system of linear equations that can express the four output bits in terms of the six input bits.

Changing one bit in the input of an S-box results in changing at least two output bits. That is, the S-boxes were designed to maximize the amount of diffusion.

The S-boxes were chosen to minimize the difference between the number of 1s and 0s when any single input bit is held constant. That is, if you hold a single bit constant and change the other five bits, the output should not have a disproportionally large number of 1s or 0s.

This didn't quell people's suspicions at all, and the debate continued [136,239, 421,849,857].

Since then, there have been many additional attempts to examine the design of the S-boxes. While those results are interesting, it is no easier to break the algorithm [796,167]. The fourth S-box, S4, has some interesting properties [250,252]: the last three output bits can be derived in the same way as the first by complementing some of the input bits. Two different, but carefully chosen, inputs to S-boxes can produce the same output [250]. It is possible to obtain the same output of a single DES cycle by changing bits in only three neighboring S-boxes [290].

As in choosing the key length, another of NSA's design criteria was based on making the algorithm resistant to differential cryptanalysis, but no one knew that yet.

Additional Results

Results of other attempts to cryptanalyze DES have been published. Feldman looked at nonrandomness based on spectral tests [344,345]. Some cryptographers have looked at sequences of linear factors in DES [731,203,323].

Differential Cryptanalysis

In 1990, Eli Biham and Adi Shamir introduced the notion of differential cryptanalysis. This was a new method of cryptanalysis, heretofore unknown to the public. Using this method, Biham and Shamir found a chosen-plaintext attack against DES that was more efficient than brute force.

Differential cryptanalysis looks at pairs of plaintexts and pairs of ciphertexts. Specifically, the attack examines **ciphertext pairs:** pairs of ciphertexts whose plaintexts have particular differences. The two plaintexts can be chosen at random, as long as they satisfy particular difference conditions, and the cryptanalyst does not have to know their values.

Certain differences in plaintext pairs have a high probability of reappearing in the resulting ciphertext pairs. These are called **characteristics.** For example, if the difference between two plaintext pairs in hexadecimal is 0080 8200 6000 0000, then (ignoring DES's initial permutation) after three rounds there is a $(1/16)^2$, or about 5%, probability that the difference between the resulting two ciphertext pairs will still be 0080 8200 6000 0000 (see Figure 10.4). Biham and Shamir found many similar characteristics.

Differential cryptanalysis uses these characteristics to assign probabilities to the possible keys and eventually to locate the most probable key. It's a statistical attack and can fail in specific rare instances.

This attack works against DES and other similar algorithms with constant S-boxes. The attack is heavily dependent on the structure of the S-boxes; the ones in DES just happen to be optimized against differential cryptanalysis. The mathematical details of the attack are beyond the scope of this book but can be found in [101,102,105,106].

The results are most interesting. Table 10.13 is a summary of the attack against DES with various numbers of rounds [297].

TABLE 10.13
Differential Cryptanalysis Attacks Against DES

NO. OF ROUNDS	CHOSEN-PLAINTEXTS	KNOWN-PLAINTEXTS	ANALYZED PLAINTEXTS	COMPLEXITY OF ANALYSIS
8	2^{14}	2^{38}	4	2^{9}
9	2^{24}	2^{44}	2	2^{32}†
10	2^{24}	2^{43}	2^{14}	2^{15}
11	2^{31}	2^{47}	2	2^{32}†·
12	2^{31}	2^{47}	2^{21}	2^{21}
13	2^{39}	2^{52}	2	2^{32}†
14	2^{39}	2^{51}	2^{29}	2^{29}
15	2^{47}	2^{56}	2^{7}	2^{37}
16	2^{47}	2^{55}	2^{36}	2^{37}

†The complexity of the analysis can be greatly reduced for these variants by using about four times as many plaintexts with the clique method.

The known-plaintext works against DES in any of its operating modes—ECB, CBC, CFB, and OFB—with the same complexity [106].

DES can be improved by increasing the number of iterations. Differential cryptanalysis (chosen-plaintext) against DES with 17 or 18 rounds takes about the

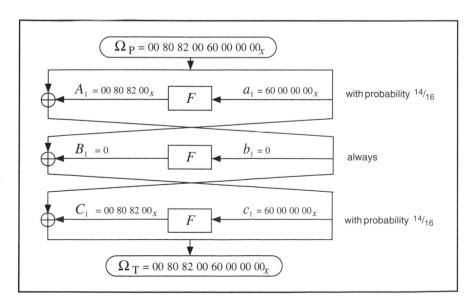

Figure 10.4
A three-round characteristic of DES with probability of 0.05.

same time as exhaustive search. At 19 rounds, exhaustive search is easier than differential cryptanalysis [107].

There are a few things to note. First, this attack is largely theoretical. The enormous time and data requirements to mount a differential cryptanalytic attack put it out of the reach of almost everyone. To get the requisite data for this attack, you have to encrypt a 1.5 Mbits/second data stream of *chosen-plaintext* for almost three years. Second, this is a chosen-plaintext attack. Differential cryptanalysis will also work as a known-plaintext attack, but you have to sift through all of the plaintext-ciphertext pairs looking for the useful ones. For full 16-round DES, this makes the attack slightly less efficient than brute force (the differential cryptanalytic attack requires $2^{55.1}$ operations, and brute force requires 2^{55}). The consensus is that DES, when implemented properly, is still secure against differential cryptanalysis.

Why is DES so resistant to differential cryptanalysis? Why are the S-boxes optimized to make this attack as difficult as possible? Why are there as many rounds as required, but no more? Because the designers knew about it. IBM's Don Coppersmith said, in an internal IBM newsgroup [798]:

> We [the IBM group] knew about differential cryptanalysis in 1974. This is why DES stood up to this line of attack; we designed the S-boxes and the permutation in such as way as to defeat it. We kept quiet about this for all these years because we knew that differential cryptanalysis was such a potent form of cryptanalysis, and we wished to avoid its discovery and use (either for designing or for attacking) on the outside. Now that the techniques are known, we felt it is time to tell our side of the story.

Adi Shamir responded to this, challenging Coppersmith to say that he hadn't found any stronger attacks since then. Coppersmith has chosen to remain silent on that question [798].

Related-Key Cryptanalysis

Table 10.3 shows the number of bits the DES key is rotated after each round: 2 bits after each round, except for 1 bit after rounds 1, 2, 9, and 16. Why?

A modified DES, where the key is rotated two bits after every round, is less secure. Eli Biham developed a related-key cryptanalytic attack that can break that variant using 2^{17} chosen-key chosen plaintexts, or 2^{33} chosen-key known plaintexts [99].

Related-key cryptanalysis examines the difference between different keys, like differential cryptanalysis. The attack is different from any discussed here before: the cryptanalyst chooses a relation between a pair of keys, but does not choose the keys themselves. Data is encrypted with both keys. In the known-plaintext version, the cryptanalyst knows the plaintext and ciphertext of random data encrypted with the key. In the chosen-plaintext version, the cryptanalyst gets to choose the plaintext encrypted with the two keys.

This attack is independent of the number of rounds of the cryptographic algorithm. It's just as effective against this DES variant with 16 rounds, 32 rounds, or 1000 rounds.

This attack is even less practical than differential cryptanalysis. Imagine that cryptanalysts know some properties of the random number generator used to create the DES keys, but not all the properties, and they have a mole inside feeding them the plaintext. Possible, but not very likely. I've heard of some banking systems using keys offset by the date; this could be problematic. In any case, DES is optimized against this attack as well. No one has stated that the algorithm's designers knew about related-key cryptanalysis in the mid-1970s, but I expect they did.

Linear Cryptanalysis

Mitsuru Matsui presented another known-plaintext attack on DES, called linear cryptanalysis [567a]. It can break 8-round DES with 2^{21} known plaintexts, and full 16-round DES with 2^{43} plaintexts. This is the most effective attack against DES at the time of writing.

10.2 DES VARIANTS

Multiple DES

Some DES implementations use triple-DES (see Figure 10.5). Since DES is not a group, then the resultant ciphertext is much harder to break using exhaustive search: 2^{112} attempts instead of 2^{56} attempts (see Section 8.2).

DES with Independent Subkeys

Another variation is to use a different subkey for each round, instead of generating them from a single 56-bit key [485]. Since 48 key bits are required for each of 16 rounds, this means that the key length for this variant is 768 bits. This variant would drastically increase the complexity of DES.

Biham and Shamir showed [101,106] that this variant can be broken with 2^{61} chosen plaintexts, instead of the 2^{768} required for a brute-force attack (see Table 10.14). It would seem that any modification of the key schedule cannot make DES much stronger.

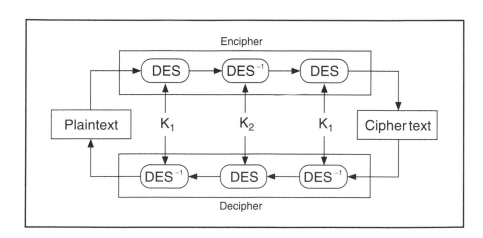

Figure 10.5
Triple DES.

DES with Alternate S-Boxes

Other DES modifications centered around the S-boxes. Some designs made the order of the S-boxes variable and dependent on the key. Other designers made the contents of the S-boxes themselves variable. Biham and Shamir showed [104,106] that the design of the S-boxes, and even the order of the S-boxes themselves, were optimized against differential cryptanalysis (see Table 10.14):

> The replacement of the order of the eight DES S-boxes (without changing their value) also makes DES much weaker: DES with 16 rounds of a particular replaced order is breakable in about 2^{38} steps. . . . DES with random S-boxes is shown to be very easy to break. Even a minimal change of one DES S-box entry can make DES easier to break.

In any case, no one has been able to show that there are no better S-boxes with respect to all known attacks.

TABLE 10.14
Differential Cryptanalysis Attacks Against DES Variants

MODIFIED OPERATION	CHOSEN PLAINTEXTS
Full DES (no modification)	2^{47} (dependent key)
P permutation	Cannot strengthen
Identity permutation	2^{19}
Order of S-boxes	2^{38}
XORs by additions	2^{39}, 2^3
S-boxes:	
Random	2^{21}
Random permutations	$2^{44} - 2^{48}$
One entry	2^{33}
Uniform tables	2^{26}
Elimination of the E expansion	2^{26}
Order of E and subkey XOR	2^{44}
GDES (width $q = 8$):	
16 rounds	6, 16
64 rounds	2^{49} (independent key)

DES with Variable S-Boxes

Differential cryptanalysis works only if the analyst knows the composition of the S-boxes. If the S-boxes are variable, dependent on the key, and secret, then differential cryptanalysis will not work.

CRYPT(3)

CRYPT(3) is a DES variant found on UNIX systems. It is primarily used as a one-way function for passwords, but sometimes can also be used for encryption. The variant is DES with a key-dependent S-box and E-box.

Generalized DES

Generalized DES (GDES) was invented both to speed up DES and to strengthen the algorithm [770,771]. The overall block size increases while function f remains constant.

Figure 10.6 is a block diagram of GDES. GDES operates on variable-sized blocks of plaintext. Encryption blocks are divided up into q 32-bit sub-blocks; the exact number depends on the total block size (this was variable in the design, but must be fixed for each implementation). In general, q equals the block size divided by 32.

Function f is calculated once per round on the right-most block. The result is XORed with all the other parts, which are then cyclically rotated to the right. GDES has a variable number of rounds, n. There is a slight modification to the last round, so that the encryption and decryption processes differ only in the order of the subkeys (just like DES). In fact, if $q = 2$ and $n = 16$, this *is* DES.

Biham and Shamir [101,102] showed that, using differential cryptanalysis, GDES with $q = 8$ and $n = 16$ is breakable with only six chosen plaintexts. If independent subkeys are also used, 16 chosen plaintexts are required. GDES with $q = 8$ and $n = 22$ is breakable with 48 chosen plaintexts, and GDES with $q = 8$ and $n = 31$ requires only 500,000 chosen plaintexts to break. Even GDES with $q = 8$ and $n = 64$ is weaker than DES; 2^{49} chosen plaintexts are required to break it. In fact, any GDES scheme that is faster than DES is also less secure (see Table 10.14).

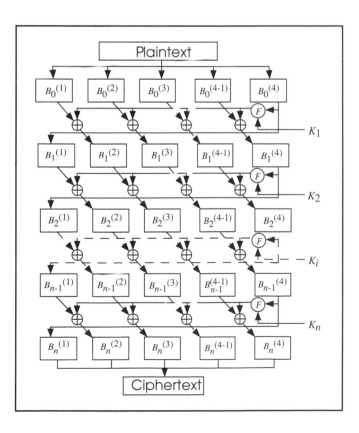

Figure 10.6
Overview of GDES.

CHAPTER
11

Other Block Algorithms

11.1 LUCIFER

Lucifer is a block algorithm designed by IBM in the early 1970s. It is also the name IBM used to denote their project to make a cryptographic algorithm. This has led to more than a little confusion.

In the beginning, the project defined a substitution-permutation network [837,839,339]. The early papers didn't define many of the algorithm's parameters permutations, S-boxes, key schedule, etc., but they gave guidelines. In DES, the output of the function f is XORed with the input of the previous round; this forms the input of the next round. In Lucifer, the input of the S-boxes is the bit-permuted output of the S-boxes of the previous round; the input of the S-boxes of the first round is the plaintext. A key bit is used to choose the actual S-box out of two possible S-boxes. Unlike DES, there is no means of swapping between rounds, and there are no halves of the blocks used.

Later on, they found a better variant [843]. This variant is more similar to DES and has considerable differences with previous variants. This variant is fully specified to have 16 rounds, 128-bit blocks, and fully defined S-boxes and key schedule. An intermediate version of Lucifer was modified to become the DES algorithm.

Using differential cryptanalysis against the first incarnation of Lucifer, Biham and Shamir showed that Lucifer, with 32-bit blocks and eight rounds, can be broken with 40 chosen plaintexts and 2^{29} steps; the same attack can break Lucifer with 128-bit blocks and eight rounds with 60 chosen plaintexts and 2^{53} steps. Another differential cryptanalytic attack broke 18-round, 128-bit Lucifer with 24 chosen plaintexts in 2^{21} steps. All of these attacks used the strong DES S-boxes.

Using differential cryptanalysis against the second incarnation, they found the S-boxes to be much weaker than DES.

Related-key cryptanalysis can break 128-bit Lucifer, with any number of rounds, with 2^{33} chosen-key chosen plaintexts or with 2^{65} chosen-key known plaintexts [99].

Patents

Lucifer is the subject of several U.S. patents: [340,341,342,838]. They have all expired.

11.2 MADRYGA

W. E. Madryga proposed this block algorithm in 1984 [562]. It is efficient for software: there are no irritating permutations, and all the operations work on 8-bit chunks of data (back then, 8 bits is what microprocessors liked).

His design objectives are worth repeating:

1. The plaintext cannot be derived from the ciphertext without use of the key. (This just means that the algorithm is secure.)

2. The number of operations required to determine the key from a sample of plaintext and ciphertext should be equal (statistically) to the product of the operations in an encipherment times the number of possible keys. (This means that there should be no plaintext attack better than brute force.)

3. Knowledge of the algorithm should not defeat the strength of the cipher. (All the security should rest in the key.)

4. A 1-bit change of the key should produce a radical change in the ciphertext using the same plaintext, and a 1-bit change of the plaintext should produce a radical change in the ciphertext using the same key. This is called the **avalanche effect.**

5. The algorithm should contain a noncommutative combination of substitution and permutation.

6. The algorithm should include substitutions and permutations under the control of both the input data and the key.

7. Redundant bit groups in the plaintext should be totally obscured in the ciphertext.

8. The length of the ciphertext should be the same length as the plaintext.

9. There should be no simple relationships between any possible keys and ciphertext effects.

10. Any possible key should produce a strong cipher. (There should be no weak keys.)

11. The length of the key and the text should be adjustable to meet application requirements and security strength requirements.

12. The algorithm should be efficiently implementable on large mainframes, minicomputers, microcomputers, and discrete logic. (In fact, the functions used in the algorithm are limited to XOR and bit-shifting.)

DES had already met objectives one through nine, but the next three were new. Assuming that the best way to break the algorithm was through brute force, a variable-length key would surely silence those who thought 56 bits was too low. They could implement this algorithm with any key length they desired. And, for anyone who has ever attempted to implement DES in software, an algorithm that took software implementations into account would be welcomed.

Description of Madryga

Madryga consists of two nested cycles. The outer cycle is repeated eight times (although this could be increased if security warrants) and consists of an application of the inner cycle to the plaintext. The inner cycle is what transforms plaintext to ciphertext and is repeated once for each 8-bit block (byte) of the plaintext. Thus, the algorithm passes through the entire plaintext eight successive times.

An iteration of the inner cycle operates on a 3-byte window of data, called the working frame (see Figure 11.1). This window advances 1 byte for each iteration. (The data is considered circular when dealing with the last 2 bytes.) The first 2 bytes of the working frame are together rotated a variable number of positions, while the last byte is XORed with some key bits. As the working frame advances, all bytes are successively rotated and XORed with key material. Successive

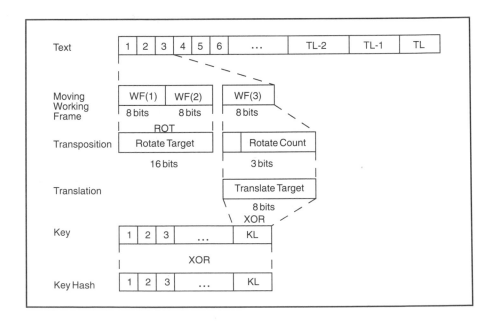

Figure 11.1
One iteration of Madryga.

rotations overlap the results of a previous XOR and rotation, and data from the XOR is used to influence the rotation. This makes the entire process reversible.

Because every byte of data influences the 2 bytes to its left and the 1 byte to its right, after eight passes every byte of the ciphertext is dependent on the 16 bytes to the right and the 8 bytes to the left.

When encrypting, each iteration of the inner cycle starts the working frame at the next-to-last byte of the plaintext and advances circularly through to the third-to-last byte of the plaintext. First, the entire key is XORed with a random constant and then rotated to the left 3 bits. The low-order 3 bits of the low-order byte of the working frame are saved; they will control the rotation of the other 2 bytes. Then, the low-order byte of the working frame is XORed with the low-order byte of the key. Next, the concatenation of the 2 high-order bytes are rotated to the left the variable number of bits (0 to 7). Finally, the working frame is shifted to the right 1 byte and the whole process repeats.

The point of the random constant is to turn whatever the key is into a pseudo-random sequence. The length of this constant must be equal to the length of the key, and must be the same for everyone who wishes to communicate with one another. For a 64-bit key, Madryga recommends the constant 0F1E2D3C4B5A6978 (in Hex).

Decryption is the reverse of this process. Each iteration of the inner cycle starts the working frame at the third-to-last byte of the ciphertext and advances in the reverse direction circularly through to the second-to-last byte of the ciphertext. Both the key and the 2 ciphertext bytes are shifted to the right. And the XOR is done before the rotations.

Cryptanalysis of the Madryga

Researchers at Queensland University of Technology [405] examined Madryga, along with several other block ciphers. They observed that the algorithm didn't exhibit the plaintext-ciphertext avalanche effect. Additionally, there was a higher percentage of 1's than 0's in many of their test ciphertexts.

Although I know of no formal analysis of the algorithm, a cursory review by Eli Biham doesn't bode well for its security [107]. The algorithm consists only of linear operations (rotations and XOR), which are slightly modified depending on the data. There is nothing like the strength of DES's S-boxes. Additionally, the parity of all the bits of the plaintext and the ciphertext is a constant, depending only on the key. So, if you have one plaintext and its corresponding ciphertext, you can predict the parity of the ciphertext for any plaintext.

None of this is damning in itself, but it doesn't leave me with a good feeling about the algorithm. I would stay away from Madryga.

11.3   NEWDES

NewDES was designed in 1985 by Robert Scott as a possible DES replacement [782,219]. It operates on 64-bit blocks of plaintext but has a 120-bit key. It is simpler than DES: there are no initial or final permutations, and all operations are on entire bytes—at no time does the algorithm read, write, or permute any particular bits.

Description of NewDES

The plaintext block is divided into eight byte-length sub-blocks: $B0$, $B1$, . . . , $B6$, $B7$. Then the sub-blocks go through 17 rounds. Each round has eight steps. In each step, one of the sub-blocks is XORed with some key material (there is one exception), substituted with another byte via an f-function, and then XORed with another sub-block to become that sub-block. The key is 120 bits long, divided into 15 key sub-blocks: $K0$, $K1$, . . . , $K13$, $K14$. The process is easier to understand visually than to describe. Figure 11.2 shows the NewDES encryption algorithm.

The f-function is derived from the Declaration of Independence. See [782] for details.

Cryptanalysis of NewDES

Scott showed that every bit of the plaintext block affects every bit of the ciphertext block after only seven rounds. He also analyzed the f-function and found no

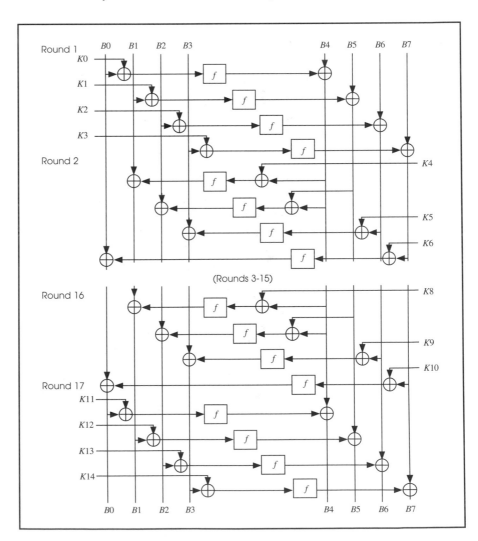

Figure 11.2
NewDES algorithm.

obvious problems. Charles Connell [219] noticed that NewDES has the same complement-key property that DES has: if $E_K(P) = C$, then $E_{K'}(P') = C'$. This reduces the time required for a brute-force attack from 2^{120} steps to 2^{119} steps. Biham noticed that any change of a full byte, applied to all the key bytes and all the data bytes except $B5$, leads to another complementation property [107]. This reduces a brute-force attack further to 2^{112} steps.

This is not damning, but Biham's related-key cryptanalytic attack can break NewDES with 2^{33} chosen-key chosen-plaintexts in 2^{48} steps [107]. While this attack is time-consuming and largely theoretical, it makes NewDES significantly weaker than old DES.

11.4   FEAL-N

FEAL-4 was designed by Akihiro Shimizu and Shoji Miyaguchi from NTT Japan [807]. It uses a 64-bit block and a 64-bit key. The idea was to make an algorithm similar to DES, but one in which each round was stronger than DES. With fewer rounds, the algorithm would run faster.

Description of FEAL

Figure 11.3 is a block diagram of the algorithm. The process starts with a 64-bit block of data (either plaintext or ciphertext). First, the data block is XORed with 64 bits of key material (the question about where the key material comes from will be addressed later). Then, the data block is split into a left half and a right half. The left half is XORed with the right half to form a new right half, and the two

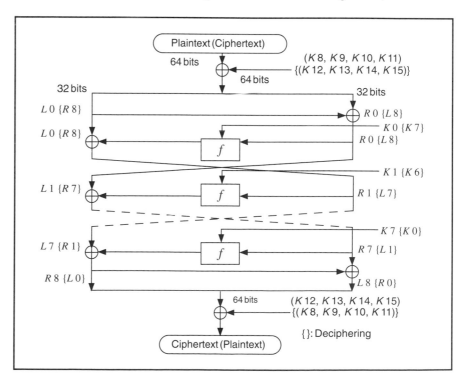

Figure 11.3
One iteration of FEAL.

halves go through N rounds (four, initially). In each round the right half is combined with 16 bits of key material (using Function f) and XORed with the left half to form the new right half. The original right half (before the round) forms the new left half. After N rounds (remember not to switch the left and right halves after the Nth round) the left half is again XORed with the right half to form a new right half, and then the left and right halves are concatenated together to form a 64-bit whole. The data block is XORed with another 64 bits of key material, and the algorithm terminates.

Function f is what takes the 32 bits of data and 16 bits of key material and mixes them together. First the data block is broken up into 8-bit chunks, and then the chunks are XORed and substituted with each other until it pops out the other end. Figure 11.4 is a block diagram of Function f. The two functions S_0 and S_1, are defined as:

$$S_0(a,b) = (\text{rotate left 2 bits } (a+b)) \bmod 256$$
$$S_1(a,b) = (\text{rotate left 2 bits } (a+b+1)) \bmod 256$$

The same algorithm can be used for both encryption and decryption. The only difference is that when decrypting the key material must be used in the reverse order.

Figure 11.5 is a block diagram of the function that generates the key material. First the 64-bit key is divided into two halves. The halves are XORed and operated on by Function f_k, as indicated in the diagram. Figure 11.6 is a block diagram of Function f_k. The two 32-bit inputs are broken up into 8-bit blocks and combined and substituted as shown. S_0 and S_1 are defined as above. The 16-bit key blocks are then used in the encryption/decryption algorithm.

On a 10MHz 80286 microprocessor, an assembly-language implementation of FEAL-32 can encrypt data at a speed of 220 kbps. FEAL-64 can encrypt data at a speed of 120 kbps [610].

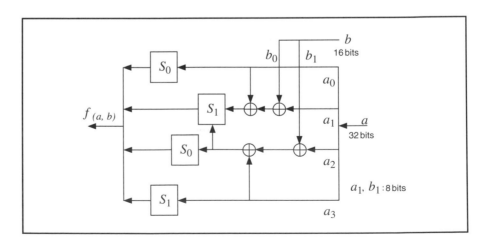

Figure 11.4
Function f.

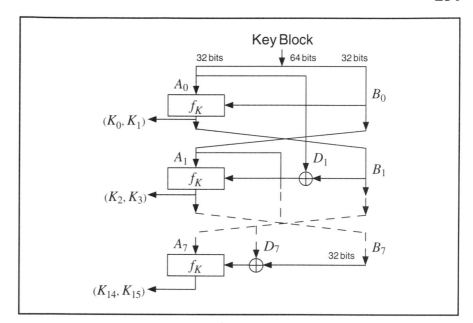

Figure 11.5
Key processing part
of FEAL.

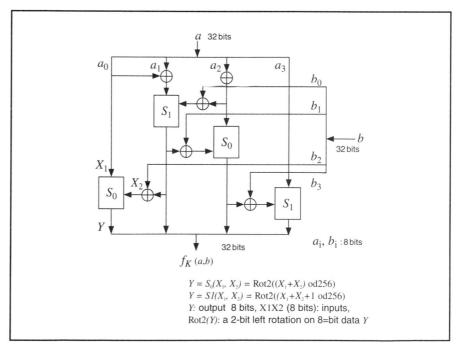

$Y = S_0(X_1, X_2) = \text{Rot2}((X_1+X_2) \text{ od256})$
$Y = S1(X_1, X_2) = \text{Rot2}((X_1+X_2+1 \text{ od256})$
Y: output 8 bits, X1X2 (8 bits): inputs,
$\text{Rot2}(Y)$: a 2-bit left rotation on 8=bit data Y

Figure 11.6
Function f_K.

Cryptanalysis of FEAL

FEAL with four rounds, called FEAL-4, was successfully cryptanalyzed with a chosen-plaintext attack in [264] and later demolished in [630]. The designers retaliated with eight-round FEAL: FEAL-8 [808,809,614]. Biham and Shamir announced a successful chosen-plaintext attack against FEAL-8 at the

SECURICOM '89 conference [797]. Another chosen-plaintext attack, using 10,000 encryptions, against FEAL-8 [370] forced the designers to throw up their hands and define FEAL-N [608,610], with a variable number of rounds (greater than eight, of course).

Biham and Shamir turned their differential cryptanalysis techniques against FEAL-N and found that they could break FEAL-N more quickly than exhaustive search (with fewer than 2^{64} chosen plaintext encryptions) for versions of the algorithm with fewer than 32 rounds [103]. FEAL-16 required 2^{28} chosen-plaintexts or $2^{46.5}$ known-plaintexts to break. FEAL-8 required 2000 chosen-plaintexts or $2^{37.5}$ known-plaintexts to break. FEAL-4 could be broken with just eight carefully selected chosen-plaintexts.

The FEAL designers also defined FEAL-NX, a modification of FEAL, to accept 128-bit keys (see Figure 11.7) [609,610]. Biham and Shamir showed that FEAL-NX with a 128-bit key is just as easy to break as FEAL-N with a 64-bit key, no matter what value N has [103].

An attack against FEAL-4, requiring only 1000 known-plaintexts, and against FEAL-8, requiring only 20,000 known-plaintexts, was published in [852]. The best attack, by Mitsuru Matsui and Atsuhiro Yamagishi [568], can break FEAL-4 with five known-plaintexts, FEAL-6 with 100 known-plaintexts, and FEAL-8 with 2^{15} known-plaintexts. This is a linear cryptanalysis attack.

Patents

FEAL is patented in the United States [810], and patents are pending in England, France, and Germany. Anyone wishing to license the algorithm should contact:

Intellectual Property Department
NTT
1-6 Uchisaiwai-cho, 1-chome, Chiyada-ku
100 Japan

A FEAL program for Maxell IC cards, NEC personal computers, and SUN workstations is available through:

Information Systems Technology Department
NTT Advance Technology Corp.
3-2-4 Miharu-cho, Yokasuka-shi
239 Japan
Tel: +81-468-27-0800
Fax: +81-468-23-3558

11.5   REDOC

REDOC II is another block algorithm, designed by Michael Wood [887,231]. It has a 20-byte (160-bit) key and operates on an 80-bit block.

REDOC II performs all of its manipulations—permutations, substitutions, and key XORs—on bytes, which makes the algorithm efficient in software. REDOC

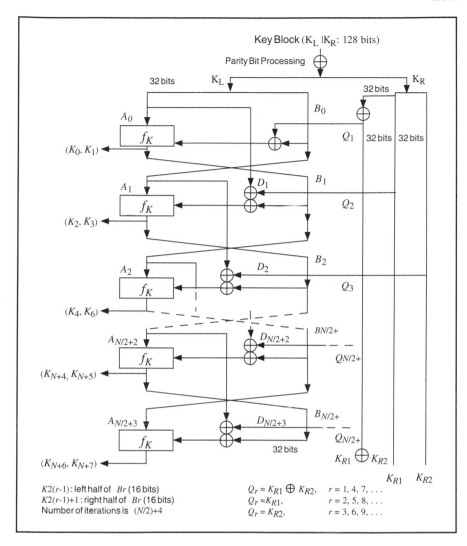

Figure 11.7
HEAL-NX key schedule.

II uses variable-function tables. Unlike DES, which has a fixed (albeit optimized for security) set of permutation and substitution tables, REDOC II uses a key-dependent and plaintext-dependent set of tables.

Another unique feature in the design is the use of MASKs. These are numbers derived from the key table that are used to select the tables in a given function within a given round. Both the value of the data and the MASKs are used together to select the function tables.

Security of REDOC II

Assuming that brute force is the most efficient means of attack, REDOC II is very secure: 2^{160} operations are required to recover the key.

Thomas Cusick cryptanalyzed one round of REDOC II, but he was unable to extend the attack to multiple rounds [231]. Using differential cryptanalysis, Biham and Shamir were able to successfully cryptanalyze one round of REDOC II with 2300 chosen-plaintexts [104]. This attack cannot be extended to multiple rounds. They were also able to obtain three MASK values after four rounds. This attack also cannot be extended.

REDOC III

REDOC III is a streamlined version of REDOC II, also designed by Michael Wood [889]. It operates on a 64-bit block. The key length is variable and can be as large as 2560 bytes (20,480 bits). The algorithm consists solely of XORing key bytes with message bytes; there are no permutations or substitutions.

(1) Create a key table of 256 10-byte keys, using the secret key.

(2) Create two 10-byte MASK blocks. MASK1 is the XOR of the first 128 10-byte keys; MASK2 is the XOR of the second 128 10-byte keys.

(3) To encrypt a 10-byte block:

(a) XOR the first byte of the data block with the first byte of MASK1. Select a key from the key table corresponding to the value obtained in step 1 (between 0 and 255). XOR each byte in the data block with the corresponding byte in the chosen key, except for the first byte.

(b) XOR the second byte of the data block with the second byte of MASK1. Select a key from the key table corresponding to the value obtained in step 1 (between 0 and 255). XOR each byte in the data block with the corresponding byte in the chosen key, except for the second byte.

(c) Continue with the entire block (bytes 3 through 10), until each byte has been used to select a key from the key table after XORing it with the corresponding MASK1 value, and then XOR each byte with the key except for the byte used to select the key.

(d) Repeat steps (a) through (c) with MASK2.

The algorithm is easy and fast. On a 33MHz 80386, the algorithm encrypts data at 2.75 Mbps. Wood estimates that a VLSI-pipelined design, with a 64-bit data path, to be able to encrypt data at over 1.28 Gbps with a 20MHz clock.

Security of REDOC III

REDOC III is still far too new to make any claims about its security. The algorithm is deceptively simple, even though it looks fairly weak.

Patents and Licenses

Both REDOC versions are patented [888]. Foreign patents are pending. Anyone interested in licensing either REDOC II or REDOC III should contact:

Randy Ordines
Cryptech, Inc.
111 West Second St.
Jamestown, NY 14701
Tel: (716) 484-0244

11.6   LOKI

LOKI is Australian and was first presented in 1990 as a potential alternative to DES [174]. It uses a 64-bit block and a 64-bit key.

Description of LOKI

The mechanics of LOKI are similar to DES. First, the data block is XORed with the key. (Unlike DES's initial permutation, this is easy to do in software, and has some cryptographic merit.) The data block is then divided into a left half and a right half and goes through 16 rounds, much like DES. In each round, the right half is first XORed with a piece of the key, then sent through an expansion permutation, an S-box substitution, and a permutation. There are four S-boxes, each of which takes a 12-bit input and produces an 8-bit output. Finally the right half is XORed with the left half to become the new left half, and the left half becomes the new right half. After 16 rounds, the block is again XORed with the key to produce the ciphertext.

The subkeys are generated from the keys in a straightforward manner. First, the 64-bit key is split into a left half and a right half. In each round, the subkey is the left half. This left half is then rotated 12 bits to the left, and then the left and right halves are exchanged. As with DES, the same algorithm can be used for both encryption and decryption, with some modification in how the subkeys are used.

Cryptanalysis of LOKI

The general structure of the algorithm and key schedule was based on [176,175], and the design of the S-boxes was based on [698].

Using differential cryptanalysis, Biham and Shamir were able to break LOKI with eleven rounds or fewer, faster than brute force [104]. Furthermore, there is an 8-bit complementation property, which reduces the complexity of a brute-force attack by a factor of 256 [104,512,513]. So, while LOKI, with 16 rounds or more, is still resistant to differential cryptanalysis, the number of encryptions necessary for a brute-force attack on the 64-bit key is only 2^{56}.

Additional differential cryptanalytic results were presented in [486]. Knudsen showed that LOKI, with 14 rounds or fewer, was vulnerable to differential cryptanalysis. Additionally, if LOKI is implemented with alternate S-boxes, it is probable that the resulting cipher will be vulnerable to differential cryptanalysis.

LOKI91

In response to these attacks, LOKI's designers went back to the drawing board and revised their algorithm. The result is LOKI91 [173]. (The previous version of LOKI was renamed LOKI89.)

To make the algorithm more resistant to differential cryptanalysis and to remove the key-complementation property, the following changes were made to the original design:

- The subkey generation algorithm was changed so that the halves were swapped every second round, not every round.

- The subkey generation algorithm was changed so that the rotation of the left subkey alternated between 12 and 13 bits to the left.

- The initial and final XOR of the block with the key was eliminated.

- The S-box function was altered.

The overall structure of LOKI91 is given in Figure 11.8.

Cryptanalysis of LOKI91

Lars Knudsen attempted to cryptanalyze LOKI91 in [487]. He was not able to use differential cryptanalysis against the revised algorithm. However, he found a chosen-plaintext attack that reduces the complexity of a brute-force search by almost a factor of four. This attack exploits a weakness in the key schedule, and it may also be a weakness if the algorithm is used as a one-way hash function.

Biham's related-key cryptanalysis can break LOKI91 with 2^{32} chosen-key chosen-plaintexts, or 2^{48} chosen-key known-plaintexts [99]. The attack is independent of the number of rounds of the algorithm. (In the same paper, Biham breaks LOKI89 with 2^{17} chosen-plaintexts or 2^{33} known-plaintexts.) It's easy to make LOKI91 resistant to this attack; just avoid the simple key schedule. A new version of LOKI should be available soon.

Patents and Licenses

LOKI is not patented. Anyone can implement the algorithm and use it. The source code implementation in this book is copyrighted by the University of New South Wales. Anyone interested in using this implementation in a commercial product (or their other implementation, which is several orders of magnitude faster), should contact:

Director CITRAD
Department of Computer Science
University College, UNSW
Australian Defense Force Academy
Canberra ACCT 2600
Australia
Fax: +61-6-268-8581

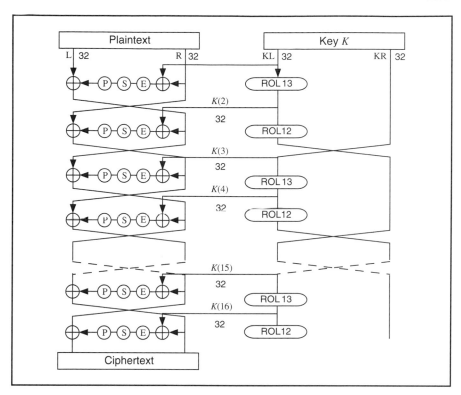

Figure 11.8
Overview of LOKI91.

11.7   KHUFU AND KHAFRE

In 1990, Ralph Merkle recognized that DES was reaching the end of its useful life and proposed a pair of cryptosystems as possible replacements. The basic design principles behind the cryptosystems are listed here in "no particular order" (as he stated) [590]:

DES's 56-bit key size is too small. Considering the negligible cost of increasing the key size (computer memory is cheap and plentiful), it should be increased.

DES's extensive use of permutations, while suitable for hardware implementations, is very difficult to implement in software. The faster software implementations of DES implement the permutations by table lookup. Table lookup can provide the same "diffusion" characteristics as permutation and can be much more flexible.

The S-boxes in DES are small, with only 64 4-bit entries per box. Now that memory is larger, S-boxes should grow. Moreover, all eight S-boxes are used simultaneously. While this is suitable for hardware, this seems like an unreasonable restriction in software. A larger S-box size and sequential (rather than parallel) S-box usage should be employed.

The initial and final permutations in DES are widely viewed as cryptographically pointless and should be discarded.

All the faster implementations of DES precompute the keys for each round. Given this fact, there is no reason not to make this computation more complicated.

Unlike DES, the design of the S-boxes should be made public.

To this list, Merkle would probably now add "resistant to differential cryptanalysis and to linear attacks," but those attacks were still unknown at the time.

Khufu

Khufu is a 64-bit block cipher. The 64-bit plaintext is first divided into two 32-bit halves, L and R. First, both halves are XORed with some key material. Then, they are subjected to a series of rounds similar to DES. In each round, the least significant byte of L is used as the input to a 256-entry S-box. Each S-box entry is 32-bits wide. The selected 32-bit entry in the S-box is then XORed with R. L is then rotated some multiple of 8 bits, L and R are swapped, and the round ends. The S-box itself is not static, but changes every eight rounds. Finally, after the last round, L and R are XORed with more key material, and then combined to form the ciphertext block.

Although parts of the key are XORed with the encryption block at the beginning and end of the algorithm, the primary purpose of the key is to generate the S-boxes. These S-boxes are secret and, in essence, part of the key. Merkle's algorithm calls for a total key size of 512 bits (64 bytes) and gives an algorithm for generating S-boxes from the key. The number of rounds for the algorithm is left open. Merkle speculated that almost all applications would use 16, 24, or 32 (he restricted the choice of rounds to a multiple of eight).

Because Khufu has key-dependent and secret S-boxes, it is immune to differential cryptanalysis. I know of no cryptanalytic results against the algorithm. If a brute-force attack is the best way to attack Khufu, it is impressively difficult to break. A 512-bit key gives a complexity of 2^{512}—inconceivable under any circumstances.

Khafre

Khafre is the second of two cryptosystems proposed by Merkle [590]. (Khufu and Khafre were named after two Egyptian pharaohs.) It is similar in design to Khufu, except that it was designed for applications where there is no precomputation time. The S-boxes are not key-dependent. Instead, Khafre uses a set of standard S-boxes. And the key is XORed with the encryption block not only before the first round and after the last round, but also after every eight rounds of encryption.

Merkle speculated that key sizes of 64- or 128-bits would be used for Khafre, and that more rounds of encryption would be required for Khafre than for Khufu. This, combined with the fact that each round of Khafre is more complex than for

Khufu, made the former algorithm slower. In compensation, Khafre does not require any precomputation and will encrypt small amounts of data more quickly.

In 1990, Biham and Shamir turned their differential cryptanalysis techniques against Khafre [104]. They were able to break 16-round Khafre with a chosen-plaintext attack using about 1500 different encryptions. It took about an hour, using their personal computer. Converting that to a known-plaintext attack would require about 2^{38} encryptions. Khafre, with 24 rounds, can be broken by a chosen-plaintext attack using 2^{53} encryptions and a known-plaintext attack using 2^{59} encryptions.

Patents

Both Khufu and Khafre are patented [591]. Source code for the algorithms are in the patent. Anyone interested in licensing either or both algorithms should contact:

Dave Petre
Director of Patent Licensing for Xerox
Tel: (203) 968-3231

11.8   RC2 AND RC4

RC2 and RC4 are variable-key-size encryption algorithms designed by Ron Rivest for RSA Data Security, Inc. (RSADI). Apparently, "RC" stands for "Ron's Code." They are proprietary, and their details have not been published. Don't think for a minute that this helps security. These algorithms have already appeared in commercial products; I am sure they have been disassembled by someone. As far as I know, these algorithms have not been patented.

RC2 is a variable-key-size block cipher, designed to be a replacement for DES. According to the company, software implementations of RC2 are three times as fast as DES. It encrypts data in blocks of 64 bits. RC2 is a "mix-and-mash" block cipher. There are no S-boxes; the two operations are mix-and-mash.

RC4 is a variable-key-size stream cipher that is, according to the company, ten times faster than DES. Both algorithms are quite compact, and their speed is independent of the key's size.

RSA Data Security claims that their algorithms are as secure as DES (with the same size key), but their refusal to make the algorithms public casts doubt on their claim. They are willing to provide details of the algorithm to scientists wishing to cryptanalyze it. I don't know of anyone who took them up on their offer, since it amounts to doing their analysis work for them. Burt Kaliski, chief scientist at RSA Data Security, said that RC2 is not vulnerable to differential cryptanalysis (there are no S-boxes) [469]. RC4, as a stream algorithm, is never used in such a way as to allow differential cryptanalysis to work. It is notable, however, that neither RC2 nor RC4 has survived the 20 years of intense cryptanalysis that DES has.

Still, Ron Rivest is not the usual "snake-oil" peddler. He's a respected and competent cryptographer. I put a fair degree of trust in the algorithm, even though I haven't personally inspected the code.

Assuming the algorithm is secure, and that brute force is the most efficient way to recover the key, then the security of the algorithms depends on the length of the key used. If a long key is used, the algorithm is more secure than DES; if a short key is used, the algorithm is less secure than DES.

A recent agreement between the Software Publishers Association (SPA) and the U.S. government gives RC2 and RC4 special export status (see Section 18.6). Products that implement one of these two algorithms have a much simpler export approval process, provided that the keys are no more than 40 bits in size.

Is a 40-bit key enough? There are a total of 2^{40} (10^{12}) possible keys. Assuming that exhaustive search is the most efficient method of cryptanalysis (a big assumption, considering that the algorithm has never been published), and assuming that cryptanalysts can test one million keys per second, it will take them 12.7 days to find the correct key. One hundred machines working in parallel can produce the key in three hours.

RSA Data Security, Inc., maintains that while encryption and decryption are quick, exhaustive key search is not. A significant amount of time is spent setting up the key schedule. While this time is negligible when encrypting and decrypting messages, it is not when trying every possible key.

The more cynical among us believe that the U.S. government would never allow export of any algorithm it couldn't, at least in theory, break. Another possibility would be to create a magnetic tape or CD of a plaintext block encrypted with every possible key. To break a given message, just run the tape and compare the ciphertext blocks in the message with the ciphertext blocks on the tape. If there is a match, try the candidate key and see if the message makes any sense. If you choose a common plaintext block (all zeros, the ASCII character for a space, etc.), this method should work. The storage requirement for a 64-bit plaintext block encrypted with all 10^{12} possible keys is 8 terabytes—certainly possible.

Current rumors are that the U.S. government will allow export of RC2 and RC4 with a 48-bit key. This implies that the NSA built 256 machines that run in parallel.

Patents and Licenses

Anyone wishing to license RC2 or RC4 should contact:

Ed Franklin
RSA Data Security, Inc.
10 Twin Dolphin Drive
Redwood City, CA 94065
Tel: (415) 595-8782

11.9   IDEA

The first incarnation of the IDEA cipher, by Xuejia Lai and James Massey, surfaced in 1990 [522]. It was called PES (Proposed Encryption Standard). The next year, after Biham and Shamir's demonstrated differential cryptanalysis, the authors strengthened their cipher against the attack [524,519]. They called the new algorithm IPES, the Improved Proposed Encryption Standard. IPES changed its

name in 1992 and became IDEA, the International Data Encryption Algorithm
[520]. In my opinion, it is the best and most secure block algorithm available to
the public at this time.

Overview of IDEA

IDEA is a block cipher; it operates on 64-bit plaintext blocks. The key is 128 bits
long. The same algorithm is used for both encryption and decryption.

As with all the other block ciphers we've seen, IDEA uses both confusion and
diffusion. The design philosophy behind the algorithm is one of "mixing
operations from different algebraic groups." There are three algebraic groups
whose operations are being mixed, and they are all easily implemented in both
hardware and software:

XOR

Addition modulo 2^{16} (addition, ignoring any overflow)

Multiplication modulo $2^{16}+1$ (multiplication, ignoring any overflow)

Even better, all these operations (and these are the only operations in the
algorithm—there are no permutations) operate on 16-bit sub-blocks. This
algorithm is even efficient on 16-bit processors.

Description of IDEA

Figure 11.9 is an overview of IDEA. The 64-bit data block is divided into four
16-bit sub-blocks: X_1, X_2, X_3, and X_4. These four sub-blocks become the input to
the first round of the algorithm. There are eight rounds total. In each round, the
four sub-blocks are XORed, added, and multiplied with one another and with six
16-bit sub-blocks of key material. Between each round, the second and third
sub-blocks are swapped.

In each round, the sequence of events is as follows:

(1) Multiply X_1 and the first key sub-block.

(2) Add X_2 and the second key sub-block.

(3) Add X_3 and the third key sub-block.

(4) Multiply X_4 and the fourth key sub-block.

(5) XOR the results of steps (1) and (3).

(6) XOR the results of steps (2) and (4).

(7) Multiply the results of step (5) with the fifth key sub-block.

(8) Add the results of steps (6) and (7).

(9) Multiply the results of step (8) with the sixth key sub-block.

(10) Add the results of steps (7) and (9).

(11) XOR the results of steps (1) and (9).

(12) XOR the results of steps (3) and (9).

(13) XOR the results of steps (2) and (10).

(14) XOR the results of steps (4) and (10).

The output of the round is the four sub-blocks that are the results of steps (11), (13), (12), and (14). Swap the two inner blocks (except for the last round), and that's the input to the next round.

After the eighth round, there is a final output transform:

(1) Multiply X_1 and the first key sub-block.

(2) Add X_2 and the second key sub-block.

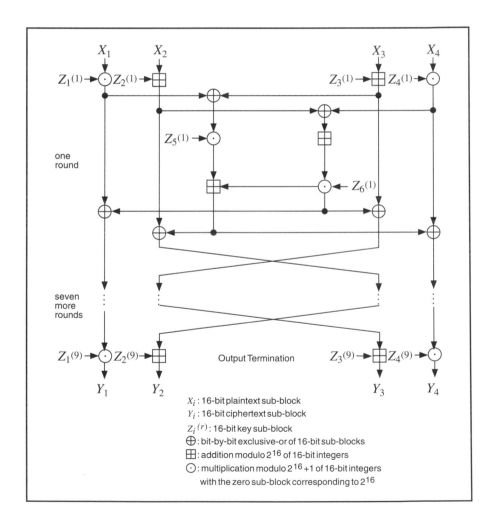

Figure 11.9
Outline of IDEA.

(3) Add X_3 and the third key sub-block.

(4) Multiply X_4 and the fourth key sub-block.

Finally, the four sub-blocks are reattached to produce the ciphertext.

Creating the key sub-blocks is also easy. The algorithm uses 52 of them (six for each of the eight rounds and four more for the output transform). First, the 128-bit key is divided into eight 16-bit subkeys. These are the first eight subkeys for the algorithm (the six for the first round, and the first two for the second round). Then, the key is rotated 25 bits to the left and again divided into eight subkeys. The first four are used in round two; the last four are used in round three. The key is rotated another 25 bits to the left for the next eight subkeys, and so on until the end of the algorithm.

Decryption is exactly the same, except that the key sub-blocks are reversed and slightly different. The decryption key sub-blocks are either the additive or multiplicative inverses of the encryption key sub-blocks. (For the purposes of IDEA, the multiplicative inverse of 0 is 0.) Calculating these takes some doing, but you only have to do it once for each decryption key. Table 11.1 shows the encryption key sub-blocks and the corresponding decryption key sub-blocks.

TABLE 11.1
IDEA Encryption and Decryption Key Sub-Blocks

ROUND	ENCRYPTION KEY SUB-BLOCKS	DECRYPTION KEY SUB-BLOCKS
1:	$Z_1^{(1)} \, Z_2^{(1)} \, Z_3^{(1)} \, Z_4^{(1)} \, Z_5^{(1)} \, Z_6^{(1)}$	$Z_1^{(9)}{-}1 \, {-}Z_2^{(9)} \, {-}Z_3^{(9)} \, Z_4^{(9)}{-}1 \, Z_5^{(8)} \, Z_6^{(8)}$
2:	$Z_1^{(2)} \, Z_2^{(2)} \, Z_3^{(2)} \, Z_4^{(2)} \, Z_5^{(2)} \, Z_6^{(2)}$	$Z_1^{(8)}{-}1 \, {-}Z_2^{(8)} \, {-}Z_3^{(8)} \, Z_4^{(8)}{-}1 \, Z_5^{(7)} \, Z_6^{(7)}$
3:	$Z_1^{(3)} \, Z_2^{(3)} \, Z_3^{(3)} \, Z_4^{(3)} \, Z_5^{(3)} \, Z_6^{(3)}$	$Z_1^{(7)}{-}1 \, {-}Z_2^{(7)} \, {-}Z_3^{(7)} \, Z_4^{(7)}{-}1 \, Z_5^{(6)} \, Z_6^{(6)}$
4:	$Z_1^{(4)} \, Z_2^{(4)} \, Z_3^{(4)} \, Z_4^{(4)} \, Z_5^{(4)} \, Z_6^{(4)}$	$Z_1^{(6)}{-}1 \, {-}Z_2^{(6)} \, {-}Z_3^{(6)} \, Z_4^{(6)}{-}1 \, Z_5^{(5)} \, Z_6^{(5)}$
5:	$Z_1^{(5)} \, Z_2^{(5)} \, Z_3^{(5)} \, Z_4^{(5)} \, Z_5^{(5)} \, Z_6^{(5)}$	$Z_1^{(5)}{-}1 \, {-}Z_2^{(5)} \, {-}Z_3^{(5)} \, Z_4^{(5)}{-}1 \, Z_5^{(4)} \, Z_6^{(4)}$
6:	$Z_1^{(6)} \, Z_2^{(6)} \, Z_3^{(6)} \, Z_4^{(6)} \, Z_5^{(6)} \, Z_6^{(6)}$	$Z_1^{(4)}{-}1 \, {-}Z_2^{(4)} \, {-}Z_3^{(4)} \, Z_4^{(4)}{-}1 \, Z_5^{(3)} \, Z_6^{(3)}$
7:	$Z_1^{(7)} \, Z_2^{(7)} \, Z_3^{(7)} \, Z_4^{(7)} \, Z_5^{(7)} \, Z_6^{(7)}$	$Z_1^{(3)}{-}1 \, {-}Z_2^{(3)} \, {-}Z_3^{(3)} \, Z_4^{(3)}{-}1 \, Z_5^{(2)} \, Z_6^{(2)}$
8:	$Z_1^{(8)} \, Z_2^{(8)} \, Z_3^{(8)} \, Z_4^{(8)} \, Z_5^{(8)} \, Z_6^{(8)}$	$Z_1^{(2)}{-}1 \, {-}Z_2^{(2)} \, {-}Z_3^{(2)} \, Z_4^{(2)}{-}1 \, Z_5^{(1)} \, Z_6^{(1)}$
output transformation	$Z_1^{(9)} \, Z_2^{(9)} \, Z_3^{(9)} \, Z_4^{(9)}$	$Z_1^{(1)}{-}1 \, {-}Z_2^{(1)} \, {-}Z_3^{(1)} \, Z_4^{(1)}{-}1$

Speed of IDEA

Current software implementations of IDEA are about as fast as DES. IDEA on a 33MHz 386 machine encrypts data at 880 kbps. On a VAX 9000, the speed is almost four times that.

A VLSI implementation of PES encrypts data at 55 Mbits/second at 25MHz [129,230]. Another VLSI chip developed at ETH Zurich, consisting of 251,000 transistors on a chip 107.8 mm on a side, encrypts data using the IDEA algorithm at a 177 Mbits/second data rate when clocked at 25Mhz [521].

Cryptanalysis of IDEA

IDEA's key length is 128 bits—over twice as long as DES. Assuming that a brute-force attack is the most efficient, it would require 2^{128} (10^{38}) encryptions to recover the key. Design a chip that can test a billion keys per second and throw a billion of them at the problem, and it will still take 10^{13} years—that's longer than the age of the universe. An array of 10^{24} such chips can find the key in a day, but there aren't enough silicon atoms in the universe to build such a machine. Now we're getting somewhere—although I'd keep my eye on the dark matter debate.

There's even another difficulty with a brute-force attack against IDEA. Generating encryption subkeys is a lot faster than generating decryption subkeys. When you're encrypting or decrypting a message, this time is generally negligible compared to the time to encrypt or decrypt the message blocks. But when you're trying a brute-force attack against a ciphertext block, every time you attempt a decryption you're going to use another key. The time required to find all of those multiplicative inverses will add up to double or triple the time (or number of parallel processors) required for a brute-force attack.

Perhaps, however, brute force isn't the best way to attack IDEA. The algorithm is still too new for any definitive cryptanalytic results. The designers have done their best to make the algorithm immune to differential cryptanalysis [524,520]. (Figure 11.10 shows the original PES algorithm, and the IDEA algorithm after it was strengthened against differential cryptanalysis. It's amazing how a few subtle changes can make such a big difference.) If you recall, differential cryptanalysis is generally more difficult the more iterations a cryptosystem has. In [520], Lai argued (he gave evidence, not a proof) that IDEA is immune from differential cryptanalysis after only four of its eight rounds. According to Eli Biham, his related-key cryptanalytic attack doesn't work against IDEA, either [107].

A recent paper "discovered" a class of weak keys for IDEA [256]. Actually, Lai described them in [520]. They are not weak keys in the sense that the DES weak keys are; i.e., the encryption function is self-inverse. They are weak in the sense that if they are used, an attacker can easily identify them in a chosen-plaintext attack. For example, a weak key is (in hex):

$$0000,0000,0F00,0000,0000,000F,FFFF,F000$$

The number at the positions of "F" can be any number.

In any case, the chance of accidentally generating one of these keys is very small: 2^{-96}. There is no danger if you choose keys at random, and I've heard of no other results.

IDEA Modes of Operation and Variants

IDEA can work within any block cipher mode discussed in Section 8.1. Any double-IDEA implementation would be susceptible to the same meet-in-the-middle attack as DES. However, because IDEA's key length is more than double DES's, the attack is impossible. It would require a storage space of 64×2^{128} bits, or 10^{39}

bytes. Maybe there's enough matter in the universe to create a memory device that large, but I doubt it.

If you're worried about parallel universes as well, use a triple-IDEA implementation:

$$C = E_{K_1}(D_{K_2}(E_{K_1}(P)))$$

It is immune to the meet-in-the-middle attack.

There's also no reason why you can't implement IDEA with independent subkeys. The algorithm needs a total of 52 16-bit keys, or a total key length of 104 bytes. There is no reason to believe this variant would be any less secure than IDEA; it might possibly even be more secure.

A naive variant might be to double the block size. The algorithm would work just as well with 32-bit sub-blocks instead of 16-bit sub-blocks, and a 256-bit key. Encryption would be quicker, and security would increase 2^{32} times. Or would it? The theory behind the algorithm hinges on the fact that $2^{16}+1$ is prime; $2^{32}+1$ is

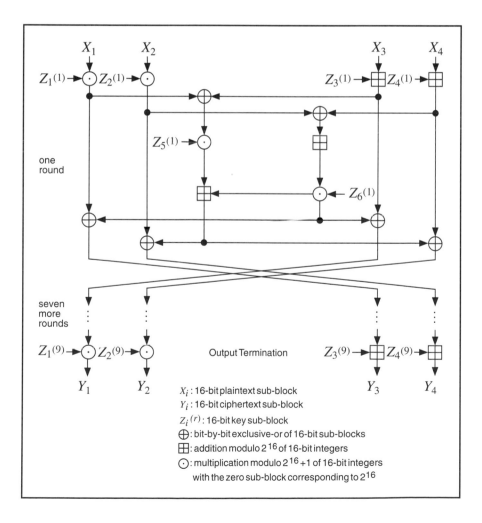

Figure 11.10
Outline of PES.

not. Perhaps the algorithm could be modified to work, but it would have very different security properties. Lai says it would be difficult to make it work [521].

While IDEA appears to be significantly more secure than DES, it isn't always easy to substitute one for the other in an existing application. If your database and message templates are hardwired to accept a 64-bit key, it may be impossible to implement IDEA's 128-bit key.

For those applications, generate a 128-bit key by concatenating the 64-bit key with itself. Remember that IDEA is weakened considerably by this modification.

Caveat Emptor

IDEA is a new algorithm. There hasn't been any paper published on the cryptanalysis of IDEA. Is IDEA a group? (Lai thinks not [521].) Are some keys stronger than others? (As far as I know, there is only one weak key: all zeros.) Are there any still-undiscovered ways of breaking this cipher? These remain unanswered questions. There are no obvious patterns in the ciphertext; IDEA looks secure. The algorithm seems resistant to differential cryptanalysis and related-key cryptanalysis; IDEA looks very secure. However, time and time again secure-looking algorithms have fallen to new forms of cryptanalysis. There are several academic and military groups currently cryptanalyzing IDEA. None of them has succeeded yet (and is willing to go public about it), but one might—someday.

Patents and Licenses

The IDEA block cipher is patented in Europe [566], and is patent-pending in the United States. The patent is held by Ascom-Tech AG. There is no license fee required for noncommercial use. Commercial users interested in licensing the algorithm should contact:

Dr. Dieter Profos
Ascom-Tech AG, Solothurn Lab
Postfach 151
4502 Solothurn, Switzerland
Tel: +41 65 242-885
Fax: +41 65 235-761

11.10   MMB

A complaint against IDEA, that it uses a 64-bit encryption block, was addressed in an algorithm called MMB (Modular Multiplication-based Block cipher) [256]. MMB is based on the same basic theory as IDEA: mixing operations of different algebraic groups. While IDEA mixes XOR of 16-bit numbers, addition modulo 2^{16}, and multiplication modulo $2^{16}+1$, MMB mixes XOR of 32-bit number with multiplication modulo $2^{32}-1$. The result is an algorithm that has both a 128-bit key and a 128-bit block size.

The algorithm operates on 32-bit sub-blocks of text (x_0, x_1, x_2, x_3) and 32-bit sub-blocks of key (k_0, k_1, k_2, k_3). This makes the algorithm well suited for implementation on modern, 32-bit processors. A nonlinear function, f, is applied six times, alternated by key XORing. Here's the overall algorithm:

$x_i = x_i$ XOR k_i, for $i = 0$ to 3
$f(x_0,x_1,x_2,x_3)$
$x_i = x_i$ XOR k_{i+1}, for $i = 0$ to 3
$f(x_0,x_1,x_2,x_3)$
$x_i = x_i$ XOR k_{i+2}, for $i = 0$ to 3
$f(x_0,x_1,x_2,x_3)$
$x_i = x_i$ XOR k_i, for $i = 0$ to 3
$f(x_0,x_1,x_2,x_3)$
$x_i = x_i$ XOR k_{i+1}, for $i = 0$ to 3
$f(x_0,x_1,x_2,x_3)$
$x_i = x_i$ XOR k_{i+2}, for $i = 0$ to 3
$f(x_0,x_1,x_2,x_3)$

The function f has three steps:

Step 1: $x_i = c_i \cdot x_i$, for $i = 0$ to 3
Step 2: if the least significant byte of $x_0 = 1$, then $x_0 = x_0$ XOR C; if the least significant byte of $x_3 = 0$, then $x_3 = x_3$ XOR C
Step 3: $x_i = x_{i-1}$ XOR x_i XOR x_{i+1}, for $i = 0$ to 3

The multiplication operation in Step 1 is modulo $2^{32}-1$. For the purposes of the algorithm, if the second operand is $2^{32}-1$, then the result is $2^{32}-1$. The various constants are (in hex):

$C = 2AAAAAAA$
$c_0 = 025F1CDB$
$c_1 = 2\ c_0$
$c_2 = 2^3 c_0$
$c_3 = 2^7 c_0$

The constant C is the "simplest" constant with a high ternary weight, a least-significant bit of zero, and no circular symmetry. The constant c_0 was chosen to have certain characteristics. The constants c_1, c_2, and c_3 are shifted versions of c_0 to prevent attacks based on symmetry. See [255] for more details.

Decryption is the reverse process. Steps 2 and 3 are their own inverse. Step 1 uses c_i^{-1} instead of c_i. The value of c_0^{-1} is 0DAD4694.

Security of MMB

This algorithm is very new; it was published in barely enough time to be included in the book. While the properties of a 128-bit key and a 128-bit block size are desirable, it is still far too early to comment on the algorithm's security. Eli Biham thinks a 128-bit block size actually weakens the algorithm [107]. The authors argue that the algorithm is not susceptible to differential cryptanalysis and that it has no weak keys.

11.11   CA-1.1

CA is a block cipher built on cellular automata, designed by Howard Gutowitz [407,408,409]. It encrypts plaintext in 384-bit blocks and has a 1088-bit key (it's really two keys, a 1024-bit key and a 64-bit key). Because of the nature of cellular automata, the algorithm is most efficient when implemented in massively parallel integrated circuits.

CA-1.1 uses both reversible and irreversible cellular automaton rules. Under a reversible rule, each state of the lattice comes from a unique predecessor state, while under an irreversible rule, each state can have many predecessor states. During encryption, irreversible rules are iterated backward in time. To go backward from a given state, one of the possible predecessor states is selected at random. This process can be repeated many times. Backward iteration thus serves to mix random information with the message information. CA-1.1 uses a particular kind of partially linear irreversible rule, which is such that a random predecessor state for any given state can be rapidly built. Reversible rules are also used for some stages of encryption. The reversible rules (simple parallel permutations on sub-blocks of the state) are fully nonlinear. The irreversible rules are derived entirely from information in the key, while the reversible rules depend both on key information and on the random information inserted during the stages of encryption with irreversible rules.

CA-1.1 features an authentication mechanism that renders chosen-ciphertext attack difficult. This authentication mechanism ensures that only ciphertext produced by the system loaded with a given key is decrypted using the same key.

CA-1.1 is built around a block-link structure. That is, the processing of the message block is partially segregated from the processing of the stream of random information inserted during encryption. This random information serves to link stages of encryption together. It can also be used to chain together the encryption of a stream of blocks. The information in the link is generated within the encryption apparatus. It is not accessible even to legitimate users of the system, hence it is not available for chosen-plaintext attacks.

Security of CA-1.1

CA-1.1 is a new algorithm, and it is too early to make any pronouncements on its security. Gutowitz discusses some possible attacks, including differential cryptanalysis, but is unable to break the algorithm. As an incentive, Gutowitz has offered a $1000 prize to "the first person who develops a tractable procedure to break CA-1.1."

Patents and Licenses

There is a patent pending in the United States for CA-1.1 [408]. Anyone interested in either licensing the algorithm or in the cryptanalysis prize should contact:

Howard Gutowitz
ESPCI
Laboratoire d'Électronique
10 rue Vauquelin
75005 Paris
FRANCE

11.12   SKIPJACK

Skipjack is the NSA-developed encryption algorithm for the Clipper and Capstone chips (see Sections 17.10 and 17.11). Since the algorithm is classified SECRET, no one knows much about it. Here's what I do know [653]:

- It's a symmetric algorithm.
- It has an 80-bit key.
- It can be used in either ECB, CFB, OFB, or CBC modes.
- There are 32 rounds of processing per single encrypt or decrypt operation.
- NSA started the design in 1985 and completed the evaluation in 1990.

No one knows if this algorithm is secure or not. If the NSA wants to produce a secure algorithm, they can certainly do it. On the other hand, if the NSA wants to design an algorithm with a trap door, they can do that as well.

The fact that the NSA is planning to use the Skipjack algorithm to encrypt their Defense Messaging System (DMS) implies that the algorithm is secure. However, many people are not convinced. Maybe the NSA purposely put a back door into the algorithm. NIST has stated that "respected experts from outside the government will be offered access to the confidential details of the algorithm to assess its capabilities and publicly report its findings" [473]. The preliminary report of these experts [163a] concluded that:

> Under an assumption that the cost of processing power is halved every eighteen months, it will be 36 years before the difficulty of breaking Skipjack by exhaustive search will be equal to the difficulty of breaking DES today. Thus, there is no significant risk that Skipjack will be broken by exhaustive search in the next 30–40 years.
>
> There is no significant risk that Skipjack can be broken through a shortcut method of attack, including differential cryptanalysis. There are no weak keys; there is no complementation property. The experts, not having time to evaluate the algorithm to any great extent, instead evaluated NSA's own design and evaluation process.
>
> The strength of Skipjack against a cryptanalytic attack does not depend on the secrecy of the algorithm.

At this writing, the final report has not been published.

11.13   USING ONE-WAY HASH FUNCTIONS

Karn

This method, invented by Phil Karn and placed in the public domain, makes an invertible encryption algorithm out of certain one-way hash functions. A similar idea was invented by Zheng, Matsumoto, and Imai [903].

The algorithm operates on plaintext and ciphertext in 32-byte blocks—that's an astounding 256 bits. The key can be any length, although certain key lengths will be more efficient for certain one-way hash functions. For the one-way hash functions MD4 and MD5, 96-byte (768-bit) keys work best.

To encrypt, first split the plaintext into two 16-byte halves: P_l and P_r. Then, split the key into two 48-byte halves: K_l and K_r. Append K_l to P_l and hash it with MD4, MD5, or Snefru, then XOR the result of the hash with P_r to produce the right half of the ciphertext: C_r. Then, append K_r to C_r and hash it with either MD4 or MD5, then XOR the result with P_l to produce C_l. Finally, append C_r to C to produce the ciphertext.

To decrypt, simply reverse the process. Append K_r to C_r, hash and XOR with C_l to produce P_l. Append K_l to P_l, hash and XOR with C_r to produce P_r.

The overall structure of the algorithm is the same as many of the other block algorithms discussed in this section. There are only two rounds, because the complexity of the algorithm is embedded in the one-way hash function. And since the key is used only as the input to the hash function, it cannot be recovered even using a chosen-plaintext attack—assuming, of course, that the one-way hash function is secure.

Luby-Rackoff

Luby and Rackoff showed that it is not secure [559]. Consider two single-block messages: AB and AC. If cryptanalysts know both the plaintext and the ciphertext of the first message, and they know the first half of the plaintext of the second message, then they can easily compute the entire second message. This is a known-plaintext attack useful only in certain circumstances, but it is a major security problem.

Luby and Rackoff suggested a four-round encryption algorithm to avoid this problem. This is Karn's algorithm with four rounds:

(1) Divide the key into two halves: K_l and K_r.

(2) Divide the plaintext block into two halves: L_0 and R_0.

(3) Append K_l to L_0 and hash it with MD4 or MD5. XOR the result of the hash with R_0 to produce R_1:

$$R_1 = R_0 \text{ XOR } H(K_l, L_0)$$

(4) Append K_r to R_1 and hash it with MD4 or MD5. XOR the result of the hash with L_0 to produce L_1:

$$L_1 = R_0 \text{ XOR } H(K_l, L_0)$$

(5) Append K_l to L_1 and hash it with MD4 or MD5. XOR the result of the hash with R_1 to produce R_2:

$$R_2 = R_1 \text{ XOR } H(K_l, L_1)$$

(6) Append K_r to R_2 and hash it with MD4 or MD5. XOR the result of the hash with L_1 to produce L_2:

$$L_2 = R_1 \text{ XOR } H(K_l, L_1)$$

(7) Append L_2 to R_2 to generate the message.

This scheme is still new, but it seems to be at least as secure as the one-way hash function. It may even be more secure than either DES or IDEA. It is certainly much faster.

Message Digest Cipher (MDC)

MDC, invented by Peter Gutmann [406], is a means of turning one-way hash functions into a block cipher that runs in CFB mode. The cipher runs virtually as fast as the hash function and is at least as secure as the hash function.

Using a one-way hash function in this manner makes more sense than using a true cipher since, when used in CFB mode, a block algorithm is simply acting as a hash function; the fact that the algorithm is reversible is irrelevant in CFB mode since the algorithm encrypts at both ends.

The MDC implementation in this book uses the MD5 message digest algorithm, although in practice any one-way hash function (for example MD2, MD5, Snefru, N-Hash, or SHA) could be used.

The transformation made by MD5 is as follows:

$$\text{data}[64] + \text{hash}[16] \rightarrow \text{hash}'[16]$$
$$\text{data} + \text{previous MD5} \rightarrow \text{current MD5}$$

However, instead of feeding in 64 bytes of data, MDC feeds in 64 bytes of key. This makes MD5 dependent on this key. The exact method is:

1. Set data[64] to zeros and hash[16] to the IV.

2. Run the cipher over the encryption key.

3. Set data[64] to the hashed key.

In normal use, step 2 would be iterated several times to slow down dictionary attacks and to distribute evenly the randomness in the encryption key over the entire 64-byte buffer.

MDC strengthens this even further by changing MD5's mysterious constants. Instead of "in step i, t_i is the integer part of $4294967296 \times \text{abs}(\sin(i))$, where i is in radians," MDC uses constants derived from a user-supplied key. This makes the MD5 transformation itself dependent on that key. Not only the data used as the encryption key but also the exact nature of the transformation itself is unknown to a potential attacker.

MDC is unpatented. The source code is unlicensed. Anyone can use it at any time, in any way, royalty-free [406].

11.14 OTHER BLOCK ALGORITHMS

Four Japanese cryptographers presented an algorithm based on chaos theory at EUROCRYPT '91 [413,414]. Biham cryptanalyzed the algorithm at the same conference [98].

There are many more block algorithms available outside the cryptology community. Some are in use by various government and military organizations. I have no information about any of those. There are also dozens of proprietary commercial algorithms. Some might be good; most are probably not. If companies do not feel that their interests are served by making their algorithms public, it is best to assume they're right and avoid the algorithm.

11.15 WHICH BLOCK ALGORITHM IS BEST?

That's a tough question. DES is still secure, unless you need your secrets to remain secret for many years or fear a major government. If you need security that lasts decades or fear the cryptanalytic efforts of major governments, use triple-DES with three independent keys.

The other algorithms aren't worthless. Assuming that there are no cryptanalytic results that are being kept secret (certainly a possibility), REDOC-II, REDOC-III, and Khufu are still secure. Even so, these algorithms have not been analyzed by enough people to make me feel safe. Khufu, which requires precomputation of the S-boxes based on the key, may not be suitable for some on-the-fly applications. The one-way hash-function-based algorithms have promise: Luby-Rackoff and MDC are as secure as their underlying one-way hash functions.

My favorite algorithm is IDEA. Its 128-bit key, combined with its resistance to any public means of cryptanalysis, gives me a warm fuzzy feeling about the algorithm. I wish it had a 128-bit block, but you can't have everything. The algorithm is new, but it is be analyzed by a lot of different groups. There could be some devastating cryptanalytic news tomorrow; today I'm betting on IDEA.

Public-Key
Algorithms

12.1 BACKGROUND

The concept of public-key cryptography was invented by Whitfield Diffie and Martin Hellman, and independently by Ralph Merkle. This contribution to the field was the notion that keys could come in pairs—an encryption key and a decryption key—and that it could be unfeasible to generate one key from the other. Diffie and Hellman first presented this concept at the 1976 National Computer Conference [298]; a few months later, their seminal paper, "New Directions in Cryptography," appeared in *IEEE Transactions on Information Theory* [299]. (Due to the glacial publishing speed of *Communications of the ACM,* Merkle's first contribution to the field didn't appear until 1978 [586].)

The first public-key algorithms became public at the same time that DES was being discussed as a proposed standard. This resulted in some partisan politics in the cryptographic community. As Diffie described it [297]:

> The excitement public key cryptosystems provoked in the popular and scientific press was not matched by corresponding acceptance in the cryptographic establishment, however. In the same year that public key cryptography was discovered, the National Security Agency (NSA), proposed a conventional cryptographic system, designed by International Business Machines (IBM), as a federal *Data Encryption Standard* DES. Marty Hellman and I criticized the proposal on the ground that its key was too small, but manufacturers were gearing up to support the proposed standard and our criticism was seen by many as an attempt to disrupt the standards-making process to the advantage of our own work. Public key cryptography in its turn was attacked, in sales literature [624] and technical

papers [483,645] alike, more as though it were a competing product than a recent research discovery. This, however, did not deter the NSA from claiming its share of the credit. Its director, in the words of the *Encyclopedia Britannica* [824], "pointed out that two-key cryptography had been discovered at the agency a decade earlier," although no evidence for this claim was ever offered publicly.

Since 1976, numerous public-key cryptography algorithms have been proposed. Many of these are insecure. Of the ones that are still considered secure, many are impractical. Either they have an impractically large key, or the ciphertext is much larger than the plaintext.

Only a few algorithms are both secure and practical. These algorithms are generally based on one of the hard problems discussed in Section 9.2. While it is theoretically possible that someone may come up with a fast solution tomorrow, not many experts think it is likely.

Of these secure and practical public-key algorithms, some are only suitable for key distribution. Others are suitable for encryption (and by extension for key distribution). Others are only suitable for digital signatures. Only two algorithms are suitable for both encryption and digital signatures: RSA and ElGamal. All of these algorithms are slow. The encryption and decryption rate is much slower than with symmetric algorithms; usually it's too slow to support bulk data encryption.

Security of Public-Key Algorithms

Since cryptanalysts have access to the public key, they can always choose any message to encrypt. This means that cryptanalysts, given $C = E_K(P)$, can guess the value of P and easily check their guess. This is a serious problem if the number of possible plaintext messages is small enough to allow exhaustive search, but can be solved by padding messages with a string of random bits. This means that identical plaintext messages will encrypt to different ciphertext messages. (For more about this concept, see Section 16.16.)

Public-key algorithms are designed to resist chosen-plaintext attacks; their security is based both on the difficulty of deducing the secret key from the public key and the difficulty of deducing the plaintext from the ciphertext. However, most public-key algorithms are particularly susceptible to what is called a **chosen-ciphertext attack:**

> A chosen-ciphertext attack is when cryptanalysts choose messages and have access to the decryption of those messages with the private key. Their job is to deduce the key or an algorithm to decrypt any new messages encrypted with the same key.
> *Given:* $C_1, P_1 = D_K(C_1), C_2, P_2 = D_K(C_2), \ldots C_i, P_i = D_K(C_i)$, where cryptanalysts choose $C_1, C_2, \ldots C_i$
> *Deduce:* K, or an algorithm to infer P_{i+1} from $C_{i+1} = E_K(P_{i+1})$

It is important to understand the significance of this attack. Even if we have a public-key cryptosystem that is provably secure and use a protocol that looks safe, cryptanalysts may still recover plaintext messages. The inherent problem is a direct result of the most useful characteristic of public-key cryptography: everyone can use the public key.

Consequently, it is important to look at the system as a whole and not just at the individual parts. Good public-key protocols are designed so that the various parties don't decrypt arbitrary messages generated by other parties—the proof-of-identity protocols are a good example (see Section 5.4).

12.2   DIFFIE-HELLMAN

Diffie-Hellman is the first public-key algorithm invented [299]. It gets its security from the difficulty of calculating discrete logarithms in a finite field, as compared with the ease of calculating exponentiation in the same field. Diffie-Hellman can be used for key distribution, but it cannot be used to encrypt and decrypt messages. Alice and Bob can use this algorithm to generate a secret key.

The math is simple. First, Alice and Bob agree on two large integers, n and g, such that g is less than n but greater than 1. These two integers don't have to be secret; Alice and Bob can agree to them over some insecure channel. They can even be common among a group of users. It doesn't matter.

Then, the protocol goes as follows:

(1) Alice chooses a random large integer x and computes

$$X = g^x \bmod n$$

(2) Bob chooses a random large integer y and computes

$$Y = g^y \bmod n$$

(3) Alice sends X to Bob, and Bob sends Y to Alice. (Note that Alice keeps x secret, and Bob keeps y secret.)

(4) Alice computes $k = Y^x \bmod n$.

(5) Bob computes $k' = X^y \bmod n$.

Both k and k' are equal to $g^{xy} \bmod n$. No one listening on the channel can compute that value; they only know n, g, X, and Y. Unless they can compute the discrete logarithm and recover x or y, they do not solve the problem. So, k is the secret key that both Alice and Bob computed independently.

The choice of g and n can have a substantial impact on the security of this system. The modulus n should be a prime; more importantly $(n-1)/2$ should also be a prime [703]. And g should be a primitive root mod n. And most important, n should be large: at least 512 bits long. Using 1028 bits would be better.

Diffie-Hellman Extended

This algorithm also works in finite fields [703]. Shmuley and Kevin McCurley studied a variant of the algorithm where the modulus is a composite number [812,578]. V. S. Miller and Neal Koblitz extended this algorithm to elliptic curves

[605,489]. Taher ElGamal used the basic idea to develop an encryption and digital signature algorithm (see Section 13.3).

This algorithm also works in the Galois field $GF(2^k)$ [812,578]. Some implementations take this approach [504,896,897], because the computation is much quicker. Similarly, cryptanalytic computation is also much quicker, so it is important to choose carefully a field large enough to ensure security.

Diffie-Hellman with Three or More Parties

The Diffie-Hellman key-exchange protocol can easily be extended to work with three or more people. In this example, Alice, Bob, and Carol together generate a secret key:

(1) Alice chooses a random large integer x and computes

$$X = g^x \bmod n$$

(2) Bob chooses a random large integer y and computes

$$Y = g^y \bmod n$$

(3) Carol chooses a random large integer z and computes

$$Z = g^z \bmod n$$

(4) Alice sends X to Bob, Bob sends Y to Carol, and Carol sends Z to Alice.

(5) Alice computes $Z' = Z^x \bmod n$.

(6) Bob computes $X' = X^y \bmod n$.

(7) Carol computes $Y' = Y^z \bmod n$.

(8) Alice sends Z' to Bob, Bob sends X' to Carol, and Carol sends Y' to Alice.

(9) Alice computes $k = Y'^x \bmod n$.

(10) Bob computes $k = Z'^y \bmod n$.

(11) Carol computes $k = X'^y \bmod n$.

The secret key, k, is equal to $g^{xyz} \bmod n$, and no one else listening in on the communications can compute that value. The protocol can be easily extended to four or more people; just add more people and more rounds of computation.

Patents

The Diffie-Hellman key-exchange algorithm is patented in the United States [426] and Canada [427]. A group called Public Key Partners (PKP) licenses the patent, along with other public-key cryptography patents. Anyone interested in obtaining a license should contact:

Robert B. Fougner
Director of Licensing
Public Key Partners

130 B Kifer Court
Sunnyvale, CA 94086
Tel: (408) 735-6779

The U.S. patent will expire on April 29, 1997.

12.3   KNAPSACK ALGORITHMS

The first algorithm for generalized public-key encryption was developed by Ralph Merkle and Martin Hellman [420,593]. It could only be used for encryption, although Shamir later adapted the system for digital signatures [787]. Knapsack algorithms get their security from the knapsack problem, an NP-complete problem. Although this algorithm was later found to be insecure, it is worth examining because it demonstrates how an NP-complete problem can be used for public-key cryptography.

The knapsack problem is a simple one. Given a pile of items, each with different weights, is it possible to put some of those items into a knapsack so that the knapsack weighs a given amount?

For example, the items might have weights of 1, 5, 6, 11, 14, and 20. It is possible to pack a knapsack that weighs 22; use weights 5, 6, and 11. It is impossible to pack a knapsack that weighs 24. In general, the time required to solve this problem seems to grow exponentially with the number of items in the pile.

In general, the problem can be defined as follows: Given a set of values, M_1, $M_2, \ldots M_n$, and a sum, S, compute the values of b such that:

$$S = b_1M_1 + b_2M_2 + \ldots + b_nM_n$$

The values of b can be either 0 or 1. A 1 indicates that the item is in the knapsack; a 0 indicates that it isn't.

The idea behind the Merkle-Hellman knapsack algorithm is to encode a message as a solution to a series of knapsack problems. A block of plaintext equal in length to the number of items in the pile would select the items (bits of the plaintext correspond to the b values: a 1 means the item was present, and a 0 means the item was absent), and the ciphertext would be the resulting sum. Figure 12.1 shows a plaintext encrypted with a sample knapsack problem.

The trick is that there are actually two different knapsack problems, one solvable in linear time and the other solvable only in exponential time. The easy knapsack can be modified to create the hard knapsack. The public key is the hard knapsack, which can easily be used to encrypt messages but cannot be used to decrypt

Plaintext:	1 1 1 0 0 1	0 1 0 1 1 0	0 0 0 0 0 0	0 1 1 0 0 0
Knapsack:	1 5 6 11 14 20	1 5 6 11 14 20	1 5 6 11 14 20	1 5 6 11 14 20
Ciphertext:	1+5+6+20=	5+11+14=	0=	5+6=
	32	30	0	11

Figure 12.1
Encryption with knapsacks.

messages. The private key is the easy knapsack, which gives an easy way to decrypt messages. People who don't know the private key are forced to try to solve the hard knapsack problem.

Superincreasing Knapsacks

What is the easy knapsack problem? If the list of weights is a **superincreasing sequence,** then the resulting knapsack problem is easy to solve. A superincreasing sequence is a sequence in which every term is greater than the sum of all the previous terms. For example, {1,3,6,13,27,52} is a superincreasing sequence, but {1,3,4,9,15,25} is not.

The solution of a **superincreasing knapsack** is easy to find. Take the total weight and compare it with the largest number in the sequence. If the total weight is less than the number, then it is not in the knapsack. If the total weight is greater than the number, then it is in the knapsack. Reduce the weight of the knapsack by the value and move to the next largest number in the sequence. Repeat until finished. If the total weight has been brought to zero, then there is a solution. If the total weight has not, there isn't.

For example, consider a total knapsack weight of 70 and a sequence of weights of {2,3,6,13,27,52}. The largest weight, 52, is less than 70, so 52 is in the knapsack. Subtracting 52 from 70 leaves 18. The next weight, 27, is greater than 18, so 27 is not in the knapsack. The next weight, 13, is less than 18, so 13 is in the knapsack. Subtracting 13 from 18 leaves 5. The next weight, 6, is greater than 5, so 6 is not in the knapsack. Continuing this process will show that both 2 and 3 are in the knapsack. Were this a Merkle-Hellman knapsack encryption block, the plaintext that resulted from a ciphertext value of 70 would be 110101.

With non-superincreasing knapsacks, there is no quick algorithm. The only way to determine which items are in the knapsack is to methodically test possible solutions until you stumble on the correct one. The fastest algorithms, taking into account the necessary heuristics, grow exponentially with the number of possible weights in the knapsack. Add one item to the sequence of weights, and it takes twice as long to find the solution. This is much more difficult than a superincreasing knapsack, when if you add one more weight to the sequence it simply takes another operation to find the solution.

The Merkle-Hellman algorithm is based on this property. The private key is a sequence of weights for a superincreasing knapsack problem. The public key is a sequence of weights for a normal knapsack problem with the same solution. Merkle and Hellman developed a technique for converting a superincreasing knapsack problem into a normal knapsack problem. They did this using modular arithmetic.

Creating the Public Key from the Private Key

Without going into the number theory, this is how the algorithm works: To get a normal knapsack sequence, take a superincreasing knapsack sequence, for example {2,3,6,13,27,52}, and multiply all of the values by a number n, mod m. The modulus should be a number greater than the largest number in the sequence, for example, 56. The multiplier should have no factors in common with any of the numbers in the sequence, for example, 31. The normal knapsack sequence would then be:

$$2 \times 31 \bmod 56 = 6$$
$$3 \times 31 \bmod 56 = 37$$
$$6 \times 31 \bmod 56 = 18$$
$$13 \times 31 \bmod 56 = 11$$
$$27 \times 31 \bmod 56 = 53$$
$$52 \times 31 \bmod 56 = 44$$

The hard knapsack would then be {6,37,18,11,53,44}.

The superincreasing knapsack sequence is the private key. The normal knapsack sequence is the public key.

Encryption

To encrypt a binary message, first break it up into blocks equal to the number of items in the knapsack sequence. Then, allowing a 1 to indicate the item is present and a 0 to indicate that the item is absent, compute the total weights of the knapsacks.

For example, if the message were 011000110101101110, encryption using the above knapsack would proceed like this:

message = 011000 110101 101110

011000 corresponds to 37+18 = 55
110101 corresponds to 6+37+11+44 = 98
101110 corresponds to 6+18+11+53 = 88

The ciphertext would be

55,98,88

Decryption

A legitimate recipient of this message knows the original superincreasing knapsack as well as the values of n and m used to transform it into a normal knapsack. To decrypt the message, the recipient must first determine n^{-1} such that $n \times n^{-1} = 1 \bmod m$. Multiply each of the ciphertext values by $n^{-1} \bmod m$ to get the plaintext values.

In our example, the superincreasing knapsack is {2,3,6,13,27,52}, m is equal to 56, and n is equal to 31. The ciphertext message is 55,98,88. In this case n^{-1} is equal to 47, so the ciphertext values must be multiplied by 47 mod 56.

$$55 \times 47 \bmod 56 = 48 = 011000$$
$$98 \times 47 \bmod 56 = 53 = 110101$$

$$88 \times 47 \bmod 56 = 46 = 101110$$

The recovered plaintext is 011000 110101 101110.

Practical Implementations

With a knapsack sequence of only six items long, it's not hard to solve the problem even if it isn't superincreasing. Real knapsacks contain about 200 items. The value for each term in the superincreasing knapsack is somewhere between 200 and 400 bits long. The modulus is chosen to be somewhere between 100 to 200 bits long. Real implementations of the algorithm use random sequence generators to produce these values.

With knapsacks like that, it's futile to try to solve them by brute force. If a computer could try a million possibilities per second, trying all possible knapsack values would take over 10^{46} years. Even a million machines working in parallel wouldn't solve this problem before the sun went nova.

Security of Knapsacks

It wasn't a million machines that broke the knapsack cryptosystem, but a pair of cryptographers. First, Herlestam noticed that often a single bit of the plaintext could be recovered [432]. Then, Shamir showed that the algorithm can be broken in certain circumstances [789,790]. There were other results—[800,21,442,313, 291]—but no one could break the general Merkle-Hellman system. Finally, Shamir and Zippel [792,793,795] found flaws in the transformation that allowed them to reconstruct the superincreasing knapsack from the normal knapsack. The exact arguments are beyond the scope of this book, but a nice summary of them can be found in [687,696]. There is also a nice story about the conference, where the results were presented in [295,297] (the attack was demonstrated on stage using an Apple II computer).

Knapsack Variants

Since the original Merkle-Hellman scheme was broken, many other knapsack systems have been proposed: multiple iterated knapsacks, Graham-Shamir knapsacks, etc. These have all been analyzed and broken, generally using the same cryptographic techniques [162,156,170,516,10,514,515,517,221,157,164,158]. (Many more proposed knapsack algorithms litter the cryptologic highway; a good overview of these systems and their cryptanalysis can be found in [168,282,160,169].)

Other cryptographic systems have been proposed that use ideas similar to those used in knapsack cryptosystems, but these too have been broken. The Lu-Lee cryptosystem [558,8] was broken in [13,372,494]. Attacks on the Niederreiter cryptosystem [648] can be found in [168,169], as can attacks against the Goodman-McAuley cryptosystem [386,387]. The Pieprzyk cryptosystem [697] can be broken by similar attacks. The Niemi cryptosystem [649], based on modular knapsacks, was broken in [209,458].

While there is still a variation of the knapsack algorithm that is currently still secure—the Chor-Rivest knapsack [213]—the amount of computation required makes it far less useful than the other algorithms discussed here. And even worse, considering the ease with which all the other variations fell, it doesn't seem prudent to trust them.

Patents

The original Merkle-Hellman algorithm is patented in the United States [428] and worldwide (see Table 12.1). PKP licenses the patent, along with other public-key cryptography patents. Anyone interested in obtaining a license should contact:

> Robert B. Fougner
> Director of Licensing
> Public Key Partners
> 130 B Kifer Court
> Sunnyvale, CA 94086
> Tel: (408) 735-6779

The U.S. patent will expire on August 19, 1997.

TABLE 12.1
Foreign Merkle-Hellman Knapsack Patents

COUNTRY	NUMBER	DATE
Belgium	871039	5 Apr 1979
Netherlands	7810063	10 Apr 1979
Great Britain	2006580	2 May 1979
Germany	2843583	10 May 1979
Sweden	7810478	14 May 1979
France	2405532	8 Jun 1979
Germany	2843583	3 Jun 1982
Germany	2857905	15 Jul 1982
Canada	1128159	20 Jul 1982
Great Britain	2006580	18 Aug 1982
Switzerland	63416114	14 Jan 1983
Italy	1099780	28 Sep 1985

12.4   RSA

Soon after Merkle's knapsack algorithm came the first full-fledged public-key algorithm, one that works for encryption as well as for digital signatures. Of all the public-key algorithms proposed over the years, it is by far the easiest to understand and implement. (Martin Gardner published an early description of the algorithm in his "Mathematical Games" column in *Scientific American* [365].) It is also the most popular. Named after the three inventors, Ron Rivest, Adi Shamir, and Leonard Adleman, who first introduced the algorithm in 1978 [749,750], it has since withstood years of extensive cryptanalysis. Although the cryptanalysis neither proved nor disproved RSA's security, it does suggest a confidence level in the theoretical underpinnings of the algorithm.

RSA gets its security from the difficulty of factoring large numbers. The public and private keys are functions of a pair of large (100 to 200 digits or even larger) prime numbers. Recovering the plaintext from one of the keys and the ciphertext is conjectured to be equivalent to factoring the product of the two primes.

To generate the two keys, choose two large prime numbers, p and q. Compute the product:

$$n = p \times q$$

Then randomly choose the encryption key, e, such that e and $(p-1) \times (q-1)$ are relatively prime. Finally, use Euclid's algorithm to compute the decryption key, d, such that

$$e \times d = 1 \ (\mathrm{mod} \ (p-1) \times (q-1))$$

In other words,

$$d = e^{-1} \ (\mathrm{mod} \ (p-1) \times (q-1))$$

Note that d and n are also relatively prime. The numbers e and n are the public key; the number d is the private key. The two primes, p and q, are no longer needed. They should be discarded, but never revealed.

To encrypt a message m, first divide it into numerical blocks such that each block has a unique representation modulo n (with binary data, choose the largest power of 2 less than n). That is, if both p and q are 100-digit primes, then n will have just under 200 digits, and each message block, m_i, should be just under 200 digits long. The encrypted message, c, will be made up of similarly sized message blocks, c_i, of about the same length. The encryption formula is simply:

$$c_i = m_i^e \ (\mathrm{mod} \ n)$$

To decrypt a message, take each encrypted block c_i and compute:

$$m_i = c_i^d \ (\mathrm{mod} \ n)$$

Since:

$$c_i^d = (m_i^e)^d = m_i^{ed} = m_i^{k(p-1)(q-1) + 1} = m_i \times m_i^{k(p-1)(q-1)} = m_i \times 1 = m_i,$$
all mod n

the formula recovers the message. This is summarized in Table 12.2.

TABLE 12.2
RSA Encryption

PUBLIC KEY:

n product of two primes, p and q (p and q must remain secret)

e relatively prime to $(p-1) \times (q-1)$

PRIVATE KEY:

d e^{-1} (mod $(p-1) \times (q-1)$)

ENCRYPTING:

$c = m^e$ (mod n)

DECRYPTING:

$m = c^d$ (mod n)

The message could just as easily have been encrypted with d and decrypted with e; the choice is arbitrary. I am not including the number theory that proves why this works; most current texts on cryptography cover the theory in detail.

A short example will probably go a long way to making this clearer. If $p = 47$ and $q = 71$, then

$$n = p \times q = 3337$$

The encryption key e must have no factors in common with:

$$(p-1) \times (q-1) = 46 \times 70 = 3220$$

Choose e (at random) to be 79. In that case:

$$d = 79^{-1} \ (\text{mod } 3220) = 1019$$

This number was calculated using the extended Euclidean algorithm (see Section 9.3). Publish e and n, and keep d secret. Discard p and q.

To encrypt the message

$$m = 6882326879666683$$

first break it into small blocks. Three-digit blocks work nicely in this case. The message will be encrypted in six blocks, m_i, in which:

$$m_1 = 688$$
$$m_2 = 232$$
$$m_3 = 687$$
$$m_4 = 966$$
$$m_5 = 668$$
$$m_6 = 3$$

The first block is encrypted as:

$$688^{79} \ (\mathrm{mod} \ 3337) = 1570 = c_1$$

Performing the same operation on the subsequent blocks generates an encrypted message:

$$c = 1570 \ 2756 \ 2714 \ 2276 \ 2423 \ 158$$

Decrypting the message requires performing the same exponentiation using the decryption key of 1019. So:

$$1570^{1019} \ (\mathrm{mod} \ 3337) = 688 = m_1$$

The rest of the message can be recovered in this manner.

Security of RSA

The security of RSA depends wholly on the problem of factoring large numbers. Technically that's not true. It is conjectured that the security of RSA depends on the problem of factoring large numbers. It has never been mathematically proven that you need to factor n to calculate m from c and e. It is conceivable that an entirely different way to cryptanalyze RSA might be discovered. However, if this new way allows the cryptanalyst to deduce d, it could also be used as a new way to factor large numbers. I wouldn't worry about it too much.

For the ultra-skeptical, there are RSA variants that have been proven to be as difficult as factoring (see Section 12.6). Also look at [20], which shows that recovering even a single bit of information from an RSA-encrypted ciphertext is as hard as decrypting the entire message.

Nevertheless, factoring n is the most obvious means of attack. Adversaries will have the public key, e, and the modulus, n. To find the decryption key, d, they have to factor n. Section 9.4 discusses the current state of factoring technology. Currently, 110-digit numbers are regularly being factored, and 120-digit numbers will be able to be factored soon. So, n must be larger than that. Some hardware implementations of RSA use 512-bit (154-digit) values for n. I've seen 664-bit (200-digit) values for n in some software implementations. The most paranoid use RSA with 1024-bit (308-digit) n's. Also read about choosing good primes (Section 9.5).

Assuming the complexity of factoring given in Section 9.4, the factoring of a 664-bit number takes 10^{23} steps. Assuming one computer can perform a million steps per second, and that a million-computer network works on the task, it will take almost 4000 years to factor the number. If n is a 1024-bit number, that same array of computers will take 10^{10} years to factor the number.

At a European Institute for System Security workshop, the participants agreed that a 1024-bit modulus should be sufficient for long-term secrets for the next ten years [93]. However, some speakers warned: "Although the participants of this workshop feel best qualified in their respective areas, this statement [with respect to lasting security] should be taken with caution." Caveat emptor.

RSA in Hardware

Much has been written on the subject of hardware implementations of RSA [739,831,819,741,840,495,682,46,786,785,753,222,801]. A good survey article is [161]. Many different chips that perform RSA encryption have been built [737,155,607,742,495,37,439,364,716,861,307,683].

A partial list of currently available RSA chips, from [93,161], is given in Table 12.3.

TABLE 12.3
Existing RSA Chips

COMPANY	CLOCK SPEED	BAUD RATE PER 512 BITS	CLOCK CYCLES PER 512 BIT ENCRYPTION	TECHNOLOGY	BITS PER CHIP	NUMBER OF TRANSISTORS
Alpha Techn.	25MHz	13 K	.98 M	2 micron	1024	180,000
AT&T	15MHz	19 K	.4 M	1.5 micron	298	100,000
British Telecom.	10MHz	5.1 K	1 M	2.5 micron	256	—
Business Sim. Ltd.	5MHz	3.8 K	.67 M	Gate Array	32	—
Calmos Syst. Inc.	20MHz	28 K	.36 M	2 micron	593	95,000
CNET	25MHz	5.3 K	2.3 M	1 micron	1024	100,000
Cryptech	14MHz	17 K	.4 M	Gate Array	120	33,000
Cylink	16MHz	6.8 K	1.2 M	1.5 micron	1024	150,000
Pijnenburg	25MHz	50 K	.256 M	1 micron	1024	400,000
Plessy Crypto.	—	10.2 K	—	—	512	—
Sandia	8MHz	10 K	.4 M	2 micron	272	86,000

Speed of RSA

At its fastest, RSA is about 1000 times slower than DES. The fastest VLSI hardware implementation for RSA with a 512-bit moduli has a throughput of 64 kbps [161]. There are also chips that perform 1024-bit RSA encryption. Currently chips are being planned that will approach 1 mbps using a 512-bit modulus; they will probably be available in 1994. Some manufacturers have implemented RSA in smart cards; these implementations are slower.

In software, DES is about 100 times faster than RSA. These numbers may change slightly as technology changes, but RSA will never approach the speed of symmetric algorithms. This is why most practical systems use RSA only to exchange DES keys, and then use DES to encrypt everything else.

Chosen Ciphertext Attack Against RSA

Scenario 1: Eve, listening in on Alice's communications, manages to collect a ciphertext message, c, encrypted with RSA in her public key. Eve wants to be able to read the message. Mathematically, she wants p, in which:

$$p = c^d$$

To recover p, she first chooses a random number, r, such that r is less than n. She gets Alice's public key, e. Then she computes:

$$x = r^e \bmod n$$
$$y = x \times c \bmod n$$
$$t = r^{-1} \bmod n$$

If $x = r^e \bmod n$, then $r = x^d \bmod n$. Therefore, $t = x^{-d} \bmod n$.

Now, Eve gets Alice to sign y with her private key, thereby decrypting y. (Alice has to sign the message, not the hash of the message.) Remember, Alice has never seen y before. Alice sends Eve:

$$u = y^d \bmod n$$

Now, Eve computes:

$$t \times u \bmod n = x^{-d} \times y^d \bmod n = x^{-d} \times x^d \times c^d \bmod n = c^d \bmod n = p$$

Eve now has p.

Scenario 2: Trent is a computer notary public. If Alice wants a document notarized, she sends it to Trent. Trent signs it with an RSA digital signature and sends it back. (No one-way hash functions are used here; Trent encrypts the entire message with his private key.)

Mallet wants Trent to sign a message he otherwise wouldn't. Maybe it has a phony timestamp; maybe it purports to be from another person. Whatever the reason, Trent would never sign it if he had a choice. Let's call this message N.

First, Mallet chooses an arbitrary value X and computes $Y = X^e$. He can easily get e; it's Trent's public key and must be public to verify his signatures. Then he computes $M = YN$, and sends M to Trent to sign. Trent returns $M^d \bmod n$. Now Mallet calculates $(M^d \bmod n)X^{-1}$, which equals $N^d \bmod n$ and is the signature of N.

Actually, there are several methods that Mallet can use to accomplish these same things [240,270,289]. The weakness they all exploit is the fact that exponentiation preserves the multiplicative structure of the input. That is:

$$(XM)^d = X^d M^d \bmod n$$

Scenario 3: Eve wants to Alice to sign M_3. She generates two messages, M_1 and M_2, such that:

$$M_3 \equiv M_1 \times M_2 \ (\mathrm{mod}\ n)$$

If she gets Alice to sign M_1 and M_2, she can calculate M_3:

$$M_3^{\ d} \ (\mathrm{mod}\ n) = M_1^{\ d} \ (\mathrm{mod}\ n) \times M_2^{\ d} \ (\mathrm{mod}\ n)$$

Moral: Never use RSA to sign a random document presented to you by a stranger. Always use a one-way hash function first or a different signature algorithm altogether.

Common Modulus Attack on RSA

Let's make life easier, and give everyone the same n. They can have different values for e and d, but the same n. Unfortunately, this doesn't work. The most obvious problem is that if the same message is ever encrypted with two different keys (both having the same modulus), and those two keys are relatively prime (which they generally would be), then the plaintext can be recovered without either of the decryption keys [820].

Let P be the plaintext message. The two encryption keys are e_1 and e_2. The common modulus is n. The two ciphertext messages are:

$$C_1 = P^{e_1} \ \mathrm{mod}\ n$$
$$C_2 = P^{e_2} \ \mathrm{mod}\ n$$

The cryptanalysts know n, e_1, e_2, C_1, and C_2. Here's how they recover P.

Since e_1 and e_2 are relatively prime, the Euclidean algorithm can find r and s, such that:

$$r \times e_1 + s \times e_2 = 1$$

Assuming r is negative (either r or s has to be), then the Euclidean algorithm can be used again to calculate C_1^{-1}. Then:

$$(C_1^{-1})^{-r} \times C_2^{\ s} = P \ \mathrm{mod}\ n$$

There are two other, more subtle, attacks against this type of system. One attack uses a probabilistic method for factoring n. The other uses a deterministic algorithm for calculating someone's secret key without factoring the modulus. Both attacks are described in detail in [260]. Moral: Don't share n among a group of users.

Low Exponent Attack Against RSA

Another suggestion to "improve" RSA is to use low values for e, the public key. This makes encryption fast and easy to perform. Unfortunately, it is also insecure. Hastad demonstrated a successful attack against RSA with a low encryption key [417]. Another attack by Michael Wiener will recover e, when e is up to one quarter the size of n [878]. A low decryption key, d, is just as serious a problem. Moral: Choose large values for e and d.

Lessons Learned

Moore lists several restrictions on the use of RSA, based on the success of these attacks [618,619]:

- Knowledge of one encryption/decryption pair of exponents for a given modulus enables an attacker to factor the modulus.

- Knowledge of one encryption/decryption pair of exponents for a given modulus enables an attacker to calculate other encryption/decryption pairs without having to factor n.

- A common modulus should not be used in a protocol using RSA in a communications network. (This should be obvious from the previous two points.)

- The exponents chosen in a protocol should not be small.

Remember, it is not enough to have a secure cryptographic algorithm. The entire cryptosystem must be secure, and the cryptographic protocol must be secure. If there is a failure in any of those three areas, the overall system is insecure.

Standards

RSA is a de facto standard in much of the world. The International Organization of Standards, ISO/IEC 9796, specifies RSA for digital signatures [446]. The French banking community has also standardized on RSA [310]. The United States currently has no standard for public-key encryption but will probably standardize on the Digital Signature Standard (see Section 13.5) for digital signatures.

Patents

The RSA algorithm is patented in the United States [751]. It is not patented in any other country. PKP licenses the patent, along with other public-key cryptography patents. Anyone interested in obtaining a license should contact:

Robert B. Fougner
Director of Licensing
Public Key Partners
130 B Kifer Court
Sunnyvale, CA 94086
Tel: (408) 735-6779

The U.S. patent will expire on September 20, 2000.

12.5   POHLIG-HELLMAN

The Pohlig-Hellman encryption scheme [703] is similar to RSA. It is not a symmetric algorithm, because different keys are used for encryption and decryption.

It is not a public-key scheme. Both the encryption and decryption keys must be kept secret.

Like RSA,

$$C = M^e \bmod n$$
$$M = C^d \bmod n$$

in which

$$ed = 1 \bmod \text{a complicated number}$$

Unlike RSA, n is not defined in terms of two large primes; it must remain part of the secret key. If someone had e and n, they could calculate d. Without knowledge of e or d, an adversary would be forced to calculate

$$e = \log_M C \bmod n$$

We have already seen that this is a hard problem.

Patents

The Pohlig-Hellman algorithm is patented in the United States [430] and also in Canada. PKP licenses the patent, along with other public-key cryptography patents. Anyone interested in obtaining a license should contact:

Robert B. Fougner
Director of Licensing
Public Key Partners
130 B Kifer Court
Sunnyvale, CA 94086
Tel: (408) 735-6779

12.6   RABIN

Rabin's scheme [724,880] gets its security from the difficulty of finding square roots modulo a composite. This problem is equivalent to factoring.

First choose two primes, p and q, both congruent to 3 mod 4. These primes are the private key; $n = pq$ is the public key.

To encrypt a message, M (M must be less than n), simply compute

$$C = M^2 \bmod n$$

Decrypting the message is just as easy, but slightly more annoying. Since the receivers know p and q, they can solve the two congruences using the Chinese remainder theorem. Compute:

$$M_1 = C^{(p+1)/4} \bmod n$$
$$M_2 = p - C^{(p+1)/4} \bmod n$$
$$M_3 = C^{(q+1)/4} \bmod n$$
$$M_4 = q - C^{(q+1)/4} \bmod n$$

One of those four results, M_1, M_2, M_3, or M_4, equals M. If the message is English text, it should be easy to choose the correct M. On the other hand, if the message is a random bit stream (say, for key generation) or a digital signature, there is no way to determine which M_i is correct.

Consequently, Rabin did not propose this as a public-key cryptography algorithm. However, ElGamal later adapted this idea for his public-key algorithm (see Section 13.3).

Williams

Williams redefined Rabin's schemes to eliminate these shortcomings [880]. In his scheme, p and q are selected such that:

$$p = -1 \pmod 4$$
$$q = -1 \pmod 4$$

and

$$N = p \times q$$

Also, there is a small integer, S, such that $J(S, N) = -1$. ("J" is the Jacobi symbol.) N and S are public. The secret key is k, such that:

$$k = 1/2 \times (1/4 \times (p-1) \times (q-1) + 1)$$

To encrypt a message, M, compute c_1 such that $J(M, N) = (-1)^{a_1}$. Then, compute $M' = S^{c_1} \times M \pmod N$. Like Rabin's scheme, $C = M'^2 \pmod N$. And $c_2 = M' \pmod 2$. The final ciphertext message is the triple:

$$(C, c_1, c_2)$$

To decrypt C, the receiver computes M'' using:

$$C^k = \pm M'' \pmod N$$

The proper sign of M'' is given by c_2. Finally:

$$M = S^{-c_1} \times (-1)^{c_1} \times M'' \pmod N$$

Williams refined this scheme further in [882,883]. Instead of squaring the plaintext message, cube it. The large primes must be congruent to 1 mod 3;

otherwise the public and private keys are the same. Even better, there is only one unique decryption for each encryption.

This algorithm has an advantage over RSA in that it is provably as secure as factoring, and it is completely insecure against a chosen-ciphertext attack. I recommend using RSA.

12.7 FEIGE-FIAT-SHAMIR

Amos Fiat and Adi Shamir's authentication and digital signature scheme is discussed in [348,349]. Uriel Feige, Fiat, and Shamir modified the algorithm to a zero-knowledge proof of identity [332,333]. This is the best-known zero-knowledge proof of identity.

On July 9, 1986, the three authors submitted a U.S. patent application [799]. Because of potential military applications, the application was reviewed by the military. The patent office had six months to respond with a secrecy order. On January 6, 1987, three days before the end of the six-month period, the patents and trademarks office imposed the order at the request of the army. They stated that ". . . the disclosure or publication of the subject matter . . . would be detrimental to the national security. . . ." The authors were ordered to notify all Americans to whom the research had been disclosed that unauthorized disclosure could lead to two years imprisonment, a ten-thousand-dollar fine, or both. Furthermore, the authors had to inform the commissioner of patents and trademarks of all foreign nationals to whom the information had been disclosed.

This was ludicrous. All through the second half of 1986, the authors had presented the work at conferences throughout Israel, Europe, and the United States. The authors weren't even American citizens; all the work had been done at the Weizmann Institute in Israel.

Word of this spread through the academic community and the press. Within two days the secrecy order was rescinded; Shamir and others believe that the NSA pulled strings to rescind the order, although they officially had no comment. Further details of this story are in [528].

Simplified Feige-Fiat-Shamir Identification Scheme

Before issuing any private keys, the arbitrator chooses a random modulus, n, which is the product of two large primes. In real life, n should be at least 512 bits long and probably closer to 1024 bits. This n can be shared among a group of provers.

To generate Peggy's public and private keys, a trusted arbitrator chooses a number, v, when v is a quadratic residue mod n. In other words, choose v such that $x^2 = v \bmod n$ has a solution and $v^{-1} \bmod n$ exists. This is the public key. Then calculate the smallest s for which $s = \mathrm{sqrt}(1/v) \bmod n$. This is the private key.

The identification protocol can now proceed:

(1) Peggy picks a random r, where r is less than n. She then computes $x = r^2 \bmod n$, and sends x to Victor.

(2) Victor sends Peggy a random bit, b.

(3) If $b = 0$, then Peggy sends Victor r. If $b = 1$, then Peggy sends Victor $y = r \times s$ mod n.

(4) If $b = 0$, Victor verifies that $x = r^2$ mod n, proving that Peggy knows sqrt(x). If $b = 1$, Victor verifies that $x = y^2 \times v$ mod n, proving that Peggy knows sqrt(x/v).

This protocol is a single **accreditation.** Peggy and Victor repeat this protocol t times, until Victor is convinced that Peggy knows s. This is a cut-and-choose protocol. If Peggy doesn't know s, she can pick r such that she can fool Victor if he sends her a 0, or she can pick r such that she can fool Victor if he sends her a 1. She can't do both. The odds of her fooling Victor once is 50%. The odds of her fooling him t times are 1 in 2^t.

Another way of attacking the protocol would be for Victor to try to impersonate Peggy. He could initiate the protocol with another verifier, Valerie. In step (1), instead of choosing a random r, he would just reuse an old r that he saw Peggy use. However, the odds of Valerie's choosing the same value for b in step (2) that Victor did in the protocol with Peggy are 1 in 2. So, the odds of his fooling Valerie are 50%. The odds of his fooling her t times are 1 in 2^t.

For this to work it is imperative that Peggy not reuse an r. If she did, and Victor sent Peggy the other random bit in step (2), then he would have both of Peggy's responses. All he has to do is to collect t of these, and then he can impersonate her.

Feige-Fiat-Shamir Identification Scheme

In their papers [332,333], Feige, Fiat, and Shamir show how parallel construction can increase the number of accreditations per round and reduce Peggy and Victor's interactions.

First generate n as above, as the product of two large primes. To generate Peggy's public and private keys, first choose k different numbers: $v_1, v_2 \ldots v_k$, where v_i is a quadratic residue mod n. In other words, choose v_i such that $x^2 = v_i$ mod n has a solution. This string, $v_1, v_2 \ldots v_k$, is the public key. Then calculate the smallest s_i such that $s_i = $ sqrt$(1/v_i)$ mod n. This string, $s_1, s_2, \ldots s_k$, is the private key.

And the protocol is:

(1) Peggy picks a random r, where r is less than n. She then computes $x = r^2$ mod n, and sends x to Victor.

(2) Victor sends Peggy a random binary string k-bits long: $b_1, b_2, \ldots b_k$.

(3) Peggy computes $y = r \times (s_1 b_1 \times s_2 b_2 \times \ldots \times s_k b_k)$ mod n. (She multiplies the values of s together based on the random binary string Victor sent her. If Victor's first bit is a 1, then s_1 is multiplied; if Victor's first bit is a 0, then s_1 is not multiplied.) She sends y to Victor.

(4) Victor verifies that $x = y^2 \times (v_1 b_1 \times v_2 b_2 \times \ldots \times v_k b_k)$ mod n. (He multiplies the values of s together based on the random binary string. If his first bit is a 1, then s_1 is multiplied; if his first bit is a 0, then s_1 is not multiplied.)

Peggy and Victor repeat this protocol t times, until Victor is convinced that Peggy knows $s_1, s_2, \ldots s_k$.

The chance that Peggy can fool Victor is 1 in 2^{kt}, where t is the number of times they repeat the protocol. They recommend a 1 in 2^{20} chance of a cheater's fooling Victor and suggest that $k = 5$ and $t = 4$. If you are more paranoid, increase these numbers.

An Example

Let's look at this protocol in action with small numbers.

If $n = 35$ (the two primes are 5 and 7), then the possible quadratic residues are:

1: $x^2 = $ 1 mod 35 has a solution: $x = 1, 6, 29$, or 34.
4: $x^2 = $ 4 mod 35 has a solution: $x = 2, 12, 23$, or 33.
9: $x^2 = $ 9 mod 35 has a solution: $x = 3, 17, 18$, or 32.
11: $x^2 = 11$ mod 35 has a solution: $x = 9, 16, 19$, or 26.
14: $x^2 = 14$ mod 35 has a solution: $x = 7$ or 28.
15: $x^2 = 15$ mod 35 has a solution: $x = 15$ or 20.
16: $x^2 = 16$ mod 35 has a solution: $x = 4, 11, 24$, or 31.
21: $x^2 = 21$ mod 35 has a solution: $x = 14$ or 21.
25: $x^2 = 25$ mod 35 has a solution: $x = 5$ or 30.
29: $x^2 = 29$ mod 35 has a solution: $x = 8, 13, 22$, or 27.
30: $x^2 = 30$ mod 35 has a solution: $x = 10$ or 25.

The inverses (mod 35) and their square roots are:

v	v^{-1}	$S=\sqrt{v^{-1}}$
1	1	1
4	9	3
9	4	2
11	16	4
16	11	9
29	29	8

Note that 14, 15, 21, 25, and 30 do not have inverses mod 35, because they are not relatively prime to 35. This makes sense, because there should be $(5-1) \times (7-1)/4$ quadratic residues mod 35 (see Section 9.3).

So, Peggy gets the public key consisting of $k = 4$ values: {4,11,16,29}. The corresponding private key is {3,4,9,8}. Here's one round of the protocol:

(1) Peggy chooses a random $r=16$, computes 16^2 mod 35 = 11, and sends it to Victor.

(2) Victor sends Peggy a random binary string {1,1,0,1}.

(3) Peggy computes $16 \times ((3^1) \times (4^1) \times (9^0) \times (8^1)) \bmod 35 = 31$ and sends it to Bob.

(4) Bob verifies that $31^2 \times ((4^1) \times (11^1) \times (16^0)) \times (29^1) \bmod 35 = 11$.

Peggy and Victor repeat the protocol, each time with a different random r, until Victor is satisfied.

With small values like these, there's no real security. But when n is 512 bits long or more, Victor cannot learn anything about Peggy's secret key except the fact that she knows it.

Enhancements

It is possible to embed identification information into the protocol. Assume that I is a binary string representing Peggy's identification: her name, address, social security number, hat size, preferred brand of soft drink, etc. Use a one-way hash function $H(x)$ to compute $H(I,j)$, where j is a small random number concatenated onto I. Find a set of j's where $H(I,j)$ is a quadratic residue mod n. These j's become $v_1, v_2 \ldots v_k$. Peggy's public key is now I and the list of j's. She sends I and the list of j's to Victor before step (1) of the protocol, and Victor generates $v_1, v_2, \ldots v_k$ from $H(I,j)$.

Now, after Victor has successfully completed the protocol with Peggy, he is assured that someone knowing the factorization of the modulus has certified the association between I and Peggy by giving her the square roots of the v_i derived from I.

The authors Feige-Fiat-Shamir also include the following implementation remarks:

> For nonperfect hash functions, it may be advisable to randomize I by concatenating it with a long random string, R. This string is chosen by the arbitrator and is revealed to Victor along with I.

> In typical implementations, k should between 1 and 18. Larger values of k can reduce the time and communication complexity by reducing the number of rounds.

> The value n should be at least 512 bits long.

> If all users choose their own n and publish it in a public key file, they can dispense with the arbitrator. However, this RSA-like variant makes the scheme considerably less convenient.

Fiat-Shamir Signature Scheme

Turning this identification scheme into a signature scheme is basically a matter of turning Victor into a hash function. The primary benefit of the Fiat-Shamir digital signature scheme over RSA is that the typical signature requires only 1% to 4% of the modular multiplications. Therefore, it is a lot faster. For this protocol, we'll use the names Alice and Bob.

The setup is the same as the identification scheme. Choose n to be the product of two large primes. Generate the public key, $v_1, v_2, \ldots v_k$, and the private key, $s_1, s_2, \ldots s_k$, such that $s_i = \mathrm{sqrt}(1/v_i) \bmod n$.

(1) Alice picks t random integers fewer than n: $r_1, r_2, \ldots, r_t$, and computes x_1, $x_2, \ldots, x_t$ such that $x_i = r_i^2 \bmod n$.

(2) Alice hashes the concatenation of the message and the string of x's to generate a bit stream: $H(m, x_1, x_2, \ldots x_t)$. She uses the first $k \times t$ bits of this string as values of b_{ij}, when i goes from 1 to t, and j goes from 1 to k.

(3) Alice computes $y_1, y_2, \ldots, y_t$, where

$$y_i = r_i \times (s_1 b_{i1} \times s_2 b_{i2} \times \ldots \times s_j b_{ij} \times s_k b_{ik}) \bmod n$$

(She multiplies the values of s together based on the random b_{ij} values. If b_{i1} is a 1, then s_1 is multiplied; if b_{i1} is a 0, then s_1 is not multiplied.)

(4) Alice sends Bob m, all the bit values of b_{ij}, and all the values of y_i. He already has Alice's public key: $v_1, v_2, \ldots, v_k$.

(5) Bob computes $z_1, z_2, \ldots, z_t$, where

$$z_i = y_i^2 \times (v_1 b_{i1} \times v_2 b_{i2} \times \ldots v_j b_{ij} \times v_k b_{ik}) \bmod n$$

(Again, Bob multiplies based on the b_{ij} values. Note that z_i should be equal to x_i.)

(6) Bob verifies that the first $k \times t$ bits of $H(m, z_1, z_2, \ldots z_t)$ are the b_{ij} values that Alice sent him.

As with the identification scheme, the security of this signature scheme is proportional to $1/2^{kt}$. It is also related to the difficulty of factoring n. Fiat and Shamir pointed out that forging a signature is easiest when the complexity of factoring n is considerably higher than 2^{kt}. And, because of birthday-type attacks (see Section 14.1), they recommend that $k \times t$ be increased from 20 to at least 72. They suggest $k = 9$ and $t = 8$.

Improved Fiat-Shamir Signature Scheme

Silvio Micali and Adi Shamir improved the Fiat-Shamir protocol in [601]. They chose $v_1, v_2, \ldots v_k$ to be the first k prime numbers. So

$$v_1 = 2, v_2 = 3, v_3 = 5, \text{ etc.}$$

This is the public key.

The private key, $s_1, s_2, \ldots s_k$ is a random square root, determined by

$$s_i = \sqrt{v_i^{-1}} \bmod n$$

In this version, every person must have a different n. The modification makes it easier to verify signatures. The time required to generate signatures, and the security of those signatures, is unaffected.

Other Enhancements

There is also an N-party identification scheme, based on the Fiat-Shamir algorithm [165]. Two other improvements to the Fiat-Shamir scheme are proposed in [679].

Ohta-Okamoto Identification Scheme

This protocol is a modification of Feige-Fiat-Shamir and gets its security from the difficulty of factoring [664,665]. The same authors also wrote a multisignature scheme, by which a number of different people can sequentially sign a message [666]. This scheme has been proposed for smart-card implementation [484].

Patents

Fiat-Shamir is patented [799]. Anyone interested in licensing the algorithm should contact:

Yeda Research and Development
The Weizmann Institute of Science
Rehovot 76100
Israel

More Public-Key Algorithms

13.1 GUILLOU-QUISQUATER

Fiat-Shamir was the first practical zero-knowledge proof of identity. It minimized the computation required in the exchange by increasing the number of iterations and accreditations per iteration. For some implementations, like smart cards, this is less than ideal. Exchanges with the outside world are time-consuming, and the storage required for each accreditation can strain the limited resources of the card.

Guillou and Quisquater developed a zero-knowledge identification algorithm more suited to applications like these [401,721]. The number of exchanges between Peggy and Victor, and the number of parallel accreditations in each exchange, are both kept to an absolute minimum: there is only one exchange of one accreditation for each proof. The computation required by Guillou-Quisquater is more than by Fiat-Shamir for the same level of security, by a factor of three.

Like Fiat-Shamir, this identification algorithm can be converted to a digital signature algorithm. For the same reasons as discussed earlier, it is also suited for smart-card applications.

Guillou-Quisquater Identification Scheme

Peggy is a smart card who wants to prove her identity to Victor. Peggy's identity consists of a set of credentials: a data string consisting of the card's name, validity period, a bank account number, and whatever else the application warrants. This bit string is called J. (Actually, the credentials can be a longer string, and hashed to a J value. This complexity does not modify the protocol in any way, however.) This is analogous to the public key. Other public information, shared by all "Peggys" who could use this application, is an exponent v and a modulus n, when

n is the product of two secret primes. The private key is B, calculated such that $JB^v \equiv 1 \pmod{n}$.

Peggy sends Victor her credentials, J. Now, she wants to prove to Victor that those credentials are hers. To do this, she has to convince Victor that she knows B. Here's the protocol:

(1) Peggy picks a random integer, r, such that r is between 1 and $n-1$. She computes $T \equiv r^v \pmod{n}$ and sends it to Victor.

(2) Victor picks a random integer, d, such that d is between zero and $v-1$. He sends d to Peggy.

(3) Peggy computes $D \equiv rB^d \pmod{n}$ and sends it to Victor.

(4) Victor computes $T' = D^v J^d \pmod{n}$. If $T \equiv T' \pmod{n}$, then the authentication succeeds.

The math isn't that complex:

$$T' = D^v J^d = (rB^d)^v J^d = r^v B^{dv} J^d = r^v (JB^v)^d = r^v \equiv T \pmod{n}$$

since B was constructed to satisfy:

$$JB^v \equiv 1 \pmod{n}$$

Guillou-Quisquater Signature Scheme

This identification can be converted to a signature scheme, also suited for smart-card implementation [402,403].

The public and private key setup is the same as before. Here's the protocol:

(1) Alice picks a random integer, r, such that r is between 1 and $n-1$. She computes $T \equiv r^v \pmod{n}$.

(2) Alice computes $d = H(M,T)$, where M is the message being signed and $H(x)$ is a one-way hash function.

(3) Alice computes $D \equiv rB^d \pmod{n}$. The signature consists of the message, M, the two calculated values, d and D, and her credentials, J.

(4) Bob computes $T' = D^v J^d \pmod{n}$. He then computes $d' = H(M,T')$. If $d \equiv d'$, then Alice must know B, and the signature is valid.

Multiple Signatures

What if many people wanted to sign the same document? There is an easy solution—each of them signs separately—but this signature scheme can do better than that. This example has Alice and Bob signing the same document and Carol verifying the signatures, but any number of people can be involved in the signature process. As before, Alice and Bob have their own unique J and B values: J_A and J_B, and B_A and B_B. The values n and v are common to the system.

(1) Alice picks a random integer, r_A, such that r_A is between 1 and $n-1$. She computes $T_A \equiv r_A{}^v \pmod{n}$.

(2) Bob picks a random integer, r_B, such that r_B is between 1 and $n-1$. He computes $T_B \equiv r_B{}^v \pmod{n}$.

(3) Alice and Bob compute $T \equiv T_A T_B \pmod{n}$.

(4) Alice and Bob compute $d = H(M,T)$, when M is the message being signed and $H(x)$ is a one-way hash function.

(5) Alice computes $D_A \equiv r_A B_A{}^d \pmod{n}$.

(6) Bob computes $D_B \equiv r_B B_B{}^d \pmod{n}$.

(7) Alice and Bob compute $D \equiv D_A D_B \pmod{n}$. The signature consists of the message, M, the two calculated values, d and D, and both of their credentials: J_A and J_B.

(8) Carol computes $J \equiv J_A J_B$.

(9) Carol computes $T' = D^v J^d \pmod{n}$. She then computes $d' = H(M,T')$. If $d \equiv d'$, then the multiple signature is valid.

This protocol can be extended to any number of people. For multiple people to sign, they all multiply their individual T_i values together in step (3) and their individual D_i values together in step (7). To verify a multiple signature, multiply all the signers' J_i values together in step (8). In banking, this ability for multiple people to cosign a document could be useful.

13.2   ONG-SCHNORR-SHAMIR

Ong, Schnorr, and Shamir developed a class of signature schemes using polynomials modulo n [680,681].

Choose a large integer n (it is not necessary to know the factorization of n). Then choose a random integer, k, such that k and n are relatively prime. Calculate h such that:

$$h = -k^{-2} \pmod{n} = -(k^{-1})^2 \pmod{n}$$

The public key is h and n; k is the private key.

To sign a message, M, first generate a random number, r, such that r and n are relatively prime. Then calculate:

$$S_1 = 1/2 \times (M/r + r) \pmod{n}$$
$$S_2 = k/2 \times (M/r - r) \pmod{n}$$

The pair, S_1 and S_2, is the signature.

To verify a signature, confirm that:

$$M \equiv S_1{}^2 + h \times S_2{}^2 \pmod{n}$$

The version of the scheme described here is based on quadratic polynomials. When it was first proposed in [678], a $100 reward was offered for successful cryptanalysis. Pollard proved it insecure [705], but its authors were not deterred. They proposed a modification of the algorithm based on cubic polynomials, which Pollard also broke [705]. The authors then proposed a quartic version [705], which was also broken [319,705]. There have been no more schemes of this type proposed since then.

13.3   ELGAMAL

The ElGamal scheme [316], first presented in [315], is a variant of Rabin (see Section 12.6). It can be used for both digital signatures and encryption and gets its security from the difficulty of calculating discrete logarithms.

To generate a key pair, first choose a prime, p, and two random numbers, g and x, such that both g and x are less than p. Then calculate

$$y = g^x \pmod{p}$$

The public key is y, g, and p. Both g and p can be shared among a group of users. The private key is x.

ElGamal Signatures

To sign a message, M, first choose a random number, k, such that k is relatively prime to $p-1$. Then compute

$$a = g^k \pmod{p}$$

and use the extended Euclidean algorithm to solve for b in the following equation:

$$M = xa + kb \pmod{p-1}$$

The signature is the pair: a and b. The random variable, k, must be kept secret. To verify a signature, confirm that

$$y^a a^b \pmod{p} = g^M \pmod{p}$$

This is summarized in Table 13.1.

For example, choose $p = 11$ and $g = 2$. Choose private key $x = 8$. Calculate:

$$y = g^x \pmod{p} = 2^8 \pmod{11} = 3$$

The public key is $y = 3$, $g = 2$, and $p = 11$.

TABLE 13.1
ElGamal Signatures

PUBLIC KEY:

p prime (can be shared among a group of users)

g $<p$ (can be shared among a group of users)

y $= g^x \pmod{p}$

PRIVATE KEY:

x $<p$

SIGNING:

k choose at random, relatively prime to $p-1$.

a (signature) $= g^k \pmod{p}$

b (signature) such that $M = xa + kb \pmod{p-1}$

VERIFYING:

Accept as valid if $y^a a^b \pmod{p} = g^M \pmod{p}$

To authenticate $M = 5$, first choose a random number, $k = 9$. Confirm that $\gcd(9,10) = 1$. Compute:

$$a = g^k \pmod{p} = 2^9 \pmod{11} = 6$$

and use the Euclidean algorithm to solve for b:

$$M = ax + kb \pmod{p-1}$$
$$5 = 8 \times 6 + 9 \times b \pmod{10}$$

The solution is $b = 3$ and the signature is the pair: $a = 6$ and $b = 3$.

To verify a signature, confirm that

$$y^a a^b \pmod{p} = g^M \pmod{p}$$
$$3^6 6^3 \pmod{11} = 2^5 \pmod{11}$$

Since the math is all correct, they do this step.

Thomas Beth invented a variant of the ElGamal scheme suitable for proofs of identity [90].

ElGamal Encryption

A modification of ElGamal can encrypt messages. To encrypt message M, first choose a random k, such that k is relatively prime to $p-1$. Then compute:

$$a = g^k \bmod p$$
$$b = y^k M \bmod p$$

The pair, a and b, is the ciphertext. Note that the ciphertext is twice the size of the plaintext.

To decrypt a and b, compute:

$$b/a^x \ (\text{mod } p)$$

Since $a^x \equiv g^{kx}$ mod p, and $b/a^x \equiv y^k M/a^x \equiv g^{xk} M/g^{xk} \equiv M$ mod p, this all works (see Table 13.2).

TABLE 13.2
ElGamal Encryption

PUBLIC KEY:

     p prime (can be shared among a group of users)

     g $< p$ (can be shared among a group of users)

     y $= g^x \ (\text{mod } p)$

PRIVATE KEY:

     x $< p$

ENCRYPTING:

     k choose at random, relatively prime to $p-1$

     a (ciphertext) $= g^k \ (\text{mod } p)$

     b (ciphertext) $= y^K M \ (\text{mod } p)$

DECRYPTING:

     M (plaintext) $= b/a^x \ (\text{mod } p)$

Patents

ElGamal is unpatented. But, before you go ahead and implement the algorithm, realize that PKP feels that this algorithm is covered under the Diffie-Hellman patent [426].

13.4   SCHNORR

Schnorr's authentication and signature scheme [776,777] combines ideas from ElGamal [316], Fiat-Shamir [348], and David Chaum, Jan-Hendrik Evertse, and Jeroen van de Graaf's interactive protocol [205,204]. It gets its security from the difficulty of calculating discrete logarithms.

To generate a key pair, first choose two primes, p and q, such that q is a prime factor of $p-1$. Then, choose an a not equal to 1, such that $a^q = 1$ mod p. All these numbers can be common to a group of users and can be freely published.

To generate a particular public/private key pair, choose a random number less than q. This is the private key, s. Then calculate $v = a^{-s}$ mod p. This is the public key.

Authentication Protocol

(1) Peggy picks a random number, r, less than q, and computes $x = a^r \bmod p$. This is the preprocessing stage and can be done long before Victor is present.

(2) Victor sends Peggy a random number, e, between 0 and 2^t-1. (I'll discuss t in a moment.)

(3) Peggy computes $y = r + s \times e \bmod q$ and sends y to Victor.

(4) Victor verifies that $x = a^y v^e \bmod p$.

The security is based on the parameter t. The difficulty of breaking the algorithm is about 2^t. Schnorr recommends that p be about 512 bits and q be about 140 bits. The value of t that is commensurate with this kind of security is $t = 72$, which Schnorr feels is secure enough.

Digital Signature Protocol

The private/public key pair is the same, but we're now adding a one-way hash function, $H(M)$.

(1) Alice picks a random number, r, less than q, and computes $x = a^r \bmod p$. This computation is the preprocessing stage.

(2) Alice concatenates the message and x, and hashes the result:

$$e = H(m,x)$$

Alice computes $y = r + s \times e \bmod q$. The signature is e and y; she sends these to Bob.

(3) Bob computes $z = a^y v^e \bmod p$. He then confirms that the concatenation of the message and z hashes to e:

$$e = H(m,z)$$

If they do, he accepts the signature as valid.

In his paper, Schnorr cites these novel features of his algorithm:

> Most of the computation for signature generation can be completed in a preprocessing stage, independent of the message being signed. Hence, it can be done during idle time and not affect the signature speed. An attack against this preprocessing stage is discussed in [279], but I don't think it's practical.

> For the same level of security, the length of signatures is less for Schnorr than for RSA. For example, with a 140-bit q, signatures are only 212-bits

long, less than half the length of RSA signatures. Schnorr's signatures are also much shorter than ElGamal's.

A modification of this algorithm, by Ernie Brickell and Kevin McCurley, enhances its security. It is in [166].

Patents

Schnorr is patented in the United States [778] and in many other countries. In 1993, PKP acquired the worldwide rights to the patent. The U.S. patent expires on February 19, 2008.

13.5   DIGITAL SIGNATURE ALGORITHM (DSA)

In August 1991, The National Institute of Standards and Technology (NIST) proposed the Digital Signature Algorithm (DSA) for use in their new Digital Signature Standard (DSS). According to the *Federal Register* [329]:

> A Federal Information Processing Standard (FIPS) for Digital Signature Standard (DSS) is being proposed. This proposed standard specifies a public-key digital signature algorithm (DSA) appropriate for Federal digital signature applications. The proposed DSS uses a public key to verify to a recipient the integrity of data and identity of the sender of the data. The DSS can also be used by a third party to ascertain the authenticity of a signature and the data associated with it.
>
> This proposed standard adopts a public-key signature scheme that uses a pair of transformations to generate and verify a digital value called a signature.

And:

> This proposed FIPS is the result of evaluating a number of alternative digital signature techniques. In making the selection NIST has followed the mandate contained in section 2 of the Computer Security Act of 1987 that NIST develop standards to ". . . assure the cost-effective security and privacy of Federal information and, among technologies offering comparable protection, on selecting the option with the most desirable operating and use characteristics.
>
> Among the factors that were considered during this process were the level of security provided, the ease of implementation in both hardware and software, the ease of export from the U.S., the applicability of patents, impact on national security and law enforcement and the level of efficiency in both the signing and verification functions.
>
> A number of techniques were deemed to provide appropriate protection for Federal systems. The technique selected has the following desirable characteristics:

—NIST expects it to be available on a royalty-free basis. Broader use of this technique resulting from public availability should be an economic benefit to the government and the public.

—The technique selected provides for efficient implementation of the signature operations in smart card applications. In these applications the signing operations are performed in the computationally modest environment of the smart card while the verification process is implemented in a more computationally rich environment such as a personal computer, a hardware cryptographic module, or a mainframe computer.

Before it gets too confusing, let me review the nomenclature: DSA is the algorithm; the DSS is the standard. The standard employs the algorithm. The algorithm is part of the standard. (NIST claimed that having DES meant that both the algorithm and the standard were too confusing—I'm not sure this is much better.)

Reaction to the Announcement

NIST's announcement created a maelstrom of criticisms and accusations. Unfortunately, it was more political than academic. RSA Data Security, Inc., purveyors of the RSA algorithm, led the criticism against DSS. They wanted RSA, not another algorithm, used as the standard. RSADSI makes a lot of money licensing the RSA algorithm, and a royalty-free digital signature standard would directly affect their bottom line. (Note: DSA is not necessarily free of any patent infringements; I'll discuss that later.)

Before the algorithm was announced, RSADSI campaigned against a "common modulus," which might have given the government the ability to forge signatures. When the algorithm was announced without this common modulus, they attacked it on other grounds [97], both in letters to NIST and statements to the press. (Four letters to NIST appeared in [747]. When reading them, keep in mind that at least two of the authors, R. Rivest and M. Hellman, have a financial interest in DSS's not being approved.)

Many large software companies that already licensed the RSA algorithm came out against the DSS. In 1982, the government solicited public-key algorithms for a standard [328]. After that, there wasn't a peep out of NIST for nine years. Companies such as IBM, Apple, Novell, Lotus, Northern Telecom, Microsoft, DEC, and Sun had already spent large amounts of money implementing the RSA algorithm. They were not interested in losing their investment.

In all, NIST received 109 comments by the end of the first comment period on February 28, 1992.

Let's look at the criticisms against DSA, one by one:

1. DSA cannot be used for encryption or key distribution.

    This is true, but that is not the point of the standard. It is a signature standard. There should be a NIST standard for public-key encryption. NIST is committing a grave injustice to the American people by not implementing a public-key encryption standard. It is suspicious that NIST proposed a digital signature standard that cannot be used for encryption. (As it turns out, though, it can—see Section 16.6.) That does not mean that a signature standard is useless.

2. DSA was developed by the NSA, and there may be a trap door in the algorithm.

   Much of the initial comments stemmed from cryptographers' paranoia: "NIST's denial of information with no apparent justification does not inspire confidence in DSS, but intensifies concern that there is a hidden agenda, such as laying the groundwork for a national public-key cryptosystem that is in fact vulnerable to being broken by NIST and/or NSA" [97]. There was one serious question about the security of DSS by Arjen Lenstra and Stuart Haber at Bellcore. This will be discussed later.

3. DSA is slower than RSA [466].

   This is true, more or less. Signature generation speeds are the same, but signature verification can be 10 to 40 times slower with DSA. Key generation is faster than RSA. Key generation is irrelevant; a user rarely does that. On the other hand, signature verification is the most common operation.

   The problem with this criticism is that there are many ways to play with the test parameters, depending on the results you want. Precomputations can speed up DSA signature generation, but they are not always applicable. Proponents of RSA use numbers optimized to make their calculations easier; proponents of DSA use their own optimizations. In any case, computers are getting faster all the time. While there is a difference, in most applications it will not be noticeable.

4. RSA is a de facto standard.

   These are two examples of the complaint. From Robert Follett, the program director of standards at IBM [351]:

   > IBM is concerned that NIST has proposed a standard with a different digital signature scheme rather than adopting the international standard. We have been convinced by users and user organizations that the international standards using RSA will be a prerequisite to the sales of security products in the very near future.

   From Les Shroyer, vice president and director, corporate MIS and telecommunications, at Motorola [813]:

   > We must have a single, robust, politically-accepted digital signature standard that is usable throughout the world, between both US and non-US, and Motorola and non-Motorola entities. The lack of other viable digital signature technology for the last eight years has made RSA a de facto standard. . . . Motorola and many other companies . . .

have committed millions of dollars to RSA. We have concern over the interoperability and support of two different standards, as that situation will lead to added costs, delays in deployment, and complication. . . .

Many companies wanted NIST to adopt the ISO/IEC 9796, the international digital signature standard that uses RSA [446]. While this is a valid complaint, it is not a sufficient justification to make it a standard. A royalty-free standard would serve the U.S. public interest to a much greater degree.

5. The DSA selection process was not public; sufficient time for analysis has not been provided.

First NIST claimed that they designed the DSA; then they admitted that NSA helped them. Finally, they confirmed that NSA designed the algorithm. This worries many people; the NSA doesn't inspire trust. Even so, the algorithm is public and available for analysis; and NIST extended the time for analysis and comment.

6. DSA may infringe on other patents.

It may. This will be discussed in the section on patents.

7. The key size is too small.

This was the only valid criticism of DSS. The original implementation set the modulus at 512 bits [650]. Since the algorithm gets its security from the difficulty of computing discrete logs in that modulus, this was worrisome to most cryptographers. There have been advances in the problem of calculating discrete logarithms in a finite field, and 512 bits is too short for long-term security. According to Brian LaMacchia and Andrew Odlyzko, ". . . even 512-bit primes appear to offer only marginal security. . . ." [526]. This isn't truly fair—512 bits provide sufficient security today. But if your security needs stretch into the far future, it's not secure. In response to this criticism, NIST made the key size variable, from 512 bits to 1024 bits. This will be discussed in more detail later.

Description of the Algorithm

DSA is a variant of the Schnorr and ElGamal signature algorithms, and is fully described in [651]. The algorithm uses the following parameters:

p = a prime number 2^L bits long, where L ranges from 512 to 1024 and is a multiple of 64. (In the original standard, the size of p was fixed at 512 bits [650]. This was the source of much criticism and was changed by NIST [651].)

q = a 160-bit prime factor of $p-1$.

$g = h^{(p-1)/q}$, when h is any number less than $p-1$ such that $h^{(p-1)/q} \bmod p$ is greater than 1.

x = a number less than q.

$y = g^x \bmod p$.

Additionally, the algorithm makes use of a one-way hash function: $H(x)$. For the DSS, this is the Secure Hash Algorithm, discussed in Section 14.7.

The first three parameters, p, q, and g, are public and can be common across a network of users. The private key is x; the public key is y.

To sign a message, m:

(1) Alice generates a random number, k, less than q.

(2) Alice generates

$$r = (g^k \bmod p) \bmod q$$
$$s = (k^{-1}(H(m) + xr)) \bmod q$$

The parameters r and s are her signature; she sends these to Bob.

(3) Bob verifies the signature by computing:

$$w = s^{-1} \bmod q$$
$$u1 = (H(m) \times w) \bmod q$$
$$u2 = (r \times w) \bmod q$$
$$v = ((g^{u1} \times y^{u2}) \bmod p) \bmod q$$

If $v = r$, then the signature is verified.

Proofs for the mathematical relationships are found in the documentation. See Table 13.3 for a summary.

TABLE 13.3
DSA Signatures

PUBLIC KEY:

    p 512-bit to 1024-bit prime (can be shared among a group of users)

    q 160-bit prime factor of $p-1$ (can be shared among a group of users)

    g $h^{(p-1)/q}$, where h is less than $p-1$ and $h^{(p-1)/q} \bmod q > 1$ (can be shared among a group of users)

    y $= g^x (\bmod p)$ (a 160-bit number)

PRIVATE KEY:

    x $< q$ (a 160-bit number)

SIGNING:

    k choose at random, less than q

    r (signature) $= (g^k \bmod p) \bmod q$

    s (signature) $= (k^{-1}(H(m) + xr)) \bmod q$

VERIFYING:

    w $= s^{-1} \bmod q$

    $u1$ $= (H(m) \times w) \bmod q$

    $u2$ $= (r \times w) \bmod q$

    v $= ((g^{u1} \times y^{u2}) \bmod p) \bmod q$

    If $v = r$, then the signature is verified.

Precomputations

Real-world implementations of DSA can be speeded up through precomputations. Notice that the value r is not dependent on the message. You can create a string of random k values and then precompute r values for each of them. You can also precompute k^{-1} for each of those k values. Then, when a message comes along, you can compute s for a given r and k^{-1}.

This precomputation speeds up the DSA considerably. Table 13.4 is a comparison of DSA and RSA computation times for a smart-card implementation [834]:

TABLE 13.4

Comparison of RSA and DSA Computation Times

	DSA	RSA	DSA with Common p,q,g
Global Computations	Off Card (P)	N/A	Off Card (P)
Key Generation	14 secs.	Off Card (S)	4 secs.
Precomputation	14 secs.	N/A	4 secs.
Signature	.03 secs.	15 secs.	.03 secs.
Verification	16 secs.	1.5 secs.	10 secs.
	1–5 secs. Off Card (P)		1–3 secs. Off Card (P)

Off-card computations were performed on an 80386, 33MHz, personal computer. (P) indicates public parameters off card, and (S) indicates secret parameters off card. Both algorithms use a 512-bit modulus.

DSA Prime Generation

Lenstra and Haber pointed out that certain moduli are much easier to crack than others [535]. If someone used one of these "cooked" moduli, then their signatures would be easy to forge. This isn't a problem for two reasons: first, the moduli for which this property holds true are easy to detect. Second, these moduli are so rare that the chances of using one when choosing a modulus randomly are negligibly small—smaller, in fact, than the chances of accidentally generating a composite number using a probabilistic prime generation routine.

NIST recommends a method for generating the two primes, p and q, such that q divides $p-1$. The prime p is between 512 and 1024 bits long, in some multiple of 64 bits. The prime q is 160 bits long. Let $L-1 = n \times 160 + b$, where L is the length of p, and n and b are two numbers.

(1) Choose an arbitrary sequence of at least 160 bits and call it S. Let g be the length of S in bits.

(2) Compute $U = \text{SHA}(S) \text{ XOR } \text{SHA}((S+1) \bmod 2^g)$.

(3) Form q from U by setting the most significant bit and the least significant bit to 1.

(4) Check whether q is prime.

(5) If q is not prime, go back to step (1).

(6) Let $C = 0$ and $N = 2$.

(7) For $k = 0, 1, \ldots, n$, let $V_k = \text{SHA}((S + N + k) \bmod 2^g)$.

(8) Let

$$W = V_0 + V_1 \times 2^{160} + \ldots + V_{n-1} \times 2^{(n-1)\times 160} + (V_n \bmod 2^b) \times 2^{n\times 160}$$

and

$X = W + 2^{L-1}$. Note that X is a 2^L-bit number.

(9) Let $p = X - ((X \bmod 2q) - 1)$. Note that p is congruent to 1 mod $2q$.

(10) If $p < 2^{L-1}$, then go to step 13.

(11) Check whether p is prime.

(12) If p is prime, go to step (15).

(13) Let $C = C + 1$ and $N = N + n + 1$.

(14) If $C = 4096$, then go to step (1). Otherwise, go to step (7).

(15) Save the value of S and the value of C used to generate p and q.

The point of this exercise is that there is a public means of generating p and q. Remember the people worried about "cooked" values of p and q that make breaking the DSA easier? For all practical purposes, this method prevents that. If someone hands you a p and a q, you might wonder where they got it. However, if someone hands you a value for S and C that generated the random p and q, you can go through this routine yourself. The use of SHA, a one-way function, prevents someone from working backwards.

This security is better than what you get with RSA. In RSA, the prime numbers are kept secret. Someone could generate a fake prime or one of a special form that makes factoring easier. Unless you know the private key, you won't know that. Here, even if you don't know the private key, you can confirm that p and q have been generated randomly.

ElGamal Encryption with DSA

There have been allegations that the government likes the DSA because it is only a digital signature algorithm and can't be used for encryption. While this is true, it is possible to use a DSA-function call to do ElGamal encryption.

Assume that the DSA algorithm is implemented with a single-function call:

```
DSAsign (p,q,g,k,x,h,r,s)
```

You supply the numbers p, q, g, k, x, and h, and the function returns the signature parameters: r and s.

To do ElGamal encryption of message *m* with public key *y,* choose a random number, *k,* and call:

```
DSAsign (p,p,g,k,0,0,r,s)
```

The value of *r* returned is *a* in the ElGamal scheme. Throw *s* away. Then, call:

```
DSAsign (p,p,y,k,0,0,r,s)
```

Rename the value of *r* to be *u;* throw *s* away. Call:

```
DSAsign (p,p,m,1,u,0,r,s)
```

Throw *r* away. The value of *s* returned is *b* in the ElGamal scheme. You now have the ciphertext, *a* and *b*.

Decryption is just as easy. Using secret key *x,* and ciphertext messages *a* and *b,* call:

```
DSAsign (p,p,a,x,0,0,r,s)
```

The value *r* is $a^x \bmod p$. Call that *e*. Then call:

```
DSAsign (p,p,1,e,b,0,r,s)
```

The value *s* is the plaintext message, *m*.

This method will not work with all implementations of DSA. Some may fix the values or *p* and *q*, or the lengths of some of the other parameters. Still, if the implementation is general enough, this is a way to encrypt with a digital signature library.

RSA Encryption with DSA

RSA encryption is even easier. With a modulus *n*, message *m*, and a public key *e*, call:

```
DSAsign (n,n,m,e,0,0,r,s)
```

The value of *r* returned is the ciphertext.

RSA decryption is the same thing:

```
DSAsign (n,n,m,d,0,0,r,s)
```

returns the plaintext as the value of *r.*

Security of DSA

At 512-bits, DSA wasn't strong enough for long-term security. At 1024 bits, it is.

The National Security Agency, in its first public interview on the subject, commented to Joe Abernathy of the *Houston Chronicle* on allegations about a trap door in DSS [218]:

> Regarding the alleged trapdoor in the DSS. We find the term trapdoor somewhat misleading since it implies that the messages sent by the DSS are encrypted and with access via a trapdoor one could somehow decrypt (read) the message without the sender's knowledge.
>
> The DSS does not encrypt any data. The real issue is whether the DSS is susceptible to someone forging a signature and therefore discrediting the entire system. We state categorically that the chances of anyone—including NSA—forging a signature with the DSS when it is properly used and implemented is infinitesimally small.
>
> Furthermore, the alleged trapdoor vulnerability is true for *any* public key-based authentication system, including RSA. To imply somehow that this only affects the DSS (a popular argument in the press) is totally misleading. The issue is one of implementation and how one goes about selecting prime numbers. We call your attention to a recent EUROCRYPT conference which had a panel discussion on the issue of trapdoors in the DSS. Included on the panel was one of the Bellcore researchers who initially raised the trapdoor allegation, and our understanding is that the panel—including the person from Bellcore—concluded that the alleged trapdoor was not an issue for the DSS. Furthermore, the general consensus appeared to be that the trapdoor issue was trivial and had been overblown in the press. However, to try to respond to the trapdoor allegation, at NIST's request, we have designed a prime generation process which will ensure that one can avoid selection of the relatively few weak primes which could lead to weakness in using the DSS. Additionally, NIST intends to allow for larger modulus sizes up to 1024 which effectively negates the need to even use the prime generation process to avoid weak primes. An additional very important point that is often overlooked is that with the DSS the primes are *public* and therefore can be subject to public examination. Not all public key systems provide for this same type of examination.
>
> The integrity of any information security system requires attention to proper implementation. With the myriad of vulnerabilities possible given the differences among users, NSA has traditionally insisted on centralized trusted centers as a way to minimize risk to the system. While we have designed technical modifications to the DSS to meet NIST's requests for a more decentralized approach, we still would emphasize that portion of the Federal Register notice for the DSS which states:
>
> > "While it is the intent of this standard to specify general security requirements for generating digital signatures, conformance to this standard does not assure that a particular implementation is secure. The responsible authority in each agency or department shall assure that an overall implementation provides an acceptable level of security. NIST will be working with government users to ensure appropriate implementations."
>
> Finally, we have read all the arguments purporting insecurities with the DSS, and we remain unconvinced of their validity. The DSS has been

subjected to intense evaluation within NSA which led to its being endorsed by our Director of Information Systems Security for use in signing unclassified data processed in certain intelligence systems and even for signing classified data in selected systems. We believe that this approval speaks to the lack of any credible attack on the integrity provided by the DSS given proper use and implementation. Based on the technical and security requirements of the U.S. government for digital signatures, we believe the DSS is the best choice. In fact, the DSS is being used in a pilot project for the Defense Message System to assure the authenticity of electronic messages of vital command and control information. This initial demonstration includes participation from the Joint Chiefs of Staff, the military services, and Defense Agencies and is being done in cooperation with NIST.

I'm not going to comment on the trustworthiness of the NSA. Take their comment for what you think it's worth.

Subliminal Channel in DSS

Gus Simmons discovered a subliminal channel in DSS [829,830] (see Section 16.7). This subliminal channel allows people to embed a secret message in their signature that can only be read by another person who knows the key. According to Simmons, it is a "remarkable coincidence" that the "apparently inherent shortcomings of subliminal channels using the ElGamal scheme can all be overcome" in the DSS, and that the DSS "provides the most hospitable setting for subliminal communications discovered to date." NIST and NSA have not commented on this subliminal channel; no one knows if they even knew about it. Since this subliminal channel allows an unscrupulous implementer of DSS to leak a piece of the private key with each signature, it is important to never use an implementation of DSS if you don't trust the implementer.

Dangers of a Common Modulus

Even though the DSS does not specify a common modulus to be shared by everyone, different implementations may. For example, the Internal Revenue Service (IRS) is considering using the DSS for the electronic submission of tax returns. What if they require every taxpayer in the country to use a common p and q? Even though the standard doesn't require a common modulus, this implementation accomplishes the same thing. The danger of a common modulus is that it becomes a tempting target. It is still too early to tell what kind of DSS implementations there will be, but there is some cause for concern.

Patents

According to NIST [329]:

> The government has applied to the U.S. Patent Office for a patent on this technique. NIST intends to make this DSS technique available world-wide on a royalty-free basis to the public interest. We believe this technique is patentable and that no other patents would apply to the DSS, but we cannot give firm assurances to such effect in advance of issuance of the patent.

Since then, the U.S. patent office has issued a patent to David Kravitz of NSA [508a]. Even so, three patentholders claim that the DSA infringes on their patents: Diffie-Hellman [426], Merkle-Hellman [428], and Schnorr [778].

The Schnorr patent is the most troublesome. The other two patents expire in 1997; the Schnorr patent is valid until 2008. The Schnorr algorithm was not developed with government money; unlike the PKP patents, the U.S. government has no rights to the Schnorr patent; and Schnorr patented his algorithm worldwide. Even if the U.S. courts rule in favor of DSA, it is unclear what other courts around the world will do. Is an international company going to adopt a standard that may be legal in some countries but infringe on a patent in others? This issue will take time to resolve; at the time of this writing it isn't even resolved in the United States.

In June 1993, NIST proposed to give Public Key Partners an exclusive patent license to DSA [331a]. All other users of DSA would have to pay royalties to PKP. This solution is the worst of both worlds: users won't conform to international signature standards, and users won't be able to implement signatures royalty-free. At this writing, nothing is final. There is at least one lawsuit pending which charges NIST of improper patent licensing [772a].

13.6   ESIGN

ESIGN is a digital signature scheme by T. Okamoto and others at NTT Japan [669,357]. According to its authors, it is at least as secure and considerably faster than either RSA or DSA, with similar key and signature lengths.

The secret key is a pair of large prime numbers, p and q. The public key is n, where

$$n = p^2 q$$

$H(x)$ is a hash function that operates on a message, m. There is also a security parameter, k, which will be discussed shortly.

(1) Alice picks a random number, x, when x is less than $p \times q$

(2) Alice computes:

  w, the least integer that is larger than $(H(m) - x^k \bmod n)/pq$

  $s = x + ((w/kx^{k-1}) \bmod p)pq$

  Alice sends s to Bob.

(3) To verify the signature, Bob computes $s^k \bmod n$. He also computes a, which is the least integer larger than the number of bits of n divided by 3. If $H(m)$ is less than or equal to $s^k \bmod n$, and if $s^k \bmod n$ is less than $H(m) + 2^a$, then the signature is considered valid.

This algorithm can be speeded up with precomputation. This precomputation can be done at any time and has nothing to do with the message being signed. After picking x, Alice could break step (2) into two partial steps. The first can be precomputed.

(2a) Alice computes:

$$u = x^k \bmod n$$
$$v = 1/(kx^{k-1}) \bmod p$$

(2b) Alice computes:

$$w = \text{the least integer that is larger than } (\mathrm{H}(m) - u)/pq$$
$$s = x + (w \times v \bmod p) \times p \times q$$

For the size numbers generally used, this precomputation speeds up the signature process by a factor of ten. Almost all the hard work is done in the precomputation stage. A discussion of modular arithmetic operations to speed the ESIGN algorithm can be found in [894,893]. This algorithm can also be extended to work with elliptic curves [670].

Security of ESIGN

When this algorithm was originally proposed, k was set to 2 [677]. This was quickly broken by Ernie Brickell and John DeLaurentis [163], who then extended their attack to $k = 3$. A modified version of this algorithm [667] was broken by Shamir [668]. The variant proposed in [668] was broken in [858]. ESIGN is the current incarnation of this family of algorithms. Another new attack [546] does not work against the ESIGN variant.

The authors currently recommend these values for k: 8, 16, 32, 64, 128, 256, 512, and 1024. They also recommend p and q to be of at least 192 bits each, making n at least 576 bits long. With these parameters, the authors conjecture that ESIGN is as secure as RSA or Rabin.

Patents

ESIGN is patented in the United States [672], Canada (patent number 255,784), England, France, Germany, and Italy. Anyone wishing to license the algorithm should contact:

Intellectual Property Department
NTT
1-6 Uchisaiwai-cho, 1-chome, Chiyada-ku
100 Japan

An ESIGN program for Maxell IC cards, NEC personal computers, and SUN workstations is available through:

Information Systems Technology Department
NTT Advance Technology Corp.
3-2-4 Miharu-cho, Yokasuka-shi
239 Japan
Tel: +81-468-27-0800
Fax: +81-468-23-3558

13.7   McELIECE

McEliece developed a public-key cryptosystem based on algebraic coding theory [580]. The algorithm makes use of the existence of a class of error-correcting codes, known as Goppa codes. His idea was to construct a Goppa code and disguise it as a general linear code. There is a fast algorithm for decoding Goppa codes, but decoding general linear codes is a hard problem. A good description of this algorithm can be found in [687]. The following is a quick summary:

Let $d_H(x)$ denote the Hamming distance. The numbers n, k, and t are system parameters.

The private key has three parts: G', is a $k \times n$ generator matrix for a Goppa code that can correct t errors. P is an $n' \times n$ permutation matrix. S is a $k' \times k$ nonsingular matrix.

The public key is a $k' \times n$ matrix G: $G = SG'P$.

Plaintext messages are strings of k bits, in the form of k-dimensional vectors over GF(2).

To encrypt a message, choose a randomly chosen n-dimensional vector over GF(2), z, with Hamming weight less than or equal to t.

$$c = mG + z$$

To decrypt the ciphertext, first compute $c' = cP^{-1}$. Then, using the decoding algorithm for the Goppa code, find m' such that $d_H(m'G, c')$ is less than or equal to t. Finally, compute $m = m'S^{-1}$.

In his original paper, McEliece suggested that $n = 1024$, $t = 50$, and $k = 524$.

Although the algorithm was one of the first public-key algorithms, and there were no successful cryptanalytic results against the algorithm, it has never gained wide acceptance in the cryptographic community. The scheme is two to three orders of magnitude faster than RSA, but there are several problems. The public key is enormous: 2^{19} bits long. The data expansion is large: the ciphertext is twice as long as the plaintext.

Some attempts at cryptanalysis of this system can be found in [5,532,860]. None of these was successful, although the similarity between the McEliece algorithm and knapsacks worried some.

In 1991, two cryptographers from the former Soviet Union, Korzhik and Turkin [502], broke the McEliece system (one of the benefits of the breakup of the Soviet Union is that ex-Soviet cryptographers are now coming to Western conferences). Their attack requires $20 \times n^3$ operations. It can break the system with the parameters that McEliece originally suggested in about 60 hours.

This scheme is extended in [241]. A variant of this scheme was proposed as a symmetric cryptosystem [730] but was quickly broken [437,848], despite the rebuttal in [729]. At this writing, though, there are still considerable doubts in the cryptologic community about this attack.

13.8   OKAMOTO 92

This signature scheme, first presented by Tatsuaki Okamoto in [670], gets its security from the discrete logarithm problem.

There are two secret primes, p and q, such that q divides $p-1$. The value of q should be at least 140 bits, and the value of p should be at least 512 bits. There are also two random numbers, g_1 and g_2, both the same length as q. The secret key is a pair of random numbers, s_1 and s_2, both less than q. The public key is v, where:

$$v = g_1{}^{-s_1} g_2{}^{-s_2} \bmod p$$

To sign a message m, first choose two random numbers, r_1 and r_2, both less than q. Then compute:

$$e = H(g_1{}^{r_1} g_2{}^{r_2} \bmod p, m), \text{ when } H(x) \text{ is a one-way hash function}$$
$$y_1 = r_1 + es_1 \bmod q$$
$$y_2 = r_2 + es_2 \bmod q$$

The signature is the triple (e, y_1, y_2).

To verify the signature, confirm that e equals:

$$H(g_1{}^{y_1} g_2{}^{y_2} v^e \bmod p, m)$$

If it does, the signature is valid.

13.9   CELLULAR AUTOMATA

A new and novel idea, studied by Guam [397], is the use of cellular automata in public-key cryptosystems. This system is still far too new and has not been studied extensively, but a preliminary examination suggests that it may have some cryptographic weaknesses [347]. Still, this is a promising area of research. Cellular automata have the property that, even if they are invertible, it is impossible to calculate the predecessor of an arbitrary state by reversing the rule for finding the successor. This sounds a lot like a trap-door one-way function.

13.10   ELLIPTIC CURVE CRYPTOSYSTEMS

Elliptic curves have been studied for many years, and there is an enormous amount of literature on the subject. In 1985, Neal Koblitz and V. S. Miller independently proposed using them for public-key cryptosystems [489,605]. They did not invent a cryptographic algorithm using elliptic curves, but they implemented existing public-key algorithms, like Diffie-Hellman, in elliptic curves over finite fields.

Elliptic curves are interesting because they provide a way of constructing "elements" and "rules of combining" that produce groups. These groups have enough familiar properties to build cryptographic algorithms, but they don't have certain properties that may facilitate cryptanalysis. For example, there is no good notion of "smooth." That is, there is no set of small elements in terms of which a random element has a good chance of being expressed by a simple algorithm. Hence, index calculus discrete logarithm algorithms do not work. See [605] for more details.

Elliptic curves over the finite field $GF(2^n)$ are particularly interesting. The arithmetic processors for the underlying field are easy to construct and are relatively simple to implement for n in the range of 130 to 200. These systems have the potential to provide small and low-cost public-key cryptosystems. Many public-key algorithms, like Diffie-Hellman, ElGamal, and Schnorr, can be implemented in elliptic curves over finite fields.

The mathematics here are complex and beyond the scope of this book. Those interested in this topic are invited to read the two references mentioned above, and [65,585,491,95,506,493,507]. Next Computer, Inc.'s Fast Elliptic Encryption (FEE) uses elliptic curves [227a]. Koblitz also proposed public-key cryptosystems using hyperelliptic curves [490,492]. See also [811,676].

13.11   OTHER PUBLIC-KEY ALGORITHMS

Many other public-key algorithms have been proposed and broken over the years. The Matsumoto-Imai algorithm [569] was broken in [261]. The Cade algorithm was first proposed in 1985, broken in 1986 [451], and then strengthened in the same year [181]. In addition to these attacks, there are general attacks for decomposing polynomials over finite fields [368]. Any algorithm that gets its security from the composition of polynomials over a finite field should be looked upon with skepticism, if not outright suspicion.

The Yagisawa algorithm combines exponentiation mod p with arithmetic mod $p-1$ [892]; it was broken in [159]. Another public-key algorithm, proposed by Tsujii, Kurosawa, Itoh, Fujioka, and Matsumoto [856] is insecure [534]. A third system, Luccio-Mazzone [560], is insecure [424].

Gustavus Simmons suggested J-algebras as a basis for public-key algorithms [818,89]. This idea was abandoned after efficient methods for factorizing polynomials was invented [536]. Special polynomial semigroups have also been studied [891,545], but so far nothing has come of it. Harald Niederreiter proposed a public-key algorithm based on shift-register sequences [647].

Some European cryptographers have developed generalizations of RSA that use various permutation polynomials instead of exponentiation. Winfried Müller and Wilfried Nöbauer use Dickson polynomials [626,627,547]. Rudolph Lidl and Müller generalized this approach in [548,625] (a variant is called the Réidi scheme), and Nöbauer looked at its security in [657,658]. Peter Smith reinvented this scheme in 1993, calling it LUC [841,318]. These variants are all as secure as

RSA; there is really no security benefit to using any of them. Tatsuaki Okamoto and Kazuo Ohta compare a number of digital signature schemes in [675].

Prospects for creating radically new and different public-key cryptography algorithms seem dim. In 1988 Diffie noted that most public-key algorithms are based on one of three hard problems [295,297]:

knapsack problem:

Given a set of unique numbers, find a subset whose sum is N.
discrete logarithm:

If p is a prime and g and M are integers, find x such that $g^x = M$ (mod p)
factoring:

If N is the product of two primes,

a) factor N,

b) given integers M and C, find d such that $M^d = C$ (mod N),

c) given integers e and C, find M such that $M^e = C$ (mod N),

d) given an integer x, decide whether there exists an integer y such that $x = y^2$ (mod N).

According to Diffie [295,297], the discrete logarithm problem was suggested by J. Gill, the factoring problem by Knuth, and the knapsack problem by Diffie himself.

This narrowness in the mathematical foundations of public-key cryptography is worrisome. A breakthrough in either the problem of factoring or of calculating discrete logarithms could render whole classes of public-key algorithms insecure. Diffie points out [295,297] that this risk is mitigated by two factors:

> The operations on which public key cryptography currently depends—multiplying, exponentiating, and factoring—are all fundamental arithmetic phenomena. They have been the subject of intense mathematical scrutiny for centuries and the increased attention that has resulted from their use in public key cryptosystems has on balance enhanced rather than diminished our confidence.
>
> Our ability to carry out large arithmetic computations has grown steadily and now permits us to implement our systems with numbers sufficient in size to be vulnerable only to a dramatic breakthrough in factoring, logarithms, or root extraction.

As we have seen, not all public-key algorithms based on these problems are secure. The strength of any public-key algorithm depends more on the computational complexity of the problem upon which it is based; a computationally difficult problem does not necessarily imply a strong algorithm. Shamir listed three reasons why this is so [789]:

1. Complexity theory usually deals with single isolated instances of a problem. A cryptanalyst often has a large collection of statistically related problems to solve—several ciphertexts encrypted with the same key.

2. The computational complexity of a problem is typically measured by its worst-case or average-case behavior. To be useful as a cipher, the problem must be hard to solve in almost all cases.

3. An arbitrarily difficult problem cannot necessarily be transformed into a cryptosystem, and it must be possible to insert trapdoor information into the problem so that a shortcut solution is possible with this information and only with this information.

13.12 WHICH PUBLIC-KEY ALGORITHM IS BEST?

This question is muddied not only by the fact that different algorithms do different things, but also by patent and licensing issues. For encryption and digital signatures, RSA is the easiest to implement. ElGamal works well for encryption, and DSA is great for digital signatures. DSA is available royalty-free, making it the obvious choice. Diffie-Hellman is the easiest algorithm for key exchange. The various identification schemes also have their uses. I would suggest that before you use any other algorithm, do a literature search to make sure it hasn't been broken.

One-Way
Hash Functions

14.1 BACKGROUND

A one-way hash function, H(M), operates on an arbitrary-length message, M. It returns a fixed-length hash value, h.

h = H(M), when h is of length m.

There are many functions that take an arbitrary-length input and return an output of fixed length, but one-way hash functions have additional characteristics:

Given M, it is easy to compute h.

Given h, it is hard to compute M.

Given M, it is hard to find another message, M', such that H(M) = H(M').

"Hard" depends on the specific security requirements of the situation, but most real-world implementations define hard as requiring on the order of 2^{64} operations, sometimes even more.

There are two basic attacks against a one-way hash function. The first is the most obvious: given the hash of message, H(M), adversaries would like to be able to create another document, M', such that H(M) = H(M'). If they could do this, it would undermine the security of every protocol that uses the one-way hash function. The point of the one-way hash function was to provide a "fingerprint" of M that is unique. If Alice signed M by using a digital signature algorithm on H(M), and Bob could produce M' such that H(M) = H(M'), then Bob could claim that Alice signed M'.

Birthday Attack

The other major attack is more subtle: it must be hard to find two random messages, M and M', such that $H(M) = H(M')$. This is a far easier attack than the previous one.

The birthday paradox is a standard statistics problem. How many people must there be in a room for there to be a greater than even chance that one of them shares your birthday? The answer is 183. Now, how many people must there be for there to be a greater than even chance that at least two of them will share the same birthday? The answer is surprisingly low: 23. There may only be 23 people in the room, but there are over 500 different *pairs* of people in the room.

Finding someone with a specific birthday is analogous to the first attack; finding two people with the same random birthday is analogous to the second attack. The second attack is commonly known as the **birthday attack.**

Assume that a one-way hash function follows all the properties listed above and the best way to attack it is by using brute force. It produces an m-bit output. Finding a message that hashes to a given hash value would require hashing 2^m random messages. Finding two messages that hash to the same value would only require hashing $2^{m/2}$ random messages. A machine that hashes a million messages per second would take 600,000 years to find a second message that matched a given 64-bit hash. The same machine could find a pair of messages that hashed to the same value in about an hour.

The following protocol, first described by Yuval [899], shows how Alice could use the birthday attack to swindle Bob.

(1) Alice prepares two versions of a contract, one favorable to Bob, and the other that takes him for everything he's worth.

(2) Alice makes several subtle changes to each document and calculates the hash value for each. (These changes could be things like: replacing a SPACE with a SPACE-BACKSPACE-SPACE, putting a space or two before a carriage return, etc. By either making or not making a single change on each of 32 lines, Alice could easily generate 2^{32} different documents.)

(3) Alice compares the set of hash values for each of the two documents, looking for a pair that matches. (If the hash function only outputs a 64-bit value, she would usually find a matching pair with 2^{32} versions of each.) She reconstructs the two documents that hash to the same value.

(4) Alice has Bob sign the version of the contract that is favorable to him, using a protocol in which he only signs the hash value.

(5) At some time in the future, Alice substitutes the contract Bob signed with the one that he didn't. Now she can convince an adjudicator that Bob signed the other contract.

This is a big problem.

There are other similar attacks that could be mounted assuming a successful birthday attack. For example, adversaries could send an automated control system (on a satellite, perhaps) random message strings with random signature strings. Eventually, one of those random messages will have a valid signature. The adversaries would have no idea what the command would do, but if their only objective was to tamper with the satellite, this would work.

Length of One-Way Hash Functions

Sixty-four-bit hash functions are just too small to survive a birthday attack. Most practical one-way hash functions produce 128-bit hashes. This forces anyone attempting the birthday attack to hash 2^{64} random documents to find two that hash to the same value. NIST, in its Secure Hash Standard (SHS), uses a 160-bit hash value. This makes the birthday attack even harder, requiring 2^{80} random hashes.

To generate a longer hash value than the hash function produces, this method has been proposed:

(1) Generate the hash value of a message, using a one-way hash function listed in this book.

(2) Append the hash value to the message.

(3) Generate the hash value of the concatenation of the message and the hash value.

(4) Create a large hash value consisting of the hash value generated in step (1) concatenated with the hash value generated in step (3).

(5) Repeat steps (1) through (3) as many times as you wish.

Although this method has never been proven, in general, to be either secure or insecure, Bart Preneel has some serious reservations about it [711].

Overview of One-Way Hash Functions

There has been a lot written on the design of one-way hash functions. For more mathematical information, consult [572,461,460,632,587,588,236]. Bart Preneel's Ph.D. thesis [711] is probably the most comprehensive treatment of one-way hash functions.

Most one-way hash functions are built on a one-way function that outputs a value of length n given two inputs of length n. Generally, the input to the function is the block of text and the hash of the previous block of text (see Figure 14.1). That is, the hash of block M_i is

$$h_i = f(M_i, h_{i-1})$$

The hash of the last block becomes the hash of the entire message.

In this way, the one-way hash function always produces a fixed-length output, whatever the size of the input.

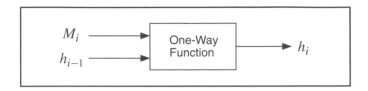

Figure 14.1
One-way hash function.

Typically, the information hashed should contain some kind of binary representation of the length of the entire message. This technique overcomes a potential security problem resulting from messages with different lengths possibly hashing to the same value [587,236].

Various researchers have theorized that if the one-way function is secure for a single block, then this method of hashing an arbitrary-length string of blocks is also secure [632,589,236]. Proven results are more limited.

14.2 SNEFRU

Snefru is a one-way hash function designed by Ralph Merkle [589]. Snefru hashes arbitrary-length messages into either 128-bit or 256-bit values.

First the message is broken into chunks, each $512-m$ in length. (The variable m is the length of the hash value.) If the output is a 128-bit hash value, then the chunks are each 384 bits long; if the output is a 256-bit hash value, then the chunks are each 256 bits long.

The heart of the algorithm is a function H, which hashes a 512-bit value into an m-bit value. H was designed so that it was easy to compute the hash of an input but computationally unfeasible to compute an input that generates a specific hash value.

The first m bits of the H's output are the hash of the block; the rest are discarded. The next block is appended to the hash of the previous block and then hashed again. (The initial block is appended to a string of zeros.) After the last block (if the message isn't an even number of blocks long, zeros are used to pad the last block), the first m bits are appended to a binary representation of the length of the message and hashed one final time.

Function H is based on another function, E, which is a reversible block cipher function that operates on 512-bit blocks. H is the last m bits of the output of E XORed with the first m bits of the input of E.

The security of Snefru resides in function E, which randomizes data in several passes. Each pass is composed of 64 randomizing rounds. In each round a different byte of the data is used as an input to an S-box; the output word of the S-box is XORed with two neighboring words of the message. The S-boxes are constructed in a manner similar to those in Khafre. There are also some rotations thrown in. Originally Snefru was designed with two passes.

Cryptanalysis of Snefru

Using differential cryptanalysis, Biham and Shamir demonstrated the insecurity of two-pass Snefru (128-bit hash value) by showing that the following messages hashed to the same value [106]:

```
3FE15E26 23B7C030 C7089999 90EFC48F A04D87EE 16493392
00046085 00003415 00000000 00000000 00000000 00000000


3FE15E26 23B7C030 C7089999 90EFC48F A04D87EE D74AF7AE
096C7885 C19EF029 00000000 00000000 00000000 00000000


Common hash value: C8FF5E2C 8F9CF7C7 F08DDAA7 E4F9B44E
```

Also, that the following four messages hashed to the same value:

```
00000000 00000000 00000000 00000000 00000000 00000000
00000000 00000000 00000000 00000000 00000000 00000000


00000000 F1301600 13DFC53E 4CC3B093 37461661 CCD8B94D
24D9D35F 71471FDE 00000000 00000000 00000000 00000000


00000000 1D197F00 2ABD3F6F CF33F3D1 8674966A 816E5D51
ACD9A905 53C1D180 00000000 00000000 00000000 00000000


00000000 E98C8300 1E777A47 B5271F34 A04974BB 44CC8B62
BE4B0EFC 18131756 00000000 00000000 00000000 00000000


Common hash value: 2E88E244 E9D4A208 B2D02FBB 72D0EEE6
```

On a personal computer, their attack finds pairs of messages that hash to the same value within three minutes and a message that hashes to a given hash value in about an hour.

On 128-bit Snefru, their attacks work better than brute force for four passes or less. A birthday attack against Snefru takes 2^{64} operations; differential cryptanalysis can find a pair of messages that hash to the same value in $2^{28.5}$ operations for three-pass Snefru and $2^{44.5}$ operations for four-pass Snefru. Finding a message that hashes to a given value by brute force requires 2^{128} operations; differential cryptanalysis takes 2^{56} operations for three-pass Snefru and 2^{88} operations for four-pass Snefru.

The results for Snefru with longer hash lengths were also better than brute force. Although Biham and Shamir didn't analyze 256-bit hash values, they extended their analysis to 224-bit hash values. Compared to a birthday attack, which requires 2^{112} operations, they can find messages that hashed to the same value in $2^{12.5}$ operations for two-pass Snefru, 2^{33} operations for three-pass Snefru, and 2^{81} operations for four-pass Snefru.

Currently, Merkle recommends using Snefru with at least eight passes [592]. However, with this many passes the algorithm is significantly slower than either MD5 or SHA.

14.3   N-HASH

N-Hash is an algorithm invented by researchers at Nippon Telephone and Telegraph, the same people who invented FEAL. It was first presented to the cryptographic community in 1990 [611,612].

N-Hash uses 128-bit message blocks, a complicated randomizing function similar to FEAL's, and produces a 128-bit hash value.

The hash of each 128-bit block is a function of the block and the hash of the previous block.

$h_o = I$, when I is a random initial value

$h_i = g(M_i, h_{i-1})$ XOR M_i XOR H_{i-1}

The hash of the entire message is the hash of the last message block. The random initial value, I, can be any value determined by the user (even all zeros).

The function g is a complicated one and is described in Figures 14.2, 14.3, and 14.4. Figure 14.2 is an overview of the algorithm. Initially, the 128-bit hash of the

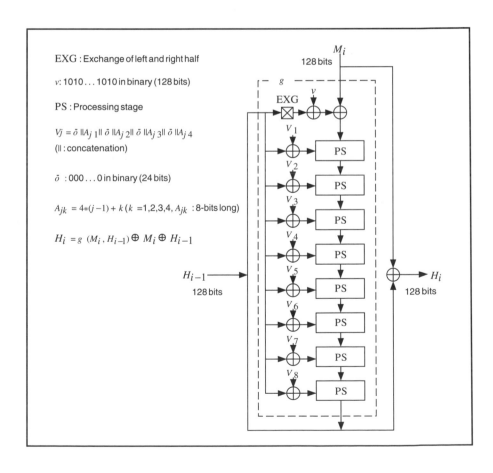

Figure 14.2
Outline of N-Hash.

previous message block, h_{i-1}, has its 64-bit left half and 64-bit right half swapped; it is then XORed with 1010 . . . 1010 (128 bits worth) in binary, and then XORed with the current message block, M_i. This value then cascades into N (N = 8 in the figures) processing stages. The other input to the processing stage is the previous hash value XORed with one of eight binary constant values.

One processing stage is given in Figure 14.3. The message block is broken into four 32-bit values. The previous hash value is also broken into four 32-bit values. The function f is given in Figure 14.4. Functions S_0 and S_1 are the same as they were in FEAL:

$$S_0(a,b) = \text{rotate left 2 bits } ((a+b) \bmod 256)$$
$$S_1(a,b) = \text{rotate left 2 bits } ((a+b+1) \bmod 256)$$

The output of one processing stage becomes the input to the next processing stage. After the last processing stage, the output is XORed with the M_i and h_{i-1}, and then the next block is ready to be hashed.

Cryptanalysis of N-Hash

Bert den Boer discovered a way to produce collisions in the round function of N-Hash [711]. Biham and Shamir used differential cryptanalysis to break six-round N-Hash [103,106]. Their particular attack (there certainly could be

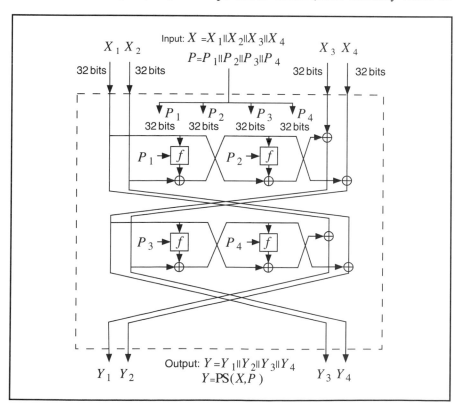

Figure 14.3
One processing stage of
N-Hash.

others) works for any N that is divisible by three, and is more efficient than the birthday attack for any N less than fifteen.

For six-round N-Hash, Biham and Shamir found the following pairs of messages the hashed to the same value:

```
CAECE595 127ABF3C 1ADE09C8 1F9AD8C2
4A8C6595 921A3F3C 1ADE09C8 1F9AD8C2
Common hash value: 12B931A6 399886B7 640B9289 36C2EF1D
```

And this pair:

```
5878BE49 F2962D67 30661E17 0C38F35E
D8183E49 72F6AD67 30661E17 0C38F35E
Common hash value: 29B0FE97 3D179E0E 5B147598 137D28CF
```

The same attack can find pairs of messages that hash to the same value for 12-round N-Hash in 2^{56} operations, compared to 2^{64} operations for a brute-force attack. N-Hash with 15 rounds is safe from differential cryptanalysis: the attack requires 2^{72} operations.

The algorithm's designers recommend using N-Hash with at least eight rounds [612]. Given the proven insecurity of N-Hash and FEAL (and its speed with eight rounds), I recommend using another algorithm entirely.

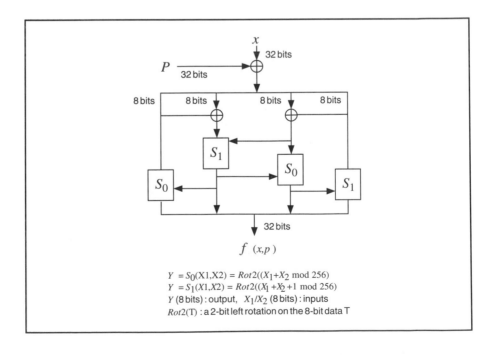

$$Y = S_0(X1,X2) = Rot2((X_1+X_2 \bmod 256)$$
$$Y = S_1(X1,X2) = Rot2((X_1+X_2+1 \bmod 256)$$
Y (8 bits) : output, X_1/X_2 (8 bits) : inputs
$Rot2(T)$: a 2-bit left rotation on the 8-bit data T

Figure 14.4
Function f.

14.4   MD4

MD4 is a one-way hash function designed by Ron Rivest [743,744,745]. MD stands for **Message Digest,** and the algorithm produces a 128-bit hash, or message digest, of the input message.

In [744], Rivest outlined his design goals for the algorithm:

Security. It is computationally infeasible to find two messages that hashed to the same value. No attack is more efficient than brute force.

Direct Security. MD4's security is not based on any assumption, like the difficulty of factoring.

Speed. MD4 is suitable for high-speed software implementations. It is based on a simple set of bit manipulations on 32-bit operands.

Simplicity and Compactness. MD4 is as simple as possible, without large data structures or a complicated program.

Favor Little-Endian Architectures. MD4 is optimized for microprocessor architectures (specifically Intel microprocessors); larger and faster computers make any necessary translations.

After the algorithm was first introduced, Bert den Boer and Antoon Bosselaers successfully cryptanalyzed two of the algorithm's three rounds [265]. Ralph Merkle successfully attacked the first two rounds [265]. Eli Biham discussed a possible differential cryptanalysis attack against two-thirds of MD4 [100]. Even though these attacks could not be extended to the full algorithm, Rivest strengthened the algorithm. The result is MD5.

14.5   MD5

MD5 is an improved version of MD4 [773,746]. Although more complex than MD4, it is similar in design and also produces a 128-bit hash.

Description of the Algorithm

After some initial processing, MD5 processes the input text in 512-bit blocks, divided into sixteen 32-bit sub-blocks. The output of the algorithm is a set of four 32-bit blocks, which concatenate to form a single 128-bit hash value.

First, the message is padded so that its length is just 64 bits short of being a multiple of 512. This padding is a single 1 added to the end of the message, followed by as many 0's as are required. Then, a 64-bit representation of the length of the message (before padding bits were added) is appended to the result. These two steps serve to make the message length an exact multiple of 512 bits in length (required for the rest of the algorithm), while ensuring that different messages will not look the same after padding.

Four 32-bit variables are initialized:

A = 01 23 45 67
B = 89 AB CD EF
C = FE DC BA 98
D = 76 54 32 10

These are called **chaining variables.**

Now, the main loop of the algorithm begins. This loop continues for as many 512-bit blocks as there are in the message.

The four variables are copied into different variables: A as AA, B as BB, C as CC, and D as DD.

The main loop has four rounds (MD4 had only three rounds), all very similar. Each round consists of 16 operations. Each operation performs a nonlinear function on three of A, B, C, and D. Then it adds that result to the fourth variable, a sub-block of the text and a constant. Then it rotates that result to the right a variable number of bits and adds the result to one of A, B, C, or D. Finally the result replaces one of A, B, C, or D.

There are four nonlinear functions, one for each round.

$F(X,Y,Z) = XY$ or (not X)Z
$G(X,Y,Z) = XZ$ or Y(not Z)
$H(X,Y,Z) = X$ XOR Y XOR Z
$I(X,Y,Z) = Y$ XOR (X or (not Z))

These functions are designed so that if the corresponding bits of X, Y, and Z are independent and unbiased, then each bit of the result will also be independent and unbiased. The function F is the bit-wise conditional: If X then Y else Z. The function H is the bit-wise parity operator.

If M_j represents the jth sub-block of the message (from 0 to 15), and $<<<s$ represents a left shift s bits, the four operations are:

FF (a,b,c,d,M_j,s,t_i) denotes $a = b + ((F(b,c,d)+M_j+t_i) <<< s)$
GG (a,b,c,d,M_j,s,t_i) denotes $a = b + ((G(b,c,d)+M_j+t_i) <<< s)$
HH (a,b,c,d,M_j,s,t_i) denotes $a = b + ((H(b,c,d)+M_j+t_i) <<< s)$
II (a,b,c,d,M_j,s,t_i) denotes $a = b + ((I(b,c,d)+M_j+t_i) <<< s)$

The four rounds (64 steps) look like:

Round 1:
FF (a, b, c, d, M[0], 7, 0xd76aa478)
FF (d, a, b, c, M[1], 12, 0xe8c7b756)
FF (c, d, a, b, M[2], 17, 0x242070db)

FF (b, c, d, a, M[3], 22, 0xc1bdceee)
FF (a, b, c, d, M[4], 7, 0xf57c0faf)
FF (d, a, b, c, M[5], 12, 0x4787c62a)
FF (c, d, a, b, M[6], 17, 0xa8304613)
FF (b, c, d, a, M[7], 22, 0xfd469501)
FF (a, b, c, d, M[8], 7, 0x698098d8)
FF (d, a, b, c, M[9], 12, 0x8b44f7af)
FF (c, d, a, b, M[10], 17, 0xffff5bb1)
FF (b, c, d, a, M[11], 22, 0x895cd7be)
FF (a, b, c, d, M[12], 7, 0x6b901122)
FF (d, a, b, c, M[13], 12, 0xfd987193)
FF (c, d, a, b, M[14], 17, 0xa679438e)
FF (b, c, d, a, M[15], 22, 0x49b40821)

Round 2:
GG (a, b, c, d, M[1], 5, 0xf61e2562)
GG (d, a, b, c, M[6], 9, 0xc040b340)
GG (c, d, a, b, M[11], 14, 0x265e5a51)
GG (b, c, d, a, M[0], 20, 0xe9b6c7aa)
GG (a, b, c, d, M[5], 5, 0xd62f105d)
GG (d, a, b, c, M[10], 9, 0x02441453)
GG (c, d, a, b, M[15], 14, 0xd8a1e681)
GG (b, c, d, a, M[4], 20, 0xe7d3fbc8)
GG (a, b, c, d, M[9], 5, 0x21e1cde6)
GG (d, a, b, c, M[14], 9, 0xc33707d6)
GG (c, d, a, b, M[3], 14, 0xf4d50d87)
GG (b, c, d, a, M[8], 20, 0x455a14ed)
GG (a, b, c, d, M[13], 5, 0xa9e3e905)
GG (d, a, b, c, M[2], 9, 0xfcefa3f8)
GG (c, d, a, b, M[7], 14, 0x676f02d9)
GG (b, c, d, a, M[12], 20, 0x8d2a4c8a)

Round 3:
HH (a, b, c, d, M[5], 4, 0xfffa3942)
HH (d, a, b, c, M[8], 11, 0x8771f681)
HH (c, d, a, b, M[11], 16, 0x6d9d6122)
HH (b, c, d, a, M[14], 23, 0xfde5380c)
HH (a, b, c, d, M[1], 4, 0xa4beea44)
HH (d, a, b, c, M[4], 11, 0x4bdecfa9)

HH (c, d, a, b, M[7], 16, 0xf6bb4b60)
HH (b, c, d, a, M[10], 23, 0xbebfbc70)
HH (a, b, c, d, M[13], 4, 0x289b7ec6)
HH (d, a, b, c, M[0], 11, 0xeaa127fa)
HH (c, d, a, b, M[3], 16, 0xd4ef3085)
HH (b, c, d, a, M[6], 23, 0x04881d05)
HH (a, b, c, d, M[9], 4, 0xd9d4d039)
HH (d, a, b, c, M[12], 11, 0xe6db99e5)
HH (c, d, a, b, M[15], 16, 0x1fa27cf8)
HH (b, c, d, a, M[2], 23, 0xc4ac5665)

Round 4:
II (a, b, c, d, M[0], 6, 0xf4292244)
II (d, a, b, c, M[7], 10, 0x411aff97)
II (c, d, a, b, M[14], 15, 0xab9423a7)
II (b, c, d, a, M[5], 21, 0xfc93a039)
II (a, b, c, d, M[12], 6, 0x655b59c3)
II (d, a, b, c, M[3], 10, 0x8f0ccc92)
II (c, d, a, b, M[10], 15, 0xffeff47d)
II (b, c, d, a, M[1], 21, 0x85845dd1)
II (a, b, c, d, M[8], 6, 0x6fa87e4f)
II (d, a, b, c, M[15], 10, 0xfe2ce6e0)
II (c, d, a, b, M[6], 15, 0xa3014314)
II (b, c, d, a, M[13], 21, 0x4e0811a1)
II (a, b, c, d, M[4], 6, 0xf7537e82)
II (d, a, b, c, M[11], 10, 0xbd3af235)
II (c, d, a, b, M[2], 15, 0x2ad7d2bb)
II (b, c, d, a, M[9], 21, 0xeb86d391)

Those constants, t_i, were chosen as follows:

In step i, t_i is the integer part of 4294967296×abs(sin(i)), when i is in radians. (Note that 4294967296 is 2^{32}.)

After all of this, *A, B, C,* and *D* are added to *AA, BB, CC, DD,* respectively, and the algorithm continues with the next block of data. The final output is the concatenation of *A, B, C,* and *D*.

Security of MD5

Ron Rivest outlined the improvements of MD5 over MD4 [746]:

1. A fourth round has been added.

2. Each step now has a unique additive constant.

3. The function g in round 2 was changed from (*XY* OR *XZ* OR *YZ*) to (*XZ* OR *Y* NOT(*Z*)) to make g less symmetric.

4. Each step now adds in the result of the previous step. This promotes a faster "avalanche effect."

5. The order in which input words are accessed in rounds 2 and 3 is changed, to make these patterns less like each other.

6. The shift amounts in each round have been approximately optimized, to yield a faster "avalanche effect." The shifts in different rounds are distinct.

Tom Berson attempted to use differential cryptanalysis against a single round of MD5 [88], but his attack is still far from being effective against all four rounds. A much more successful attack by Bert den Boer and Antoon Bosselaers can produce collisions using the compression function in MD5 [266]. This does not lend itself to attacks against MD5 in practical applications; it does mean that one of the basic design principles of MD5—to design a collision-resistant compression function—has been violated. It is enough of a weakness in MD5 to make me wary of using it.

14.6   MD2

MD2 is yet another one-way hash function designed by Ron Rivest [467]. It, along with MD5, is used in the PEM protocols (see Section 17.7). It produces a 128-bit hash value for an arbitrary input. It's similar in structure to MD4 and MD5, slower, and less secure. I don't recommend it.

14.7   SECURE HASH ALGORITHM (SHA)

The National Institute of Standards and Technology, along with the National Security Agency, designed the Secure Hash Algorithm (SHA) for use with the DSA [652,653]. (The standard is the Secure Hash Standard (SHS); SHA is the algorithm used in the standard.)

According to the *Federal Register* [330]:

A Federal Information Processing Standard (FIPS) for Secure Hash Standard (SHS) is being proposed. This proposed standard specified a Secure Hash Algorithm (SHA) for use with the proposed Digital Signature Standard. Additionally, for applications not requiring a digital signature, the SHA is to be used whenever a secure hash algorithm is required for Federal applications.

And:

This Standard specifies a Secure Hash Algorithm (SHA), which is necessary to ensure the security of the Digital Signature Algorithm (DSA). When a message of any length $<2^{64}$ bits is input, the SHA produces a 160-bit output called a message digest. The message digest is then input to the DSA, which computes the signature for the message. Signing the message digest rather than the message often improves the efficiency of the process, because the message digest is usually much smaller than the message. The same message digest should be obtained by the verifier of the signature when the received version of the message is used as input to SHA. The SHA is called secure because it is designed to be computationally infeasible to recover a message corresponding to a given message digest, or to find two different messages which produce the same message digest. Any change to a message in transit will, with a very high probability, result in a different message digest, and the signature will fail to verify. The SHA is based on principles similar to those used by Professor Ronald L. Rivest of MIT when designing the MD4 message digest algorithm [744], and is closely modelled after that algorithm.

SHA produces a 160-bit hash, longer than any of the other algorithms in this chapter.

Description of SHA

First, the message is padded so that it is a multiple of 512 bits long. Padding is exactly the same as in MD5: first append a 1, then as many 0's as necessary to make it 64 bits short of a multiple of 512, and finally a 64-bit representation of the length of the message before padding.

Five 32-bit variables (MD5 has four variables, but this algorithm needs to produce a 160-bit hash) are initialized as follows:

$$A = \text{67 45 23 01}$$
$$B = \text{EF CD AB 89}$$
$$C = \text{98 BA DC FE}$$
$$D = \text{10 32 54 76}$$
$$E = \text{C3 D2 E1 F0}$$

The main loop of the algorithm then begins. It processes the message 512 bits at a time and continues for as many 512-bit blocks as are in the message.

First the five variables are copied into different variables: A as AA, B as BB, C as CC, D as DD, and E as EE.

The main loop has four rounds of 20 operations each (MD5 has four rounds of 16 operations each). Each operation performs a nonlinear operation on three of A, B, C, and D, and then does shifting and adding similar to MD5.

SHA's set of nonlinear functions is:

$$f_t(X,Y,Z) = XY \text{ OR (NOT } X)Z, \text{ for the first 20 operations.}$$
$$f_t(X,Y,Z) = X \text{ XOR } Y \text{ XOR } Z, \text{ for the second 20 operations.}$$
$$f_t(X,Y,Z) = XY \text{ OR } XZ \text{ OR } YZ, \text{ for the third 20 operations.}$$
$$f_t(X,Y,Z) = X \text{ XOR } Y \text{ XOR } Z, \text{ for the fourth 20 operations.}$$

There are also four constants used in the algorithm:

K_t = 5A827999, for the first 20 operations.
K_t = 6ED9EBA1, for the second 20 operations.
K_t = 8F1BBCDC, for the third 20 operations.
K_t = CA62C1D1, for the fourth 20 operations.

The message block is transformed from sixteen 32-bit words (M_0 to M_{15}) to eighty 32-bit words (W_0 to W_{79}) using the following algorithm:

$W_t = M_t$, for t = 0 to 15
$W_t = W_{t-3}$ XOR W_{t-8} XOR W_{t-14} XOR W_{t-16}, for t = 16 to 79

If t is the operation number (from 1 to 80), M_j represents the jth sub-block of the message (from 0 to 15), and $<<<s$ represents a left shift s bits, then the 80 operations look like:

$$TEMP = (A <<< 5) + f_t(B,C,D) + E + W_t + K_t$$
$$E = D$$
$$D = C$$
$$C = (B <<< 30)$$
$$B = A$$
$$A = TEMP$$

After all of this, A, B, C, D, and E are added to AA, BB, CC, DD, and EE, respectively, and the algorithm continues with the next block of data. The final output is the concatenation of A, B, C, D, and E.

Security of SHA

SHA is very similar to MD4. The main changes are the addition of an expand transformation, the addition of the previous round's output into the next round for a faster avalanche effect, and the increase of the whole transformation to fit the DSS block size. SHA is very much an MD4-variant rather than a redesign, like MD5.

Ron Rivest made public the design decisions behind MD5, but SHA's designers did not. Here are Rivest's MD5 improvements to MD4 and how they compare with SHA's:

1. "A fourth round has been added." SHA does this too. However, in SHA the fourth round uses the same f-function as the second round.

2. "Each step now has a unique additive constant." SHA keeps the MD4 scheme when it reuses the constants for each group of 20 rounds.

3. "The function g in round 2 was changed from (XY or XZ or YZ) to (XZ or Y not(Z)) to make g less symmetric." SHA uses the MD4 version (XY or XZ or YZ).

4. "Each step now adds in the result of the previous step. This promotes a faster 'avalanche effect.'" This change has been made in SHA as well. The difference in SHA is that a fifth variable is added, and not B, C, or D, which are already used in f_i. This subtle change makes the den Boer-Bosselaers attack against MD5 impossible against SHA.

5. "The order in which input words are accessed in rounds 2 and 3 is changed, to make these patterns less like each other." SHA is completely different, since it uses a cyclic error correcting code.

6. "The shift amounts in each round have been approximately optimized, to yield a faster 'avalanche effect.' The shifts in different rounds are distinct." SHA uses a constant shift amount in each round. This shift amount is relatively prime to the word size, as in MD4.

This leads to the following situation:

SHA = MD4 + "expand" transformation + extra round + better-avalanche

MD5 = MD4 + improved bit-bashing + extra round + better-avalanche

There are no known cryptographic attacks against SHA. And because it produces a 160-bit hash, it is more resistant to brute-force attacks (including birthday attacks) than are the other algorithms covered in this chapter.

14.8   RIPE-MD

RIPE-MD was developed for the European Community's RACE project (see Section 18.8). The algorithm is a variation of MD4, designed to be resistant to known cryptanalytic attacks. The rotations of and the order of the message words are modified. Additionally, two instances of the algorithm, differing only in the constants, run in parallel. After each block, the output of both instances are added to the chaining variables.

14.9   HAVAL

HAVAL is a variable-length one-way hash function, invented by Yuliang Zheng, Josef Pieprzyk, and Jennifer Seberry [904]. It is a modification of MD5. HAVAL processes messages in blocks of 1024 bits, twice that of MD5. It has eight 32-bit chaining variables, twice that of MD5. It has a variable number of rounds, from three to five (each round has 16 steps), and it can produce a hash length of 128, 160, 92, 224, or 256 bits.

HAVAL replaces MD5's simple nonlinear functions with highly nonlinear 7-variable functions. Each round uses a single function, but in every step a different permutation is applied to the inputs. There is a new message order, and every step (except those in the first round) uses a different additive constant. There are also two rotations.

The core of the algorithm is:

$$TEMP = (\mathrm{f}(j,A,B,C,D,E,F,G) <<< 7) + (H <<< 11) + M[i][r(j)] + K(j);$$
$$H = G;$$
$$G = F;$$
$$F = E;$$
$$E = D;$$
$$D = C;$$
$$C = B;$$
$$B = A;$$
$$A = TEMP$$

HAVAL is faster than MD5: 60% faster with three rounds, 15% faster with four rounds, and as fast with five rounds.

The variable number of rounds and variable-length output means there are 15 different versions of this algorithm. Den Boer and Bosselaers's attack against MD5 [266] is not applicable to HAVAL because of the rotation applied to H.

14.10   OTHER ONE-WAY HASH FUNCTIONS

A group of researchers at the University of Waterloo have proposed a one-way hash function based on iterated exponentiation in $GF(2^{593})$ [16]. In this scheme, a message is divided into 593-bit blocks. The blocks are successively exponentiated, beginning with the first block. Each exponent is the result of the computation with the previous block; the first exponent is given by an initialization vector.

Ivan Damgård designed a one-way hash function based on the knapsack problem [236]; it can be broken in about 2^{32} operations [182].

Steve Wolfram's cellular automata [885] have been proposed as a basis for one-way hash functions. An early implementation by Ivan Damgård [236] is insecure [844,233]. There is a one-way hash function, Cellhash [233], and an improved version, Subhash [234], which are based on cellular automata.

C. P. Schnorr proposed a one-way hash function based on the discrete Fourier transform, called FFT-Hash, in the summer of 1991 [779]; it was broken a few months later by two independent groups [232,43]. Schnorr proposed a revised version, called FFT-Hash II (the previous version was renamed FFT-Hash I) [780], which was broken a few weeks later [862]. Schnorr has proposed further modifications but, as it stands, the algorithm is much slower than the others in this chapter.

Additional theoretical work on constructing one-way hash functions from one-way functions and one-way permutations can be found in [632,752].

14.11   USING SYMMETRIC BLOCK ALGORITHMS

It is possible to use a symmetric block cipher algorithm as a one-way hash function. The thought is that if we know that the block algorithm is secure, then the one-way hash function will also be secure.

The most obvious method is to use the algorithm in CBC mode, with the Initialization Vector set to 0 and to make the last ciphertext block into the hash value. This method is described in Federal Information Processing Standard 113 [639] using DES, although any block algorithm will work.

However, there are two problems with this approach. DES, and most block algorithms, generate 64-bit blocks; this is often too small for a useful hash value. Second, this method entails specifying an encryption key for the algorithm, and then keeping it secret. Otherwise, an attacker could run the algorithm in reverse: decrypting the hash value with the known key.

A more clever approach is to use the message block as the key, the previous hash value as the input, and the current hash value as the output.

The details of the hash function are more complex. There are often XORs and things added in for good measure. This means that the block size is the key length, and the size of the hash value is the block size. Since most block algorithms are 64 bits, several schemes are designed around a hash that is twice the block size.

What follows is a smattering of the various hash functions that have appeared in the literature. Summaries of these functions can be found in [520,828]. Statements about attacks against these schemes assume that the underlying block cipher is secure; i.e., the best attack against them is brute force.

Davies-Meyer

This scheme was proposed independently by Davies and Meyer [248,572,884]. It works with any block cipher. The length of the hash is the size of the block—64 bits with most of the block algorithms in this book.

In each round, one block of the message is hashed using the following formula:

$$H_0 = I, \text{ where } I \text{ is a random initial value}$$
$$H_i = E_{M_i}(H_{i-1}) \text{ XOR } H_{i-1}$$

Figure 14.5 illustrates this technique. The message block, M_i, is used as the encryption key. The previous message block is encrypted using that key and then XORed with itself. (That seemingly superfluous XOR is added to thwart a meet-in-the-middle attack.) The result becomes the input to the next round. And at the end, the length of the message becomes the last M_i.

So far, this one-way hash function is as secure as the underlying encryption algorithm. It only produces a 64-bit hash, so it is not suitable for applications susceptible to the birthday attack.

Using DES, M is first broken down into 56-bit blocks (the length of the DES key). The first message block, M_1, becomes the DES key; the plaintext input to the DES algorithm is H_0, the random initial value. The ciphertext output of the DES algorithm is H_1. This is XORed with H_0 and becomes the input to the hash

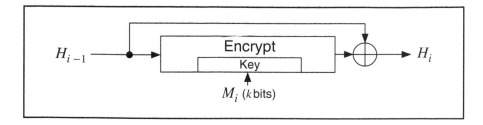

Figure 14.5
Davies-Meyer.

of the second block. M_2, the next 56-bit message block, becomes the new DES key. H_1 is the plaintext input to the algorithm; H_2 is the ciphertext output. H_2 XOR H_1 is the input to the hash of the third block, and so on.

This algorithm is slower than any of the one-way hash functions discussed previously because the DES algorithm gets a new key for each block. All of the subkeys have to be generated every time. And even worse, this algorithm only generates a 64-bit hash value.

LOKI Single-Block

This algorithm was designed by the creators of LOKI [174]. It creates a hash the length of the block.

$$H_0 = I_H, \text{ where } I_H \text{ is a random initial value}$$
$$H_i = E_{H_{i-1} \text{ XOR } M_i}(H_{i-1}) \text{ XOR } H_{i-1} \text{ XOR } M_i$$

Figure 14.6 illustrates this algorithm. Because of LOKI's complementation property [486], it is insecure when used with the LOKI algorithm. And it could be insecure regardless.

Miyaguchi

This algorithm, described in [611,612], produces a hash value equal in length to the block.

$$H_0 = I_H, \text{ where } I_H \text{ is a random initial value}$$
$$H_i = E_{H_{i-1}}(M_i) \text{ XOR } H_{i-1} \text{ XOR } M_i$$

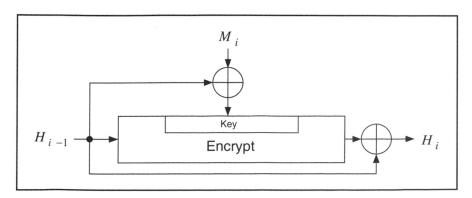

Figure 14.6
LOKI single-block hash.

Figure 14.7 illustrates this algorithm.

There is no known way to attack this scheme that is easier than by using brute force.

Other Schemes Where the Block and Key Sizes Are Equal

Bart Preneel identified twelve secure schemes based on block ciphers, where the block and key sizes are equal [711]. Davies-Meyer and Miyaguchi are two. Here are the other ten:

$$H_i = E_{H_{i-1}} (M_i) \text{ XOR } M_i$$
$$H_i = E_{H_{i-1}} (M_i \text{ XOR } H_{i-1}) \text{ XOR } M_i \text{ XOR } H_{i-1}$$
$$H_i = E_{H_{i-1}}(M_i \text{ XOR } H_{i-1}) \text{ XOR } M_i$$
$$H_i = E_{M_i} (M_i \text{ XOR } H_{i-1}) \text{ XOR } M_i \text{ XOR } H_{i-1}$$
$$H_i = E_{M_i} (H_{i-1}) \text{ XOR } M_i \text{ XOR } H_{i-1}$$
$$H_i = E_{M_i} (M_i \text{ XOR } H_{i-1}) \text{ XOR } H_{i-1}$$
$$H_i = E_{M_i \text{ XOR } H_{i-1}} (M_i) \text{ XOR } X_i$$
$$H_i = E_{M_i \text{ XOR } H_{i-1}} (H_{i-1}) \text{ XOR } H_{i-1}$$
$$H_i = E_{M_i \text{ XOR } H_{i-1}} (M_i) \text{ XOR } H_{i-1}$$
$$H_i = E_{M_i \text{ XOR } H_{i-1}} (H_{i-1}) \text{ XOR } X_i$$

They all assume that

$$H_0 = I_H, \text{ where } I_H \text{ is a random initial value.}$$

A more detailed discussion of these schemes and their properties can be found in [711].

Modified Davies-Meyer

Xuejia Lai and James Massey modified the Davies-Meyer technique to work with the IDEA cipher [523,520]. IDEA has a 64-bit block size and 128-bit key size. Their scheme is:

$$H_0 = I, \text{ where } I \text{ is a random initial value}$$
$$H_i = E_{H_{i-1},M_i}(H_{i-1})$$

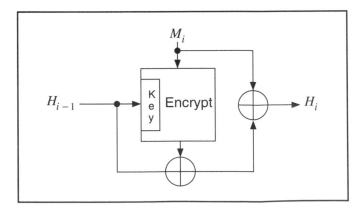

Figure 14.7
Miyaguchi.

This function hashes the message in blocks of 64 bits. At each round, the key to the IDEA cipher is the 64-bit hash from the previous round followed by the 64-bit block of the message. The input to the algorithm is the hash of the previous round; the output is the hash of the current round. Note that unlike the original Davies-Meyer technique, the output is not XORed with the input (see Figure 14.8).

There is no known way to attack this scheme that's easier than brute force.

Preneel-Bosselaers-Govaerts-Vandewalle

This hash function, first proposed in [712], generates a hash that is twice the length of the block cipher algorithm: a 64-bit algorithm produces a 128-bit hash.

With a 64-bit block algorithm, the scheme produces two 64-bit hash values, G_i and H_i, which are concatenated to produce the 128-bit hash. With most block algorithms, the block size is 64 bits. Two adjacent message blocks, L_i and R_i, each the size of the key, are hashed together.

$G_0 = I_G$, where I_G is a random initial value

$H_0 = I_H$, where I_H is another random initial value

$G_i = E_{L_i \text{ XOR } H_{i-1}}(R_i \text{ XOR } G_{i-1}) \text{ XOR } R_i \text{ XOR } G_{i-1} \text{ XOR } H_{i-1}$

$H_i = E_{L_i \text{ XOR } R_i}(H_{i-1} \text{ XOR } G_{i-1}) \text{ XOR } L_i \text{ XOR } G_{i-1} \text{ XOR } H_{i-1}$

Lai demonstrates attacks against this scheme that, in some instances, make the birthday attack trivially solvable [520,521]. Preneel [711] and Don Coppersmith [224a] also have successful attacks against this scheme. Do not use it.

Quisquater-Girault

This scheme, first proposed in [720], also produces a hash value twice the length of the block algorithm. Two blocks, L_i and R_i, each the size of the key, are hashed together.

$G_0 = I_G$, where I_G is a random initial value

$H_0 = I_H$, where I_H is another random initial value

$W_i = E_{L_i}(G_{i-1} \text{ XOR } R_i) \text{ XOR } R_i \text{ XOR } H_{i-1}$

$G_i = E_{R_i}(W_i \text{ XOR } L_i) \text{ XOR } G_{i-1} \text{ XOR } H_{i-1} \text{ XOR } L_i$

$H_i = W_i \text{ XOR } G_{i-1}$

This scheme appeared in a 1989 draft ISO standard but was dropped in a later version [448]. Security problems with this scheme were identified in [613,520,224a,711]. An attack can, in some instances, make the birthday attack solvable with a complexity of 2^{32}, not 2^{64} through brute force. Do not use this scheme.

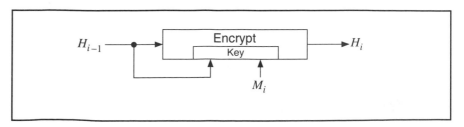

Figure 14.8
Modified Davies-Meyer.

LOKI Double-Block

This algorithm is a modification of Quisquater-Girault, specifically designed to work with LOKI [174]. Two blocks, L_i and R_i, each the size of the key, are hashed together.

$G_0 = I_G$, where I_G is a random initial value

$H_0 = I_H$, where I_H is another random initial value

$W_i = E_{L_i \text{ XOR } G_{i-1}}(G_{i-1} \text{ XOR } R_i) \text{ XOR } R_i \text{ XOR } H_{i-1}$

$G_i = E_{R_i \text{ XOR } H_{i-1}}(W_i \text{ XOR } L_i) \text{ XOR } G_{i-1} \text{ XOR } H_{i-1} \text{ XOR } L_i$

$H_i = W_i \text{ XOR } G_{i-1}$

Figure 14.9 illustrates this algorithm.

There are attacks that, again, in some instances, make the birthday attack trivially solvable [520,521,224a,711]. Do not use this scheme.

Tandem Davies-Meyer

Due to the inherent limitations of a block cipher with a 64-bit key, the only solution is to use an algorithm with a 128-bit key, like IDEA. This technique produces a 128-bit hash value [523,520]. Two modified Davies-Meyer functions work in tandem (see Figure 14.10).

The scheme produces two 64-bit hash values, G_i and H_i, which are concatenated to produce the 128-bit hash. The block size is 64 bits (at least with IDEA).

$G_0 = I_G$, where I_G is a random initial value

$H_0 = I_H$, where I_H is another random initial value

$W_i = E_{G_{i-1},M_i}(H_{i-1})$

$G_i = G_{i-1} \text{ XOR } E_{M_i W_i}(G_{i-1})$

$H_i = W_i \text{ XOR } H_{i-1}$

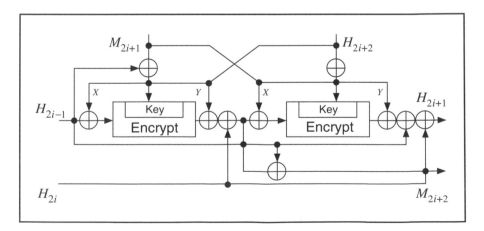

Figure 14.9
LOKI double-block hash.

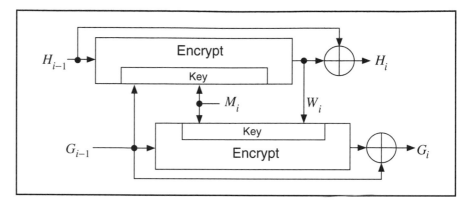

Figure 14.10
Tandem Davies-Meyer.

Note that the algorithm uses two IDEA encryptions to hash each 64-bit message block.

As far as anyone knows, this algorithm has ideal security for a 128-bit hash function: finding a message that hashes to a given message requires 2^{128} attempts, and finding two random messages that hash to the same value requires 2^{64} attempts—assuming that there is no better way to attack the block algorithm than by using brute force, that is.

Abreast Davies-Meyer

This technique, also invented by Lai and Massey to work with IDEA, uses two modified Davies-Meyer schemes side-by-side [523,520]. It also uses two 64-bit hash values, G_i and H_i, which are concatenated to perform the 128-bit hash. It also performs two encryptions for each 64-bit message block.

The scheme is as follows (see Figure 14.11):

$$G_0 = I_G, \text{ where } I_G \text{ is a random initial value}$$
$$H_0 = I_H, \text{ where } I_H \text{ is another random initial value}$$
$$G_i = G_{i-1} \text{ XOR } E_{M_i H_{i-1}} (\text{NOT } G_{i-1})$$
$$H_i = H_{i-1} \text{ XOR } E_{G_{i-1} M_i} (H_{i-1})$$

Like the previous algorithm, this one has ideal security (at least, so far).

MDC-4

MDC-4 was developed for the RIPE project [727] (see Section 18.8). The MDC-4 specification uses DES as the block function (four DES encryptions are required to process a single, 64-bit, message block), although any encryption algorithm could be used in theory. MDC-4 produces a hash twice the length of the encryption block.

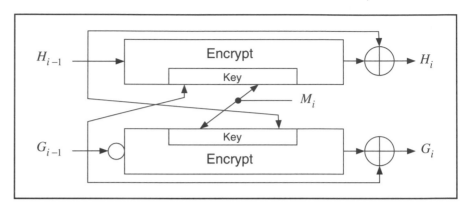

Figure 14.11
Abreast Davies-Meyer.

Other Schemes

The design of fast and secure hash functions (which process one block per encryption) is still under study. They are probably hard to design, and should not be trusted for the time being.

Ralph Merkle proposed a scheme using DES, but it's slow; it only processes 7 message-bits at a time [587]. It is secure, though, if you add some precautions against weak-key attacks. Another scheme, called Meyer-Schilling [597], also has problems [520]. A variant of this is likely to become an ISO standard in 1993 or 1994. There are probably still others.

14.12   USING PUBLIC-KEY ALGORITHMS

It is possible to use a public-key encryption algorithm in a block chaining mode as a digital signature. If you throw away the private key, breaking the hash would be as difficult as reading the message without the private key.

For example, here is how RSA can be turned into a one-way hash function. If M is the message to be hashed, n is the product of two primes, p and q, and e is another large number relatively prime to $(p-1) \times (q-1)$, then the hash function, $H(M)$, would be:

$$H(M) = M^e \bmod n$$

An even easier solution would be to use a single strong prime as the modulus, p. Then:

$$H(M) = M^e \bmod p$$

Breaking this problem is probably as difficult as finding the discrete logarithm of e. If e and p are large enough, the one-way hash function is secure. The problem with this algorithm is that it's far slower than any others discussed here. I don't recommend it for that reason.

14.13   WHICH ONE-WAY HASH FUNCTION IS BEST?

I vote for SHA; it's longer than the others and was developed by an organization that knows what it's doing (the NSA). The Davies-Meyer variants that work with IDEA are also probably secure, but read the warnings in Section 11.9 before you begin.

14.14   KEY-DEPENDENT ONE-WAY HASH FUNCTIONS

A key-dependent one-way hash function is often called a MAC, for Message Authentication Code. MACs have the same properties as the one-way hash functions discussed previously, but they also include a key. Only someone with the identical key can verify the hash. They are very useful to protect authenticity without providing secrecy.

Block Cipher MAC

The simplest way to make a key-dependent one-way hash function is to encrypt a message with a block algorithm in CFB mode. The hash is the last encrypted block, encrypted once more in CFB mode. This method is specified in ANSI X9.9 [29] and ISO 9797 [447].

RIPE-MAC was invented by Bart Preneel [711] and adopted by the RIPE project [727] (see Section 18.8). It is based on ISO 9797 [447], and uses DES as a block encryption function. There are two flavors of RIPE-MAC: one using normal DES, called RIPE-MAC1, and another using triple-DES for even greater security, called RIPE-MAC3. RIPE-MAC1 uses one DES encryption per 64-bit message block; RIPE-MAC3 uses three.

The algorithm consists of three parts. First, the message is expanded to a length that is a multiple of 64 bits. Next, the expanded message is divided up into 64-bit blocks. A keyed compression function is used to hash these blocks, under the control of a secret key, into a single block of 64 bits. This is the step that uses either DES or triple-DES. Finally, the output of this compression is subjected to another DES-based encryption with a different key, derived from the key used in the compression. See [727] for details.

One-Way Hash Function MAC

A one-way hash function can also be used as a MAC [855]. Assume Alice and Bob share a key, K, and Alice wants to send Bob a MAC for message M. Alice concatenates M and K and computes the one-way hash of the concatenation. This hash is the MAC. Since Bob knows K, he can reproduce Alice's result. Mallet, who does not know K, cannot.

Stream Cipher MAC

A truly elegant MDC scheme, by Xuejia Lai, Ranier Rueppel, and Jack Woollven, uses stream ciphers (see Figure 14.12) [525]. A cryptographically secure pseudo-random bit generator demultiplexes the message stream into two substreams. If the output bit of the bit generator, k_i, is 1, then the current message

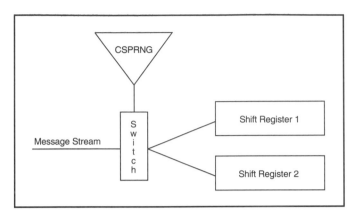

Figure 14.12
Stream cipher MAC.

bit, m_i, is routed to the first substream; if the k_i is 0, the m_i is routed to the second substream. The substreams are each fed into a different feedback shift register (see Section 15.1). The output of the MAC is simply the final states of the shift registers.

This scheme is elegant because it can hash a message on the fly; there are no multiple iterations or lengthy rounds. It's probably the best way to hash high-speed data streams.

# CHAPTER 15

Random Sequence Generators and Stream Ciphers

15.1 PSEUDO-RANDOM SEQUENCE GENERATORS

Linear Congruential Generators

Linear congruential generators are pseudo-random sequence generators of the form:

$$X_n = (aX_{n_1} + b) \bmod m$$

in which X_n is the nth number of the sequence, and X_{n_1} is the previous number of the sequence. The variables a, b, and m are constants: a is the **multiplier**, b is the **increment**, and m is the modulus. The seed is the initial value of X.

This generator has a period no greater than m. If a, b, and m are properly chosen, then the generator will be a **maximal length generator,** and have period m. (For example, m should be chosen to be a prime number.) Details on choosing constants to ensure maximal length can be found in [488,531]. Another good article on linear congruential generators and their theory is [814].

Table 15.1, taken from [713], gives a list of good constants for linear congruential generators. They all produce maximal length generators and, even more important, pass Knuth's spectral test for randomness for dimensions 2, 3, 4, 5, and 6 [488]. They are organized by the largest product that does not overflow a specific word length.

The advantage of linear congruential generators is that they are fast, requiring few operations per bit.

TABLE 15.1
Constants for Linear Congruential Generators

OVERFLOW AT	a	b	m
2^{20}	106	1283	6075
2^{21}	211	1663	7875
2^{22}	421	1663	7875
2^{23}	430	2531	11979
	936	1399	6655
	1366	1283	6075
2^{24}	171	11213	53125
	859	2531	11979
	419	6173	29282
	967	3041	14406
2^{25}	141	28411	134456
	625	6571	31104
	1541	2957	14000
	1741	2731	12960
	1291	4621	21870
	205	29573	139968
2^{26}	421	17117	81000
	1255	6173	29282
	281	28411	134456
2^{27}	1093	18257	86436
	421	54773	259200
	1021	24631	116640
	1021	25673	121500
2^{28}	1277	24749	117128
	741	66037	312500
	2041	25673	121500
2^{29}	2311	25367	120050
	1807	45289	214326
	1597	51749	244944
	1861	49297	233280
	2661	36979	175000
	4081	25673	121500
	3661	30809	145800
2^{30}	3877	29573	139968
	3613	45289	214326
	1366	150889	714025
2^{31}	8121	28411	134456
	4561	51349	243000
	7141	54773	259200
2^{32}	9301	49297	233280
	4096	150889	714025
2^{33}	2416	374441	1771875
2^{34}	17221	107839	510300
	36261	66037	312500
2^{35}	84589	45989	217728

Unfortunately, linear congruential generators cannot be used for stream-cipher cryptography; they are predictable. Linear congruential generators were first broken by Joan Boyar [701]. She also broke quadratic generators:

$$X_n = (aX_{n-1}^2 + bX_{n-1} + c) \bmod m$$

and cubic generators:

$$X_n = (aX_{n-1}^3 + bX_{n-1}^2 + cX_{n-1} + d) \bmod m$$

Other researchers extended Boyar's work to break any polynomial congruential generator [518,509,510], and Stern and Boyar demonstrated how to break linear congruential generators even if the entire sequence is unknown [846,130].

Still, linear congruential generators remain useful for noncryptographic applications, such as simulations. They are efficient and show good statistical behavior with respect to most reasonable empirical tests. Considerable information on linear congruential generators and their implementations can be found in [531].

Combining Linear Congruential Generators

Wichmann and Hill [877], and later Pierre L'Écuyer [530], examine combining linear congruential generators. Their results are no more cryptographically secure, but they have longer periods and perform better in some randomness tests.

L'Écuyer gives [530] a generator for 32-bit computers.

```
static long s1 = 1 ; /* A "long" must be 32 bits long. */
static long s2 = 1 ;

#define MODMULT(a,b,c,m,s) q = s/a; s = b*(s-a*q) - c*q; if (s<0)
s+=m;
/* MODMULT(a,b,c,m,s) computes s*b mod m, provided that m=a*b+c
and 0 <= c < m. */

/* combinedLCG returns a pseudorandom real value in the range
 * (0,1).  It combines linear congruential generators with
 *  periods of 2^31-85 and 2^31-249, and has a period that is the
 * product of these two prime numbers.  */

double combinedLCG ( void )
{
  long q ;
  long z ;

  MODMULT ( 53668, 40014, 12211, 2147483563L, s1 )
  MODMULT ( 52774, 40692, 3791,  2147483399L, s2 )
  z = s1 - s2 ;
  if ( z < 1 )
```

```
      z += 2147483562 ;
   return z * 4.656613e-10 ;
}

/* In general, call initLCG before using combinedLCG. */
void initLCG ( long InitS1, long InitS2 )
{
   s1 = InitS1 ;
   s2 = InitS2 ;
}
```

This generator works as long as the machine can represent all integers between $-2^{31}+85$ and $2^{31}-85$. The variables, $s1$ and $s2$, are global; they hold current state of the generator. Before the first call, they must be initialized. The variable $s1$ needs an initial value between 1 and 2147483562; the variable $s2$ needs an initial value between 1 and 2147483398. The generator has a period somewhere in the neighborhood of 10^{18}.

If you only have a 16-bit computer, use this generator instead:

```
static int s1 = 1 ;   /* An "int" must be 16 bits long. */
static int s2 = 1 ;
static int s3 = 1 ;

#define MODMULT(a,b,c,m,s) q = s/a; s = b*(s-a*q) - c*q; if (s<0)
s+=m;

/* combinedLCG returns a pseudorandom real value in the range
 * (0,1).  It combines linear congruential generators with
 * periods of 2^15-405, 2^15-1041, and 2^15-1111, and has a period
 * that is the product of these three prime numbers. */

double combinedLCG ( void )
{
   int q ;
   int z ;

   MODMULT ( 206, 157, 21,  32363, s1 )
   MODMULT ( 217, 146, 45,  31727, s2 )
   MODMULT ( 222, 142, 133, 31657, s3 )
   z = s1 - s2 ;
   if ( z > 706 )
      z -= 32362 ;
   z += s3 ;
   if ( z < 1 )
      z += 32362 ;
   return z * 3.0899e-5 ;
}

/* In general, call initLCG before using combinedLCG. */
void initLCG ( int InitS1, int InitS2, InitS3 )
{
```

```
        s1 = InitS1 ;
        s2 = InitS2 ;
        s3 = InitS3 ;
    }
```

This generator works as long as the machine can represent all integers between −32363 and 32363. The variables, $s1$, $s2$, and $s3$, are global; they hold current state of the generator. Before the first call, they must be initialized. The variable $s1$ needs an initial value between 1 and 32362. The variable $s2$ needs an initial value between 1 and 31762. The variable $s3$ needs an initial value between 1 and 31656. This generator has a period of 1.6×10^{13}.

For both of these generators, the constant term, b, is 0.

Linear Feedback Shift Registers

A **linear feedback shift register,** or LFSR, is made up of two parts: a shift register and a **tap sequence** (see Figure 15.1). The shift register is sequence of bits. Each time a bit is needed (sometimes called a **clock pulse,** since this scheme is often implemented in hardware), all of the bits in the shift register are shifted right and the LFSR outputs the least significant bit. The new left-most bit is computed by XORing the other bits in the register, in accordance with the tap sequence.

In theory, an n-bit LFSR can generate a 2^n-1-bit-long pseudo-random sequence before repeating [385]. To do this, the shift register must cycle through all 2^n-1 internal states. (It's 2^n-1 and not 2^n because a shift register filled with zeros will cause the LFSR to output a never-ending stream of zeros—this is not particularly useful.) Only LFSRs with certain tap sequences will cycle through all 2^n-1 internal states; these are called **maximal length** LFSRs.

For example, a 4-bit LFSR, tapped at the first and fourth bit (see Figure 15.2) and initialized with the value 1111, produces the following sequence of internal states before repeating:

```
        1 1 1 1
        0 1 1 1
        1 0 1 1
        0 1 0 1
        1 0 1 0
        1 1 0 1
        0 1 1 0
        0 0 1 1
        1 0 0 1
        0 1 0 0
        0 0 1 0
        0 0 0 1
        1 0 0 0
        1 1 0 0
        1 1 1 0
```

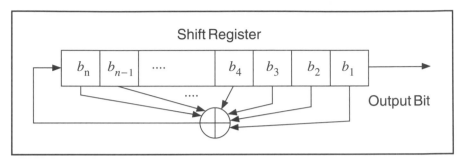

Figure 15.1
Linear feedback shift register.

The output sequence is the string of least significant bits:

$$1\ 1\ 1\ 1\ 0\ 1\ 0\ 1\ 1\ 0\ 0\ 1\ 0\ 0\ 0\ \ldots.$$

In order for an LFSR to be a maximal-length LFSR, the polynomial formed from the elements of the tap sequence plus the constant 1 must be a **primitive polynomial** mod 2. A primitive polynomial of degree n is an irreducible polynomial that divides $x^{2^{\wedge}n-1}+1$, but not x^d+1 for any d that divides 2^n-1 (see Section 9.3). For more mathematics, consult [385,906,905].

Table 15.2 is a list of degrees of primitive polynomials mod 2 [870]. For example, the listing (32, 7, 5, 3, 2, 1, 0) means that the following polynomial is primitive modulo 2:

$$x^{32} + x^7 + x^5 + x^3 + x^2 + x + 1$$

It's easy to turn this into a maximal-length LFSR. The first number is the degree and the length of the LFSR. The last number is always 0 and can be ignored. All the numbers, except the 0, specify the tap sequence.

To continue the example, the listing (32, 7, 5, 3, 2, 1, 0) means that if you take a 32-bit shift register and generate the new bit by XORing the thirty-second, seventh, fifth, third, second, and first bits together (see Figure 15.3), the resultant LFSR will be maximal length; it will cycle through $2^{32}-1$ values before repeating.

The C code for this LFSR looks like:

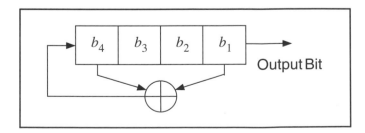

Figure 15.2
4-bit LFSR.

```
int LFSR ()  {
  static unsigned long ShiftRegister = 1 /* Anything but 0. */
  ShiftRegister = ((((ShiftRegister >> 7)
        ^ (ShiftRegister >> 5)
        ^ (ShiftRegister >> 3)
        ^ (ShiftRegister >> 2)
        ^ (ShiftRegister >> 1)
        ^ (ShiftRegister)
        & 0x00000001)
        < 31)
        | (ShiftRegister >> 1);
  return ShiftRegister & 0x00000001;
}
```

The code is a little more complicated when the shift register is longer than the computer's word size, but not significantly so.

Table 15.2 lists some, but by no means all, primitive polynomials modulo 2 [385,906,905,713,415]. Note that all have an odd number of coefficients. I have provided such a large table because LFSRs are often used from stream-cipher cryptography, and I wanted so many different examples so that different people would pick different primitive polynomials. Since, if $p(x)$ is primitive, then so is $x^n p(1/x)$; each entry on the table is actually two primitive polynomials.

For example, if $(a, b, 0)$ is primitive, then $(a, a-b, 0)$ is also primitive. If $(a, b, c, d, 0)$ is primitive, then $(a, a-d, a-c, a-b, 0)$ is also primitive. Mathematically:

$$\text{if } x^a + x^b + 1 \text{ is primitive, so is } x^a + x^{a-b} + 1$$
$$\text{if } x^a + x^b + x^c + x^d + 1 \text{ is primitive, so is } x^a + x^{a-d} + x^{a-c} + x^{a-b} + 1$$

Primitive trinomials are particularly useful, because only two bits of the shift register have to be XORed. However, they are also a lot easier to attack.

LFSRs are competent random sequence generators all by themselves, but they have some annoying nonrandom properties. Sequential bits are linear, which makes them all but useless for encryption. For an LFSR of length n, the internal state is the previous n output bits of the generator. Even if the feedback scheme is unknown, it only takes $2n$ output bits of the generator to determine it [598,599].

Large random numbers generated from sequential bits of this sequence are highly correlated and, for certain types of applications, not random at all. Even so, LFSRs are often used as building blocks in encryption algorithms.

Figure 15.3
32-bit long maximal-length LFSR.

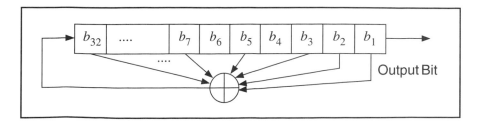

TABLE 15.2
Some Primitive Polynomials Mod 2

(1, 0)	(32, 7, 6, 2, 0)	(58, 6, 5, 1, 0)	(85, 8, 2, 1, 0)
(2, 1, 0)	(33, 13, 0)	(59, 7, 4, 2, 0)	(86, 6, 5, 2, 0)
(3, 1, 0)	(33, 16, 4, 1, 0)	(59, 6, 5, 4, 3, 1, 0)	(87, 13, 0)
(4, 1, 0)	(34, 8, 4, 3, 0)	(60, 1, 0)	(87, 7, 5, 1, 0)
(5, 2, 0)	(34, 7, 6, 5, 2, 1, 0)	(61, 5, 2, 1, 0)	(88, 11, 9, 8, 0)
(6, 1, 0)	(35, 2, 0)	(62, 6, 5, 3, 0)	(88, 8, 5, 4, 3, 1, 0)
(7, 1, 0)	(36, 11, 0)	(63, 1, 0)	(89, 38, 0)
(7, 3, 0)	(36, 6, 5, 4, 2, 1, 0)	(64, 4, 3, 1, 0)	(89, 51, 0)
(8, 4, 3, 2, 0)	(37, 6, 4, 1, 0)	(65, 18, 0)	(89, 6, 5, 3, 0)
(9, 4, 0)	(37, 5, 4, 3, 2, 1, 0)	(65, 4, 3, 1, 0)	(90, 5, 3, 2, 0)
(10, 3, 0)	(38, 6, 5, 1, 0)	(66, 9, 8, 6, 0)	(91, 8, 5, 1, 0)
(11, 2, 0)	(39, 4, 0)	(66, 8, 6, 5, 3, 2, 0)	(91, 7, 6, 5, 3, 2, 0)
(12, 6, 4, 1, 0)	(40, 5, 4, 3, 0)	(67, 5, 2, 1, 0)	(92, 6, 5, 2, 0)
(13, 4, 3, 1, 0)	(41, 3, 0)	(68, 9, 0)	(93, 2, 0)
(14, 5, 3, 1, 0)	(42, 7, 4, 3, 0)	(68, 7, 5, 1, 0)	(94, 21, 0)
(15, 1, 0)	(42, 5, 4, 3, 2, 1, 0)	(69, 6, 5, 2, 0)	(94, 6, 5, 1, 0)
(16, 5, 3, 2, 0)	(43, 6, 4, 3, 0)	(70, 5, 3, 1, 0)	(95, 11, 0)
(17, 3, 0)	(44, 6, 5, 2, 0)	(71, 6, 0)	(95, 6, 5, 4, 2, 1, 0)
(17, 5, 0)	(45, 4, 3, 1, 0)	(71, 5, 3, 1, 0)	(96, 10, 9, 6, 0)
(17, 6, 0)	(46, 8, 7, 6, 0)	(72, 10, 9, 3, 0)	(96, 7, 6, 4, 3, 2, 0)
(18, 7, 0)	(46, 8, 5, 3, 2, 1, 0)	(72, 6, 4, 3, 2, 1, 0)	(97, 6, 0)
(18, 5, 2, 1, 0)	(47, 5, 0)	(73, 25, 0)	(98, 11, 0)
(19, 5, 2, 1, 0)	(48, 9, 7, 4, 0)	(73, 4, 3, 2, 0)	(98, 7, 4, 3, 1, 0)
(20, 3, 0)	(48, 7, 5, 4, 2, 1, 0)	(74, 7, 4, 3, 0)	(99, 7, 5, 4, 0)
(21, 2, 0)	(49, 9, 0)	(75, 6, 3, 1, 0)	(100, 37, 0)
(22, 1, 0)	(49, 6, 5, 4, 0)	(76, 5, 4, 2, 0)	(100, 8, 7, 2, 0)
(23, 5, 0)	(50, 4, 3, 2, 0)	(77, 6, 5, 2, 0)	(101, 7, 6, 1, 0)
(24, 4, 3, 1, 0)	(51, 6, 3, 1, 0)	(78, 7, 2, 1, 0)	(102, 6, 5, 3, 0)
(25, 3, 0)	(52, 3, 0)	(79, 9, 0)	(103, 9, 0)
(26, 6, 2, 1, 0)	(53, 6, 2, 1, 0)	(79, 4, 3, 2, 0)	(104, 11, 10, 1, 0)
(27, 5, 2, 1, 0)	(54, 8, 6, 3, 0)	(80, 9, 4, 2, 0)	(105, 16, 0)
(28, 3, 0)	(54, 6, 5, 4, 3, 2, 0)	(80, 7, 5, 3, 2, 1, 0)	(106, 15, 0)
(29, 2, 0)	(55, 24, 0)	(81, 4, 0)	(107, 9, 7, 4, 0)
(30, 6, 4, 1, 0)	(55, 6, 2, 1, 0)	(82, 9, 6, 4, 0)	(108, 31, 0)
(31, 3, 0)	(56, 7, 4, 2, 0)	(82, 8, 7, 6, 1, 0)	(109, 5, 4, 2, 0)
(31, 6, 0)	(57, 7, 0)	(83, 7, 4, 2, 0)	(110, 6, 4, 1, 0)
(31, 7, 0)	(57, 5, 3, 2, 0)	(84, 13, 0)	(111, 10, 0)
(31, 13, 0)	(58, 19, 0)	(84, 8, 7, 5, 3, 1, 0)	(111, 49, 0)

TABLE 15.2 (continued)
Some Primitive Polynomials Mod 2

(112, 11, 6, 4, 0)	(142, 21, 0)	(164, 12, 6, 5, 0)	(236, 5, 0)
(113, 9, 0)	(143, 5, 3, 2, 0)	(165, 9, 8, 3, 0)	(250, 103, 0)
(113, 15, 0)	(144, 7, 4, 2, 0)	(166, 10, 3, 2, 0)	(255, 52, 0)
(113, 30, 0)	(145, 52, 0)	(167, 6, 0)	(255, 56, 0)
(114, 11, 2, 1, 0)	(145, 69, 0)	(170, 23, 0)	(255, 82, 0)
(115, 8, 7, 5, 0)	(146, 5, 3, 2, 0)	(172, 2, 0)	(258, 83, 0)
(116, 6, 5, 2, 0)	(147, 11, 4, 2, 0)	(174, 13, 0)	(266, 47, 0)
(117, 5, 2, 1, 0)	(148, 27, 0)	(175, 6, 0)	(270, 133, 0)
(118, 33, 0)	(149, 10, 9, 7, 0)	(175, 16, 0)	(282, 35, 0)
(119, 45, 0)	(150, 53, 0)	(175, 18, 0)	(282, 43, 0)
(119, 8, 0)	(151, 3, 0)	(175, 57, 0)	(286, 69, 0)
(120, 9, 6, 2, 0)	(151, 9, 0)	(177, 8, 0)	(286, 73, 0)
(121, 18, 0)	(151, 15, 0)	(177, 22, 0)	(294, 61, 0)
(122, 6, 2, 1, 0)	(151, 31, 0)	(177, 88, 0)	(322, 67, 0)
(123, 2, 0)	(151, 39, 0)	(178, 87, 0)	(333, 2, 0)
(124, 37, 0)	(151, 43, 0)	(183, 56, 0)	(350, 53, 0)
(125, 7, 6, 5, 0)	(151, 46, 0)	(194, 87, 0)	(366, 29, 0)
(126, 7, 4, 2, 0)	(151, 51, 0)	(198, 65, 0)	(378, 43, 0)
(127, 1, 0)	(151, 63, 0)	(201, 14, 0)	(378, 107, 0)
(127, 7, 0)	(151, 66, 0)	(201, 17, 0)	(390, 89, 0)
(127, 15, 0)	(151, 67, 0)	(201, 59, 0)	(462, 73, 0)
(127, 30, 0)	(151, 70, 0)	(201, 79, 0)	(521, 32, 0)
(127, 63, 0)	(152, 6, 3, 2, 0)	(202, 55, 0)	(521, 48, 0)
(128, 7, 2, 1, 0)	(153, 1, 0)	(207, 43, 0)	(521, 158, 0)
(129, 5, 0)	(153, 8, 0)	(212, 105, 0)	(521, 168, 0)
(130, 3, 0)	(154, 9, 5, 1, 0)	(218, 11, 0)	(607, 105, 0)
(131, 8, 3, 2, 0)	(155, 7, 5, 4, 0)	(218, 15, 0)	(607, 147, 0)
(132, 29, 0)	(156, 9, 5, 3, 0)	(218, 71, 0)	(607, 273, 0)
(133, 9, 8, 2, 0)	(157, 6, 5, 2, 0)	(218, 71, 0)	(1279, 216, 0)
(134, 57, 0)	(158, 8, 6, 5, 0)	(218, 83, 0)	(1279, 418, 0)
(135, 11, 0)	(159, 31, 0)	(225, 32, 0)	(2281, 715, 0)
(135, 16, 0)	(159, 34, 0)	(225, 74, 0)	(2281, 915, 0)
(135, 22, 0)	(159, 40, 0)	(225, 88, 0)	(2281, 1029, 0)
(136, 8, 3, 2, 0)	(160, 5, 3, 2, 0)	(225, 97, 0)	(3217, 67, 0)
(137, 21, 0)	(161, 18, 0)	(225, 109, 0)	(3217, 576, 0)
(138, 8, 7, 1, 0)	(161, 39, 0)	(231, 26, 0)	(4423, 271, 0)
(139, 8, 5, 3, 0)	(161, 60, 0)	(231, 34, 0)	(9689, 84, 0)
(140, 29, 0)	(162, 8, 7, 4, 0)	(234, 31, 0)	
(141, 13, 6, 1, 0)	(163, 7, 6, 3, 0)	(234, 103, 0)	

Modified LFSRs

It is possible to modify the LFSR's feedback scheme. The resultant generator is
no better cryptographically, but it is still maximal length and is easier to implement
in software [713].

Instead of using the bits in the tap sequence to generate the new left-most bit,
each bit in the tap sequence is XORed with the output of the generator and
replaced, and then the output of the generator becomes the new left-most bit (see
Figure 15.4).

In C, this looks like:

```
#define mask 0x80000057

static unsigned long ShiftRegister=1;

void seed_LFSR (unsigned long seed)
{
  if (seed == 0)/* avoid calamity */
    seed = 1;
  ShiftRegister = seed;
}

int modified_LFSR (void)
{
  if (ShiftRegister & 0x00000001) {
    ShiftRegister = (ShiftRegister ^ (mask >> 1)) | 0x8000000;
    return 1;
  } else {
    ShiftRegister >>= 1;
    return 0;
  }
}
```

The savings here is that all the XORs can be done as a single operation. If the tap sequence
is a primitive polynomial mod 2, then the sequence generator is maximal length.

15.2   STREAM CIPHERS

The main point behind cryptographically secure pseudo-random sequence
generators (CSPRSGs) is that they are perfect for stream ciphers. The output of
these generators is indistinguishable (at least, in any reasonable amount of time)

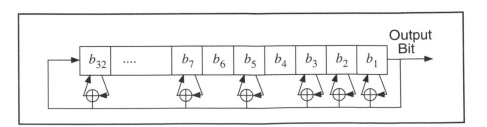

Figure 15.4
Modified 32-bit LFSR.

from real-random bit generators. Simply XOR the output of the generator with the plaintext stream, and you have a good stream cipher.

According to Rainer Rueppel, there are four practical approaches to the construction of CSPRSGs [759,761]: an information-theoretic approach, a system-theoretic approach, a complexity-theoretic approach, and a randomized approach. The approaches differ in their assumptions about the capabilities and opportunities of the cryptanalyst, the definition of cryptographic success, and the notion of security. Most of the research in this field is theoretical, but there are some good CS generators that exist among the impractical ones. (A good overview of clock-controlled stream ciphers is in [384].)

15.2.1 System-Theoretic Approach

In this approach to stream ciphers, the cryptographer designs keystream generators that have testable security properties—period, distribution of bit patterns, linear complexity, etc., instead of mathematical theory. The cryptographer also studies various cryptanalytic techniques against these generators and makes sure the generators are immune to these attacks.

Over the years, the approach has resulted in a set of design criteria for keystream generators [804,54,756,699]. These were delineated by Rueppel in [761], where he details the theory behind them.

Long period, no repetitions.

Linear complexity criteria: large linear complexity, linear complexity profile, local linear complexity, etc. (The **linear complexity** of a generator is the length of the shortest LFSR that can generate the output of the generator—linear complexity is a measure of the randomness of the generator.)

Statistical criteria such as ideal k-tuple distributions.

Confusion: every keystream bit must be a complex transformation of all or most of the key bits.

Diffusion: redundancies in substructures must be dissipated into long-range statistics.

Nonlinearity criteria for Boolean functions like mth-order correlation immunity, distance to linear functions, avalanche criterion, etc.

This list of design criteria is not unique for stream ciphers designed by the system-theoretic approach; it is true for all stream ciphers. It is even true for all block ciphers. What is unique about the system-theoretic approach is that stream ciphers are designed to satisfy these goals directly.

The major problem with these cryptosystems is that nothing can be proven about their security; the design criteria have never been proven to be either necessary or sufficient for security. A keystream generator may satisfy all the design principles but could still turn out to be insecure. Another could turn out to be secure. There is still some magic to the process.

On the other hand, breaking each of these keystream generators is a different problem for cryptanalysts. If there are enough different generators out there, it may not be worth the cryptanalysts' time to try to break each one. They may have to achieve fame and glory by figuring out better ways to factor large numbers or calculate discrete logarithms.

In the end, stream ciphers are no different from any of the symmetric block algorithms in this book. There are no proofs of security. There are a number of systematic ways of attacking them, but resistance to them does not guarantee resistance to new attacks. This field is expanding quickly, and it is politically charged, since most military encryption systems in use today are based on LFSRs. Still, it seems that an astonishingly large number of seemingly complex shift-register-based generators have been cracked. It's amazing that people keep trying to use them.

Geffe Generator

This keystream generator uses three LFSRs, combined in a nonlinear manner (see Figure 15.5) [369]. Two of the LFSRs are inputs into a multiplexer, and the third LFSR controls the output of the multiplexer. If a_1, a_2, and a_3 are the outputs of the three LFSRs, the output of Geffe's generator can be described by:

$$b = a_2a_1 \text{ XOR (NOT } a_2)a_3$$

If the primitive feedback polynomials of the three LFSRs have degrees n_1, n_2, and n_3, respectively, then the linear complexity of the generator is:

$$(n_1 + 1)n_2 + n_1n_3$$

The period of the generator is the least common multiple of the periods of the three generators. Assuming the degrees of the three primitive feedback polynomials are relatively prime, the period of this generator is the product of the periods of the three LFSRs.

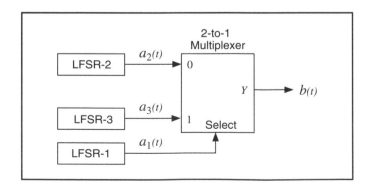

Figure 15.5
Geffe's generator.

Although this generator looks good on paper, it is cryptographically weak. If you run through the probabilities, you will see that the output of the generator equals the output of LFSR-1 75% of the time. Similarly, the output of the generator equals the output of LFSR-2 75% of the time. With that kind of correlation, the keystream generator can be cracked fairly easily. For example, if the primitive polynomials only have three terms each, and the largest degree polynomial is of degree n, it only takes a segment of the output sequence $37 \times n$-bits long to reconstruct the internal states of all three LFSRs [901].

Pless Generator

This generator is designed around the capabilities of the J–K flip-flop [700]. It consists of eight LFSRs driving four J–K flip-flops. Each flip-flop acts as a nonlinear combiner for two of the LFSRs. To avoid the problem of knowing that an output of the flip-flop identifies both the source and value of the next output bit, the four flip-flops are decimated by four and then interleaved to yield the final keystream.

This algorithm has been cryptanalyzed by attacking each of the four flip-flops independently [754]. Additionally, combining J–K flip-flops is cryptographically weak, and generators of this type succumb to what is called a correlation attack [815].

Multiplexer Generator

This scheme uses a multiplexer to combine two LFSRs [454,455]. For each output bit the multiplexer, controlled by LFSR-1, selects one bit of LFSR-2. There is also a function that maps the output of LFSR-2 to the input of the multiplexer (see Figure 15.6).

The key is the initial state of the two LFSRs and the mapping function. Although this generator has great statistical properties, it fell to Ross Anderson's cryptanalysis [22]. Additional results are in [900,255]. The mathematics are too complicated to reproduce here; don't use this generator.

Beth-Piper Stop-and-Go Generator

This generator, shown in Figure 15.7, uses the output of one LFSR to control the clock of another LFSR [94]. The clock input of LFSR-2 is controlled by the output of LFSR-1, so that LFSR-2 can change its state at time t only if the output of LFSR-1 was 1 at time $t-1$.

Assuming all lengths of the three LFSRs are relatively prime and the feedback sequences are primitive polynomials, this generator has a dramatically large linear complexity:

$$(2^{n_1}-1)n_2+n_3$$

However, its security is as poor as the Geffe generator [901].

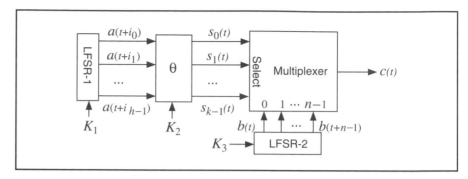

Figure 15.6
The Jennings multiplexer generator.

Gollmann Cascade

The Gollmann Cascade, described in [382,383,190], is a strengthened version of the Beth-Piper generator (see Figure 15.8). It consists of a series of LFSRs, with the clock of each controlled by the previous LFSR. If the output of LFSR-1 is 1 at time $t-1$, then LFSR-2 steps. If the output of LFSR-2 is 1 at time $t-1$, then LFSR-3 steps, and so on. The output of the final LFSR is the output of the generator. If all the LFSRs have the same length, l, the linear complexity of a system with n LFSRs is:

$$l(2^l-1)^{n-1}$$

This is a huge number. Although I have seen no successful cryptanalysis of this generator, the authors in [901] wrote: "The proposer of this scheme is himself aware of a certain weakness related to it. Efforts are being made to estimate its influence on the security of the keystream thus generated." I haven't been able to track down exactly what that "certain weakness" is, but the hint of it is reason to worry.

Alternating Stop-and-Go Generator

This generator uses three LFSRs of different length. LFSR-2 is clocked when the output of LFSR-1 is 1; LFSR-3 is clocked when the output of LFSR-1 is 0. The output of the generator is the XOR of LFSR-2 and LFSR-3 (see Figure 15.9) [404].

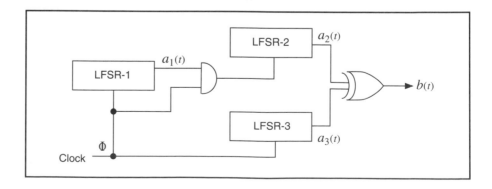

Figure 15.7
The Beth-Piper stop-and-go generator.

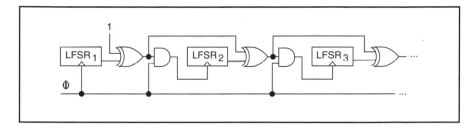

Figure 15.8
Gollmann Cascade.

This generator has a long period and large linear complexity. The authors found a correlation attack against LFSR-1, but it does not substantially reduce the effort required to break the generator.

Bilateral Stop-and-Go Generator

This generator uses two LFSRs, both of length 1 (see Figure 15.10) [900]. The output of the generator is the XOR of the outputs of each LFSR. If the output of LFSR-A at time $t-1$ is 0 and the output at time $t-2$ is 1, then LFSR-B does not step at time t. Conversely, if the output of LFSR-B at time $t-1$ is 0 and the output at time $t-2$ is 1, and if LFSR-B stepped at time t, then LFSR-A does not step at time t.

The linear complexity of this system is roughly equal to the period. According to [900], "no evident key redundancy has been observed in this system."

Threshold Generator

This generator tries to get around the security problems of the previous generators by using a variable number of LFSRs [178]. The theory is that if you use a lot of LFSRs, it's harder to break the cipher.

This generator is illustrated in Figure 15.11. Take the output of a large number of LFSRs (make it an odd number of them). Make sure the lengths of all the LFSRs are relatively prime and all the feedback polynomials are primitive—to maximize the period. If more than half the output bits are 1, then the output of the generator is 1. If more than half the output bits are 0, then the output of the generator is 0.

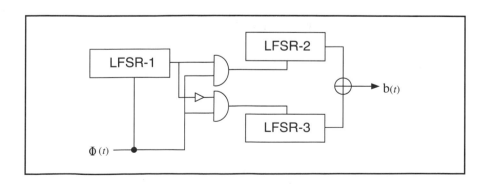

Figure 15.9
Alternating stop-and-go generator.

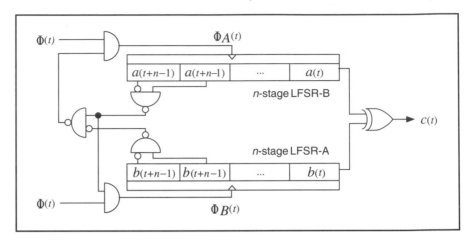

Figure 15.10
Bilateral stop-and-go
generator.

With three LFSRs, the output generator can be written as:

$$b = a_1 a_2 \text{ OR } a_1 a_3 \text{ OR } a_2 a_3$$

This is very similar to the Geffe generator, except that it has a larger linear complexity of

$$L_1 L_2 + L_1 L_3 + L_2 L_3$$

in which L_1, L_2, and L_3 are the lengths of the first, second, and third LFSRs.

This generator isn't great. Each output bit of the generator yields some information about the state of the LFSRs, 0.189 bits to be exact. I don't recommend using it.

Self-Decimated Generators

Self-decimated generators are generators that control their own clock. Two have been proposed, one by Rueppel (see Figure 15.12) [758] and another by Chambers and Gollmann [189] (see Figure 15.13). In Rueppel's generator, when the output of

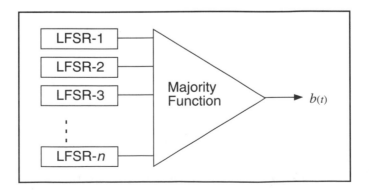

Figure 15.11
Threshold generator.

the LFSR is 0, the LFSR is clocked d times. When the output of the LFSR is 1, the LFSR is clocked k times. Chambers's and Gollmann's generator is more complicated, but the idea is the same. Unfortunately, both generators are insecure [901].

Multispeed Inner-Product Generator

This generator, by Massey and Rueppel [567], uses two LFSRs clocked at two different speeds (see Figure 15.14). LFSR-2 is clocked d times as fast as LFSR-1. Then the individual bits of the two LFSRs are ANDed together and then XORed with each other to produce the final output bit of the generator.

Although the linear complexity is high and the generator possesses excellent statistical properties, it is still insecure [901]. If l is the length of LFSR-1, n is the length of the LFSR-2, and d is the speed multiple between the two, then the internal state of the generator can be recovered from an output sequence of length

$$l + n + \log_2 d$$

Cellular Automaton Generator

In [885,886], Steve Wolfram proposed using a one-dimensional cellular automaton, such as a CSPRNG. A discussion of the mechanics of cellular automata is beyond the scope of this book, but, in brief, Wolfram's generator consisted of a one-dimensional array of bits, $a_1, a_2, a_3, \ldots a_k, \ldots a_n$, and an update function:

$$a'_k = a_{k-1} \text{ XOR } (a_k \text{ OR } a_{k+1})$$

The bit is extracted from one of the a_k values; which one really doesn't matter.

This generator's behavior appears to be quite random. However, there is a known-plaintext attack against these generators [582]. This attack works on a PC with values of n up to 500 bits. Additionally, Paul Bardell proved that the output of a cellular automaton is identical to the output of a linear-feedback shift register and is therefore no more secure [42].

$1/p$ Generator

This generator was proposed, and then cryptanalyzed, in [121]. If the internal state of the generator at time t is x_t, then

$$x_{t+1} = bx_t \bmod p$$

The output of the generator is the least significant bit of

$$x_t \text{ div } p, \text{ when div is truncated integer division}$$

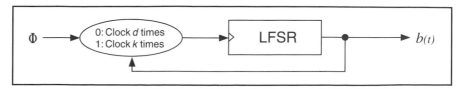

Figure 15.12
Rueppel's self-decimated generator.

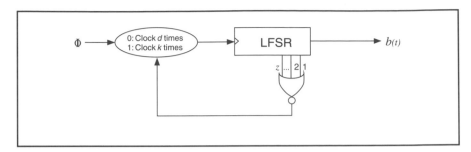

Figure 15.13
Chambers's and Gollmann's
self-decimated generator.

For maximum period, the constants b and p should be chosen so that p is prime and b is a primitive root mod p. It is a pity that the generator isn't at all secure.

Summation Generator

This generator, devised by Rainer Rueppel [757,756]. Basically, the generator takes the output of two LFSRs through an adder (with carry). This operation is highly nonlinear, and through the late 1980s the generator was the security front-runner. Recently it fell to a correlation attack [583,584,602].

crypt (1)

The original UNIX encryption algorithm, crypt(1), is a stream cipher based on the same technology as the Enigma. It is a 256-element, single-rotor substitution cipher with a reflector. Both the rotor and the reflector are generated from the key. This algorithm is far simpler than the World War II German Enigma and, for a skilled cryptanalyst, very easy to break [868,732]. A public-domain UNIX program, called Crypt Breakers Workbench (CBW), can be used to break files encrypted with crypt(1).

Other Schemes

RC4 is a stream cipher developed by RSA Data Security, Inc. (see Section 11.8). There is also a generator based on the knapsack problem [755].

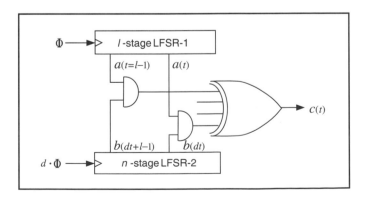

Figure 15.14
Multispeed inner-product
generator.

15.2.2 Complexity-Theoretic Approach

In this approach to stream ciphers, the cryptographer attempts to use complexity theory to prove that his generators are secure. Consequently, the generators tend to be more complicated, based on the same sorts of hard problems we saw in public-key cryptography. And like public-key algorithms, they tend to be slow and cumbersome.

Shamir's Pseudo-Random Number Generator

Shamir used the RSA algorithm as a pseudo-random number generator [791]. While Shamir showed that predicting the output of the pseudo-random number generator is equivalent to breaking RSA, potential biases in the output were demonstrated in [781,127].

Blum-Micali Generator

This generator gets its security from the difficulty of computing discrete logarithms [127]. Let a be a prime and p be an odd prime. A random seed, x_0, starts off the process:

$$x_{i+1} = a_{x_i} \bmod p$$

The output of the generator is 1 if $x < (p-1)/2$, and 0 otherwise.

If p is large enough so that computing discrete logarithms mod p is unfeasible, then this generator is secure. Additional theoretical results can be found in [895,556,557,690,508,465].

RSA

This RSA generator [19,20] is a modification of [127]. The initial parameters are N, the product of two large primes, and a random seed x_0, where x_0 is less than N.

$$x_{i+1} = x_i^e \bmod N$$

The output of the generator is the least significant bit of x_i. The security of this generator is based on the difficulty of breaking RSA. If N is large enough, then the generator is secure. Additional theory can be found in [863,864,865,17,211].

Blum Blum Shub

Currently the simplest and most efficient generator is called the Blum, Blum, and Shub generator, after its inventors. We shall mercifully abbreviate it as BBS, although it is sometimes called the quadratic residue generator [121].

The theory behind the BBS generator has to do with quadratic residues modulo n (see Section 9.3). Here's how it works:

First find two large prime numbers, p and q, that are congruent to 3 modulo 4. The product of those numbers, $n = p \times q$, is a Blum integer. Choose another random integer, x, which is relatively prime to n. Compute

$$x_0 = x^2 \bmod n$$

That's the seed for the generator.

Now you can start computing bits. The ith pseudo-random bit is the least significant bit of x_i, when

$$x_i = x_{i-1}^{\,2} \bmod n$$

The most intriguing property of this generator is that you don't have to iterate through all $i-1$ bits to get the ith bit. If you know p and q, you can compute the ith bit directly:

b_i is the least significant bit of x_i, when
$$x_i = x_0^{\,(2^i) \bmod ((p-1)(q-1))} \bmod n$$

This property means you can use this cryptographically strong pseudo-random bit generator as a stream cryptosystem for a random-access file.

The security of this scheme rests on the difficulty of factoring n. You can make n public, so anyone can generate bits using the generator. However, unless cryptanalysts can factor n, they can never predict the output of the generator—not even with a statement like: "The next bit has a 51% chance of being a 1."

More strongly, the BBS generator is **unpredictable to the left** and **unpredictable to the right.** This means that, given a sequence generated by the generator, cryptanalysts cannot predict the next bit in the sequence or the previous bit in the sequence. This is not security based on a complicated bit generator that no one understands, but on the mathematics behind factoring n. For those who are concerned about cryptographically secure pseudo-random bits, this is the best choice.

This algorithm is slow, but there are speedups. As it turns out, you can use more than the least significant bit of each x_i as a pseudo-random bit. According to [863,864,865,19,20], if l is the length of x_i, the least significant $\log_2 l$ bits of x_i can be used.

The BBS generator is comparatively slow and isn't useful for stream ciphers. However, for high-security applications, such as key generation, this generator is the best.

15.2.3 Information-Theoretic Approach

In an information-theoretic approach to stream ciphers, the cryptanalyst is assumed to have unlimited time and computing power. The only practical stream cipher that is secure against an adversary like this is a one-time pad (see Section 1.2.4). Since a one-time pad of bits would be impractical on a pad, this is sometimes called a **one-time tape.** Two magnetic tapes, one at the encryption end and the other at the decryption end, would have the same random keystream on them. To encrypt, simply XOR the plaintext with the bits on the tape. To decrypt, XOR the ciphertext with the bits on the other, identical, tape. Since the keystream bits are truly random, you never use the same keystream bits twice. If you burn the tapes when you are through with them, you've got perfect secrecy.

Ueli Maurer described a scheme based on XORing the plaintext with several large public random bit sequences [577,573,574]. The key is the starting position within each sequence. This turns out to be provably almost secure, with a calculable probability of being broken based on how much memory the attacker has (not how much computing power). Maurer claims that this scheme would be practical with about 100 different sequences of 10^{20} random bits each. Digitizing the face of the moon might be one way to get this volume of bits.

Another stream cipher, developed by Schnorr, assumes that the cryptanalyst only has access to a limited number of ciphertext bits [775]. The results are highly theoretical and have no practical value, at least not yet. For more details, consult [760,902,663].

15.2.4 Randomized Stream Ciphers

In a randomized stream cipher, the cryptographer tries to ensure that the cryptanalyst has a problem of unfeasible size to solve. The objective is to increase the number of bits the cryptanalyst has to work with, while keeping the secret key small. This can be done by making use of a large public random string for encryption and decryption. The key would specify which parts of the large random string are to be used for encryption and decryption. The cryptanalyst, not knowing the key, is forced to pursue a brute-force search through the random string.

The security of this sort of cipher can be expressed by the average number of bits a cryptanalyst must examine before the chances of determining the key improve over pure guessing.

While there has been some theoretical work on ciphers of this type, nothing has been implemented. James Massey and Ingmar Ingemarsson proposed the Rip van Winkle cipher [565], so named because the receiver has to receive 2^n bits of ciphertext before attempting decryption. The algorithm, illustrated in Figure 15.15, is simple to implement, provably secure, and completely impractical. In Massey's words: "One can easily guarantee that the enemy cryptanalyst will need thousands of years to break the cipher, if one is willing to wait millions of years to read the plaintext." Further work on this idea is in [869].

Ueli Maurer improved on this sort of scheme [574]. His algorithm is based on the XOR of several large public-random bit sequences. The key is the set of starting positions within each sequence. This turns out to be provably almost secure; the probability of the algorithm being broken is based on the amount of memory the attackers have at their disposal, without regard to the amount of their computing power. In order to make this scheme practical, you need about 100 bit sequences of 10^{20} bits each.

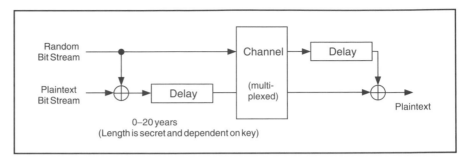

Figure 15.15
Rip van Winkle cipher.

15.3   REAL RANDOM SEQUENCE GENERATORS

Sometimes cryptographically secure pseudo-random numbers are not good enough. There are many times in cryptography when you want real random numbers. Key generation is a prime example. It's fine to generate random cryptographic keys based on a CSPRNG, but if an adversary gets a copy of that CSPRNG and whatever secret information you used to produce the numbers, the adversary can create the same keys and break your cryptosystem, no matter how secure your algorithms are. A random sequence generator's sequences cannot be reproduced. No one, not even you, can reproduce the bit sequence out of those generators.

There is a large philosophical debate over whether any of these techniques actually produces real random bits. I am not going to address that debate. The point here is to produce bits that have the same statistical properties as random bits and are not reproducible.

The important thing about any real random sequence generator is that it be tested. There is a wealth of literature on this topic. Tests of randomness can be found in [488,54]. Ueli Maurer showed that all these tests can be derived from trying to compress the sequence [575,576]. If you can compress a random sequence, then it is not truly random.

Anyhow, what we have here is a whole lot of black magic. The primary point is to generate a sequence of bits that your adversary is not unusually likely to guess. It doesn't sound like much, but it's harder than you might think. I can't prove that any of these techniques generates random bits. These techniques produce a sequence of bits that cannot easily be reproduced. For some details, see [765,766].

RAND Tables

Back in 1955, when computers were still new, the Rand Corporation published a book that contained a million random digits [728]. Their method is described in the book:

> The random digits in the book were produced by rerandomization of a basic table generated by an electronic roulette wheel. Briefly, a random frequency

pulse source, providing on the average about 100,000 pulses per second, was gated about once per second by a constant frequency pulse. Pulse standardization circuits passed the pulses through a 5-place binary counter. In principle the machine was a 32-place roulette wheel which made, on the average, about 3000 revolutions per trial and produced one number per second. A binary-to-decimal converter was used which converted 20 of the 32 numbers (the other twelve were discarded) and retained only the final digit of two-digit numbers; this final digit was fed into an IBM punch to produce finally a punched card table of random digits.

The book goes on to discuss the results of various randomness tests on the data. It also suggests how to use the book to find a random number:

The lines of the digit table are numbered from 00000 to 19999. In any use of the table, one should first find a random starting position. A common procedure for doing this is to open the book to an unselected page of the digit table and blindly choose a five-digit number; this number with the first digit reduced modulo 2 determines the starting line; the two digits to the right of the initially selected five-digit number are reduced modulo 50 to determine the starting column in the starting line. To guard against the tendency of books to open repeatedly at the same page and the natural tendency of a person to choose a number toward the center of the page: every five-digit number used to determine a starting position should be marked and not used a second time for this purpose.

The meat of the book is the "Table of Random Digits." It lists them in five-digit groups—"10097 32533 76520 13586 . . . "—50 on a line and 50 lines on a page. The table goes on for 400 pages and, except for a particular racy section on page 283 which reads "69696," makes for a boring read. The book also includes a table of 100,000 normal deviates.

The interesting thing about the RAND book is not that there are a million random digits, but that they were created before the computer revolution. Many cryptographic algorithms use arbitrary constants—so-called "magic numbers." Choosing magic numbers from the RAND tables ensures that they haven't been specially chosen for some nefarious reason. Khafre does this, for example.

Using the Computer's Clock

If you want a single random bit (or even a few), take the least significant bit from any clock register. This might not be terribly random in a UNIX system because of various potential synchronizations, but it will work on personal computers.

Beware of getting too many bits this way. Executing the same subroutine several times in succession could easily skew bits generated in this manner. For example, if each bit-generation subroutine takes an even number of clock ticks to execute, you will get an endless stream of the same bit out of the generator. If each bit generation takes an odd number of clock ticks to execute, you will get an endless stream of alternating bits out of the generator. Even if the resonance isn't this obvious, the resultant bit stream will be far from random.

Measuring Keyboard Latency

People's typing patterns are quite random. Measure the time between successive keystrokes, then take the least significant bits of those measurements. This technique may not work on a UNIX terminal, because they pass through filters and other mechanisms before they get to your program, but it will work on a personal computer.

Ideally, you only want to collect one random bit per keystroke. Collecting more may skew the results, depending on how good a typist is sitting at the keyboard. This technique is limited, though. While it's easy to have someone type 100 words or so when it is time to generate a key, it isn't reasonable to ask the typist to type a 100,000-word essay to generate a keystream for a one-time pad.

Using Random Noise

The best way to collect a large number of random bits is to tap the natural randomness of the real world. This way often requires specialized hardware, but there are tricks you can play with computers.

Find an event that happens regularly but randomly: atmospheric noise peaking a certain threshold, a toddler falling while learning to walk, etc. Measure the time interval between one event and the next event. Record it. Measure the time interval between the next event and the third event. Record it as well. If the first time interval is greater than the second, output 1 as the bit. If the second time interval is greater than the first, output 2 as the event. Do it again for the next bit.

G. B. Agnew proposes a real-random-bit generator, suitable for integration into a VLSI device [15]. It is a metal insulator semiconduction capacitor (MISC). Two of them are placed in close proximity, and the random bit is a function of the difference in charge between the two. Another LSI random number generator generates a random-bit stream based on the frequency instability in a free-running oscillator [326]. A commercial chip from AT&T generates random numbers from the same phenomenon [36]. M. Gude built a random number generator that collected random bits from physical phenomena, such as radioactive decay [399,400]. Manfield Richter developed a random number generator based on thermal noise from a semiconductor diode [736].

There is also a random number generator that uses the computer's disk drive. The generator measures the time required to read a disk block and uses the variation in that time as a random number source. A large part of the variation in disk rotation speed is caused by air turbulence, so there is some randomness in the system.

There are other sources of randomness available in some computer systems:

time of day

actual mouse position

number of current scanline of monitor

contents of the actually displayed image

contents of FATs, kernel tables, etc.

access/modify times of/dev/tty

CPU load

arrival times of network packets

input from a microphone

The problem isn't in actually finding the sources of randomness; the problem is in sampling the sources in a way that preserves the randomness.

Biases and Correlations

A major problem with all these systems is that there could be correlations and biases in the generated sequence. The underlying physical processes might be random, but there many types of measuring instruments between the digital part of the computer and the physical process. Those instruments could easily introduce biases and correlations. A way to eliminate correlations is to XOR several bits together. If a random bit is biased toward 0 by a factor e, then the probability of 0 can be written as:

$$P(0) = .5 + e$$

XORing two of these bits together yields:

$$P(0) = (.5 + e)^2 + (.5 - e)^2 = .5 + 2 \times e^2$$

By the same calculation, XORing 4 bits together yields:

$$P(0) = .5 + 8 \times e^4$$

XORing m bits will exponentially converge to an equal probability of 0 and 1.

An even better method can remove all bias from an otherwise random source. Look at the bits in pairs. If the two bits are the same, discard them and look at the next pair. If the two bits are different, take the first bit as the output of the generator.

The potential problem with both methods is that if there is a correlation between adjacent bits, then these methods will *increase* the bias. One way to correct this is to use multiple random sources. Take four different random sources and XOR the bits together; or take two random sources, and look at those bits in pairs.

For example, take a radioactive source and hook a Geiger counter to your computer. Take a pair of noisy diodes and record as an event every time the noise exceeds a certain peak. Measure atmospheric noise. Get a random bit from each, and XOR them together to produce the random bit. The possibilities are endless.

The mere fact that a random number generator has a bias does not necessarily mean that it is unusable. It just means that it is less secure. For example, consider the problem of Alice generating a triple-DES 112-bit key. All she has is a random bit generator with a bias toward 0: it produces 55% 0's and 45% 1's. This means that there are only 0.99277 bits of entropy per key bit, as opposed to 1 bit if the generator were perfect. Mallet, trying to break the key, can optimize his brute-force search to try the most probable key first (000 . . . 0), and work toward the least probable key (111 . . . 1). Because of the bias, Mallet can expect to find the key in 2^{109} attempts. If there were no bias, Mallet would expect to make 2^{111} attempts. The resultant key is less secure, but not appreciably so.

Diffusing Randomness with a One-Way Hash Function

Another technique is to operate on the random bits with a one-way hash function. This has the effect of distilling the entropy from the input. It also helps eliminate the low-order biases or correlations of the physical generator.

For example, if you need 128 random bits for a key, generate a large number of random bits using any of the above sources and operate on them with a good one-way hash function. As long as there are at least 128 bits of total entropy somewhere in the random bit sequence, then the output of the one-way hash function should also have 128 bits of entropy, i.e., it will be perfectly random. This should be true even if each individual bit has considerably less than 1 bit of entropy.

15.4   GENERATING NUMBERS AND NONUNIFORM DISTRIBUTIONS

If your needs for pseudo-random or random numbers are more complicated than uniformly distributed bits, start with bits and work your way up. If you need a random digit between 0 and 9, collect 4 bits and ignore numbers greater than 9. If you need a random number between 1 and 1,000,000, collect 20 random bits and ignore numbers greater than 1,000,000 (it will only happen about 5% of the time).

There are far simpler approaches. These functions assume the existence of the function:

```
rand_bit()
```

which returns a random bit.

To generate an unsigned long integer:

```
unsigned long long_rand (void)
{
  ulong v;
  int i;

  for (i=0; i<BITS.PER.ULONG; i++)
  {
  v <<= 1;
  v |= rand_bit();
  }
  return v;
}
```

To generate an unsigned short integer:

```
unsigned short short_rand (void)
{
  return (long_rand() & 0xFFFF);
}
```

To generate a positive double between 0.0 and 1.0:

```
# define MAXLONG 4294967296.0
double frac_rand (void)
{
  return (long_rand() / MAXLONG);
}
```

To generate a random integer in the range *a* through *b:*

```
int range_rand (int a, int b)
{
  return ((int) (long_rand() % (b-a+1) +a ));
}
```

To generate a random double in the range double_*a* through double_*b:*

```
# define MAXLONG 4294967296.0
int range_double_rand (double double_a, double double_b)
{
  return ((long_rand() / MAXLONG) * (double_b - double_a) +
  double_a );
}
```

To generate a random double with a normal distribution, defined by a given mean and standard deviation:

```
# define MAXLONG 4294967296.0
# define PI 3.141592653589793
int normal_rand (double mean, double std_dev)
{
  double a,b,x;
  a = long_rand() / MAXLONG;
  b = long_rand() / MAXLONG;
  x = sqrt (-2.0 * log(a)) * cos (2 * PI * b);
  return (mean + std_dev * x);
}
```

To generate a random double with an exponential distribution, defined by a given mean:

```
# define MAXLONG 4294967296.0
int exponential_rand (double mean)
{
  return ( -mean * log( long_rand() / MAXLONG ));
}
```

15.5 GENERATING RANDOM PERMUTATIONS

Given a random number generator, it is easy to create a random permutation generator. This is sometimes called **shuffling**, since shuffling a deck of cards is nothing more than randomly permuting it.

This algorithm comes from Durstenfeld [306]. In C, it's:

```
shuffle a[1....n]  /* the array of things to be shuffled */
  for i = (n-1) downto 1
    z = random (i);   /*  This function produces a     */
                      /*  random # between 0 and i.  */
    temp = a[i];
    a[i] = a[z];
    a[z] = temp;
  next i;
```

This function can produce any sort of random permutation you want. If the function random is deterministic, then the permutation can be reproduced (and even reversed). If the function random produces a cryptographically secure random sequence, then the resulting permutation will be cryptographically secure. If the function random produces a real-random sequence, then the permutation will be truly random.

Sorting and shuffling are, in some sense, inverse operations. If you have a good sorting routine, you can easily adapt it to shuffle a file [23]. For example, perform the mergesort algorithm with the modification that whenever the algorithm needs to make a decision, use the next bit of your random bit generator rather than checking whether $a<b$. If your file is n items long, this algorithm uses $n \log n$ random bits, and O($n \log n$) operations, so it's fairly efficient.

CHAPTER
16

Special Algorithms for Protocols

16.1 KEY EXCHANGE

Shamir's Three-Pass Protocol

This protocol, invented by Shamir but never published, enables Alice and Bob to communicate securely without any advance exchange of either secret keys or public keys [564].

This assumes the existence of a symmetric cipher that is commutative, that is:

$$E_A(E_B(P)) = E_B(E_A(P))$$

Alice's secret key is $A;$ Bob's secret key is B. Alice wants to send a message, $M,$ to Bob. Here's the protocol:

(1) Alice encrypts P with her key and sends the ciphertext to Bob.

$$C_1 = E_A(P)$$

(2) Bob encrypts C_1 with his key and sends the ciphertext to Alice.

$$C_2 = E_B(E_A(P))$$

(3) Alice decrypts C_2 with her key and sends the ciphertext to Bob.

$$C_3 = D_A(E_B(E_A(P))) = D_A(E_A(E_B(P))) = E_B(P)$$

(4) Bob decrypts C_3 with his key to recover the plaintext message.

One-time pads are commutative and have perfect secrecy, but they will not work with this protocol. With a one-time pad, the three ciphertext messages would be:

$$C_1 = P \text{ XOR } A$$
$$C_2 = P \text{ XOR } A \text{ XOR } B$$
$$C_3 = P \text{ XOR } B$$

Eve, who can record the three messages as they pass between Alice and Bob, simply XORs them together to retrieve the message:

$$C_1 \text{ XOR } C_2 \text{ XOR } C_3 = (P \text{ XOR } A) \text{ XOR } (P \text{ XOR } A \text{ XOR } B) \text{ XOR } (P \text{ XOR } B) = P$$

This clearly doesn't work.

Shamir described an encryption algorithm that will work with this protocol; one similar to RSA. Let p be a large prime for which $p-1$ has a large prime factor (to frustrate solving the discrete logarithm mod p). Choose an encryption key, e, and a decryption key, d, as you would choose them in RSA. The encryption key, e, has to be relatively prime to $p-1$. If you already have a prime testing routine and not a greatest-common-divisor routine, the easiest solution is to choose a large prime for e. Calculate d using Euclid's algorithm such that $de = 1 \pmod{p-1}$.

To encrypt a message, calculate:

$$C = P^e \pmod{p}$$

To decrypt a message, calculate:

$$P = C^d \pmod{p}$$

There seems to be no way for Eve to recover P without solving the discrete logarithm problem, but (like so many other things in public-key cryptography) this has never been proved.

This protocol does something that simple public-key encryption does not. It allows Alice to initiate a secure communication with Bob without knowing any of his keys. For Alice to use a public-key algorithm, she has to know his public key. With Shamir's three-pass protocol, she just sends him a ciphertext message. The same thing with a public-key algorithm looks like:

(1) Alice asks Bob (or a KDC) for his public key.

(2) Bob (or the KDC) sends Alice his public key.

(3) Alice encrypts P with Bob's public key and sends it to Bob.

COMSET

COMSET (COMmunications SETup) is a mutual identification and key exchange protocol developed for the RIPE project [727] (see Section 18.8). Using public-key cryptography, it allows Alice and Bob to identify themselves to each other, and also to exchange a secret key.

The mathematical principle behind COMSET is Rabin's scheme [724] (see Section 12.6). The scheme itself was originally proposed in [135a]. See [727] for details.

16.2 ENCRYPTED KEY EXCHANGE

The encrypted key exchange (EKE) protocol was designed by Steve Bellovin and Michael Merritt [59]. It provides security and authentication on computer networks, using both symmetric and public-key cryptography in a novel way: a shared secret key is used to encrypt a randomly generated public key.

The Basic Protocol

Alice and Bob (two users, a user and the host, or whomever) share a common password, P. Using this protocol, they can authenticate each other and generate a common session key, K.

(1) Alice generates a random public key, K'. She encrypts it using a symmetric algorithm and key P: $E_P(K')$. She sends Bob:

$Alice, E_P(K')$

(2) Bob knows P. He decrypts the message to obtain K'. Then, he generates a random session key, K, and encrypts it with the public key he received from Alice and the secret key, P:

$E_P(E_{K'}(K))$

He sends this to Alice.

(3) Alice decrypts the message to obtain K. She generates a random string, R_A, encrypts it with K, and sends the result to Bob:

$E_K(R_A)$

(4) Bob decrypts the message to obtain R_A. He generates another random string, R_B, encrypts both strings with K, and sends the result to Alice:

$E_K(R_A, R_B)$

(5) Alice decrypts the message to obtain R_A and R_B. Assuming the R_A she received from Bob is the same as the one she sent to Bob in step (3), she encrypts R_B with K and sends it to Bob.

$E_K(R_B)$

(6) Bob decrypts the message to obtain R_B. Assuming the R_B he received from Alice is the same as the one he sent to Alice in step (4), the protocol is complete. Both parties now communicate using K as the session key.

At step (3), both Alice and Bob know K' and K. K is the session key and can be used to encrypt all other messages between Alice and Bob. Eve, sitting between

Alice and Bob, only knows $E_P(K')$, $E_P(E_{K'}(K))$, and some messages encrypted with K. In other protocols, Eve could make guesses at P (people choose bad passwords all the time, and if Eve is clever she can make some good guesses) and then test her guesses. In this protocol, Eve cannot test her guess without cracking the public-key algorithm as well. And if both K' and K are chosen randomly, this can be an insurmountable problem.

The challenge-response portion of the protocol, steps (3) through (6), validate the protocol. Steps (3) through (5) prove to Alice that Bob knows K; steps (4) through (6) prove to Bob that Alice knows K. The Kerberos protocol timestamp exchange accomplishes the same thing.

Implementing EKE with RSA

The RSA algorithm seems perfect for this application, but there are some subtle problems. The authors recommend encrypting only the encryption exponent in step (1) and sending the modulus in the clear. An explanation of the reasoning behind this explanation, as well as other subtleties involved in using RSA, are in [59].

Implementing EKE with ElGamal

Implementing EKE with the ElGamal algorithm is straightforward, and there is even a simplification of the basic protocol. Using the notation from Section 13.3, g and p are parts of the public key and are common to all users. The private key is a random number r. The public key is g^r (mod p). The message Alice sends to Bob in step (1) becomes:

$$\text{Alice}, g^r \ (\text{mod } p)$$

Note that this public key does not have to be encrypted with P. This is not true in general, but it is true for the ElGamal algorithm. Details are in [59].

Bob chooses a random number, R (this is for the ElGamal algorithm and is independent of any random numbers chosen for EKE), and the message he sends to Alice in step (2) becomes:

$$P(g^R \ (\text{mod } p), Kg^{Rr} \ (\text{mod } p))$$

Refer back to Section 13.3 for restrictions on choosing the variables for ElGamal.

Implementing EKE with Diffie-Hellman

With the Diffie-Hellman protocol, K is generated automatically. The final protocol is even simpler. A value for g and n is set for all users on the network.

(1) Alice picks a random number, r_A, and sends Bob:

$$\textit{Alice}, \ g^{r_A} \ (\text{mod } n)$$

With Diffie-Hellman, Alice does not have to encrypt her first message with P.

(2) Bob picks a random number, r_B, and calculates:

$$K = g^{r_A \times r_B} \pmod{n}$$

He generates a random string, R_B, then calculates and sends Alice:

$$P(g^{r_B}(\bmod\ n)),\ K(R_B)$$

(3) Alice decrypts the first half of Bob's message to obtain g^{r_B} (mod n). Then she calculates K and uses K to decrypt R_B. She generates another random string, R_A, encrypts both strings with K, and sends the result to Bob:

$$K(R_A, R_B)$$

(4) Bob decrypts the message to obtain R_A and R_B. Assuming the R_B he received from Alice is the same as the one he sent to Alice in step (2), he encrypts R_A with K and sends it to Alice.

$$K(R_B)$$

(5) Bob decrypts the message to obtain R_A. Assuming the R_A he received from Alice is the same as the one she sent to Bob in step (3), the protocol is complete. Both parties now communicate using K as the session key.

Strengthening EKE

Bellovin and Merritt suggest an enhancement of the challenge-and-response portion of the protocol—to prevent a possible attack if a cryptanalyst recovers an old K value.

Look at the basic EKE protocol. In step (3), Alice generates another random number, S_A, and sends Bob:

$$K(R_A, S_A)$$

In step (4), Bob generates another random number, S_B, and sends Alice:

$$K(R_A, R_B, S_B)$$

Alice and Bob now can both calculate the true session key, S_A XOR S_B. This key is used for all future messages between Alice and Bob; K is just used as a key-exchange key.

Look at the levels of protection. A recovered value of S gives Eve no information about P, because P is never used to encrypt anything that leads directly to S. A cryptanalytic attack on K is also not feasible; K is used only to encrypt random data, and S is never directly encrypted.

Applications of EKE

Bellovin and Merritt suggest that this protocol could be used for secure public telephones [59]:

> Let us assume that encrypting public telephones are deployed. If someone wishes to use one of these phones, some sort of keying information must be provided. Conventional solutions . . . require that the caller possess a physical

key. This is undesirable in many situations. EKE permits use of a short, keypad-entered password, but uses a much longer session key for the call.

EKE would also be useful with cellular phones. Fraud has been a problem in the cellular industry; EKE can defend against it (and ensure the privacy of the call) by rendering a phone useless if a PIN has not been entered. Since the PIN is not stored within the phone, it is not possible to retrieve one from a stolen unit.

EKE's primary strength is that both symmetric and public-key cryptography work together in a manner that strengthens them both [59]:

> From a general perspective, EKE functions as a *privacy amplifier.* That is, it can be used to strengthen comparatively weak symmetric and asymmetric systems when used together. Consider, for example, the key size needed to maintain security when using exponential key exchange. As LaMacchia and Odlyzko have shown [526], even modulus sizes once believed to be safe (to wit, 192 bits) are vulnerable to an attack requiring only a few minutes of computer time. But their attack is not feasible if one must first guess a password before applying it.
>
> Conversely, the difficulty of cracking exponential key exchange can be used to frustrate attempts at password-guessing. Password-guessing attacks are feasible because of how rapidly each guess may be verified. If performing such verification requires solving an exponential key exchange, the total time, if not the conceptual difficulty, increases dramatically.
>
> EKE is patented [59a].

16.3   MULTIPLE-KEY PUBLIC-KEY CRYPTOGRAPHY

This algorithm, found in [134], is a generalization of RSA. The modulus, n, is the product of two primes, p and q. However, instead of choosing e and d such that $e \times d \equiv 1 \bmod (p-1) \times (q-1)$, choose t keys, k_i, such that:

$$k_1 \times k_2 \times \ldots \times k_t \equiv 1 \bmod (p-1) \times (q-1)$$

Since:

$$M^{k_1 \times k_2 \times \ldots \times k_t} = M$$

this is a multiple-key scheme as described in Section 3.4.

If, for example, there are five keys, a message encrypted with k_3 and k_5 can be decrypted with k_1, k_2, and k_4:

$$C = M^{k_3 \times k_5} \bmod n$$
$$M = C^{k_1 \times k_2 \times k_4} \bmod n$$

An improvement to this algorithm can be found in [135].

16.4   SECRET BROADCASTING

Alice wants to broadcast a message, *M,* from a single transmitter. However, she doesn't want it to be intelligible by every listener. In fact, she only wants a select subset of listeners to be able to recover *S*. Everyone else should get nonsense.

Alice can share a different key (secret or public) with each listener. She encrypts the message in some random key, *K*. Then she encrypts *K* with the keys of all her intended recipients, a different copy of *K* each time. Finally, she broadcasts the encrypted message and then all of the encrypted *K*'s. Bob, who is listening, either tries to decrypt all the *K*'s with his secret key, looking for one that is correct; or, if Alice doesn't mind everyone knowing whom her message is for, he looks for his name followed by an encrypted key. Multiple-key cryptography works.

Another method is suggested in [210]. First, each listener shares a secret key with Alice, one that is larger than any possible encrypted message. She encrypts the message in a random key, *K*. Then, she computes a single integer, *R,* such that *R* modulo a secret key is congruent to *K* when that secret key is supposed to decrypt the message, and *R* modulo a secret key is otherwise congruent to zero.

For example, if Alice wants the secret to be received by Bob, Carol, and Ellen, but not by Dave and Frank, she encrypts the message with *K* and then computes *R* such that:

$$R \bmod K_B \equiv K$$
$$R \bmod K_C \equiv K$$
$$R \bmod K_D \equiv 0$$
$$R \bmod K_E \equiv K$$
$$R \bmod K_F \equiv 0$$

This is a straightforward algebra problem, one that Alice can solve easily. When listeners receive the broadcast, they compute the received key modulo their secret key. If they were intended to receive the message, they recover the key. Otherwise, they recover nothing.

Yet a third way, using a threshold scheme, is suggested by Shimshon Berkovitz in [86]. Like the others, every potential receiver gets a secret key. This key is a shadow in a yet-uncreated threshold scheme. Alice saves some secret keys for herself, to add some randomness into the system. Let's say there are *k* people out there.

Then, to broadcast *M,* Alice encrypts *M* with key *K* and does the following:

(1) Alice chooses a random number, *j*. This number serves to hide the number of recipients of the message. It doesn't have to be very large; it can be as small as 0.

(2) Alice creates a $(k + j + 1, 2k + j + 1)$ threshold scheme, with:

K as the secret

The secret keys of the intended recipients as shadows

The secret keys of nonrecipients not as shadows

j randomly chosen shadows, not the same as any of the secret keys

(3) Alice broadcasts $k + j$ randomly chosen shadows, none of which is any of the shadows listed in step (2).

(4) All listeners who receive the broadcast add their shadow to the $k + j$ shadows they received. If the addition of their shadow allows them to calculate the secret, then they have recovered the key. If it does not, then they haven't.

16.5   SECRET SHARING ALGORITHMS

A secret sharing scheme, also called a **threshold scheme,** works like this: A message is divided into n pieces, called **shadows,** such that any m shadows can be used to reconstruct the message, but any $m - 1$ of them cannot. This is called an **(m,n)-threshold scheme.**

Although I describe four different schemes here, Kothari has shown that they are all particular cases of a more general scheme [503].

LaGrange Interpolating Polynomial Scheme

Adi Shamir uses polynomial equations in a finite field to construct a threshold scheme [788]. First, choose a prime, p, which is larger than the number of possible shadows and the largest possible secret. To share a secret, generate an arbitrary polynomial of degree $m - 1$. For example, if you want to create a $(3,n)$-threshold scheme (three shadows are necessary to reconstruct M), generate a quadratic polynomial:

$$ax^2 + bx + M \ (\text{mod } p)$$

in which p is a random prime larger than any of the coefficients. The coefficients a and b are chosen randomly; they are kept secret and discarded after the shadows are handed out. M is the message. The prime must be made public.

The shadows are obtained by evaluating the polynomial at n different points:

$$k_i = F(x_i)$$

In other words, the first shadow could be the polynomial evaluated at $x = 1$, the second shadow could be the polynomial evaluated at $x = 2$, etc.

Since the quadratic polynomial has three unknown coefficients, a, b, and m, any three shadows can be used to create three equations; then linear algebra can be used to solve for M. Two shadows cannot. One shadow cannot. Four or five shadows are redundant.

For example, let M be 11. To construct a (3–5)-threshold scheme, in which any three of five people can reconstruct M, first generate a quadratic equation (7 and 8 were chosen randomly):

$$F(x) = 7x^2 + 8x + 11 \ (\text{mod } 13)$$

The five shadows are:

$$k_1 = F(1) = 7 + 8 + 11 = 0 \ (\text{mod } 13)$$
$$k_2 = F(2) = 28 + 16 + 11 = 3 \ (\text{mod } 13)$$
$$k_3 = F(3) = 63 + 24 + 11 = 7 \ (\text{mod } 13)$$
$$k_4 = F(4) = 112 + 32 + 11 = 12 \ (\text{mod } 13)$$
$$k_5 = F(5) = 175 + 40 + 11 = 5 \ (\text{mod } 13)$$

To reconstruct M from three of the shadows, for example, k_2, k_3, and k_5, solve the set of linear equations:

$$3 = a \times 2^2 + b \times 2 + M \ (\text{mod } 13)$$
$$7 = a \times 3^2 + b \times 3 + M \ (\text{mod } 13)$$
$$5 = a \times 5^2 + b \times 5 + M \ (\text{mod } 13)$$

The solution will be $a = 7$, $b = 8$, and $M = 11$. So M is recovered.

This sharing scheme can be easily implemented for larger numbers. If you want to divide the message in 30 equal parts such that any six can get together and reproduce the message, give each of the 30 people the evaluation of a polynomial of degree 5:

$$F(x) = ax^6 + bx^5 + cx^4 + dx^3 + ex^2 + fx + M \ (\text{mod } p)$$

Six people can solve for the six unknowns (including M); five people cannot learn anything about M.

The most mind-boggling aspect of secret sharing is that if the coefficients were picked randomly, five people with infinite computing power can't learn anything more than the length of the message (which each of them knows, anyway). This is as secure as a one-time pad; an attempt at exhaustive search (i.e., trying all possible sixth shadows) will reveal that any conceivable message could be the secret. This is true for all four secret-sharing schemes.

Vector Scheme

Blakley invented a scheme using points in space [117]. The message is defined as a point in m-dimensional space. Each shadow is the equation of an $(m-1)$-dimensional hyperplane that includes the point. The intersection of any m of the hyperplanes exactly determines the point.

For example, if three shadows are required to reconstruct the message, then it is a point in three-dimensional space. Each shadow is a different plane. With one shadow, you know the point is somewhere on the plane. With two shadows, you know the point is somewhere on the line formed where the two planes intersect. With three shadows, you can determine the point exactly: the intersection of the three planes.

Asmuth-Bloom

Asmuth and Bloom invented another scheme using prime numbers [35]. For an (m,n)-threshold scheme, choose a large prime, p, greater than M. Then choose n numbers less than p, d_1, d_2, ... d_n, such that the d values are in increasing order; $d_i < d_{i+1}$; and each d_i is relatively prime to every other d_j.

$$d_1 \times d_2 \times \ \ldots \ \times d_m > p \times d_{n-m+2} \times d_{n-m+3} \times \ \ldots \ \times d_n$$

To distribute the shadows, first choose a random value, r, and compute

$$M' = M + rp$$

The shadows, k_i, are

$$k_i = M' \ (\text{mod} \ d_i)$$

Any m shadows can get together and reconstruct M using the Chinese remainder theorem, but any $m - 1$ cannot. See [35] for details.

Karnin-Greene-Hellman

Karnin, Greene, and Hellman's scheme uses matrix multiplication [474]. Choose $n + 1$ m-dimensional vectors, V_0, V_1, ... V_n, such that any possible $m \times m$ matrix formed out of those vectors has rank m. The vector U is a row vector of dimension $m + 1$.

M is the matrix product $U \cdot V_0$. The shadows are the products $U \cdot V_i$, when i is a number from 1 to n.

Any m shadows can be used to solve the $m \times m$ system of linear equations, where the unknowns are the coefficients of U. Knowing U, UV_0 can be computed. Any $m - 1$ shadows cannot solve the system of linear equations and therefore cannot recover the secret.

Advanced Threshold Schemes

The previous examples illustrate only the simplest threshold schemes: divide a secret into n shadows such that any m can be used to recover the secret. These algorithms can be used to create far more complicated schemes. The following examples will use Shamir's algorithm, although any of the previous algorithms will work.

To create a scheme in which one person is more important than another, give that person more shadows. Let's say it takes five shadows to recreate a secret. If one person has three different shadows while everyone else has only one, then that person and two other people can recreate the secret. Without that person, it takes five to recreate the secret.

Two or more people could get multiple shadows. Each different person could get a different number of shadows. In whatever way the shadows are distributed, any m of them can be used to reconstruct the secret. Someone with $m - 1$ shadows, whether one person or a roomful of people, cannot do it.

Other types of schemes can also be created. Imagine a scenario in which there are two hostile delegations. You can share the secret so that two people from the seven in Delegation A and three people from the 12 in Delegation B are required to reconstruct the secret. Make a polynomial of degree 3 that is the product of a linear equation and a quadratic equation. Give everyone from Delegation A a shadow that is the evaluation of the linear equation; give everyone from Delegation B a shadow that is the evaluation of the quadratic equation.

Any two shadows from Delegation A can be used to reconstruct the linear equation, but no matter how many other shadows the group has, they cannot get any information about the secret. The same is true for Delegation B: they can get three shadows together to reconstruct the quadratic equation, but they cannot get any more information necessary to reconstruct the secret. Only when the two delegations share their equations can they be multiplied to reconstruct the secret.

In general, any type of sharing scheme that can be imagined can be implemented. All you have to do is to envision a system of equations that corresponds to the particular scheme. Some excellent papers on generalized secret-sharing schemes are [825,826,827].

Sharing a Secret Without Revealing the Shares

The problem with these schemes is that when everyone gets together to reconstruct their secret, they reveal their shares. Using the LaGrange scheme, this does not have to be the case. If the shared secret is a private key (to a digital signature, for example), then n shareholders can each complete partial signature of the document. After the nth partial signature, the document is signed with the shared private key, and none of the shareholders learns any other shares. This concept is explored further by Yvo Desmedt and Yair Frankel [286,287].

This method has also been suggested for applications similar to Micali's fair cryptosystems (see Section 16.10).

Sharing a Secret with Cheaters

This algorithm modifies the standard $(m\text{-}n)$-threshold scheme to detect cheaters [854]. It can work with any of the schemes, but I am going to demonstrate this using the LaGrange scheme.

Choose a prime, $p,$ that is larger than n and larger than

$$(s-1) \times (m-1)/e + m$$

when s is the largest possible secret, and e is the probability of successful cheating. You can make e as small as you want; it just makes the math more complex. Construct your shadows as before, except instead of using $1,2,3,\ldots n$ for $x_i,$ choose random numbers between 1 and $p-1$ for $x_i.$

Now, when Mallet sneaks into the secret reconstruction meeting with his false share, his share has a high probability of not being possible. An impossible secret is, of course, a fake secret. See [854] for the math.

Unfortunately, while Mallet is exposed as a cheater, he still learns the secret (assuming that there are m other valid shares). Another protocol, from [854,550], prevents that. The basic idea is to have a series of k secrets such that none of the participants knows beforehand which is the correct secret. Each secret is larger than the one before, except for the real secret. The participants combine their shadows to generate one secret after the other, until they create a secret that is less than the previous secret. That's the correct one.

This scheme will expose cheaters early on in the process, before the secret is generated. There are complications when the participants deliver their shadows one at a time; refer to the papers for details. Other papers on the detection and prevention of cheaters in threshold schemes are [212,62,171].

Secret Sharing Schemes with Prevention

A secret is divided up among 50 people so that any ten can get together and reconstruct the secret. That's easy. Now, can we implement the same secret sharing scheme with the added constraint that 20 people can get together and *prevent* the others from reconstructing the secret, no matter how many of them there are? As it turns out, we can [96].

The math is complicated, but the basic idea is that everyone gets two shares: a "yes" share and a "no" share. When it comes time to reconstruct the secret, people submit one of their shares. The actual share they submit depends on whether or not they wish the secret reconstructed. If there are m or more "yes" shares and fewer than n "no" shares, the secret can be reconstructed. Otherwise, it cannot.

Of course, there's nothing preventing the "yes" people from going off in a corner without the "no" people and reconstructing the secret, assuming there are enough of them. But in a situation when everyone submits their shares into a central computer, this scheme will work.

16.6   SUBLIMINAL CHANNEL

Ong-Schnorr-Shamir

This subliminal channel scheme, designed by Gustavus Simmons [821,822,823], uses the Ong-Schnorr-Shamir identification scheme (see Section 13.2). As in the original scheme, the sender (Alice) chooses a public modulus, n, and a secret key, k, such that n and k are relatively prime. Unlike the original scheme, k is shared between Alice and Bob, the recipient of the subliminal message.

The public key is also calculated the same way:

$$h = -k^{-2 \text{ (mod n)}}$$

If Alice wants to send the subliminal message M by means of the innocuous message M', she first confirms that M' and n are relatively prime, and that M and n are relatively prime.

Alice calculates:

$$S_1 = 1/2 \times (M'/M + M) \pmod{n}$$
$$S_2 = k/2 \times (M'/M - M) \pmod{n}$$

Together, the pair, S_1 and S_2, is the signature under the traditional Ong-Schnorr-Shamir scheme and the carrier of the subliminal message.

Walter, the prison warden, can authenticate the message as described by the Ong-Schnorr-Shamir signature scheme, but Bob can do better. He can authenticate the message (it is always possible that Walter can make his own messages). He confirms that

$$M' = S_1{}^2 - S_2{}^2/k^2 \pmod{n}$$

If the message is authentic, the receiver can recover the subliminal message using this formula:

$$M = M'/(S_1 + S_2/k) \pmod{n}$$

This works, but remember that Ong-Schnorr-Shamir has been broken.

ElGamal

Simmons's second subliminal channel [822], described in [784], is based on the ElGamal signature scheme.

Key generation is the same as the basic ElGamal signature scheme. First choose a prime, p, and two random numbers, g and r, such that both g and r are less than p. Then calculate:

$$K = g^r \pmod{p}$$

The public key is $K, g,$ and p. The private key is r. Besides Alice, Bob also knows r; it is the key that is used to send and read the subliminal message in addition to being the key used to sign the innocuous message.

To send a subliminal message, M, using the innocuous message, M', M, and p must be relatively prime, and M and $p - 1$ must be relatively prime. Alice calculates:

$$X = g^M \pmod{p}$$

and solves the following equation for Y (using the Euclidean algorithm):

$$M' = rX + MY \pmod{p - 1}$$

As in the basic ElGamal scheme, the signature is the pair: X and Y.

Walter can verify the ElGamal signature. He confirms that

$$K^X X^Y \pmod{p} = g^{M'} \pmod{p}$$

Bob can recover the subliminal message. First he confirms that

$$(g^r)^X X^Y \pmod{p} = g^{M'} \pmod{p}$$

If it does, he accepts the message as genuine (and not one from Walter).

Then, to recover M, he computes

$$M = Y^{-1} (M' - rX) \pmod{p - 1}$$

For example, let $p = 11$ and $g = 2$. The secret key, r, is chosen to be 8. This means the public key, which Walter can use to verify the signature, is $g^r \pmod{p} = 2^8 \pmod{11} = 3$.

To send the subliminal message, $M = 9$, using innocuous message, $M' = 5$, Alice confirms that 9 and 11 are relatively prime and that 5 and 11 are relatively prime. She also confirms that 9 and 11−1 are relatively prime. They are, so she calculates:

$$X = g^M \pmod{p} = 2^9 \pmod{11} = 6$$

Then, she solves the following equation for Y:

$$5 = 8 \times 6 + 9 \times Y \pmod{10}$$

$Y=3$, so the signature is the pair, X and Y: 6 and 3.

Bob confirms that

$$(g^r)^X X^Y \pmod{p} = g^C \pmod{p}$$
$$(2^8)^6 6^3 \pmod{11} = 2^5 \pmod{11}$$

It does, so he then recovers the subliminal message by calculating:

$$M = Y^{-1} (M' - rX) \pmod{p - 1} = 3^{-1}(5 - 8 \times 6) \pmod{10} = 7(7) \pmod{10} = 49 \pmod{10} = 9$$

ESIGN

A subliminal channel can be added to ESIGN [823] (see Section 13.6).

In ESIGN, the secret key is a pair of large prime numbers, p and q, and the public key is $n = p^2 q$. With a subliminal channel, the secret key is three primes, p, q, and r, and the public key is n, such that:

$$n = p^2 q r$$

The variable, r, is the extra piece of information that Bob needs to read the subliminal message.

To sign a normal message, Alice first picks a random number, $x < p \times q \times r$, and computes:

w, the least integer that is larger than

$$(\mathrm{H}(m) - x^k \bmod n)/pqr)$$
$$s = x + ((w/kx^{k-1}) \bmod p)pqr$$

$\mathrm{H}(m)$ is the hash of the message; k is a security parameter. The value s is the signature.

To verify the signature, Bob computes $s^k \bmod n$. He also computes a, which is the least integer larger than the number of bits of n divided by three. If $\mathrm{H}(m)$ is less than or equal to $s^k \bmod n$, and if $s^k \bmod n$ is less than $\mathrm{H}(m) + 2^a$, then the signature is considered valid.

To send a subliminal message, M, using the innocuous message, M', Alice calculates s using M in place of $\mathrm{H}(m)$. This means that the message must be smaller than p^2qr. She then chooses a random value, u, and calculates:

$$x' = M' + ur$$

Then, use this x' value as the "random number" x to sign M'. This second s value is sent as a signature.

Walter can verify that s (the second s) is a valid signature of M'.

Bob can also authenticate the message in the same way. But, since he also knows r, he can calculate:

$$\mathrm{s} = x' + ypqr = M + ur + ypqr \equiv M \ (\bmod\ r)$$

This implementation of a subliminal channel is far better than the previous two. In the Ong-Schnorr-Shamir and ElGamal implementations, Bob has Alice's private key. Besides being able to read subliminal messages from Alice, Bob can impersonate Alice and sign normal documents. Alice can do nothing about this; her trust in Bob is required to set up this subliminal channel.

The ESIGN scheme doesn't suffer from this problem. Alice's private key is the set of three primes: p, q, and r. Bob's secret key is just r. He knows $n = p^2qr$, but to recover p and q, he has to factor that number. If the primes are large enough, Bob has just as much trouble impersonating Alice as would Walter, or anyone else.

DSA

There is also a subliminal channel in the DSA [829,830]. In fact, there are several. The simplest subliminal channel involves the choice of k. It is supposed to be a 160-bit random number. However, if Alice chooses a particular k, then Bob, who also knows Alice's private key, can recover it. Alice can send Bob a 160-bit subliminal message in each DSA signature. Everyone else can simply verify Alice's signature. There are further complications. Since k should be random, Alice and Bob need to share a one-time pad and encrypt the subliminal message with the one-time pad to generate a k. And, like the ElGamal subliminal channel scheme, Bob must know Alice's private key.

There are subliminal channels with DSA that do not require Bob to know Alice's private key. They also involve choosing particular values of k, but cannot be used to send 160 bits of information. This scheme, presented in [829,830], allows Alice and Bob to exchange 1 bit of subliminal information per signed message:

(1) Alice and Bob agree on a random prime, P (different from the parameter p in the signature scheme). This is their secret key for the subliminal channel.

(2) Alice signs an innocuous message, M. If she wants to send Bob the subliminal bit, 1, she makes sure the r parameter of the signature is a quadratic residue modulo P. If she wants to send him a 0, she makes sure the r parameter is a quadratic nonresidue modulo P. She does this by signing the message with random k values until she gets a signature with an r with the requisite property. Since quadratic residues and quadratic nonresidues are equally likely, this shouldn't be too difficult.

(3) Alice sends the signed message to Bob.

(4) Bob verifies the signature to make sure the message is authentic. Then he checks whether r is a quadratic residue or a quadratic nonresidue modulo P and recovers the subliminal bit.

There are ways to send multiple bits via this method that involve making r either a quadratic residue or a quadratic nonresidue modulo a variety of parameters. See [829,830] for details.

This scheme can be easily extended to send multiple subliminal bits per signature. If Alice and Bob agree on two random primes, P and Q, Alice can send two bits by choosing a random k such that r is either a quadratic residue mod P or a quadratic nonresidue mod P, and either a quadratic residue mod Q or a quadratic nonresidue mod Q. A random value of k has a 25% chance of producing an r of the correct form.

Here's how Mallet, an unscrupulous implementer of DSS, can have the algorithm leak ten bits of Alice's private key every time she signs a document:

(1) Mallet puts his implementation of DSS in a tamper-proof VLSI chip, so that no one can examine its inner workings. He creates a 14-bit subliminal channel in his implementation of DES. That is, he chooses fourteen random primes, and has the chip choose a value of k such that r is either q quadratic residue or a quadratic nonresidue modulo each of those fourteen primes, depending on the subliminal message.

(2) Mallet distributes the chips to Alice, Bob, and everyone else who wants them.

(3) Alice signs a message normally, using her 160-bit secret key, y.

(4) The chip randomly chooses a 10-bit block of y: the first ten bits, the second ten bits, etc. Since there are 16 possible 10-bit blocks, a 4-bit

number can identify which block it is. This 4-bit identifier, plus the ten bits of the key, is the 14-bit subliminal message.

(5) The chip tries random values of k until it finds one that has the correct quadratic residue properties to send the subliminal message. The odds of a random k being of the correct form are 1 in 16,384. Assuming the chip can test 10,000 values of k per second, it will take less than two seconds to find one. This computation does not involve the message and can be performed off line, before Alice wants to sign a message.

(6) The chip signs the message normally, using the value of k chosen in step (5).

(7) Alice sends the digital signature to Bob, or publishes it on the network, or whatever.

(8) Mallet recovers r and, because he knows the fourteen primes, decrypts the subliminal message.

The scary part of this is that even if Alice knows that this is happening, she cannot prove it. As long as those fourteen secret primes stay secret, Mallet is safe.

Other Schemes

There are other schemes for embedding a subliminal channel in a signature scheme [821,823,783]. A protocol for embedding a subliminal channel in the Fiat-Shamir and Feige-Fiat-Shamir protocols, as well as possible abuses of the subliminal channel, can be found in [288]. In fact, any signature scheme can be converted into a subliminal channel.

16.7 UNDENIABLE DIGITAL SIGNATURES

This algorithm is by David Chaum [207]. First, a large prime, p, and a primitive element, g, are made public, and used by a group of signers. Alice has a private key, x, and a public key, g^x.

To sign a message, Alice computes $z = m^x$. That's all she needs to do.

Verification is a little more complicated:

(1) Bob chooses two random numbers, a and b, both less than p, and sends Alice:

$$c = z^a(g^x)^b \pmod{p}$$

(2) Alice computes $x^{-1} \pmod{p-1}$, and sends Bob:

$$d = c^{x^{-1}} \pmod{p}$$

(3) Bob confirms that

$$d \equiv m^a g^b \pmod{p}$$

If it is, he accepts the signature as genuine.

Imagine that Alice and Bob go through this protocol, and Bob is now convinced that Alice signed the message. Now, Bob wants to convince Carol. He shows Carol a transcript of the protocol. Dave wants to convince Carol that some other person signed the document. He creates a fake transcript of the protocol. First he generates the message in step (1). Then he does the calculation in step (3) to generate d and the fake transmission from this other person in step (2). Finally, he creates the message in step (3). To Carol, both Bob's and Dave's transcripts are identical. She cannot be convinced of the signature's validity unless she goes through the protocol herself.

Of course, if she were watching over Bob's shoulder as he completed the protocol, she would be convinced. Carol has to see the steps done in order, just as Bob does.

Another protocol is presented by Chaum [199]. This protocol not only has a confirmation protocol, by which Alice convinces Bob that her signature is valid, it also has a disavowal protocol, in which Alice uses a zero-knowledge interactive protocol to convince him that the signature is not valid, if it is not.

Like the previous protocol, a large prime, p, and a primitive element, g, are made public, and used by a group of signers. Alice has a private key, x, and a public key, g^x. To sign a message, Alice computes $z = m^x$.

To verify a signature:

(1) Bob chooses two random numbers, a and b, both less than p, and sends Alice:

$$c = m^a g^b$$

(2) Alice chooses a random number, q, less than p, and computes and sends to Bob:

$$s_1 = c \times g^q, \; s_2 = (c \times g^q)^x$$

(3) Bob sends Alice a and b, so that Alice can confirm that Bob did not cheat in step (1).

(4) Alice sends Bob q, so that Bob can use m^x and reconstruct s_1 and s_2. If

$$s_1 = c \times g^q$$
$$s_2 = (g^x)^{b+q} \times z^a$$

then the signature is valid.

Alice can also disavow a signature, z, for a message, m. See [199] for details.

Additional protocols for undeniable signatures can be found in [358,208]. Lein Harn and Shoubao Yang proposed a group undeniable signature scheme [416].

Convertible Undeniable Signatures

An algorithm for a **convertible undeniable signature,** which can be verified, disavowed, and also converted to a conventional digital signature is given in [131]. It's based on the ElGamal digital signature algorithm.

Like ElGamal, first choose two primes, p and q, such that q divides $p - 1$. Now you have to create a number, g, less than q. First choose a random number, h, between 2 and $p - 1$. Calculate

$$g = h^{(p-1)/q}$$

If g equals the identity, choose another random h. If it doesn't, keep the g you have.

The private keys are two different random numbers, x and z, both less than q. The public keys are p, q, g, y, and u, when:

$$y = g^x \pmod p$$
$$u = g^z \pmod p$$

To compute the convertible undeniable signature of message m (which is actually the hash of a message), first choose a random number, t, between 1 and $q - 1$. Then compute:

$$T = g^t \bmod p$$

and

$$m' = Ttzm \bmod q$$

Now, compute the standard ElGamal signature on m'. Choose a random number, R, such that R is less than $(p - 1)$ and relatively prime to $p - 1$. Then compute $r = g^R$, and use the Euclidean algorithm to compute s, such that:

$$m' = rx + Rs \pmod q$$

Finally, choose another random number, t. The signature is the ElGamal signature (r,s), and T.

Here's how Alice verifies her signature to Bob:

(1) Bob generates two random numbers, a and b. He computes $c = T^{Tma}g^b$ $(\bmod\ p)$ and sends that to Alice.

(2) Alice generates a random number, k, and computes $h_1 = cg^k \pmod p$, and $h_2 = h_1^z \pmod p$, and sends both of those numbers to Bob.

(3) Bob sends Alice a and b.

(4) Alice verifies that $c = T^{Tma}g^b \pmod p$. She sends k to Bob.

(5) Bob verifies that $h_1 = T^{Tma}g^{b+k} \pmod p$, and that $H_2 = y^{ra}r^{sa}u^{b+k} \pmod p$.

Alice can convert all of her undeniable signatures to normal signatures by publishing *z*. Now, anyone can verify her signature without her help.

Torben Pederson combined this notion with secret sharing schemes to create **distributed convertible undeniable signatures** [688]. People can sign messages and then distribute the ability to confirm that the signature is valid. They might, for example, require three out of five people to participate in the protocol in order to convince Bob that the signature is valid.

16.8   COMPUTING WITH ENCRYPTED DATA

The Discrete Logarithm Problem

There is a large prime, *p,* and a generator, *g.* Alice has a particular value of *x,* and wants to know *e,* such that:

$$g^e \equiv x \bmod p$$

This is normally a hard problem, and Alice lacks the computational power to compute the result. Bob has the computational power to solve the problem—he's in the government, for example, or at a large computing organization. Here's how Alice can let him do it without revealing *x* [335,4]:

(1) Alice chooses a random number, *r,* less than *p.*

(2) Alice computes

$$x' = xg^r \bmod p$$

(3) Alice asks Bob to solve

$$g^{e'} \equiv x' \bmod p$$

(4) Bob computes *e'* and sends it to Alice.

(5) Alice recovers *e* by computing

$$e = e' - r \bmod p - 1$$

There are similar protocols for the quadratic residuosity problem and for the primitive root problem [3,4].

16.9   FAIR COIN FLIPS

The following protocols allow Alice and Bob to flip a fair coin over modem. This is an example of flipping a coin into a well (see Section 4.7). At first, only Bob knows the result of the coin toss and tells it to Alice. Later, Alice may check to make sure that Bob told her the correct outcome of the toss.

Coin Flipping Using Square Roots

Coin-flip subprotocol:

(1) Alice chooses two large primes, p and q, and computes their product.

$$n = pq$$

Alice sends n to Bob.

(2) Bob chooses a random positive integer, r, such that r is less than or equal to $n/2$. Bob computes

$$z = r^2 \bmod n$$

and sends z to Alice.

(3) Alice computes the four square roots of z (mod n). She can do this because she knows the factorization of n. Let's call them $+x$, $-x$, $+y$, and $-y$. Call x' the smaller of these two numbers:

$x \bmod n$
$-x \bmod n$

Similarly, call y' the smaller of these two numbers:

$y \bmod n$
$-y \bmod n$

Note that r is equal either to x' or y'.

(4) Alice guesses whether $r = x'$ or $r = y'$, and sends 1 bit of her guess to Bob. (The way she does this is to find the smallest bit of x' and y' that is different. Then she tells Bob, "the ith bit of your number, r, is 0," or "the ith bit of your number, r, is 1."

(5) If Alice's guess is correct, the result of the coin flip is heads. If Alice's guess is incorrect, the result of the coin flip is tails. Bob announces the result of the coin flip.

Verification subprotocol:

(6) Bob sends r to Alice.

(7) Alice sends p and q to Bob.

Alice has no way of knowing r, so her guess is real. She only tells Bob 1 bit of her guess in step (4) to prevent Bob from getting both x' and y'. If Bob has both of those numbers, he can factor n, and thereby change u after step (4). Other than that way of cheating, the security of this protocol relies on the fact that factoring is difficult.

Coin Flipping Using Exponentiation Modulo p

Exponentiation modulo a prime number, p, is used as a one-way function in this protocol [733]:

Coin-flip subprotocol:

(1) Alice and Bob mutually choose a prime number, p, in such a way that the factorization of $p - 1$ is known.

(2) Bob selects two primitive elements, h and t, in GF(p). He sends them to Alice.

(3) Alice chooses a random integer, x, relatively prime to $p - 1$. She then computes one of the two values:

$$y = h^x \pmod{p} \text{ or } y = t^x \pmod{p}$$

She sends y to Bob.

(4) Bob guesses whether y is a function of h or t and sends his guess to Alice.

(5) If Bob's guess is correct, the result of the coin flip is heads. If Bob's guess is incorrect, the result of the coin flip is tails. Alice announces the result of the coin flip.

Verification subprotocol:

(6) Alice reveals x to Bob. Bob computes $h^x \pmod{p}$ and $t^x \pmod{p}$ to both confirm that Alice has played fairly and to verify the result of the toss.

Step (1) can be easily completed by having Alice and Bob each suggest a few large primes, multiply them together publicly, and then check the product times two plus one for primality. Knowing the factorization of $p - 1$ helps access the difficulty of calculating discrete logarithms modulo p. It is in Bob's interest to make sure that $p - 1$ isn't made up of small prime factors.

For Alice to cheat, she has to know two integers, x and x', such that $h^x \equiv t^{x'} \pmod{p}$. To be able to compute x' given x, she has to compute:

$$log_t h^x \pmod{p}$$

Alice would be able to do this if she knew $log_t h$, but Bob chooses h and t in step (2). Alice has no other recourse except to try to compute the discrete logarithm. Alice could also attempt to cheat by choosing an x that is not relatively prime to $p - 1$, but Bob will detect that in step (6).

Bob can cheat if h and t are not primitive in GF(p), but Alice can easily check that after step (2) because she knows the prime factorization of $p - 1$.

One nice thing about this protocol is that if Alice and Bob want to flip multiple coins, they can use the same values for p, h, and t. Alice just generates a new x, and the protocol continues from step (3).

Coin Flipping Using Blum Integers
Blum integers can be used in a coin-flipping protocol:

(1) Alice generates a Blum integer, n, a random x relatively prime to n, $x_0 = x^2$ mod n, and $x_1 = x_0^2$ mod n. She sends n and x_1 to Bob.

(2) Bob guesses whether or not x_0 is even or odd.

(3) Alice sends x and x_0 to Bob.

(4) Bob checks that n is a Blum integer (Alice would have to give Bob the factors of n or execute some zero-knowledge protocol to convince him that n is a Blum integer), and he verifies that $x_0 = x^2 \bmod n$ and $x_1 = x_0^2 \bmod n$. If all this checks out, Bob wins the flip if he guessed correctly.

It is crucial that n be a Blum integer. Otherwise, Alice can find an x' such that $x_0 \equiv x^2 \bmod n = x'^2 \bmod n$, when $x_0^2 \bmod n$ is also a quadratic residue. If x were even and x' were odd (or vice versa), Alice could freely cheat.

16.10 FAIR CRYPTOSYSTEMS

This example is from Silvio Micali [600].

Fair Diffie-Hellman

In the basic Diffie-Hellman scheme, a group of users share a prime, p, and a generator, g. Alice's private key is s, and her public key is $t = g^s \bmod p$.

Here's how to make Diffie-Hellman fair (this example uses five trustees).

(1) Alice chooses five integers, s_1, s_2, s_3, s_4, and s_5, each less than p. Alice's private key is

$$S = (s_1 + s_2 + s_3 + s_4 + s_5) \bmod p$$

and her public key is

$$T = g^s \ (\bmod p)$$

Alice also computes

$$t_i = g^{s_i} \ (\bmod p), \text{ for } i = 1 \text{ to } 5$$

Alice's public shares are t_i, and her private shares are s_i.

(2) Alice sends a private piece and corresponding public piece to each trustee. For example, she sends s_1 and t_1 to trustee 1. She sends T to the KDC.

(3) Each trustee verifies that

$$t_i = g^{s_i} \ (\bmod p)$$

If it does, the trustee signs t_i and sends it to the KDC. The trustee then stores s_i in a secure place.

(4) After receiving all five public pieces, the KDC verifies that

$$T = (t_1 \times t_2 \times t_3 \times t_4 \times t_5) \bmod p$$

If it does, the KDC approves the public key.

At this point, the KDC knows that each trustee has a valid piece, and that they can reconstruct the private key if required. However, neither the KDC nor any individual trustee can reconstruct Alice's private key.

Micali's paper [600] also contains a procedure for making RSA fair and for combining a threshold scheme with the fair cryptosystem, so that m out of n trustees can reconstruct the private key.

16.11   ALL-OR-NOTHING DISCLOSURE OF SECRETS

This protocol, by Arto Salomaa and Lila Santean [764,659], allows multiple parties (at least two are required for the protocol to work) to buy individual secrets from a single seller.

First, a definition. Take two bit strings, x and y. The **fixed-bit index (FBI)** of x and y are the bits when the ith bit of x equals the ith bit of y.

For example:

> $x = 110101001011$
>
> $y = 101010000110$
>
> $FBI(x,y) = \{1,4,5,11\}$. (We're reading the bits from right to left, with the right-most index of zero.)

Now, the protocol. Alice is the seller. Bob and Carol are buyers. Alice has k n-bit secrets: $S_1, S_2, \ldots, S_k$. Bob wants to buy secret S_b; Carol wants to buy secret S_c.

(1) Alice generates a public/private key pair and tells Bob (but not Carol) the public key. She generates another public/private key pair and tells Carol (but not Bob) the public key.

(2) Bob generates k n-bit random numbers, $B_1, B_2, \ldots, B_k$, and tells them to Carol. Carol generates k n-bit random numbers, $C_1, C_2, \ldots, C_k$, and tells them to Bob.

(3) Bob encrypts C_b (remember, S_b is the secret he wants to buy) with the public key from Alice. He computes the FBI of C_b and the result he just encrypted. He sends this FBI to Carol.

Carol encrypts B_c (remember, S_c is the secret she wants to buy) with the public key from Alice. She computes the FBI of B_c and the result she just encrypted. She sends this FBI to Bob.

(4) Bob takes each of the n-bit numbers $B_1, B_2, \ldots B_k$, and replaces every bit whose index is not in the FBI he received from Carol with its complement. He sends this new list of n-bit numbers, $B'_1, B'_2, \ldots, B'_k$, to Alice.

Carol takes each of the n-bit numbers $C_1, C_2, \ldots C_k$, and replaces every bit whose index is not in the FBI she received from Bob with its complement. She sends this new list of n-bit numbers, $C'_1, C'_2, \ldots, C'_k$, to Alice.

(5) Alice decrypts all C'_i with the private key associated with the public key she gave to Bob, giving her k n-bit numbers: $C''_1, C''_2, \ldots, C''_k$. She computes S_i XOR C''_i, for $i = 1$ to k, and sends the results to Bob.

Alice decrypts all B'_i with the private key associated with the public key she gave to Carol, giving her k n-bit numbers: $B''_1, B''_2, \ldots, B''_k$. She computes S_i XOR B''_i, for $i = 1$ to k, and sends the results to Carol.

(6) Bob computes S_b by XORing C_b and the bth number he received from Alice.

Carol computes S_c by XORing B_c and the cth number she received from Alice.

This is complicated. An example will go a long way to help.

Alice has the following eight 12-bit secrets for sale: $S_1 = 1990$, $S_2 = 471$, $S_3 = 3860$, $S_4 = 1487$, $S_5 = 2235$, $S_6 = 3751$, $S_7 = 2546$, and $S_8 = 4043$. Bob wants to buy S_7. Carol wants to buy S_2.

(1) Alice uses the RSA algorithm. The key pair she will use with Bob is: $n = 7387$, $e = 5145$, and $d = 777$. The key pair she will use with Carol is: $n = 2747$, $e = 1421$, and $d = 2261$. She tells Bob and Carol each their public key.

(2) Bob generates eight 12-bit random numbers: $B_1 = 743$, $B_2 = 1988$, $B_3 = 4001$, $B_4 = 2942$, $B_5 = 3421$, $B_6 = 2210$, $B_7 = 2306$, and $B_8 = 222$, and tells them to Carol. Carol generates eight 12-bit random numbers: $C_1 = 1708$, $C_2 = 711$, $C_3 = 1969$, $C_4 = 3112$, $C_5 = 4014$, $C_6 = 2308$, $C_7 = 2212$, and $C_8 = 222$, and tells them to Bob.

(3) Bob wants to buy S_7, so he encrypts C_7 with the public key that Alice gave him:

$$2212^{5145} \pmod{7387} = 5928$$

Now:

$$2212 = 0100010100100$$
$$5928 = 1011100101000$$

So, the FBI of those two numbers is $\{0, 1, 4, 5, 6\}$. He sends this to Carol.

Carol wants to buy S_2, so she encrypts B_2 with the public key that Alice gave her and computes the FBI of B_2 with the result of her encryption. She sends $\{0, 1, 2, 6, 9, 10\}$ to Bob.

(4) Bob takes $B_1, B_2, \ldots, B_8$, and replaces every bit whose index is not in the set $\{0, 1, 2, 6, 9, 10\}$ with its complement. For example:

$$B_2 = 111111000100 = 1988$$
$$B'_2 = 011001111100 = 1660$$

He sends $B'_1, B'_2, \ldots, B'_8$, to Alice.

Carol takes $C_1, C_2, \ldots, C_8$, and replaces every bit whose index is not in the set $\{0, 1, 4, 5, 6\}$ with its complement. For example:

$$C_7 = 0100010100100 = 2212$$
$$C'_7 = 1011100101000 = 5928$$

She sends $C'_1, C'_2, \ldots, C'_8$, to Alice.

(5) Alice decrypts all C'_i with the private key associated with Bob and XORs the results with S_i. For example, for $i = 7$:

$$5928^{777} \pmod{7387} = 2212; \ 2546 \text{ XOR } 2212 = 342$$

She sends the results to Bob.

Alice decrypts all B'_i with the private key associated with Carol and XORs the results with S_i. For example, for $i = 2$:

$$1660^{2261} \pmod{2747} = 1988; \ 471 \text{ XOR } 1988 = 1555$$

She sends the results to Carol.

(6) Bob computes S_7 by XORing C_7 and the seventh number he received from Alice:

$$2212 \text{ XOR } 342 = 2546$$

Carol computes S_2 by XORing B_2 and the second number she received from Alice.

$$1988 \text{ XOR } 1555 = 471$$

The protocol works for any number of buyers. If Bob, Carol, and Dave want to buy secrets, Alice gives each buyer two public keys, one for each of the others. Each buyer gets a set of numbers from each other buyer. Then, they complete the protocol with Alice for each of their sets of numbers and XOR all of their final results from Alice to get their secret. More details are in [764,659]. Another ANDOS algorithm is given in [148].

16.12   ZERO-KNOWLEDGE PROOFS OF KNOWLEDGE

Zero-Knowledge Proof of a Discrete Logarithm

Peggy wants to prove to Victor that she knows an x that satisfies:

$$A^x \equiv B \pmod{P}$$

when p is a prime, and x is relatively prime to $P-1$. The numbers A, B, and P are public, and x is randomly chosen. Here's how Peggy can prove she knows x without revealing it [205]:

(1) Peggy generates t random numbers, $r_1, r_2, \ldots, r_t$, when all values of r are less than $p-1$.

(2) Peggy computes $h_i = A^{r_i} \pmod{p}$, for all values of r, and sends them to Bob.

(3) Peggy and Victor engage in a coin-flipping protocol to generate t bits: b_1, $b_2, \ldots, b_t$.

(4) For all t bits, Peggy does one of the following:

> (a) If $b_i = 0$, she sends Victor r_i.
> (b) If $b_i = 1$, she sends Victor $s_i = r_i - r_j \pmod{p-1}$, when j is the lowest value of i for which $b_i = 1$

(5) For all t bits, Victor confirms one of the following:

> (a) If $b_i = 0$, that $A^{r_i} = h_i$
> (b) If $b_i = 1$, that $A^{s_i} = h_i h_j^{-1}$

(6) Peggy sends Victor Z, when:

$$Z = x - r_j \pmod{p-1}$$

(7) Victor confirms that:

$$A^Z = B \times h_j^{-1}$$

Peggy's probability of cheating is 2^t.

Improved Zero-Knowledge Proof of a Discrete Logarithm

Like the previous protocol, A, B, and P are public. Peggy wants to prove to Victor that she knows an x that satisfies:

$$A^x \equiv B \pmod{p}$$

Here's the protocol [204]:

(1) Peggy chooses a random number, r, such that r is less than $p - 1$. She computes $h = A^r$, and sends h to Victor.

(2) Victor sends Peggy a random bit, b.

(3) Peggy computes and sends Victor:

$$s = r + bx \pmod{p - 1}$$

(4) Victor confirms that:

$$A^s = hB^b$$

(5) Repeat steps (1) through (4) t times.

The chances of Peggy's cheating are one in 2^t. Check the reference for proof that it works.

The proof can be modified to work with a composite modulus n, when n is the product of two primes, p and q. In step (1), Peggy chooses a number less than $(p - 1) \times (q - 1)$; and in step (3), Peggy computes and sends Victor $s = r + bx$ (mod $((p - 1) \times (q - 1))$.

Zero-Knowledge Proof of the Ability to Break RSA

Alice knows Carol's private key. Maybe she has broken RSA; maybe she has broken into Carol's house and stolen the key. Alice wants to convince Bob that she knows Carol's key. However, she doesn't want to tell Bob the key or even decrypt one of Carol's messages for Bob. Here's a zero-knowledge protocol by which Alice convinces Bob that she knows Carol's private key [505].

Carol's public key is e. Her private key is d. The RSA modulus is n.

(1) Alice and Bob agree on a random k and m, such that

$$km = e$$

They should choose the numbers randomly, using any coin-flip protocol to generate k and then compute m. If both k and m are greater than 3, the protocol continues. Otherwise, choose again.

(2) Alice and Bob generate a random ciphertext, C. Again, they should use a coin-flip protocol.

(3) Alice, using Carol's private key, computes:

$$M = C^d \bmod n$$

She then computes:

$$X = M^k \bmod n$$

and sends X to Bob.

(4) Bob confirms that $X^m \bmod n = C$. If it does, he believes Alice.

A similar protocol can be used to demonstrate the ability to break a discrete logarithm problem [505].

16.13   BLIND SIGNATURES

The notion of blind signatures was invented by David Chaum [192], who also invented their first implementation [193]. It uses the RSA algorithm.

Bob has a public key, e, a private key, d, and a public modulus, n. Alice wants Bob blindly to sign message m.

Alice chooses a random value, k, between 1 and n. Then she blinds m by computing:

$$t \equiv mk^e \pmod{n}$$

Bob signs t:

$$t^d \equiv (mk^e)^d \pmod{n}$$

Alice unblinds t^d by computing:

$$s \equiv t^d/k \pmod{n}$$

and the result is:

$$s \equiv m^d \pmod{n}$$

This can easily be shown:

$$t^d \equiv (mk^e)^d \equiv m^d k \pmod{n}, \text{ so } t^d/k = m^d \times k/k \equiv m^d \pmod{n}.$$

Of course, any implementation of this blind signature algorithm in a protocol will include the cut-and-choose technique discussed in Section 5.3.

Chaum invented a family of more complicated blind signature algorithms in [195].

16.14 OBLIVIOUS TRANSFER

In this protocol by Rabin [122], Alice has a 50% chance of sending Bob two primes, p and q. Alice will not know whether or not the transfer is successful.

(1) Alice sends Bob the product of the two primes: $n = p \times q$.

(2) Bob chooses a random x less than n, such that x is relatively prime to n. He sends Alice:

$$a = x^2 \bmod n$$

(3) Alice, knowing p and q, computes the four roots of a: x, $n - x$, y, and $n - y$. She chooses one of these roots at random and sends it to Bob.

(4) If Bob receives y or $n - y$, he can compute the greatest common divisor of $x + y$ and n, which is either p or q. Then, of course, $n/p = q$.

If Bob receives x or $n - x$, he can't compute anything.

16.15 SECURE MULTIPARTY COMPUTATION

This protocol is from [763]. Alice knows the integer i; Bob knows the integer j. Alice and Bob together wish to know whether $i \geq j$ or if $i < j$, but Alice and Bob don't wish to reveal their integer.

For this example, assume that i and j range from 1 to 100. Bob has a public key and a private key.

(1) Alice chooses a large random number, x, and encrypts it in Bob's public key.

$$c = E_B(x)$$

(2) Alice computes $c - i$ and sends the result to Bob.

(3) Bob computes the following 100 numbers:

$$y_u = D_B(c{-}i{+}u), \text{ for } 1 \leq u \leq 100$$

D_B is the decryption algorithm with Bob's private key.

He chooses a large random prime, p. (The size of p should be somewhat smaller than the size of x. Bob doesn't know x, but Alice could easily tell him the size of x.) He then computes the following 100 numbers:

$$z_u = (y_u \bmod p), \text{ for } 1 \leq u \leq 100$$

He then verifies that, for all $u \neq v$

$$\mid z_u{-}z_v \mid \geq 2$$

and that for all u

$$0 < z_u < p{-}1$$

If this is not true, Bob chooses another prime and tries again.

(4) Bob sends Alice this sequence of numbers in this exact order:

$$z_1, z_2, \ldots, z_j, z_{j+1}{+}1, z_{j+2}{+}1, \ldots, z_{100}{+}1, p$$

(5) Alice checks whether the ith number in the sequence is congruent to x mod p. If it is, she concludes that $i \leq j$. If it is not, she concludes that $i > j$.

(6) Alice tells Bob the conclusion.

All the verification that Bob goes through in step (3) is to guarantee that no number appears twice in the sequence generated in step (4). Otherwise, if $z_a = z_b$, Alice knows that $a \leq j < b$.

The one drawback to this protocol is that Alice learns the result of the computation before Bob does. There's nothing to stop her from completing the protocol up to step (5) and then refusing to tell Bob the results in step (6). She could even lie to Bob in step (6).

Example of the Protocol

Assume that RSA is the public-key algorithm used. Bob's public key is 7 and his private key is 23; $n = 55$. Alice's secret value, i, is 4; Bob's secret value, j, is 2. (Assume that only the values 1, 2, 3, and 4 are possible for i and j.)

(1) Alice chooses $x = 39$, and $c = E_B(39) = 19$.

(2) Alice computes $c - i = 19 - 4 = 15$. She sends 15 to Bob.

(3) Bob computes the following four numbers:

$$y_1 = D_B(15+1) = 26$$
$$y_2 = D_B(15+2) = 18$$
$$y_3 = D_B(15+3) = 2$$
$$y_4 = D_B(15+4) = 39$$

He chooses a large $p = 31$ and calculates:

$$z_1 = (26 \bmod 31) = 26$$
$$z_2 = (18 \bmod 31) = 18$$
$$z_3 = (2 \bmod 31) = 2$$
$$z_4 = (39 \bmod 31) = 8$$

He does all the verifications and confirms that the sequence is fine.

(4) Bob sends Alice this sequence of numbers in this exact order:

$$26,18,2+1,8+1,31 = 26,18,3,9,31$$

(5) Alice checks whether the fourth number in the sequence is congruent to x mod p. Since $9 \not\equiv 39 \bmod 31$, then $i < j$.

(6) Alice tells Bob.

16.16   PROBABILISTIC ENCRYPTION

The notion of **probabilistic encryption** was invented by Shafi Goldwasser and Silvio Micali [377]. Although its theory makes it the most secure cryptosystem invented, its early implementation was impractical [378]. More recent implementations have changed that.

The point behind probabilistic encryption is to eliminate the last trickle of information leaked with public-key cryptography. Because cryptanalysts can always encrypt random messages with a public key, they can get some information. Assuming they have ciphertext $C = E_K(P)$ and are trying to recover plaintext P, they can pick a random message P' and encrypt it: $C' = E_K(P')$. If $C'=C$, then they guessed the correct plaintext. If it's wrong, they just guess again.

Also, there is no partial information leaked about the original message. With public-key cryptography, sometimes cryptanalysts can learn things about the bits: the XOR of bits 5, 17, and 39 is 1, etc. With probabilistic encryption, even this type of information remains hidden.

True, there is not a lot of new information in this. Still, there are potential problems with allowing cryptanalysts to encrypt random messages with your public key. Some information is being leaked to the cryptanalysts every time they encrypt a message. No one really knows how much, but it is something.

Probabilistic encryption tries to eliminate that leakage. The goal is that no computation on the ciphertext, or on any other trial plaintexts, can give cryptanalysts any information about the corresponding plaintext.

In probabilistic encryption, the encrypting algorithm is probabilistic rather than deterministic. In other words, there are a large number of ciphertexts that correspond to a given plaintext, and the particular ciphertext used in any given encryption is randomly chosen. All of those ciphertexts decrypt to the same plaintext.

$$C_1 = E_K(P), C_2 = E_K(P), C_3 = E_K(P), \ldots C_i = E_K(P)$$
$$P = D_K(C_1) = D_K(C_2) = D_K(C_3) = \ldots = D_K(C_i)$$

With probabilistic encryption, cryptanalysts can no longer encrypt random plaintexts looking for the correct one. To illustrate, assume the cryptanalysts have ciphertext $C_i = E_K(P)$. Even if they guess P correctly, when they encrypt $E_K(P)$, the result will be a completely different C: C_j. They cannot compare C_i and C_j, and so they cannot know that they have guessed the message correctly.

This is amazingly cool stuff. Even if cryptanalysts have the public encryption key, the plaintext, and the ciphertext, they cannot prove that the ciphertext is the encryption of the plaintext without the private decryption key. Even if they try exhaustive search, they can only prove that every conceivable plaintext is a possible plaintext.

Using this sort of scheme, the ciphertext will always be larger than the plaintext. You can't get around this; it's a result of the fact that many ciphertexts decrypt to the same plaintexts. The first probabilistic encryption scheme [378] resulted in a ciphertext so much larger than the plaintext that it was unusable.

However, there is an efficient implementation of probabilistic encryption by Manuel Blum and Shafi Goldwasser [126]. It uses the Blum Blum Shub (BBS) random bit generator described in Section 15.2.2.

The BBS generator is based on the theory of quadratic residues. In English, there are two primes, p and q, that are congruent to 3 modulo 4. That's the private key. Their product, $p \times q = n$, is the public key. (Mind your p's and q's; the security of this scheme rests in the difficulty of factoring n.)

To encrypt a message, P, first choose a random x, relatively prime to n. Then compute

$$x_0 = x^2 \bmod n$$

Use x_0 as the seed of the BBS pseudo-random bit generator and XOR P, 1 bit at a time, with the output of the generator. The generator spits out bits b_i, so

$P = P_1, P_2, P_3, \ldots P_t$
$C = P_1 \text{ XOR } b_1, P_2 \text{ XOR } b_2, P_3 \text{ XOR } b_3, \ldots P_t \text{ XOR } b_t$ when t is the length of the plaintext

Then append the value of x at the end of this process, x_t, to the end of the message and you're done.

The only way to decrypt this message is to recover x_0 and then set up the same BBS generator to XOR with the ciphertext. Because the BBS generator is secure to the left, the value x_t is of no use to the cryptanalyst. Only someone who knows p and q can decrypt the message.

The C algorithm to recover x_0 from x_t is as follows:

```
/*  pow(x,y) returns x to the power of y.  */
int x0 (int p, int q, int n, int t, int xt)
{
  int a, b, u, v, w, z;

    /* we already know that gcd(p, q) == 1 */
    (void)extended_euclidian(p, q, &a, &b);
    u = pow ( (p+1)/4, t ) % (p-1);
    v = pow ( (q+1)/4, t ) % (q-1);
    w = pow ( xt, u ) % p;
    z = pow ( xt % q, v  ) % q;
    return (b*q*w + a*p*z) % n;
}
```

Once you have x_0, decryption is easy. Just set up the BBS generator and XOR the output with the ciphertext.

You can make this scheme go even faster by using all the secure bits of x_i, not just the least significant bit. Using this improvement, Blum-Goldwasser probabilistic encryption is faster than RSA, and it leaks no partial information about the plaintext. You can also prove that the difficulty of breaking this scheme is the same as the difficulty of factoring n.

On the other hand, this scheme is totally insecure against a chosen-ciphertext attack. From the least significant bits of the right quadratic residues, it is possible to calculate the square root of any quadratic residue. If you can do this, then you can factor. For details, consult [864,865,19,20].

16.17   QUANTUM CRYPTOGRAPHY

Quantum cryptography taps the natural uncertainty of the quantum world. You can create a communications channel with it in which it is impossible to eavesdrop without disturbing the transmission. The laws of physics secure this quantum channel—even if the eavesdroppers can do whatever they want, even if the eavesdroppers have unlimited computing power, and even if **P=NP.** Charles Bennett and Gilles Brassard have taken this idea as far as they can, describing quantum key distribution, quantum coin flipping, and quantum bit commitment. Their work is described in [73,743,68,69,70,78,71,79,150,314,77,75]. The best overview of quantum cryptography can be found in [76]; [907] is another popular overview.

This would still be on the lunatic fringe of cryptography, but Bennett and Brassard actually went and built a working model of the thing [72,67]. Now we have *experimental* quantum cryptography.

So sit back, get yourself something to drink, and relax. I'm going to explain what this is all about.

According to quantum mechanics, particles don't actually exist in any single place. They exist in several places at once, with probabilities of being in different places if someone looks. However, it isn't until a scientist comes along and measures the particle that it "collapses" into a single location. But you can't measure every aspect of a particle at the same time: position and velocity, for example. If you measure one of those two quantities, the very act of measuring them destroys any possibility of measuring the other quantity. There is a fundamental uncertainty in the quantum world, and there's no avoiding it.

That uncertainty can be used to generate a secret key. Photons vibrate as they travel. This vibration is in some direction; up and down, left to right, or more likely at some angle. Normal sunlight is unpolarized; the photons vibrate every which way. When a large group of photons vibrate in the same direction, they are polarized. Polarization filters only allow photons that are polarized in a certain direction through; they block all the rest. For example, a horizontal polarization filter only allows horizontally polarized photons through. Turn the filter 90 degrees, and only vertically polarized photons can come through.

Let's say you have a pulse of horizontally polarized photons. If they try to pass through a horizontally polarized filter, they all get through. Slowly turn that filter to 90 degrees; the number of photons getting through gets smaller and smaller, until none gets through. This is counterintuitive. You'd think that turning the filter just a little will block all the photons, since the photons are horizontally polarized. That would make sense in our world, not in quantum mechanics. Each particle has a probability of suddenly switching its polarization to match the filter. If the angle is a little bit off, it has a good probability. If the angle is 90 degrees off, it has no probability. If the angle is 45 degrees off, it has a 50% probability. We're going to use this property to generate a secret key:

(1) Alice sends Bob a string of photon pulses. Each of the pulses is randomly polarized in one of four directions: horizontal, vertical, left-diagonal, and right-diagonal.

   For example, Alice sends Bob:

   | |/ - -\ -|-/

(2) Bob has a polarization detector. He can set his detector to measure horizontal and vertical polarization, or he can set his detector to measure diagonal polarization. He can't do both; quantum mechanics won't let him. Measuring one destroys any possibility of measuring the other. So, he sets his detectors at random, for example:

   X + + X X X + X + +

Now, when Bob sets his detector correctly, he will record the correct answer. If he sets his detector to measure horizontal or vertical and the pulse is polarized either horizontally or vertically, he will learn which way Alice polarized the photon. If he sets his detector incorrectly, he will get a random result. He won't know the difference. In this example, he might get the result:

   | | / - - \ - | - /

(3) Bob tells Alice, over an insecure channel, what settings he used.

(4) Alice tells Bob which settings were correct. In our example, pulses 2, 6, 7, and 9 were set correctly.

(5) Alice and Bob keep only those settings that were correct. In our example, they keep:

   * | * * * \ _ * _ *

Using a pre-arranged code, Alice and Bob each translate those settings into bits. For example, horizontal and left-diagonal might be 1, and vertical and right-diagonal might be 0. In our example, they both have:

   0 0 1 1

So, Alice and Bob have generated 4 bits. They can generate as many as they like using this system. On the average, Bob will guess the correct setting 50% of the time, so Alice has to send $2 \times n$ photon pulses to generate n bits. They can use these bits as a secret key for a conventional algorithm, or they can guarantee perfect secrecy and generate enough bits for a one-time pad.

Using this system, Eve cannot eavesdrop. If she tries to detect the photons as they go by, Bob will notice. Her only hope is to capture and measure the photons and then to try to send Bob identical ones. But just like Bob, she has to guess which type of polarization to measure; and, like Bob, half of her guesses will be wrong. She can't help introducing errors in the pulses she sends to Bob.

If she does, Alice and Bob will have different bit strings. So, they finish the protocol like this:

(6) Alice and Bob compare a few bits in their strings. If there are discrepancies, they know they are being bugged. If there are none, they discard the bits they used for comparison and use the rest.

There are enhancements to this protocol that allow Alice and Bob to use their bits even if Eve is bugging them, and even if Eve is just trying to catch a few bits out of thousands.

As I said, Bennett and Brassard built a working model. The last I heard, some folks at British Telcom were sending bits over a ten-kilometer fiber-optic link [177].

The mind boggles.

PART
FOUR

The Real World

Example Implementations

It is one thing to design protocols and algorithms for key management, authentication, and encryption, but another thing entirely to implement them in operational systems. Often ideas that look good on paper don't work in real life. Maybe the bandwidth requirements are too large; maybe there is just too much delay in the protocol.

Most of the following key management systems have been implemented, at least in a test bed.

17.1 IBM SECRET-KEY MANAGEMENT PROTOCOL

This is a complete key management system for communications and file security on a computer network, using only symmetric cryptography. It was designed at IBM in the late 1970s by Ehrsam, Matyas, Meyer, and Tuchman [312,571].

This protocol has three main features: secure communications between a server and several terminals, secure file storage at the server, and secure communication among servers. The protocol doesn't really provide for direct terminal-to-terminal communication, although it can be modified to do that.

Each server on the network is attached to a cryptographic facility, which does all of the encrypting and decrypting. Each server has a **master key,** KM0, and two variants, KM1 and KM2. Both KM1 and KM2 are simple variants of KM0. These keys are used to encrypt other keys and to generate new keys. Each terminal has a **master terminal key,** KMT, which is used to facilitate key exchange among different computers.

The servers store KMT, encrypted with KM1. All other keys, such as those used to encrypt files of keys (called KNF), are stored in encrypted form under KM2.

The master key, KM0, is stored in some nonvolatile security module. Today it could be either a ROM key or a magnetic card, or it could be typed in manually by the user (probably as a text string and then key-crunched). KM1 and KM2 are not stored anywhere in the system, but they are computed from KM0 whenever they are needed. Session keys, for communication among servers, are generated with a pseudo-random process in the server. Keys to encrypt files for storage (KNF) are generated in the same manner.

The heart of the protocol is a tamper-resistant module, called a **cryptographic facility.** At both the server and the terminal, all encryption and decryption takes place within this facility. The most important keys, the keys used to generate the actual encryption keys, are also stored in this module. These keys can never be read once they are stored. Davies and Price [249] discuss this key management protocol in detail.

A Variation

A variation on this scheme of master and session keys can be found in [833]. This scheme is built around network nodes with key notarization facilities that serve local terminals. It is designed to provide:

- Secure two-way communication between any two terminal users.

- Secure communications using encrypted mail.

- Protection of personal files.

- Provision of a digital signature capability.

For communication and file transfer among users, the scheme uses keys generated in the key notarization facility and sent to the users encrypted under a master key. The identities of the users are incorporated with the key, to provide evidence that the session key has been used between a particular pair of users. This is the **key notarization** feature that is central to the system. Although the system does not use public-key cryptography, there is a digital-signature-like capability, in that the key could have only come from a particular source and could only be read at a particular destination.

17.2   MITRENET

One of the earliest implementations of public-key cryptography is the experimental system MEMO (MITRE Encrypted Mail Office). MITRE is a DoD contractor, a government think-tank. MEMO was a secure electronic-mail system for users in the MITRENET network. MEMO uses public-key cryptography for key exchange and DES for file encryption.

In the MEMO system, a Public Key Distribution Center is a separate node on the network. It contains all public keys, stored in EPROM, to prevent anyone from changing them. Private keys are generated by users or by the system.

Every time users log on to the network, they first establish a secure communications path with the Public Key Distribution Center. The users request a file of all the public keys from the Center. If the users pass an identification test using their individual private keys, the Center sends this list to each user's workstation. This list is encrypted using DES to ensure file integrity.

When users want to send a message to other users, they first generate a random DES key (actually, the system does this itself). Then they encrypt the file with the DES key and encrypt the DES key with the recipient's public key. Both the DES-encrypted file and the public-key-encrypted key are sent to the recipient.

MEMO makes no provision for lost keys. There is some provision for integrity checking of the messages, using checksums. There is no authentication built into the system.

The particular public-key implementation used for this system (Diffie-Hellman key exchange over $GF(2^{127})$) was proven insecure before the system was implemented (see Section 9.6), although it is easy to modify the system to use larger numbers. MEMO was intended mainly for experimental purposes and was never made operational on the real MITRENET system.

17.3   ISDN

Bell-Northern Research developed a prototype secure Integrated Services Digital Network (ISDN) Terminal [302,662,296,303]. The terminal can transmit and receive voice and data at 64 kbps. The terminal uses Diffie-Hellman key exchange, RSA digital signatures, and DES data encryption.

Keys

There is a long-term public/private key pair embedded in the phone. The private key is stored in a tamper-resistant area of the phone. The public key serves as the identification of the phone. These keys are part of the phone itself and cannot be altered in any way.

Additionally, there are two other public keys stored in the phone. One of these keys is the owner's public key. This key is used to authenticate commands from the owner. This key can be changed via a command signed by the owner. In this way one owner can transfer ownership of the phone to another person.

Another public key stored in the phone is the public key of the network. This key is used to authenticate commands from the network's key management facility. It is used to authenticate calls from other users on the network. This key can also be changed via a signed command from the owner. This permits the owners to move their phone from one network to another.

These keys are considered long-term keys: they are rarely, if ever, changed. There is also a short-term public/private key pair stored on the phone. These are encapsulated in a certificate signed by the key management facility. When two phones set up a call, they exchange certificates. The public key of the network is used to authenticate these certificates.

This exchange and verification of certificates only sets up a secure call from phone to phone. To set up a secure call from person to person, there is an additional piece of the protocol. The private key of the owner is stored on a hardware "ignition key," which is inserted into the telephone by the owner. This ignition key contains the owner's private key, encrypted under a secret password known only by the owner (not by the phone, not by the network's key management facility, not by anybody). It also contains a certificate signed by the network's key management facility that contains the owner's public key and some identifying information (name, company, security clearance, job title, favorite pizza toppings, etc.). This is also encrypted. To decrypt this information and enter it into the phone, the owners must type their secret password on the phone's touchpad. After the phone uses this information to set up calls, it is destroyed when the owners remove their ignition key.

The phone also stores a set of certificates from the network's key management facility. These certificates authorize particular users to use particular phones.

Calling

A call from Alice to Bob works as follows:

(1) Alice inserts her ignition key into the phone and enters her password.

(2) The phone interrogates the ignition key to determine Alice's identity.

(3) The phone checks its set of certificates to ensure that the user is authorized to use the particular phone.

(4) Alice dials the number; the phone places the call.

(5) The two telephones use a public-key cryptography key-exchange protocol to generate a unique and random session key. All subsequent protocol steps are encrypted using this key.

(6) The calling phone transmits its certificate and user authentication.

(7) The called phone authenticates the signatures on both the certificate and the user authentication using the network's public key.

(8) Bob's phone initiates a challenge-and-reply sequence. It demands real-time signed responses to time-dependent challenges. (This prevents an adversary from using certificates copied from a previous exchange.) One response must be signed by Alice's phone's private key; another must be signed by Alice's user's private key.

(9) Bob's phone rings.

(10) If he is home, he inserts his ignition key into the phone. His phone interrogates the ignition key and checks the certificate as in steps (2) and (3).

(11) Alice's phone transmits its certificate and user authentication.

(12) Alice's phone authenticates Bob's signatures as in step (7) and initiates a challenge-and-reply sequence as in step (8).

(13) Both phones display the identities of the other user and phone on their displays.

(14) The secure conversation begins.

(15) When one party hangs up, the session key is deleted, as are the certificates the called phone received from the calling phone and the certificates the calling phone received from the called phone.

Each DES key is unique to each call. It exists only inside the two phones for the duration of the call and is destroyed immediately afterward. If an adversary captures one of the phones involved in the call—or even both phones—the adversary will not be able to decrypt any of the previous calls between the two phones.

17.4   KERBEROS

Kerberos is a trusted third-party authentication protocol designed for UNIX TCP/IP networks. A Kerberos service, sitting on the network, acts as a trusted arbitrator. Kerberos provides secure network authentication, allowing a person to access different machines on the network. Kerberos is based on symmetric cryptography (DES as implemented, but other algorithms could be used instead); Kerberos shares a different secret key with every entity on the network. Knowledge of the secret key is used as proof of identity.

The Kerberos authentication service was originally developed at MIT for Project Athena. The UNIX software has been put in the public domain and can be used by anybody. The Kerberos model is based in part on Needham and Schroeder's trusted third-party protocol [645] and on modifications by Denning and Sacco [272]. The original version of Kerberos, Version 4, is specified in [604,845]. (Versions 1 through 3 were internal development versions.) Version 5, modified from Version 4, is specified in [497,498]. Two good articles on using Kerberos in the real world are [456,457].

The Kerberos Model

The basic Kerberos protocol was outlined in Section 3.3. In the Kerberos model, there are entities—clients and servers—sitting on the network. Clients can be users, but they can also be independent software programs that need to do things: download files, send messages, access databases, whatever.

Kerberos is a service Kerberos on the network. This is the trusted arbiter mentioned above. Kerberos keeps a database of clients and their secret keys. For a human user, the secret key is an encrypted password. Network services that require authentication, as well as clients who wish to use these services, register their secret key with Kerberos.

Because Kerberos knows everyone's secret key, it can create messages that convince one entity of another entity's identity. Kerberos also creates temporary secret keys, called **session keys,** which are given to a client and a server (or to two clients) and no one else. A session key is used to encrypt messages between the two parties, after which it is destroyed.

Kerberos provides three different levels of protection. (In mythology, Kerberos was a mythical three-headed guard dog.) It provides authentication at the beginning of a network connection, after which all further communications are assumed to come from the authenticated entity. It also provides authentication for each message sent from one entity to another. Finally, it provides both authentication and encryption for each message sent from one entity to another.

Software Modules

The implementation of Kerberos generally available contains several software modules. These are:

Kerberos applications library provides an interface for application clients and servers. It contains routines for creating and reading authentication requests and routines for creating authenticated and encrypted messages.

Encryption library: a DES implementation is provided with Kerberos (users outside the United States may find this removed when the code is exported, but they can easily add it back in). The DES included with the source code may be replaced with other DES implementations or a different encryption routine. Kerberos Version 4 provided a nonstandard **Propagating Cipher Block Chaining (PCBC)** mode for authentication. This mode is insecure (see Section 8.1.7). Kerberos Version 5 uses CBC mode.

Database library: Kerberos has simple database needs—a record for each entity containing its name, secret key, expiration date of the secret key, and some administrative information. Since the security of the whole system depends on the security of this database, it must run on a secure machine.

Database administration programs administer the Kerberos database.

Administration server provides a read-write network interface to the database. It is used to add, delete, and update entries in the database. For integrity reasons, the server side of this program must run on the machine housing the Kerberos database. Of course, this machine must be secure.

Authentication server provides a read-only network interface to the database. It is used to authenticate entities and to generate session keys. Since this server does not modify the database, it can run on machines with a read-only copy of the Kerberos database. These machines must also be secure.

Database propagation software. This manages replication of the Kerberos database. To keep Kerberos from collapsing under all the requests for authentication, it is often desirable to have multiple authentication servers on multiple machines. Each of these servers receives a copy of the Kerberos database at regular intervals.

User programs. These are programs for logging into Kerberos, changing a Kerberos password, and displaying and destroying authentication information.

Applications.

How Kerberos Works

This section discusses Kerberos Version 5. I will outline the differences between Version 4 and Version 5 in a later section. The Kerberos protocol is straightforward (see Figure 17.1). A client requests a ticket for a **Ticket-Granting Service (TGS ticket)** from the Kerberos service. This ticket is sent to the client, encrypted in the client's secret key. To use a particular service, the client requests a ticket for that service from the **Ticket-Granting Server (TGS).** Assuming everything is in order, the TGS sends the ticket back to the client. The client then presents this ticket to the server along with an authenticator. Again, if there's nothing wrong with the client's credentials, the server lets the client have access to the service.

Credentials

There are two types of credentials used in Kerberos: **tickets** and **authenticators.** (The rest of this section uses the notation used in Kerberos documents—see Table 17.1.) A ticket is used to pass securely the identity of the client for whom the ticket was issued to the server. It also contains information that the server can use to ensure that the client using the ticket is the same client to which the ticket was issued. An authenticator is an additional credential, presented with the ticket.

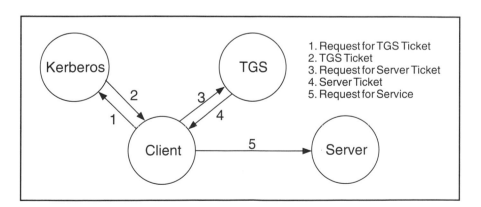

Figure 17.1
Kerberos authentication protocols.

TABLE 17.1
Kerberos Table of Abbreviations

c	= client
s	= server
addr	= client's network address
times	= beginning and ending validity time for a ticket
Kerberos	= authentication server
K_x	= x's secret key
$K_{x,y}$	= session key for x and y
$\{m\}K_x$	= m encrypted in x's secret key
$T_{x,y}$	= x's ticket to use y
$A_{x,y}$	= authenticator from x to y

A Kerberos ticket looks like this:

$$T_{c,s} = s, \{c, \text{addr}, \text{times}, K_{c,s}\}K_s$$

A ticket is good for a single server and a single client. It contains the name of the client, the name of the server, the network address of the client, a timestamp, and a session key. This information is encrypted with the server's secret key. Once the client gets this ticket, she can use it multiple times to gain access to the server, until the ticket expires. The client cannot decrypt the ticket (she does not know the server's secret key), but she can present it to the server in its encrypted form. No one listening on the network can read or modify the ticket as it passes through the network.

A Kerberos authenticator looks like:

$$A_{c,s} = \{c, \text{time}, \text{key}\}K_{c,s}$$

The client generates it every time she wishes to use a service on the server. It contains the name of the client, a timestamp, an optional additional session key, all encrypted with the session key shared between the client and the server. Unlike a ticket, it can only be used once. However, since the client can generate authenticators as needed (it knows the shared secret key), this is not a problem.

The authenticator serves two purposes. First, it contains some plaintext encrypted in the session key. This proves that the sender of the authenticator also knows the key. Just as important, the sealed plaintext includes the time of day; an eavesdropper who records both the ticket and the authenticator can't replay them two days later.

Getting an Initial Ticket

The client has one piece of information that can prove her identity: her password. Obviously we don't want the client to send this password over the network. The Kerberos protocol minimizes the chance that this password will be compromised, while at the same time not allowing a user to properly authenticate herself unless she knows the password.

The client sends a message to the Kerberos authentication server, containing the user's name and the name of her TGS server. (There can be many TGS servers.) In reality, the user probably just enters her username onto the system, and the log-in program sends the request.

The Kerberos authentication server looks up the client in his database. If the client is in the database, Kerberos generates a session key to be used between the client and the TGS. This is called a **Ticket Granting Ticket,** or a **TGT.** It encrypts that session key with the client's secret key. Then it creates a TGT for the client to authenticate herself to the TGS and encrypts that in the TGS's secret key. The authentication server sends both of these encrypted messages back to the client. Figure 17.2 shows this exchange.

The client now decrypts the first message and retrieves the session key. The secret key is a one-way hash of the user's password, so a legitimate user will have no trouble doing this. If the user were an imposter, she would not know the correct password and therefore could not decrypt the response from the Kerberos authentication server. Access would be denied, and she wouldn't be able to get the ticket or the session key.

The client saves the TGT and session key and erases the password and the one-way hash. This information is erased to reduce the chance of compromise. If an adversary manages to copy the client's memory, the result will only be the TGT and the session key. These are valuable pieces of information, but only during the lifetime of the TGT. After the TGT expires, they will be worthless.

If everyone is who they say they are, the client can now prove her identity to the TGS for the lifetime of the TGT.

Getting Server Tickets

A client has to obtain a separate ticket for each service she wants to use. The TGS grants tickets for individual servers.

When a client requires a ticket that she does not already have, she sends a request to the TGS. (In reality, the program would do this automatically, and it would be invisible to the user.) Figure 17.3 shows the exchange.

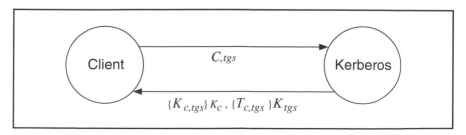

Figure 17.2
Getting a TGS ticket.

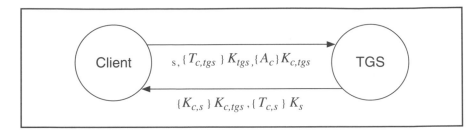

Figure 17.3

Getting a server ticket.

First, the client creates an authenticator. The authenticator consists of the client's name, the client's address, and a timestamp, encrypted with the session key generated by the Kerberos authentication server. The request consists of the name of the server, the TGT received from Kerberos (already encrypted with the TGS's secret key), and the encrypted authenticator.

The TGS, upon receiving the request, decrypts the TGT with his secret key. Then he uses the session key included in the TGT to decrypt the authenticator. Finally, he compares the information in the authenticator with the information in the ticket, the network address of the client with the address the request was sent from, and the timestamp with the current time. If everything matches, he allows the request to proceed.

Checking timestamps assumes that all machines have synchronized clocks, at least to within several minutes. If the time in the request is too far in the future or the past, the TGS treats the request as an attempt to replay a previous request. The TGS should also keep track of all live authenticators, i.e., past requests with timestamps that are still valid. Another request received with the same ticket and timestamp as one already received can be ignored.

The TGS responds to a valid request by returning a valid ticket for the client to present to the server. The ticket contains the name of the client, the network address of the client, a timestamp, an expiration time for the ticket, and the session key it just created, all encrypted with the server's secret key, and the name of the server. The TGS also creates a new session key for the client and the server, encrypted with the session key shared by the client and the TGS. Both of these messages are then sent back to the client.

The client decrypts the message and extracts the session key.

Requesting a Service

Now the client is ready to authenticate herself to the server. She creates a message very similar to the one sent to the TGS (which makes sense, since the TGS is a service). Figure 17.4 shows this.

The client creates an authenticator, consisting of the client's name, the client's network address, and a timestamp, encrypted with the session key for the client and the server that the TGS generated. The request consists of the ticket received from Kerberos (already encrypted with the server's secret key) and the encrypted authenticator.

The server decrypts and checks the ticket and the authenticator, as discussed previously, and also checks the client's address and the timestamp. If everything

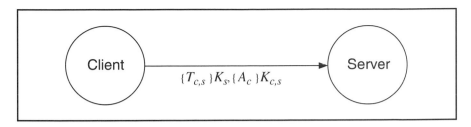

Figure 17.4
Requesting a service.

checks out, the server knows that, according to Kerberos, the client is who she says she is.

For applications that require mutual authentication, the server sends the client back a message consisting of the timestamp plus one, encrypted with the session key (see Figure 17.5). This proves that the server knew his secret key and could decrypt the ticket and therefore the authenticator.

The client and the server can encrypt future messages with the shared key, if desired. Since only the client and the server share this key, they both can assume that a recent message encrypted in that key originated with the other party.

Kerberos Version 4

The previous sections discussed Kerberos Version 5. Kerberos Version 4 differed slightly in the messages and the construction of the tickets and authenticators.

In Kerberos Version 4, the five messages looked like:

1. Client to Kerberos: c, tgs

2. Kerberos to client: $\{K_{c,tgs}, \{T_{c,tgs}\}K_{tgs}\}K_c$

3. Client to TGS: $\{A_c\}K_{c,tgs}, \{T_{c,tgs}\}K_{tgs}, s$

4. TGS to client: $\{K_{c,s}, \{T_{c,s}\}K_s\}K_{c,tgs}$

5. Client to server: $\{A_c\}K_{c,s}, \{T_{c,s}\}K_s$

$T_{c,s} = \{s, c, \text{addr}, \text{time}, \text{life}, K_{c,s}\}K_s$

$A_{c,s} = \{c, \text{addr}, \text{time}\}K_{c,s}$

Messages 1, 3, and 5 are identical. The double encryption of the ticket in steps 2 and 4 has been removed in Version 5. The Version 5 ticket adds the ability to have

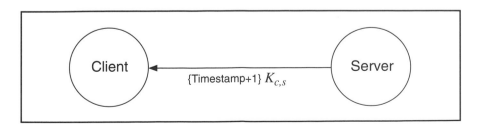

Figure 17.5
Mutual authentication.

multiple addresses, and it replaces a "lifetime" field with a beginning and ending time. The Version 5 authenticator adds the option of including an additional key.

Security of Kerberos

Steve Bellovin and Michael Merritt, in their paper "Limitations of the Kerberos Protocol" [58], discuss several potential security vulnerabilities of Kerberos. Although this paper was written about the Version 4 protocols, many of their comments also apply to Version 5.

It may be possible to cache and replay old authenticators. Although timestamps are supposed to prevent this, replays can be done during the lifetime of the ticket. Servers are supposed to store all valid tickets to prevent replays, but this is not always possible.

Authenticators rely on the fact that all the clocks in the network are more or less synchronized. If a host can be fooled about the correct time, then an old authenticator can be replayed without any problem. Most network time protocols are insecure, so this can be a serious problem.

Kerberos is also vulnerable to password-guessing attacks. An intruder can collect tickets and then try to decrypt them. Remember that the average user doesn't usually choose good passwords. If Mallet collects enough tickets, his chances of recovering a password are good.

Perhaps the most serious attack involves malicious software. The Kerberos protocols rely on the fact that the Kerberos software is trustworthy. There's nothing to stop Mallet surreptitiously replacing all client Kerberos software with a version that, in addition to completing the Kerberos protocols, records passwords. This is a problem with any cryptographic software package on an insecure computer, but the widespread use of Kerberos in these environments makes it a particularly tempting target.

Future of Kerberos

In [497], Kohl discusses items that may be incorporated into future versions of Kerberos:

> Public-key cryptosystems. The current Kerberos protocols are designed for symmetric algorithms. There is some work towards incorporating public-key algorithms into Kerberos, but public-key algorithms have very different characteristics. Taking advantage of public-key cryptography would require a complete reworking of the protocol.

> Smart Cards. These are hand-held devices which would augment normal password security methods.

> Remote Administration. This feature would provide a standard interface to the Kerberos database for system administrators.

> Directional inter-realm keys. This would increase security across different networks.

> Database propagations. There is thought of turning the Kerberos database into a distributed database.

Validation suites. There is currently no complete validation suite to verify that the protocol is properly implemented. Such a suite could prevent security problems resulting from faulty implementation of the protocols, and would help insure interoperability between implementations.

Applications. There are many applications that would benefit from the addition of Kerberos authentication (this is known as "Kerberizing" an application).

Licenses

Kerberos is public domain, and free source code is available from MIT's Project Athena. Actually implementing this code into a working environment is another story. The Open Computer Security Group sells and supports a commercial version of the Kerberos Version 5 protocols for SUN, RS/6000, NeXT, HP 9000, Sequent, Pyramid, NCR, IBM mainframes, VMS, MS-DOS, and Macintosh. Interested parties should contact:

Gene Egan
Open Computing Security Group
2451 152nd Avenue NE
Redmond, WA 98052
Tel: (206) 883-8721

17.5   KRYPTOKNIGHT

KryptoKnight (Kryptonite—get it?) is an authentication and key distribution system designed by IBM. It is a secret-key protocol and uses either DES in CBC mode (see Section 8.1.3) or a modified version MD5 (see Section 14.5).
    KryptoKnight supports four security services:

- User authentication (called Single Sign-On)

- Two-party authentication

- Key distribution

- Authentication of origin and content of data

From a user's perspective, KryptoKnight is similar to Kerberos. For further information on KryptoKnight and its protocols, read [615,108,109,110].

17.6   ISO AUTHENTICATION FRAMEWORK

Public-key cryptography has been recommended for use with the ISO authentication framework, also known as the X.509 protocols [188]. This framework provides for authentication across networks. Although no particular algorithms have been specified for either security or authentication, the specification calls for an algorithm that can be used for both security and authentication, and one in which the encryption and decryption processes are inverses of each other. (This precludes ElGamal and DSA and strongly implies the RSA algorithm.) There are provisions, however, for multiple algorithms and hash functions.

Certificates

The framework is certificate-based. Each user has a distinct name. A trusted certification authority assigns a unique name to each user and issues a certificate containing the name and the user's public key.

An X.509 certificate looks like [188]:

```
certificate ::= SIGNED SEQUENCE (
  signature   AlgorithmIdentifier,
  issuer   Name,
  validity    Validity ::= SEQUENCE (
    notBefore   UTCTime,
    notAfter    UTCTime)
  subject    Name,
  subjectPublicKeyInfo   SubjectPublicKeyInfo ::= SEQUENCE (
    algorithm   AlgorithmIdentifier,
    subjectPublicKey   BIT STRING))
```

A Certifying Authority (CA) signs all certificates. If Alice and Bob want to communicate, each of them has to verify the signature of the other person's certificate. If they use the same CA, this is easy. If they use different CAs, this is more complicated. Think of a tree structure, with different CAs certifying other CAs and users. On the top there is one master CA. Each CA stores the certificate obtained from its superior CA, as well as all the certificates issued by it. Alice and Bob have to traverse the certification tree, looking for a common trusted point.

Figure 17.6 illustrates this. Alice's certificate is certified by CA_A; Bob's is certified by CA_B. CA_A's certificate (needed to verify CA_A's signature on Alice's certificate) is certified by CA_C. CA_C's certificate is certified by CA_E; CA_E's certificate is certified by CA_F. CA_B's certificate is certified by CA_D; CA_D's certificate is certified by CA_F. This is a common trusted point and one that can certify Alice to Bob and Bob to Alice.

This procedure becomes complicated if Alice and Bob have to search the network for the different certificates, but in reality they can both cache all the certificates to speed up the process.

Certificates have a specific validity period. When a certificate expires, it should be removed from any public directories maintained by the CAs. The issuing CA, however, should maintain a copy of the certificate. It will be required to resolve any disputes that might arise.

The Protocols

Alice wants to communicate with Bob. First she goes to a directory and obtains what is called a "certification path" from Alice to Bob, and Bob's public key. At

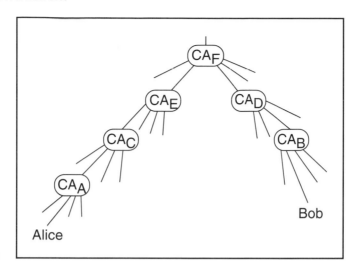

Figure 17.6
Sample certification hierarchy.

this point Alice can initiate either a one-way, two-way, or three-way authentication protocol.

The one-way protocol is a single communication from Alice to Bob. It establishes the identities of both Alice and Bob and the integrity of any information communicated by Alice to Bob. It also prevents any replay attacks in the communication.

The two-way protocol is identical to the one-way protocol, but it also adds a reply from Bob. It establishes that Bob, and not an imposter, sent the reply. It also establishes the secrecy of both communications and prevents replay attacks.

Both the one-way and two-way protocols use timestamps. A three-way protocol adds another message from Alice to Bob and obviates the need for timestamps.

The one-way protocol is:

(1) Alice generates a random number, R_A.

(2) Alice constructs a message, $M = (T_A, R_A, I_B, \text{data})$, in which T_A is Alice's timestamp, I_B is Bob's identity, and data is an arbitrary piece of information. The data may be encrypted with Bob's public key, E_B, for security.

(3) Alice sends $(C_A, D_A(M))$ to Bob.

(4) Bob verifies C_A and obtains E_A. He makes sure these keys have not expired.

(5) Bob uses E_A to decrypt $D_A(M)$. This verifies both Alice's signature and the integrity of the signed information.

(6) Bob checks the I_B in M for accuracy.

(7) Bob checks the T_A in M and confirms that the message is current.

(8) As an option, Bob can check R_A in M against a database of old random numbers to ensure the message is not an old one being replayed.

The two-way protocol consists of the one-way protocol and then a similar one-way protocol from Bob to Alice. After executing steps (1) through (8) of the one-way protocol, the two-way protocol continues with:

(9) Bob generates another random number, R_B.

(10) Bob constructs a message, $M' = (T_B, R_B, I_A, R_A, \text{data})$, in which T_B is Bob's timestamp, I_A is Alice's identity, and data is arbitrary. The data may be encrypted with Alice's public key, E_A, for security. R_A is the random number Alice generated in step (1).

(11) Bob sends $D_B(M')$ to Alice.

(12) Alice uses E_B to decrypt $D_B(M')$. This verifies both Bob's signature and the integrity of the signed information.

(13) Alice checks the I_A in M' for accuracy.

(14) Alice checks the T_B in M' and confirms that the message is current.

(15) As an option, Alice can check the R_B in M' to ensure the message is not an old one being replayed.

The three-way protocol accomplishes the same thing as the two-way protocol, but without timestamps. Steps (1) through (15) are identical to the two-way protocol, with $T_A = T_B = 0$.

(16) Alice checks the received version of R_A against the R_A she sent to Bob in step (3).

(17) Alice sends $D_A(R_B)$ to Bob.

(18) Bob uses E_A to decrypt $D_A(R_B)$. This verifies both Alice's signature and the integrity of the signed information.

(19) Bob checks the received version of R_B against the R_B he sent to Alice in step (10).

17.7   PRIVACY-ENHANCED MAIL (PEM)

PEM is the Internet Privacy-Enhanced Mail standard, adapted by the Internet Architecture Board (IAB) to provide secure electronic mail over the Internet. It was initially designed by the Internet Resources Task Force (IRTF) Privacy and Security Research Group (PSRG), and then handed over to the Internet Engineering Task Force (IETF) PEM Research Group. The PEM protocols provide for encryption, authentication, message integrity, and key management.

The complete PEM protocols were initially detailed in a series of RFCs (Requests for Comment) in [551] and then revised in [552]. The third iteration of the protocols [553,477,554] are summarized in a paper by Matthew Bishop [112,113], a member of the PSRG. The protocols were modified and improved, and the final protocols are detailed in another series of RFCs [555,476,39,468]. Another paper by Matthew Bishop [114] details the changes.

PEM is an inclusive standard. The PEM procedures and protocols are intended to be compatible with a wide range of key-management approaches, including both secret-key and public-key approaches for encryption of data encrypting keys. Symmetric cryptography is used for message-text encryption. Cryptographic hash algorithms are used for message integrity. Other documents specify supporting key-management mechanisms based on the use of public-key certificates; algorithms, modes, and associated identifiers; and details of paper and electronic formats and procedures for the key-management infrastructure being established in support of these services.

Initially, PEM supports only certain algorithms. Messages are encrypted with DES in CBC mode. Authentication, provided by something called a **Message Integrity Check (MIC),** uses either MD2 or MD5. Symmetric key management can use either DES in ECB mode or triple-DES, using two keys (called EDE mode). PEM also supports the use of public-key certificates for key management, using the RSA algorithm (key length up to 1024 bits) and the X.509 standard for certificate structure.

End-to-end cryptography provides three "privacy-enhancement services": confidentiality, authentication, and message integrity. There are no special processing requirements imposed on the electronic mail system. PEM can be incorporated selectively, by site or by user, without impacting the rest of the network.

PEM Documents

There are four PEM documents:

RFC 1421, Part I, Message Encryption and Authentication Procedures: This document defines message encryption and authentication procedures in order to provide privacy-enhanced mail services for electronic mail transfer in the Internet.

RFC 1422, Part II, Certificate-Based Key Management: This document defines a supporting key management architecture and infrastructure, based on public-key certificate techniques to provide keying information to message originators and recipients.

RFC 1423, Part III, Algorithms, Modes, and Identifiers: This document provides definitions, formats, references, and citations for cryptographic algorithms, usage modes, and associated identifiers and parameters.

RFC 1424, Part IV, Key Certification and Related Services: This document describes three types of service in support of PEM: key certification, certificate revocation list (CRL) storage, and CRL retrieval.

Certificates

PEM is compatible with the authentication framework described in [188]. PEM is a superset of X.509; it establishes procedures and conventions for a key management infrastructure for use with PEM and with other protocols, from both the TCP/IP and OSI suites, in the future.

The key-management infrastructure establishes a single root for all certification within the Internet: the Internet Policy Registration Authority (IPRA). The IPRA establishes global policies that apply to all certification effected under this hierarchy. Beneath the IPRA root are Policy Certification Authorities (PCAs), each of which establishes and publishes its policies for registration of users or organizations. Each PCA is certified by the IPRA. Below PCAs, Certification Authorities (CAs) are established to certify users and subordinate organizational entities (e.g., departments, offices, subsidiaries, etc.). Initially, the majority of users are expected to be registered with some organization.

Some PCAs are expected to provide certification for users who wish to register independent of any organization. For users who wish anonymity while taking advantage of PEM privacy facilities, one or more PCAs are expected to be established with policies that allow for registration of users, under subordinate PCAs, who do not wish to disclose their identities.

PEM Messages

The heart of PEM is its message format. Figure 17.7 shows an encrypted message using symmetric key management, Figure 17.8 shows an encrypted message using public-key key management, and Figure 17.9 shows an authenticated (but unencrypted) message using public-key key management.

```
---BEGIN PRIVACY-ENHANCED MESSAGE---
Proc-Type: 4,ENCRYPTED
Content-Domain: RFC822
DEK-Info: DES-CBC,F8143EDE5960C597
Originator-ID-Symmetric: linn@zendia.enet.dec.com,,
Recipient-ID-Symmetric: linn@zendia.enet.dec.com,ptf-kmc,3
Key-Info: DES-ECB,RSA-MD2,9FD3AAD2F2691B9A,B70665BB9BF7CBCDA60195DB94F727D3
Recipient-ID-Symmetric: pem-dev@tis.com,ptf-kmc,4
Key-Info: DES-ECB,RSA-MD2,161A3F75DC82EF26,E2EF532C65CBCFF79F83A2658132DB47

LLrHBOeJzyhP+/fSStdW8okeEnv47jxe7SJ/iN72ohNcUk2jHEUSoH1nvNSIWL9M
8tEjmF/zxB+bATMtPjCUWbz8Lr9wloXIkjHUlBLpvXROUrUzYbkNpkOagV2IzUpk
J6UiRRGcDSvzrsoK+oNvqu6z7Xs5Xfz5rDqUcM1K1Z6720dcBWGGsDLpTpSCnpot
dXd/H5LMDWnonNvPCwQUHt==
---END PRIVACY-ENHANCED MESSAGE---
```

Figure 17.7
Example encapsulated message (symmetric case).

```
——-BEGIN PRIVACY-ENHANCED MESSAGE——-
Proc-Type: 4,ENCRYPTED
Content-Domain: RFC822
DEK-Info: DES-CBC,BFF968AA74691AC1
Originator-Certificate:
 MIIB1TCCAScCAWUwDQYJKoZIhvcNAQECBQAwUTELMAkGA1UEBhMCVVMxIDAeBgNV
 BAoTF1JTQSBEYXRhIFN1Y3VyaXR5LCBJbmMuMQ8wDQYDVQQLEwZCZXRhIDExDzAN
 BgNVBAsTBk5PVEFSWTAeFw05MTA5MDQxODM4MTdaFw05MzA9MDMxODM4MTZaMEUx
 CzAJBgNVBAYTA1VTMSAwHgYDVQQKExdSU0EgRGF0YSBTZWN1cm10eSwgSW5jLjEU
 MBIGA1UEAxMLVGVzdCBVc2VyIDEwWTAKBgRVCAEBAgICAANLADBIAkEAwHZH17i+
 yJcqDtjJCowzTdBJrdAiLAnSC+CnnjOJELyuQiBgkGrgIh3j8/xOfM+YrsyF1u3F
 LZPVtzlndhYFJQIDAQABMAOGCSqGSIb3DQEBAgUAA1kACKrOPqphJYw1j+YPtcIq
 iWlFPuN5jJ79Khfg7ASFxskYkEMjRNZV/HZDZQEhtVaU7Jxfzs2wfX5byMp2X3U/
 5XUXGx7qusDgHQGs7Jk9W8CW1fuSWUgN4w==
Key-Info: RSA,
 I3rRIGXUGWAF8js5wCzRTkdhO34PTHdRZY9Tuvm03M+NM7fx6qc5udixps2LngO+
 wGrtiUm/ovtKdinz6ZQ/aQ==
Issuer-Certificate:
 MIIB3DCCAUgCAQowDQYJKoZIhvcNAQECBQAwTzELMAkGA1UEBhMCVVMxIDAeBgNV
 BAoTF1JTQSBEYXRhIFN1Y3VyaXR5LCBJbmMuMQ8wDQYDVQQLEwZCZXRhIDExDTAL
 BgNVBAsTBFRMQQEwHhcNOTEwOTAxMDgwMDAwWhcNOTIwOTAxMDc1OTU5WjBRMQsw
 CQYDVQQGEwJVUzEgMB4GA1UEChMXUlNBIERhdGEgU2VjdXJpdHksIEluYy4xDzAN
 BgNVBAsTBkJldGEgMTEPMAOGA1UECxMGTk9UQVJZMHAwCgYEVQgBAQICArwDYgAw
 XwJYCsnp61QCxYykN1ODwutF/jMJ3kL+3PjYyHOwk+/9rLg6X65B/LD4bJHtO5XW
 cqAz/7R7XhjYCmOPcqbdzoACZtIlETrKrcJiDYoP+DkZ8k1gCk7hQHpbIwIDAQAB
 MAOGCSqGSIb3DQEBAgUAA38AAICPv4f9Gx/tY4+p+4DB7MV+tKZnvBoy8zgoMGOx
 dD2jMZ/3HsyWKWgSFOeH/AJB3qr9zosG47pyMnTf3aSy2nBO7CMxpUWRBcXUpE+x
 EREZd9++32ofGBIXaialnOgVUn0OzSYgugiQO77nJLDUjOhQehCizEs5wUJ35a5h
MIC-Info: RSA-MD5,RSA,
 UdFJR8u/TIGhfH65ieewe21OW4tooa3vZCvVNGBZirf/7nrgzWDABz8w9NsXSexv
 AjRFbHoNPzBuxwmOAFeAOHJszL4yBvhG
Recipient-ID-Asymmetric:
 MFExCzAJBgNVBAYTA1VTMSAwHgYDVQQKExdSU0EgRGF0YSBTZWN1cm10eSwgSW5j
 LjEPMAOGA1UECxMGQmVOYSAxMQ8wDQYDVQQLEwZOT1RBU1k=,
 66
Key-Info: RSA,
 O6BS1ww9CTyHPtS3bMLD+LOhejdvX6Qv1HK2ds2sQPEaXhX8EhvVphHYTjwekdWv
 7xOZ3Jx2vTAhOYHMcqqCjA==

 qeWlj/YJ2Uf5ng9yznPbtDOmYloSwIuV9FRYx+gzY+8iXd/NQrXHfi6/MhPfPF3d
 jIqCJAxvld2xgqQimUzoS1a4r7kQQ5c/Iua4LqKeq3ciFzEv/MbZhA==
——-END PRIVACY-ENHANCED MESSAGE——-
```

Figure 17.8
Example encapsulated message (asymmetric case).

```
      —-BEGIN PRIVACY-ENHANCED MESSAGE—-
   Proc-Type: 4,MIC-ONLY
   Content-Domain: RFC822
   Originator-Certificate:
    MIIB1TCCAScCAWUwDQYJKoZIhvcNAQECBQAwUTELMAkGA1UEBhMCVVMxIDAeBgNV
    BAoTF1JTQSBEYXRhIFN1Y3VyaXR5LCBJbmMuMQ8wDQYDVQQLEwZCZXRhIDExDzAN
    BgNVBAsTBk5PVEFSWTAeFw05MTA5MDQxODM4MTdaFw05MzA5MDMxODM4MTZaMEUx
    CzAJBgNVBAYTA1VTMSAwHgYDVQQKExdSU0EgRGF0YSBTZWN1cml0eSwgSW5jLjEU
    MBIGA1UEAxMLVGVzdCBVc2VyIDEwWTAKBgRVCAEBAgICAANLADBIAkEAwHZH17i+
    yJcqDtjJCowzTdBJrdAiLAnSC+CnnjOJELyuQiBgkGrgIh3j8/xOfM+YrsyF1u3F
    LZPVtz1ndhYFJQIDAQABMAOGCSqGSIb3DQEBAgUAA1kACKrOPqphJYw1j+YPtcIq
    iW1FPuN5jJ79Khfg7ASFxskYkEMjRNZV/HZDZQEhtVaU7Jxfzs2wfX5byMp2X3U/
    5XUXGx7qusDgHQGs7Jk9W8CW1fuSWUgN4w==
   Issuer-Certificate:
    MIIB3DCCAUgCAQowDQYJKoZIhvcNAQECBQAwTzELMAkGA1UEBhMCVVMxIDAeBgNV
    BAoTF1JTQSBEYXRhIFN1Y3VyaXR5LCBJbmMuMQ8wDQYDVQQLEwZCZXRhIDExDTAL
    BgNVBAsTBFRMQ0EwHhcNOTEwOTAxMDgwMDAwWhcNOTIwOTAxMDc1OTU5WjBRMQsw
    CQYDVQQGEwJVUzEgMB4GA1UEChMXU1NBIERhdGEgU2VjdXJpdHksIE1uYy4xDzAN
    BgNVBAsTBkJ1dEgEgMTEPMAOGA1UECxMGTk9UQVJZMHAwCgYEVQgBAQICArwDYgAw
    XwJYCsnp61QCxYykN1ODwutF/jMJ3kL+3PjYyHOwk+/9rLg6X65B/LD4bJHtO5XW
    cqAz/7R7XhjYCmOPcqbdzoACZtI1ETrKrcJiDYoP+DkZ8k1gCk7hQHpbIwIDAQAB
    MAOGCSqGSIb3DQEBAgUAA38AAICPv4f9Gx/tY4+p+4DB7MV+tKZnvBoy8zgoMGOx
    dD2jMZ/3HsyWKWgSFOeH/AJB3qr9zosG47pyMnTf3aSy2nBO7CMxpUWRBcXUpE+x
    EREZd9++32ofGBIXaialnOgVUnOOzSYgugiQ077nJLDUjOhQehCizEs5wUJ35a5h
   MIC-Info: RSA-MD5,RSA,
    jV2OfH+nnXHU8bnL8kPAad/mSQ1TDZ1bVuxvZAOVRZ5q5+Ej15bQvqNeqOUNQjr6
    EtE7K2QDeVMCyXsdJlA8fA==

    LSBBIG11c3NhZ2UgZm9yIHVzZSBpbiBOZXN0aW5nLgOKLSBGb2xsb3dpbmcgaXMg
    YSBibGFuayBsaW51OgOKDQpUaGlzIG1zIHRoZSBlbmQuDQo=
      —-END PRIVACY-ENHANCED MESSAGE—-
```

Figure 17.9
Example encapsulated MIC-ONLY message (asymmetric case).

The first field is "Proc-Type," and identifies the type of processing performed on the message. There are three types of messages. The "ENCRYPTED" specifier signifies that the message is encrypted and authenticated. The "MIC-ONLY" and "MIC-CLEAR" specifier indicates that the message is signed, but not encrypted. MIC-CLEAR messages are not encoded, and can be read using non-PEM software. MIC-ONLY messages must be transformed to a human-readable form before being read, so PEM software is needed. A PEM message is always signed; it is optionally encrypted.

The next field, "Content-Domain," has nothing to do with security. It specifies the type of mail message.

The "DEK-Info" field specifies information pertaining to the **Data Exchange Key (DEK),** the encryption algorithm used to encrypt the text and any parameters associated with the encryption algorithm. Only one algorithm is currently specified: DES in CBC mode. This is specified by "DES-CBC." The second field specifies the Initialization Vector, used by DES in CBC mode. Other algorithms may be specified by PEM in the future; their use will be noted in the DEK-Info and in other fields that identify algorithms.

For messages with symmetric key management, the next field is "Originator-ID-Symmetric." There are three subfields. The first subfield identifies the sender by a unique electronic mail address. The second subfield is optional and identifies the authority that issued the interchange key. The third subfield is an optional Version/Expiration subfield.

Continuing with the symmetric key-management case, the next field deals with the recipients. There are two fields for each recipient: "Recipient-ID-Symmetric" and "Key-Info." The "Recipient-ID-Symmetric" field has three subfields; it identifies the receiver in the same way that "Originator-ID-Symmetric identified the sender.

The "Key-Info" field specifies the key-management parameters. This field has four subfields. The first subfield specifies the algorithm used to encrypt the DEK. Since the key management in this message is symmetric, the sender and receiver have to share a common key. This is called the **Interchange Key (IK),** which is used to encrypt the DEK. The DEK can be either encrypted using DES in Electronic Codebook Mode (denoted by "DES-ECB") or triple-DES (denoted by "DES-EDE") for DES-Encrypt Decrypt Encrypt. The second subfield specifies the MIC algorithm. It can be either MD2 (denoted by "RSA-MD2") or MD5 (denoted by "RSA-MD5"). The third subfield is the DEK, encrypted with the IK. The fourth field is the MIC, also encrypted with the IK.

For messages with public-key (asymmetric) key management, the headers are different. After the "DEK-Info" field comes the "Originator-Certificate" field. The certificate follows the X.509 standard (see Section 17.6). The next field is "Key-Info." There are two subfields. The first subfield specifies the public-key algorithm used to encrypt the DEK; currently only RSA is supported. The next subfield is the DEK, encrypted in the originator's public key. This is an optional field, intended to permit the originator to decrypt an individual message in the event that it is returned by the mail system. The next field "Issuer-Certificate," is the certificate of whomever signed the Originator-Certificate.

Continuing with the asymmetric key-management case, the next field is "MIC-Info." The first subfield specifies the algorithm under which the MIC was computed. The second subfield specifies the algorithm under which the MIC was signed. The third subfield consists of the MIC, signed by the sender's private key.

Still continuing with asymmetric key management, the next fields deal with the recipients. There are two fields for each recipient: "Recipient-ID-Asymmetric" and "Key-Info." The "Recipient-ID-Asymmetric" field has two subfields. The first identifies the authority that issued the receiver's public key; the second is an optional Version/Expiration subfield. The "Key-Info" field specifies the key-management parameters. The first subfield identifies the algorithm used to encrypt the message; the second subfield is the DEK, encrypted with the receiver's public key.

Security of PEM

RSA keys in PEM can range from 508 bits to 1024 bits. This should be long enough for anyone's security needs. A more likely attack would be against the key-management protocols. Mallet could steal your private key—it should never be written down anywhere—or attempt to fool you into accepting a bogus public key. The key certification provisions of PEM make this unlikely if everyone follows proper procedures, but people have been known to be sloppy.

A more insidious attack would be for Mallet to modify the implementation of PEM running on your system. The modified implementation could surreptitiously send Mallet all of your mail, encrypted with his public key. It could even send him a copy of your private key. If the modified implementation works well, you will never know what is happening.

There's no real way to prevent this kind of attack. You could use a one-way hash function and fingerprint the PEM code. Then, each time you run it, you could check the fingerprint for modification. But Mallet could modify the fingerprint code at the same time he modifies the PEM code. You could fingerprint the fingerprint code, but Mallet could modify that as well. If Mallet can get access to your machine, he can subvert the security of PEM.

The moral is that you can never really trust a piece of software if you cannot trust the hardware it is running on. For most people, this kind of paranoia is unwarranted. For some, it is very real.

TIS-PEM

Trusted Information Systems, partially supported by the U.S. government Advanced Research Projects Agency, has designed and implemented a reference implementation of Privacy-Enhanced Mail (TIS/PEM). The implementation was developed for UNIX-based platforms but has also been ported to VMS. A DOS and MS Windows port is under development.

The PEM specifications currently indicate that RSA and DES are to be used in PEM. However, there is provision within the specifications for additional suites of algorithms to be used within the same framework, and whenever an algorithm is used, it is labeled with an identifier. In keeping with this architecture, the TIS/PEM system is modular and is written to accommodate multiple suites of algorithms.

Including support for other algorithms in TIS/PEM only requires a cryptographic library to perform the actual operation, a small set of routines to interface TIS/PEM to the cryptographic library, and an entry in a table of cryptographic algorithms supported. In the Internet distribution of TIS/PEM, the RSA routines are provided via RSAREF.

Although the PEM specifications indicate a single certification hierarchy for use by the Internet, TIS/PEM supports the existence of multiple certification hierarchies. This is accomplished by allowing sites to specify a set of certificates that are to be considered valid, including all certificates issued by them. In addition, sites are not required to join the Internet hierarchy in order to acquire TIS/PEM.

TIS/PEM is currently available to all U.S. and Canadian organizations and citizens upon request (see contact information below). It will be distributed in source code form. Distribution via anonymous FTP is currently being investigated. Interested parties should contact:

Privacy-Enhanced Mail
Trusted Information Systems, Inc.
3060 Washington Road (Rte. 97)
Glenwood, MD 21738
Tel: (301) 854-6889
Fax: (301) 854-5363
Internet: pem-info@tis.com

RIPEM

RIPEM is a program, written by Mark Riorden, that implements the PEM protocols. Although technically not public domain, the program is publicly available and can be used royalty-free for personal, noncommercial applications. A license for its use is included with the documentation.

The code cannot be exported. To quote from the program's documentation:

> Please do not export the cryptographic code in this distribution outside the USA or Canada. This a personal request from me, the author of RIPEM, and a condition of your use of RIPEM.

Of course, U.S. government laws don't apply outside the United States, and people have ignored the export rules. RIPEM code has found its way outside the country and it is available worldwide.

RIPEM uses RSA Data Security's reference implementation of the RSA algorithm: RSA-REF. At this writing, RIPEM is not a complete implementation of the PEM protocols; it does not implement certificates for authenticating keys. Riorden plans to implement this feature, and it will be completed soon after this book is published.

Before writing RIPEM, Riorden wrote a similar program called RPEM. This was intended to be a public-domain electronic-mail encryption program. To try to avoid patent issues, Riorden used Rabin's algorithm (see Section 12.6). Public Key Partners claimed that their patents were broad enough to cover all of public-key cryptography and threatened to sue; Riorden stopped distributing the program.

RPEM isn't really used anymore. It is not compatible with RIPEM. Since RIPEM can be used with the full blessing of Public Key Partners, there is no reason to use RPEM instead.

17.8   MESSAGE SECURITY PROTOCOL (MSP)

The Message Security Protocol (MSP) is the military equivalent of PEM. It was developed by the NSA in the late 1980s under the Secure Data Network System (SDNS) program. It is an X.400-compatible application-level protocol for securing electronic mail. It will be used for signing and encrypting messages in the Department of Defense's planned Defense Message System (DMS) network.

The Preliminary Message Security Protocol (PMSP), to be used for "unclassified but sensitive" messages, is a version of MSP adapted for use with both X.400 and TCP/IP. This protocol is also called "Mosaic."

Like PEM, MSP and PMSP software applications are flexibly designed to accommodate a variety of algorithms for a variety of security functions, including signing, hashing, and encryption. PMSP will work with the Capstone chip (see Section 17.11).

17.9   PRETTY GOOD PRIVACY (PGP)

Pretty Good Privacy (PGP) is a public-domain encryption program designed by Philip Zimmermann [908]. It uses IDEA for data encryption, RSA (with a 512-bit, 1024-bit, or 1280-bit key) for key management, and MD5 as a one-way hash function. PGP also compresses files before encryption.

PGP's random public keys uses a probabilistic primality tester, and gets its initial seeds from measuring the user's keyboard latency while typing. PGP generates random IDEA keys using the method delineated in ANSI X9.17, Appendix C [30], with IDEA as the symmetric algorithm instead of DES. PGP also encrypts the user's private key using a hashed pass phrase instead of a password.

PGP-encrypted messages have layered security. The only thing cryptanalysts can learn about an encrypted message is who the recipient is, assuming they know the recipient's key ID. Only after the recipient decrypts the message do they learn who signed the message, if it is signed. After verifying the signature they decrypt the message and learn what it says. Contrast this approach with PEM, which leaves quite a bit of information about the sender, recipient, and message in the unencrypted header.

The most interesting aspect of PGP is its distributed approach to key management (see Section 7.3). There are no key certification authorities. All users generate and distribute their own public key. Users can sign one another's public keys, adding extra confidence to the key's validity. Someone who signs another's public key becomes an introducer for that person. When users receive a new public key, they examine the list of introducers who have signed the key. If one of the introducers is someone they trust, then they have reason to accept the new key as valid. If two of the introducers are people they trust marginally, then they have some reason to accept it as valid. This is all automatic: Tell PGP who you trust and how much, assess your own trust level, and proceed. PGP is well designed, nicely coded, and in the public domain. It's the closest you're likely to get to military-grade encryption.

17.10 CLIPPER

Clipper is an NSA-designed, tamper-resistant VLSI chip that uses the Skipjack encryption algorithm (see Section 11.12). Each chip has a special key, not needed for messages. It is used only to encrypt a copy of each user's message key. Anyone knowing the special key can decrypt wiretapped communications protected with this chip. This ensures government personnel the ability to conduct electronic surveillance. The claim is that only the government will know this key and will use it only if/when authorized by a court.

This special key is split (see Section 3.5) and stored in two key-escrow databases. According to the director of NIST [472]:

> A "key-escrow" system is envisioned that would ensure that the "Clipper Chip" is used to protect the privacy of law-abiding Americans. Each device containing the chip will have two unique "keys," numbers that will be needed by authorized government agencies to decode messages encoded by the device. When the device is manufactured, the two keys would be deposited separately in two "key-escrow" data bases established by the Attorney General. Access to these keys would be limited to government officials with legal authorization to conduct a wiretap.

At this writing, much about the Clipper chip, including the actual key-escrow mechanism, is undefined. The following section describes what I do know [472,653,876,270,56].

The Clipper chip is designed for the AT&T commercial secure voice products. The functionality of the chip is specified by NSA, the logic is designed by Mykotronx, Inc., and the chip is fabricated by VLSI, Inc. (at this writing there is talk of a second source for the chips).

Each chip is uniquely programmed before being sold to customers. The chip programming equipment writes the following information into a special memory (called VROM or VIA-Link) on the chip:

- A serial number, unique to the chip

- A unit key, unique to the chip

- A family key, common to a family of chips

- Any specialized control software

Upon generation (or entry) of a session key in the chip, the chip performs the following actions:

(1) Encrypts the 80-bit session key under the unit key, producing an 80-bit intermediate result;

(2) Concatenates the 80-bit result with the 25-bit serial number and a 23-bit authentication pattern (total of 128 bits);

(3) Encrypts this 128 bits with the family key to produce a 128-bit cipher block chain called the Law Enforcement Field (LEF);

(4) Transmits the LEF at least once to the intended receiving Clipper chip;

(5) The two communicating Clipper chips use this field together with a random IV to establish synchronization.

(6) Once synchronized, the Clipper chips use the session key to encrypt/decrypt data in both directions.

The point of this complicated process is to allow someone with the unique serial number and unique unit key to decrypt messages encrypted with this chip. This is the back door that the government is embedding into the system; it is not a back door to the Skipjack algorithm, but a back door to Clipper's key-management scheme. To prevent someone from circumventing this scheme, the chips can be programmed not to enter secure mode if the LEF field has been tampered with (e.g., modified, superencrypted, replaced). The chip also is resistant to reverse-engineering "against a very sophisticated, well funded adversary" [653].

There are enormous privacy issues associated with this scheme. Both the Computer Professionals for Social Responsibility and the Electronic Frontier Foundation are actively campaigning against any key-escrow mechanism that gives the government the right to eavesdrop on citizens.

17.11 CAPSTONE

CAPSTONE is an NSA-developed VLSI cryptographic chip that implements the Skipjack algorithm as well as the same key-escrow features as the Clipper chip. In addition, the Capstone chip includes the following functions [654]:

- The Digital Signature Algorithm (DSA).

- The Secure Hashing Algorithm (SHA).

- A general purpose exponentiation algorithm.

- A general purpose, random number generator that uses a pure noise source.

A key exchange algorithm (probably Diffie-Hellman) is also programmable on the chip and uses the above four functions.

CHAPTER
18

Politics

18.1 NATIONAL SECURITY AGENCY (NSA)

The NSA is the National Security Agency (although, among professionals, it's been jokingly referred to as "No Such Agency" and "Never Say Anything"), the official security body of the U.S. government. President Harry Truman created the agency in the late 1940s under the Department of Defense, and for many years its very existence was kept secret. The NSA's mandate is to listen in on and decode all foreign communications of interest to the security of the United States.

NSA conducts research in cryptology, both in designing secure algorithms to protect our communications, and in designing cryptanalytic techniques to listen in on their communications. The NSA is known to be the largest employer of mathematicians in the world; it is also the largest purchaser of computer hardware in the world. Governments in general have always been prime employers of cryptologists. The NSA probably possesses cryptographic expertise many years ahead of the public state of the art and can undoubtedly break many of the systems used in practice; but for reasons of national security almost all information about the NSA is classified.

The NSA uses its power to restrict the public availability of cryptography, so as to prevent national enemies from employing encryption methods too strong for the NSA to break. James Massey [563] discusses this struggle between academic and military research in cryptography:

> If one regards cryptology as the prerogative of government, one accepts that most cryptologic research will be conducted behind closed doors. Without doubt, the number of workers engaged today in such secret research in cryptology far exceeds that of those engaged in open research in cryptology.

For only about 10 years has there in fact been widespread open research in cryptology. There have been, and will continue to be, conflicts between these two research communities. Open research is common quest for knowledge that depends for its vitality on the open exchange of ideas via conference presentations and publications in scholarly journals. But can a government agency, charged with responsibilities of breaking the ciphers of other nations, countenance the publication of a cipher that it cannot break? Can a researcher in good conscience publish such a cipher that might undermine the effectiveness of his own government's code-breakers? One might argue that publication of a provably-secure cipher would force all governments to behave like Stimson's "gentlemen," but one must be aware that open research in cryptography is fraught with political and ethical considerations of a severity more than in most scientific fields. The wonder is not that some conflicts have occurred between government agencies and open researchers in cryptology, but rather that these conflicts (at least those of which we are aware) have been so few and so mild.

James Bamford wrote a fascinating book about the NSA [40].

18.2 NATIONAL COMPUTER SECURITY CENTER (NCSC)

The National Computer Security Center is a branch of the NSA that is responsible for the government's trusted computer program. Currently, the center evaluates commercial security products (both hardware and software), sponsors and publishes research, develops technical guidelines, and generally provides advice, support, and training. Government reorganizations may change who does what, but the NCSC is always a good place to start.

The NCSC publishes the infamous "Orange Book" [273]. Its actual title is the *Department of Defense Trusted Computer System Evaluation Criteria,* but that's a mouthful to say and the book has an orange cover. The Orange Book attempts to define security requirements, gives computer manufacturers an objective way to measure the security of their systems, and guides them as to what to build into their secure products.

The Orange Book defines four broad divisions of security protection. It also defines classes of protection within some of those divisions. They are, in order of increasing security:

D: Minimal Security

C: Discretionary Protection
    C1: Discretionary Security Protection
    C2: Controlled Access Protection

B: Mandatory Protection
    B1: Labeled Security Protection
    B2: Structured Protection
    B3: Security Domains

       A: Verified Protection
        A1: Verified Design

Sometimes manufacturers say things like "we have C2 security." This is what they're talking about. For more information on this, read [762].

The NCSC has published a whole series of books on computer security. Sometimes called the "Rainbow Books" (because all the covers have different colors), they all discuss some aspect of computer security. For example, *Trusted Network Interpretation of the Trusted Computer System Evaluation Criteria* [640], sometimes called the "Red Book," interprets the Orange Book for networks and network equipment. The *Trusted Database Management System Interpretation of the Trusted Computer System Evaluation Criteria* [641] does the same for databases. There are now 30 of these books.

For a complete set of the Rainbow Books, write:

Director, National Security Agency
INFOSEC Awareness
Attention: C81
9800 Savage Road
Fort George G. Meade, MD 20755-6000
Tel: (301) 766-8729

18.3   NATIONAL INSTITUTE OF STANDARDS AND TECHNOLOGY (NIST)

The NIST is the National Institute of Standards and Technology, a division of the U.S. Department of Commerce. Formerly the NBS (National Bureau of Standards), it changed its name in 1988. Through its Computer Systems Laboratory (CSL), NIST promotes open standards and interoperability that it hopes will spur the economic development of computer-based industries. To this end, it issues standards and guidelines that it hopes will be adopted by all computer systems in the United States. Official standards are published as FIPS (Federal Information Processing Standards) publications.

If you want copies of any FIPS (or any other NIST publication), contact:

National Technical Information Service (NTIS)
U.S. Department of Commerce
5285 Port Royal Road
Springfield, VA 22161
Tel: (703) 487-4650

NIST also runs a public-access BBS for computer security, at (301) 948-5717 (2400,n,8,1).

In 1987 Congress passed the Computer Security Act, which gives NIST a mandate to define standards for ensuring the security of sensitive but unclassified information in government computer systems. (Classified information and

"Warner Amendment" data is under the jurisdiction of the NSA.) The Act authorizes NIST to work with other government agencies and private industry in evaluating proposed technology standards.

NIST issues standards for cryptographic functions. U.S. government agencies are required to use them for sensitive but unclassified information. Often the private sector adopts these standards as well. NIST adopted DES as the standard for data encryption; they have proposed DSS and SHS as the digital signature standard and the one-way hash function standard.

All these algorithms were developed with the help of the NSA. Some people have criticized NIST for allowing the NSA to have too much control over these standards, since the NSA's interests may not coincide with those of NIST. It is unclear how much actual influence NSA has on the design and development of the algorithms.

Given NIST's limited staff, budget, and resources, NSA's involvement is probably considerable. With a budget rumored of about $20+ billion, the NSA has significant resources to bring to the table, including a computer facility second to none.

The official "Memorandum of Understanding" (MOU) between the two agencies reads:

MEMORANDUM OF UNDERSTANDING BETWEEN THE DIRECTOR OF THE NATIONAL INSTITUTE OF STANDARDS AND TECHNOLOGY AND THE DIRECTOR OF THE NATIONAL SECURITY AGENCY CONCERNING THE IMPLEMENTATION OF PUBLIC LAW 100-235
Recognizing that:

A. Under Section 2 of the Computer Security Act of 1987 (Public Law 100-235), (the Act), the National Institute of Standards and Technology (NIST) has the responsibility within the Federal Government for:

1. Developing technical, management, physical, and administrative standards and guidelines for the cost-effective security and privacy of sensitive information in Federal computer systems as defined in the Act; and,

2. Drawing on the computer system technical security guidelines of the National Security Agency (NSA) in this regard where appropriate.

B. Under Section 3 of the Act, the NIST is to coordinate closely with other agencies and offices, including the NSA, to assure:

1. Maximum use of all existing and planned programs, materials, studies, and reports relating to computer systems security and privacy, in order to avoid unnecessary and costly duplication of effort; and,

2. To the maximum extent feasible, that standards developed by the NIST under the Act are consistent and compatible with standards and procedures developed for the protection of classified information in Federal computer systems.

C. Under the Act, the Secretary of Commerce has the responsibility, which he has delegated to the Director of NIST, for appointing the members of the Computer System Security and Privacy Advisory Board, at least one of whom shall be from the NSA.

Therefore, in furtherance of the purposes of this MOU, the Director of the NIST and the Director of the NSA hereby agree as follows:

I. The NIST will:

1. Appoint to the Computer Security and Privacy Advisory Board at least one representative nominated by the Director of the NSA.

2. Draw upon computer system technical security guidelines developed by the NSA to the extent that the NIST determines that such guidelines are consistent with the requirements for protecting sensitive information in Federal computer systems.

3. Recognize the NSA-certified rating of evaluated trusted systems under the Trusted Computer Security Evaluation Criteria Program without requiring additional evaluation.

4. Develop telecommunications security standards for protecting sensitive unclassified computer data, drawing upon the expertise and products of the National Security Agency, to the greatest extent possible, in meeting these responsibilities in a timely and cost-effective manner.

5. Avoid duplication where possible in entering into mutually agreeable arrangements with the NSA for the NSA support.

6. Request the NSA's assistance on all matters related to cryptographic algorithms and cryptographic techniques including but not limited to research, development valuation, or endorsement.

II. The NSA will:

1. Provide the NIST with technical guidelines in trusted technology, telecommunications security, and personal identification that may be used in cost-effective systems for protecting sensitive computer data.

2. Conduct or initiate research and development programs in trusted technology, telecommunications security, cryptographic techniques and personal identification methods.

3. Be responsive to the NIST's requests for assistance in respect to all matters related to cryptographic algorithms and cryptographic techniques including but not limited to research, development, evaluation, or endorsement.

4. Establish the standards and endorse products for application to secure systems covered in 10 USC Section 2315 (the Warner Amendment).

5. Upon request by Federal agencies, their contractors and other government-sponsored entities, conduct assessments of the hostile intelligence threat to federal information systems, and provide technical assistance and recommend endorsed products for application to secure systems against that threat.

III. The NIST and the NSA shall:

1. Jointly review agency plans for the security and privacy of computer systems submitted to NIST and NSA pursuant to section 6(b) of the Act.

2. Exchange technical standards and guidelines as necessary to achieve the purposes of the Act.

3. Work together to achieve the purposes of this memorandum with the greatest efficiency possible, avoiding unnecessary duplication of effort.

4. Maintain an ongoing, open dialogue to ensure that each organization remains abreast of emerging technologies and issues affecting automated information system security in computer-based systems.

5. Establish a Technical Working Group to review and analyze issues of mutual interest pertinent to protection of systems that process sensitive or other unclassified information. The Group shall be composed of six federal

employees, three each selected by NIST and NSA and to be augmented as necessary by representatives of other agencies. Issues may be referred to the group by either the NSA Deputy Director for Information Security or the NIST Deputy Director or may be generated and addressed by the group upon approval by the NSA DDI or NIST Deputy Director. Within days of the referral of an issue to the Group by either the NSA Deputy Director for Information Security or the NIST Deputy Director, the Group will respond with a progress report and plan for further analysis, if any.

6. Exchange work plans on an annual basis on all research and development projects pertinent to protection of systems that process sensitive or other unclassified information, including trusted technology, for protecting the integrity and availability of data, telecommunications security and personal identification methods. Project updates will be exchanged quarterly, and project reviews will be provided by either party upon request of the other party.

7. Ensure the Technical Working Group reviews prior to public disclosure all matters regarding technical systems security techniques to be developed for use in protecting sensitive information in federal computer systems to ensure they are consistent with the national security of the United States. If NIST and NSA are unable to resolve such an issue within 60 days, either agency may elect to raise the issue to the Secretary of Defense and the Secretary of Commerce. It is recognized that such an issue may be referred to the President through the NSC for resolution. No action shall be taken on such an issue until it is resolved.

8. Specify additional operational agreements in annexes to this MOU as they are agreed to by NSA and NIST.

IV. Either party may elect to terminate this MOU upon six months written notice. This MOU is effective upon approval of both signatories.

/signed/

RAYMOND G. KAMMER

Acting Director, National Institute of Standards and Technology, 24 March 1989

W. O. STUDEMAN

Vice Admiral, U.S. Navy; Director, National Security Agency, 23 March 1989

18.4   RSA DATA SECURITY, INC.

RSA Data Security, Inc. (RSADSI) was founded in 1982 to develop, license, and market the RSA patent. It has some commercial products, including a stand-alone E-mail security package and various cryptographic libraries (available in either source or object form). RSADSI also markets the RC2 and RC4 symmetric algorithms (see Section 11.8). RSA Laboratories provides cryptographic consulting services.

Anyone interested in either their patents or products should contact:

Edward Franklin, Jr.
Director of Sales
RSA Data Security, Inc.
100 Marine Parkway
Redwood City, CA 94065

Tel: (415) 595-8782
Fax: (415) 595-1873

18.5 INTERNATIONAL ASSOCIATION OF CRYPTOGRAPHIC RESEARCH (IACR)

The International Association of Cryptographic Research is the worldwide cryptographic research organization. Its stated purpose is to advance the theory and practice of cryptology and related fields. Membership is open to any person. The association sponsors two annual conferences, Crypto and Eurocrypt, and publishes *The Journal of Cryptology* and the *IACR Newsletter*.

The address of the IACR Business Office changes whenever the president does. The current address is:

IACR Business Office
Aarhus Science Park
Gustav Wieds Vej 10
DK-8000 Aarhus C
Denmark

18.6 SCI.CRYPT

Sci.crypt is the Internet newsgroup for cryptography. Most of the postings are political, and most of the rest are requests for information or basic questions. Occasionally there are nuggets of new and useful information in the field.

18.7 CYPHERPUNKS

The cypherpunks are an informal group of people interested in teaching and learning about cryptography. They also experiment with cryptography and try to put it into use. In their opinion, all the cryptographic research in the world doesn't do society any good unless it gets used.

Interested parties can send electronic mail to:

cypherpunks-request@toad.com

18.8   RESEARCH AND DEVELOPMENT IN ADVANCED COMMUNICATION TECHNOLOGIES IN EUROPE (RACE)

The RACE program was launched by the European Community to support pre-competitive and pre-normative work in communications standards and technologies to support Integrated Broad-band Communication (IBC). As part of that effort, RACE established the RIPE (RACE Integrity Primitives Evaluation) to put together a portfolio of techniques to meet the anticipated security requirements of IBC.

Six leading European cryptography research groups made up the RIPE consortium: Center for Mathematics and Computer Science, Amsterdam; Siemens AG; Philips Crypto BV; Royal PTT Nederland NV, PTT Research; Katholieke Universiteit Leuven; and Arhus Universitet. After a 350 man-month project, the consortium published *RIPE Integrity Primitives* [727]. The report included an introduction and some basic integrity concepts, and these primitives: MDC-4 (see Section 14.11), RIPE-MD (see Section 14.8), RIPE-MAC (see Section 14.14), IBC Hash, SKID (see Section 3.2), RSA, COMSET (see Section 16.1), and RSA key generation.

18.9   ELECTRONIC FRONTIER FOUNDATION (EFF)

The Electronic Frontier Foundation (EFF) is protecting civil rights into cyberspace. With respect to cryptographic policy in the United States, they believe that information and access to cryptography are fundamental rights, and therefore should be free of government restriction. They organize the Digital Privacy and Security Working Group, a coalition of fifty organizations. This working group successfully opposed the digital telephony initiative of the Bush administration, and is working on opposing the CLIPPER initiative of the Clinton administration. The EFF has also been examining into the 1st Amendment implications on export controls in cryptography.

Anyone interested in joining the EFF should contact:

Electronic Frontier Foundation
1001 G Street NW, Suite 950E
Washington D.C. 20001

Tel: (202) 347-5400
Fax: (202) 393-5509
Internet: eff@eff.org

18.10   COMPUTER PROFESSIONALS FOR SOCIAL RESPONSIBILITY (CPSR)

The Computer Professionals for Social Responsibility (CPSR) is a national membership organization concerned with the application of technology and its social implications. They try to represent the public's interest in policy debates that usually involve the government and large corporations.

The CPSR's interest in cryptography is part of its Project on Civil Liberties and Computing. They believe that the process of developing cryptographic policy be as open as possible. To that end, they seek to obtain information on United States cryptographic policy. They have successfully sued NIST and NSA for information concerning the respective roles of the two agencies in development of DSA. In May 1993 the CPSR filed suit against NSA under the Freedom of Information Act, seeking the disclosure of documentation concerning the CLIPPER chip proposal.

Anyone interested in joining the CPSR should contact:

Computer Professionals for Social Responsibility
P.O. Box 717
Palo Alto, CA 94301

Tel: (415) 322-3778
Internet: cpsr@cpsr.org

18.11   PATENTS

Software patents are an issue much larger than the scope of this book. Whether they're good or bad, they exist. Algorithms, cryptographic algorithms included, can be patented in the United States. IBM patented the DES algorithm [311]. Almost every public-key algorithm is patented. NIST has even applied for patents for DSS. Some cryptography patents have been blocked by intervention by the NSA, under the authority of the Invention Secrecy Act of 1940 and the National Security Act of 1947.

There are a lot of public-key cryptography patents in existence. The first public-key patent was issued in 1980 to Hellman, Diffie, and Merkle [426]. Another 1980 patent covers Merkle-Hellman knapsacks [428]. The RSA patent was issued in 1983 [751]; the Pohlig-Hellman patent in 1984 [430].

These five patents (see Table 18.1) are held by Public Key Partners (PKP) of Sunnyvale, California, a consortium of RSADSI, Cylink, Inc., Stanford University, and MIT. The details of how the consortium operates is secret, along with the percentage ownership of each entity. They claim that the patents, and 4,218,582 in particular, apply to *all uses* of public-key cryptography.

TABLE 18.1
Public Key Partners' Patents

PATENT #	DATE	INVENTORS	PATENT COVERS:
4,200,770	3/29/80	Hellman, Diffie, Merkle	Diffie-Hellman Key Exchange
4,218,582	8/19/80	Hellman, Merkle	Merkle-Hellman Knapsacks
4,405,829	9/20/83	Rivest, Shamir, Adleman	RSA
4,424,414	3/3/84	Hellman, Pohlig	Pohlig-Hellman
4,995,082	2/19/91	Schnorr	Schnorr Signatures

In [353], PKP writes:

> These patents [4,200,770, 4,218,582, 4,405,829, and 4,424,414] cover all known methods of practicing the art of Public Key, including the variations collectively known as ElGamal.
>
> Due to the broad acceptance of RSA digital signatures throughout the international community, Public Key Partners strongly endorses its incorporation in a digital signature standard. We assure all interested parties that Public Key Partners will comply with all of the policies of ANSI and the IEEE concerning the availability of licenses to practice this art. Specifically, in support of any RSA signature standard which may be adopted, Public Key Partners hereby gives its assurance that licenses to practice RSA signatures will be available under reasonable terms and conditions on a non-discriminatory basis.

Whether or not this is true depends on with whom you talk. PKP's licenses have mostly been secret, so there is no way to check if the licenses are standard. Although they claim to have never denied a license to anyone, at least two companies have been denied a license. PKP guards its patents closely, threatening anyone who tries to use public-key cryptography without a license. In part, this is brought about by U.S. patent law. If you hold a patent and fail to prosecute an infringement, you can lose your patent. There has been much talk about whether the patents are legal, but so far it has all been talk. All legal challenges to PKP's patents have been settled before judgment.

I am not going to dispense legal advice in this book. Maybe the RSA patent will not hold up in court. Maybe the patents do not apply to the entirety of public-key cryptography. Perhaps someone will eventually win a suit against PKP or RSADSI. However, keep in mind that corporations with large legal departments like IBM, Microsoft, Lotus, Apple, Novell, Digital, and Sun have all licensed RSA for use in their products rather than fight them in court. And Boeing, Shell Oil, DuPont, Raytheon, and Citicorp have licensed RSA for their own internal use.

In a recent case, PKP brought suit against the TRW Corporation for using the ElGamal algorithm without a license. TRW claimed they did not need a license. PKP and TRW reached a settlement in June 1992. The details of the settlement are unknown, but they included an agreement by TRW to license the patents. This does not bode well; TRW can afford good lawyers, and I can only assume that if they thought they could win the suit without spending an unreasonable amount of money, they would have fought.

Patents are good for only 17 years. On September 20, 2000, RSA will enter the public domain.

18.12 EXPORT RULES

According to the U.S. government, cryptography is a munition. This means it is covered under the same rules as a TOW missile or an F-16. If you sell cryptography overseas without the proper export license, then you're an international arms trafficker. Unless you think time in a Federal penitentiary would look good on your resume, pay attention to the rules.

There are two government agencies that control export of encryption software. One is the Bureau of Export Administration (BXA) in the Department of Commerce, authorized by the Export Administration Regulations (EAR). Another is the Office of Defense Trade Controls (DTC) in the State Department, authorized by the Defense Trade Regulations. As a rule of thumb, BXA (which works with COCOM) has less stringent requirements, but DTC (which takes orders from NSA) wants to see everything first and can refuse to transfer jurisdiction to BXA.

The Defense Trade Regulations [275] (formerly called the International Traffic in Arms Regulation (ITAR) [274]) regulates this stuff. (The Office of Defense Trade Controls used to be called the Office of Munitions Controls; presumably this is a massive public relations effort designed to make us forget that we're dealing with guns and bombs.) Historically, the DTC has been reluctant to grant export licenses for encryption products stronger than a certain level—not that they are ever public about exactly what that level is.

The following sections, which are relevant to cryptography, are excerpted from the Defense Trade Regulations [274,275]:

Part 120—Purpose, Background and Definitions
§ 120.1 General.
(a) Purpose. Section 38 of the Arms Export Control Act (22 U.S.C. 2778) authorizes the President to control the export and import of defense articles and defense services. It is the purpose of this subchapter to implement this authority. The statutory authority of the President to promulgate regulations with respect to exports of defense articles and defense services was delegated to the Secretary of State by Executive Order 11958, as amended (42 FR 4311). By virtue of delegations of authority by the Secretary of State, these regulations are primarily administered by the Director of the Office of Defense Trade Controls, Bureau of Politico-Military Affairs, Department of State (35 FR 5422).
§ 120.10 Export—permanent and temporary.
Export means:
(1) Sending or taking defense articles out of the United States in any manner, except by mere travel outside of the United States by a person whose personal knowledge includes technical data; or
(2) Transferring registration, control or ownership to a foreign person of any aircraft, vessel, or satellite covered by the U.S. Munitions List, whether in the United States or abroad; or
(3) Disclosing or transferring in the United States any defense articles to an embassy, any agency or subdivision of a foreign government (e.g., diplomatic missions); or
(4) Disclosing or transferring technical data to a foreign person, whether in the United States or abroad; or
(5) Performing a defense service on behalf of, or for the benefit of, a foreign person, whether in the United States or abroad.
A launch vehicle or payload shall not, by the launching of such vehicle, be considered export for the purposes of this subchapter. Most of the

requirements of the subchapter relate only to exports, as defined above. However, for certain limited purposes, the controls of this subchapter apply to sales and other transfers of defense articles and defense services (see, e.g., Section 126.1) of this subchapter.

§ 120.11 Foreign person.

Foreign person means any natural person who is not a "citizen or intending citizen" of the United States within the meaning of 8 U.S.C. 1324 b(a)(3). It also means any foreign corporation, business association, partnership, society, trust, or any other entity or group that is not incorporated or organized to do business in the United States, as well as *international* organizations, foreign governments and any agency or subdivision of foreign governments (e.g., diplomatic missions). The term "intending citizen" means a person who has been lawfully admitted to the United States for permanent residence (and maintains such residence) under the Immigration and Naturalization Act (8 U.S.C. 101(a), 1101(a), 60 Stat. 163).

§ 120.17 Person.

Person means a natural person as well as a corporation, business association, partnership, society, trust, or any other entity, organization or group, including governmental entitles. If a provision in this subchapter does not refer exclusively to a foreign person (Section 120.11) or U.S. person (Section 120.27), then it refers to both.

§ 120.19 Public domain.

Public domain means information which is published and which is generally accessible or available to the *public*:

(1) Through sales at newsstands and bookstores;

(2) Through subscriptions which are available without restriction to any individual who desires to obtain or purchase the published information;

(3) Through second class mailing privileges granted by the U.S. Government;

(4) At libraries open to the *public* or from which the *public* can obtain documents;

(5) Through patents available at any patent office;

(6) Through unlimited distribution at a conference, meeting, seminar, trade show or exhibition, generally accessible to the *public*, in the United States;

(7) Through *public* release (i.e., unlimited distribution) in any form (e.g., not necessarily in published form) after approval by the cognizant U.S. government department or agency (see also Sec. 125.4(b)(13)).

§ 120.23 Technical data.

Technical data means, for purposes of this subchapter:

(a) Classified information relating to defense articles and defense services;

(b) Information covered by an invention secrecy order;

(c) *Software* as defined in Sec. 121.8(f) directly related to defense articles;

(d) Information, other than *software* as defined in 120.23(c), which is required for the design, development, production, processing, manufacture, assembly, operation, repair, maintenance or modification of defense articles. This includes, for example, information in the form of blueprints, drawings, photographs, plans, instructions and documentation. This also includes information that advances the state of the art of articles on the U.S. Munitions

List. This definition does not include information concerning general scientific, mathematical or engineering principles commonly taught in schools, colleges and universities. It also does not include basic marketing information on function or purpose or general system descriptions of defense articles.

§ 120.23 U.S. Person.

U.S. person means a person (as defined in Sec. 120.17 of this part) who is a citizen or national of the United States, or has been lawfully admitted to the United States for permanent residence (and maintains such a residence) under the Immigration and Nationality Act (8 U.S.C. 1101(a), 101(a), 60 Stat. 163). It also means any corporation, business association, partnership, society, trust, or any other entity, organization or group that is incorporated or organized to do business in the United States. It also includes any governmental (federal, state or local) entity. It does not include any foreign person as defined in Sec. 120.11 of this part.

Part 121—The United States Munitions List

§ 121.1 General. The United States Munitions List

Category XIII—Auxiliary Military Equipment

(b) Speech scramblers, privacy devices, cryptographic devices and software (encoding and decoding), and components specifically designed to be modified therefore, ancillary equipment, and protective apparatus specifically designed or modified for such devices, components, and equipment.

§ 121.8 End-items, components, accessories, attachment parts, firmware, software, and systems.

(e) "Software" includes but is not limited to the system functional design, operating systems and support software for design, implementation, test, operation, diagnosis and repair.

Part 125—Licenses for the Export of Technical Data and Classified Defense Articles

§ 125.1 Exports subject to this part.

(a) The export controls of this part apply to the export of technical data and the export of classified defense articles. Information which is in the "*public* domain" (see Sections 120.19 and 125.4(b)(13)) is not subject to the controls of this subchapter.

§ 125.2 Exports of unclassified technical data.

(a) General. A license (DSP-5) issued by the Office of Defense Trade Controls is required for the export (and return to the U.S. if applicable) of unclassified technical data unless the export is exempt from the licensing requirements of this subchapter. If the unclassified technical data is related to a classified defense article, any classified technical data or defense articles that may subsequently be required to be exported must be described, along with the address and telephone number of the U.S. Government office that classified the information. In the case of a plant visit, details of the proposed discussions must be transmitted to the Office of Defense Trade Controls for an appraisal of the technical data. Seven copies of the technical data or the details of the discussions must be provided. Only one copy must be provided if a renewal of the license is requested.

(b) Patents. A license issued by the Office of Defense Trade Controls is required for the export of technical data whenever the data exceeds that which is used to support a domestic filing of a patent application or to support a foreign filing of a patent application whenever no domestic application has been filed. Requests for the filing of patent applications in a foreign country, and requests for the filing of amendments, modifications or supplements to such patents, should follow the regulations of the U.S. Patent and Trademark Office in accordance with 37 CFR part 5. The export of technical data to support the filing and processing of patent applications in foreign countries is subject to regulations issued by the U.S. Patent and Trademark Office pursuant to 35 U.S.C. 184.

(c) Disclosures. Unless otherwise expressly exempted in this subchapter, a license is required for the oral, visual or documentary disclosure of technical data by U.S. persons to foreign persons. A license is required regardless of the manner in which the technical data is transmitted (e.g., in person, by telephone, correspondence, electronic means, etc.). A license is required for such disclosures by U.S. persons in connection with visits to foreign diplomatic missions and consular offices.

And so on. There's a whole lot more information in this document. If you're going to try to export cryptography, I suggest you get both a copy of the entire document and a lawyer who speaks the language.

In reality, the NSA has control over the export of cryptographic products. If you want an export license, you must first submit your product to the NSA for approval and the export license application to the State Department. After State Department approval, the matter moves under the jurisdiction of the Commerce Department, which has never cared much about the export of cryptography. However, the State Department will never grant approval without NSA approval, and they are not known to refuse a license after NSA approval.

In 1977 an NSA employee named Joseph A. Meyer wrote a letter—unauthorized, according to the official story of the incident—to the IEEE, warning them that the scheduled presentation of the original RSA paper would violate the ITAR. From *The Puzzle Palace:*

He had a point. The ITAR did cover any "unclassified information that can be used, or adapted for use, in the design, production, manufacture, repair, overhaul, processing, engineering, development, operation, maintenance, or reconstruction" of the listed materials, as well as "any technology which advances the state-of-the-art or establishes a new art in an area of significant military applicability in the United States." And export did include transferring the information both by writing and by either oral or visual means, including briefings and symposia in which foreign nationals are present.

But followed literally, the vague, overly broad regulations would seem to require that anyone planning to write or speak out publicly on a topic touching the Munitions List must first get approval from the State Department—a chilling prospect clearly at odds with the First Amendment and one as yet untested by the Supreme Court.

In the end NSA disavowed Meyer's actions and the RSA paper was presented as planned. No actions were taken against any of the inventors, although their work arguably enhanced foreign cryptography capabilities far more than anything released since.

In addition, the following is a statement by NSA regarding the export of cryptography [218]:

> Cryptographic technology is deemed vital to national security interests. This includes economic, military, and foreign policy interests.
>
> We do not agree with the implications from the House Judiciary Committee hearing of 7 May 1992 and recent news articles that allege that U.S. export laws prevent U.S. firms' manufacture and use of top encryption equipment. We are unaware of any case where a U.S. firm has been prevented from manufacturing and using encryption equipment within this country or for use by the U.S. firm or its subsidiaries in locations outside the U.S. because of U.S. export restrictions. In fact, NSA has always supported the use of encryption by U.S. businesses operating domestically and overseas to protect sensitive information.
>
> For export to foreign countries, NSA as a component of the Department of Defense (along with the Department of State and the Department of Commerce) reviews export licenses for information security technologies controlled by the Export Administration Regulations or the International Traffic in Arms Regulations. Similar export control systems are in effect in all the Coordinating Committee for Multilateral Export Controls (CoCom) countries as well as many non-CoCom countries as these technologies are universally considered as sensitive. Such technologies are not banned from export and are reviewed on a case-by-case basis. As part of the export review process, licenses may be required for these systems and are reviewed to determine the effect such export could have on national security interests—including economic, military, and political security interests. Export licenses are approved or denied based upon the type of equipment involved, the proposed end-use and the end-user.
>
> Our analysis indicates that the U.S. leads the world in the manufacture and export of information security technologies. Of those cryptologic products referred to NSA by the Department of State for export licenses, we consistently approve over 90%. Export licenses for information security products under the jurisdiction of the Department of Commerce are processed and approved without referral to NSA or DoD. This includes products using such techniques as the DSS and RSA which provide authentication and access control to computers or networks. In fact, in the past NSA has played a major role in successfully advocating the relaxation of export controls on RSA and related technologies for authentication purposes. Such techniques are extremely valuable against the hacker problem and unauthorized use of resources.

It is the stated policy of the NSA not to restrict the export of authentication products, only encryption products. If you have an authentication-only product you want to export, approval may merely be a matter of showing that the device cannot easily be converted to an encryption device. Furthermore, the bureaucratic procedures are much simpler for authentication products than for encryption products. An authentication product needs NSA and State Department approval only once; an encryption product may need approval for every product revision or even every sale.

The State Department does not approve the export of products with the DES algorithm. The Software Publishers Association (SPA) has recently been negotiating with the government to get export license restrictions eased. A 1992 agreement eased the export license rules for two ciphers, RC2 and RC4, as long as the key size is 40 bits or less. Refer to Section 7.1 for more information.

Meanwhile, the Computer Security and Privacy Advisory Board, an official advisory board to NIST, voted in March 1992 to recommend a national policy review of cryptographic issues, including export policy. They said that export policy is decided solely by agencies concerned with national security, without input from agencies concerned with encouraging commerce. Expect U.S. export policy to change frequently over the next few years.

18.13   LEGAL ISSUES

Are digital signatures real signatures? Will they stand up in court? Some preliminary legal research has resulted in the opinion that digital signatures would meet the requirements of legally binding signatures for most purposes, including commercial use as defined in the Uniform Commercial Code (UCC). A GAO (Government Accounting Office) decision, made at the request of NIST, opines that digital signatures will meet the legal standards of handwritten signatures [217].

Even so, the validity of digital signatures has not been challenged in court; their legal status is still undefined. In order for digital signatures to carry the same authority as handwritten signatures, they must first be used to sign a legally binding document, and then be challenged in court by one party. The court would then consider the security of the signature scheme and issue a ruling. Over time, as this happened repeatedly, a body of precedent rulings would emerge regarding which digital signature methods and what key sizes are required for a digital signature to be legally binding.

Until then, if two people wish to use digital signatures for contracts (or purchase requests, or work orders, etc.), it is recommended that they sign a paper contract in which they agree in the future to be bound by any documents digitally signed by them with a given signature scheme and a given key size.

PART
FIVE

Source Code

Source Code

VIGENERE, BEAUFORD, VARIANT BEAUFORD

```
#include <stdio.h>

/* This program enciphers files using one of Vigenere, Beauford or
   Variant Beauford ciphers. Note inverses means this code also
   decrypts - eg encipherment by Vigenere can be deciphered by
   enciphering with Variant Beauford with the same key. Similarly,
   Beauford is its own inverse.

   Author: Dr Leisa Condie, December 1992.
   phoenix@neumann.une.edu.au
   Dept of Mathematics, Statistics and Computing Science,
   University of New England - Armidale,
   New South Wales, 2351, AUSTRALIA.
*/

#define ALPHA         26          /* length of alphabet for modulo */
#define MAXKEYLENGTH 10           /* maximum length of the key used */
#define BLOCKLENGTH   5         /* for output, how many chars in a block */
#define LINELENGTH   80           /* maximum output characters per line */

char key[MAXKEYLENGTH+1];         /* encipherment key: +1 for possible newline */
int  blockcount = 0;              /* counts of chars in printed block */
int  linechars = 0;               /* count of chars printed on current line */
int  keylength = 0;               /* holds actual length of the key */
```

```
int  vigenere=0,beauford=0,varbeau=0;
        /* cipher type is set to 1 (TRUE) if chosen */
FILE *fp;                        /* set to stdin if interactive, else file */

void getsetup(void)
{
  char ch;                 /* generic character variable */
  char *tmp = key;         /* pointer to key array */

  /* find cipher type */
  ch = getc(fp);
  if (ch == 'V' || ch == 'v')         vigenere =1;
  else if (ch == 'B'|| ch == 'b')     beauford =1;
  else if (ch == 'A'|| ch == 'a')     varbeau  =1;
  else {  /* otherwise error, so notify by stderr and use Vigenere */
    fprintf(stderr,"V/B/A ciphers only - Vigenere assumed\n");
    vigenere =1;
  }

  while ((ch=getc(fp)) != '\n');       /* if extraneous input, clear it! */


  /* get key - anything after the MAXKEYLENGTH'th char is discarded */

  for (keylength=0; keylength < MAXKEYLENGTH; keylength++)
    if ((key[keylength]= getc(fp)) == '\n') break;

  if (key[keylength] != '\n'){
    while ((ch=getc(fp)) != '\n');  /* if excess key, clear it! */
    fprintf(stderr,"Key truncated to %d characters\n",keylength);
  }
}


int encipher(int i)
{
  /* Takes argument i - where we are in the key,
     Returns tmp - the ciphertext equivalent of the input if
     the input was alphabetic, else the input character unchanged */
  char ch;                 /* character read in */
  int tmp;                 /* for cipher char calculation */

  ch = getc(fp);
  if (ch >= 'A' && ch <= 'Z') {   /* convert to lowercase */
    ch = ch - 'A' + 'a';    /* don't trust tolower() */
  }
  if (ch >= 'a' && ch <= 'z') {   /* encipher */
```

```
    if (vigenere)
      tmp = (ch + key[i] - 2*'a') % ALPHA;
    else if (beauford)
      tmp = (key[i] - ch) % ALPHA;
    else    tmp = (ch - key[i]) % ALPHA;

    /* make offset positive and convert to lowercase char */
    while (tmp < 0) tmp += ALPHA;
    tmp += 'a';
  }
  else    tmp = ch;                 /* else return character unchanged */
  return(tmp);
}

void outputcipher(void)
{
  int cipherch, i=0;                /* cipher character */

  while (!feof(fp)) {               /* keep going whilst there is input */
    cipherch = encipher(i); /* generate cipher character */
    if (cipherch < 'a' || cipherch > 'z') /* invalid char in */
      continue;         /* ignore code below - restart loop */

    /* check we haven't finished key and need to restart it */
    if (i == keylength-1)   i=0;
    else                    i++;

    /* if a BLOCKLENGTH block is finished print a space */
    if (blockcount == BLOCKLENGTH) {
      /* check whether a newline is needed yet */
      if (linechars > LINELENGTH - BLOCKLENGTH) {
        putchar('\n');
        linechars = 0;
      }
      else {
        putchar(' ');
        linechars++;
      }
      blockcount = 0;
    }
    /* print enciphered character */
    putchar(cipherch);
    blockcount++;
    linechars++;
  }
  putchar('\n');
```

```
}

/* This version of main is set for input to come from the keyboard either
   directly or through file redirection: e.g. program < input_file
*/
/*
void main(void)
{
  fp = stdin;
  getsetup();
  outputcipher();
}
*/

/* This version of main looks for an input file whose name is specified on
   the argument line: e.g. program input_file
*/
void main(int argc, char *argv[])
{
  if (argc != 2) {
    fprintf(stderr,"Usage: program <input_file>\n");
    exit(1);
  }

  if ((fp = fopen(argv[1],"r")) == NULL) {
    fprintf(stderr,"File %s cannot be read from\n",argv[1]);
    exit(1);
  }

  getsetup();
  outputcipher();
}
```

ENIGMA

```
/*
 * enigma simulation
 *
 * author: Henry Tieman
 *
 * references:
 *     "How Polish Mathematicians Deciphered the Enigma", Marian Rejewski,
 *     Annals of the History of Computing, Vol 3, no 3, July 1981, Pg 213 ff
 *     appendix by C. A. Devours.
 *
 *     "Machine Cryptography and Modern Crypyanalysis", C.A. Deavours and L.
```

```
*       Kurh, Artech House, Dedham, Mass 1985.
 */


#include <stdio.h>
#include <ctype.h>

#ifndef TRUE
#define TRUE  1
#define FALSE 0
#endif


#define LINE_LEN  80

/*
 * rotor data
 *        reference "Machine Cryptography and Modern Cryptanalysis" pg. 100
 *
 * note: rotor stepping is associated with each @PROGCODE = rotor instead of
position
 *        or being constant.
 */


#define NUM_ROTORS 5

char ref_rotor[27] = "YRUHQSLDPXNGOKMIEBFZCWVJAT";

char rotor[NUM_ROTORS][27] = {      /* pre defined rotors */
  "EKMFLGDQVZNTOWYHXUSPAIBRCJ",
  "AJDKSIRUXBLHWTMCQGZNPYFVOE",
  "BDFHJLCPRTXVZNYEIWGAKMUSQO",
  "ESOVPZJAYQUIRHXLNFTGKDCMWB",
  "VZBRGITYUPSDNHLXAWMJQOFECK",
};

int step_data[NUM_ROTORS] = {
  16,  4, 21,  9, 25               /* steps at: q, e, v, j, z */
};

/*
 * enigma key default settings
 */

int  order[3] = { 0, 1, 2};         /* rotor order, user input is +1 */
char ring[8] = {                    /* ring settings */
 '\0', 'A', 'A', 'A',               /* default: AAA */
 '\0', '\0', '\0', '\0' };
```

```
int  n_plugs = 0;                   /* number of plugs */
char plugs[80] = "";                /* plug string */
int  pos[3] = { 0, 0, 0 };          /* rotor positions */

/*
 * simulation data and machine state data
 */

int  data[8][26];                   /* working array for machine */
int  step[3];                       /* steps coresponding to rotors */
int  double_step;                   /* rotor 2 step twice */

/*
 *  encipher - c implementation of the enigma cipher function
 */

int
encipher(int c)

  int j;                            /* index for counting */
  int idx;                          /* rotor index */

  if (isalpha(c))
    {

     pos[0] = (pos[0] + 1) % 26; /* first, advances the rotors */
     if (pos[0] == step[0])
    pos[1] = (pos[1] + 1) % 26;
     if (double_step)
    {
      pos[1] = (pos[1] + 1) % 26;
      pos[2] = (pos[2] + 1) % 26;
      double_step = FALSE;
    }
     if (pos[1] == step[1])
    double_step = TRUE;

     c -= 'A';                      /* start to encipher */
     if (n_plugs != 0)
    c = data[0][c];
     for (j=0;j<3;j++)              /* do rotors forward */
    {
      idx = (c + pos[j]) % 26;
      c   = (c + data[j+1][idx]) % 26;
    }
     c = (data[4][c]) % 26;         /* reflecting rotor */
```

```
      for (j=0;j<3;j++)                /* do rotors reverse */
      {
        idx = (c + pos[2-j]) % 26;
        c   = (c + data[j+5][idx]) % 26;
      }
       if (n_plugs != 0)
      c = data[0][c];
        c += 'A';
      }
    return (c);
}


/*
 * encipher_file - open and encipher a file
 */

void
encipher_file(char *file_name)
{
  FILE *fp;                         /* plaintext/ciphertext FILE pointer */
  char line[LINE_LEN + 1];          /* input data line, inc. '\n' */
  char *ret_val;                    /* value from fgets(), used for EOF check */
  char c;                           /* character from data line */
  int  len;                         /* length of data line */
  int  idx;                         /* index/counter */

  fp = fopen(file_name, "r");
  ret_val = fgets(line, LINE_LEN, fp);
  while(ret_val != NULL)
    {
      len = strlen(line);
      for(idx=0;idx<len;idx++)
        {
          c = line[idx];
          if (isalpha(c))
            {
              c = encipher((int)(toupper(c)));
              line[idx] = c;
            }
        }
      printf("%s", line);
      ret_val = fgets(line, LINE_LEN, fp);
    }
  fclose(fp);
}
```

```
/*
 * init_mach - set up data according to the input data
 */

void
init_mach( void )
{
  int i, j;                          /* indexes */
  int ds;                            /* used durring ring settings */
  int u, v;                          /* temps for plugboard input */

  /* setup rotor data */
  for (j=0;j<26;j++)
    data[4][j] = ((int)ref_rotor[j]-'A'+26)%26;

  for (i=1;i<4;i++)
    {
      step[i-1] = step_data[order[i-1]];
      for (j=0;j<26;j++)
        {
          data[i][j] = ((int)(rotor[order[i-1]][j])-'A' + 26) % 26;
          data[8-i][data[i][j]] = j;
        }
    }

  /* setup ring settings */
  ring[7] = ring[1];
  ring[6] = ring[2];
  ring[5] = ring[3];
  for (i=1;i<8;i++)
    if (i !=4)
      {
        ds = (int)(ring[i]) - 'A';
        if (ds != 0)
          {
            for (j=0;j<26;j++)
              data[0][j] = data[i][j];
            for (j=0;j<26;j++)
              data[i][j] = data[0][(26-ds+j)%26];
          }
      }

  /* setup plug data */
  if (n_plugs != 0)
    {
      j = 0;
```

```
        for (i=0;i<26;i++)
          data[0][i] = i;
        for (i=0;i<n_plugs;i++)
          {
            while(!isalpha(plugs[j]))
              {
                j++;
                if (plugs[j] == '\0')
                  break;
              }
            u = toupper(plugs[j++]) - 'A';
            v = toupper(plugs[j++]) - 'A';
            data[0][u] = v;
            data[0][v] = u;
          }
      }

  /* convert all moving rotor data to displacements */
  for (i=1;i<8;i++)
    {
      if (i!=4)
      for(j=0;j<26;j++)
        data[i][j] = (data[i][j] - j + 26) % 26;
    }

  /* setup rotor starting positions */
  double_step = FALSE;            /* no previous rotor position */
  /* input function has already done the rotor positions */
}

/*
 * read_keyfile - a simple function to read in the key file.
 */

void
read_keyfile( char *str)
{
  FILE *kf;                       /* input key FILE pointer */
  int num;                        /* dummy returned from fscanf() */
  int idx;                        /* index/counter */
  char a[3];                      /* dummy for input */

  kf = fopen(str, "r");
  num = fscanf(kf, "%d %d %d\n", &order[0], &order[1], &order[2]);
  num = fscanf(kf, "%c %c %c\n", &ring[1], &ring[2], &ring[3]);
  num = fscanf(kf, "%d\n", &n_plugs);
```

```
  if (n_plugs != 0)
    num = fscanf(kf, "%[^\n]\n", plugs);
  num = fscanf(kf, "%c %c %c\n", &a[0], &a[1], &a[2]);

  for (idx = 0; idx < 3; idx ++)
    {
      (order[idx])-;
      ring[idx+1] = toupper(ring[idx+1]);
      pos[idx]   = toupper(a[idx]) - 'A';
    }
  fclose(kf);
}

/*
 * usage - function to print out the correct usage of the program
 */

void
usage( char *str )
{
  fprintf(stderr, "usage: %s [<keyfile>] <infile>\n\n", str);
  fprintf(stderr, "\tkeyfile has the form:\n");
  fprintf(stderr, "\t\tn n n\t\t- for rotor order, 1 <= n <=5\n");
  fprintf(stderr, "\t\tx x x\t\t- for ring settings, x alpha\n");
  fprintf(stderr, "\t\tn\t\t- number of plugs, 0 <= n <= 13\n");
  fprintf(stderr, "\t\txx xx xx ...\t- plug letter pairs, one pair"
          " for each n\n");
  fprintf(stderr, "\t\tx x\t\t- initial rotor position, x alpha\n\n");
  fprintf(stderr, "\toutput is to stdout\n");
  exit(0);
}

/*
 * main - the main function, nothing special here
 */

void
main( int argc, char ** argv)
{
  char *infile;                    /* plaintext/cphertext file name ptr */

  if ((argc < 2) || (argc > 3))
    usage(argv[0]);

  if(argc == 2)
    {
```

```
      infile = argv[1];
    }
  else
    {
      infile = argv[2];
      read_keyfile(argv[1]);
    }

  init_mach();
  encipher_file(infile);
}

/*
 * end of enigma simulation
 */
```

DES

```
/* d3des.h -
 *
 * Headers and defines for d3des.c
 * Graven Imagery, 1992.
 *
 * THIS SOFTWARE PLACED IN THE PUBLIC DOMAIN BY THE AUTHOUR
 * 920825 19:42 EDST
 *
 * Copyright (c) 1988,1989,1990,1991,1992 by Richard Outerbridge
 *      (GEnie : OUTER; CIS : [71755,204])
 */

#define D2_DES                  /* include double-length support */
#define D3_DES                  /* include triple-length support */

#ifdef D3_DES
#ifndef D2_DES
#define D2_DES                  /* D2_DES is needed for D3_DES */
#endif
#endif

#define EN0    0                /* MODE == encrypt */
#define DE1    1                /* MODE == decrypt */

/* Useful on 68000-ish machines, but NOT USED here. */

typedef union {
  unsigned long blok[2];
```

```
   unsigned short word[4];
   unsigned char byte[8];
   } M68K;

typedef union {
   unsigned long dblok[4];
   unsigned short dword[8];
   unsigned char dbyte[16];
   } M68K2;

extern void deskey(unsigned char *, short);
/*                 hexkey[8]      MODE
 * Sets the internal key register according to the hexadecimal
 * key contained in the 8 bytes of hexkey, according to the DES,
 * for encryption or decryption according to MODE.
 */

extern void usekey(unsigned long *);
/*                 cookedkey[32]
 * Loads the internal key register with the data in cookedkey.
 */

extern void cpkey(unsigned long *);
/*                 cookedkey[32]
 * Copies the contents of the internal key register into the storage
 * located at &cookedkey[0].
 */

extern void des(unsigned char *, unsigned char *);
/*                 from[8]           to[8]
 * Encrypts/Decrypts (according to the key currently loaded in the
 * internal key register) one block of eight bytes at address 'from'
 * into the block at address 'to'.  They can be the same.
 */

#ifdef D2_DES

#define desDkey(a,b) des2key((a),(b))
extern void des2key(unsigned char *, short);
/*                 hexkey[16]     MODE
 * Sets the internal key registerS according to the hexadecimal
 * keyS contained in the 16 bytes of hexkey, according to the DES,
 * for DOUBLE encryption or decryption according to MODE.
 * NOTE: this clobbers all three key registers!
 */
```

```
extern void Ddes(unsigned char *, unsigned char *);
/*                 from[8]           to[8]
 * Encrypts/Decrypts (according to the keyS currently loaded in the
 * internal key registerS) one block of eight bytes at address 'from'
 * into the block at address 'to'.  They can be the same.
 */


extern void D2des(unsigned char *, unsigned char *);
/*                 from[16]          to[16]
 * Encrypts/Decrypts (according to the keyS currently loaded in the
 * internal key registerS) one block of SIXTEEN bytes at address 'from'
 * into the block at address 'to'.  They can be the same.
 */


extern void makekey(char *, unsigned char *);
/*               *password,    single-length key[8]
 * With a double-length default key, this routine hashes a NULL-terminated
 * string into an eight-byte random-looking key, suitable for use with the
 * deskey() routine.
 */


#define makeDkey(a,b)make2key((a),(b))
extern void make2key(char *, unsigned char *);
/*               *password,    double-length key[16]
 * With a double-length default key, this routine hashes a NULL-terminated
 * string into a sixteen-byte random-looking key, suitable for use with the
 * des2key() routine.
 */


#ifndef D3_DES/* D2_DES only */

#define useDkey(a)    use2key((a))
#define cpDkey(a)     cp2key((a))

extern void use2key(unsigned long *);
/*               cookedkey[64]
 * Loads the internal key registerS with the data in cookedkey.
 * NOTE: this clobbers all three key registers!
 */


extern void cp2key(unsigned long *);
/*               cookedkey[64]
 * Copies the contents of the internal key registerS into the storage
 * located at &cookedkey[0].
 */
```

```
#else   /* D3_DES too */

#define useDkey(a)    use3key((a))
#define cpDkey(a)     cp3key((a))

extern void des3key(unsigned char *, short);
/*                 hexkey[24]    MODE
 * Sets the internal key registerS according to the hexadecimal
 * keyS contained in the 24 bytes of hexkey, according to the DES,
 * for DOUBLE encryption or decryption according to MODE.
 */

extern void use3key(unsigned long *);
/*              cookedkey[96]
 * Loads the 3 internal key registerS with the data in cookedkey.
 */

extern void cp3key(unsigned long *);
/*              cookedkey[96]
 * Copies the contents of the 3 internal key registerS into the storage
 * located at &cookedkey[0].
 */

extern void make3key(char *, unsigned char *);
/*              *password,    triple-length key[24]
 * With a triple-length default key, this routine hashes a NULL-terminated
 * string into a twenty-four-byte random-looking key, suitable for use with
 * the des3key() routine.
 */

#endif /* D3_DES */
#endif /* D2_DES */

/* d3des.h V5.09 rwo 9208.04 15:06 Graven Imagery


  ***************************D3DES.C**********************************/


/* D3DES (V5.0A) -
 *
 * A portable, public domain, version of the Data Encryption Standard.
 *
 * Written with Symantec's THINK (Lightspeed) C by Richard Outerbridge.
 * Thanks to: Dan Hoey for his excellent Initial and Inverse permutation
 * code;  Jim Gillogly & Phil Karn for the DES key schedule code; Dennis
```

```
 * Ferguson, Eric Young and Dana How for comparing notes; and Ray Lau,
 * for humouring me on.
 *
 * THIS SOFTWARE PLACED IN THE PUBLIC DOMAIN BY THE AUTHOUR
 * 920825 19:42 EDST
 *
 * Copyright (c) 1988,1989,1990,1991,1992 by Richard Outerbridge.
 * (GEnie : OUTER; CIS : [71755,204]) Graven Imagery, 1992.
  */

#include "d3des.h"

static void scrunch(unsigned char *, unsigned long *);
static void unscrun(unsigned long *, unsigned char *);
static void desfunc(unsigned long *, unsigned long *);
static void cookey(unsigned long *);

static unsigned long KnL[32] = { 0L };
static unsigned long KnR[32] = { 0L };
static unsigned long Kn3[32] = { 0L };
static unsigned char Df_Key[24] = {
      0x01,0x23,0x45,0x67,0x89,0xab,0xcd,0xef,
      0xfe,0xdc,0xba,0x98,0x76,0x54,0x32,0x10,
      0x89,0xab,0xcd,0xef,0x01,0x23,0x45,0x67 };

static unsigned short bytebit[8]= {
      0200, 0100, 040, 020, 010, 04, 02, 01 };

static unsigned long bigbyte[24] = {
  0x800000L,    0x400000L,    0x200000L,    0x100000L,
  0x80000L,     0x40000L,     0x20000L,     0x10000L,
  0x8000L,      0x4000L,      0x2000L,      0x1000L,
  0x800L,          0x400L,                  0x200L,                   0x100l,
  0x80L,        0x40L,        0x20L,        0x10L,
  0x8L,         0x4L,         0x2L,         0x1L   };

/* Use the key schedule specified in the Standard (ANSI X3.92-1981). */

static unsigned char pc1[56] = {
  56, 48, 40, 32, 24, 16,  8,   0, 57, 49, 41, 33, 25, 17,
   9,  1, 58, 50, 42, 34, 26,  18, 10,  2, 59, 51, 43, 35,
  62, 54, 46, 38, 30, 22, 14,   6, 61, 53, 45, 37, 29, 21,
  13,  5, 60, 52, 44, 36, 28, 20, 12,  4, 27, 19, 11,  3 };

static unsigned char totrot[16] = {
  1,2,4,6,8,10,12,14,15,17,19,21,23,25,27,28 };
```

```
static unsigned char pc2[48] = {
  13, 16, 10, 23,  0,  4, 2, 27, 14,  5, 20,  9,
   2, 18, 11,  3, 25,  7,15,  6, 26, 19, 12,  1,
  40, 51, 30, 36, 46, 54,29, 39, 50, 44, 32, 47,
  43, 48, 38, 55, 33, 52,45, 41, 49, 35, 28, 31 };

void deskey(key, edf)/* Thanks to James Gillogly & Phil Karn! */
unsigned char *key;
short edf;
{
  int i, j, l, m, n;
  unsigned char pc1m[56], pcr[56];
  unsigned long kn[32];

  for ( j = 0; j < 56; j++ ) {
    l = pc1[j];
    m = l & 07;
    pc1m[j] = (key[l >> 3] & bytebit[m]) ? 1 : 0;
    }
  for( i = 0; i<<16; i++ ) {
    if( edf == DE1 ) m = (15 - i) << 1;
    else m = i << 1;
    n = m + 1;
    kn[m] = kn[n] = 0L;
    for( j = 0; j < 28; j++ ) {
      l = j + totrot[i];
      if( l < 28 ) pcr[j] = pc1m[l];
      else pcr[j] = pc1m[l - 28];
      }
    for( j = 28; j < 56; j++ ) {
      l = j + totrot[i];
      if( l < 56 ) pcr[j] = pc1m[l];
      else pcr[j] = pc1m[l - 28];
      }
    for( j = 0; j < 24; j++ ) {
      if( pcr[pc2[j]] ) kn[m] |= bigbyte[j];
      if( pcr[pc2[j+24]] ) kn[n] |= bigbyte[j];
      }
    }
  cookey(kn);
  return;
  }

static void cookey(raw1)
unsigned long *raw1;
```

```
    {
      unsigned long *cook, *raw0;
      unsigned long dough[32];
      int i;

      cook = dough;
      for( i = 0; i < 16; i++, raw1++ ) {
        raw0 = raw1++;
        *cook    = (*raw0 & 0x00fc0000L) << 6;
        *cook   |= (*raw0 & 0x00000fc0L) << 10;
        *cook   |= (*raw1 & 0x00fc0000L) >> 10;
        *cook++          |= (*raw1 & 0x00000fc0L) >> 6;
        *cook    = (*raw0 & 0x0003f000L) << 12;
        *cook   |= (*raw0 & 0x0000003fL) << 16;
        *cook   |= (*raw1 & 0x0003f000L) >> 4;
        *cook++          |= (*raw1 & 0x0000003fL);
        }
      usekey(dough);
      return;
      }

void cpkey(into)
unsigned long *into;
    {
      unsigned long *from, *endp;

      from = KnL, endp = &KnL[32];
      while( from  endp ) *into++ = *from++;
      return;
      }

void usekey(from)
unsigned long *from;
    {
      unsigned long *to, *endp;

      to = KnL, endp = &KnL[32];
      while( to < endp ) *to++ = *from++;
      return;
      }

void des(inblock, outblock)
unsigned char *inblock, *outblock;
    {
      unsigned long work[2];
```

```
  scrunch(inblock, work);
  desfunc(work, KnL);
  unscrun(work, outblock);
  return;
  }

static void scrunch(outof, into)
unsigned char *outof;
unsigned long *into;
{
  *into   = (*outof++ & 0xffL) << 24;
  *into  |= (*outof++ & 0xffL) << 16;
  *into  |= (*outof++ & 0xffL) << 8;
  *into++ |= (*outof++ & 0xffL);
  *into   = (*outof++ & 0xffL) << 24;
  *into  |= (*outof++ & 0xffL) << 16;
  *into  |= (*outof++ & 0xffL) << 8;
  *into  |= (*outof   & 0xffL);
  return;
  }

static void unscrun(outof, into)
unsigned long *outof;
unsigned char *into;
{
  *into++ = (unsigned char) ((*outof >> 24) & 0xffL);
  *into++ = (unsigned char) ((*outof >> 16) & 0xffL);
  *into++ = (unsigned char) ((*outof >>  8) & 0xffL);
  *into++ = (unsigned char) ( *outof++      & 0xffL);
  *into++ = (unsigned char) ((*outof >> 24) & 0xffL);
  *into++ = (unsigned char) ((*outof >> 16) & 0xffL);
  *into++ = (unsigned char) ((*outof >>  8) & 0xffL);
  *into   = (unsigned char) ( *outof        & 0xffL);
  return;
  }

static unsigned long SP1[64] = {
  0x01010400L, 0x00000000L, 0x00010000L, 0x01010404L,
  0x01010004L, 0x00010404L, 0x00000004L, 0x00010000L,
  0x00000400L, 0x01010400L, 0x01010404L, 0x00000400L,
  0x01000404L, 0x01010004L, 0x01000000L, 0x00000004L,
  0x00000404L, 0x01000400L, 0x01000400L, 0x00010400L,
  0x00010400L, 0x01010000L, 0x01010000L, 0x01000404L,
  0x00010004L, 0x01000004L, 0x01000004L, 0x00010004L,
  0x00000000L, 0x00000404L, 0x00010404L, 0x01000000L,
  0x00010000L, 0x01010404L, 0x00000004L, 0x01010000L,
```

```
  0x01010400L, 0x01000000L, 0x01000000L, 0x00000400L,
  0x01010004L, 0x00010000L, 0x00010400L, 0x01000004L,
  0x00000400L, 0x00000004L, 0x01000404L, 0x00010404L,
  0x01010404L, 0x00010004L, 0x01010000L, 0x01000404L,
  0x01000004L, 0x00000404L, 0x00010404L, 0x01010400L,
  0x00000404L, 0x01000400L, 0x01000400L, 0x00000000L,
  0x00010004L, 0x00010400L, 0x00000000L, 0x01010004L };

static unsigned long SP2[64] = {
  0x80108020L, 0x80008000L, 0x00008000L, 0x00108020L,
  0x00100000L, 0x00000020L, 0x80100020L, 0x80008020L,
  0x80000020L, 0x80108020L, 0x80108000L, 0x80000000L,
  0x80008000L, 0x00100000L, 0x00000020L, 0x80100020L,
  0x00108000L, 0x00100020L, 0x80008020L, 0x00000000L,
  0x80000000L, 0x00008000L, 0x00108020L, 0x80100000L,
  0x00100020L, 0x80000020L, 0x00000000L, 0x00108000L,
  0x00008020L, 0x80108000L, 0x80100000L, 0x00008020L,
  0x00000000L, 0x00108020L, 0x80100020L, 0x00100000L,
  0x80008020L, 0x80100000L, 0x80108000L, 0x00008000L,
  0x80100000L, 0x80008000L, 0x00000020L, 0x80108020L,
  0x00108020L, 0x00000020L, 0x00008000L, 0x80000000L,
  0x00008020L, 0x80108000L, 0x00100000L, 0x80000020L,
  0x00100020L, 0x80008020L, 0x80000020L, 0x00100020L,
  0x00108000L, 0x00000000L, 0x80008000L, 0x00008020L,
  0x80000000L, 0x80100020L, 0x80108020L, 0x00108000L };

static unsigned long SP3[64] = {
  0x00000208L, 0x08020200L, 0x00000000L, 0x08020008L,
  0x08000200L, 0x00000000L, 0x00020208L, 0x08000200L,
  0x00020008L, 0x08000008L, 0x08000008L, 0x00020000L,
  0x08020208L, 0x00020008L, 0x08020000L, 0x00000208L,
  0x08000000L, 0x00000008L, 0x08020200L, 0x00000200L,
  0x00020200L, 0x08020000L, 0x08020008L, 0x00020208L,
  0x08000208L, 0x00020200L, 0x00020000L, 0x08000208L,
  0x00000008L, 0x08020208L, 0x00000200L, 0x08000000L,
  0x08020200L, 0x08000000L, 0x00020008L, 0x00000208L,
  0x00020000L, 0x08020200L, 0x08000200L, 0x00000000L,
  0x00000200L, 0x00020008L, 0x08020208L, 0x08000200L,
  0x08000008L, 0x00000200L, 0x00000000L, 0x08020008L,
  0x08000208L, 0x00020000L, 0x08000000L, 0x08020208L,
  0x00000008L, 0x00020208L, 0x00020200L, 0x08000008L,
  0x08020000L, 0x08000208L, 0x00000208L, 0x08020000L,
  0x00020208L, 0x00000008L, 0x08020008L, 0x00020200L };

static unsigned long SP4[64] = {
  0x00802001L, 0x00002081L, 0x00002081L, 0x00000080L,
```

```
    0x00802080L, 0x00800081L, 0x00800001L, 0x00002001L,
    0x00000000L, 0x00802000L, 0x00802000L, 0x00802081L,
    0x00000081L, 0x00000000L, 0x00800080L, 0x00800001L,
    0x00000001L, 0x00002000L, 0x00800000L, 0x00802001L,
    0x00000080L, 0x00800000L, 0x00002001L, 0x00002080L,
    0x00800081L, 0x00000001L, 0x00002080L, 0x00800080L,
    0x00002000L, 0x00802080L, 0x00802081L, 0x00000081L,
    0x00800080L, 0x00800001L, 0x00802000L, 0x00802081L,
    0x00000081L, 0x00000000L, 0x00000000L, 0x00802000L,
    0x00002080L, 0x00800080L, 0x00800081L, 0x00000001L,
    0x00802001L, 0x00002081L, 0x00002081L, 0x00000080L,
    0x00802081L, 0x00000081L, 0x00000001L, 0x00002000L,
    0x00800001L, 0x00002001L, 0x00802080L, 0x00800081L,
    0x00002001L, 0x00002080L, 0x00800000L, 0x00802001L,
    0x00000080L, 0x00800000L, 0x00002000L, 0x00802080L };

static unsigned long SP5[64] = {
    0x00000100L, 0x02080100L, 0x02080000L, 0x42000100L,
    0x00080000L, 0x00000100L, 0x40000000L, 0x02080000L,
    0x40080100L, 0x00080000L, 0x02000100L, 0x40080100L,
    0x42000100L, 0x42080000L, 0x00080100L, 0x40000000L,
    0x02000000L, 0x40080000L, 0x40080000L, 0x00000000L,
    0x40000100L, 0x42080100L, 0x42080100L, 0x02000100L,
    0x42080000L, 0x40000100L, 0x00000000L, 0x42000000L,
    0x02080100L, 0x02000000L, 0x42000000L, 0x00080100L,
    0x00080000L, 0x42000100L, 0x00000100L, 0x02000000L,
    0x40000000L, 0x02080000L, 0x42000100L, 0x40080100L,
    0x02000100L, 0x40000000L, 0x42080000L, 0x02080100L,
    0x40080100L, 0x00000100L, 0x02000000L, 0x42080000L,
    0x42080100L, 0x00080100L, 0x42000000L, 0x42080100L,
    0x02080000L, 0x00000000L, 0x40080000L, 0x42000000L,
    0x00080100L, 0x02000100L, 0x40000100L, 0x00080000L,
    0x00000000L, 0x40080000L, 0x02080100L, 0x40000100L };

static unsigned long SP6[64] = {
    0x20000010L, 0x20400000L, 0x00004000L, 0x20404010L,
    0x20400000L, 0x00000010L, 0x20404010L, 0x00400000L,
    0x20004000L, 0x00404010L, 0x00400000L, 0x20000010L,
    0x00400010L, 0x20004000L, 0x20000000L, 0x00004010L,
    0x00000000L, 0x00400010L, 0x20004010L, 0x00004000L,
    0x00404000L, 0x20004010L, 0x00000010L, 0x20400010L,
    0x20400010L, 0x00000000L, 0x00404010L, 0x20404000L,
    0x00004010L, 0x00404000L, 0x20404000L, 0x20000000L,
    0x20004000L, 0x00000010L, 0x20400010L, 0x00404000L,
    0x20404010L, 0x00400000L, 0x00004010L, 0x20000010L,
    0x00400000L, 0x20004000L, 0x20000000L, 0x00004010L,
```

```
    0x20000010L, 0x20404010L, 0x00404000L, 0x20400000L,
    0x00404010L, 0x20404000L, 0x00000000L, 0x20400010L,
    0x00000010L, 0x00004000L, 0x20400000L, 0x00404010L,
    0x00004000L, 0x00400010L, 0x20004010L, 0x00000000L,
    0x20404000L, 0x20000000L, 0x00400010L, 0x20004010L };

static unsigned long SP7[64] = {
    0x00200000L, 0x04200002L, 0x04000802L, 0x00000000L,
    0x00000800L, 0x04000802L, 0x00200802L, 0x04200800L,
    0x04200802L, 0x00200000L, 0x00000000L, 0x04000002L,
    0x00000002L, 0x04000000L, 0x04200002L, 0x00000802L,
    0x04000800L, 0x00200802L, 0x00200002L, 0x04000800L,
    0x04000002L, 0x04200000L, 0x04200800L, 0x00200002L,
    0x04200000L, 0x00000800L, 0x00000802L, 0x04200802L,
    0x00200800L, 0x00000002L, 0x04000000L, 0x00200800L,
    0x04000000L, 0x00200800L, 0x00200000L, 0x04000802L,
    0x04000802L, 0x04200002L, 0x04200002L, 0x00000002L,
    0x00200002L, 0x04000000L, 0x04000800L, 0x00200000L,
    0x04200800L, 0x00000802L, 0x00200802L, 0x04200800L,
    0x00000802L, 0x04000002L, 0x04200802L, 0x04200000L,
    0x00200800L, 0x00000000L, 0x00000002L, 0x04200802L,
    0x00000000L, 0x00200802L, 0x04200000L, 0x00000800L,
    0x04000002L, 0x04000800L, 0x00000800L, 0x00200002L };

static unsigned long SP8[64] = {
    0x10001040L, 0x00001000L, 0x00040000L, 0x10041040L,
    0x10000000L, 0x10001040L, 0x00000040L, 0x10000000L,
    0x00040040L, 0x10040000L, 0x10041040L, 0x00041000L,
    0x10041000L, 0x00041040L, 0x00001000L, 0x00000040L,
    0x10040000L, 0x10000040L, 0x10001000L, 0x00001040L,
    0x00041000L, 0x00040040L, 0x10040040L, 0x10041000L,
    0x00001040L, 0x00000000L, 0x00000000L, 0x10040040L,
    0x10000040L, 0x10001000L, 0x00041040L, 0x00040000L,
    0x00041040L, 0x00040000L, 0x10041000L, 0x00001000L,
    0x00000040L, 0x10040040L, 0x00001000L, 0x00041040L,
    0x10001000L, 0x00000040L, 0x10000040L, 0x10040000L,
    0x10040040L, 0x10000000L, 0x00040000L, 0x10001040L,
    0x00000000L, 0x10041040L, 0x00040040L, 0x10000040L,
    0x10040000L, 0x10001000L, 0x10001040L, 0x00000000L,
    0x10041040L, 0x00041000L, 0x00041000L, 0x00001040L,
    0x00001040L, 0x00040040L, 0x10000000L, 0x10041000L };

static void desfunc(block, keys)
unsigned long *block, *keys;
{
    unsigned long fval, work, right, leftt;
```

```
    int round;

    leftt = block[0];
    right = block[1];
    work = ((leftt > 4) ^ right) & 0x0f0f0f0fL;
    right ^= work;
    leftt ^= (work << 4);
    work = ((leftt > 16) ^ right) & 0x0000ffffL;
    right ^= work;
    leftt ^= (work << 16);
    work = ((right >> 2) ^ leftt) & 0x33333333L;
    leftt ^= work;
    right ^= (work << 2);
    work = ((right >> 8) ^ leftt) & 0x00ff00ffL;
    leftt ^= work;
    right ^= (work << 8);
    right = ((right << 1) | ((right >> 31) & 1L)) & 0xffffffffL;
    work = (leftt ^ right) & 0xaaaaaaaaL;
    leftt ^= work;
    right ^= work;
    leftt = ((leftt << 1) | ((leftt > 31) & 1L)) & 0xffffffffL;

    for( round = 0; round < 8; round++ ) {
      work  = (right << 28) | (right >> 4);
      work ^= *keys++;
      fval  = SP7[ work             & 0x3fL];
      fval |= SP5[(work >> 8) & 0x3fL];
      fval |= SP3[(work >> 16) & 0x3fL];
      fval |= SP1[(work >> 24) & 0x3fL];
      work  = right ^ *keys++;
      fval |= SP8[ work             & 0x3fL];
      fval |= SP6[(work >> 8) & 0x3fL];
      fval |= SP4[(work >> 16) & 0x3fL];
      fval |= SP2[(work >> 24) & 0x3fL];
      leftt ^= fval;
      work  = (leftt << 28) | (leftt >> 4);
      work ^= *keys++;
      fval  = SP7[ work             & 0x3fL];
      fval |= SP5[(work >> 8) & 0x3fL];
      fval |= SP3[(work >> 16) & 0x3fL];
      fval |= SP1[(work >> 24) & 0x3fL];
      work  = leftt ^ *keys++;
      fval |= SP8[ work             & 0x3fL];
      fval |= SP6[(work >> 8) & 0x3fL];
      fval |= SP4[(work >> 16) & 0x3fL];
      fval |= SP2[(work >> 24) & 0x3fL];
```

```
      right ^= fval;
      }

   right = (right << 31) | (right >> 1);
   work = (leftt ^ right) & 0xaaaaaaaaL;
   leftt ^= work;
   right ^= work;
   leftt = (leftt << 31) | (leftt >> 1);
   work = ((leftt >> 8) ^ right) & 0x00ff00ffL;
   right ^= work;
   leftt ^= (work << 8);
   work = ((leftt >> 2) ^ right) & 0x33333333L;
   right ^= work;
   leftt ^= (work << 2);
   work = ((right >> 16) ^ leftt) & 0x0000ffffL;
   leftt ^= work;
   right ^= (work << 16);
   work = ((right >> 4) ^ leftt) & 0x0f0f0f0fL;
   leftt ^= work;
   right ^= (work << 4);
   *block++ = right;
   *block = leftt;
   return;
   }

#ifdef D2_DES

void des2key(hexkey, mode)          /* stomps on Kn3 too */
unsigned char *hexkey;              /* unsigned char[16] */
short mode;
{
   short revmod;

   revmod = (mode == EN0) ? DE1 : EN0;
   deskey(&hexkey[8], revmod);
   cpkey(KnR);
   deskey(hexkey, mode);
   cpkey(Kn3);                                  /* Kn3 = KnL */
   return;
   }

void Ddes(from, into)
unsigned char *from, *into;         /* unsigned char[8] */
{
   unsigned long work[2];
```

```
  scrunch(from, work);
  desfunc(work, KnL);
  desfunc(work, KnR);
  desfunc(work, Kn3);
  unscrun(work, into);
  return;
  }

void D2des(from, into)
unsigned char *from;                    /* unsigned char[16] */
unsigned char *into;                    /* unsigned char[16] */
{
  unsigned long *right, *ll, swap;
  unsigned long leftt[2], bufR[2];

  right = bufR;
  ll = &leftt[1];
  scrunch(from, leftt);
  scrunch(&from[8], right);
  desfunc(leftt, KnL);
  desfunc(right, KnL);
  swap = *ll;
  *ll = *right;
  *right = swap;
  desfunc(leftt, KnR);
  desfunc(right, KnR);
  swap = *ll;
  *ll = *right;
  *right = swap;
  desfunc(leftt, Kn3);
  desfunc(right, Kn3);
  unscrun(leftt, into);
  unscrun(right, &into[8]);
  return;
  }

void makekey(aptr, kptr)
char *aptr;                                        /* NULL-terminated  */
unsigned char *kptr;                    /* unsigned char[8] */
{
  unsigned char *store;
  int first, i;
  unsigned long savek[96];

  cpDkey(savek);
  des2key(Df_Key, EN0);
```

```
  for( i = 0; i < 8; i++ ) kptr[i] = Df_Key[i];
  first = 1;
  while( (*aptr != '\0') || first ) {
    store = kptr;
    for( i = 0; i < 8 && (*aptr != '\0'); i++ ) {
      *store++ ^= *aptr & 0x7f;
      *aptr++ = '\0';
      }
    Ddes(kptr, kptr);
    first = 0;
    }
  useDkey(savek);
  return;
  }

void make2key(aptr, kptr)
char *aptr;                                    /* NULL-terminated   */
unsigned char *kptr;                 /* unsigned char[16] */
{
  unsigned char *store;
  int first, i;
  unsigned long savek[96];

  cpDkey(savek);
  des2key(Df_Key, EN0);
  for( i = 0; i < 16; i++ ) kptr[i] = Df_Key[i];
  first = 1;
  while( (*aptr != '\0') || first ) {
    store = kptr;
    for( i = 0; i < 16 && (*aptr != '\0'); i++ ) {
      *store++ ^= *aptr & 0x7f;
      *aptr++ = '\0';
      }
    D2des(kptr, kptr);
    first = 0;
    }
  useDkey(savek);
  return;
  }

#ifndef D3_DES/* D2_DES only */

void cp2key(into)
unsigned long *into;                 /* unsigned long[64] */
{
  unsigned long *from, *endp;
```

```
  cpkey(into);
  into = &into[32];
  from = KnR, endp = &KnR[32];
  while( from < endp ) *into++ = *from++;
  return;
  }

void use2key(from)                                    /* stomps on Kn3 too */
unsigned long *from;                          /* unsigned long[64] */
{
  unsigned long *to, *endp;

  usekey(from);
  from = &from[32];
  to = KnR, endp = &KnR[32];
  while( to < endp ) *to++ = *from++;
  cpkey(Kn3);                                         /* Kn3 = KnL */
  return;
  }

#else  /* D3_DES too */

void des3key(hexkey, mode)
unsigned char *hexkey;                    /* unsigned char[24] */
short mode;
{
  unsigned char *first, *third;
  short revmod;

  if( mode == EN0 ) {
    revmod = DE1;
    first = hexkey;
    third = &hexkey[16];
    }
  else {
    revmod = EN0;
    first = &hexkey[16];
    third = hexkey;
    }
  deskey(&hexkey[8], revmod);
  cpkey(KnR);
  deskey(third, mode);
  cpkey(Kn3);
  deskey(first, mode);
  return;
```

```
  }

void cp3key(into)
unsigned long *into;                   /* unsigned long[96] */
{
  unsigned long *from, *endp;

  cpkey(into);
  into = &into[32];
  from = KnR, endp = &KnR[32];
  while( from < endp ) *into++ = *from++;
  from = Kn3, endp = &Kn3[32];
  while( from < endp ) *into++ = *from++;
  return;
  }

void use3key(from)
unsigned long *from;                   /* unsigned long[96] */
{
  unsigned long *to, *endp;

  usekey(from);
  from = &from[32];
  to = KnR, endp = &KnR[32];
  while( to < endp ) *to++ = *from++;
  to = Kn3, endp = &Kn3[32];
  while( to < endp ) *to++ = *from++;
  return;
  }

static void D3des(unsigned char *, unsigned char *);

static void D3des(from, into)/* amateur theatrics */
unsigned char *from;                   /* unsigned char[24] */
unsigned char *into;                   /* unsigned char[24] */
{
  unsigned long swap, leftt[2], middl[2], right[2];

  scrunch(from, leftt);
  scrunch(&from[8], middl);
  scrunch(&from[16], right);
  desfunc(leftt, KnL);
  desfunc(middl, KnL);
  desfunc(right, KnL);
  swap = leftt[1];
  leftt[1] = middl[0];
```

```
    middl[0] = swap;
    swap = middl[1];
    middl[1] = right[0];
    right[0] = swap;
    desfunc(leftt, KnR);
    desfunc(middl, KnR);
    desfunc(right, KnR);
    swap = leftt[1];
    leftt[1] = middl[0];
    middl[0] = swap;
    swap = middl[1];
    middl[1] = right[0];
    right[0] = swap;
    desfunc(leftt, Kn3);
    desfunc(middl, Kn3);
    desfunc(right, Kn3);
    unscrun(leftt, into);
    unscrun(middl, &into[8]);
    unscrun(right, &into[16]);
    return;
    }

void make3key(aptr, kptr)
char *aptr;                                   /* NULL-terminated   */
unsigned char *kptr;           /* unsigned char[24] */
{
    unsigned char *store;
    int first, i;
    unsigned long savek[96];

    cp3key(savek);
    des3key(Df_Key, EN0);
    for( i = 0; i < 24; i++ ) kptr[i] = Df_Key[i];
    first = 1;
    while( (*aptr != '\0') || first ) {
        store = kptr;
        for( i = 0; i < 24 && (*aptr != '\0'); i++ ) {
            *store++ ^= *aptr & 0x7f;
            *aptr++ = '\0';
            }
        D3des(kptr, kptr);
        first = 0;
        }
    use3key(savek);
    return;
    }
```

```
#endif /* D3_DES */
#endif /* D2_DES */

/* Validation sets:
 *
 * Single-length key, single-length plaintext -
 * Key    : 0123 4567 89ab cdef
 * Plain  : 0123 4567 89ab cde7
 * Cipher : c957 4425 6a5e d31d
 *
 * Double-length key, single-length plaintext -
 * Key    : 0123 4567 89ab cdef fedc ba98 7654 3210
 * Plain  : 0123 4567 89ab cde7
 * Cipher : 7f1d 0a77 826b 8aff
 *
 * Double-length key, double-length plaintext -
 * Key    : 0123 4567 89ab cdef fedc ba98 7654 3210
 * Plain  : 0123 4567 89ab cdef 0123 4567 89ab cdff
 * Cipher : 27a0 8440 406a df60 278f 47cf 42d6 15d7
 *
 * Triple-length key, single-length plaintext -
 * Key    : 0123 4567 89ab cdef fedc ba98 7654 3210 89ab cdef 0123 4567
 * Plain  : 0123 4567 89ab cde7
 * Cipher : de0b 7c06 ae5e 0ed5
 *
 * Triple-length key, double-length plaintext -
 * Key    : 0123 4567 89ab cdef fedc ba98 7654 3210 89ab cdef 0123 4567
 * Plain  : 0123 4567 89ab cdef 0123 4567 89ab cdff
 * Cipher : ad0d 1b30 ac17 cf07 0ed1 1c63 81e4 4de5
 *
 * d3des V5.0A rwo 9211.09 13:55 Graven Imagery
 **********************************************************************/
```

LUCIFER

```
/*
 * lucifer.c
 *
 * C implementation of IBM lucifer cipher
 *
 * This version: 3/16/91, Jonathan M. Smith
 */

#include <stdio.h>
```

```
#define ENCIPHER 0
#define DECIPHER 1

#define L_BLOCK 128                    /* bits in a lucifer block */
#define BPB 8                          /* bits per byte */

int m[L_BLOCK];                                    /* message vector */
int k[L_BLOCK];                                    /* key vector */

int o[8] = { 7, 6, 2, 1, 5, 0, 3, 4 };  /* diffusion pattern */
int pr[8] = { 2, 5, 4, 0, 3, 1, 7, 6 }; /* inverse of fixed permutation */

/* S-box permutations */
int s0[16] = { 12, 15, 7, 10, 14, 13, 11, 0, 2, 6, 3, 1, 9, 4, 5, 8 };
int s1[16] = { 7, 2, 14, 9, 3, 11, 0, 4, 12, 13, 1, 10, 6, 15, 8, 5 };

lucifer( direction )
int direction;
{
  int tcbindex, tcbcontrol; /* transfer control byte indices */
  int round, hi, lo, h_0, h_1;
  register int bit, temp1;
  int byte, index, v, tr[BPB];

  h_0 = 0;
  h_1 = 1;

  if( direction == DECIPHER )
    tcbcontrol = 8;
  else
    tcbcontrol = 0;


  for( round=0; round < 16; round += 1 )
  {
    if( direction == DECIPHER )
      tcbcontrol = (tcbcontrol+1) & 0xF;
    tcbindex = tcbcontrol;
    for( byte = 0; byte < 8; byte +=1 )
    {
      lo = (m[(h_1*64)+(BPB*byte)+7])*8
        +(m[(h_1*64)+(BPB*byte)+6])*4
        +(m[(h_1*64)+(BPB*byte)+5])*2
        +(m[(h_1*64)+(BPB*byte)+4]);
      hi = (m[(h_1*64)+(BPB*byte)+3])*8
        +(m[(h_1*64)+(BPB*byte)+2])*4
```

```
          +(m[(h_1*64)+(BPB*byte)+1])*2
          +(m[(h_1*64)+(BPB*byte)+0]);

    v = (s0[lo]+16*s1[hi])*(1-k[(BPB*tcbindex)+byte])
        +(s0[hi]+16*s1[lo])*k[(BPB*tcbindex)+byte];

    for( temp1 = 0; temp1 < BPB; temp1 += 1 )
    {
      tr[temp1] = v & 0x1;
      v = v>>1;
    }

    for( bit = 0; bit < BPB; bit += 1 )
    {
      index = (o[bit]+byte) & 0x7;
      temp1 = m[(h_0*64)+(BPB*index)+bit]
        +k[(BPB*tcbcontrol)+pr[bit]]
        +tr[pr[bit]];
      m[(h_0*64)+(BPB*index)+bit] = temp1 & 0x1;
    }

    if( byte<7 || direction == DECIPHER )
      tcbcontrol = (tcbcontrol+1) & 0xF;
  }

  temp1 = h_0;
  h_0 = h_1;
  h_1 = temp1;
}

/* final swap */
for( byte = 0; byte < 8; byte += 1 )
{
  for( bit = 0; bit < BPB; bit += 1 )
  {
    temp1 = m[(BPB*byte)+bit];
    m[(BPB*byte)+bit] = m[64+(BPB*byte)+bit];
    m[64+(BPB*byte)+bit] = temp1;
  }
}

return;

}

/*
```

```
 * mygetpw()
 * essentially getpass() with modifiable length parms
 */

#include <sys/ioctl.h>
#include <termio.h>
#include <fcntl.h>

#ifndef EOS
#define EOS '\0'
#endif

#ifndef EOL
#define EOL '\n'
#endif

mygetpw( buf, len, prompt )
char *buf, *prompt;
int len;
{
  int i, fd;
  struct termio t;
  unsigned short save;

  fd = open( "/dev/tty", O_RDWR );
  if( fd >= 0 )
  {
    write( fd, prompt, strlen( prompt ) );
    ioctl( fd, TCGETA, &t );
    save = t.c_lflag;
    t.c_lflag &= ~ECHO;
    ioctl( fd, TCSETAW, &t );

    for( i = 0; i < len; i += 1 )
    {
      if( read( fd, &buf[i], sizeof(char) ) < sizeof(char) )
        break;
      if( buf[i] == EOL )
      {
        write( fd, &buf[i], sizeof(char) );
        break;
      }
    }
    for( ; i < len; i += 1 )
      buf[i] = EOS;
```

```
    t.c_lflag = save;
    ioctl( fd, TCSETAF, &t );
    close( fd );
  }
  else
  {
    fprintf( stderr, "Can't open /dev/tty. Exiting!\n" );
    exit( 1 );
  }

  return;
}


/*
 * this front-end uses mygetpw() to get a key, and then
 * loads the key into k,
 * and then operates on the message 128 bits at a time,
 * by putting it in "m" and calling lucifer().
 * encryption/decryption controlled by a command line argument.
 */


main( argc, argv )
int argc;
char *argv[];
{
  int i, c, output, counter, direction;
  char buf[16];

  if( argc != 2 )
    usage();
  if( argv[1][0] != '-' || argv[1][2] != '\0' )
    usage();
  if( argv[1][1] == 'd' )
    direction = DECIPHER;
  else if( argv[1][1] == 'e' )
    direction = ENCIPHER;
  else
    usage();

  mygetpw( buf, 16, "Password: " );
  for( counter = 0; counter < 16; counter += 1 )
  {
    c = buf[counter] & 0xFF;
    for( i = 0; i < BPB; i += 1 )
```

```
    {
      k[(BPB*counter)+i] = c & 0x1;
      c = c>>1;
    }
  }

  counter = 0;

  while( (c=getchar()) != EOF )
  {
    if( counter == 16 )
    {
      lucifer( direction );
      for( counter = 0; counter < 16; counter += 1 )
      {
        output = 0;
        for( i = BPB-1; i >= 0; i -= 1 )
        {
          output = (output<<1) + m[(BPB*counter)+i];
        }
        putchar( output );
      }
      counter = 0;

    }

    for( i = 0; i < BPB; i += 1 )
    {
      m[(BPB*counter)+i] = c & 0x1;
      c = c>>1;
    }
    counter += 1;
  }
  for( ;counter < 16; counter += 1 )
    for( i = 0; i < BPB; i += 1 )
      m[(BPB*counter)+i] = 0;

  lucifer( direction );
  for( counter = 0; counter < 16; counter += 1 )
  {
    output = 0;
    for( i = BPB-1; i >= 0; i -= 1 )
    {
      output = (output<<1) + m[(BPB*counter)+i];
    }
    putchar( output );
```

```
  }

  exit( 0 );

}

usage()
{
  fprintf( stderr, "Usage: lucifer -[e|d]\n" );
  exit( 1 );
}
```

NEWDES

●
```
/*-- newdes2.c — Program to implement the NEWDES algorithm.
 *   Mark Riordan     12 August 1990.
 */
#include "newdes2p.h"

#define SIZE_ROTOR       256
#define SIZE_KEY_UNRAV    60
#define SIZE_USER_KEY     15
#define BLOCK_BYTES        8

#if 0
unsigned int newdes_buf(unsigned char *buf,unsigned int block_length);
void newdes_block(unsigned char *block);
void newdes_set_key_encipher(unsigned char *key);
void newdes_set_key_decipher(unsigned char *key);
#endif

unsigned char newdes_rotor[SIZE_ROTOR]
 = {
   32,137,239,188,102,125,221, 72,212, 68, 81, 37, 86,237,147,149,
   70,229, 17,124,115,207, 33, 20,122,143, 25,215, 51,183,138,142,
  146,211,110,173,  1,228,189, 14,103, 78,162, 36,253,167,116,255,
  158, 45,185, 50, 98,168,250,235, 54,141,195,247,240, 63,148,  2,
  224,169,214,180, 62, 22,117,108, 19,172,161,159,160, 47, 43,171,
  194,175,178, 56,196,112, 23,220, 89, 21,164,130,157,  8, 85,251,
  216, 44, 94,179,226, 38, 90,119, 40,202, 34,206, 35, 69,231,246,
   29,109, 74, 71,176,  6, 60,145, 65, 13, 77,151, 12,127, 95,199,
   57,101,  5,232,150,210,129, 24,181, 10,121,187, 48,193,139,252,
  219, 64, 88,233, 96,128, 80, 53,191,144,218, 11,106,132,155,104,
   91,136, 31, 42,243, 66,126,135, 30, 26, 87,186,182,154,242,123,
   82,166,208, 39,152,190,113,205,114,105,225, 84, 73,163, 99,111,
```

```
    204,  61,200,217,170,  15,198,  28,192,254,134,234,222,   7,236,248,
    201,  41,177,156,  92,131,  67,249,245,184,203,   9,241,   0,  27,  46,
    133,174,  75,  18,  93,209,100,120,  76,213,  16,  83,   4,107,140,  52,
     58,  55,   3,244,  97,197,238,227,118,  49,  79,230,223,165,153,  59
};

unsigned char newdes_key_unravelled[SIZE_KEY_UNRAV];


/*-- function newdes_buf ─────────────────-
 *
 * Encipher or decipher a buffer of data.
 *
 *     Entry     buf                points to the buffer.
 *               block_length   is the number of bytes in the buffer.
 *                                  If it is not a multiple of 8, it will be
 *                                  rounded up to the next multiple of 8—
 *                                  so make sure that the buffer is long enough.
 *               newdes_key_unravelled   points to the key.  It has
 *                      been "unravelled" as necessary for either
 *                      enciphering or deciphering.
 *               newdes_rotor   is the fundamental mapping function
 *                      (array) for NEWDES.
 *
 *     Exit     Returns the number of bytes now in the buffer
 *                (rounded up as described above).
 */
unsigned int
newdes_buf(buf,block_length)
unsigned char *buf;
unsigned int block_length;
{
  unsigned int mylen, mylen2;

  if(block_length > 0) {
    mylen2 = mylen = (((block_length - 1) / BLOCK_BYTES) + 1) * BLOCK_BYTES;
  }

  for(;mylen; mylen -= BLOCK_BYTES){
    newdes_block(buf);
    buf += BLOCK_BYTES;
  }

  return(mylen2);
}
```

```c
/*-- function newdes_block ----------------------
 *
 *   Encipher or decipher an 8-byte block.
 *
 *      Entry     block    points to the block.
 *                newdes_key_unravelled   points to the key.  It has
 *                          been "unravelled" as necessary for either
 *                          enciphering or deciphering.
 *                newdes_rotor   is the fundamental mapping function
 *                          (array) for NEWDES.
 */
void
newdes_block(block)
unsigned char *block;
{
  unsigned char *keyptr = newdes_key_unravelled;
  register unsigned char *byteptr = block;
  int count;

#define B0 (*byteptr)
#define B1 (*(byteptr+1))
#define B2 (*(byteptr+2))
#define B3 (*(byteptr+3))
#define B4 (*(byteptr+4))
#define B5 (*(byteptr+5))
#define B6 (*(byteptr+6))
#define B7 (*(byteptr+7))

  for(count=8; count-;) {
    B4 = B4 ^ newdes_rotor[B0 ^ *(keyptr++)];
    B5 = B5 ^ newdes_rotor[B1 ^ *(keyptr++)];
    B6 = B6 ^ newdes_rotor[B2 ^ *(keyptr++)];
    B7 = B7 ^ newdes_rotor[B3 ^ *(keyptr++)];

    B1 = B1 ^ newdes_rotor[B4 ^ *(keyptr++)];
    B2 = B2 ^ newdes_rotor[B4 ^ B5];
    B3 = B3 ^ newdes_rotor[B6 ^ *(keyptr++)];
    B0 = B0 ^ newdes_rotor[B7 ^ *(keyptr++)];
  }
  B4 = B4 ^ newdes_rotor[B0 ^ *(keyptr++)];
  B5 = B5 ^ newdes_rotor[B1 ^ *(keyptr++)];
  B6 = B6 ^ newdes_rotor[B2 ^ *(keyptr++)];
  B7 = B7 ^ newdes_rotor[B3 ^ *(keyptr++)];
}


/*-- function newdes_set_key_encipher ----------------
```

```
*
*      Set newdes to encipher using a given key.
*
*      Entry    key   points to a 15-byte key.
*
*      Exit     newdes_key_unravelled   contains the key set up properly
*                      for use in newdes_block, for enciphering.
*/
void
newdes_set_key_encipher(key)
unsigned char *key;
{
  unsigned char *kuserptr, *kunravptr;
  int outloopct = SIZE_KEY_UNRAV / SIZE_USER_KEY;
  int inloopct;

  kunravptr = newdes_key_unravelled;
  for(;outloopct—;) {
    kuserptr = key;
    for(inloopct=SIZE_USER_KEY; inloopct—;) {
     *(kunravptr++) = *(kuserptr++);
    }
  }
}


/*—- function newdes_set_key_decipher ————————————-
 *
 *      Set newdes to decipher using a given key.
 *
 *      Entry    key   points to a 15-byte key.
 *
 *      Exit     newdes_key_unravelled   contains the key set up properly
 *                      for use in newdes_block, for deciphering.
 */
void
newdes_set_key_decipher(key)
unsigned char *key;
{
  unsigned char *kunravptr;
  int outloopct = SIZE_KEY_UNRAV / SIZE_USER_KEY;
  int userkeyidx;

  kunravptr = newdes_key_unravelled;
  userkeyidx = 11;
  while (1) {
```

```
   *(kunravptr++) = key[userkeyidx];
   userkeyidx++;
   if(userkeyidx == SIZE_USER_KEY) userkeyidx = 0;

   *(kunravptr++) = key[userkeyidx];
   userkeyidx++;
   if(userkeyidx == SIZE_USER_KEY) userkeyidx = 0;

   *(kunravptr++) = key[userkeyidx];
   userkeyidx++;
   if(userkeyidx == SIZE_USER_KEY) userkeyidx = 0;

   *(kunravptr++) = key[userkeyidx];
   userkeyidx = (userkeyidx+9) % 15;

   if(userkeyidx == 12) break;

   *(kunravptr++) = key[userkeyidx++];
   *(kunravptr++) = key[userkeyidx++];

   *(kunravptr++) = key[userkeyidx];

   userkeyidx = (userkeyidx+9) % 15;
  }
}
```

FEAL-8

```
/* FEAL8.H——————————————————————————————
Version of 20 September 1989.
*/

typedef unsigned char ByteType ;

void SetKey( ByteType * ) ;
void Encrypt( ByteType *Plain, ByteType *Cipher ) ;
void Decrypt( ByteType *Cipher, ByteType *Plain ) ;
/* FEAL8 - Implementation of NTT's FEAL-8 cipher.——————————-
Version of 11 September 1989.
*/

#include "feal8.h"
#ifdef DEBUG
#include <stdio.h>
#endif
```

```
typedef unsigned long HalfWord ;

typedef unsigned int QuarterWord ;

QuarterWord K[16] ;
HalfWord K89, K1011, K1213, K1415 ;

void Decrypt( ByteType *Cipher, ByteType *Plain )
/*
   Decrypt a block, using the last key set.
*/
{
  HalfWord L, R, NewL ;
  int r ;
  HalfWord MakeH1( ByteType * ) ;
  HalfWord f( HalfWord, QuarterWord ) ;
  void DissH1( HalfWord, ByteType * ) ;

  R = MakeH1( Cipher ) ;
  L = MakeH1( Cipher+4 ) ;
  R ^= K1213 ;
  L ^= K1415 ;
  L ^= R ;

  for ( r = 7 ; r >= 0 ; -r )
  {
   NewL = R ^ f( L, K[r] ) ;
   R = L ;
   L = NewL ;
  }

  R ^= L ;
  R ^= K1011 ;
  L ^= K89 ;

  DissH1( L, Plain ) ;
  DissH1( R, Plain + 4 ) ;
}

void DissH1( HalfWord H, ByteType *D )
/*
   Disassemble the given halfword into 4 bytes.
*/
{
  union {
```

```
   HalfWord All ;
   ByteType Byte[4] ;
  } T ;

  T.All = H ;
  *D++ = T.Byte[0] ;
  *D++ = T.Byte[1] ;
  *D++ = T.Byte[2] ;
  *D   = T.Byte[3] ;
}

void DissQ1( QuarterWord Q, ByteType *B )
/*
   Disassemble a quarterword into two Bytes.
*/
{
  union {
   QuarterWord All ;
   ByteType Byte[2] ;
  } QQ ;

  QQ.All = Q ;
  *B++ = QQ.Byte[0] ;
  *B   = QQ.Byte[1] ;
}

void Encrypt( ByteType *Plain, ByteType *Cipher )
/*
   Encrypt a block, using the last key set.
*/
{
  HalfWord L, R, NewR ;
  int r ;
  HalfWord MakeH1( ByteType * ) ;
  HalfWord f( HalfWord, QuarterWord ) ;
  void DissH1( HalfWord, ByteType * ) ;

  L = MakeH1( Plain ) ;
  R = MakeH1( Plain+4 ) ;
  L ^= K89 ;
  R ^= K1011 ;
  R ^= L ;

#ifdef DEBUG
  printf( "p:  %08lx %08lx\n", L, R ) ;
#endif
```

```
  for ( r = 0 ; r < 8 ; ++r )
  {
   NewR = L ^ f( R, K[r] ) ;
   L = R ;
   R = NewR ;
#ifdef DEBUG
  printf( "%2d: %08lx %08lx\n", r, L, R ) ;
#endif
  }

  L ^= R ;
  R ^= K1213 ;
  L ^= K1415 ;

  DissH1( R, Cipher ) ;
  DissH1( L, Cipher + 4 ) ;
}

HalfWord f( HalfWord AA, QuarterWord BB )
/*
   Evaluate the f function.
*/
{
  ByteType f1, f2 ;
  union {
   unsigned long All ;
   ByteType Byte[4] ;
  } RetVal, A ;
  union {
   unsigned int All ;
   ByteType Byte[2] ;
  } B ;
  ByteType S0( ByteType, ByteType ) ;
  ByteType S1( ByteType, ByteType ) ;

  A.All = AA ;
  B.All = BB ;
  f1 = A.Byte[1] ^ B.Byte[0] ^ A.Byte[0] ;
  f2 = A.Byte[2] ^ B.Byte[1] ^ A.Byte[3] ;
  f1 = S1( f1, f2 ) ;
  f2 = S0( f2, f1 ) ;
  RetVal.Byte[1] = f1 ;
  RetVal.Byte[2] = f2 ;
  RetVal.Byte[0] = S0( A.Byte[0], f1 ) ;
  RetVal.Byte[3] = S1( A.Byte[3], f2 ) ;
  return RetVal.All ;
```

```
}

HalfWord FK( HalfWord AA, HalfWord BB )
/*
    Evaluate the FK function.
*/
{
  ByteType FK1, FK2 ;
  union {
   unsigned long All ;
   ByteType Byte[4] ;
  } RetVal, A, B ;
  ByteType S0( ByteType, ByteType ) ;
  ByteType S1( ByteType, ByteType ) ;

  A.All = AA ;
  B.All = BB ;
  FK1 = A.Byte[1] ^ A.Byte[0] ;
  FK2 = A.Byte[2] ^ A.Byte[3] ;
  FK1 = S1( FK1, FK2 ^ B.Byte[0] ) ;
  FK2 = S0( FK2, FK1 ^ B.Byte[1] ) ;
  RetVal.Byte[1] = FK1 ;
  RetVal.Byte[2] = FK2 ;
  RetVal.Byte[0] = S0( A.Byte[0], FK1 ^ B.Byte[2] ) ;
  RetVal.Byte[3] = S1( A.Byte[3], FK2 ^ B.Byte[3] ) ;
  rcturn RetVal.All ;
}

HalfWord MakeH1( ByteType *B )
/*
   Assemble a HalfWord from the four bytes provided.
*/
{
  union {
   unsigned long All ;
   ByteType Byte[4] ;
  } RetVal ;

  RetVal.Byte[0] = *B++ ;
  RetVal.Byte[1] = *B++ ;
  RetVal.Byte[2] = *B++ ;
  RetVal.Byte[3] = *B ;
  return RetVal.All ;
}

HalfWord MakeH2( QuarterWord *Q )
```

```
/*
   Make a halfword from the two quarterwords given.
*/
{
  ByteType B[4] ;
  void DissQ1( QuarterWord, ByteType * ) ;

  DissQ1( *Q++, B ) ;
  DissQ1( *Q, B+2 ) ;
  return MakeH1( B ) ;
}

ByteType Rot2( ByteType X )
/*
   Evaluate the Rot2 function.
*/
{
  static int First = 1 ;
  static ByteType RetVal[ 256 ] ;

  if ( First )
  {
   int i, High, Low ;
   for ( i = 0, High = 0, Low = 0 ; i < 256 ; ++i )
   {
    RetVal[ i ] = High + Low ;
    High += 4 ;
    if ( High > 255 )
    {
    High = 0 ;
    ++Low ;
    }
   }
   First = 0 ;
  }
  return RetVal[ X ] ;
}

ByteType S0( ByteType X1, ByteType X2 )
{
  ByteType Rot2( ByteType X ) ;

  return Rot2( ( X1 + X2 ) & 0xff ) ;
}

ByteType S1( ByteType X1, ByteType X2 )
```

```
{
  ByteType Rot2( ByteType X ) ;

  return Rot2( ( X1 + X2 + 1 ) & 0xff ) ;
}

void SetKey( ByteType *KP )
/*
   KP points to an array of 8 bytes.
*/
{
  union {
   HalfWord All ;
   ByteType Byte[4] ;
  } A, B, D, NewB ;
  union {
   QuarterWord All ;
   ByteType Byte[2] ;
  } Q ;
  int i ;
  QuarterWord *Out ;
  HalfWord FK( HalfWord, HalfWord ) ;
  HalfWord MakeH2( QuarterWord * ) ;

  A.Byte[0] = *KP++ ;
  A.Byte[1] = *KP++ ;
  A.Byte[2] = *KP++ ;
  A.Byte[3] = *KP++ ;
  B.Byte[0] = *KP++ ;
  B.Byte[1] = *KP++ ;
  B.Byte[2] = *KP++ ;
  B.Byte[3] = *KP ;
  D.All = 0 ;

  for ( i = 1, Out = K ; i <= 8 ; ++i )
  {
   NewB.All = FK( A.All, B.All ^ D.All ) ;
   D = A ;
   A = B ;
   B = NewB ;
   Q.Byte[0] = B.Byte[0] ;
   Q.Byte[1] = B.Byte[1] ;
   *Out++ = Q.All ;
   Q.Byte[0] = B.Byte[2] ;
   Q.Byte[1] = B.Byte[3] ;
   *Out++ = Q.All ;
```

```
  }
  K89 = MakeH2( K+8 ) ;
  K1011 = MakeH2( K+10 ) ;
  K1213 = MakeH2( K+12 ) ;
  K1415 = MakeH2( K+14 ) ;
}
```

FEAL-NX

```
/* FEALNX.H - Specification for FEALNX package.
Version of 92.12.28 by Peter Pearson.
*/

/* Definitions
 * ────-
 * The user of this package is discouraged from referring to the internals
 * of these data types, in order that the implementation may be changed
 * without affecting client programs.
 */

typedef struct {
        int NRounds ;
        unsigned char *KSchedule ;
    } *KeyScheduleType ;

typedef unsigned char DataBlockType[8] ;

/* Services
 * ────
 * The intended usage of this package:
 *      #include "fealnx.h"
 *      KeyScheduleType KS ;
 *      unsigned char Key[16] = { ... } ;
 *      KS = NewKeySchedule( 32, Key ) ;
 *      Encrypt( KS, Plain, Cipher ) ;
 *      free( KS ) ;
 */


/************************************************************************
 * NewKeySchedule takes a 16-byte key, builds a key schedule, and
 * returns a pointer to that key schedule. The caller should free
 * the key schedule (using the standard C runtime routine "free")
 * when it is no longer needed.
 * NewKeySchedule returns the value NULL (stdlib.h) if memory cannot
 * be allocated for the key schedule.
```

```
 ********************************************************************/

KeyScheduleType NewKeySchedule( int Rounds, unsigned char *Key ) ;

/*******************************************************************
 * Encrypt and Decrypt to the obvious. Note that the key schedule must
 * have been established by prior call to NewKeySchedule.
 ********************************************************************/

void Encrypt( KeyScheduleType K, DataBlockType Plain, DataBlockType Cipher ) ;
void Decrypt( KeyScheduleType K, DataBlockType Cipher, DataBlockType Plain ) ;


 ――――――――――― begin file FEALNX.C ――――――――――-
/* FEALNX.C - Implementation of the FEALNX package.
Version of 92.12.28 by Peter Pearson.

This implementation strives primarily for portability and secondarily for
clarity, with execution speed only a tertiary consideration. On
processors with 16-bit or 32-bit registers, the quickest way to boost
execution speed is to lump the data into pieces bigger than 8 bits.
*/

#include <alloc.h> /* For "malloc".              */
#include <mem.h>   /* For "memcpy" and "memset".*/
#include "fealnx.h"

#define S0(x,y)Rot2((x)+(y))
#define S1(x,y)Rot2((x)+(y)+1)

void CalcFk( unsigned char Output[4], unsigned char Alpha[4],
                     unsigned char Beta[4] )
/*
    Calculate the function "fk" of the two specified inputs,
    and write the resulting four bytes to the provided output.
*/
{
  unsigned char t1, t2 ;
  unsigned char Rot2( int A ) ;

  t1 = Alpha[0] ^ Alpha[1] ;
  t2 = Alpha[2] ^ Alpha[3] ;
  t1 = S1( t1, t2 ^ Beta[0] ) ;
  t2 = S0( t2, t1 ^ Beta[1] ) ;
  Output[1] = t1 ;
  Output[2] = t2 ;
```

```
  Output[0] = S0( Alpha[0], t1 ^ Beta[2] ) ;
  Output[3] = S1( Alpha[3], t2 ^ Beta[3] ) ;
}


void Decrypt( KeyScheduleType K, DataBlockType Cipher, DataBlockType Plain )
{
  int Rounds ;
  int i ;
  unsigned char L[4], R[4], NewR[4] ;
  unsigned char *KP ;
  unsigned char *Xor4( unsigned char A[4], unsigned char B[4] ) ;
  unsigned char *F( unsigned char K[2], unsigned char R[4] ) ;

  Rounds = K->NRounds ;
  KP = K->KSchedule + 2 * Rounds ;
  movmem(             Xor4( KP + 8,  Cipher        ), L, 4 ) ;
  movmem( Xor4( L, Xor4( KP + 12, Cipher + 4 ) ), R, 4 ) ;
  for ( i = 0 ; i < Rounds ; ++i )
  {
    KP -= 2 ;
    movmem( Xor4( L, F( KP, R ) ), NewR, 4 ) ;
    movmem( R, L, 4 ) ;
    movmem( NewR, R, 4 ) ;
  }  /* Fall out with KP pointing to KSchedule.*/
  KP = K->KSchedule + 2 * Rounds ;
  movmem( Xor4( KP     , R            ), Plain, 4 ) ;
  movmem( Xor4( KP + 4, Xor4( R, L ) ), Plain + 4, 4 ) ;
}


void Encrypt( KeyScheduleType K, DataBlockType Plain, DataBlockType Cipher )
{
  int Rounds ;
  int i ;
  unsigned char L[4], R[4], NewR[4] ;
  unsigned char *KP ;
  unsigned char *Xor4( unsigned char A[4], unsigned char B[4] ) ;
  unsigned char *F( unsigned char K[2], unsigned char R[4] ) ;

  KP = K->KSchedule ;
  Rounds = K->NRounds ;
  movmem(             Xor4( KP + 2 * Rounds,     Plain        ), L, 4 ) ;
  movmem( Xor4( L, Xor4( KP + 2 * Rounds + 4, Plain + 4 ) ), R, 4 ) ;
  for ( i = 0 ; i < Rounds ; ++i, KP += 2 )
  {
    movmem( Xor4( L, F( KP, R ) ), NewR, 4 ) ;
    movmem( R, L, 4 ) ;
```

```
      movmem( NewR, R, 4 ) ;
    }  /* Fall out with KP pointing to KSchedule[ 2*Rounds ].*/
    movmem( Xor4( KP + 8,  R             ), Cipher, 4 ) ;
    movmem( Xor4( KP + 12, Xor4( R, L ) ), Cipher + 4, 4 ) ;
}


unsigned char *F( unsigned char Beta[2], unsigned char Alpha[4] )
/*
    This function implements the "f" box in the Feal-N
    flowchart.

The result is returned in a static array, and will be overwritten
when this function is next called.
*/
{
    unsigned char t1, t2 ;
    static unsigned char Result[4] ;
    unsigned char Rot2( int A ) ;

    t1 = Alpha[0] ^ Alpha[1] ^ Beta[0] ;
    t2 = Alpha[2] ^ Alpha[3] ^ Beta[1] ;
    t1 = S1( t1, t2 ) ;
    t2 = S0( t2, t1 ) ;
    Result[1] = t1 ;
    Result[2] = t2 ;
    Result[0] = S0( t1, Alpha[0] ) ;
    Result[3] = S1( t2, Alpha[3] ) ;
    return Result ;
}


KeyScheduleType NewKeySchedule( int Rounds, unsigned char *Key )
{
    KeyScheduleType Result ;
    int Step ;
    unsigned char *KSP ;
    unsigned char a[4], b[4], c[4], d[4] ;
    void CalcFk( unsigned char Output[4], unsigned char In1[4],
                        unsigned char In2[4] ) ;
    unsigned char *Xor4( unsigned char A[4], unsigned char B[4] ) ;

    Result = malloc( ( sizeof( *Result ) + Rounds + 8 ) * 2 ) ;
    if ( Result != NULL )
    {
        Result->NRounds = Rounds ;
        Result->KSchedule = ( unsigned char *) ( Result + 1 ) ;
        memcpy( a, Key,   4 ) ;
```

```
      memcpy( b, Key+4, 4 ) ;
      memcpy( c, Xor4( Key + 8, Key + 12 ), 4 ) ;
      memset( d, 0, 4 ) ;
      KSP = Result->KSchedule ;
      for ( Step = 0 ; Step < Rounds/2 + 4 ; ++Step, KSP += 4 )
      {
        switch( Step % 3 )
        {
         case 0:
          CalcFk( KSP, a, Xor4( d, Xor4( b, c ) ) ) ;
          break ;

         case 1:
          CalcFk( KSP, a, Xor4( d, Xor4( b, Key + 8 ) ) ) ;
          break ;

         case 2:
          CalcFk( KSP, a, Xor4( d, Xor4( b, Key + 12 ) ) ) ;
          break ;
        }
        memcpy( d, a, 4 ) ;
        memcpy( a, b, 4 ) ;
        memcpy( b, KSP, 4 ) ;
      }
  }
  return Result ;
}

unsigned char Rot2( int X )
/*
    Return X (an 8-bit quantity) rotated left by two bits.

    (In an uncharacteristic concession to execution speed, we
    implement this function by table lookup.)
*/
{
  static First = 1 ;
  static unsigned char Result[ 256 ] ;

  if ( First )
  {
    int i ;

    for ( i = 0 ; i < 256 ; ++i )
      Result[i] = ( i << 2 ) + ( i >> 6 ) ;
    First = 0 ;
```

```
  }

  return Result[ X & 0xFF ] ;
}

unsigned char *Xor4( unsigned char A[4], unsigned char B[4] )
/*
    Exclusive-or two 4-byte quantities. Return a pointer to
    the result.

    The pointer returned points to a static variable that will
    be overwritten the next time this function is called. We
    guarantee that calls to this function may be nested simply
    (e.g., Xor4( a, Xor4( b, Xor4( c, d ) ) ) ) but anything
    more complex may behave badly. (For example,
    Xor4( Xor4( a, b ), Xor4( c, d ) ) will result in all 0s) .
*/
{
    static unsigned char Result[4] ;

    Result[0] = A[0] ^ B[0] ;
    Result[1] = A[1] ^ B[1] ;
    Result[2] = A[2] ^ B[2] ;
    Result[3] = A[3] ^ B[3] ;
    return Result ;
}
```

REDOC III

```
•
#include <stdio.h>
#include <stdlib.h>


#define byte unsigned char


union U_INT
{
    byte    b_int[2];
    int     i_int;
};

int i;

byte  key_table[2560];
```

```
byte  mask_table[16];

byte  key_length = 6;
byte  master_key[70] = {89, 66, 128, 231, 18, 43};

byte  the_data[8];

byte  initialize_key_table ()
{
  int   data_point, pi, pii;
  union  U_INTseed, data_value;
  unsigned int prime[35] = {  1,    3,    5,    7,  11,  13,  17,
             19,   23,   29,   31,  37,  41,  43,
             47,   53,   59,   61,  67,  71,  73,
             79,   83,   89,   97, 101, 103, 107,
            109, 113, 127, 131, 137, 139, 149};

  for (pi = 1; pi <= key_length; ++pi)
  {
  if (pi != key_length)
  {   seed.b_int[0] = master_key[pi-1];
   seed.b_int[1] = master_key[pi];
  }
   else
  {   seed.b_int[0] = master_key[pi-1];
   seed.b_int[1] = master_key[0];
  }

  srand (seed.i_int);
  data_point = 0;

  for (pii = 0; pii < 2560; ++pii)
  { data_point += prime[pi];
   if (data_point > 2559) data_point -= 2560;

   data_value.i_int = rand ();

   key_table[data_point] = data_value.b_int[0];
   if ( (data_point + 1) != 2559)
   key_table[data_point + 1] = data_value.b_int[1];
    else
   key_table[0] = data_value.b_int[1];
  }

  }
```

```
   return (0);
}

byte  create_mask_table ()
{
   int pi, mask_counter;
   byte  *mask_pointer;

   mask_pointer = mask_table;
   mask_counter = 0;

   for (pi = 0; pi < 16; ++pi) mask_table[pi] = 0;

   for (pi = 0; pi < 2560; ++pi)
   { *mask_pointer ^= key_table[pi];
   ++mask_pointer;
   ++mask_counter;
   if (mask_counter == 16)
     {   mask_counter = 0;
         mask_pointer = mask_table;
     }
   }

   return (0);
}




byte encrypt_data (data)
   byte *data;
{
   int pi, pii, key_value;
   byte  *mask_point, *data_point, *valu_point;

   valu_point = data;
   mask_point = mask_table;

   for (pi = 0; pi < 8; ++pi)
   {   key_value = *valu_point ^ *mask_point;
    key_value *= 8;
    ++valu_point;
    ++mask_point;

    data_point = data;
    for (pii = 0; pii < 8; ++pii)
    { if (pi != pii) *data_point ^= key_table[key_value + pii];
```

```
    ++data_point;
   }
  }


  valu_point = data;

  for (pi = 0; pi < 8; ++pi)
  {
   key_value = *valu_point ^ *mask_point;
   key_value *= 8;
   ++valu_point;
   ++mask_point;

   data_point = data;
   for (pii = 0; pii < 8; ++pii)
   { if (pi != pii) *data_point ^= key_table[key_value + pii];
     ++data_point;
   }
  }

  return (0);
}

byte decrypt_data (data)
  byte *data;
{
  int pi, pii, key_value;
  byte *mask_point, *data_point, *valu_point;

  valu_point = data+7;
  mask_point = mask_table+15;

  for (pi = 7; pi >= 0; -pi)
  {  key_value = *valu_point ^ *mask_point;
   key_value *= 8;
   -valu_point;
   -mask_point;

   data_point = data;
   for (pii = 0; pii < 8; ++pii)
   { if (pi != pii) *data_point ^= key_table[key_value + pii];
     ++data_point;
   }
  }
```

```
  valu_point = data + 7;

  for (pi = 7; pi >= 0; --pi)
  {   key_value = *valu_point ^ *mask_point;
   key_value *= 8;
   --valu_point;
   --mask_point;

   data_point = data;
   for (pii = 0; pii < 8; ++pii)
   { if (pi != pii) *data_point ^= key_table[key_value + pii];
     ++data_point;
   }
  }

  return (0);
}


byte  main ()
{
  initialize_key_table ();
  create_mask_table ();


  encrypt_data (the_data);
  decrypt_data (the_data);

  return (0);
}
```

LOKI 91

```
/*
 *  loki.h - specifies the interface to the LOKI encryption routines.
 *      This library proviloki routines to expand a key, encrypt and
 *      decrypt 64-bit data blocks.  The LOKI Data Encryption Algorithm
 *      is a block cipher which ensures that its output is a complex
 *      function of its input and the key.
 *
 *  Authors:      Lawrie Brown <Lawrie.Brown@adfa.oz.au>          Aug 1989
 *                Matthew Kwan <mkwan@cs.adfa.oz.au>              Sep 1991
 *
 *      Computer Science, UC UNSW, Australian Defence Force Academy,
 *          Canberra, ACT 2600, Australia.
```

```
 *
 *   Version:
 *       v1.0 - of loki64.o is current 7/89 lpb
 *        v2.0 - of loki64.c is current 9/91 mkwan
 *        v3.0 - now have loki89.c & loki91.c 10/92 lpb
 *
 *   Copyright 1989 by Lawrie Brown and UNSW. All rights reserved.
 *       This program may not be sold or used as inducement to buy a
 *       product without the written permission of the author.
 *
 *   Description:
 *   The routines provided by the library are:
 *
 *   lokikey(key)      - expands a key into subkey, for use in
 *     char  key[8];          encryption and decryption operations.
 *
 *   enloki(b)               - main LOKI encryption routine, this routine
 *     char  b[8];            encrypts one 64-bit block b with subkey
 *
 *   deloki(b)               - main LOKI decryption routine, this routine
 *     char  b[8];            decrypts one 64-bit block b with subkey
 *
 *   The 64-bit data & key blocks used in the algorithm are specified as eight
 *       unsigned chars. For the purposes of implementing the LOKI algorithm,
 *       these MUST be word aligned with bits are numbered as follows:
 *         [63..56] [55..48]              ...              [7..0]
 *       in b[0]    b[1]  b[2]  b[3]  b[4]  b[5]  b[6]  b[7]
 */
#define LOKIBLK          8               /* No of bytes in a LOKI data-block    */
#define ROUNDS           16              /* No of LOKI rounds                   */
typedef unsigned long      Long;   /* type specification for aligned LOKI blocks */
extern Long        lokikey[2];     /* 64-bit key used by LOKI routines        */
extern char        *loki_lib_ver;  /* String with version no. & copyright     */
#ifdef __STDC__                          /* declare prototypes for library
functions   */
extern void enloki(char b[LOKIBLK]);
extern void deloki(char b[LOKIBLK]);
extern void setlokikey(char key[LOKIBLK]);
#else                            /* else just declare library functions extern */
extern void enloki(), deloki(), setlokikey();
#endif __STDC__


*************************************************************************
**
/*
 *      loki91.c - library routines for a 64 bit LOKI89 implementation
```

```
  *
  * Designed by  Matthew Kwan <mkwan@crypto.cs.adfa.oz.au> and
  *               Lawrence Brown <lpb@cs.adfa.oz.au>
  *   Modifications:
  *               v2.0 - original set of code by mkwan 9/91
  *               v3.0 - support both LOKI89 & LOKI91 versions   10/92 lpb
  *
  *   Copyright 1991 by Lawrence Brown and UNSW. All rights reserved.
  *       This program may not be sold or used as inducement to buy a
  *       product without the written permission of the author.
  *
  *        nb: if this program is compiled on a little-endian machine (eg Vax)
  *               #define LITTLE ENDIAN
  *               in order to enable the byte swapping  routines
  *
  *           if a detailed trace of LOKI91 function f is required for debugging
  *               #define TRACE=n                         n=1 print blocks, n=2 print
fn f also
  *                                   n=3 print individual S-box calcs also
  *
  *           these routines assume that the 8-byte char arrays used to pass
  *               the 64-bit blocks fall on a word boundary, so that the blocks
  *               may be read as longwords for efficiency reasons. If this is
  *               not true, the load & save of the parameters will need changing.
  */

#include <stdio.h>
#include "loki.h"          /* include Interface Specification header file */
#include "loki.i" /* include Interface Specification header file */
/*
  *       string specifying version and copyright message
  */
char    *loki_lib_ver = "LOKI91 library v3.0, Copyright (C) 1991 Lawrence Brown &
UNSW";
Long    loki_subkeys[ROUNDS];               /* subkeys at the 16 rounds */
static Long     f();                        /* declare LOKI function f */
static short    s();                        /* declare LOKI S-box fn s */

/*
  *       ROL12(b) - macro to rotate 32-bit block b left by 12 bits
  *       ROL13(b) - macro to rotate 32-bit block b left by 13 bits
  */
#define ROL12(b) b = ((b << 12) | (b >> 20));
#define ROL13(b) b = ((b << 13) | (b >> 19));
/*
  *       bswap(b) - exchanged bytes in each longword of a 64-bit data block
```

```
 *                      on little-endian machines where byte order is reversed
 */
#ifdef  LITTLE_ENDIAN
#define bswap(cb) {                                      \
  register char   c;                          \
  c = cb[0]; cb[0] = cb[3]; cb[3] = c;    \
  c = cb[1]; cb[1] = cb[2]; cb[2] = c;    \
  c = cb[4]; cb[4] = cb[7]; cb[7] = c;    \
  c = cb[5]; cb[5] = cb[6]; cb[6] = c;    \
}
#endif
/*
 *       setlokikey(key) - save 64-bit key for use in encryptions & decryptions
 *                       and compute sub-keys using the key schedule
 */
void
setlokikey(key)
char    key[LOKIBLK];               /* Key to use, stored as an array of Longs    */
{
   register i;
   register Long    KL, KR;
#ifdef LITTLE_ENDIAN
   bswap(key);                              /* swap bytes round if little-endian */
#endif
#if     TRACE >= 1
   fprintf(stderr," keyinit(%08lx, %08lx)\n", ((Long *)key)[0], ((Long *)key)[1]);
#endif
        KL = ((Long *)key)[0];
   KR = ((Long *)key)[1];
        for (i=0; i<ROUNDS; i+=4) {          /* Generate the 16 subkeys */
   loki_subkeys[i] = KL;
   ROL12 (KL);
   loki_subkeys[i+1] = KL;
   ROL13 (KL);
   loki_subkeys[i+2] = KR;
   ROL12 (KR);
   loki_subkeys[i+3] = KR;
   ROL13 (KR);
   }
#ifdef LITTLE_ENDIAN
   bswap(key);                                  /* swap bytes back if little-endian */
#endif
}

/*
 *       enloki(b) - main LOKI91 encryption routine, this routine encrypts one
```

```
 *                       64-bit block b using the LOKI91 algorithm with loki_subkeys
 *
 *                       nb: The 64-bit block is passed as two longwords. For the
 *                           purposes of the LOKI89 algorithm, the bits are numbered:
 *                           [63 62 .. 33 32] [31 30 ... 1 0]
 *                           The L (left) half is b[0], the R (right) half is b[1]
 *
 */
void
enloki (b)
char      b[LOKIBLK];
{
   register i;
   register Long     L, R;                  /* left & right data halves  */
#ifdef LITTLE_ENDIAN
   bswap(b);                                 /* swap bytes round if little-endian */
#endif
#if     TRACE >= 1
   fprintf(stderr," enloki(%08lx, %08lx)\n", ((Long *)b)[0], ((Long *)b)[1]);
#endif
        L = ((Long *)b)[0];
   R = ((Long *)b)[1];
        for (i=0; i<ROUNDS; i+=2) {         /* Encrypt with the 16 subkeys */
    L ^= f (R, loki_subkeys[i]);
    R ^= f (L, loki_subkeys[i+1]);
   }
        ((Long *)b)[0] = R;                  /* Y = swap(LR) */
   ((Long *)b)[1] = L;
#if     TRACE >= 1
   fprintf(stderr," enloki returns %08lx, %08lx\n", ((Long *)b)[0], ((Long
 *)b)[1]);
#endif
#ifdef LITTLE_ENDIAN
   bswap(b);                                 /* swap bytes round if little-endian */
#endif
}

/*
 *      deloki(b) - main LOKI91 decryption routine, this routine decrypts one
 *              64-bit block b using the LOKI91 algorithm with loki_subkeys
 *
 *              Decryption uses the same algorithm as encryption, except that
 *              the subkeys are used in reverse order.
 */
void
deloki(b)
```

```
char       b[LOKIBLK];
{
   register i;
   register Long     L, R;                         /* left & right data halves  */
#ifdef LITTLE_ENDIAN
   bswap(b);                          /* swap bytes round if little-endian */
#endif
#if     TRACE >= 1
   fprintf(stderr," deloki(%08lx, %08lx)\n", ((Long *)b)[0], ((Long *)b)[1]);
#endif
       L = ((Long *)b)[0];                          /* LR = X XOR K */
   R = ((Long *)b)[1];
       for (i=ROUNDS; i>0; i-=2) {                 /* subkeys in reverse order */
   L ^= f(R, loki_subkeys[i-1]);
   R ^= f(L, loki_subkeys[i-2]);
   }
       ((Long *)b)[0] = R;                          /* Y = LR XOR K */
   ((Long *)b)[1] = L;
#if     TRACE >= 1
   fprintf(stderr," deloki returns %08lx, %08lx\n", ((Long *)b)[0], ((Long
 *)b)[1]);
#endif
#ifdef LITTLE_ENDIAN
   bswap(b);                          /* swap bytes round if little-endian */
#endif
}


/*
 *      f(r, k) - is the complex non-linear LOKI function, whose output
 *              is a complex function of both input data and sub-key.
 *
 *      The data is XORed with the subkey, then expanded into 4 x 12-bit
 *      values, which are fed into the S-boxes. The 4 x 8-bit outputs
 *      from the S-boxes are permuted together to form the 32-bit value
 *      which is returned.
 *
 *      In this implementation the outputs from the S-boxes have been
 *      pre-permuted and stored in lookup tables.
 */
#define MASK12           0x0fff                      /* 12 bit mask for expansion
E */
static Long
f(r, k)
register Long     r;         /* Data value R(i-1) */
Long              k;         /* Key     K(i)    */
{
```

```
    Long     a, b, c;            /* 32 bit S-box output, & P output */
        a = r ^ k;                          /* A = R(i-1) XOR K(i) */
        /* want to use slow speed/small size version */
    b = ((Long)s((a            & MASK12))      ) | /* B = S(E(R(i-1))^K(i)) */
    ((Long)s(((a >> 8) & MASK12)) << 8) |
    ((Long)s(((a >> 16) & MASK12)) << 16) |
    ((Long)s((((a >> 24) | (a << 8)) & MASK12)) << 24;
        perm32(&c, &b, P);                   /* C = P(S( E(R(i-1)) XOR K(i))) */
#if     TRACE >= 2         /* If Tracing, dump A, K(i), and f(R(i-1),K(i)) */
    fprintf(stderr," f(%08lx, %08lx) = P.S(%08lx) = P(%08lx) = %08lx\n",
      r, k, a, b, c);
#endif
        return(c);                          /* f returns the result C */
}


/*
 *      s(i) - return S-box value for input i
 */
static short s(i)
register Long i;  /* return S-box value for input i */
{
    register short    r, c, v, t;
    short     exp8();            /* exponentiation routine for GF(2^8) */

    r = ((i>>8) & 0xc) | (i & 0x3);                       /* row value-top 2 &
  bottom 2 */
    c = (i>>2) & 0xff;                       /* column value-middle 8 bits */
    t = (c + ((r * 17) ^ 0xff)) & 0xff;      /* base value for Sfn */
    v = exp8(t, sfn[r].exp, sfn[r].gen);     /* Sfn[r] = t ^ exp mod gen */
#if TRACE >= 3
    fprintf(stderr, "   s(%lx=[%d,%d]) = %x sup %d mod %d = %x\n",
        i, r, c, t, sfn[r].exp, sfn[r].gen, v);
#endif
    return(v);
}
/*
 *      perm32(out, in, perm) is the general permutation of a 32-bit input
 *              block to a 32-bit output block, under the control of a
 *              permutation array perm. Each element of perm specifies which
 *              input bit is to be permuted to the output bit with the same
 *              index as the array element.
 *
 *      nb: to set bits in the output word, as mask with a single 1 in it is
 *              used. On each step, the 1 is shifted into the next location
 */
#define  MSB      0x80000000L                    /* MSB of 32-bit word */
```

```
perm32(out, in , perm)
Long     *out;              /* Output 32-bit block to be permuted          */
Long     *in;              /* Input  32-bit block after permutation         */
char     perm[32];          /* Permutation array                           */
{
   Long     mask = MSB;                 /* mask used to set bit in output    */
   register int     i, o, b; /* input bit no, output bit no, value */
   register char     *p = perm;         /* ptr to permutation array  */
        *out = 0;                        /* clear output block */
   for (o=0; o < 32; o++) {                       /* For each output bit position o
 */
    i =(int)*p++;              /* get input bit permuted to output o */
    b = (*in >> i) & 01;       /* value of input bit i */
    if (b)                     /* If the input bit i is set */
      *out |= mask;              /*  OR in mask to output i */
    mask >>= 1;                       /* Shift mask to next bit     */
    }
}


/*
 *      mult8(a, b, gen) - returns the product of two binary
 *               strings a and b using the generator gen as the modulus
 *                    mult = a * b mod gen
 *               gen generates a suitable Galois field in GF(2^8)
 */
#define SIZE 256                 /* 256 elements in GF(2^8) */
short mult8(a, b, gen)
short    a, b;              /* operands for multiply */
short    gen;              /* irreducible polynomial generating Galois Field */
{
   short     product = 0;                 /* result of multiplication */
        while(b != 0) {                       /* while multiplier is non-zero */
    if (b & 01)
      product ^= a;       /*   add multiplicand if LSB of b set */
    a <<= 1;                   /*    shift multiplicand one place */
    if (a >= SIZE)
      a ^= gen;            /*    and modulo reduce if needed */
    b >>= 1;                   /*    shift multiplier one place  */
    }
   return(product);
}
/*
 *      exp8(base, exponent, gen) - returns the result of
 *               exponentiation given the base, exponent, generator of GF,
 *                    exp = base ^ exp mod gen
 */
```

```
short exp8(base, exponent, gen)
short    base;              /* base of exponentiation          */
short    exponent;          /* exponent                        */
short    gen;               /* irreducible polynomial generating Galois Field */
{
   short    accum = base;     /* superincreasing sequence of base */
   short    result = 1;       /* result of exponentiation          */
    if (base == 0)            /* if zero base specified then      */
    return(0);           /* the result is "0" if base = 0    */
    while (exponent != 0) {    /* repeat while exponent non-zero */
    if (( exponent & 0x0001) == 0x0001)          /* multiply if exp 1 */
      result = mult8(result, accum, gen);
    exponent >>= 1;                     /* shift exponent to next digit */
    accum = mult8(accum, accum, gen);          /* & square  */
    }
    return(result);
}
```

IDEA

```
/*****************************IDEA.H***************************/
*/
/*      idea.h - header file for idea.c
*/

#include "usuals.h"  /* typedefs for byte, word16, boolean, etc. */

#define IDEAKEYSIZE 16
#define IDEABLOCKSIZE 8


void initcfb_idea(word16 iv0[4], byte key[16], boolean decryp);
void ideacfb(byteptr buf, int count);
void close_idea(void);

void init_idearand(byte key[16], byte seed[8], word32 tstamp);
byte idearand(void);
void close_idearand(void);


/* prototypes for passwd.c */

/* GetHashedPassPhrase - get pass phrase from user, hashes it to an IDEA key. */
int GetHashedPassPhrase(char *keystring, char *hash, boolean noecho);

/* hashpass - Hash pass phrase down to 128 bits (16 bytes). */
```

```
void hashpass (char *keystring, int keylen, byte *hash);


/*****************************IDEA.C*****************************/

/*      idea.c - C source code for IDEA block cipher.
 *      IDEA (International Data Encryption Algorithm), formerly known as
 *      IPES (Improved Proposed Encryption Standard).
 *      Algorithm developed by Xuejia Lai and James L. Massey, of ETH Zurich.
 *      This implementation modified and derived from original C code
 *      developed by Xuejia Lai.
 *      Zero-based indexing added, names changed from IPES to IDEA.
 *      CFB functions added.  Random number routines added.
 *
 *   Optimized for speed 21 Oct 92 by Colin Plumb <colin@nsq.gts.org>
 *
 *      This code assumes that each pair of 8-bit bytes comprising a 16-bit
 *      word in the key and in the cipher block are externally represented
 *      with the Most Significant Byte (MSB) first, regardless of the
 *      internal native byte order of the target CPU.
 */

#include "idea.h"

#ifdef TEST
#include <stdio.h>
#include <time.h>
#endif

#define ROUNDS      8               /* Don't change this value, should be 8 */
#define KEYLEN      (6*ROUNDS+4)        /* length of key schedule */

typedef word16 IDEAkey[KEYLEN];

#ifdef IDEA32/* Use > 16-bit temporaries */
#define low16(x) ((x) & 0xFFFF)
typedef unsigned int uint16;/* at LEAST 16 bits, maybe more */
#else
#define low16(x) (x)/* this is only ever applied to uint16's */
typedef word16 uint16;
#endif

#ifdef _GNUC_
/* __const__ simply means there are no side effects for this function,
 * which is useful info for the gcc optimizer */
#define CONST __const__
```

```
#else
#define CONST
#endif


static void en_key_idea(word16 userkey[8], IDEAkey Z);
static void de_key_idea(IDEAkey Z, IDEAkey DK);
static void cipher_idea(word16 in[4], word16 out[4], CONST IDEAkey Z);

/*
 *      Multiplication, modulo (2**16)+1
 * Note that this code is structured like this on the assumption that
 * untaken branches are cheaper than taken branches, and the compiler
 * doesn't schedule branches.
 */
#ifdef SMALL_CACHE
CONST static uint16 mul(register uint16 a, register uint16 b)
{
  register word32 p;

  if (a)
  {     if (b)
    {       p = (word32)a * b;
      b = low16(p);
      a = p>>16;
      return b - a + (b < a);
    }
    else
    {       return 1-a;
    }
  }
  }
  else
  {     return 1-b;
  }
}         /* mul */
#endif /* SMALL_CACHE */

/*
 *      Compute multiplicative inverse of x, modulo (2**16)+1,
 *      using Euclid's GCD algorithm.  It is unrolled twice to
 *      avoid swapping the meaning of the registers each iteration,
 *      and some subtracts of t have been changed to adds.
 */
CONST static uint16 inv(uint16 x)
{
  uint16 t0, t1;
```

```
  uint16 q, y;

  if (x <= 1)
    return x;     /* 0 and 1 are self-inverse */
  t1 = 0x10001 / x;   /* Since x >= 2, this fits into 16 bits */
  y = 0x10001 % x;
  if (y == 1)
    return low16(1-t1);
  t0 = 1;
  do
  {     q = x / y;
    x = x % y;
    t0 += q * t1;
    if (x == 1)
      return t0;
    q = y / x;
    y = y % x;
    t1 += q * t0;
  } while (y != 1);
  return low16(1-t1);
} /* inv */

/*     Compute IDEA encryption subkeys Z */
static void en_key_idea(word16 *userkey, word16 *Z)
{
  int i,j;

  /*
   * shifts
   */
  for (j=0; j<8; j++)
    Z[j] = *userkey++;

  for (i=0; j<KEYLEN; j++)
  {     i++;
    Z[i+7] = Z[i & 7] << 9 | Z[i+1 & 7] >> 7;
    Z += i & 8;
    i &= 7;
  }
}          /* en_key_idea */

/*     Compute IDEA decryption subkeys DK from encryption subkeys Z */
/* Note: these buffers *may* overlap! */
static void de_key_idea(IDEAkey Z, IDEAkey DK)
{
  int j;
```

```
   uint16 t1, t2, t3;
   IDEAkey T;
   word16 *p = T + KEYLEN;

   t1 = inv(*Z++);
   t2 = -*Z++;
   t3 = -*Z++;
   *--p = inv(*Z++);
   *--p = t3;
   *--p = t2;
   *--p = t1;

   for (j = 1; j < ROUNDS; j++)
   {
     t1 = *Z++;
     *--p = *Z++;
     *--p = t1;

     t1 = inv(*Z++);
     t2 = -*Z++;
     t3 = -*Z++;
     *--p = inv(*Z++);
     *--p = t2;
     *--p = t3;
     *--p = t1;
   }
   t1 = *Z++;
   *--p = *Z++;
   *--p = t1;

   t1 = inv(*Z++);
   t2 = -*Z++;
   t3 = -*Z++;
   *--p = inv(*Z++);
   *--p = t3;
   *--p = t2;
   *--p = t1;
/* Copy and destroy temp copy */
   for (j = 0, p - T; j<KEYLEN; j++)
   {
     *DK++ = *p;
     *p++ = 0;
   }
} /* de_key_idea */

/*
```

```
 * MUL(x,y) computes x = x*y, modulo 0x10001.  Requires two temps,
 * t16 and t32.  x must me a side-effect-free lvalue.  y may be
 * anything, but unlike x, must be strictly 16 bits even if low16()
 * is #defined.
 * All of these are equivalent - see which is faster on your machine
 */
#ifdef SMALL_CACHE
#define MUL(x,y) (x = mul(low16(x),y))
#else
#ifdef AVOID_JUMPS
#define MUL(x,y) (x = low16(x-1), t16 = low16((y)-1), \
    t32 = (word32)x*t16+x+t16+1, x = low16(t32), \
    t16 = t32>>16, x = x-t16+(x<t16) )
#else
#define MUL(x,y) ((t16 = (y)) ? (x=low16(x)) ? \
   t32 = (word32)x*t16, x = low16(t32), t16 = t32>>16, \
   x = x-t16+(x<t16) : \
   (x = 1-t16) : (x = 1-x))
#endif
#endif

/*      IDEA encryption/decryption algorithm */
/* Note that in and out can be the same buffer */
static void cipher_idea(word16 in[4], word16 out[4], register CONST IDEAkey Z)
{
  register uint16 x1, x2, x3, x4, t1, t2;
  register uint16 t16;
  register word32 t32;

  int r = ROUNDS;

  x1 = *in++;   x2 = *in++;
  x3 = *in++;   x4 = *in;
  do
  {
    MUL(x1,*Z++);
    x2 += *Z++;
    x3 += *Z++;
    MUL(x4, *Z++);

    t2 = x1^x3;
    MUL(t2, *Z++);
    t1 = t2 + (x2^x4);
    MUL(t1, *Z++);
    t2 = t1+t2;
```

```
      x1 ^= t1;
      x4 ^= t2;

      t2 ^= x2;
      x2 = x3^t1;
      x3 = t2;
    } while (-r);
  MUL(x1, *Z++);
  *out++ = x1;
  *out++ = x3 + *Z++;
  *out++ = x2 + *Z++;
  MUL(x4, *Z);
  *out = x4;
} /* cipher_idea */


/*- - - - - - - - - - - - - - - - - - - - - - - - - - - - - - - - - */

#ifdef TEST
/*
 * This is the number of Kbytes of test data to encrypt.
 * It defaults to 1 MByte.
 */
#ifndef KBYTES
#define KBYTES 1024
#endif

void main(void)
{       /* Test driver for IDEA cipher */
  int i, j, k;
  IDEAkey Z, DK;
  word16 XX[4], TT[4], YY[4];
  word16 userkey[8];
  clock_t start, end;
  long l;

  /* Make a sample user key for testing... */
  for(i=0; i<8; i++)
    userkey[i] = i+1;

  /* Compute encryption subkeys from user key... */
  en_key_idea(userkey,Z);
  printf("\nEncryption key subblocks: ");
  for(j=0; j<ROUNDS+1; j++)
  {
    printf("\nround %d:    ", j+1);
    if (j==ROUNDS)
```

```
    for(i=0; i<4; i++)
            printf(" %6u", Z[j*6+i]);
  else
    for(i=0; i<6; i++)
            printf(" %6u", Z[j*6+i]);
}

/* Compute decryption subkeys from encryption subkeys... */
de_key_idea(Z,DK);
printf("\nDecryption key subblocks: ");
for(j=0; j<ROUNDS+1; j++)
{
  printf("\nround %d:    ", j+1);
  if (j==ROUNDS)
    for(i=0; i<4; i++)
            printf(" %6u", DK[j*6+i]);
  else
    for(i=0; i<6; i++)
        printf(" %6u", DK[j*6+i]);
}

/* Make a sample plaintext pattern for testing... */
for (k=0; k<4; k++)
  XX[k] = k;

printf("\n Encrypting %d KBytes (%ld blocks)...", KBYTES, KBYTES*64l);
fflush(stdout);
start = clock();
cipher_idea(XX,YY,Z);        /* encrypt plaintext XX, making YY */
for (l = 1; l < 64*KBYTES; l++)
  cipher_idea(YY,YY,Z);/* repeated encryption */
cipher_idea(YY,TT,DK);       /* decrypt ciphertext YY, making TT */
for (l = 1; l < 64*KBYTES; l++)
  cipher_idea(TT,TT,DK);/* repeated decryption */
end = clock() - start;
l = end * 1000. / CLOCKS_PER_SEC + 1;
i = l/1000;
j = l%1000;
l = KBYTES * 1024. * CLOCKS_PER_SEC / end;
printf("%d.%03d seconds = %ld bytes per second\n", i, j, l);

printf("\nX %6u   %6u  %6u  %6u \n",
  XX[0], XX[1],  XX[2], XX[3]);
printf("Y %6u   %6u  %6u  %6u \n",
  YY[0], YY[1],  YY[2], YY[3]);
printf("T %6u   %6u  %6u  %6u \n",
```

```
      TT[0], TT[1],  TT[2], TT[3]);

   /* Now decrypted TT should be same as original XX */
   for (k=0; k<4; k++)
     if (TT[k] != XX[k])
     {
       printf("\n\07Error!  Noninvertable encryption.\n");
       exit(-1);    /* error exit */
     }
   printf("\nNormal exit.\n");
   exit(0);/* normal exit */
}         /* main */


#endif        /* TEST */



/**************************************************************************/


/*
 *      xorbuf - change buffer via xor with random mask block
 *      Used for Cipher Feedback (CFB) or Cipher Block Chaining
 *      (CBC) modes of encryption.
 *      Can be applied for any block encryption algorithm,
 *      with any block size, such as the DES or the IDEA cipher.
 */
static void xorbuf(register byteptr buf, register byteptr mask,
       register int count)
/*      count must be > 0 */
{
   if (count)
     do
       *buf++ ^= *mask++;
     while (-count);
}       /* xorbuf */



/*
 *      cfbshift - shift bytes into IV for CFB input
 *      Used only for Cipher Feedback (CFB) mode of encryption.
 *      Can be applied for any block encryption algorithm with any
 *      block size, such as the DES or the IDEA cipher.
 */
static void cfbshift(register byteptr iv, register byteptr buf,
    register int count, int blocksize)
```

```
/*      iv is the initialization vector.
 *      buf is the buffer pointer.
 *      count is the number of bytes to shift in...must be > 0.
 *      blocksize is 8 bytes for DES or IDEA ciphers.
 */
{
  int retained;
  if (count)
  {
    retained = blocksize-count;/* number bytes in iv to retain */
    /* left-shift retained bytes of IV over by count bytes to make room */
    while (retained--)
    {
      *iv = *(iv+count);
      iv++;
    }
    /* now copy count bytes from buf to shifted tail of IV */
    do     *iv++ = *buf++;
    while (--count);
  }
}      /* cfbshift */



/* Key schedules for IDEA encryption and decryption */
static IDEAkey Z, DK;
static word16 *iv_idea;   /* pointer to IV for CFB or CBC */
static boolean cfb_dc_idea; /* TRUE iff CFB decrypting */



/* initkey_idea initializes IDEA for ECB mode operations */
void initkey_idea(byte key[16], boolean decryp)
{
  word16 userkey[8]; /* IDEA key is 16 bytes long */
  int i;
  /* Assume each pair of bytes comprising a word is ordered MSB-first. */
  for (i=0; i<8; i++)
  {
    userkey[i] = (key[0]<<8) + key[1];
    key++; key++;
  }
  en_key_idea(userkey,Z);
  if (decryp)
  {
    de_key_idea(Z,Z);   /* compute inverse key schedule DK */
  }
```

```
  for (i=0; i<8; i++)/* Erase dangerous traces */
    userkey[i] = 0;
} /* initkey_idea */


/*      Run a 64-bit block thru IDEA in ECB (Electronic Code Book) mode,
  using the currently selected key schedule.
*/
void idea_ecb(word16 *inbuf, word16 *outbuf)
{
  /* Assume each pair of bytes comprising a word is ordered MSB-first. */
#ifndef HIGHFIRST   /* If this is a least-significant-byte-first CPU */
  word16 x;

  /* Invert the byte order for each 16-bit word for internal use. */
  x = inbuf[0]; outbuf[0] = x >> 8 | x << 8;
  x = inbuf[1]; outbuf[1] = x >> 8 | x << 8;
  x = inbuf[2]; outbuf[2] = x >> 8 | x << 8;
  x = inbuf[3]; outbuf[3] = x >> 8 | x << 8;
  cipher_idea(outbuf, outbuf, Z);
  x = outbuf[0]; outbuf[0] = x >> 8 | x << 8;
  x = outbuf[1]; outbuf[1] = x >> 8 | x << 8;
  x = outbuf[2]; outbuf[2] = x >> 8 | x << 8;
  x = outbuf[3]; outbuf[3] = x >> 8 | x << 8;
#else   /* HIGHFIRST */
  /* Byte order for internal and external representations is the same. */
  cipher_idea(inbuf, outbuf, Z);
#endif /* HIGHFIRST */
} /* idea_ecb */


/*
 *      initcfb - Initializes the IDEA key schedule tables via key,
 *      and initializes the Cipher Feedback mode IV.
 *      References context variables cfb_dc_idea and iv_idea.
 */
void initcfb_idea(word16 iv0[4], byte key[16], boolean decryp)
/*      iv0 is copied to global iv_idea, buffer will be destroyed by ideacfb.
  key is pointer to key buffer.
  decryp is TRUE if decrypting, FALSE if encrypting.
*/
{
  iv_idea = iv0;
  cfb_dc_idea = decryp;
  initkey_idea(key,FALSE);
} /* initcfb_idea */
```

```
/*
 *      ideacfb - encipher a buffer with IDEA enciphering algorithm,
 *          using Cipher Feedback (CFB) mode.
 *
 *      Assumes initcfb_idea has already been called.
 *      References context variables cfb_dc_idea and iv_idea.
 */
void ideacfb(byteptr buf, int count)
/*      buf is input, output buffer, may be more than 1 block.
 *      count is byte count of buffer.  May be > IDEABLOCKSIZE.
 */
{
  int chunksize;/* smaller of count, IDEABLOCKSIZE */
  word16 temp[IDEABLOCKSIZE/2];

  while ((chunksize = min(count,IDEABLOCKSIZE)) > 0)
  {
    idea_ecb(iv_idea,temp);  /* encrypt iv_idea, making temp. */

    if (cfb_dc_idea)/* buf is ciphertext */
      /* shift in ciphertext to IV... */
      cfbshift((byte *)iv_idea,buf,chunksize,IDEABLOCKSIZE);

    /* convert buf via xor */
    xorbuf(buf,(byte *)temp,chunksize); /* buf now has enciphered output */

    if (!cfb_dc_idea)/* buf was plaintext, is now ciphertext */
      /* shift in ciphertext to IV... */
      cfbshift((byte *)iv_idea,buf,chunksize,IDEABLOCKSIZE);

    count -= chunksize;
    buf += chunksize;
  }
} /* ideacfb */


/*
  close_idea function erases all the key schedule information when
  we are all done with a set of operations for a particular IDEA key
  context.  This is to prevent any sensitive data from being left
  around in memory.
*/
void close_idea(void)/* erase current key schedule tables */
{
```

```
  short i;
  for (i = 0; i < KEYLEN; i++)
    Z[i] = 0;
}       /* close_idea() */


/*********************************************************************/

/*
 *      These buffers are used by init_idearand, idearand, and close_idearand.
 */
static word16 dtbuf_idea[4] = {0}; /* buffer for enciphered timestamp */
static word16 randseed_idea[4] = {0}; /* seed for IDEA random # generator */
static word16 randbuf_idea[4] = {0}; /* buffer for IDEA random # generator */
static byte randbuf_idea_counter = 0;/* # of random bytes left in randbuf_idea */

/*
 *      init_idearand - initialize idearand, IDEA random number generator.
 *           Used for generating cryptographically strong random numbers.
 *           Much of the design comes from Appendix C of ANSI X9.17.
 *           key is pointer to IDEA key buffer.
 *           seed is pointer to random number seed buffer.
 *           tstamp is a 32-bit timestamp
 */
void init_idearand(byte key[16], byte seed[8], word32 tstamp)
{
  int i;
  initkey_idea(key, FALSE); /* initialize IDEA */

  for (i=0; i<; i++)        /* capture timestamp material */
  {     dtbuf_idea[i] = tstamp;/* get bottom word */
    tstamp = tstamp >> 16;    /* drop bottom word */
    /* tstamp has only 4 bytes- last 4 bytes will always be 0 */
  }
  /* Start with enciphered timestamp: */
  idea_ecb(dtbuf_idea,dtbuf_idea);

  /* initialize seed material */
  for (i=0; i<8; i++)
    ((byte *)randseed_idea)[i] = seed[i];

  randbuf_idea_counter = 0; /* # of random bytes left in randbuf_idea */

} /* init_idearand */


/*
```

```
*       idearand - IDEA pseudo-random number generator
*           Used for generating cryptographically strong random numbers.
*           Much of the design comes from Appendix C of ANSI X9.17.
*/
byte idearand(void)
{
  int i;
  if (randbuf_idea_counter==0)/* if random buffer is spent...*/
  {     /* Combine enciphered timestamp with seed material: */
    for (i=0; i<4; i++)
      randseed_idea[i] ^= dtbuf_idea[i];
    idea_ecb(randseed_idea,randbuf_idea); /* fill new block */

    /* Compute new seed vector: */
    for (i=0; i<4; i++)
      randseed_idea[i] = randbuf_idea[i] ^ dtbuf_idea[i];
    idea_ecb(randseed_idea,randseed_idea); /* fill new seed */

    randbuf_idea_counter = 8; /* reset counter for full buffer */
  }
  /* Take a byte from randbuf_idea: */
  return(((byte *)randbuf_idea)[--randbuf_idea_counter]);
} /* idearand */


void close_idearand(void)
{     /* Erase random IDEA buffers and wipe out IDEA key info */
  int i;
  for (i=0; i<4; i++)
  {     randbuf_idea[i] = 0;
    randseed_idea[i] = 0;
    dtbuf_idea[i] = 0;
  }
  close_idea();/* erase current key schedule tables */
}     /* close_idearand */

/* end of idea.c */
```

N-HASH

```
/* NHASH.C - Implementation of N-Hash.
Version of 93.02.15.
*/

#include <stdio.h>
```

```c
static unsigned char BN = { 2 } ;/* Block number */
static unsigned char MESSAGE[32] = {
    0x00, 0x00, 0x00, 0x00, 0x00, 0x00, 0x00, 0x00,
    0x00, 0x00, 0x00, 0x00, 0x00, 0x00, 0x00, 0x00,
    0x01, 0x23, 0x45, 0x67, 0x89, 0xab, 0xcd, 0xef,
    0x01, 0x23, 0x45, 0x67, 0x89, 0xab, 0xcd, 0xef } ;

static unsigned char INITIAL[16] = {
    0x00, 0x00, 0x00, 0x00, 0x00, 0x00, 0x00, 0x00,
    0x00, 0x00, 0x00, 0x00, 0x00, 0x00, 0x00, 0x00 } ;

static unsigned char INITIAL2[16] = {
    0x52, 0x52, 0x52, 0x52, 0x52, 0x52, 0x52, 0x52,
    0x25, 0x25, 0x25, 0x25, 0x25, 0x25, 0x25, 0x25 } ;


static unsigned char OUT[16] ;

void main()
{
   register i, loop ;
   void HASH128( unsigned char BN, unsigned char *MSGIN,
      unsigned char *INIT, unsigned char *OUT ) ;

   printf( "\n\nInitial Value (No.1) \n" ) ;
   for ( i = 0 ; i < 16 ; i++ )
   printf( " %02X", INITIAL[i] ) ;
  printf( "\n\nMessage" ) ;
  for ( loop = 0 ; loop < BN ; loop++ )
  {
   printf( "\n" ) ;
   for ( i = 0 ; i < 16 ; i++ )
    printf( " %02X", MESSAGE[ 16 * loop + i ] ) ;
  }

  HASH128( BN, MESSAGE, INITIAL, OUT ) ;
  printf( "\n\nOutput of N-Hash\n" ) ;
  for ( i = 0 ; i < 16 ; i++ )
   printf( " %02X", OUT[i] ) ;


  printf( "\n\n\nInitial Value (No.2) \n" ) ;
  for ( i = 0 ; i < 16 ; i++ )
   INITIAL[i] = INITIAL2[i] ;
```

```
 for ( i = 0 ; i < 16 ; i++ )
  printf( " %02X", INITIAL[i] ) ;
 printf( "\n\nMessage" ) ;
 for ( loop = 0 ; loop < BN ; loop++ )
 {
  printf( "\n" ) ;
  for ( i = 0 ; i < 16 ; i++ )
   printf( " %02X", MESSAGE[ 16 * loop + i ] ) ;
 }

 HASH128( BN, MESSAGE, INITIAL, OUT ) ;
 printf( "\n\nOutput of N-Hash\n" ) ;
 for ( i = 0 ; i < 16 ; i++ )
  printf( " %02X", OUT[i] ) ;
}

void HASH128( unsigned char BN, unsigned char *MSGIN, unsigned char *INIT,
  unsigned char *OUT )
{
 register i, loop ;
 unsigned char X2[16], X1[16], Y[16] ;
 void setkey( unsigned char *key ) ;
 void encrypt( unsigned char *data, unsigned char *output ) ;

 for ( i = 0 ; i < 16 ; i++ )
  X2[i] = INIT[i] ;
 for ( loop = 0 ; loop < BN ; loop++ )
 {
  for ( i = 0 ; i < 16 ; i++ )
   X1[i] = MSGIN[16*loop + i ] ;
  printf( "\n\nH%X     ", loop ) ;
  for ( i = 0 ; i < 16 ; i++ )
   printf( " %02X", X2[i] ) ;
  printf( "\nM%x      ", loop + 1 ) ;
  for ( i = 0 ; i < 16 ; i++ )
   printf( " %02X", X1[i] ) ;

  setkey( X2 ) ;

  encrypt( X1, Y ) ;

  printf( "\nH%x      ", loop + 1 ) ;
  for ( i = 0 ; i < 16 ; i++ )
   printf( " %02X", Y[i] ) ;
  for ( i = 0 ; i < 16 ; i++ )
   X2[i] = Y[i] ;
```

```
  }
  for ( i = 0 ; i < 16 ; i++ )
   OUT[i] = Y[i] ;
}

static unsigned char X1[16], X2[16] ;

void setkey( unsigned char *key )
{
  register int i ;

  for ( i = 0 ; i < 16 ; i++ )
   X2[i] = key[i] ;
}

void encrypt( unsigned char *data, unsigned char *output )
{
  unsigned char block[16], work[4], V ;
  register int loop, i ;
  int sbox( unsigned char data ) ;

  for ( i = 0 ; i < 16 ; i++ )
   X1[i] = data[i] ;

  printf( "\nInput X1 of IP function\n" ) ;
  for ( i = 0 ; i < 16 ; i++ )
   printf( " %02X", X1[i] ) ;
  printf( "\nInput X2 of IP function\n" ) ;
  for ( i = 0 ; i < 16 ; i++ )
   printf( " %02X", X2[i] ) ;
  for ( i = 0 ; i < 8 ; i++ )
   block[i] = X2[i] ^ X1[i+8] ^ 0xaa ;
  for ( i = 0 ; i < 8 ; i++ )
   block[i+8] = X2[i+8] ^ X1[i] ^ 0xaa ;
  V = 0 ;
  for ( loop = 0 ; loop < 8 ; loop++ )
  {
   for ( i = 0 ; i < 4 ; i++ )
    work[i] = block[i] ^ X1[i] ;

   /* P1 */

   ++V ;
   work[3] ^= V ;
   work[1] ^= work[0] ;
   work[2] ^= work[3] ;
```

```
work[1] = sbox( work[1] + work[2] + 1 ) ;
work[2] = sbox( work[2] + work[1] ) ;
work[0] = sbox( work[0] + work[1] ) ;
work[3] = sbox( work[3] + work[2] + 1 ) ;

for ( i = 0 ; i < 4 ; i++ )
 work[i] ^= block[i+4] ;
for ( i = 0 ; i < 4 ; i++ )
 block[i+12] ^= work[i] ;
for ( i = 0 ; i < 4 ; i++ )
 work[i] ^= X1[i+4] ;

/* P2 */

++V ;
work[3] ^= V ;
work[1] ^= work[0] ;
work[2] ^= work[3] ;
work[1] = sbox( work[1] + work[2] + 1 ) ;
work[2] = sbox( work[2] + work[1] ) ;
work[0] = sbox( work[0] + work[1] ) ;
work[3] = sbox( work[3] + work[2] + 1 ) ;

for ( i = 0 ; i < 4 ; i++ )
 block[i+8] ^= work[i] ^ block[i] ;

/*****************************/

for ( i = 0 ; i < 4 ; i++ )
 work[i] = block[i+8] ^ X1[i+8] ;

/* P3 */

++V ;
work[3] ^= V ;
work[1] ^= work[0] ;
work[2] ^= work[3] ;
work[1] = sbox( work[1] + work[2] + 1 ) ;
work[2] = sbox( work[2] + work[1] ) ;
work[0] = sbox( work[0] + work[1] ) ;
work[3] = sbox( work[3] + work[2] + 1 ) ;

for ( i = 0 ; i < 4 ; i++ )
 work[i] ^= block[i+12] ;
for ( i = 0 ; i < 4 ; i++ )
 block[i+4] ^= work[i] ;
```

```
   for ( i = 0 ; i < 4 ; i++ )
    work[i] ^= X1[i+12] ;

   /* P4 */

   ++V ;
   work[3] ^= V ;
   work[1] ^= work[0] ;
   work[2] ^= work[3] ;
   work[1] = sbox( work[1] + work[2] + 1 ) ;
   work[2] = sbox( work[2] + work[1] ) ;
   work[0] = sbox( work[0] + work[1] ) ;
   work[3] = sbox( work[3] + work[2] + 1 ) ;

   for ( i = 0 ; i < 4 ; i++ )
    block[i] ^= work[i] ^ block[i+8] ;
   }

  for ( i = 0 ; i < 16 ; i++ )
   output[i] = block[i] ^ X1[i] ^ X2[i] ;

  printf( "\nOutput Y of IP function\n" ) ;
  for ( i = 0 ; i < 16 ; i++ )
   printf( " %02X", output[i] ) ;
}

int sbox( unsigned char data )
{
  union {
   unsigned int DATA ;
   struct {
    unsigned char low ;
    unsigned char high ;
   } reg ;
  } s ;

  s.reg.high = 0 ;
  s.reg.low = data ;
  s.DATA <<- 2 ;
  return ( s.reg.high | s.reg.low ) ;
}

#include <stdio.h>
#include <stdlib.h>
```

```c
#define byte unsigned char


union U_INT
{
    byte    b_int[2];
    int    i_int;
};

int i;

byte  key_table[2560];
byte  mask_table[16];

byte  key_length=6;
byte  master_key[70]={89, 66, 128, 231, 18, 43};

byte  the_data[8];

byte  initialize_key_table ()
{
  int   data_point, pi, pii;
  union   U_INTseed, data_value;
  unsigned int prime[35] = {  1,   3,   5,   7,  11,  13,  17,
            19,  23,  29,  31,  37,  41,  43,
            47,  53,  59,  61,  67,  71,  73,
            79,  83,  89,  97, 101, 103, 107,
           109, 113, 127, 131, 137, 139, 149};

  for (pi = 1; pi <= key_length; ++pi)
  {
  if (pi != key_length)
  {   seed.b_int[0] = master_key[pi-1];
    seed.b_int[1] = master_key[pi];
  }
   else
  {   seed.b_int[0] = master_key[pi-1];
    seed.b_int[1] = master_key[0];
  }

  srand (seed.i_int);
  data_point = 0;

  for (pii = 0; pii < 2560; ++pii)
  { data_point += prime[pi];
    if (data_point > 2559) data_point -= 2560;
```

```
      data_value.i_int = rand ();

      key_table[data_point] = data_value.b_int[0];
      if ( (data_point + 1) != 2559)
      key_table[data_point + 1] = data_value.b_int[1];
       else
      key_table[0] = data_value.b_int[1];
    }

    }

    return (0);
}

byte  create_mask_table ()
{
    int pi, mask_counter;
    byte *mask_pointer;

    mask_pointer = mask_table;
    mask_counter = 0;

    for (pi = 0; pi < 16; ++pi) mask_table[pi] = 0;

    for (pi - 0; pi < 2560; ++pi)
    { *mask_pointer ^= key_table[pi];
    ++mask_pointer;
    ++mask_counter;
    if (mask_counter == 16)
      {  mask_counter = 0;
         mask_pointer = mask_table;
      }
    }

    return (0);
}



byte encrypt_data (data)
    byte *data;
{
    int pi, pii, key_value;
    byte *mask_point, *data_point, *valu_point;
```

```
   valu_point = data;
   mask_point = mask_table;

   for (pi = 0; pi < 8; ++pi)
   {  key_value = *valu_point ^ *mask_point;
    key_value *= 8;
    ++valu_point;
    ++mask_point;

    data_point = data;
    for (pii = 0; pii < 8; ++pii)
    { if (pi != pii) *data_point ^= key_table[key_value + pii];
      ++data_point;
    }
   }


   valu_point = data;

   for (pi = 0; pi < 8; ++pi)
   {
    key_value = *valu_point ^ *mask_point;
    key_value *= 8;
    ++valu_point;
    ++mask_point;

    data_point = data;
    for (pii = 0; pii < 8; ++pii)
    { if (pi != pii) *data_point ^= key_table[key_value + pii];
      ++data_point;
    }
   }

   return (0);
}

byte decrypt_data (data)
  byte *data;
{
   int pi, pii, key_value;
   byte  *mask_point, *data_point, *valu_point;

   valu_point = data+7;
   mask_point = mask_table+15;

   for (pi = 7; pi >= 0; --pi)
```

```
{  key_value = *valu_point ^ *mask_point;
   key_value *= 8;
 - - valu_point;
 - - mask_point;

   data_point = data;
   for (pii = 0; pii < 8; ++pii)
   { if (pi != pii) *data_point ^= key_table[key_value + pii];
     ++data_point;
   }
 }

valu_point = data + 7;

for (pi = 7; pi >= 0; -pi)
{  key_value = *valu_point ^ *mask_point;
   key_value *= 8;
 - - valu_point;
 - - mask_point;

   data_point = data;
   for (pii = 0; pii < 8; ++pii)
   { if (pi != pii) *data_point ^= key_table[key_value + pii];
     ++data_point;
   }
 }

return (0);
}



byte  main ()
{
  initialize_key_table ();
  create_mask_table ();


  encrypt_data (the_data);
  decrypt_data (the_data);

  return (0);
}
```

MD5

```
/* MD5.H - header file for MD5C.C
 */
```

```
/* MD5 context. */
typedef struct {
  UINT4 state[4];                                        /* state (ABCD) */
  UINT4 count[2];                      /* number of bits, modulo 2^64 (lsb first) */
  unsigned char buffer[64];                              /* input buffer */
} MD5_CTX;

void MD5Init PROTO_LIST ((MD5_CTX *));
void MD5Update PROTO_LIST ((MD5_CTX *, unsigned char *, unsigned int));
void MD5Final PROTO_LIST ((unsigned char [16], MD5_CTX *));

**************************************************************************

/* MD5C.C - RSA Data Security, Inc., MD5 message-digest algorithm
 */

#include "global.h"
#include "md5.h"

/* Constants for MD5Transform routine.
 */
```

```
#define S11 7
#define S12 12
#define S13 17
#define S14 22
#define S21 5
#define S22 9
#define S23 14
#define S24 20
#define S31 4
#define S32 11
#define S33 16
#define S34 23
#define S41 6
#define S42 10
#define S43 15
#define S44 21


static void MD5Transform PROTO_LIST ((UINT4 [4], unsigned char [64]));
static void Encode PROTO_LIST ((unsigned char *, UINT4 *, unsigned int));
static void Decode PROTO_LIST ((UINT4 *, unsigned char *, unsigned int));
static void MD5_memcpy PROTO_LIST ((POINTER, POINTER, unsigned int));
static void MD5_memset PROTO_LIST ((POINTER, int, unsigned int));

static unsigned char PADDING[64] = {
  0x80, 0, 0, 0, 0, 0, 0, 0, 0, 0, 0, 0, 0, 0, 0, 0, 0, 0, 0, 0, 0, 0,
  0, 0, 0, 0, 0, 0, 0, 0, 0, 0, 0, 0, 0, 0, 0, 0, 0, 0, 0, 0, 0, 0,
  0, 0, 0, 0, 0, 0, 0, 0, 0, 0, 0, 0, 0, 0, 0, 0, 0, 0, 0, 0
};

/* F, G, H and I are basic MD5 functions.
 */
#define F(x, y, z) (((x) & (y)) | ((~x) & (z)))
#define G(x, y, z) (((x) & (z)) | ((y) & (~z)))
#define H(x, y, z) ((x) ^ (y) ^ (z))
#define I(x, y, z) ((y) ^ ((x) | (~z)))

/* ROTATE_LEFT rotates x left n bits.
 */
#define ROTATE_LEFT(x, n) (((x) < (n)) | ((x) > (32-(n))))

/* FF, GG, HH, and II transformations for rounds 1, 2, 3, and 4.
  Rotation is separate from addition to prevent recomputation.
 */
#define FF(a, b, c, d, x, s, ac) { \
    (a) += F ((b), (c), (d)) + (x) + (UINT4)(ac); \
  (a) = ROTATE_LEFT ((a), (s)); \
```

```
  (a) += (b); \
  }
#define GG(a, b, c, d, x, s, ac) { \
  (a) += G ((b), (c), (d)) + (x) + (UINT4)(ac); \
  (a) = ROTATE_LEFT ((a), (s)); \
  (a) += (b); \
  }
#define HH(a, b, c, d, x, s, ac) { \
  (a) += H ((b), (c), (d)) + (x) + (UINT4)(ac); \
  (a) = ROTATE_LEFT ((a), (s)); \
  (a) += (b); \
  }
#define II(a, b, c, d, x, s, ac) { \
  (a) += I ((b), (c), (d)) + (x) + (UINT4)(ac); \
  (a) = ROTATE_LEFT ((a), (s)); \
  (a) += (b); \
  }


 * MD5 initialization. Begins an MD5 operation, writing a new context.
 */
void MD5Init (context)
MD5_CTX *context;                                          /* context */
 {
  context->count[0] = context->count[1] = 0;

  /* Load magic initialization constants.
   */
  context->state[0] = 0x67452301;
  context->state[1] = 0xefcdab89;
  context->state[2] = 0x98badcfe;
  context->state[3] = 0x10325476;
 }


 * MD5 block update operation. Continues an MD5 message-digest operation,
   processing another message block, and updating the context.
 */
void MD5Update (context, input, inputLen)
MD5_CTX *context;                                          /* context */
unsigned char *input;                                  /* input block */
unsigned int inputLen;                        /* length of input block */
 {
  unsigned int i, index, partLen;

  /* Compute number of bytes mod 64 */
  index = (unsigned int)((context->count[0] >> 3) & 0x3F);
```

```
  /* Update number of bits */
  if ((context->count[0] += ((UINT4)inputLen << 3)) < ((UINT4)inputLen << 3))
  context->count[1]++;
  context->count[1] += ((UINT4)inputLen > 29);

  partLen = 64 - index;

  /* Transform as many times as possible.
   */
  if (inputLen >= partLen) {
  MD5_memcpy ((POINTER)&context->buffer[index], (POINTER)input, partLen);
  MD5Transform (context->state, context->buffer);

  for (i = partLen; i + 63 < inputLen; i += 64)
    MD5Transform (context->state, &input[i]);

  index = 0;
  }
  else
  i = 0;

  /* Buffer remaining input */
  MD5_memcpy
  ((POINTER)&context->buffer[index], (POINTER)&input[i], inputLen-i);
  }

 * MD5 finalization. Ends an MD5 message-digest operation, writing the
   the message digest and zeroizing the context.
 */
void MD5Final (digest, context)
unsigned char digest[16];                               /* message digest */
MD5_CTX *context;                                        /* context */
 {
  unsigned char bits[8];
  unsigned int index, padLen;

  /* Save number of bits */
  Encode (bits, context->count, 8);

  /* Pad out to 56 mod 64.
   */
  index = (unsigned int)((context->count[0] >> 3) & 0x3f);
  padLen = (index < 56) ? (56 - index) : (120 - index);
  MD5Update (context, PADDING, padLen);

  /* Append length (before padding) */
```

```
  MD5Update (context, bits, 8);

  /* Store state in digest */
  Encode (digest, context->state, 16);

  /* Zeroize sensitive information.
   */
  MD5_memset ((POINTER)context, 0, sizeof (*context));
}

 * MD5 basic transformation. Transforms state based on block.
 */
static void MD5Transform (state, block)
UINT4 state[4];
unsigned char block[64];
{
  UINT4 a = state[0], b = state[1], c = state[2], d = state[3], x[16];

  Decode (x, block, 64);

  /* Round 1 */
  FF ( a, b, c, d, x[ 0], S11, 0xd76aa478); /* 1 */
  FF ( d, a, b, c, x[ 1], S12, 0xe8c7b756); /* 2 */
  FF ( c, d, a, b, x[ 2], S13, 0x242070db); /* 3 */
  FF ( b, c, d, a, x[ 3], S14, 0xc1bdceee); /* 4 */
  FF ( a, b, c, d, x[ 4], S11, 0xf57c0faf); /* 5 */
  FF ( d, a, b, c, x[ 5], S12, 0x4787c62a); /* 6 */
  FF ( c, d, a, b, x[ 6], S13, 0xa8304613); /* 7 */
  FF ( b, c, d, a, x[ 7], S14, 0xfd469501); /* 8 */
  FF ( a, b, c, d, x[ 8], S11, 0x698098d8); /* 9 */
  FF ( d, a, b, c, x[ 9], S12, 0x8b44f7af); /* 10 */
  FF ( c, d, a, b, x[10], S13, 0xffff5bb1); /* 11 */
  FF ( b, c, d, a, x[11], S14, 0x895cd7be); /* 12 */
  FF ( a, b, c, d, x[12], S11, 0x6b901122); /* 13 */
  FF ( d, a, b, c, x[13], S12, 0xfd987193); /* 14 */
  FF ( c, d, a, b, x[14], S13, 0xa679438e); /* 15 */
  FF ( b, c, d, a, x[15], S14, 0x49b40821); /* 16 */

  /* Round 2 */
  GG ( a, b, c, d, x[ 1], S21, 0xf61e2562); /* 17 */
  GG ( d, a, b, c, x[ 6], S22, 0xc040b340); /* 18 */
  GG ( c, d, a, b, x[11], S23, 0x265e5a51); /* 19 */
  GG ( b, c, d, a, x[ 0], S24, 0xe9b6c7aa); /* 20 */
  GG ( a, b, c, d, x[ 5], S21, 0xd62f105d); /* 21 */
  GG ( d, a, b, c, x[10], S22,  0x2441453); /* 22 */
  GG ( c, d, a, b, x[15], S23, 0xd8a1e681); /* 23 */
```

```
GG ( b, c, d, a, x[ 4], S24, 0xe7d3fbc8); /* 24 */
GG ( a, b, c, d, x[ 9], S21, 0x21e1cde6); /* 25 */
GG ( d, a, b, c, x[14], S22, 0xc33707d6); /* 26 */
GG ( c, d, a, b, x[ 3], S23, 0xf4d50d87); /* 27 */
GG ( b, c, d, a, x[ 8], S24, 0x455a14ed); /* 28 */
GG ( a, b, c, d, x[13], S21, 0xa9e3e905); /* 29 */
GG ( d, a, b, c, x[ 2], S22, 0xfcefa3f8); /* 30 */
GG ( c, d, a, b, x[ 7], S23, 0x676f02d9); /* 31 */
GG ( b, c, d, a, x[12], S24, 0x8d2a4c8a); /* 32 */

/* Round 3 */
HH ( a, b, c, d, x[ 5], S31, 0xfffa3942); /* 33 */
HH ( d, a, b, c, x[ 8], S32, 0x8771f681); /* 34 */
HH ( c, d, a, b, x[11], S33, 0x6d9d6122); /* 35 */
HH ( b, c, d, a, x[14], S34, 0xfde5380c); /* 36 */
HH ( a, b, c, d, x[ 1], S31, 0xa4beea44); /* 37 */
HH ( d, a, b, c, x[ 4], S32, 0x4bdecfa9); /* 38 */
HH ( c, d, a, b, x[ 7], S33, 0xf6bb4b60); /* 39 */
HH ( b, c, d, a, x[10], S34, 0xbebfbc70); /* 40 */
HH ( a, b, c, d, x[13], S31, 0x289b7ec6); /* 41 */
HH ( d, a, b, c, x[ 0], S32, 0xeaa127fa); /* 42 */
HH ( c, d, a, b, x[ 3], S33, 0xd4ef3085); /* 43 */
HH ( b, c, d, a, x[ 6], S34,  0x4881d05); /* 44 */
HH ( a, b, c, d, x[ 9], S31, 0xd9d4d039); /* 45 */
HH ( d, a, b, c, x[12], S32, 0xe6db99e5); /* 46 */
HH ( c, d, a, b, x[15], S33, 0x1fa27cf8); /* 47 */
HH ( b, c, d, a, x[ 2], S34, 0xc4ac5665); /* 48 */

/* Round 4 */
II ( a, b, c, d, x[ 0], S41, 0xf4292244); /* 49 */
II ( d, a, b, c, x[ 7], S42, 0x432aff97); /* 50 */
II ( c, d, a, b, x[14], S43, 0xab9423a7); /* 51 */
II ( b, c, d, a, x[ 5], S44, 0xfc93a039); /* 52 */
II ( a, b, c, d, x[12], S41, 0x655b59c3); /* 53 */
II ( d, a, b, c, x[ 3], S42, 0x8f0ccc92); /* 54 */
II ( c, d, a, b, x[10], S43, 0xffeff47d); /* 55 */
II ( b, c, d, a, x[ 1], S44, 0x85845dd1); /* 56 */
II ( a, b, c, d, x[ 8], S41, 0x6fa87e4f); /* 57 */
II ( d, a, b, c, x[15], S42, 0xfc2cc6e0); /* 58 */
II ( c, d, a, b, x[ 6], S43, 0xa3014314); /* 59 */
II ( b, c, d, a, x[13], S44, 0x4e0811a1); /* 60 */
II ( a, b, c, d, x[ 4], S41, 0xf7537e82); /* 61 */
II ( d, a, b, c, x[11], S42, 0xbd3af235); /* 62 */
II ( c, d, a, b, x[ 2], S43, 0x2ad7d2bb); /* 63 */
II ( b, c, d, a, x[ 9], S44, 0xeb86d391); /* 64 */
```

```
state[0] += a;
state[1] += b;
state[2] += c;
state[3] += d;

/* Zeroize sensitive information.
 */
MD5_memset ((POINTER)x, 0, sizeof (x));
}


* Encodes input (UINT4) into output (unsigned char). Assumes len is
  a multiple of 4.
*/
static void Encode (output, input, len)
unsigned char *output;
UINT4 *input;
unsigned int len;
{
  unsigned int i, j;

  for (i = 0, j = 0; j < len; i++, j += 4) {
  output[j] = (unsigned char)(input[i] & 0xff);
  output[j+1] = (unsigned char)((input[i] >> 8) & 0xff);
  output[j+2] = (unsigned char)((input[i] >> 16) & 0xff);
  output[j+3] = (unsigned char)((input[i] >> 24) & 0xff);
  }
}


* Decodes input (unsigned char) into output (UINT4). Assumes len is
  a multiple of 4.
*/
static void Decode (output, input, len)
UINT4 *output;
unsigned char *input;
unsigned int len;
{
  unsigned int i, j;

  for (i = 0, j = 0; j < len; i++, j += 4)
  output[i] = ((UINT4)input[j]) | (((UINT4)input[j+1]) << 8) |
    (((UINT4)input[j+2]) << 16) | (((UINT4)input[j+3]) << 24);
}


* Note: Replace "for loop" with standard memcpy if possible.
*/
static void MD5_memcpy (output, input, len)
```

```
POINTER output;
POINTER input;
unsigned int len;
 {
  unsigned int i;

  for (i = 0; i < len; i++)
  output[i] = input[i];
 }

 * Note: Replace "for loop" with standard memset if possible.
 */
static void MD5_memset (output, value, len)
POINTER output;
int value;
unsigned int len;
 {
  unsigned int i;

  for (i = 0; i < len; i++)
  ((char *)output)[i] = (char)value;
 }
•
```

SECURE HASH ALGORITHM

```
/* - - - - - - - - - - - - - - -  SHS.H - - - - - - - - - - - - - - -  */

/* NIST Secure Hash Standard.

  Written 2 September 1992, Peter C. Gutmann.
  This implementation placed in the public domain.*/

/* Useful defines/typedefs */

typedef unsigned char   BYTE;
typedef unsigned long   LONG;

/* The SHS block size and message digest sizes, in bytes */

#define SHS_BLOCKSIZE           64
#define SHS_DIGESTSIZE          20

/* The structure for storing SHS info */

typedef struct {
```

```
        LONG digest[ 5 ];       /* Message digest */
        LONG countLo, countHi;          /* 64-bit bit count */
        LONG data[ 16 ];        /* SHS data buffer */
        } SHS_INFO;

/* Whether the machine is little-endian or not */

#define LITTLE_ENDIAN

/* - - - - - - - - - - - - - - - - SHS.C - - - - - - - - - - - - - - - - - - */

/* NIST proposed Secure Hash Standard.

   Written 2 September 1992, Peter C. Gutmann.
   This implementation placed in the public domain.

   Comments to pgut1@cs.aukuni.ac.nz */

#include <stdio.h>
#include <stdlib.h>
#include <time.h>
#include <string.h>

/* The SHS f()-functions */

#define f1(x,y,z)    ( ( x & y ) | ( ~x & z ) )                 /* Rounds  0-19 */
#define f2(x,y,z)    ( x ^ y ^ z )                  /* Rounds 20-39 */
#define f3(x,y,z)    ( ( x & y ) | ( x & z ) | ( y & z ) )   /* Rounds 40-59 */
#define f4(x,y,z)    ( x ^ y ^ z )                  /* Rounds 60-79 */

/* The SHS Mysterious Constants */

#define K1  0x5A827999L      /* Rounds  0-19 */
#define K2  0x6ED9EBA1L      /* Rounds 20-39 */
#define K3  0x8F1BBCDCL      /* Rounds 40-59 */
#define K4  0xCA62C1D6L      /* Rounds 60-79 */

/* SHS initial values */

#define h0init  0x67452301L
#define h1init  0xEFCDAB89L
#define h2init  0x98BADCFEL
#define h3init  0x10325476L
#define h4init  0xC3D2E1F0L

/* 32-bit rotate - kludged with shifts */
```

```
#define S(n,X)  ( ( X << n ) | ( X >> ( 32 - n ) ) )

/* The initial expanding function */

#define expand(count)    W[ count ] = W[ count - 3 ] ^ W[ count - 8 ] ^ W[ count -
14 ] ^ W[ count - 16 ]

/* The four SHS sub-rounds */

#define subRound1(count)    \
  { \
  temp = S( 5, A ) + f1( B, C, D ) + E + W[ count ] + K1; \
  E = D; \
  D = C; \
  C = S( 30, B ); \
  B = A; \
  A = temp; \
  }

#define subRound2(count)    \
  { \
  temp = S( 5, A ) + f2( B, C, D ) + E + W[ count ] + K2; \
  E = D; \
  D = C; \
  C = S( 30, B ); \
  B = A; \
  A = temp; \
  }

#define subRound3(count)    \
  { \
  temp = S( 5, A ) + f3( B, C, D ) + E + W[ count ] + K3; \
  E = D; \
  D = C; \
  C = S( 30, B ); \
  B = A; \
  A = temp; \
  }

#define subRound4(count)    \
  { \
  temp = S( 5, A ) + f4( B, C, D ) + E + W[ count ] + K4; \
  E = D; \
  D = C; \
  C = S( 30, B ); \
```

```
  B = A; \
  A = temp; \
  }

/* The two buffers of 5 32-bit words */

LONG h0, h1, h2, h3, h4;
LONG A, B, C, D, E;

/* Initialize the SHS values */

void shsInit( shsInfo )
  SHS_INFO *shsInfo;
  {
  /* Set the h-vars to their initial values */
  shsInfo->digest[ 0 ] = h0init;
  shsInfo->digest[ 1 ] = h1init;
  shsInfo->digest[ 2 ] = h2init;
  shsInfo->digest[ 3 ] = h3init;
  shsInfo->digest[ 4 ] = h4init;

  /* Initialise bit count */
  shsInfo->countLo = shsInfo->countHi = 0L;
  }

/* Perform the SHS transformation.  Note that this code, like MD5, seems to
   break some optimizing compilers - it may be necessary to split it into
   sections, eg based on the four subrounds */

void shsTransform( shsInfo )
  SHS_INFO *shsInfo;
  {
  LONG W[ 80 ], temp;
  int i;

  /* Step A.  Copy the data buffer into the local work buffer */
  for( i = 0; i < 16; i++ )
    W[ i ] = shsInfo->data[ i ];

  /* Step B.  Expand the 16 words into 64 temporary data words */
  expand( 16 ); expand( 17 ); expand( 18 ); expand( 19 ); expand( 20 );
  expand( 21 ); expand( 22 ); expand( 23 ); expand( 24 ); expand( 25 );
  expand( 26 ); expand( 27 ); expand( 28 ); expand( 29 ); expand( 30 );
  expand( 31 ); expand( 32 ); expand( 33 ); expand( 34 ); expand( 35 );
  expand( 36 ); expand( 37 ); expand( 38 ); expand( 39 ); expand( 40 );
  expand( 41 ); expand( 42 ); expand( 43 ); expand( 44 ); expand( 45 );
```

```
   expand( 46 ); expand( 47 ); expand( 48 ); expand( 49 ); expand( 50 );
   expand( 51 ); expand( 52 ); expand( 53 ); expand( 54 ); expand( 55 );
   expand( 56 ); expand( 57 ); expand( 58 ); expand( 59 ); expand( 60 );
   expand( 61 ); expand( 62 ); expand( 63 ); expand( 64 ); expand( 65 );
   expand( 66 ); expand( 67 ); expand( 68 ); expand( 69 ); expand( 70 );
   expand( 71 ); expand( 72 ); expand( 73 ); expand( 74 ); expand( 75 );
   expand( 76 ); expand( 77 ); expand( 78 ); expand( 79 );

   /* Step C.  Set up first buffer */
   A = shsInfo->digest[ 0 ];
   B = shsInfo->digest[ 1 ];
   C = shsInfo->digest[ 2 ];
   D = shsInfo->digest[ 3 ];
   E = shsInfo->digest[ 4 ];

   /* Step D.  Serious mangling, divided into four sub-rounds */
   subRound1( 0 ); subRound1( 1 ); subRound1( 2 ); subRound1( 3 );
   subRound1( 4 ); subRound1( 5 ); subRound1( 6 ); subRound1( 7 );
   subRound1( 8 ); subRound1( 9 ); subRound1( 10 ); subRound1( 11 );
   subRound1( 12 ); subRound1( 13 ); subRound1( 14 ); subRound1( 15 );
   subRound1( 16 ); subRound1( 17 ); subRound1( 18 ); subRound1( 19 );
   subRound2( 20 ); subRound2( 21 ); subRound2( 22 ); subRound2( 23 );
   subRound2( 24 ); subRound2( 25 ); subRound2( 26 ); subRound2( 27 );
   subRound2( 28 ); subRound2( 29 ); subRound2( 30 ); subRound2( 31 );
   subRound2( 32 ); subRound2( 33 ); subRound2( 34 ); subRound2( 35 );
   subRound2( 36 ); subRound2( 37 ); subRound2( 38 ); subRound2( 39 );
   subRound3( 40 ); subRound3( 41 ); subRound3( 42 ); subRound3( 43 );
   subRound3( 44 ); subRound3( 45 ); subRound3( 46 ); subRound3( 47 );
   subRound3( 48 ); subRound3( 49 ); subRound3( 50 ); subRound3( 51 );
   subRound3( 52 ); subRound3( 53 ); subRound3( 54 ); subRound3( 55 );
   subRound3( 56 ); subRound3( 57 ); subRound3( 58 ); subRound3( 59 );
   subRound4( 60 ); subRound4( 61 ); subRound4( 62 ); subRound4( 63 );
   subRound4( 64 ); subRound4( 65 ); subRound4( 66 ); subRound4( 67 );
   subRound4( 68 ); subRound4( 69 ); subRound4( 70 ); subRound4( 71 );
   subRound4( 72 ); subRound4( 73 ); subRound4( 74 ); subRound4( 75 );
   subRound4( 76 ); subRound4( 77 ); subRound4( 78 ); subRound4( 79 );

   /* Step E.  Build message digest */
   shsInfo->digest[ 0 ] += A;
   shsInfo->digest[ 1 ] += B;
   shsInfo->digest[ 2 ] += C;
   shsInfo->digest[ 3 ] += D;
   shsInfo->digest[ 4 ] += E;
   }

#ifdef LITTLE_ENDIAN
```

```
/* When run on a little-endian CPU we need to perform byte reversal on an
   array of longwords.   It is possible to make the code endianness-
   independant by fiddling around with data at the byte level, but this
   makes for very slow code, so we rely on the user to sort out endianness
   at compile time */

static void byteReverse( buffer, byteCount )
  LONG *buffer;
  int byteCount;

  {
  LONG value;
  int count;

  byteCount /= sizeof( LONG );
  for( count = 0; count < byteCount; count++ )
    {
    value = ( buffer[ count ] << 16 ) | ( buffer[ count ] >> 16 );
    buffer[ count ] = ( ( value & 0xFF00FF00L ) >> 8 ) | ( ( value & 0x00FF00FFL ) << 8 );
    }
  }
#endif /* LITTLE_ENDIAN */

/* Update SHS for a block of data.  This code assumes that the buffer size
   is a multiple of SHS_BLOCKSIZE bytes long, which makes the code a lot
   more efficient since it does away with the need to handle partial blocks
   between calls to shsUpdate() */

void shsUpdate( shsInfo, buffer, count )
  SHS_INFO *shsInfo;
  BYTE *buffer;
  int count;

  {
  /* Update bitcount */
  if( ( shsInfo->countLo + ( ( LONG ) count << 3 ) ) < shsInfo->countLo )
    shsInfo->countHi++; /* Carry from low to high bitCount */
  shsInfo->countLo += ( ( LONG ) count << 3 );
  shsInfo->countHi += ( ( LONG ) count >> 29 );

  /* Process data in SHS_BLOCKSIZE chunks */
  while( count >= SHS_BLOCKSIZE )
    {
    memcpy( shsInfo->data, buffer, SHS_BLOCKSIZE );
#ifdef LITTLE_ENDIAN
```

```
      byteReverse( shsInfo->data, SHS_BLOCKSIZE );
#endif /* LITTLE_ENDIAN */
      shsTransform( shsInfo );
      buffer += SHS_BLOCKSIZE;
      count  -= SHS_BLOCKSIZE;
      }

   /* Handle any remaining bytes of data.  This should only happen once
      on the final lot of data */
   memcpy( shsInfo->data, buffer, count );
   }

void shsFinal( shsInfo )
   SHS_INFO *shsInfo;

   {
   int count;
   LONG lowBitcount = shsInfo->countLo, highBitcount = shsInfo->countHi;

   /* Compute number of bytes mod 64 */
   count = ( int ) ( ( shsInfo->countLo >> 3 ) & 0x3F );

   /* Set the first char of padding to 0x80.  This is safe since there is
      always at least one byte free */
   ( ( BYTE * ) shsInfo->data )[ count++ ] = 0x80;

   /* Pad out to 56 mod 64 */
   if( count > 56 )
      {
      /* Two lots of padding:  Pad the first block to 64 bytes */
      memset( ( BYTE * ) &shsInfo->data + count, 0, 64 - count );
#ifdef LITTLE_ENDIAN
      byteReverse( shsInfo->data, SHS_BLOCKSIZE );
#endif /* LITTLE_ENDIAN */
      shsTransform( shsInfo );

      /* Now fill the next block with 56 bytes */
      memset( &shsInfo->data, 0, 56 );
      }
   else
      /* Pad block to 56 bytes */
      memset( ( BYTE * ) &shsInfo->data + count, 0, 56 - count );
#ifdef LITTLE_ENDIAN
   byteReverse( shsInfo->data, SHS_BLOCKSIZE );
#endif /* LITTLE_ENDIAN */
```

```
  /* Append length in bits and transform */
  shsInfo->data[ 14 ] = highBitcount;
  shsInfo->data[ 15 ] = lowBitcount;

  shsTransform( shsInfo );
#ifdef LITTLE_ENDIAN
  byteReverse( shsInfo->data, SHS_DIGESTSIZE );
#endif /* LITTLE_ENDIAN */
  }

/* – – – – – – – – – – – – – -  SHS Test code – – – – – – – – – – – – – -  */

/* Size of buffer for SHS speed test data */

#define TEST_BLOCK_SIZE      ( SHS_DIGESTSIZE * 100 )

/* Number of bytes of test data to process */

#define TEST_BYTES             10000000L
#define TEST_BLOCKS            ( TEST_BYTES / TEST_BLOCK_SIZE )

void main( )
  {
  SHS_INFO shsInfo;
  time_t endTime, startTime;
  BYTE data[ TEST_BLOCK_SIZE ];
  long i;

  /* Test output data (this is the only test data given in the SHS
     document, but chances are if it works for this it'll work for
     anything) */
  shsInit( &shsInfo );
  shsUpdate( &shsInfo, ( BYTE * ) "abc", 3 );
  shsFinal( &shsInfo );
  if( shsInfo.digest[ 0 ] != 0x0164B8A9L ||
    shsInfo.digest[ 1 ] != 0x14CD2A5EL ||
    shsInfo.digest[ 2 ] != 0x74C4F7FFL ||
    shsInfo.digest[ 3 ] != 0x082C4D97L ||
    shsInfo.digest[ 4 ] != 0xF1EDF880L )
    {
    puts( "Error in SHS implementation" );
    exit( -1 );
    }

  /* Now perform time trial, generating MD for 10MB of data.   First,
     initialize the test data */
```

```
memset( data, 0, TEST_BLOCK_SIZE );

/* Get start time */
printf( "SHS time trial.  Processing %ld characters...\n", TEST_BYTES );
time( &startTime );

/* Calculate SHS message digest in TEST_BLOCK_SIZE byte blocks */
shsInit( &shsInfo );
for( i = TEST_BLOCKS; i > 0; i- )
  shsUpdate( &shsInfo, data, TEST_BLOCK_SIZE );
shsFinal( &shsInfo );

/* Get finish time and time difference */
time( &endTime );
printf( "Seconds to process test input: %ld\n", endTime - startTime );
printf( "Characters processed per second: %ld\n", TEST_BYTES / ( endTime -
startTime ) );
}
```

●

SECRET SHARING

```
- - - - - - - - - - COMBINE.C - - - - - - - - - - - - - - -
/* COMBINE.C - Program to "combine" the files of a Threshhold Information
    Protection Scheme.
Author: Peter Pearson.
Version of 93.02.15.

This program is the complement of DISPERSE. See DISPERSE.C for literature
references.

This program EXITs with errorlevel 0 normally,
                       2 if it couldn't find enough files.

Revision history:
    87.07.06 - Initial version.
  93.02.15 - Move argument names into function definitions.
*/


#include <stdio.h>
#include <time.h>
#include <fcntl.h>
#include <io.h>
#include <process.h>
#include <string.h>
```

```c
#include "g13.h"

#defineBOOLEAN int
#defineFALSE0
#defineTRUE(1==1)

void main( int argc, char *argv[] )
{
  FILE *InputFiles[15] ;
  int Positions[15] ;
  int NumberInputs ;
  BOOLEAN InputsOK( char *FamilyName, int Positions[], FILE *InputFiles[],
      int *RequiredPtr ) ;
  void Combine( int Positions[], FILE *InputFiles[], int NumberInputs ) ;
  int ExitCode ;

  ExitCode = 2 ;/* Unless things go just right, return an unhappy
        exit code.  */
  if ( argc != 2 )
  {
   fprintf( stderr,
    "Usage: COMBINE filename\n" ) ;
   fprintf( stderr,
    "where 'filename' identifies a family of files named\n" ) ;
   fprintf( stderr,
    "filename.f0, filename.f4, etc.\n" ) ;
  }
  else
  {
   if ( InputsOK( argv[1], Positions, InputFiles, &NumberInputs ) )
   {
    Combine( Positions, InputFiles, NumberInputs ) ;
    ExitCode = 0 ;
   }
  }
  exit( ExitCode ) ;
}

BOOLEAN InputsOK( char *FamilyName,/* Input. */
      int   Positions[],/* Output. */
      FILE *InputFiles[],/* Output. */
      int  *RequiredPtr )/* Output. */
/*
   Try to open as many files of the input "family" as are necessary
   to reconstitute the output file.
```

Returns with a list of open files in the InputFiles array, and the
number in *RequiredPtr. The array Positions returns the "sequence number"
of each file within the family.

Returns:
    TRUE if everything goes OK,
    FALSE if there aren't enough input files, or some inconsistency
        is found.

Details:
    Files of the input family are expected to have names of the form
    FAMILYNAME.F1, FAMILYNAME.F2, ..., FAMILYNAME.F15.
    The first byte of each input file contains the number of files
    required to reconstitute the output file. These first bytes must all
    agree.

    The second byte of each input file gives the "sequence number"
    of that file in the family. It must be greater than zero, and must not
    be greater than the first byte.
    Neither the first byte nor the second byte may exceed 15.
    The first two bytes are read from each input file inside this
    routine.
*/
{
```
  char TryName[100] ;
  char FirstName[100] ;
  BOOLEAN FoundSequence[16] ;
  int i ;
  int Count ;
  int Required ;
  BOOLEAN Acceptable ;

  Count = 0 ;
  for ( i = 0; i < 16; i++ ) FoundSequence[i] = FALSE ;
  for ( i = 1; i <= 15; i++ )
  {
   sprintf( TryName, "%s.f%d", FamilyName, i ) ;
   if ( ( *InputFiles = fopen( TryName, "r" ) ) != NULL )
   {
    Acceptable = TRUE ;
    setmode( fileno( *InputFiles ), O_BINARY ) ;
    if ( Count == 0 )
    {
     if ( ( Required = getc( *InputFiles ) ) > 15
     || Required < 2 )
     {
```

```
        fprintf( stderr,
      "The first byte of '%s' is not what I expect."
      " '%s' will be ignored.\n",
       TryName, TryName ) ;
          Acceptable = FALSE ;
     }
}
else if ( Required != getc( *InputFiles ) )
{
  fprintf( stderr,
        "Input files '%s' and '%s' come from different sets.\n",
        FirstName, TryName ) ;
  fprintf( stderr, "'%s' will be ignored.\n", TryName ) ;
  Acceptable = FALSE ;
}
if ( Acceptable )
{
  *Positions = getc( *InputFiles ) ;
  if ( *Positions < 1 || *Positions > 15 )
  {
        fprintf( stderr,
      "The second byte of '%s' isn't what I expect."
      " I'll ignore '%s'.\n",
       TryName, TryName ) ;
          Acceptable = FALSE ;
  }
  else if ( FoundSequence[ *Positions ] )
  {
        fprintf( stderr,
      "'%s' has the same sequence number as somebody else."
      " I'll ignore '%s'.\n",
       TryName, TryName ) ;
          Acceptable = FALSE ;
  }
}
if ( Acceptable )
{
  if ( Count == 0 ) strcpy( FirstName, TryName ) ;
  FoundSequence[ *Positions ] = TRUE ;
  ++Positions ;
  ++InputFiles ;
  ++Count ;
}
else
{
  fclose( *InputFiles ) ;
```

```
    }
   }
   if ( Count > 2 && Count >= Required ) break ;
  }

  if ( Count <= 0 )
  {
   fprintf( stderr, "Didn't find any input files. Sorry.\n" ) ;
   return FALSE ;
  }
  else if ( Count < Required )
  {
   fprintf( stderr, "I have %d of the %d files needed.\n",
    Count, Required ) ;
   return FALSE ;
  }
  else
  {
   *RequiredPtr = Required ;
   return TRUE ;
  }
}

void Combine( int Positions[], FILE *InputFiles[], int NumberInputs )
{
  int OddNibble ;
  BOOLEAN Odd ;
  int i ;
  int j ;
  G13 C[15] ;
  G13 c ;
  G13 Y[15] ;
  BOOLEAN FillNibbles( G13 *Nibbles, FILE *InputFiles[], int NumberInputs );

  setmode( fileno( stdout ), O_BINARY ) ;

  /* Compute the coefficients by which the nibbles from the
   * various input files can be combined to produce the output
   * file.
   *     If X(i) is the "position" of the ith input file, and
   * Y(i) is the value of a particular nibble in the ith file,
   * we will find coefficients C(i) such that
   *
   *     p = C(1) * Y(1) + C(2) * Y(2) + ...
   *
   * where p is the appropriate nibble for the output file.
```

```
 *
 *       The formula for the Cs is:
 *
 *       C(i) = product of (    X(j) / ( X(i) - X(j) )    ) for all j != i .
 *
 *
 */

  for ( i = 0; i < NumberInputs; i++ )
  {
   c = 1 ;
   for ( j = 0; j < NumberInputs; j++ )
    if ( j != i )
     c = Mult( c,
      Div( Positions[j], Positions[i] ^ Positions[j] ) ) ;
   C[i] = c ;
  }

  /*
   *  Now, process the input files:
   */

  Odd = TRUE ;
  while ( FillNibbles( Y, InputFiles, NumberInputs ) )
  {
   c = 0 ;
   for ( i = 0; i < NumberInputs; i++ )
    c ^= Mult( C[i], Y[i] ) ;

   if ( Odd )
    OddNibble = c ;
   else
    putchar( ( OddNibble << 4 ) | c ) ;

   Odd = !Odd ;
  }
}

BOOLEAN FillNibbles( G13  *Nibbles,  /* Output. */
     FILE *InputFiles[],  /* Input. */
     int   NumberInputs ) /* Input. */
/*
   Fill the output array with nibbles, one from each
   input file.                       .

Returns
```

```
    TRUE  normally,
    FALSE if an error or end-of-file condition is encountered.
*/
{
  static BOOLEAN Odd = TRUE ;
  static G13 Holdover[15] ;
  int c ;
  int i ;

  if ( Odd )
  {
   for ( i = 0; i < NumberInputs; i++, InputFiles++ )
   {
    if ( ( c = getc( *InputFiles ) ) == EOF )
    {
     if ( i != 0 ) fprintf( stderr,
         "Warning: Input files weren't all the same length!\n" ) ;
     return FALSE ;
    }
    else
    {
     *Nibbles++ = ( c >> 4 ) & 0xF ;
     Holdover[i] = c & 0xF ;
    }
   }
  }
  else
  {
   for ( i = 0; i < NumberInputs; i++ )
    *Nibbles++ = Holdover[i] ;
  }
  Odd = !Odd ;
  return TRUE ;
}
– – – – – – – – – – DISPERSE.C – – – – – – – – – – – – – –
/* DISPERSE.C - Program to "disperse" the information from an
input file into a number of output files.
Author: Peter Pearson.
Version of 93.02.15.

*/

#include <stdio.h>
#include <fcntl.h>
#include <io.h>
#include <ctype.h>
```

```
#include <stdlib.h>
#include <string.h>
#include <time.h>
#include "g13.h"

#define BOOLEANint
#define FALSE0
#defineTRUE(1==1)

void main( int argc, char *argv[] )
{
  BOOLEAN Help ;
  char FileName[100] ;
  int Total ;
  int Required ;
  void Disperse( char *FileName, int Total, int Required ) ;

  srand((unsigned)(time(0) & 0xffff));
  FileName[0] = '\0' ;
  Total = 0 ;
  Required = 0 ;

  Help = ( argc != 4 ) ;
  if ( Help == FALSE )
  {
   strcpy( FileName, *++argv ) ;
   if ( sscanf( *++argv, "%d", &Total ) != 1
   ||    sscanf( *++argv, "%d", &Required ) != 1 )
     Help = TRUE ;
  }
  if ( Help )
  {
   fprintf( stderr, "Usage:\n    DISPERSE filename 5 3\n" ) ;
   fprintf( stderr, "where\n    filename is the name of the input file,\n" ) ;
   fprintf( stderr, "    5 is the total number of files to be output,\n" ) ;
   fprintf( stderr, "    3 is the number of files required for reconstruction.\n" ) ;
  }
  else
  {
   if ( Total < Required )
   {
    int Temp ;

    Temp = Total ;
    Total = Required ;
    Required = Temp ;
```

```
     fprintf( stderr,
      "(I assume you mean %d files total and", Total ) ;
     fprintf( stderr,
      " %d files required for reconstruction.)\r\n", Required ) ;
   }
   Disperse( FileName, Total, Required ) ;
 }
}

BOOLEAN ArgsOK( char *FileName, int Total, int Required )
{
  BOOLEAN ArgError ;

  ArgError = FALSE ;
  if ( FileName[0] == '\0' )
  {
   ArgError = TRUE ;
   fprintf( stderr, "You must specify a non-null file name.\n" ) ;
  }
  if ( Total < 2 || Total > 15 || Required < 2 || Required > 15 )
  {
   ArgError = TRUE ;
   fprintf( stderr,
    "Both Total and Required file numbers must be in 2 .. 15.\n" ) ;
  }
  if ( Total < Required )
  {
   ArgError = TRUE ;
   fprintf( stderr,
    "Required File Number cannot exceed Total File Number.\n" ) ;
  }
  return ( ArgError == FALSE ) ;
}

BOOLEAN CreatedOutput( char *FileName, int Number, FILE *FileList[] )
/*
   Create several output files with names derived from one
   specified name.

Returns:
   TRUE if everything went OK,
   FALSE if something went wrong. (An error message has been issued.)

Algorithm:
   We strip the FileName of any leading "\xxx\xxx" and any
   trailing ".ext", and append .f0, .f1, .f2, et cetera.
```

```
        If a file exists already with any of these names, it will
        be overwritten.
*/
{
  int  i ;
  char Stripped[100] ;
  char NewName[100] ;
  void Strip( char *Stripped, char *Full ) ;

  Strip( Stripped, FileName ) ;
  if ( Stripped[0] == '\0' )
  {
    fprintf( stderr,
      "There's something wrong with the input file name.\n" ) ;
    return FALSE ;
  }

  for ( i = 0; i < Number; i++ )
  {
    sprintf( NewName, "%s.f%d", Stripped, i+1 ) ;
    fprintf( stderr, "Creating file %s.\n", NewName ) ;
    FileList[i] = fopen( NewName, "w" ) ;
    if ( FileList[i] == NULL )
    {
      fprintf( stderr,
        "Sorry, I had trouble creating the %dth output file.\n",
        i ) ;
      return FALSE ;
    }
    setmode( fileno( FileList[i] ), O_BINARY ) ;
  }
  return TRUE ;
}

void Disperse( char *FileName, int Total, int Required )
{
  int Byte ;
  G13 HighNibble[15] ;
  G13 LowNibble[15] ;
  int i ;
  FILE *OutFile[15] ;
  FILE *InFile ;
  long StartTime ;
  long EndTime ;
  long ByteCount ;
```

```
  BOOLEAN ArgsOK( char *FileName, int Total, int Required ) ;
  FILE *OpenedInput( char * ) ;
  BOOLEAN CreatedOutput( char *, int, FILE * * ) ;
  void Process( int Nibble, int *OutArray, int Total, int Required ) ;

  if ( ArgsOK( FileName, Total, Required )
  &&   ( InFile = OpenedInput( FileName ) ) != NULL
  &&   CreatedOutput( FileName, Total, OutFile ) )
  {
   ByteCount = 0 ;
   StartTime = time( NULL ) ;

   for ( i = 0; i < Total; i++ ).
   {
    putc( Required, OutFile[i] ) ; /* Say how many files required. */
    putc( i+1     , OutFile[i] ) ; /* Say which file this is.      */
   }

   while ( ( Byte = getc( InFile ) ) != EOF )
   {
    ++ByteCount ;
    Process( Byte >> 4, HighNibble, Total, Required ) ;
    Process( Byte     , LowNibble,  Total, Required ) ;
    for ( i = 0; i < Total; i++ )
     putc( ( HighNibble[i] << 4 ) + LowNibble[i], OutFile[i] ) ;
   }
   EndTime = time( NULL ) ;
   if ( EndTime > StartTime )
    fprintf( stderr, "\
%ld seconds elapsed time.\r\n\
%ld bytes read, %ld bytes written.\r\n\
%d bytes read per second, %d bytes written per second.\r\n",
     EndTime - StartTime,
     ByteCount, Total * ByteCount,
     (int) ( ByteCount / ( EndTime - StartTime ) ),
     (int) ( ( Total * ByteCount ) / ( EndTime - StartTime ) ) ) ;
  }
}

FILE *OpenedInput( char *FileName )
{
  FILE *F ;

  if ( ( F = fopen( FileName, "r" ) ) == NULL )
   fprintf( stderr, "Error opening file \"%s\" for input.\n",
    FileName ) ;
```

```
  setmode( fileno( F ), O_BINARY ) ;
  return F ;
}


void Process( int Nibble, int *OutArray, int Total, int Required )
/*
   Given one nibble of the input file, fill an array with
   the values that go into the output files.
*/
{
  G13 C[15] ;
  int i ;
  int j ;
  G13 y ;
  G13 Rand4( void ) ;

  C[0] = Nibble & 0xF ;
  for ( i = 1; i < Required; i++ ) C[i] = Rand4() ;
  for ( i = 1; i <= Total; i++ )
  {
   y = C[ Required-1 ] ;
   for ( j = Required-2 ; j >= 0 ; j- ) y = C[j] ^ Mult( i, y ) ;
   *OutArray++ = y ;
  }
}


G13 Rand4( void )
/*
   Return a random G13-thing (4-bits).
```

Important note:
   The output from this program will resist intelligent, informed
   cryptanalysis only to the extent that the random number sequence
   resists analysis. If the random number sequence is truly random,
   as could be achieved by attaching special hardware to your
   computer, then the output from this program will resist decryption
   even by an infinitely-intelligent cryptanalyst knowing all the
   algorithms involved.
    Such perfection is not likely to be achieved. Second-best is
   a pseudorandom-number generator whose future outputs cannot be
   predicted even when given a long sequence of past outputs. Any
   encryption scheme (e.g. DES) resistant to known-plaintext attack
   might be harnessed to this purpose.

    This version of this program, however, settles for a very
   predictable pseudorandom-number generator.

```
*/
{
  return ( rand() > 11 ) & 0xF ;
}


void Strip( char *Stripped, char *Full )
/*
   Strip a file name of preceding directory-path information
   (\xxxx\xxxx\xxx\) and trailing "extension" information (.ext).

   Stripped : output
   Full     : input
*/
{
  char *fp ;
  char *sp ;

  sp = Full ;
  for ( fp = Full ; *fp ; ) if ( *fp++ == '\\' ) sp = fp ;
  while ( *sp && *sp != '.' ) *Stripped++ = *sp++ ;
  *Stripped = '\0' ;
}
- - - - - - - - - - G13.H - - - - - - - - - - - - - - - - - -
/* G13.H - Header file for package for arithmetic in field G(2^4),
reduced modulo x^4 + x + 1.

Version of 19 May 1987.
*/

#ifndef G13
#define G13int
G13 Add( G13, G13 ) ;
G13 Mult( G13, G13 ) ;
G13 Div( G13, G13 ) ;
#endif
- - - - - - - - - - G13.C - - - - - - - - - - - - - - - - - -
/* G13.C - Functions for arithmetic in G(2^4) reduced modulo x^4 + x + 1.
Author: Peter Pearson
Version of 93.02.15.

Revision history:
   87.05.19 - Initial version.
   93.02.15 - Adapted to Turbo C.
*/

#include <stdio.h>
```

```c
#include "g13.h"

int Offset[16] = { 0,1,3,6,10,15,21,28,36,45,55,66,78,91,105,120 } ;
int Product[136] = {
0x0,
0x0, 0x1,
0x0, 0x2, 0x4,
0x0, 0x3, 0x6, 0x5,
0x0, 0x4, 0x8, 0xc, 0x3,
0x0, 0x5, 0xa, 0xf, 0x7, 0x2,
0x0, 0x6, 0xc, 0xa, 0xb, 0xd, 0x7,
0x0, 0x7, 0xe, 0x9, 0xf, 0x8, 0x1, 0x6,
0x0, 0x8, 0x3, 0xb, 0x6, 0xe, 0x5, 0xd, 0xc,
0x0, 0x9, 0x1, 0x8, 0x2, 0xb, 0x3, 0xa, 0x4, 0xd,
0x0, 0xa, 0x7, 0xd, 0xe, 0x4, 0x9, 0x3, 0xf, 0x5, 0x8,
0x0, 0xb, 0x5, 0xe, 0xa, 0x1, 0xf, 0x4, 0x7, 0xc, 0x2, 0x9,
0x0, 0xc, 0xb, 0x7, 0x5, 0x9, 0xe, 0x2, 0xa, 0x6, 0x1, 0xd, 0xf,
0x0, 0xd, 0x9, 0x4, 0x1, 0xc, 0x8, 0x5, 0x2, 0xf, 0xb, 0x6, 0x3, 0xe,
0x0, 0xe, 0xf, 0x1, 0xd, 0x3, 0x2, 0xc, 0x9, 0x7, 0x6, 0x8, 0x4, 0xa, 0xb,
0x0, 0xf, 0xd, 0x2, 0x9, 0x6, 0x4, 0xb, 0x1, 0xe, 0xc, 0x3, 0x8, 0x7, 0x5, 0xa
} ;
int Reciprocal[16] = {  0, 1, 9, 0xe, 0xd, 0xb, 7, 6,
      0xf, 2, 0xc, 5, 0xa, 4, 3, 8 } ;

G13 Add( G13 a, G13 b )
{
  return a^b ;
}

G13 Div( G13 a, G13 b )
{
  if ( ( a | b ) > 15 )
    fprintf( stderr, "Illegal argument in G13 Divide.\n" ) ;

  return Mult( a, Reciprocal[b] ) ;
}

G13 Mult( G13 a, G13 b )
{
  if ( ( a | b ) > 15 )
    fprintf( stderr, "Illegal argument in G13 Multiply.\n" ) ;

  return ( a < b ) ? Product[ Offset[ b ] + a ]
      : Product[ Offset[ a ] + b ] ;
}
```
•

References

1. ABA Bank Card Standard, "Management and Use of Personal Information Numbers," Aids from ABA, Catalog no. 207213, American Bankers Association, 1979.
2. ABA Document 4.3, "Key Management Standard," American Bankers Association, 1980.
3. M. Abadi, J. Feigenbaum, and J. Kilian, "On Hiding Information from an Oracle," *Proceedings of the 19th ACM Symposium on the Theory of Computing,* 1987, pp. 195-203.
4. M. Abadi, J. Feigenbaum, and J. Kilian, "On Hiding Information from an Oracle," *Journal of Computer and System Sciences,* v. 39, n. 1, Aug 1989, pp. 21–50.
5. C. M. Adams and H. Meijer, "Security-Related Comments Regarding McEliece's Public-Key Cryptosystem," *Advances in Cryptology—CRYPTO '87 Proceedings,* Berlin: Springer-Verlag, 1988, pp. 224–230.
6. W. Adams and D. Shanks, "Strong Primality Tests That Are Not Sufficient," *Mathematics of Computation,* v. 39, 1982, pp. 255-300.
7. W. W. Adams and L. J. Goldstein, *Introduction to Number Theory,* Prentice-Hall, 1976.
8. B. S. Adiga and P. Shankar, "Modified Lu-Lee Cryptosystem," *Electronics Letters,* v. 21, n. 18, 29 Aug 1985, pp. 794–795.
9. L. M. Adleman, "A Subexponential Algorithm for the Discrete Logarithm Problem with Applications to Cryptography," *Proceedings of the IEEE 20th Annual Symposium of Foundations of Computer Science, 1979,* pp. 55–60.
10. L. M. Adleman, "On Breaking Generalized Knapsack Public Key Cryptosystems," *Proceedings of the 15th ACM Symposium on Theory of Computing,* 1983, pp. 402–412.
11. L. M. Adleman, "Factoring Numbers Using Singular Integers," *Proceedings of the 23rd Annual ACM Symposium on the Theory of Computing,* 1991, pp. 64–71.
12. L. M. Adleman, C. Pomerance, and R. S. Rumley, "On Distinguishing Prime Numbers from Composite Numbers," *Annals of Mathematics,* v. 117, n. 1, 1983, pp. 173–206.
13. L. M. Adleman and R. L. Rivest, *How to Break the Lu-Lee (COMSAT) Public-Key Cryptosystem,* MIT Laboratory for Computer Science, Jul 1979.
14. A. Aho, J. Hopcraft, and J. Ullman, *The Design and Analysis of Computer Algorithms,* Addison-Wesley, 1974.
15. G. B. Agnew, "Random Sources for Cryptographic Systems," *Advances in Cryptology—EUROCRYPT '87 Proceedings,* Berlin: Springer-Verlag, 1988, pp. 77–81.
16. G. B. Agnew, R. C. Mullin, I. M. Onyszchuk, and S. A. Vanstone, "An Implementation for a Fast Public-Key Cryptosystem," *Journal of Cryptology,* v. 3, n. 2, 1991, pp. 63–79.

17. S. G. Akl and H. Meijer, "A Fast Pseudo Random Permutation Generator with Applications to Cryptology," *Advances in Cryptology—Proceedings of CRYPTO, 84,* Berlin: Springer-Verlag, 1985, pp. 269–275.

18. K. Alagappan and J. Tardo, *SPX Guide: Prototype Public-Key Authentication Service,* Digital Equipment Corp., May 1991.

19. W. Alexi, B.-Z. Chor, O. Goldreich, and C. P. Schnorr, "RSA and Rabin Functions: Certain Parts Are as Hard as the Whole," *Proceedings of the 25th IEEE Symposium on the Foundations of Computer Science,* 1984, pp. 449–457.

20. W. Alexi, B.-Z. Chor, O. Goldreich, and C. P. Schnorr, "RSA and Rabin Functions: Certain Parts Are as Hard as the Whole," *SIAM Journal on Computing,* v. 17, n. 2, Apr 1988, pp. 194–209.

21. H. R. Amirazizi, E. D. Karnin, and J. M. Reyneri, "Compact Knapsacks are Polynomial Solvable," *ACM SIGACT News,* v. 15, 1983, pp. 20–22.

22. R. Anderson, "Solving a Class of Stream Ciphers," *Cryptologia,* v. 14, n. 3, Jul 1990, pp. 285–288.

23. R. Anderson, personal communication.

24. D. Andleman and J. Reeds, "On the Cryptanalysis of Rotor Machines and Substitution-Permutation Networks," *IEEE Transactions on Information Theory,* v. IT-28, n. 4, Jul 1982, pp. 578–584.

25. ANSI X3.92, "American National Standard for Data Encryption Algorithm (DEA)," American National Standards Institute, 1981.

26. ANSI X3.105, "American National Standard for Information Systems—Data Link Encryption," American National Standards Institute, 1983.

27. ANSI X3.106, "American National Standard for Information Systems—Data Encryption Algorithm—Modes of Operation," American National Standards Institute, 1983.

28. ANSI X9.8, "American National Standard for Personal Information Number (PIN) Management and Security," American Bankers Association, 1982.

29. ANSI X9.9 (Revised), "American National Standard for Financial Institution Message Authentication (Wholesale)," American Bankers Association, 1986.

30. ANSI X9.17 (Revised), "American National Standard for Financial Institution Key Management (Wholesale)," American Bankers Association, 1985.

31. ANSI X9.19, "American National Standard for Retail Message Authentication," American Bankers Association, 1985.

32. ANSI X9.23, "American National Standard for Financial Institution Message Encryption," American Bankers Association, 1988.

33. ANSI X9.24, "Draft Proposed American National Standard for Retail Key Management," American Bankers Association, 1988.

34. ANSI X9.26 (Revised), "American National Standard for Financial Institution Sign-On Authentication for Wholesale Financial Transaction," American Bankers Association, 1990.

35. C. Asmuth and J. Bloom, "A Modular Approach to Key Safeguarding," *IEEE Transactions on Information Theory,* v. IT-30, Mar 1983, pp. 208–210.

36. AT&T, *T7001 Random Number Generator,* Data Sheet, Aug 1986.

37. AT&T, *T7002/T7003 Bit Slice Multiplier,* product announcement, 1987.

38. R. G. Ayoub, *An Introduction to the Theory of Numbers,* American Mathematical Society: Providence RI, 1963.

39. D. Balenson, "Privacy Enhancement for Internet Electronic Mail: Part III: Algorithms, Modes, and Identifiers," RFC 1423, Feb 1993.

40. J. Bamford, *The Puzzle Palace, Boston:* Houghton Mifflin, 1982.

41. S. K. Banerjee, "High Speed Implementation of DES," *Computers and Security,* v. 1, 1982, pp. 261–267.

42. P. H. Bardell, "Analysis of Cellular Automata Used as Pseudorandom Pattern Generators," *Proceedings of 1990 International Test Conference,* pp. 762–768.

43. T. Baritaud, H. Gilbert, and M. Girault, "FFT Hashing Is Not Collision-Free," *Advances in Cryptology—EUROCRYPT '92 Proceedings,* Berlin: Springer-Verlag, 1993, pp. 35–44.

44. C. Barker, "An Industry Perspective of the CCEP," *2nd Annual AIAA Computer Security Conference Proceedings,* 1986.

45. W. G. Barker, *Cryptanalysis of the Haglen Cryptograph,* Aegean Park Press, 1977.

46. P. Barrett, "Impelementing the Rivest, Shamir, and Adleman Public-Key Encryption Algorithm on a Standard Digital Signal Processor," *Advances in Cryptology—CRYPTO '86 Proceedings,* Berlin: Springer-Verlag, 1987, pp. 311–323.

47. K. R. Bauer, T. A. Bersen, and R. J. Feiertag, "A Key Distribution Protocol Using Event Markers," *ACM Transactions on Computer Systems,* v. 1, n. 3, 1983, pp. 249–255.

48. D. Bayer, S. Haber, and W. S. Stornetta, "Improving the Efficiency and Reliability of Digital

Time-Stamping," *Sequences II: Methods in Communication, Security, and Computer Science,* Berlin: Springer-Verlag, 1993, pp. 329–334.

49. R. Bayer and J. K. Metzger, "On the Encipherment of Search Trees and Random Access Files," *ACM Transactions on Database Systems,* v. 1, n. 1, Mar 1976, pp. 37–52.

50. P. Beauchemin and G. Brassard, "A Generalization of Hellman's Extension to Shannon's Approach to Cryptography," *Journal of Cryptology,* v. 1, n. 2, 1988, pp. 129–132.

51. P. Beauchemin, G. Brassard, C. Crépeau, C. Goutier, and C. Pomerance, "The Generation of Random Numbers That Are Probably Prime," *Journal of Cryptology,* v. 1, n. 1, 1988, pp. 53–64.

52. D. Beaver, J. Feigenbaum, and V. Shoup, "Hiding Instances in Zero-Knowledge Proofs," *Advances in Cryptology—CRYPTO '90 Proceedings,* Berlin: Springer-Verlag, 1991, pp. 326–338.

53. H. Beker, J. Friend, and P. Halliden, "Simplifying Key Management in Electronic Funds Transfer Points of Sale Systems," *Electronics Letters,* v. 19, n. 12, Jun 1983, pp. 442–444.

54. H. Beker and F. Piper, *Cipher Systems: The Protection of Communications, London:* Northwood Books, 1982.

55. N. Bellare and S. Goldwasser, "New Paradigms for Digital Signatures and Message Authentication Based on Non-Interactive Zero Knowledge Proofs," *Advances in Cryptology—CRYPTO '89 Proceedings,* Berlin: Springer-Verlag, 1990, pp. 194–211.

56. M. Bellare and S. Micali, "Non-Interactive Oblivious Transfer and Applications," *Advances in Cryptology—CRYPTO '89 Proceedings,* Berlin: Springer-Verlag, 1990, pp. 547–557

57. S. M. Bellovin, "A Preliminary Technical Analysis of Clipper and Skipjack," unpublished manuscript, 20 Apr 1993.

58. S. M. Bellovin and M. Merritt, "Limitations of the Kerberos Protocol," *Winter 1991 USENIX Conference Proceedings,* 1991, pp. 253–267.

59. S. M. Bellovin and M. Merritt, "Encrypted Key Exchange: Password-Based Protocols Secure Against Dictionary Attacks," *Proceedings of the 1992 IEEE Computer Society Conference on Research in Security and Privacy,* 1992, pp. 72–84.

59a. S. M. Bellovin and M. Merritt, "Cryptographic Protocol for Secure Communications," U.S. Patent # 5,241,599, 31 Aug 93.

60. S. M. Bellovin and M. Merritt, "An Attack on the Interlock Protocol When Used for Authentication," *IEEE Transactions on Information Theory,* forthcoming.

61. J. C. Benaloh, "Cryptographic Capsules: A Disjunctive Primitive for Interactive Protocols," *Advances in Cryptology—CRYPTO '86 Proceedings,* Berlin: Springer-Verlag, 1987, pp. 213–222.

62. J. C. Benaloh, "Secret Sharing Homorphisms: Keeping Shares of a Secret Secret," *Advances in Cryptology—CRYPTO '86 Proceedings,* Berlin: Springer-Verlag, 1987, pp. 251–260.

63. J. C. Benaloh, "Verifiable Secret-Ballot Elections," Ph.D. diss., Yale University, YALEU/DCS/TR-561, Dec 1987.

64. J. C. Benaloh and M. Yung, "Distributing the Power of a Government to Enhance the Privacy of Voters," *Proceedings of the 5th ACM Symposium on the Principles in Distributed Computing,* 1986, pp. 52–62.

65. A. Bender and G. Castagnoli, "On the Implementation of Elliptic Curve Cryptosystems," *Advances in Cryptology—CRYPTO '89 Proceedings,* Berlin: Springer-Verlag, 1990, pp. 186–192.

66. S. Bengio, G. Brassard, Y. G. Desmedt, C. Goutier, and J.-J. Quisquater, "Secure Implementation of Identification Systems," *Journal of Cryptology,* v. 4, n. 3, 1991, pp. 175–184.

67. C. H. Bennett, F. Bessette, G. Brassard, L. Salvail, and J. Smolin, "Experimental Quantum Cryptography," *Advances in Cryptology—EUROCRYPT '90 Proceedings,* Berlin: Springer-Verlag, 1991, pp. 253–265.

68. C. H. Bennett and G. Brassard, "Quantum Cryptography: Public Key Distribution and Coin Tossing," *Proceedings of the IEEE International Conference on Computers, Systems, and Signal Processing,* Banjalore, India, Dec 1984, pp. 175–179.

69. C.H. Bennett and G. Brassard, "An Update on Quantum Cryptography," *Advances in Cryptology—Proceedings of CRYPTO '84,* Berlin: Springer-Verlag, 1985, pp. 475–480.

70. C. H. Bennett and G. Brassard, "Quantum Public-Key Distribution System," *IBM Technical Disclosure Bulletin,* v. 28, 1985, pp. 3153–3163.

71. C. H. Bennett and G. Brassard, "Quantum Public Key Distribution Reinvented," *SIGACT News,* v. 18, n. 4, 1987, pp. 51–53.

72. C. H. Bennett and G. Brassard, "The Dawn of a New Era for Quantum Cryptography: The Experimental

Prototype Is Working!" *SIGACT News,* v. 20, n. 4, Fall 1989, pp. 78–82.

73. C. H. Bennett, G. Brassard, and S. Breidbart, *Quantum Cryptography II: How to Re-Use a One-Time Pad Safely Even if P=NP,* unpublished manuscript, Nov 1982.

74. C. H. Bennett, G. Brassard, S. Breidbart, and S. Weisner, "Quantum Cryptography, or Unforgeable Subway Tokens," *Advances in Cryptology: Proceedings of Crypto 82,* Plenum Press, 1983, pp. 267–275.

75. C. H. Bennett, G. Brassard, C. Crépeau, and M.-H. Skubiszewska, "Practical Quantum Oblivious Transfer," *Advances in Cryptology—CRYPTO '91 Proceedings,* Berlin: Springer-Verlag, 1992, pp. 351–366.

76. C. H. Bennett, G. Brassard, and A. K. Ekert, "Quantum Cryptography," *Scientific American,* v. 267, n. 4, Oct 1992, pp. 50–57.

77. C. H. Bennett, G. Brassard, and N. D. Mermin, "Quantum Cryptography Without Bell's Theorem," *Physical Review Letters,* v. 68, n. 5, 3 Feb 1992, pp. 557–559.

78. C. H. Bennett, G. Brassard, and J.-M. Robert, "How to Reduce Your Enemy's Information," *Advances in Cryptology—CRYPTO '85 Proceedings,* Berlin: Springer-Verlag, 1986, pp. 468–476.

79. C. H. Bennett, G. Brassard, and J.-M. Robert, "Privacy Amplification by Public Discussion," *SIAM Journal on Computing,* v. 17, n. 2, Apr 1988, pp. 210–229.

80. J. Bennett, "Analysis of the Encryption Algorithm Used in WordPerfect Word Processing Program," *Cryptologia,* v. 11, n. 4, Oct 1987, pp. 206–210.

81. M. Ben-Or, S. Goldwasser, and A. Wigderson, "Completeness Theorems for Non-Cryptographic Fault-Tolerant Distributed Computation," *Proceedings of the 20th ACM Symposium on the Theory of Computing,* 1988, pp. 1–10.

82. M. Ben-Or, O. Godreich, S. Goldwasser, J. Håstad, J. Kilian, S. Micali, and P. Rogaway, "Everything Provable is Provable in Zero-Knowledge," *Advances in Cryptology—CRYPTO '88 Proceedings, Berlin:* Springer-Verlag, 1990, pp. 37–56.

83. M. Ben-Or, O. Goldreich, S. Micali, and R. L. Rivest, "A Fair Protocol for Signing Contracts," *IEEE Transactions on Information Theory,* v. 36, n. 1, Jan 1990, pp. 40–46.

84. H. A. Bergen and W. J. Caelli, "File Security in WordPerfect 5.0," *Cryptologia,* v. 15, n. 1, Jan 1991, pp. 57–66.

85. E. R. Berklecamp, *Algebraic Coding Theory,* Aegean Park Press, 1984.

86. S. Berkovitz, "How to Broadcast a Secret," *Advances in Cryptology—EUROCRYPT '91 Proceedings,* Berlin: Springer-Verlag, 1991, pp. 535–541.

87. S. Berkovitz, J. Kowalchuk, and B. Schanning, "Implementing Public-Key Scheme," *IEEE Communications Magazine,* v. 17, n. 3, May 1979, pp. 2–3.

88. T. Berson, "Differential Cryptanalysis Mod 2^{32} with Applications to MD5," *Advances in Cryptology—EUROCRYPT '92 Proceedings,* Berlin: *Springer-Verlag,* 1992, pp. 71–80.

89. T. Beth, *Verfahren der schnellen Fourier-Transformation,* Stuttgart: Teubner, 1984. (in German)

90. T. Beth, "Efficient Zero-Knowledge Identification Scheme for Smart Cards," *Advances in Cryptology—EUROCRYPT '88 Proceedings,* Berlin: Springer-Verlag, 1988, pp. 77–84.

91. T. Beth, B. M. Cook, and D. Gollmann, "Architectures for Exponentiation in $GF(2^n)$," *Advances in Cryptology—CRYPTO '86 Proceedings,* Berlin: Springer-Verlag, 1987, pp. 302–310.

92. T. Beth and Y. Desmedt, "Identification Tokens or: Solving the Chess Grandmaster Problem," *Advances in Cryptology—CRYPTO '90 Proceedings,* Berlin: Springer-Verlag, 1991, pp. 169–176.

93. T. Beth, M. Frisch, and G. J. Simmons, eds., *Lecture Notes in Computer Science 578; Public-Key Cryptography: State of the Art and Future Directions,* Springer-Verlag, 1992.

94. T. Beth and F. C. Piper, "The Stop-and-Go Generator," *Advances in Cryptology—EUROCRYPT '84 Proceedings,* Berlin: Springer-Verlag, 1984, pp. 88–92.

95. T. Beth and F. Schaefer, "Non-Supersingular Elliptic Curves for Public Key Cryptosystems," *Advances in Cryptology—EUROCRYPT '91 Proceedings,* Berlin: Springer-Verlag, 1991, pp. 316–327.

96. A. Beutelspacher, "How to Say 'No'," *Advances in Cryptology—EUROCRYPT '89 Proceedings,* Berlin: Springer-Verlag, 1990, pp. 491–496.

97. J. Bidzos, Letter to NIST regarding DSS, 20 Sep 1991.

98. E. Biham, "Cryptanalysis of the Chaotic-Map Cryptosystem Suggested at EUROCRYPT '91," *Advances in Cryptology—EUROCRYPT '91 Proceedings,* Berlin: Springer-Verlag, 1991, pp. 532–534.

99. E. Biham, *New Types of Cryptanalytic Attacks Using Related Keys,* Technical Report #753, Computer Science Department, Technion—Israel Institute of Technology, Sep 1992.

100. E. Biham, "On the Applicability of Differential Cryptanalysis to Hash Functions," lecture at *Workshop on Cryptographic Hash Functions,* Mar 1992.

101. E. Biham and A. Shamir, "Differential Cryptanalysis of DES-like Cryptosystems," *Advances in Cryptology—CRYPTO '90 Proceedings,* Berlin: Springer-Verlag, 1991, pp. 2 21.

102. E. Biham and A. Shamir, "Differential Cryptanalysis of DES-like Cryptosystems," *Journal of Cryptology,* v. 4, n. 1, 1991, pp. 3–72.

103. E. Biham and A. Shamir, "Differential Cryptanalysis of Feal and N-Hash," *Advances in Cryptology—EUROCRYPT '91 Proceedings,* Berlin: Springer-Verlag, 1991, pp. 1–16.

104. E. Biham and A. Shamir, "Differential Cryptanalysis of Snefru, Khafre, REDOC-II, LOKI, and Lucifer," *Advances in Cryptology—CRYPTO '91 Proceedings,* Berlin: Springer-Verlag, 1992, pp. 156–171.

105. E. Biham and A. Shamir, "Differential Cryptanalysis of the Full 16-Round DES," *Advances in Cryptology—CRYPTO '92 Proceedings,* Berlin: Springer-Verlag, 1993, forthcoming.

106. E. Biham and A. Shamir, *Differential Cryptanalysis of the Data Encryption Standard,* Berlin: Springer-Verlag, 1993.

107. E. Biham, personal communication.

108. R. Bird, I. Gopal, A. Herzberg, P. Janson, S. Kutten, R. Molva, and M. Yung, "Systematic Design of Two-Party Authentication Protocols," *Advances in Cryptology—CRYPTO '91 Proceedings,* Berlin: Springer-Verlag, 1992, pp. 44–61.

109. R. Bird, I. Gopal, A. Herzberg, P. Janson, S. Kutten, R. Molva, and M. Yung, "Systematic Design of a Family of Attack-Resistant Authentication Protocols," *IEEE Journal of Selected Areas in Communication,* forthcoming.

110. R. Bird, I. Gopal, A. Herzberg, P. Janson, S. Kutten, R. Molva, and M. Yung, "A Modular Family of Secure Protocols for Authentication and Key Distribution," *IEEE/ACM Transactions on Networking,* forthcoming.

111. M. Bishop, "An Application for a Fast Data Encryption Standard Implementation," *Computing Systems,* v. 1, n. 3, 1988, pp. 221–254.

112. M. Bishop, "Privacy-Enhanced Electronic Mail," in *Distributed Computing and Cryptography,* J. Feigenbaum and M. Merritt, eds., American Mathematical Society, 1991, pp. 93–106.

113. M. Bishop, "Privacy-Enhanced Electronic Mail," *Internetworking: Research and Experience,* v. 2, 1991, pp. 199–233.

114. M. Bishop, "Recent Changes to Privacy Enhanced Electronic Mail," *Internetworking: Research and Experience,* 1993, forthcoming.

115. I. F. Blake, R. Fuji-Hara, R. C. Mullin, and S. A. Vanstone, "Computing Logarithms in Finite Fields of Characteristic Two," *SIAM Journal on Algebraic Discrete Methods,* v. 5, 1984, pp. 276–285.

116. I. F. Blake, R. C. Mullin, and S. A. Vanstone, "Computing Logarithms in $GF(2^n)$," *Advances in Cryptology—Proceedings of CRYPTO '84,* Berlin: Springer-Verlag, 1985, pp. 73–82.

117. G. R. Blakley, "Safeguarding Cryptographic Keys," *Proceedings of the National Computer Conference, 1979,* American Federation of Information Processing Societies, v. 48, 1979, pp. 242–268.

118. G. R. Blakley, "One-Time Pads Are Key Safeguarding Schemes, Not Cryptosystems. Fast Key Safeguarding Schemes (Threshold Schemes) Exist," *Proceedings of the 1980 Symposium on Security and Privacy,* IEEE Computer Society, Apr 1980, pp. 108–113.

119. G. R. Blakley and I. Borosh, "Rivest-Shamir-Adleman Public-Key Cryptosystems Do Not Always Conceal Messages," *Computers and Mathematics with Applications,* v. 5, n. 3, 1979, pp. 169–178.

120. G. R. Blakley and C. Meadows, "A Database Encryption Scheme Which Allows the Computation of Statistics Using Encrypted Data," *Proceedings of the 1985 Symposium on Security and Privacy,* IEEE Computer Society, Apr 1985, pp. 116–122.

121. L. Blum, M. Blum, and M. Shub, "A Simple Unpredictable Pseudo-Random Number Generator," *SIAM Journal on Computing,* v. 15, n. 2, 1986, pp. 364–383.

122. M. Blum, "Coin Flipping by Telephone: A Protocol for Solving Impossible Problems," *Proceedings of the 24th IEEE Computer Conference (CompCon),* 1982, pp. 133–137.

123. M. Blum, "How to Prove a Theorem So No One Else Can Claim It," *Proceedings of the International Congress of Mathematicians,* Berkeley, CA, 1986, pp. 1444–1451.

124. M. Blum, A. De Santis, S. Micali, and G. Persiano, "Noninteractive Zero-Knowledge," *SIAM Journal on Computing,* v. 20, n. 6, Dec 1991, pp. 1084–1118.

125. M. Blum, P. Feldman, and S. Micali, "Non-Interactive Zero-Knowledge and Its Applications," *Proceedings*

of the 20th ACM Symposium on Theory of Computing, 1988, pp. 103–112.

126. M. Blum and S. Goldwasser, "An *Efficient* Probabilistic Public-Key Encryption Scheme Which Hides All Partial Information," *Advances in Cryptology: Proceedings of CRYPTO 84,* Berlin: Springer-Verlag, 1985, pp. 289–299.

127. M. Blum and S. Micali, "How to Generate Cryptographically Strong Sequences of Pseudo-Random Bits," *SIAM Journal of Computing,* v. 13, n. 4, Nov 1984, pp. 850–864.

128. D. J. Bond, "Practical Primality Testing," *Proceedings of IEEE International Conference on Secure Communications Systems,* 22–23 Feb 1984, pp. 50–53.

129. H. Bonnenberg, A. Curiger, N. Felber, H. Kaeslin, and X. Lai, "VLSI Implementation of a New Block Cipher," *Proceedings of the IEEE International Conference on Computer Design: VLSI in Computers and Processors (ICCD 91),* Oct 1991, pp. 510–513.

130. J. Boyar, "Inferring Sequences Produced by a Linear Congruential Generator Missing Low-Order Bits," *Journal of Cryptology,* v. 1, n. 3, 1989, pp. 177–184.

131. J. Boyar, D. Chaum, and I. Damgård, "Convertible Undeniable Signatures," *Advances in Cryptolog—CRYPTO '90 Proceedings,* Berlin: Springer-Verlag, 1991, pp. 189–205.

132. J. Boyar, K. Friedl, and C. Lund, "Practical Zero-Knowledge Proofs: Giving Hints and Using Deficiencies," *Advances in Cryptology—EUROCRYPT '89 Proceedings,* Berlin: Springer-Verlag, 1990, pp. 155–172.

133. J. Boyar and R. Peralta, "On the Concrete Complexity of Zero-Knowledge Proofs," *Advances in Cryptology—CRYPTO '89 Proceedings,* Berlin: Springer-Verlag, 1990, pp. 507–525.

134. C. Boyd, "Some Applications of Multiple Key Ciphers," *Advances in Cryptology—EUROCRYPT '88 Proceedings,* Berlin: Springer-Verlag, 1988, pp. 455–467.

135. C. Boyd, "A New Multiple Key Cipher and an Improved Voting Scheme," *Advances in Cryptology—EUROCRYPT '89 Proceedings,* Berlin: Springer-Verlag, 1990, pp. 617–625.

135a. J. Brandt, I.B. Damgård, P. Landrock, and T. Pederson, "Zero-Knowledge Authentication Scheme with Secret Key Exchange," *Advances in Cryptology—CRYPTO '88,* Berlin: Springer-Verlag, 1990, pp. 583–588.

136. D. K. Branstead, "Hellman's Data Does Not Support His Conclusion," *IEEE Spectrum,* v. 16, n. 7, Jul 1979, p. 39.

137. D. K. Branstead, J. Gait, and S. Katzke, *Report on the Workshop on Cryptography in Support of Computer Security,* NBSIR 77-1291, National Bureau of Standards, Sep 21–22, 1976, September 1977.

138. G. Brassard, "A Note on the Complexity of Cryptography," *IEEE Transactions on Information Theory,* v. IT-25, n. 2, Mar 1979, pp. 232–233.

139. G. Brassard, "Relativized Cryptography," *Proceedings of the IEEE 20th Annual Symposium on the Foundations of Computer Science,* 1979, pp. 383–391.

140. G. Brassard, "A Time-Luck Tradeoff in Relativized Cryptography," *Proceedings of the IEEE 21st Annual Symposium on the Foundations of Computer Science,* 1980, pp. 380–386.

141. G. Brassard, "A Time-Luck Tradeoff in Relativized Cryptography," *Journal of Computer and System Sciences,* v. 22, n. 3, Jun 1981, pp. 280–311.

142. G. Brassard, "An Optimally Secure Relativized Cryptosystem," *SIGACT/NEWS,* v. 15, n. 1, 1983, pp. 28–33.

143. G. Brassard, "Relativized Cryptography," *IEEE Transactions on Information Theory,* v. IT-29, n. 6, Nov 1983, pp. 877–894.

144. G. Brassard, *Modern Cryptology: A Turorial,* Berlin: Springer-Verlag, 1988.

145. G. Brassard, D. Chaum, and C. Crépeau, "An Introduction to Minimum Disclosure," *CWI Quarterly,* v. 1, 1988, pp. 3–17.

146. G. Brassard and C. Crépeau, "Non-Transitive Transfer of Confidence: A *Perfect* Zero-Knowledge Interactive Protocol for SAT and Beyond," *Proceedings of the 27th IEEE Symposium on Foundations of Computer Science,* 1986, pp. 188–195.

147. G. Brassard and C. Crépeau, "Zero-Knowledge Simulation of Boolean Circuits," *Advances in Cryptology—CRYPTO '86 Proceedings,* Berlin: Springer-Verlag, 1987, pp. 223–233.

148. G. Brassard and C. Crépeau, "All-or-Nothing Disclosure of Secrets," *Advances in Cryptology—CRYPTO '86 Proceedings,* Berlin: Springer-Verlag, 1987, pp. 234–238.

149. G. Brassard and C. Crépeau, "Sorting Out Zero-Knowledge," *Advances in Cryptology—EUROCRYPT '89 Proceedings,* Berlin: Springer-Verlag, 1990, pp. 181–191.

150. G. Brassard and C. Crépeau, "Quantum Bit Commitment and Coin Tossing Protocols, *Advances in Cryptology—CRYPTO '90 Proceedings,* Berlin: Springer-Verlag, 1991, pp. 49–61.

151. G. Brassard, C. Crépeau, and D. Chaum, "Minimum Disclosure Proofs of Knowledge," *Journal of Computer and System Sciences,* v. 37, n. 2, Oct 1988, pp. 156–189.

152. R. P. Brent, "An Improved Monte-Carlo Factorization Algorithm," *BIT,* v. 20, 1980, pp. 176–184.

153. R. P. Brent, *Parallel Algorithms for Integer Factorization,* Research Report CMA-R49-89, Computer Science Laboratory, The Australian National University, Oct 1989.

154. D. M. Bressoud, *Factorization and Primality Testing,* Springer-Verlag, 1990.

155. E. F. Brickell, "A Fast Modular Multiplication Algorithm with Applications to Two-Key Cryptography," *Advances in Cryptology: Proceedings of Crypto 82,* Plenum Press, 1982, pp. 51–60.

156. E. F. Brickell, "Are Most Low Density Polynomial Knapsacks Solvable in Polynomial Time?" *Proceedings of the 14th Southeastern Conference on Combinatorics, Graph Theory, and Computing,* 1983.

157. E. F. Brickell, "Solving Low Density Knapsacks," *Advances in Cryptology: Proceedings of Crypto 83,* Plenum Press, 1984, pp. 25–37.

158. E. F. Brickell, "Breaking Iterated Knapsacks," *Advances in Cryptology—Proceedings of Crypto '84,* Berlin: Springer-Verlag, 1985, pp. 342–358.

159. E. F. Brickell, "Cryptanalysis of the Uagisawa Public-Key Cryptosystem," *Abstracts of Papers, EUROCRYPT '86,* 20–22 May 1986.

160. E. F. Brickell, "The Cryptanalysis of Knapsack Cryptosystems," in *Applications of Discrete Mathematics,* R. D. Ringeisen and F. S. Roberts, Eds., Philadelphia: Society for Industrial and Applied Mathematics, 1988, p. 3–23.

161. E. F. Brickell, "Survey of Hardware Implementations of RSA," *Advances in Cryptology—CRYPTO '89 Proceedings,* Berlin: Springer-Verlag, 1990, pp. 368–370.

162. E. F. Brickell, J. A. Davis, and G. J. Simmons, "A Preliminary Report on the Cryptanalysis of Merkle-Hellman Knapsack," *Advances in Cryptology: Proceedings of Crypto 82,* Plenum Press, 1983, pp. 289–303.

163. E. F. Brickell and J. DeLaurentis, "An Attack on a Signature Scheme Proposed by Okamoto and Shiraishi," *Advances in Cryptology—CRYPTO '85 Proceedings,* Berlin: Springer-Verlag, 1986, pp. 28–32.

163a. E.F. Bricknell, D. E. Denning, S. T. Kent, D. P. Maher, and W. Tuchman, "SKIP JACK Review—Interim Report," 28 Jul 1993.

164. E. F. Brickell, J. C. Lagarias, and A. M. Odlyzko, "Evaluation of the Adleman Attack of Multiple Iterated Knapsack Cryptosystems," *Advances in Cryptology: Proceedings of Crypto 83,* Plenum Press, 1984, pp. 39–42.

165. E. F. Brickell, P. J. Lee, and Y. Yacobi, "Secure Audio Teleconference," *Advances in Cryptology—CRYPTO '87 Proceedings,* Berlin: Springer-Verlag, 1988, pp. 418–426.

166. E. F. Brickell and K. S. McCurley, "An Interactive Identification Scheme Based on Discrete Logarithms and Factoring," *Advances in Cryptology— EUROCRYPT '90 Proceedings,* Berlin: Springer-Verlag, 1991, pp. 63–71.

167. E. F. Brickell, J. H. Moore, and M. R. Purtill, "Structure in the S-Boxes of the DES," *Advances in Cryptology—CRYPTO '86 Proceedings,* Berlin: Springer-Verlag, 1987, pp. 3–8.

168. E. F. Brickell and A. M. Odlyzko, "Cryptanalysis: A Survey of Recent Results," *Proceedings of the IEEE,* v. 76, n. 5, May 1988, pp. 578–593.

169. E. F. Brickell and A. M. Odlyzko, "Cryptanalysis: A Survey of Recent Results," in *Contemporary Cryptology: The Science of Information Integrity,* G. J. Simmons, ed., Piscatoway, N.J.: IEEE Press, 1991, pp. 501–540.

170. E. F. Brickell and G. J. Simmons, "A Status Report on Knapsack Based Public-Key Cryptosystems," *Congressus Numerantium,* v. 7, 1983, pp. 3–72.

171. E. F. Brickell and D. R. Stinson, "The Detection of Cheaters in Threshold Schemes," *Advances in Cryptology—CRYPTO '88 Proceedings,* Berlin: Springer-Verlag, 1990, pp. 564–577.

172. A. G. Broscius and J. M. Smith, "Exploiting Parallelism in Hardware Implementation of the DES," *Advances in Cryptology—CRYPTO '91 Proceedings,* Berlin: Springer-Verlag, 1992, pp. 367–376.

173. L. Brown, M. Kwan, J. Pieprzyk, and J. Seberry, "Improving Resistance to Differential Cryptanalysis and the Redesign of LOKI," *ASIACRYPT '91 Abstracts,* 1991, pp. 25–30.

174. L. Brown, J. Pieprzyk, and J. Seberry, "LOKI: A Cryptographic Primitive for Authentication and Secrecy Applications," *Advances in*

Cryptology—AUSCRYPT '90 Proceedings, Berlin: Springer-Verlag, 1990, pp. 229–236.

175. L. Brown, J. Pieprzyk, and J. Seberry, "Key Scheduling in DES Type Cryptosystems," *Advances in Cryptology—AUSCRYPT '90 Proceedings,* Berlin: Springer-Verlag, 1990, pp. 221–228.

176. L. Brown and J. Seberry, "On the Design of Permutation P in DES Type Cryptosystems," *Advances in Cryptology—EUROCRYPT '89 Proceedings, Berlin:* Springer-Verlag, 1990, pp. 696–705.

177. W. Brown, "A Quantum Leap in Secret Communications," *New Scientist,* n. 1585, 30 Jan 1993, p. 21.

178. J. O. Bruer, "On Pseudo Random Sequences as Crypto Generators," *Proceedings of the International Zurich Seminar on Digital Communication,* Zurich, Switzerland, 1984.

179. M. Burmester and Y. Desmedt, "Broadcast Interactive Proofs," *Advances in Cryptology—EUROCRYPT '91 Proceedings,* Berlin: Springer-Verlag, 1991, pp. 81–95.

180. M. Burrows, M. Abadi, and R. Needham, *A Logic of Authentication,* Digital Equipment Corp. Systems Research Center, Feb 1990.

181. J. J. Cade, "A Modification of a Broken Public-Key Cipher," *Advances in Cryptology—CRYPTO '86 Proceedings,* Berlin: Springer-Verlag, 1987, pp. 64–83.

182. P. Camion and J. Patarin, "The Knapsack Hash Function Proposed at Crypto '89 Can Be Broken," *Advances in Cryptology—EUROCRYPT '91 Proceedings,* Berlin: Springer-Verlag, 1991, pp. 39–53.

183. C. M. Campbell, "Design and Specification of Cryptographic Capabilities," *IEEE Computer Society Magazine,* v. 16, n. 6, Nov 1978, pp. 15–19.

184. K. W. Campbell and M. J. Wiener, "Proof That DES Is Not a Group," *Advances in Cryptology—CRYPTO '92 Proceedings,* Berlin: Springer-Verlag, 1993, pp. 518–526.

185. J. M. Carroll, *Computer Security,* 2nd edition, Butterworths, 1987.

186. J. M. Carroll, "The Three Faces of Information Security," *Advances in Cryptology—AUSCRYPT '90 Proceedings,* Berlin: Springer-Verlag, 1990, pp. 433–450.

187. T. R. Caron and R. D. Silverman, "Parallel Implementation of the Quadratic Scheme," *Journal of Supercomputing,* v. 1, n. 3, 1988, pp. 273–290.

188. CCITT, Recommendation X.509, *The Directory-Authentication Framework,* Blue Book—Melbourne 1988, Fascicle VIII.8: Data Communication networks: Directory, International Telecommunications Union, Geneva, Switzerland, 1989, pp. 127–141.

189. W. G. Chambers and D. Gollmann, "Generators for Sequences with Near-Maximal Linear Equivalence," *IEEE Proceedings,* v. 135, Pt. E, n. 1, Jan 1988, pp. 67–69.

190. W. G. Chambers and D. Gollmann, "Lock-In Effect in Cascades of Clock-Controlled Shift Registers," *Advances in Cryptology—EUROCRYPT '88 Proceedings,* Berlin: Springer-Verlag, 1988, pp. 331–343.

191. D. Chaum, "Untraceable Electronic Mail, Return Addresses, and Digital Pseudonyms," *Communications of the ACM,* v. 24, n. 2, Feb 1981, pp. 84–88.

192. D. Chaum, "Blind Signatures for Untraceable Payments," *Advances in Cryptology: Proceedings of Crypto 82,* Plenum Press, 1983, pp. 199–203.

193. D. Chaum, "Security Without Identification: Transaction Systems to Make Big Brother Obsolete," *Communications of the ACM,* v. 28, n. 10, Oct 1985, pp. 1030–1044.

194. D. Chaum, "Demonstrating That a Public Predicate Can Be Satisfied Without Revealing Any Information Aboout How," *Advances in Cryptology—CRYPTO '86 Proceedings,* Berlin: Springer-Verlag, 1987, pp. 159–199.

195. D. Chaum, "Blinding for Unanticipated Signatures," *Advances in Cryptology—EUROCRYPT '87 Proceedings, Berlin:* Springer-Verlag, 1988, pp. 227–233.

196. D. Chaum, "The Dining Cryptographers Problem: Unconditional Sender and Receiver Untraceability," *Journal of Cryptology,* v. 1, n. 1, 1988, pp. 65–75.

197. D. Chaum, "Elections with Unconditionally Secret Ballots and Disruptions Equivalent to Breaking RSA," *Advances in Cryptology,—EUROCRYPT '88 Proceedings,* Berlin: Springer-Verlag, 1988, pp. 177–181.

198. D. Chaum, "Online Cash Checks," *Advances in Cryptology—EUROCRYPT '89 Proceedings,* Berlin: Springer-Verlag, 1990, pp. 288–293.

199. D. Chaum, "Zero-Knowledge Undeniable Signatures," *Advances in Cryptology—EUROCRYPT '90 Proceedings,* Berlin: Springer-Verlag, 1991, pp. 458–464.

200. D. Chaum, "Group Signatures," *Advances in Cryptology—EUROCRYPT '91 Proceedings,* Berlin: Springer-Verlag, 1991, pp. 257–265.

201. D. Chaum, C. Crépeau, and I. Damgård, "Multiparty Unconditionally Secure Protocols," *Proceedings of the 20th ACM Symposium on the Theory of Computing,* 1988, pp. 11–19.

202. D. Chaum, B. den Boer, E. van Heyst, S. Mjølsnes, and A. Steenbeek, "Efficient Offline Electronic Checks," *Advances in Cryptology—EUROCRYPT '89 Proceedings,* Berlin: Springer-Verlag, 1990, pp. 294–301.

203. D. Chaum and J.-H. Evertse, "Cryptanalysis of DES with a Reduced Number of Rounds: Sequences of Linear Factors in Block Ciphers," *Advances in Cryptology—CRYPTO '85 Proceedings,* Berlin: Springer-Verlag, 1986, pp. 192–211.

204. D. Chaum, J.-H. Evertse, and J. van de Graff, "An Improved Protocol for Demonstrating Possession of Discrete Logarithms and Some Generalizations," *Advances in Cryptology—EUROCRYPT '87 Proceedings,* Berlin: Springer-Verlag, 1988, pp. 127–141.

205. D. Chaum, J.-H. Evertse, J. van de Graff, and R. Peralta, "Demonstrating Possession of a Discrete Logarithm Without Revealing It," *Advances in Cryptology—CRYPTO '86 Proceedings,* Berlin: Springer-Verlag, 1987, pp. 200–212.

206. D. Chaum, A. Fiat, and M. Naor, "Untraceable Electronic Cash," *Advances in Cryptology—CRYPTO '88 Proceedings,* Berlin: Springer-Verlag, 1990, pp. 319–327.

207. D. Chaum and H. van Antwerpen, "Undeniable Signatures," *Advances in Cryptology—CRYPTO '89 Proceedings,* Berlin: Springer-Verlag, 1990, pp. 212–216.

208. D. Chaum, E. van Heijst, and B. Pfitzmann, "Cryptographically Strong Undeniable Signatures, Unconditionally Secure for the Signer," *Advances in Cryptology—CRYPTO '91 Proceedings,* Berlin: Springer-Verlag, 1992, pp. 470–484.

209. T. M. Chee, "The Cryptanalysis of a New Public-Key Cryptosystem Based on Modular Knapsacks," *Advances in Cryptology—CRYPTO '91 Proceedings,* Berlin: Springer-Verlag, 1992, pp. 204–212.

210. G. C. Chiou and W. C. Chen, "Secure Broadcasting Using the Secure Lock," *IEEE Transactions on Software Engineering,* v. SE-15, n. 8, Aug 1989, pp. 929–934.

211. B. Chor and O. Goldreich, "RSA/Rabin Least Significant Bits Are 1/2+1/poly(log N) Secure," *Advances in Cryptology—CRYPTO '84 Proceedings,* Berlin: Springer Verlag, 1985, pp. 303–313.

212. B. Chor, S. Goldwasser, S. Micali, and B. Awerbuch, "Verifiable Secret Sharing and Achieving Simultaneity in the Presence of Faults," *Proceedings of the 26th Annual IEEE Symposium on the Foundations of Computer Science,* 1985, pp. 383–395.

213. B. Chor and R. L. Rivest, "A Knapsack Type Public-Key Cryptosystem Based on Arithmetic in Finite Fields," *Advances in Cryptology—CRYPTO '84 Proceedings,* Berlin: Springer-Verlag, 1985, pp. 54–65.

214. P. Christoffersson, S.-A. Ekahll, V. Fäk, S. Herda, P. Mattila, W. Price, and H.-O. Widman, *Crypto Users' Handbook: A Guide for Implementors of Cryptographic Protection in Computer Systems,* North Holland: Elsivier Science Publishers, 1988.

215. J. D. Cohen, *Improving Privacy in Cryptographic Elections,* Yale University Computer Science Department Technical Report YALEU/DCS/TR-454, Feb 1986.

216. J. D. Cohen and M. H. Fischer, "A Robust and Verifiable Cryptographically Secure Election Scheme," *Proceedings of the 26th Annual IEEE Symposium on the Foundations of Computer Science,* 1985, pp. 372–382.

217. Comptroller General of the United States, *Matter of National Institute of Standards and Technology—Use of Electronic Data Interchange Technology to Create Valid Obligations,* File B-245714, 13 Dec 1991.

218. M. S. Conn, letter to Joe Abernathy, National Security Agency, Ser: Q43-111-92, 10 Jun 1992.

219. C. Connell, "An Analysis of NewDES: A Modified Version of DES," *Cryptologia,* v. 14, n. 3, Jul 1990, pp. 217–223.

220. S. A. Cook, "The Complexity of Theorem-Proving Procedures," *Proceedings of the 3rd Annual ACM Symposium on the Theory of Computing,* 1971, pp. 151–158.

221. R. H. Cooper and W. Patterson, "A Generalization of the Knapsack Method Using Galois Fields," *Cryptologia,* v. 8, n. 4, Oct 1984, pp. 343–347.

222. R. H. Cooper and W. Patterson, "RSA as a Benchmark for Multiprocessor Machines," *Advances in Cryptology—AUSCRYPT '90 Proceedings,* Berlin: Springer-Verlag, 1990, pp. 356–359.

223. D. Coppersmith, "Fast Evaluation of Logarithms in Fields of Characteristic Two," *IEEE Transactions on Information Theory,* v. 30, n. 4, Jul 1984, pp. 587–594.

224. D. Coppersmith, "Cheating at Mental Poker," *Advances in Cryptology—CRYPTO '85 Proceedings,* Berlin: Springer-Verlag, 1986, pp. 104–107.

224a. D. Coppersmith, "Two Broken Hash Functions," Research Report RD 18397, IBM T.J. Watson Center, Oct. 1992.

225. D. Coppersmith and E. Grossman, "Generators for Certain Alternating Groups with Applications to Cryptography," *SIAM Journal on Applied Mathematics,* v. 29, n. 4, Dec 1975, pp. 624–627.

226. D. Coppersmith, A. Odlykzo, and R. Schroeppel, "Discrete Logarithms in GF(p)," *Algorithmica,* v. 1, n. 1, 1986, pp. 1–16.

227. C. Couvreur and J. -J. Quisquater, "An Introduction to Fast Generation of Large Prime Numbers," *Philips Journal Research,* v. 37, n. 5–6, 1982, pp. 231–264; erratum in ibid, v. 38, 1983, p. 77.

227a. R.E. Crandell, "Method and Apparatus for Public Key Exchange in a Cryptographic System," U.S. Patent #5,159,632,27 October 1992.

228. C. Crépeau, "A Secure Poker Protocol That Minimizes the Effect of Player Coalitions," *Advances in Cryptology—CRYPTO '85 Proceedings,* Berlin: Springer-Verlag, 1986, pp. 73–86.

229. C. Crépeau, "A Zero-Knowledge Poker Protocol That Achieves Confidentiality of the Players' Strategy, *or* How to Achieve an Electronic Poker Face," *Advances in Cryptology—CRYPTO '86 Proceedings,* Berlin: Springer-Verlag, 1987, pp. 239–247.

230. A. Curiger and B. Stuber, "Specification for the IDEA Chip," *Technical Report No. 92/03,* ETH Zurich: Institut für Integrierte Systeme, Feb 1992.

231. T. W. Cusick and M. C. Wood, "The REDOC-II Cryptosystem." *Advances in Cryptology—CRYPTO '90 Proceedings,* Berlin: Springer-Verlag, 1991, pp. 545–563.

232. J. Daeman, A. Bosselaers, R. Govaerts, and J. Vandewalle, "Collisions for Schnorr's Hash Function FFT-Hash Presented at Crypto '91," *ASIACRYPT '91,* 1991, presented at rump session.

233. J. Daeman, R. Govaerts, and J. Vandewalle, "A Framework for the Design of One-Way Hash Functions Including Cryptanalysis of Damgård's One-Way Function Based on Cellular Automata," *ASIACRYPT '91 Abstracts,* 1991, pp. 49–54.

234. J. Daeman, R. Govaerts, and J. Vandewalle, "A Hardware Design Model for Cryptographic Algorithms," *ESORICS 92, Proceedings of the Second European Symposium on Research in Computer Security,* Berlin: Springer-Verlag, 1992, pp. 419–434.

235. I. B. Damgård, "Payment Systems and Credential Mechanisms with Provable Security Against Abuse by Individuals," *Advances in Cryptology—CRYPTO '88 Proceedings,* Berlin: Springer-Verlag, 1990, pp. 328–335.

236. I. B. Damgård, "A Design Principle for Hash Functions," *Advances in Cryptology—CRYPTO '89 Proceedings,* Berlin: Springer-Verlag, 1990, pp. 416–427.

237. H. Davenport, *The Higher Arithmetic,* Dover Books, 1983.

238. G. I. Davida, "Inverse of Elements of a Galois Field," *Electronics Letters,* v. 8, n. 21, 19 Oct 1972, pp. 518–520.

239. G. I. Davida, "Hellman's Scheme Breaks DES in its Basic Form," *IEEE Spectrum,* v. 16, n. 7, Jul 1979, p. 39.

240. G. I. Davida, "Chosen Signature Cryptanalysis of the RSA (MIT) Public-Key Cryptosystem," *Technical Report TR-CS-82-2,* Department of EECS, University of Wisconsin, 1982.

241. G. I. Davida and G. G. Walter, "A Public-Key Analog Cryptosystem," *Advances in Cryptology—EUROCRYPT '87 Proceedings,* Berlin: Springer-Verlag, 1988, pp. 143–147.

242. G. I. Davida, D. Wells, and J. Kam, "A Database Encryption System with Subkeys," *ACM Transactions on Database Systems,* v. 6, n. 2, Jun 1981, pp. 312–328.

243. D. W. Davies, "Some Regular Properties of the DES," *Advances in Cryptology: Proceedings of Crypto 82,* Plenum Press, 1983, pp. 89–96.

244. D. W. Davies and G. I. P. Parkin, "The Average Size of the Key Stream in Output Feedback Encipherment," *Cryptography: Proceedings of the Workshop on Cryptography, Burg Feuerstein, Germany, March 29–April 2, 1982,* Berlin: Springer-Verlag, 1983, pp. 263–279.

245. D. W. Davies and G. I. P. Parkin, "The Average Size of the Key Stream in Output Feedback Mode," *Advances in Cryptology: Proceedings of Crypto 82,* Plenum Press, 1983, pp. 97–98.

246. D. W. Davies and W. L. Price, "The Application of Digital Signatures Based on Public-Key Cryptosystems," *Proceedings of the Fifth International Computer Communications Conference,* Oct 1980, pp. 525–530.

247. D. W. Davies and W. L. Price, *The Application of Digital Signatures Based on Public-Key Cryptosystems,* National Physical Laboratory Report DNACS 39/80, Dec 1980.

248. D. W. Davies and W. L. Price, "Digital Signature—An Update," *Proceedings of International Conference on Computer Communications, Sydney, Oct 1984, North Holland:* Elsevier Science Publishers, 1985, pp. 843–847.

249. D. W. Davies and W. L. Price, *Security for Computer Networks,* second edition, New York: John Wiley & Sons, 1989.

250. M. Davio, Y. Desmedt, M. Fosseprez, R. Govaerts, J. Hulsbrosch, P. Neutjens, P. Piret, J.-J. Quisquater, J. Vandewalle, and S. Wouters, "Analytical Characteristics of the Data Encryption Standard," *Advances in Cryptology: Proceedings of Crypto 83,* Plenum Press, 1984, pp. 171–202.

251. M. Davio, Y. Desmedt, J. Goubert, F. Hoornaert, and J.-J. Quisquater, "Efficient Hardware and Software Implementation of the DES," *Advances in Cryptology—CRYPTO '84 Proceedings,* Berlin: Springer-Verlag, 1985, pp. 144–146.

252. M. Davio, Y. Desmedt, and J.-J. Quisquater, "Propagation Characteristics of the DES," *Advances in Cryptology—EUROCRYPT '84 Proceedings,* Berlin: Springer-Verlag, 1985, pp. 62–73.

253. J. A. Davis, D. B. Holdbridge, and G. J. Simmons, "Status Report on Factoring (at the Sandia National Laboratories)," *Advances in Cryptology—CRYPTO '84 Proceedings,* Berlin: Springer-Verlag, 1985, pp. 183–215.

254. R. M. Davis, "The Data Encryption Standard in Perspective," *Computer Security and the Data Encryption Standard,* National Bureau of Standards Special Publication 500-27, Feb 1978.

255. E. Dawson and A. Clard, "Cryptanalysis of Universal Logic Sequences," *Advances in Cryptology—EUROCRYPT '93 Proceedings,* Berlin: Springer-Verlag, forthcoming.

256. J. Deamen, R. Govaerts, and J. Vandewalle, "Block Ciphers Based on Modular Arithmetic," *Proceedings of the 3rd Symposium on State and Progress of Research in Cryptography,* Rome, Italy, 15–16 Feb 1993, pp. 80–89.

257. C. A. Deavours, "Unicity Points in Cryptanalysis," *Cryptologia,* v. 1, n. 1, 1977, pp. 46–68.

258. C. A. Deavours, "The Black Chamber: A Column; How the British Broke Enigma," *Cryptologia,* v. 4, n. 3, Jul 1980, pp. 129–132.

259. C. A. Deavours, "The Black Chamber: A Column; La Methode des Batons," *Cryptologia,* v. 4, n. 4, Oct 1980, pp. 240–247.

260. J. M. DeLaurentis, "A Further Weakness in the Common Modulus Protocol for the RSA Cryptosystem," *Cryptologia,* v. 8, n. 3, Jul 1984, pp. 253–259.

261. P. Delsarte, Y. Desmedt, A. Odlyzko, and P. Piret, "Fast Cryptanalysis of the Matsumoto-Imai Public-Key Scheme," *Advances in Cryptology—EUROCRYPT '84 Proceedings,* Berlin: Springer-Verlag, 1985, pp. 142–149.

262. R. DeMillo, N. Lynch, and M. Merritt, "Cryptographic Protocols," *Proceedings of the 14th Annual Symposium on the Theory of Computing,* 1982, pp. 383–400.

263. R. DeMillo and M. Merritt, "Protocols for Data Security," *Computer,* v. 16, n. 2, Feb 1983, pp. 39–50.

264. B. den Boer, "Cryptanalysis of F.E.A.L.," *Advances in Cryptology—EUROCRYPT '88 Proceedings,* Berlin: Springer-Verlag, 1988, pp. 293–300.

265. B. den Boer and A. Bosselaers, "An Attack on the Last Two Rounds of MD4," *Advances in Cryptology—CRYPTO '91 Proceedings,* Berlin: Springer-Verlag, 1992, pp. 194–203.

266. B. den Boer and A. Bosselaers, "Collisions for the Compression Function of MD5," *Advances in Cryptology—EUROCRYPT '93 Proceedings,* Berlin: Springer-Verlag, forthcoming.

267. D. E. Denning, "Secure Personal Computing in an Insecure Network," *Communications of the ACM,* v. 22, n. 8, Aug 1979, pp. 476–482.

268. D. E. Denning, *Cryptography and Data Security,* Addison-Wesley, 1982.

269. D. E. Denning, "Protecting Public Keys and Signature Keys," *Computer,* v. 16, n. 2, Feb 1983, pp. 27–35.

270. D. E. Denning, "Digital Signatures with RSA and Other Public-Key Cryptosystems," *Communications of the ACM,* v. 27, n. 4, Apr 1984, pp. 388–392.

271. D. E. Denning, "The Clipper Chip: A Technical Summary," unpublished manuscript, 21 Apr 1993.

272. D. E. Denning and G. M. Sacco, "Timestamps in Key Distribution Protocols," *Communications of the ACM,* v. 24, n. 8, Aug 81, pp. 533–536.

273. Department of Defense, *Department of Defense Trusted Computer System Evaluation Criteria,* DOD 5200.28-STD, Dec 1985.

274. Department of State, *International Traffic in Arms Regulations (ITAR),* 22 CFR 120–130, Office of Munitions Control, Nov 1989.

275. Department of State, *Defense Trade Regulations,* 22 CFR 120–130, Office of Defense Trade Controls, May 1992.

276. Department of the Treasury, "Electronic Funds and Securities Transfer Policy," *Department of the Treasury Directives Manual,* Chapter TD-81, Section 80, Department of the Treasury, Aug 16, 1984.

277. Department of the Treasury, *Criteria and Procedures for Testing, Evaluating, and Certifying Message Authentication Decision for Federal E.F.T. Use,* Department of the Treasury, May 1, 1985.

278. Department of the Treasury, *Electronic Funds and Securities Transfer Policy—Message Authentication and Enhanced Security,* Order No. 106-09, Department of the Treasury, Oct 2, 1986.

279. P. de Rooij, "On the Security of the Schnorr Scheme Using Preprocessing," *Advances in Cryptology—EUROCRYPT '91 Proceedings,* Berlin: Springer-Verlag, 1991, pp. 71–80.

280. A. De Santis, S. Micali, and G. Persiano, "Non-Interactive Zero-Knowledge Proof Systems," *Advances in Cryptology—CRYPTO '87 Proceedings,* Berlin: Springer-Verlag, pp. 52–72.

281. A. De Santis, S. Micali, and G. Persiano, "Non-Interactive Zero-Knowledg ewith Preprocessing," *Advances in Cryptology—CRYPTO '88 Proceedings,* Berlin: Springer-Verlag, 1990, pp. 269–282.

282. Y. Desmedt, "What Happened with Knapsack Cryptographic Schemes" *Performance Limits in Communication, Theory and Practice,* NATO ASI Series E: Applied Sciences, V. 142, Boston: Kluwer Academic Publishers, 1988, pp. 113–134.

283. Y. Desmedt, "Subliminal-Free Authentication and Signature," *Advances in Cryptology—EUROCRYPT '88 Proceedings,* Berlin: Springer-Verlag, 1988, pp. 23–33.

284. Y. Desmedt, "Abuses in Cryptography and How to Fight Them," *Advances in Cryptology—CRYPTO '88 Proceedings, Berlin:* Springer-Verlag, 1990, pp. 375–389.

285. Y. Desmedt and M. Burmester, "An Efficient Zero-Knowledge Scheme for the Discrete Logarithm Based on Smooth Numbers," *ASIACRYPT '91 Abstracts,* 1991, pp. 215–220.

286. Y. Desmedt and Y. Frankel, "Threshold Cryptosystems," *Advances in Cryptology—CRYPTO '90 Proceedings,* Berlin: Springer-Verlag, 1990, pp. 307–315.

287. Y. Desmedt and Y. Frankel, "Shared Generation of Authentication and Signatures," *Advances in Cryptology—CRYPTO '91 Proceedings,* Springer-Verlag, *Berlin:* 1992, pp. 457–469.

288. Y. Desmedt, C. Goutier, and S. Bengio, "Special Uses and Abuses of the Fiat-Shamir Passport Protocol," *Advances in Cryptology—CRYPTO '87 Proceedings,* Berlin: Springer-Verlag, 1988, pp. 21–39.

289. Y. Desmedt and A. M. Odlykzo, "A Chosen Text Attack on the RSA Cryptosystem and Some Discrete Logarithm Problems," *Advances in Cryptology—CRYPTO '85 Proceedings,* Berlin: Springer-Verlag, 1986, pp. 516–522.

290. Y. Desmedt, J.-J. Quisquater, and M. Davio, "Dependence of Output on Input in DES: Small Avalanche Characteristics," *Advances in Cryptology—CRYPTO '84 Proceedings,* Berlin: Springer-Verlag, 1985, pp. 359–376.

291. Y. Desmedt, J. Vandewalle, and R. Govaerts, "Critical Analysis of the Security of Knapsack Public-Key Algorithms," *IEEE Transactions on Information Theory,* v. IT-30, n. 4, Jul 1984, pp. 601–611.

292. Y. Desmedt and M. Yung, "Weaknesses of Undeniable Signature Schemes," *Advances in Cryptology—EUROCRYPT '91 Proceedings,* Berlin: Springer-Verlag, 1991, pp. 205–220.

293. W. Diffie, lecture at IEEE Information Theory Workshop, Ithaca, N.Y., 1977.

294. W. Diffie, "Cryptographic Technology: Fifteen Year Forecast," BNR Inc., Jan 1981.

295. W. Diffie, "The First Ten Years of Public-Key Cryptography," *Proceedings of the IEEE,* v. 76, n. 5, May 1988, pp. 560–577.

296. W. Diffie, "Authenticated Key Exchange and Secure Interactive Communication," *Proceedings of SECURICOM '90,* 1990.

297. W. Diffie, "The First Ten Years of Public-Key Cryptography," in *Contemporary Cryptology: The Science of Information Integrity,* G. J. Simmons, ed., Piscatoway, N.J.: IEEE Press, 1992, pp. 65–134.

298. W. Diffie and M. E. Hellman, "Multiuser Cryptographic Techniques," *Proceedings of AFIPS National Computer Conference,* 1976, pp. 109–112.

299. W. Diffie and M. E. Hellman, "New Directions in Cryptography," *IEEE Transactions on Information Theory,* v. IT-22, n. 6, Nov 1976, pp. 644–654.

300. W. Diffie and M. E. Hellman, "Exhaustive Cryptanalysis of the NBS Data Encryption Standard," *Computer,* v. 10, n. 6, Jun 1977, pp. 74–84.

301. W. Diffie and M. E. Hellman, "Privacy and Authentication: An Introduction to Cryptography,"

Proceedings of the IEEE, v. 67, n. 3, Mar 1979, pp. 397–427.

302. W. Diffie, L. Strawczynski, B. O'Higgins, and D. Steer, "An ISDN Secure Telephone Unit," *Proceedings of the National Telecommunications Forum,* v. 41, n. 1, 1987, pp. 473–477.

303. W. Diffie, P. C. van Oorschot, and M. J. Wiener, "Authentication and Authenticated Key Exchanges," *Designs, Codes and Cryptography,* v. 2, 1992, pp. 107–125.

304. J. D. Dixon, "Factorization and Primality Tests," *American Mathematical Monthly,* v. 91, n. 6, 1984, pp. 333–352.

305. D. Dolev and A. Yao, "On the Security of Public-Key Protocols," *Proceedings of the 22nd Annual Symposium on the Foundations of Computer Science,* 1981, pp. 350–357.

306. R. Durstenfeld, "Algorithm 235: Random Permutation," *Communications of the ACM,* v. 7, n. 7, Jul 1964, p. 420.

307. S. Dussé and B. Kaliski, Jr., "A Cryptographic Library for the Motorola DSP56000," *Advances in Cryptology—EUROCRYPT '90 Proceedings,* Berlin: Springer-Verlag, 1991, pp. 230–244.

308. C. Dwork and L. Stockmeyer, "Zero-Knowledge with Finite State Verifiers," *Advances in Cryptology—CRYPTO '88 Proceedings,* Berlin: Springer-Verlag, 1990, pp. 71–75.

309. H. Eberle, "A High-Speed DES Implementation for Network Applications," *Advances in Cryptology—CRYPTO '92 Proceedings,* Berlin: Springer-Verlag, 1993, pp. 527–545.

310. Échanges Télématiques Entre Les Banques et Leurs Clients," Standard ETEBAC 5, *Comité Français d'Organisation et de Normalisation Bancaires,* Apr 1989. (in French)

311. W. F. Ehrsam, C. H. W. Meyer, R. L. Powers, J. L. Smith, and W. L. Tuchman, "Product Block Cipher for Data Security," U.S. Patent #3,962,539, 8 Jun 1976.

312. W. F. Ehrsam, C. H. W. Meyer, and W. L. Tuchman, "A Cryptographic Key Management Scheme for Implementing the Data Encryption Standard, *IBM Systems Journal,* v. 17, n. 2, 1978, pp. 106–125.

313. R. Eier and H. Lagger, "Trapdoors in Knapsack Cryptosystems," *Lecture Notes in Computer Science 149; Cryptography—Proceedings, Burg Feuerstein, 1982,* Berlin: Springer-Verlag, 1983, pp. 316–322.

314. A. K. Ekert, "Quantum Cryptography Based on Bell's Theorem," *Physical Review Letters,* v. 67, n. 6, Aug 1991, pp. 661–663.

315. T. ElGamal, "A Public-Key Cryptosystem and a Signature Scheme Based on Discrete Logarithms," *Advances in Cryptology—CRYPTO '84 Proceedings,* Berlin: Springer-Verlag, 1985, pp. 10–18.

316. T. ElGamal, "A Public-Key Cryptosystem and a Signature Scheme Based on Discrete Logarithms," *IEEE Transactions on Information Theory,* v. IT-31, n. 4, 1985, pp. 469–472.

317. T. ElGamal, "On Computing Logarithms over Finite Fields," *Advances in Cryptology—CRYPTO '85 Proceedings,* Berlin: Springer-Verlag, 1986, pp. 396–402.

318. T. ElGamal and B. Kaliski, Letter to the editor regarding LUC, *Dr. Dobbs Journal,* v. 18, n. 5, May 1993, p. 10.

319. D. Estes, L. M. Adleman, K. Konpella, K. S. McCurley, and G. L. Miller, "Breaking the Ong-Schnorr-Shamir Signature Schemes for Quadratic Number Fields," *Advances in Cryptology—CRYPTO '85 Proceedings,* Berlin: Springer-Verlag, 1986, pp. 3–13.

320. A. Evans, W. Kantrowitz, and E. Weiss, "A User Identification Scheme Not Requiring Secrecy in the Computer," *Communications of the ACM,* v. 17, n. 8, Aug 1974, pp. 437–472.

321. S. Even, O. Goldreich, and A. Lempel, "A Randomizing Protocol for Signing Contracts," *Communications of the ACM,* v. 28, n. 6, Jun 1985, pp. 637–647.

322. S. Even and Y. Yacobi, "Cryptography and NP-Completeness," *Proceedings of the 7th International Colloquium on Automata, Languages, and Programming,* Berlin: Springer-Verlag, 1980, pp. 195–207.

323. H.-H. Evertse, "Linear Structures in Block Ciphers," *Advances in Cryptology—EUROCRYPT '87 Proceedings,* Berlin: Springer-Verlag, 1988, pp. 249–266.

324. R. C. Fairfield, A. Matusevich, and J. Plany, "An LSI Digital Encryption Processor (DEP)," *Advances in Cryptology—CRYPTO '84 Proceedings,* Berlin: Springer-Verlag, 1985, pp. 115–143.

325. R. C. Fairfield, A. Matusevich, and J. Plany, "An LSI Digital Encryption Processor (DEP)," *IEEE Communications,* v. 23, n. 7, Jul 1985, pp. 30–41.

326. R. C. Fairfield, R. L. Mortenson, and K. B. Koulthart, "An LSI Random Number Generator (RNG)," *Advances in Cryptology—CRYPTO '84 Proceedings,* Berlin: Springer-Verlag, 1985, pp. 203–230.

327. "International Business Machines Corp. License Under Patents," *Federal Register,* v. 40, n. 52, 17 Mar 1975, p. 12067.

328. "Solicitation for Public-Key Cryptographic Algorithms," *Federal Register,* v. 47, n. 126, 30 Jun 1982, p. 28445.

329. "Proposed Federal Information Processing Standard for Digital Signature Standard (DSS)," *Federal Register,* v. 56, n. 169, 30 Aug 1991, pp. 42980–42982.

330. "Proposed Federal Information Processing Standard for Secure Hash Standard," *Federal Register,* v. 57, n. 21, 31 Jan 1992, pp. 3747–3749.

331. "Proposed Reaffirmation of Federal Information Processing Standard (FIPS) 46-1, Data Encryption Standard (DES)," *Federal Register,* v. 57, n. 177, 11 Sep 1992, p. 41727.

331a. "Notice of Proposal for Grant of Exclusive Patent License," Federal Register, v. 8, n. 108, 8 Jun 1993.

332. U. Feige, A. Fiat, and A. Shamir, "Zero Knowledge Proofs of Identity," *Proceedings of the 19th Annual ACM Symposium on the Theory of Computing,* 1987, pp. 210–217.

333. U. Feige, A. Fiat, and A. Shamir, "Zero Knowledge Proofs of Identity," *Journal of Cryptology,* v. 1, n. 2, 1988, pp. 77–94.

334. U. Feige and A. Shamir, "Zero Knowledge Proofs of Knowledge in Two Rounds," *Advances in Cryptology—CRYPTO '89 Proceedings,* Berlin: Springer-Verlag, 1990, pp. 526–544.

335. J. Feigenbaum, "Encrypting Problem Instances, or, . . . , Can You Take Advantage of Someone Without Having to Trust Him?" *Advances in Cryptology—CRYPTO '85 Proceedings,* Berlin: Springer-Verlag, 1986, pp. 477–488.

336. J. Feigenbaum, E. Grosse, and J. A. Reeds, "Cryptographic Protection of Membership Lists," *Newsletter of the International Association of Cryptologic Research,* v. 9, 1992, pp. 16–20.

337. J. Feigenbaum, M. Y. Liverman, and R. N. Wright, "Cryptographic Protection of Databases and Software," in *Distributed Computing and Cryptography,* J. Feigenbaum and M. Merritt, eds., American Mathematical Society, 1991, pp. 161–172.

338. H. Feistel, *Cryptographic Coding for Data-Bank Privacy,* RC 2827, Yorktown: IBM Research, Mar 1970.

339. H. Feistel, "Cryptography and Computer Privacy," *Scientific American,* v. 228, n. 5, May 1973, pp. 15–23.

340. H. Feistel, "Block Cipher Cryptographic System," U.S. Patent #3,798,359, 19 Mar 1974.

341. H. Feistel, "Step Code Ciphering System," U.S. Patent #3,798,360, 19 Mar 1974.

342. H. Feistel, "Centralized Verification System," U.S. Patent #3,798,605, 19 Mar 1974.

343. H. Feistel, W. A. Notz, and J. L. Smith, "Some Cryptographic Techniques for Machine to Machine Data Communications," *Proceedings of the IEEE,* v. 63, n. 11, Nov 1975, pp. 1545–1554.

344. F. A. Feldman, "A New Spectral Test for Nonrandomness and the DES," *IEEE Transactions on Software Engineering,* v. 16, n. 3, Mar 1990, pp. 261–267.

345. R. A. Feldman, "Fast Spectral Test for Measuring Nonrandomness and the DES," *Advances in Cryptology—CRYPTO '87 Proceedings,* Berlin: Springer-Verlag, 1988, pp. 243–254.

346. D. C. Feldmeier and P. R. Karn, "UNIX Password Security—Ten Years Later," *Advances in Cryptology—CRYPTO '89 Proceedings,* Berlin: Springer-Verlag, 1990, pp. 44–63.

347. H. Fell and W. Diffie, "Analysis of a Public-Key Approach Based on Polynomial Substitution," *Advances in Cryptology—CRYPTO '85 Proceedings,* Berlin: Springer-Verlag, 1986, pp. 427–437.

348. A. Fiat and A. Shamir, "How to Prove Yourself: Practical Solutions to Identification and Signature Problems," *Advances in Cryptology—CRYPTO '86 Proceedings,* Berlin: Springer-Verlag, 1987, pp. 186–194.

349. A. Fiat and A. Shamir, "Unforgeable Proofs of Identity," *Proceedings of SECURICOM '87,* Paris, 1987, pp. 147–153.

350. R. Flynn and A. S. Campasano, "Data Dependent Keys for Selective Encryption Terminal," *Proceedings of NCC,* v. 47, AFIPS Press, 1978, pp. 1127–1129.

351. R. H. Follett, Letter to NIST regarding DSS, 25 Nov 1991.

352. S. Fortune and M. Merritt, "Poker Protocols," *Advances in Cryptology—CRYPTO '84 Proceedings,* Berlin: Springer-Verlag, 1985, pp. 454–464.

353. R. B. Fougner, "Public-Key Standards and Licenses," RFC 1170, Jan 1991.

354. W. F. Friedman, *Methods for the Solution of Running-Key Ciphers,* Riverbank Publication No. 16, Riverbank Labs, 1918.

355. W. F. Friedman, *The Index of Coincidence and Its Applications in Cryptography,* Riverbank Publication No. 22, Riverbank Labs, 1920.

356. W. F. Friedman, "Cryptology," *Encyclopedia Britannica,* v. 6, pp. 844–851, 1967.

357. A. Fujioka, T. Okamoto, and S. Miyaguchi, "ESIGN: An Efficient Digital Signature Implementation for Smart Cards," *Advances in Cryptology—EUROCRYPT '91 Proceedings,* Berlin: Springer-Verlag, 1991, pp. 446–457.

358. A. Fujioka, T. Okamoto, and K. Ohta, "Interactive Bi-Proof Systems and Undeniable Signature Schemes," *Advances in Cryptology—EUROCRYPT '91 Proceedings,* Berlin: Springer-Verlag, 1991, pp. 243–256.

359. A. Fujioka, T. Okamoto, and K. Ohta, "A Practical Secret Voting Scheme for Large Scale Elections," *Advances in Cryptology—AUSCRYPT '92 Proceedings,* Berlin: Springer-Verlag, forthcoming.

360. H. F. Gaines, *Cryptanalysis,* American Photographic Press, 1937 (Reprinted by Dover Publications, 1956.)

361. J. Gait, "A New Nonlinear Pseudorandom Number Generator," *IEEE Transactions on Software Engineering,* v. SE-3, n. 5, Sep 1977, pp. 359–363.

362. Z. Galil, S. Haber, and M. Yung, "A Private Interactive Test of a Boolean Predicate and Minimum-Knowledge Public-Key Cryptosystems," *Proceedings of the 26th IEEE Symposium on Foundations of Computer Science,* 1985, pp. 360–371.

363. R. G. Gallager, *Information Theory and Reliable Communications,* New York: John Wiley & Sons, 1968.

364. P. Gallay and E. Depret, "A Cryptography Microprocessor," *1988 IEEE International Solid-State Circuits Conference Digest of Technical Papers,* 1988, pp. 148–149.

365. M. Gardner, "A New Kind of Cipher That Would Take Millions of Years to Break," *Scientific American,* v. 237, n. 8, Aug 1977, pp. 120–124.

366. M. R. Garey and D. S. Johnson, *Computers and Intractability: A Guide to the Theory of NP-Completeness,* W. H. Freeman and Co., 1979.

367. G. Garon and R. Outerbridge, "DES Watch: An Examination of the Sufficiency of the Data Encryption Standard for Financial Institution Information Security in the 1990's," *Cryptologia,* v. 15, n. 3, Jul 1991, pp. 177–193.

368. J. von zur Gathen, D. Kozen, and S. Landau, "Functional Decomposition of Polynomials," *Proceedings of the 28th IEEE Symposium on the Foundations of Computer Science,* Piscatoway, N.Y.: IEEE Press, 1987, pp. 127–131.

369. P. R. Geffe, "How to Protect Data with Ciphers That Are Really Hard to Break," *Electronics,* v. 46, n. 1, Jan 1973, pp. 99–101.

370. H. Gilbert and G. Chase, "A Statistical Attack on the Feal-8 Cryptosystem," *Advances in Cryptology—CRYPTO '90 Proceedings,* Berlin: Springer-Verlag, 1991, pp. 22–33.

371. J. Gleick, "A New Approach to Protecting Secrets Is Discovered," *New York Times,* 18 Feb 1987, pp. C1 and C3.

372. J. M. Goethals and C. Couvreur, "A Cryptanalytic Attack on the Lu-Lee Public-Key Cryptosystem," *Philips Journal of Research,* v. 35, 1980, pp. 301–306.

373. O. Goldreich and E. Kushilevitz, "A Perfect Zero-Knowledge Proof for a Problem Equivalent to Discrete Logarithm," *Advances in Cryptology—CRYPTO '88 Proceedings,* Berlin: Springer-Verlag, 1990, pp. 58–70.

374. O. Goldreich, S. Micali, and A. Wigderson, "Proofs That Yield Nothing but Their Validity and a Methodology of Cryptographic Protocol Design," *Proceedings of the 27th IEEE Symposium on the Foundations of Computer Science,* 1986, pp. 174–187.

375. O. Goldreich, S. Micali, and A. Wigderson, "How to Prove All NP Statements in Zero Knowledge and a Methodology of Cryptographic Protocol Design," *Advances in Cryptology—CRYPTO '86 Proceedings,* Berlin: Springer-Verlag, 1987, pp. 171–185.

376. S. Goldwasser and J. Kilian, "All Primes Can Be Quickly Certified," *Proceedings of the 18th ACM Symposium on the Theory of Computing,* 1986.

377. S. Goldwasser and S. Micali, "Probabilistic Encryption and How to Play Mental Poker Keeping Secret All Partial Information," *Proceedings of the 14th ACM Symposium on the Theory of Computing,* 1982, pp. 270–299.

378. S. Goldwasser and S. Micali, "Probabilistic Encryption," *Journal of Computer and System Sciences,* v. 28, n. 2, Apr 1984, pp. 270–299.

379. S. Goldwasser, S. Micali, and C. Rackoff, "The Knowledge Complexity of Interactive Proof Systems," *Proceedings of the 17th ACM Symposium on the Theory of Computing,* 1985, pp. 291–304.

380. S. Goldwasser, S. Micali, and C. Rackoff, "The Knowledge Complexity of Interactive Proof Systems," *SIAM Journal on Computing,* v. 18, n. 1, Feb 1989, pp. 186–208.

381. S. Goldwasser, S. Micali, and A. C. Yao, "On Signatures and Authentication," *Advances in Cryptology: Proceedings of Crypto 82,* Plenum Press, 1983, pp. 211–215.

382. D. Gollmann, "Kaskadenschaltungen taktgesteuerter Schieberegister als Pseudozufallszahlengeneratoren," Ph.D. diss., Universität Linz, 1983.(in German)

383. D. Gollmann, "Pseudo Random Properties of Cascade Connections of Clock-Controlled Shift Registers," *Advances in Cryptology—EUROCRYPT '84 Proceedings,* Berlin: Springer-Verlag, 1985, pp. 93–98.

384. D. Gollmann and W. G. Chambers, "Clock-Controlled Shift Registers: A Review," *IEEE Journal on Selected Areas in Communications,* v. 7, n. 4, May 1989, pp. 525–533.

385. S. W. Golomb, *Shift Register Sequences,* San Francisco: Holden-Day, 1967. (Reprinted by Aegean Park Press, 1982.)

386. R. M. Goodman and A. J. McAuley, "A New Trapdoor Knapsack Public-Key Cryptosystem," *Advances in Cryptology—EUROCRYPT '84 Proceedings,* Berlin: Springer-Verlag, 1985, pp. 150–18.

387. R. M. Goodman and A. J. McAuley, "A New Trapdoor Knapsack Public-Key Cryptosystem," *IEEE Proceedings,* v. 132, pt. E, n. 6, Nov 1985, pp. 289–292.

388. D. M. Gordon, "Discrete Logarithms Using the Number Field Sieve," preprint, 28 Mar 1991.

389. D. M. Gordon and K. S. McCurley, "Computation of Discrete Logarithms in Fields of Characteristic Two," Presented at the rump session of CRYPTO '91.

390. D. M. Gordon and K. S. McCurley, "Massively Parallel Computation of Discrete Logarithms," *Advances in Cryptology—CRYPTO '92 Proceedings,* Berlin: Springer-Verlag, 1993, pp. 315–329.

391. J. A. Gordon, "Strong Primes Are Easy to Find," *Advances in Cryptology—EUROCRYPT '84 Proceedings,* Berlin: Springer-Verlag, 1985, pp. 216–223.

392. J. van de Graff and R. Peralta, "A Simple and Secure Way to Show the Validity of Your Public Key," *Advances in Cryptology—CRYPTO '87 Proceedings,* Berlin: Springer-Verlag, 1988, pp. 128–134.

393. J. Grollman and A. L. Selman, "Complexity Measures for Public-Key Cryptosystems," *Proceedings of the 25th IEEE Symposium on the Foundations of Computer Science,* 1984, pp. 495–503.

394. GSA Federal Standard 1026, "Telecommunications: General Security Requirements for Equipment Using the Data Encryption Standard," General Services Administration, Apr 1982.

395. GSA Federal Standard 1027, "Telecommunications: Interoperability and Security Requirements for Use of the Data Encryption Standard in the Physical and Data Link Layers of Data Communications," General Services Administration, Jan 1983.

396. GSA Federal Standard 1028, "Interoperability and Security Requirements for Use of the Data Encryption Standard with CCITT Group 3 Facsimile Equipment," General Services Administration, Apr 1985.

397. P. Guam, "Cellular Automaton Public-Key Cryptosystems," *Complex Systems,* v. 1, pp. 51–56.

398. G. Guanella, "Means for and Method for Secret Signalling," U.S. Patent #2,405,500, 6 Aug 1946.

399. M. Gude, "Concept for a High-Performance Random Number Generator Based on Physical Random Phenomena," *Frequenz,* v. 39, 1985, pp. 187–190.

400. M. Gude, "Ein quasi-idealer Gleichverteilungsgenerator basierend auf physikalischen Zufallsphänomenen," Ph.D. diss., Aachen University of Technology, 1987. (in German)

401. L. C. Guillou and J.-J. Quisquater, "A Practical Zero-Knowledge Protocol Fitted to Security Microprocessor Minimizing Both Transmission and Memory," *Advances in Cryptology—EUROCRYPT '88 Proceedings,* Berlin: Springer-Verlag, 1988, pp. 123–128.

402. L. C. Guillou and J.-J. Quisquater, "A 'Paradoxical' Identity-Based Signature Scheme Resulting from Zero-Knowledge," *Advances in Cryptology—CRYPTO '88 Proceedings,* Berlin: Springer-Verlag, 1990, pp. 216–231.

403. L. C. Guillou, M. Ugon, and J. J. Quisquater, "The Smart Card: A Standardized Security Device Dedicated to Public Cryptology," *Contemporary Cryptology: The Science of Information Integrity,* Piscataway, N.J.: IEEE Press, 1992, pp. 561–613.

404. C. G. Günther, "Alternating Step Generators Controlled by de Bruijn Sequences," *Advances in Cryptology—EUROCRYPT '87 Proceedings,* Berlin: Springer-Verlag, 1988, pp. 5–14.

405. H. Gustafson, E. Dawson, and B. Caelli, "Comparison of Block Ciphers," *Advances in Cryptology—AUSCRYPT '90 Proceedings,* Berlin: Springer-Verlag, 1990, pp. 208–220.

406. P. Gutmann, personal communication.

407. H. Gutowitz, "A Cellular Automaton Cryptosystem: Specification and Call for Attack," unpublished, Aug 1992.

408. H. Gutowitz, "Method and Apparatus for Encryption, Decryption, and Authentication Using Dynamical Systems," U.S. patent pending, 1992.

409. H. Gutowitz, "Cryptography with Dynamical Systems," *Cellular Automata and Cooperative Phenomena*, Kluwer Academic Press, 1993.

410. R. K. Guy, *Unsolved Problems in Number Theory*, Berlin: Springer-Verlag, 1981.

411. S. Haber and W. S. Stornetta, "How to Time-Stamp a Digital Document," *Advances in Cryptology—CRYPTO '90 Proceedings*, Berlin: Springer-Verlag, 1991, pp. 437–455.

412. S. Haber and W. S. Stornetta, "How to Time-Stamp a Digital Document," *Journal of Cryptology*, v. 3, n. 2, 1991, pp. 99–112.

413. T. Habutsu, Y. Nishio, I. Sasase, and S. Mori, "A Secret Key Cryptosystem by Iterating a Chaotic Map," *Transactions IEICE Japan*, v. E73, n. 7, Jul 1990, pp. 1041–1044.

414. T. Habutsu, Y. Nishio, I. Sasase, and S. Mori, "A Secret Key Cryptosystem by Iterating a Chaotic Map," *Advances in Cryptology—EUROCRYPT '91 Proceedings*, Berlin: Springer-Verlag, 1991, pp. 127–140.

415. T. Hansen and G. L. Mullen, "Primitive Polynomials over Finite Fields," *Mathematics of Computation*, v. 59, n. 200, Oct 1992, pp. 639–643.

416. L. Harn and S. Yang, "Group-Oriented Undeniable Signature Schemes Without the Assistance of a Mutually Trusted Party," *Advances in Cryptology—AUSCRYPT '92 Proceedings*, Berlin: Springer-Verlag, forthcoming.

417. J. Hastad, "On Using RSA with Low Exponent in a Public-Key Network," *Advances in Cryptology—CRYPTO '85 Proceedings*, Berlin: Springer-Verlag, 1986, pp. 403–408.

418. B. Hayes, "Anonymous OneTime Signatures and Flexible Untraceable Electronic Cash," *Advances in Cryptology—AUSCRYPT '90 Proceedings*, Berlin: Springer-Verlag, 1990, pp. 294–305.

418a. E.H. Hebern, "Electric Coding Machine," U.S. Patent #1,510,441, 30 Sep 1924.

419. M. E. Hellman, "An Extension of the Shannon Theory Approach to Cryptography," *IEEE Transactions on Information Theory*, v. IT-23, n. 3, May 1977, pp. 289–294.

420. M. E. Hellman, "The Mathematics of Public-Key Cryptography," *Scientific American*, v. 241, n. 8, Aug 1979, pp. 146–157.

421. M. E. Hellman, "DES Will Be Totally Insecure Within Ten Years," *IEEE Spectrum*, v. 16, n. 7, Jul 1979, pp. 32–39.

422. M. E. Hellman, *On DES-Based Synchronous Encryption*, Department of Electrical Engineering, Stanford University, 1980.

423. M. E. Hellman, "A Cryptanalytic Time-Memory Trade-Off," *IEEE Transactions on Information Theory*, v. 26, n. 4, Jul 1980, pp. 401–406.

424. M. E. Hellman, "Another Cryptanalytic Attack on 'A Cryptosystem for Multiple Communications'," *Information Processing Letters*, v. 12, 1981, pp. 182–183.

425. M. E. Hellman, Comments at 1993 RSA Data Security conference, 14–15 Jan 1993.

426. M. E. Hellman, W. Diffie, and R. C. Merkle, "Cryptographic Apparatus and Method," U.S. Patent 4,200,770, 29 Apr 1980.

427. M. E. Hellman, W. Diffie, and R. C. Merkle, "Cryptographic Apparatus and Method," Canada Patent 1,121,480, 6 Apr 1982.

428. M. E. Hellman and R. C. Merkle, "Public-Key Cryptographic Apparatus and Method," U.S. Patent 4,218,582, 19 Aug 1980.

429. M. E. Hellman, R. C. Merkle, R. Schroeppel, L. Washington, W. Diffie, S. Pohlig, and P. Schweitzer, "Results of an Initial Attempt to Cryptanalyze the NBS Data Encryption Standard," Technical Report SEL 76-042, Information Systems Lab., Department of Electrical Engineering, Stanford University, 1976.

430. M. E. Hellman and S. C. Pohlig, "Exponentiation Cryptographic Apparatus and Method," U.S. Patent 4,424,414, 3 Jan 1984.

431. M. E. Hellman and J. M. Reyneri, "Distribution of Drainage in the DES," *Advances in Cryptology: Proceedings of Crypto 82*, Plenum Press, 1983, pp. 129–131.

432. T. Herlestam, "Critical Remarks on Some Public-Key Cryptosystems," *BIT*, v. 18, 1978, pp. 493–496.

433. T. Herlestam and R. Johannesson, "On Computing Logarithms over $GF(2^p)$," *BIT*, v. 21, 1981, pp. 326–334.

434. E. Heyst and T. P. Pederson, "How to Make Fail-Stop Signatures," *Advances in Cryptology—EUROCRYPT '92 Proceedings*, Berlin: Springer-Verlag, 1993, pp. 366–377.

435. E. Heyst, T. P. Pederson, and B. Pfitzmann, "New Construction of Fail-Stop Signatures and Lower Bounds," *Advances in Cryptology—CRYPTO '92 Proceedings*, Berlin: Springer-Verlag, 1993, forthcoming.

436. L. S. Hill, "Cryptography in an Algebraic Alphabet," *American Mathematical Monthly,* v. 36, Jun–Jul 1929, pp. 306–312.

437. P. J. M. Hin, "Channel-Error-Correcting Privacy Cryptosystems," Ph.D. diss., Delft University of Technology, 1986. (in Dutch)

438. A. Hodges, *Alan Turing: The Enigma,* Simon and Schuster, 1983.

439. F. Hoornaert, M. Decroos, J. Vandewalle, and R. Govaerts, "Fast RSA-Hardware: Dream or Reality?" *Advances in Cryptology—EUROCRYPT '88 Proceedings,* Berlin: Springer-Verlag, 1988, pp. 257–264.

440. F. Hoornaert, J. Goubert, and Y. Desmedt, "Efficient Hardware Implementation of the DES," *Advances in Cryptology—CRYPTO '84 Proceedings,* Berlin: Springer-Verlag, 1985, pp. 147–173.

441. L. K. Hua, *Introduction to Number Theory,* Berlin: Springer-Verlag, 1982.

442. I. Ingemarsson, "A New Algorithm for the Solution of the Knapsack Problem," *Lecture Notes in Computer Science 149; Cryptography: Proceedings of the Workshop on Cryptography,* Berlin: Springer-Verlag, 1983, pp. 309–315.

443. I. Ingemarsson and G. J. Simmons, "A Protocol to Set Up Shared Secret Schemes Without the Assistance of a Mutually Trusted Party," *Advances in Cryptology—EUROCRYPT '90 Proceedings,* Berlin: Springer-Verlag, 1991, pp. 266–282.

444. ISO DIS 8730, "BankingRequirements for Message Authentication (Wholesale)," Association for Payment Clearing Services, London, Jul 1987.

445. ISO DIS 8732, "BankingKey Management (Wholesale)," Association for Payment Clearing Services, London, Dec 1987.

446. ISO/IEC 9796, "Information TechnologySecurity TechniquesDigital Signature Scheme Giving Message Recovery," International Organization for Standardization, Jul 1991.

447. ISO/IEC 9797, "Data Cryptographic TechniquesData Integrity Mechanism Using a Cryptographic Check Function Employing a Block Cipher Algorithm," International Organization for Standardization, 1989.

448. ISO DIS 10118 DRAFT, "Information Technology Security Techniques Hash Functions," International Organization for Standardization, April 1991.

449. K. R. Iversen, "The Application of Cryptographic Zero-Knowledge Techniques in Computerized Secret Ballot Election Schemes," Ph.D. diss., IDT-report 1991:3, Norwegian Institute of Technology, Feb 1991.

450. K. R. Iversen, "A Cryptographic Scheme for Computerized General Elections," *Advances in Cryptology—CRYPTO '91 Proceedings,* Berlin: Springer-Verlag, 1992, pp. 405–419.

451. N. S. James, R. Lidi, and H. Niederreiter, "Breaking the Cade Cipher," *Advances in Cryptology—CRYPTO '86 Proceedings,* Berlin: Springer-Verlag, pp. 60–63.

452. C. Jansen, "On the Key Storage Requirements for Secure Terminals," *Computers and Security,* v. 5, n. 2, Jun 1986, pp. 145–149.

453. C. Jansen and D. E. Boekee, "Modes of Blockcipher Algorithms and Their Protection Against Active Eavesdropping," *Advances in Cryptology—EUROCRYPT '87 Proceedings,* Berlin: Springer-Verlag, 1988, pp. 281–286.

454. S. M. Jennings, "Multiplexed Sequences: Some Properties of the Minimum Polynomial," *Lecture Notes in Computer Science 149; Cryptography: Proceedings of the Workshop on Cryptography,* Berlin: Springer-Verlag, 1983, pp. 189–206.

455. S. M. Jennings, "Autocorrelation Function of the Multiplexed Sequence," *IEEE Proceedings,* v. 131, n. 2, Apr 1984, pp. 169–172.

456. T. Jin, *Care and Feeding of Your Three-Headed Dog,* Document Number IAG-90-011, Hewlett-Packard, May 1990.

457. T. Jin, *Living with Your Three-Headed Dog,* Document Number IAG-90-012, Hewlett-Packard, May 1990.

458. A. Joux and J. Stern, "Cryptanalysis of Another Knapsack Cryptosystem," *ASIACRYPT '91 Abstracts,* 1991, pp. 280–284.

459. R. R. Jueneman, "Analysis of Certain Aspects of Output-Feedback Mode," *Advances in Cryptology: Proceedings of Crypto 82,* Plenum Press, 1983, pp. 99–127.

460. R. R. Jueneman, "A High-Speed Manipulation Detection Code," *Advances in Cryptology—CRYPTO '85 Proceedings,* Berlin: Springer-Verlag, 1987, pp. 327–346.

461. R. R. Jueneman, S. M. Matyas, and C. H. Meyer, "Message Authentication," *IEEE Communications Magazine,* v. 23, n. 9, Sep 1985, pp. 29–40.

462. D. Kahn, *The Codebreakers: The Story of Secret Writing,* New York: Macmillan, 1967.

463. D. Kahn, *Kahn on Codes,* New York: Macmillan, 1983.

464. D. Kahn, *Seizing the Enigma,* Boston: Houghton Mifflin, 1991.

465. B. S. Kaliski, "A Pseudo-Random Bit Generator Based on Elliptic Logarithms," Master's thesis, Massachusetts Institute of Technology, 1987.

466. B. S. Kaliski, Letter to NIST regarding DSS, 4 Nov 1991.

467. B. S. Kaliski, "The MD2 Message Digest Algorithm," RFC 1319, Apr 1992.

468. B. S. Kaliski, "Privacy Enhancement for Internet Electronic Mail: Part IV: Key Certificates and Related Services," RFC 1424, Feb 1993.

469. B. S. Kaliski, personal communication.

470. B. S. Kaliski, R. L. Rivest, and A. T. Sherman, "Is the Data Encryption Standard a Group?", *Advances in Cryptology—EUROCRYPT '85,* Berlin: Springer-Verlag, 1986, pp. 81–95.

471. B. S. Kaliski, R. L. Rivest, and A. T. Sherman, "Is the Data Encryption Standard a Pure Cipher? (Results of More Cycling Experiments in DES)," *Advances in Cryptology—CRYPTO '85 Proceedings,* Berlin: Springer-Verlag, 1986, pp. 212–226.

472. B. S. Kaliski, R. L. Rivest, and A. T. Sherman, "Is the Data Encryption Standard a Group? (Results of Cycling Experiments on DES)," *Journal of Cryptology,* v. 1, n. 1, 1988, pp. 3–36.

473. R. G. Kammer, Statement before the Subcommittee on Telecommunications and Finance, Committee on Energy and Commerce, 29 Apr 1993.

474. E. D. Karnin, J. W. Greene, and M. E. Hellman, "On Sharing Secret Systems," *IEEE Transactions on Information Theory,* v. IT-29, 1983, pp. 35–41.

475. F. W. Kasiski, *Die Geheimschriften und die Dechiffrir-kunst,* Miller & Son, 1963. (in German)

476. S. Kent, "Privacy Enhancement for Internet Electronic Mail: Part II: Certificate-Based Key Management," RFC 1422, Feb 1993.

477. S. Kent and J. Linn, "Privacy Enhancement for Internet Electronic Mail: Part II: Certificate-Based Key Management," RFC 1114, Aug 1989.

478. S. T. Kent, "Encryption-Based Protection Protocols for Interactive User-Computer Communications," MIT/LCS/TR-162, MIT Lab for Computer Science, May 1976.

479. J. Kilian, *Uses of Randomness in Algorithms and Protocols,* Cambridge: MIT Press, 1990.

480. J. Kilian, "Achieving Zero-Knowledge Robustly," *Advances in Cryptology—CRYPTO '90 Proceedings,* Berlin: Springer-Verlag, 1991, pp. 313–325.

481. P. Kinnucan, "Data Encryption Gurus: Tuchman and Meyer," *Cryptologia,* v. 2, n. 4, Oct 1978.

482. D. V. Klein, "'Foiling the Cracker': A Survey of, and Implications to, Password Security," *Proceedings of the USENIX UNIX Security Workshop,* Aug 1990, pp. 5–14.

483. C. S. Kline and G. J. Popek, "Public-Key vs. Conventional Key Cryptosystems," *Proceedings of AFIPS National Computer Conference,* pp. 831–837.

484. H.-J. Knobloch, "A Smart Card Implementation of the Fiat-Shamir Identification Scheme," *Advances in Cryptology—EUROCRYPT '88 Proceedings,* Berlin: Springer-Verlag, 1988, pp. 87–95.

485. T. Kroph, J. FRößL, W. Beller, and T. Giesler, "A Hardware Implementation of a Modified DES Algorithm," *Microprocessing and Microprogramming,* v. 30, 1990, pp. 59–66.

486. L. R. Knudsen, "Cryptanalysis of LOKI," *ASIACRYPT '91 Abstracts,* 1991, pp. 19–30.

487. L. R. Knudsen, "Cryptanalysis of LOKI91," *Advances in Cryptology—AUSCRYPT '92 Proceedings,* Berlin: Springer-Verlag, forthcoming.

488. D. Knuth, *The Art of Computer Programming: Volume 2, Seminumerical Algorithms,* 2nd edition, Addison-Wesley, 1981.

489. N. Koblitz, "Elliptic Curve Cryptosystems," *Mathematics of Computation,* v. 48, n. 177, 1987, pp. 203–209.

490. N. Koblitz, "A Family of Jacobians Suitable for Discrete Log Cryptosystems," *Advances in Cryptology—CRYPTO '88 Proceedings,* Berlin: Springer-Verlag, 1990, pp. 94–99.

491. N. Koblitz, "Constructing Elliptic Curve Cryptosystems in Characteristic 2," *Advances in Cryptology—CRYPTO '90 Proceedings,* Berlin: Springer-Verlag, 1991, pp. 156–167.

492. N. Koblitz, "Hyperelliptic Cryptosystems," *Journal of Cryptology,* v. 1, n. 3, 1989, pp. 129–150.

493. N. Koblitz, "CM-Curves with Good Cryptographic Properties," *Advances in Cryptology—CRYPTO '91 Proceedings,* Berlin: Springer-Verlag, 1992, pp. 279–287.

494. M. J. Kochanski, "Remarks on Lu and Lee's Proposals," *Cryptologia,* v. 4, n. 4, 1980, pp. 204–207.

495. M. J. Kochanski, "Developing an RSA Chip," *Advances in Cryptology—CRYPTO '85 Proceedings,* Berlin: Springer-Verlag, 1986, pp. 350–357.

496. J. T. Kohl, "The Use of Encryption in Kerberos for Network Authentication," *Advances in Cryptology—CRYPTO '89 Proceedings,* Berlin: Springer-Verlag, 1990, pp. 35–43.

497. J. T. Kohl, "The Evolution of the Kerberos Authentication Service," *EurOpen Conference Proceedings,* May 1991, pp. 295–313.

498. J. T. Kohl and B. C. Neuman, "The Kerberos Network Authentication Service," unpublished manuscript.

499. Kohnfelder, "Toward a Practical Public-Key Cryptosystem," Bachelor's thesis, MIT Department of Electrical Engineering, May 1978.

500. A. G. Konheim, *Cryptography: A Primer,* New York: John Wiley & Sons, 1981.

501. A. G. Konheim, M. H. Mack, R. K. McNeill, B. Tuckerman, and G. Waldbaum, "The IPS Cryptographic Programs," *IBM Systems Journal,* v. 19, n. 2, 1980, pp. 253–283.

502. V. I. Korzhik and A. I. Turkin, "Cryptanalysis of McEliece's Public-Key Cryptosystem," *Advances in Cryptology—EUROCRYPT '91 Proceedings,* Berlin: Springer-Verlag, 1991, pp. 68–70.

503. S. C. Kothari, "Generalized Linear Threshold Scheme," *Advances in Cryptology—Proceedings of CRYPTO '84,* Berlin: Springer-Verlag, 1985, pp. 231–241.

504. J. Kowalchuk, B. P. Schanning, and S. Powers, "Communication Privacy: Integration of Public and Secret Key Cryptography," *Proceedings of the National Telecommunication Conference,* Piscatoway, N.J.: IEEE Press, 1980, pp. 49.1.1–49.1.5.

505. K. Koyama, "Direct Demonstration of the Power to Break Public-Key Cryptosystems," *Advances in Cryptology—AUSCRYPT '90 Proceedings,* Berlin: Springer-Verlag, 1990, pp. 14–21.

506. K. Koyama, U. M. Maurer, T. Okamoto, and S. A. Vanstone, "New Public-Key Schemes Based on Elliptic Curves over the Ring Z_n," *Advances in Cryptology—CRYPTO '91 Proceedings,* Berlin: Springer-Verlag, 1992, pp. 252–266.

507. K. Koyama and Y. Tsuruoka, "Speeding Up Elliptic Cryptosystems Using a Singled Binary Window Method," *Advances in Cryptology—CRYPTO '92 Proceedings,* Berlin: Springer-Verlag, 1993, pp. 351–364.

508. E. Kranakis, *Primality and Cryptography,* Wiler-Tuebner Series in Computer Science, 1986.

508a. D. Kravitz, "Digital Signature Algorithm," U.S. Patent pending.

509. H. Krawczyk, "How to Predict Congruential Generators," *Advances in Cryptology—CRYPTO '89 Proceedings,* Berlin: Springer-Verlag, 1990, pp. 138–153.

510. H. Krawczyk, "How to Predict Congruential Generators," *Journal of Algorithms,* v. 13, n. 4, Dec 1992, pp. 527–545.

511. G. C. Kurtz, D. Shanks, and H. C. Williams, "Fast Primality Tests for Numbers Less than $50*10^9$," *Mathematics of Computation,* v. 46, n. 174, Apr 86, pp. 691–701.

512. M. Kwan, "An Eight-Bit Weakness in the LOKI Cryptosystem," technical report, Australian Defense Force Academy, Apr 1991.

513. M. Kwan and J. Pieprzyk, "A General Purpose Technique for Locating Key Scheduling Weakness in DES-like Cryptosystems," *ASIACRYPT '91,* Berlin: Springer-Verlag, 1991, pp. 136–139.

514. J. C. Lagarias, "Knapsack Public-Key Cryptosystems and Diophantine Approximations," *Advances in Cryptology: Proceedings of Crypto 83,* Plenum Press, 1984, pp. 3–23.

515. J. C. Lagarias, "Performance Analysis of Shamir's Attack on the Basic Merkle-Hellman Knapsack Cryptosystem," *Lecture Notes in Computer Science 172; Proceedings of the 11th International Colloquium on Automata, Languages, and Programming (ICALP),* Berlin: Springer-Verlag, 1984, pp. 312–323.

516. J. C. Lagarias and A. M. Odlyzko, "Solving Low-Density Subset Sum Problems," *Proceedings of the 24th IEEE Symposium on the Foundations of Computer Science,* 1983, pp. 1–10.

517. J. C. Lagarias and A. M. Odlyzko, "Solving Low-Density Subset Sum Problems," *J. Assoc. Comp. Mach.,* v. 32, 1985, pp. 229–246.

518. J. C. Lagarias and J. Reeds, "Unique Extrapolation of Polynomial Recurrences," *SIAM Journal on Computing,* v. 17, n. 2, Apr 1988, pp. 342–362.

519. X. Lai, *Detailed Description and a Software Implementation of the IPES Cipher,* preprint 8 Nov 1991.

520. X. Lai, "On the Design and Security of Block Ciphers," ETH Series in Information Processing, v. 1, Konstanz: Hartung-Gorre Verlag, 1992.

521. X. Lai, personal communication.

522. X. Lai and J. Massey, "A Proposal for a New Block Encryption Standard," *Advances in Cryptology—EUROCRYPT '90 Proceedings,* Berlin: Springer-Verlag, 1991, pp. 389–404.

523. X. Lai and J. Massey, "Hash Functions Based on Block Ciphers," *Advances in Cryptology—EUROCRYPT '92 Proceedings,* Berlin: Springer-Verlag, 1992, pp. 55–70.

524. X. Lai, J. Massey, and S. Murphy, "Markov Ciphers and Differential Cryptanalysis," *Advances in Cryptology—EUROCRYPT '91 Proceedings,* Berlin: Springer-Verlag, 1991, pp. 17–38.

525. X. Lai, R. A. Rueppel, and J. Woollven, "A Fast Cryptographic Checksum Algorithm Based on Stream Ciphers," *Advances in Cryptology—AUSCRYPT '92 Proceedings,* forthcoming.

526. B. A. LaMacchia and A. M. Odlyzko, "Computation of Discrete Logarithms in Prime Fields," *Designs, Codes, and Cryptography,* v. 1, 1991, pp. 46–62.

527. L. Lamport, "Password Identification with Insecure Communications," *Communications of the ACM,* v. 24, n. 11, Nov 1981, pp. 770–772.

528. S. Landau, "Zero-Knowledge and the Department of Defense," *Notices of the American Mathematical Society,* v. 35, n. 1, Jan 1988, pp. 5–12.

529. D. Lapidot and A. Shamir, "Publicly Verifiable Non-Interactive Zero-Knowledge Proofs," *Advances in Cryptology—CRYPTO '90 Proceedings,* Berlin: Springer-Verlag, 1991, pp. 353–365.

530. P. L'Écuyer, "Efficient and Portable Combined Random Number Generators," *Communications of the ACM,* v. 31, n. 6, Jun 1988, pp. 742–749, 774.

531. P. L'Écuyer, "Random Numbers for Simulation," *Communications of the ACM,* v. 33, n. 10, Oct 1990, pp. 85–97.

532. P. J. Lee and E. F. Brickell, "An Observation on the Security of McEliece's Public-Key Cryptosystem," *Advances in Cryptology—EUROCRYPT'88 Proceedings,* Berlin: Springer-Verlag, 1988, pp. 275–280.

533. D. J. Lehmann, "On Primality Tests," *SIAM Journal on Computing,* v. 11, n. 2, May 1982, pp. 374–275.

534. A. K. Lenstra, "Factoring Multivariate Polynomials over Finite Fields," *Journal of Computer System Science,* v. 30, n. 2, Apr 1985, pp. 235–248.

535. A. K. Lenstra and S. Haber, Letter to NIST regarding DSS, 26 Nov 1991.

536. A. K. Lenstra, H. W. Lenstra, Jr., and L. Lovácz, "Factoring Polynomials with Rational Coefficients, *Mathematische Annalen,* v. 261, n. 4, 1982, pp. 515–534.

537. A. K. Lenstra, H. W. Lenstra, Jr., M. S. Manasse, and J. M. Pollard, "The Number Field Sieve," *Proceedings of the 22nd ACM Symposium on the Theory of Computing,* 1990, pp. 564–572.

538. A. K. Lenstra, H. W. Lenstra, Jr., M. S. Manasse, and J. M. Pollard, "The Factorisation of the Ninth Fermat Number," *Mathematics of Computation,* v. 61, n. 203, Jul 1993, pp. 319–350.

539. A. K. Lenstra and M. S. Manasse, "Factoring by Electronic Mail," *Advances in Cryptology— EUROCRYPT '89 Proceedings,* Berlin: Springer-Verlag, 1990, pp. 355–371.

540. A. K. Lenstra and M. S. Manasse, "Factoring with Two Large Primes," *Advances in Cryptology— EUROCRYPT '90 Proceedings,* Berlin: Springer-Verlag, 1991, pp. 72–82.

541. H. W. Lenstra, Jr., "Elliptic Curves and Number-Theoretic Algorithms," Report 86-19, Mathematisch Instituut, Universiteit van Amsterdam, 1986.

542. L. A. Levin, "One-Way Functions and Pseudo-Random Generators," *Proceedings of the 17th ACM Symposium on the Theory of Computing,* 1985, pp. 363–365.

543. W. J. LeVeque, *Fundamentals of Number Theory,* Addison-Wesley, 1977.

544. Lexar Corporation, *An Evaluation of the DES,* Sep 1976.

545. D.-X. Li, "Cryptanalysis of Public-Key Distribution Systems Based on Dickson Polynomials," *Electronics Letters,* v. 27, n. 3, 1991, pp. 228–229.

546. F.-X. Li, "How to Break Okamoto's Cryptosystems by Continued Fraction Algorithm," *ASIACRYPT '91 Abstracts,* 1991, pp. 285–289.

547. R. Lidl, G. L. Mullen, and G. Turwald, *Pitman Monographs and Surveys in Pure and Applied Mathematics 65: Dickson Polynomials,* London: Longman Scientific and Technical, 1993.

548. R. Lidl and W. B. Müller, "Permutation Polynomials in RSA-Cryptosystems," *Advances in Cryptology: Proceedings of Crypto 83,* Plenum Press, 1984, pp. 293–301.

549. R. Lidl and H. Niederreiter, *Introduction to Finite Fields and Their Applications,* London: Cambridge University Press, 1986.

550. H.-Y. Lin and L. Harn, "A Generalized Secret Sharing Scheme with Cheater Detection," *ASIACRYPT '91 Abstracts, 1991* pp. 83–87.

551. J. Linn, "Privacy Enhancement for Internet Electronic Mail: Part IMessage Encipherment and Authentication Procedures," RFC 989, Feb 1987.

552. J. Linn, "Privacy Enhancement for Internet Electronic Mail: Part IMessage Encipherment and Authentication Procedures," RFC 1040, Jan 1988.

553. J. Linn, "Privacy Enhancement for Internet Electronic Mail: Part IMessage Encipherment and Authentication Procedures," RFC 1113, Aug 1989.

554. J. Linn, "Privacy Enhancement for Internet Electronic Mail: Part IIIAlgorithms, Modes, and Identifiers," RFC 1115, Aug 1989.

555. J. Linn, "Privacy Enhancement for Internet Electronic Mail: Part IMessage Encipherment and Authentication Procedures," RFC 1421, Feb 1993.

556. D. L. Long and A. Wigderson, "How Discrete Is the Discrete Log," *Proceedings of the 15th Annual ACM Syposium on the Theory of Computing,* Apr 1983.

557. D. L. Long, "The Security of Bits in the Discrete Logarithm," Ph.D. diss., Princeton University, Jan 1984.

558. S. C. Lu and L. N. Lee, "A Simple and Effective Public-Key Cryptosystem," *COMSAT Technical Review,* 1979, pp. 15–24.

559. M. Luby and C. Rackoff, "How to Construct Pseudo-Random Permutations from Pseudorandom Functions," *SIAM Journal on Computing,* Apr 1988, pp. 373–386.

560. F. Luccio and S. Mazzone, "A Cryptosystem for Multiple Communications," *Information Processing Letters,* v. 10, 1980, pp. 180–183.

561. D. MacMillan, "Single Chip Encrypts Data at 14Mb/s," *Electronics,* v. 54, n. 12, 16 June 1981, pp. 161–165.

562. W. E. Madryga, "A High Performance Encryption Algorithm," *Computer Security: A Global Challenge,* North Holland: Elsevier Science Publishers, 1984, pp. 557–570.

563. J. L. Massey, "An Introduction to Contemporary Cryptology," *Proceedings of the IEEE,* v. 76, n. 5, May 1988, pp. 533–549.

564. J. L. Massey, "Contemporary Cryptology: An Introduction," *Contemporary Cryptology: The Science of Information Integrity,* G. J. Simmons, ed., Piscatoway, N.J.: IEEE Press, 1992, pp. 1–39.

565. J. L. Massey and I. Ingemarsson, "The Rip van Winkle CipherA Simple and Provably Computationally Secure Cipher with a Finite Key," *IEEE International Symposium on Information Theory,* Brighton, UK, May 1985.

566. J. L. Massey and X. Lai, "Device for Converting a Digital Block and the Use Thereof," International Patent PCT/CH91/00117, 28 Nov 1991.

567. J. L. Massey and R. A. Rueppel, "Linear Ciphers and Random Sequence Generators with Multiple Clocks," *Advances in Cryptology—EUROCRYPT '84 Proceedings,* Berlin: Springer-Verlag, 1985, pp. 74–87.

567a. M. Matsui, "Linear Cryptanalysis Method dor DES Cipher," *Advances in Cryptology—EUROCRYPT '93 Proceedings,* Berlin: Springer-Verlag, 1994, forthcoming.

568. M. Matsui and A. Yamagishi, "A New Method for Known Plaintext Attack of FEAL Cipher," *Advances in Cryptology—EUROCRYPT '92 Proceedings,* Berlin: Springer-Verlag, 1993, pp. 81–91.

569. T. Matsumoto and H. Imai, "A Class of Asymmetric Cryptosystems Based on Polynomials over Finite Rings," *IEEE International Symposium on Information Theory,* 1983, pp. 131–132.

570. S. M. Matyas, "Digital SignaturesAn Overview," *Computer Networks,* v. 3, n. 2, Apr 1979, pp. 87–94.

571. S. M. Matyas and C. H. Meyer, "Generation, Distribution, and Installation of Cryptographic Keys," *IBM Systems Journal,* v. 17, n. 2, 1978, pp. 126–137.

572. S. M. Matyas, C. H. Meyer, and J. Oseas, "Generating Strong One-Way Functions with Cryptographic Algorithms," *IBM Technical Disclosure Bulletin,* v. 27, n. 10A, Mar 1985, pp. 5658–5659.

573. U. M. Maurer, "Provable Security in Cryptography," Ph.D. diss., ETH No. 9260, Swiss Federal Instiutute of Technology, Zürich, Switzerland, 1990.

574. U. M. Maurer, "A Provable-Secure Strongly-Randomized Cipher," *Advances in Cryptology—EUROCRYPT '90 Proceedings,* Berlin: Springer-Verlag, 1990, pp. 361–373.

575. U. M. Maurer, "A Universal Statistical Test for Random Bit Generators," *Advances in Cryptology—CRYPTO '90 Proceedings,* Berlin: Springer-Verlag, 1991, pp. 409–420.

576. U. M. Maurer, "A Universal Statistical Test for Random Bit Generators," *Journal of Cryptology,* v. 5, n. 2, 1992, pp. 89–106.

577. U. M. Maurer and J. L. Massey, "Perfect Local Randomness in Pseudo-Random Sequences," *Advances in Cryptology—CRYPTO '89 Proceedings,* Berlin: Springer-Verlag, 1990, pp. 110–112.

578. K. S. McCurley, "A Key Distribution System Equivalent to Factoring," *Journal of Cryptology,* v. 1, n. 2, 1988, pp. 95–106.

579. K. S. McCurley, "The Discrete Logarithm Problem," *Cryptography and Computational Number Theory (Proceedings of the Symposium on Applied Mathematics),* American Mathematical Society, 1990, pp. 49–74.

580. R. J. McEliece, "A Public-Key Cryptosystem Based on Algebraic Coding Theory," Deep Space Network Progress Report 42-44, Jet Propulsion Laboratory, California Institute of Technology, 1978, pp. 42–44.

581. R. J. McEliece, *Finite Fields for Computer Scientists and Engineers,* Boston: Kluwer Academic Publishers, 1987.

582. W. Meier and O. Staffelbach, "Analysis of Pseudo Random Sequences Generated by Cellular Automata," *Advances in Cryptology—EUROCRYPT'91 Proceedings,* Berlin: Springer-Verlag, 1991, pp. 186–199.

583. W. Meier and O. Staffelbach, "Correlation Properties of Combiners with Memory in Stream Ciphers," *Advances in Cryptology—EUROCRYPT'90 Proceedings,* Berlin: Springer-Verlag, 1991, pp. 204–213.

584. W. Meier and O. Staffelbach, "Correlation Properties of Combiners with Memory in Stream Ciphers," *Journal of Cryptology,* v. 5, n. 1, 1992, pp. 67–86.

585. A. Menezes and S. Vanstone, "The Implementation of Elliptic Curve Cryptosystems," *Advances in Cryptology—AUSCRYPT '90 Proceedings,* Berlin: Springer-Verlag, 1990, pp. 2–13.

586. R. C. Merkle, "Secure Communication over Insecure Channels," *Communications of the ACM,* v. 21, n. 4, 1978, pp. 294–299.

587. R. C. Merkle, "One-Way Hash Functions and DES," *Advances in Cryptology—CRYPTO '89 Proceedings,* Berlin: Springer-Verlag, 1990, pp. 428–446.

588. R. C. Merkle, "A Certified Digital Signature," *Advances in Cryptology—CRYPTO '89 Proceedings,* Berlin: Springer-Verlag, 1990, pp. 218–238.

589. R. C. Merkle, "A Fast Software One-Way Hash Function," *Journal of Cryptology,* v. 3, n. 1, 1990, pp. 43–58.

590. R. C. Merkle, "Fast Software Encryption Functions," *Advances in Cryptology—CRYPTO '90 Proceedings,* Berlin: Springer-Verlag, 1991, pp. 476–501.

591. R. C. Merkle, "Method and Apparatus for Data Encryption," U.S. Patent 5,003,597, 26 Mar 1991.

592. R. C. Merkle, personal communication.

593. R. C. Merkle and M. Hellman, "Hiding and Signatures in Trapdoor Knapsacks," *IEEE Transactions on Information Theory,* v. 24, n. 5, Sep 1978, pp. 525–530.

594. R.C. Merkle and M. Hellman, "On the Security of Multiple Encryption," *Communications of the ACM,* v. 24, n. 7, 1981, pp. 465–467.

595. M. Merritt, *Cryptographic Protocols,* Ph.D. diss., Georgia Institute of Technology, GIT-ICS-83/6, Feb 1983.

596. M. Merritt, "Towards a Theory of Cryptographic Systems: A Critique of Crypto-Complexity," *Distributed Computing and Cryptography,* J. Feigenbaum and M. Merritt, eds., American Mathematical Society, 1991, pp. 203–212.

597. C. H. Meyer and S. M. Matyas, *Cryptography: A New Dimension in Computer Data Security,* New York: John Wiley & Sons, 1982.

598. C. H. Meyer and W. L. Tuchman, "Pseudo-Random Codes Can Be Cracked," *Electronic Design,* v. 23, Nov 1972.

599. C. H. Meyer and W. L. Tuchman, "Design Considerations for Cryptography," *Proceedings of the NCC,* v. 42, Montvale, N.J.: AFIPS Press, Nov 1979, pp. 594–597.

600. S. Micali, "Fair Public-Key Cryptosystems," *Advances in Cryptology—CRYPTO '92 Proceedings,* Berlin: Springer-Verlag, 1993, forthcoming.

601. S. Micali and A. Shamir, "An Improvement on the Fiat-Shamir Identification and Signature Scheme," *Advances in Cryptology—CRYPTO '88 Proceedings,* Berlin: Springer-Verlag, 1990, pp. 244–247.

602. M. J. Mihajlevic and J. D. Golic , "Convergence of a Bayesian Iterative Error-Correction Procedure to a Noisy Shift Register Sequence," *Advances in Cryptology—EUROCRYPT '92 Proceedings,* Berlin: Springer-Verlag, 1993, pp. 124–137.

603. G. L. Miller, "Riemann's Hypothesis and Tests for Primality," *Journal of Computer Systems Science,* v. 13, n. 3, Dec 1976, pp. 300–317.

604. S. P. Miller, B. C. Neuman, J. I. Schiller, and J. H. Saltzer, "Section E.2.1: Kerberos Authentication and Authorization System," MIT Project Athena, Dec 1987.

605. V. S. Miller, "Use of Elliptic Curves in Cryptography," *Advances in Cryptology—CRYPTO '85 Proceedings,* Berlin: Springer-Verlag, 1986, pp. 417–426.

606. M. Minsky, *Computation: Finite and Infinite Machines,* Prentice-Hall, 1967.

607. S. Miyaguchi, "Fast Encryption Algorithm for the RSA Cryptographic System," *Proceedings of Compcon 82,* IEEE, 1982, pp. 672–678.

608. S. Miyaguchi, "The FEAL-8 Cryptosystem and Call for Attack," *Advances in Cryptology—CRYPTO '89 Proceedings,* Berlin: Springer-Verlag, 1990, pp. 624–627.

609. S. Miyaguchi, "Expansion of the FEAL Cipher," *NTT Review,* v. 2, n. 6, Nov 1990.

610. S. Miyaguchi, "The FEAL Cipher Family," *Advances in Cryptology—CRYPTO'90 Proceedings,* Berlin: Springer-Verlag, 1991, pp. 627–638.

611. S. Miyaguchi, K. Ohta, and M. Iwata, "128-bit Hash Function (N-Hash)," *Proceedings of SECURICOM '90,* 1990, pp. 127–137.

612. S. Miyaguchi, K. Ohta, and M. Iwata, "128-bit Hash Function (N-Hash)," *NTT Review*, v. 2, n. 6, Nov 1990, pp. 128–132.

613. S. Miyaguchi, K. Ohta, and M. Iwata, "Confirmation That Some Hash Functions Are Not Collision Free," *Advances in Cryptology—EUROCRYPT '90 Proceedings*, Berlin: Springer-Verlag, 1991, pp. 326–343.

614. S. Miyaguchi, A. Shiraishi, and A. Shimizu, "Fast Data Encipherment Algorithm FEAL-8," *Review of the Electrical Communication Laboratories*, v. 36, n. 4, 1988.

615. R. Molva, G. Tsudik, E. van Herreweghen, and S. Zatti, "*KryptoKnight* Authentication and Key Distribution System," *Proceedings of European Symposium on Research in Computer Security*, Toulouse, France, Nov 1992.

616. P. Montgomery, "Speeding the Pollard and Elliptic Curve Methods of Factorization," *Mathematics of Computation*, v. 48, n. 177, Jan 1987, pp. 243–264.

617. P. Montgomery and R. Silverman, "An FFT Extension to the $p1$ Factoring Algorithm," *Mathematics of Computation*, v. 54, n. 190, 1990, pp. 839–854.

618. J. H. Moore, "Protocol Failures in Cryptosystems," *Proceedings of the IEEE*, v. 76, n. 5, May 1988.

619. J. H. Moore, "Protocol Failures in Cryptosystems," in *Contemporary Cryptology: The Science of Information Integrity*, G. J. Simmons, ed., Piscatoway, N.J.: IEEE Press, 1992, pp. 541–558.

620. J. H. Moore and G. J. Simmons, "Cycle Structure of the DES with Weak and Semi-Weak Keys," *Advances in Cryptology—CRYPTO '86 Proceedings*, Berlin: Springer-Verlag, 1987, pp. 3–32.

621. R. Morris and K. Thompson, "Password Security: A Case History," *Communications of the ACM*, v. 22, n. 11, Nov 1979, pp. 594–597.

622. R. Morris, N. J. A. Soane, and A. D. Wyner, "Assessment of the NBS Proposed Data Encryption Standard," *Cryptologia*, v. 1, n. 3, Jul 1977, pp. 281–291.

623. M. N. Morrison and J. Brillhart, "A Method of Factoring and the Factorization of F_7," *Mathematics of Computation*, v. 29, n. 129, Jan 1975, pp. 183–205.

624. Motorola Government Electronics Division, *Advanced Techniques in Network Security*, Scottsdale, AZ, 1977.

625. W. B. Müller, "Polynomial Functions in Modern Cryptology," *Contributions to General Algebra 3: Proceedings of the Vienna Conference*, Vienna: Verlag Hölder-Pichler-Tempsky, 1985, pp. 7–32.

626. W. Müller and W. Nöbauer, "Some Remarks on Public-Key Cryptography," *Studia Scientiarum Mathematicarum Hungarica*, v. 16, 1981, pp. 71–76.

627. W. Müller and W. Nöbauer, "Cryptanalysis of the Dickson-Scheme," *Advances in Cryptology—EUROCRYPT '85 Proceedings*, Berlin: Springer-Verlag, 1986, pp. 50–61.

628. C. Muller-Scholer, "A Microprocessor-Based Cryptoprocessor," *IEEE Micro*, Oct 1983, pp. 5–15.

629. R. C. Mullin, E. Nemeth, and N. Weidenhofer, "Will Public Key Cryptosystems Live Up to Their Expectations?, HEP Implementation of the Discrete Log Codebreaker," *ICPP 85*, pp. 193–196.

630. S. Murphy, "The Cryptanalysis of FEAL-4 with 20 Chosen Plaintexts," *Journal of Cryptology*, v. 2, n. 3, 1990, pp. 145–154.

631. M. Naor, "Bit Commitment Using Pseudo-Randomness," *Advances in Cryptology—CRYPTO '89 Proceedings*, Berlin: Springer-Verlag, 1990, pp. 128–136.

632. M. Naor and M. Yung, "Universal One-Way Hash Functions and Their Cryptographic Application," *Proceedings of the 21st Annual ACM Symposium on the Theory of Computing*, 1989, pp. 203–210.

633. National Bureau of Standards, Report of the Workshop on Estimation of Significant Advances in Computer Technology," NBSIR76-1189, 21–22 Sep 1976, Dec 1977.

634. NBS FIPS PUB 46, "Data Encryption Standard," National Bureau of Standards, U.S. Department of Commerce, Jan 1977.

635. NBS FIPS PUB 46-1, "Data Encryption Standard," National Bureau of Standards, U.S. Department of Commerce, Jan 1988.

636. NBS FIPS PUB 74, "Guidelines for Implementing and Using the NBS Data Encryption Standard," National Bureau of Standards, U.S. Department of Commerce, Apr 1981.

637. NBS FIPS PUB 81, "DES Modes of Operation," National Bureau of Standards, U.S. Department of Commerce, Dec 1980.

638. NBS FIPS PUB 112, "Password Usage," National Bureau of Standards, U.S. Department of Commerce, May 1985.

639. NBS FIPS PUB 113, "Computer Data Authentication," National Bureau of Standards, U.S. Department of Commerce, May 1985.

640. National Computer Security Center, *Trusted Network Interpretation of the Trusted Computer System*

Evaluation Criteria, NCSC-TG-005 Version 1, Jul 1987.

641. National Computer Security Center, *Trusted Database Management System Interpretation of the Trusted Computer System Evaluation Criteria,* NCSC-TG-021 Version 1, Apr 1991.

642. National Computer Security Center, *A Guide to Understanding Data Remanence in Automated Information Systems,* NCSC-TG-025 Version 2, Sep 1991.

643. J. Nechvatal, "Public-Key Cryptography," NIST Special Publication 800-2, National Institute of Standards and Technology, U.S. Department of Commerce, Apr 1991.

644. J. Nechvatal, "Public-Key Cryptography," in *Contemporary Cryptology: The Science of Information Integrity,* G. J. Simmons, ed., Piscataway, N.J.: IEEE Press, 1992, pp. 177–288.

645. R. M. Needham and M. D. Schroeder, "Using Encryption for Authentication in Large Networks of Computers," *Communications of the ACM,* v. 21, n. 12, Dec 1978, pp. 993–999.

646. R. M. Needham and M. D. Schroeder, "Authentication Revisited," *Operating Systems Review,* v. 21, n. 1, 1987, p. 7.

647. H. Niederreiter, "A Public-Key Cryptosystem Based on Shift Register Sequences," *Advances in Cryptology—EUROCRYPT '85 Proceedings,* Berlin: Springer-Verlag, 1986, pp. 35–39.

648. H. Niederreiter, "Knapsack-Type Cryptosystems and Algebraic Coding Theory," *Problems of Control and Information Theory,* v. 15, n. 2, 1986, pp. 159–166.

649. V. Niemi, "A New Trapdoor in Knapsacks," *Advances in Cryptology—EUROCRYPT '90 Proceedings,* Berlin: Springer-Verlag, 1991, pp. 405–411.

650. NIST FIPS PUB XX, "Digital Signature Standard," National Institute of Standards and Technology, U.S. Department of Commerce, DRAFT, 19 Aug 1991.

651. NIST FIPS PUB XX, "Digital Signature Standard," National Institute of Standards and Technology, U.S. Department of Commerce, DRAFT, 1 Feb 1993.

652. NIST FIPS PUB YY, "Secure Hash Standard," National Institute of Standards and Technology, U.S. Department of Commerce, DRAFT, 22 Jan 1992.

653. NIST FIPS PUB 180, "Secure Hash Standard," National Institute of Standards and Technology, U.S. Department of Commerce, DRAFT, Apr 1993.

654. NIST, "Clipper Chip Technology," 30 Apr 1993.

655. NIST, "Capstone Chip Technology," 30 Apr 1993.

656. I. Niven and H. A. Zuckerman, *An Introduction to the Theory of Numbers,* New York: John Wiley & Sons, 1972.

657. R. Nöbauer, "Cryptanalysis of the Rédei-Scheme," *Contributions to General Algebra 3: Proceedings of the Vienna Conference,* Vienna: Verlag Hölder-Pichler-Tempsky, 1985, pp. 255–264.

658. R. Nöbauer, "Cryptanalysis of a Public-Key Cryptosystem Based on Dickson Polynomials," *Mathematica Slovaca,* v. 38, 1989.

659. H. Nurmi, A. Salomaa, and L. Santean, "Secret Ballot Elections in Computer Networks," *Computers & Security,* v. 10, 1991, pp. 553–560.

660. A. Odlyzko, "Discrete Logarithms in Finite Fields and Their Cryptographic Significance,"*Advances in Cryptology: Proceedings of EUROCRYPT '84 Proceedings,* Berlin: Springer-Verlag, 1985, pp. 224–314.

661. Office of Technology Assessment, U.S. Congress, "Defending Secrets, Sharing Data: New Locks and Keys for Electronic Communication," OTA-CIT-310, U.S. Government Printing Office, Oct 1987.

662. B. O'Higgins, W. Diffie, L. Strawczynski, and R. de Hoog, "Encryption and ISDNa Natural Fit," *Proceedings of the 1987 International Switching Symposium,* 1987, pp. 863–869.

663. Y. Ohnishi, "A Study on Data Security," Master's thesis, Tohuku University, Japan, 1988. (in Japanese)

664. K. Ohta and T. Okamoto, "Practical Extension of Fiat-Shamir Scheme," *Electronics Letters,* v. 24, n. 15, 1988, pp. 955–956.

665. K. Ohta and T. Okamoto, "A Modification of the Fiat-Shamir Scheme," *Advances in Cryptology—CRYPTO '88 Proceedings,* Berlin: Springer-Verlag, 1990, pp. 232–243.

666. K. Ohta and T. Okamoto, "A Digital Multisignature Scheme Based on the Fiat-Shamir Scheme," *ASIACRYPT '91 Abstracts,* 1991, pp. 75–79.

667. T. Okamoto, "Fast Public-Key Cryptosystems Using Congruent Polynomial Equations," *Electronics Letters,* v. 22, n. 11, 1986, pp. 581–582.

668. T. Okamoto, "Modification of a Public-Key Cryptosystem," *Electronics Letters,* v. 23, n. 16, 1987, pp. 814–815.

669. T. Okamoto, "A Fast Signature Scheme Based on Congruential Polynomial Operations," *IEEE Transactions on Information Theory,* v. 36, n. 1, 1990, pp. 47–53.

670. T. Okamoto, "Provably Secure and Practical Identification Schemes and Corresponding Signature

Schemes," *Advances in Cryptology—CRYPTO '92 Proceedings,* Berlin: Springer-Verlag, 1993, pp. 31–53.

671. T. Okamoto, A. Fujioka, and E. Fujisaki, "An Efficient Digital Signature Scheme Based on Elliptic Curve over the Ring Z_n," *Advances in Cryptology—CRYPTO '92 Proceedings,* Berlin: Springer-Verlag, 1993, pp. 54–65.

672. T. Okamoto, S. Miyaguchi, A. Shiraishi, and T. Kawoaka, "Signed Document Transmission System," U.S. Patent 4,625,076, 25 Nov 1986.

673. T. Okamoto and K. Ohta, "Disposable Zero-Knowledge Authentication and Their Applications to Untraceable Electronic Cash," *Advances in Cryptology—CRYPTO '89 Proceedings,* Berlin: Springer-Verlag, 1990, pp. 134–149.

674. T. Okamoto and K. Ohta, "Universal Electronic Cash," *Advances in Cryptology—CRYPTO '91 Proceedings,* Berlin: Springer-Verlag, 1992, pp. 324–337.

675. T. Okamoto and K. Ohta, "Survey of Digital Signature Schemes," *Proceedings of the Third Symposium on: State and Progress of Research in Cryptography,* Rome: Fondazone Ugo Bordoni, 1993, pp. 17–29.

676. T. Okamoto and K. Sakurai, "Efficient Algorithms for the Construction of Hyperelliptic Cryptosystems," *Advances in Cryptology—CRYPTO '91 Proceedings,* Berlin: Springer-Verlag, 1992, pp. 267–278.

677. T. Okamoto and A. Shiraishi, "A Fast Signature Scheme Based on Quadratic Inequalities," *Proceedings of the 1985 Symposium on Security and Privacy,* IEEE, Apr 1985, pp. 123–132.

678. H. Ong and C. P. Schnorr, "Signatures Through Approximate Representations by Quadratic Forms," *Advances in Cryptology: Proceedings of Crypto 83,* Plenum Press, 1984.

679. H. Ong and C. P. Schnorr, "Fast Signature Generation with a Fiat Shamir-like Scheme," *Advances in Cryptology—EUROCRYPT '90 Proceedings,* Berlin: Springer-Verlag, 1991, pp. 432–440.

680. H. Ong, C. P. Schnorr, and A. Shamir, "An Efficient Signature Scheme Based on Polynomial Equations," *Proceedings of the 16th Annual Symposium on the Theory of Computing,* 1984, pp. 208–216.

681. H. Ong, C. P. Schnorr, and A. Shamir, "Efficient Signature Schemes Based on Polynomial Equations," *Advances in Cryptology: Proceedings of CRYPTO '84,* Berlin: Springer-Verlag, 1985, pp. 37–46.

682. G. A. Orton, M. P. Roy, P. A. Scott, L. E. Peppard, and S. E. Tavares, "VLSI Implementation of Public-Key Encryption Algorithms," *Advances in Cryptology—CRYPTO '86 Proceedings,* Berlin: Springer-Verlag, 1987, pp. 277–301.

683. H. Orup, E. Svendsen, and E. Andreasen, "VICTOR—An Efficient RSA Hardware Implementation," *Advances in Cryptology—EUROCRYPT '90 Proceedings,* Berlin: Springer-Verlag, 1991, pp. 245–252.

684. D. Otway and O. Rees, "Efficient and Timely Mutual Authentication," *Operating Systems Review,* v. 21, n. 1, 1987, pp. 8–10.

685. G. Pagels-Fick, "Implementation Issues for Master Key Distribution and Protected Keyload Procedures," *Computers and Security: A Global Challenge, Proceedings of IFIP/SEC '83,* North Holland,Elsevier Science Publishers, 1984, pp. 381–390.

686. S. K. Park and K. W. Miller, "Random Number Generators: Good Ones Are Hard to Find," *Communications of the ACM,* v. 31, n. 10, Oct 1988, pp. 1192–1201.

687. W. Patterson, *Mathematical Cryptology for Computer Scientists and Mathematicians,* Totowa, N.J.: Rowman & Littlefield, 1987.

688. T. P. Pederson, "Distributed Provers with Applications to Undeniable Signatures," *Advances in Cryptology—EUROCRYPT '91 Proceedings,* Berlin: Springer-Verlag, 1991, pp. 221–242.

689. S. Peleg and A. Rosenfield, "Breaking Substitution Ciphers Using a Relaxation Algorithm," *Communications of the ACM,* v. 22, n. 11, Nov 1979, pp. 598–605.

690. R. Peralta, "Simultaneous Security of Bits in the Discrete Log," *Advances in Cryptology— EUROCRYPT '85 Proceedings,* Berlin: Springer-Verlag, 1986, pp. 62–72.

691. I. Peterson, "Monte Carlo Physics: A Cautionary Lesson," *Science News,* v. 142, n. 25, 19 Dec 1992, p. 422.

692. B. Pfitzmann, "Fail-Stop Signatures: Principles and Applications," *Proceedings of COMPUSEC '91, Eighth World Conference on Computer Security, Audit, and Control,* North Holland: Elsevier Science Publishers, 1991, pp. 125–134.

693. B. Pfitzmann and M. Waidner, "Formal Aspects of Fail-Stop Signatures," Fakultät für Informatik, University Karlsruhe, Deutschland, Report 22/90, 1990.

694. B. Pfitzmann and M. Waidner, "Fail-Stop Signatures and Their Application," *SECURICOM '91,* 1991, pp. 145–160.

695. B. Pfitzmann and M. Waidner, "How to Break and Repair a 'Provably Secure' Untraceable Payment System," *Advances in Cryptology—CRYPTO '91*

Proceedings, Berlin: Springer-Verlag, 1992, pp. 338–350.

696. C. P. Pfleeger, *Security in Computing,* Prentice-Hall, 1989.

697. J. Pieprzyk, "On Public-Key Cryptosystems Built Using Polynomial Rings," *Advances in Cryptology—EUROCRYPT '85,* Berlin: Springer-Verlag, 1986, pp. 73–80.

698. J. Pieprzyk, "Error Propagation Property and Applications in Cryptography," *IEEE Proceedings-E, Computers and Digital Techniques,* v. 136, n. 4, Jul 1989, pp. 262–270.

699. F. Piper, "Stream Ciphers," *Elektrotechnic und Maschinenbau,* v. 104, n. 12, 1987, pp. 564–568.

700. V. S. Pless, "Encryption Schemes for Computer Confidentiality," *IEEE Transactions on Computing,* v. C-26, n. 11, Nov 1977, pp. 1133–1136.

701. J. Boyar Plumstead, "Inferring a Sequence Generated by a Linear Congruence," *Proceedings of the 23rd IEEE Symposium on the Foundations of Computer Science,* 1982, pp. 153–159.

702. R. Poet, "The Design of Special Purpose Hardware to Factor Large Integers," *Computer Physics Communications,* v. 37, 1985, pp. 337–341.

703. S. C. Pohlig and M. E. Hellman, "An Improved Algorithm for Computing Logarithms in GF(p) and Its Cryptographic Significance," *IEEE Transactions on Information Theory,* v. 24, n. 1, Jan 1978, pp. 106–111.

704. J. M. Pollard, "A Monte Carlo Method for Factorization," *BIT,* v. 15, 1975, pp. 331–334.

705. J. M. Pollard and C. P. Schnorr, "An Efficient Solution of the Congruence $x^2 + ky^2 = m \pmod{n}$," *IEEE Transactions on Information Theory,* v. IT-33, n. 5, Sep 1987, pp. 702–709.

706. C. Pomerance, "Recent Developments in Primality Testing," *Mathematics Intelligence,* v. 3, 1981, pp. 97–105.

707. C. Pomerance, "The Quadratic Sieve Factoring Algorithm," *Advances in Cryptology—EUROCRYPT '84 Proceedings,* Berlin: Springer-Verlag, 1985, pp. 169–182.

708. C. Pomerance, "Fast, Rigorous Factorization and Discrete Logarithm Algorithms," *Discrete Algorithms and Complexity,* New York: Academic Press, 1987, pp. 119–143.

709. C. Pomerance, J. W. Smith, R. Tuler, "A Pipe-Line Architecture for Factoring Large Integers with the Quadratic Sieve Algorithm," *SIAM Journal on Computing,* v. 17, n. 2, Apr 1988, pp. 387–403.

710. F. Pratt, *Secret and Urgent,* Blue Ribbon Books, 1942.

711. B. Preneel, "Analysis and Design of Cryptographic Hash Functions," Ph.D. diss., Katholieke Universiteit Leuven, Jan 1993.

712. B. Preneel, A. Bosselaers, R. Govaerts, and J. Vanderwalle, "Collision-Free Hash Functions Based on Blockcipher Algorithms," *Proceedings of the 1989 Carnahan Conference on Security Technology,* 1989, pp. 203–210.

713. W. H. Press, B. P. Flannery, S. A. Teukolsky, and W. T. Vetterling, *Numerical Recipes in* C: *The Art of Scientific Computing,* Cambridge University Press, 1988.

714. W. Price, "Key Management for Data Encipherment," *Security: Proceedings of IFIP/SEC '83,* North Holland: Elsevier Science Publishers, 1983.

715. G. P. Purdy, "A High-Security Log-in Procedure," *Communications of the ACM,* v. 17, n. 8, Aug 1974, pp. 442–445.

716. J.-J. Quisquater, "Announcing the Smart Card with RSA Capability," *Proceedings of the Conference: IC Cards and Applications, Today and Tomorrow,* Amsterdam, the Netherlands, 1989.

717. J.-J. Quisquater and C. Couvreur, "Fast Decipherment Algorithm for RSA Public-Key Cryptosystem," *Electronic Letters,* v. 18, 1982, pp. 155–168.

718. J.-J. Quisquater and Y. G. Desmedt, "Chinese Lotto as an Exhaustive Code-Breaking Machine," *Computer,* v. 24, n. 11, Nov 1991, pp. 14–22.

719. J.-J. Quisquater and J.-P. Delescaille, "Other Cycling Tests for DES," *Advances in Cryptology—CRYPTO '87 Proceedings,* Berlin: Springer-Verlag, 1988, pp. 255–256.

720. J.-J. Quisquater and M. Girault, "2n-bit Hash Functions Using n-bit Symmetric Block Cipher Algorithms," *Advances in Cryptology—EUROCRYPT '89 Proceedings,* Berlin: Springer-Verlag, 1990, pp. 102–109.

721. J.-J. Quisquater and L. C. Guillou, "Des Procédés d'Authentification Basés sur une Publication de Problèmes Complexes et Personnalisés dont les Solutions Maintenues Secrètes Constituent Autant d'Accréditations," *Proceedings of SECURICOM '89: 7th Worldwide Congress on Computer and Communications Security and Protection,* Société d'Édition et d'Organisation d'Éxpositions Professionelles, 1989, pp. 149–158.

722. J.-J., Myriam, Muriel, and Michaël Quisquater: L., Marie Annick, Gaïd, Anna, Gwenolé, and Soazig Guillou; and T. Berson, "How to Explain Zero-Knowledge Protocols to Your Children,"

Advances in Cryptology—CRYPTO '89 Proceedings, Berlin: Springer-Verlag, 1990, pp. 628–631.

723. M. O. Rabin, "Digital Signatures," *Foundations of Secure Communication,* New York: Academic Press, 1978, pp. 155–168.

724. M. O. Rabin, "Digital Signatures and Public-Key Functions as Intractable as Factorization," MIT Laboratory of Computer Science, Technical Report, MIT/LCS/TR-212, Jan 1979.

725. M. O. Rabin, "Probabilistic Algorithm for Testing Primality," *Journal of Number Theory,* v. 12, n. 1, Feb 1980, pp. 128–138.

726. T. Rabin and M. Ben-Or, "Verifiable Secret Sharing and Multiparty Protocols with Honest Majority," Proceedings of the 21st ACM Symposium on the Theory of Computing, 1989, pp. 73–85.

727. RACE, *RIPE Integrity Primitives: Final Report of RACE Integrity Primitives Evaluation (R1040),* June 1992.

728. RAND Corporation, *A Million Random Digits with 100,000 Normal Deviates,* Glencoe, IL: Free Press Publishers, 1955.

729. T. R. N. Rao, "On Struit-Tilburg Cryptanalysis of Rao-Nam Scheme," *Advances in Cryptology—CRYPTO '87 Proceedings,* Berlin: Springer-Verlag, 1988, pp. 458–460.

730. T. R. N. Rao and K. H. Nam, "Private-Key Algebraic-Coded Cryptosystems," *Advances in Cryptology—CRYPTO '86 Proceedings,* Berlin: Springer-Verlag, 1987, pp. 35–48.

731. J. A. Reeds and J. L. Manferdelli, "DES Has No Per Round Linear Factors," *Advances in Cryptology—CRYPTO '84 Proceedings,* Berlin: Springer-Verlag, 1985, pp. 377–389.

732. J. A. Reeds and B. J. Weinberger, "File Security and the UNIX Crypt Command," *AT&T Technical Journal,* v. 63, n. 8, Oct 1984, pp. 1673–1683.

733. J. M. Reyneri and E. D. Karnin, "Coin Flipping by Telephone," *IEEE Transactions on Information Theory,* v. IT-30, n. 5, Sep 1984, pp. 775–776.

734. P. Ribenboim, *The Book of Prime Number Records,* Berlin: Springer-Verlag, 1988.

735. P. Ribenboim, *The Little Book of Big Primes,* Berlin: Springer-Verlag, 1991.

736. M. Richter, "Ein Rauschgenerator zur Gewinnung von quasi-idealen Zufallszahlen für die stochastische Simulation," Ph.D. diss., Aachen University of Technology, 1992. (in German)

737. R. F. Rieden, J. B. Snyder, R. J. Widman, and W. J. Barnard, "A Two-Chip Implementation of the RSA Public Encryption Algorithm," *Proceedings of GOMAC (Government Microcircuit Applications Conference),* Nov 1982, pp. 24–27.

738. H. Riesel, *Prime Numbers and Computer Methods for Factorization,* Boston: Birkhäuser, 1985.

739. R. Rivest, "A Description of a Single-Chip Implementation of the RSA Cipher," *LAMBDA Magazine,* v. 1, n. 3, Fall 1980, pp. 14–18.

740. R. Rivest, "Statistical Analysis of the Hagelin Cryptograph," *Cryptologia,* v. 5, n. 1, Jan 1981, pp. 27–32.

741. R. Rivest, "A Short Report on the RSA Chip," *Advances in Cryptology: Proceedings of Crypto 82,* Plenum Press, 1983, p. 327.

742. R. Rivest, "RSA Chips (Past/Present/Future)," *Advances in Cryptology—EUROCRYPT '84 Proceedings,* Berlin: Springer-Verlag, 1985, pp. 159–168.

743. R. Rivest, "The MD4 Message Digest Algorithm," RFC 1186, Oct 1990.

744. R. Rivest, "The MD4 Message Digest Algorithm," *Advances in Cryptology—CRYPTO '90 Proceedings,* Berlin: Springer-Verlag, 1991, pp. 303–311.

745. R. Rivest, "The MD4 Message Digest Algorithm," RFC 1320, Apr 1992.

746. R. Rivest, "The MD5 Message Digest Algorithm," RFC 1321, Apr 1992.

747. R. Rivest, M. E. Hellman, J. C. Anderson, and J. W. Lyons, "Responses to NIST's Proposal," *Communications of the ACM,* v. 35, n. 7, Jul 1992, pp. 41–54.

748. R. Rivest and A. Shamir, "How to Expose an Eavesdropper," *Communications of the ACM,* v. 27, n. 4, Apr 1984, pp. 393–395.

749. R. Rivest, A. Shamir, and L. Adleman, "A Method for Obtaining Digital Signatures and Public-Key Cryptosystems," *Communications of the ACM,* v. 21, n. 2, Feb 1978, pp. 120–126.

750. R. Rivest, A. Shamir, and L. Adleman, "On Digital Signatures and Public-Key Cryptosystems," MIT Laboratory for Computer Science, Technical Report, MIT/LCS/TR-212, Jan 1979.

751. R. Rivest, A. Shamir, and L. M. Adleman, "Cryptographic Communications System and Method," U.S. Patent 4,405,829, 20 Sep 1983.

752. J. Rompel, "One-Way Functions Are Necessary and Sufficient for Secure Signatures," *Proceedings of the 22nd Annual ACM Symposium on the Theory of Computing,* 1990, pp. 387–394.

753. T. Rosati, "A High Speed Data Encryption Processor for Public-Key Cryptography," *Proceedings of the*

IEEE Custom Integrated Circuits Conference, 1989, pp. 12.3.1–12.3.5.

754. F. Rubin, "Decrypting a Stream Cipher Based on J–K Flip-Flops," *IEEE Transactions on Computing,* v. C-28, n. 7, Jul 1979, pp. 483–487.

755. R. A. Rueppel and J. L. Massey, "The Knapsack as a Nonlinear Function," *IEEE International Symposium on Information Theory,* Brighton, UK, May 1985.

756. R. A. Rueppel, *Analysis and Design of Stream Ciphers,* Berlin: Springer-Verlag, 1986.

757. R. A. Rueppel, "Correlation Immunity and the Summation Combiner," *Advances in Cryptology—EUROCRYPT '85 Proceedings,* Berlin: Springer-Verlag, 1986, pp. 260–272.

758. R. A. Rueppel, "When Shift Registers Clock Themselves," *Advances in Cryptology—EUROCRYPT '87 Proceedings,* Berlin: Springer-Verlag, 1987, pp. 53–64.

759. R. A. Rueppel, "Security Models and Notions for Stream Ciphers," *Proceedings of the 2nd IMA Conference on Cryptography and Coding,* Cirencester, England, 1989.

760. R. A. Rueppel, "On the Security of Schnorr's Pseudo-Random Sequence Generator," *Advances in Cryptology—EUROCRYPT '89 Proceedings,* Berlin: Springer-Verlag, 1990, pp. 423–428.

761. R. A. Rueppel, "Stream Ciphers," in *Contemporary Cryptology: The Science of Information Integrity,* G. J. Simmons, ed., IEEE Press, 1992, pp. 65–134.

762. D. Russell and G. T. Gangemi, *Computer Security Basics,* O'Reilly and Associates, Inc., 1991.

763. A. Salomaa, *Public-Key Cryptography,* Berlin: Springer-Verlag, 1990.

764. A. Salomaa and L. Santean, "Secret Selling of Secrets with Many Buyers," *ETACS Bulletin,* v. 42, 1990, pp. 178–186.

765. M. Santha and U. V. Vizirani, "Generating Quasi-Random Sequences from Slightly Random Sources," *Proceedings of the 25th Annual Symposium on the Foundations of Computer Science,* 1984, pp. 434–440.

766. M. Santha and U. V. Vizirani, "Generating Quasi-Random Sequences from Slightly Random Sources," *Journal of Computer and System Sciences,* v. 33, 1986, pp. 75–87.

767. J. E. Savage, "Some Simple Self-Synchronizing Digital Data Scramblers," *Bell System Technical Journal,* v. 46, n. 2, Feb 1967, pp. 448–487.

768. B. P. Schanning, "Applying Public-Key Distribution to Local Area Networks," *Computers & Security,* v. 1, n. 3, Nov 1982, pp. 268–274.

769. B. P. Schanning, S. A. Powers, and J. Kowalchuk, "MEMO: Privacy and Authentication for the Automated Office," *Proceedings of the 5th Conference on Local Computer Networks,* Piscatoway, N.J.: IEEE Press, 1980, pp. 21–30.

770. Schaumuller-Bichl, "Zur Analyse des Data Encryption Standard und Synthese Verwandter Chiffriersysteme," Ph.D. diss., Linz University, May 1981. (in German)

771. Schaumuller-Bichl, "On the Design and Analysis of New Cipher Systems Related to the DES," Technical Report, Linz University, 1983.

772. A. Scherbius, "Ciphering Machine," U.S. Patent 1,657,411, 24 Jan 1928.

772a. R. Schlafly, "Complaint Against Exclusive Federal Patent License," Civil Action File No. C–93 20450, United States District Court for the Northern District of California.

773. B. Schneier, "One-Way Hash Functions," *Dr. Dobbs Journal,* v. 16, n. 9, Sep 1991, pp. 148–151.

774. B. Schneier, "Data Guardians," *MacWorld,* v. 10, n. 2, Feb 1993, pp. 145–151.

775. C. P. Schnorr, "On the Construction of Random Number Generators and Random Function Generators," *Advances in Cryptology—EUROCRYPT '88 Proceedings,* Berlin: Springer-Verlag, 1988, pp. 225–232.

776. C. P. Schnorr, "Efficient Signature Generation for Smart Cards," *Advances in Cryptology—CRYPTO '89 Proceedings,* Berlin: Springer-Verlag, 1990, pp. 239–252.

777. C. P. Schnorr, "Efficient Signature Generation for Smart Cards," *Journal of Cryptology,* v. 4, n. 3, 1991, pp. 161–174.

778. C. P. Schnorr, "Method for Identifying Subscribers and for Generating and Verifying Electronic Signatures in a Data Exchange System," U.S. Patent 4,995,082, 19 Feb 1991.

779. C. P. Schnorr, "An Efficient Cryptographic Hash Function," presented at the rump session of *CRYPTO '91.*

780. C. P. Schnorr, "FFT-Hash II, Efficient Cryptographic Hashing," *Advances in Cryptology—EUROCRYPT '92 Proceedings,* Berlin: Springer-Verlag, 1993, pp. 45–54.

781. C. P. Schnorr and W. Alexi, "RSA-bits Are 0.5 + Secure," *Advances in Cryptology—EUROCRYPT '84*

Proceedings, Berlin: Springer-Verlag, 1985, pp. 113–126.

782. R. Scott, "Wide Open Encryption Design Offers Flexible Implementations," *Cryptologia,* v. 9, n. 1, Jan 85, pp. 75–90.

783. J. Seberry, "A Subliminal Channel in Codes for Authentication Without Secrecy," *Ars Combinatorica,* v. 19A, 1985, pp. 337–342.

784. J. Seberry and J. Pieprzyk, *Cryptography: An Introduction to Computer Security,* Prentice-Hall, 1989.

785. H. Sedlack, "The RSA Cryptography Processor: The First High Speed One-Chip Solution," *Advances in Cryptology—EUROCRYPT '87 Proceedings,* Berlin: Springer-Verlag, 1988, pp. 95–105.

786. H. Sedlack and U. Golze, "An RSA Cryptography Processor," *Microprocessing and Microprogramming,* v. 18, 1986, pp. 583–590.

787. A. Shamir, "A Fast Signature Scheme," MIT Library for Computer Science, Technical Memorandum, MIT/LCS/TM-107, Jul 1978.

788. A. Shamir, "How to Share a Secret," *Communications of the ACM,* v. 24, n. 11, Nov 1979, pp. 612–613.

789. A. Shamir, "On the Cryptocomplexity of Knapsack Systems," *Proceedings of the 11th ACM Symposium on the Theory of Computing,* 1979, pp. 118–129.

790. A. Shamir, "The Cryptographic Security of Compact Knapsacks," MIT/LCS/TM-164, Massachusetts Institute of Technology, 1980.

791. A. Shamir, "On the Generation of Cryptographically Strong Pseudo-Random Sequences," *Lecture Notes in Computer Science 62: 8th International Colloquium on Automata, Languages, and Programming,* Berlin: Springer-Verlag, 1981.

792. A. Shamir, "A Polynomial Time Algorithm for Breaking the Basic Merkle-Hellman Cryptosystem," *Advances in Cryptology: Proceedings of Crypto 82,* Plenum Press, 1983, pp. 339–340.

793. A. Shamir, "A Polynomial Time Algorithm for Breaking the Basic Merkle-Hellman Cryptosystem," *Proceedings of the 23rd IEEE Symposium on the Foundations of Computer Science,* 1982, pp. 145–152.

794. A. Shamir, "On the Generation of Cryptographically Strong Pseudo-Random Sequences," *ACM Transactions on Computer Systems,* v. 1, 1983, pp. 38–44.

795. A. Shamir, "A Polynomial Time Algorithm for Breaking the Basic Merkle-Hellman Cryptosystem," *IEEE Transactions on Information Theory,* v. IT-30, n. 5, Sep 1984, pp. 699–704.

796. A. Shamir, "On the Security of DES," *Advances in Cryptology—CRYPTO '85 Proceedings,* Berlin: Springer-Verlag, 1986, pp. 280–281.

797. A. Shamir, lecture at *SECURICOM '89.*

798. A. Shamir, personal communication.

799. A. Shamir and A. Fiat, "Method, Apparatus and Article for Identification and Signature," U.S. Patent 4,748,668, 31 May 1988.

800. A. Shamir and R. Zippel, "On the Security of the Merkle-Hellman Cryptographic Scheme," *IEEE Transactions on Information Theory,* v. 26, n. 3, May 1980, pp. 339–340.

801. M. Shand, P. Bertin, and J. Vuillemin, "Hardware Speedups in Long Integer Multiplication," *Proceedings of the 2nd Annual ACM Symposium on Parallel Algorithms and Architectures,* 1990, pp. 138–145.

802. D. Shanks, *Solved and Unsolved Problems in Number Theory,* Washington, D.C.: Spartan, 1962.

803. C. E. Shannon, "A Mathematical Theory of Communication," *Bell System Technical Journal,* v. 27, n. 4, 1948, pp. 379–423, 623–656.

804. C. E. Shannon, "Communication Theory of Secret Systems," *Bell System Technical Journal,* v. 28, n. 4, 1949, pp. 656–715.

805. C. E. Shannon, *Collected Papers: Claude Elmwood Shannon,* N. J. A. Sloane and A. D. Wyner, eds., New York: IEEE Press, 1993.

806. C. E. Shannon, "Predication and Entropy in Printed English," *Bell System Technical Journal,* v. 30, n. 1, 1951, pp. 50–64.

807. A. Shimizu and S. Miyaguchi, "Fast Data Encipherment Algorithm FEAL," *Transactions of IECE of Japan,* v. J70-D, n. 7, Jul 87, pp. 1413–1423. (in Japanese)

808. A. Shimizu and S. Miyaguchi "Fast Data Encipherment Algorithm FEAL," *Advances in Cryptology—EUROCRYPT '87 Proceedings,* Berlin: Springer-Verlag, 1988, pp. 267–278.

809. A. Shimizu and S. Miyaguchi, "FEAL—Fast Data Encipherment Algorithm," *Systems and Computers in Japan,* v. 19, n. 7, 1988, pp. 20–34, 104–106.

810. A. Shimizu and S. Miyaguchi, "Data Randomization Equipment," U.S. Patent 4,850,019, 18 Jul 1989.

811. H. Shizuya, T. Itoh, and K. Sakurai, "On the Complexity of Hyperelliptic Discrete Logarithm Problem," *Advances in Cryptology—EUROCRYPT '91 Proceedings,* Berlin: Springer-Verlag, 1991, pp. 337–351.

812. Z. Shmuley, "Composite Diffie-Hellman Public-Key Generating Systems Are Hard to Break," Computer

Science Department, Technion, Haifa, Israel, Technical Report 356, Feb 1985.

813. L. Shroyer, Letter to NIST regarding DSS, 17 Feb 1992.

814. E. H. Sibley, "Random Number Generators:Good Ones Are Hard to Find," *Communications of the ACM,* v. 31, n. 10, Oct 1988, pp. 1192–1201.

815. T. Siegenthaler, "Decrypting a Class of Stream Ciphers Using Ciphertext Only," *IEEE Transactions on Computing,* v. C-34, Jan 1985, pp. 81–85.

816. R. D. Silverman, "The Multiple Polynomial Quadratic Sieve," *Mathematics of Computation,* v. 48, n. 177, Jan 1987, pp. 329–339.

817. G. J. Simmons, "Authentication Without Secrecy: A Secure Communication Problem Uniquely Solvable by Asymmetric Encryption Techniques," *Proceedings of IEEE EASCON '79,* 1979, pp. 661–662.

818. G. J. Simmons, "Some Number Theoretic Questions Arising in Asymmetric Encryption Techniques, *Annual Meeting of the American Mathematical Society,* AMS Abstract 763.94.1, 1979, pp. 136–151.

819. G. J. Simmons, "High Speed Arithmetic Using Redundant Number Systems," *Proceedings of the National Telecommunications Conference,* 1980, pp. 49.3.1–49.3.2.

820. G. J. Simmons, "A 'Weak' Privacy Protocol Using the RSA Cryptosystem," *Cryptologia,* v. 7, n. 2, Apr 1983, pp. 180–182.

821. G. J. Simmons, "The Prisoner's Problem and the Subliminal Channel," *Advances in Cryptology: Proceedings of Crypto 83,* Plenum Press, 1984, pp. 51–67.

822. G. J. Simmons, "The Subliminal Channel and Digital Signatures," *Advances in Cryptology—Proceedings of EUROCRYPT '84,* Berlin: Springer-Verlag, 1985, pp. 364–378.

823. G. J. Simmons, "A Secure Subliminal Channel (?)," *Advances in Cryptology—CRYPTO '85 Proceedings,* Berlin: Springer-Verlag, 1986, pp. 33–41.

824. G. J. Simmons, "Cryptology," *Encyclopedia Britannica,* Sixteenth edition, 1986, pp. 913–924B.

825. G. J. Simmons, "How to (Really) Share a Secret," *Advances in Cryptology—CRYPTO '88 Proceedings,* Berlin: Springer-Verlag, 1990, pp. 390–448.

826. G. J. Simmons, "Prepositioned Secret Sharing Schemes and/or Shared Control Schemes," *Advances in Cryptology—EUROCRYPT '89 Proceedings,* Berlin: Springer-Verlag, 1990, pp. 436–467.

827. G. J. Simmons, "Geometric Shared Secret and/or Shared Control Schemes," *Advances in Cryptology—CRYPTO '90 Proceedings,* Berlin: Springer-Verlag, 1991, pp. 216–241.

828. G. J. Simmons, ed., *Contemporary Cryptology: The Science of Information Integrity,* Piscataway, N.J.: IEEE Press, 1992.

829. G. J. Simmons, "The Subliminal Channels of the U.S. Digital Signature Algorithm (DSA)," *Proceedings of the 3rd Symposium on: State and Progress of Research in Cryptography,* Fondazone Ugo Bordoni, Rome, 1993, pp. 35–54.

830. G. J. Simmons, "Subliminal Communication Is Easy Using the DSA," *Advances in Cryptology—EUROCRYPT '93 Proceedings,* Berlin: Springer-Verlag, forthcoming.

831. G. J. Simmons and M. J. Norris, *How to Cipher Fast Using Redundant Number Systems,* SAND-80-1886, Sandia National Laboratories, Aug 1980.

832. A. Sinkov, *Elementary Cryptanalysis,* Mathematical Association of America, 1966.

833. M. E. Smid, "A Key Notarization System for Computer Networks," NBS. Special Report 500-54, U.S. Department of Commerce, Oct 1979.

834. M. E. Smid, "The DSS and the SHS," *Federal Digital Signature Applications Symposium,* Rockville, MD., 17–18 Feb 1993.

835. M. E. Smid and D. K. Branstead, "The Data Encryption Standard: Past and Future," *Proceedings of the IEEE,* v. 76, n. 5, May 1988, pp. 550–559.

836. M. E. Smid and D. K. Branstead, "The Data Encryption Standard: Past and Future," in *Contemporary Cryptology: The Science of Information Integrity,* G. J. Simmons, ed., Piscataway, N.J.: IEEE Press, 1992, pp. 43–64.

837. J. L. Smith, "The Design of Lucifer, A Cryptographic Device for Data Communications," IBM Research Report RC3326, 1971.

838. J. L. Smith, "Recirculating Block Cipher Cryptographic System," U.S. Patent #3,796,830, 12 Mar 1974.

839. J. L. Smith, W. A. Notz, and P. R. Osseck, "An Experimental Application of Cryptography to a Remotely Accessed Data System," *Proceedings of the ACM Annual Conference,* Aug 1972, pp. 282–290.

840. K. Smith, "Watch Out, Hackers, Public Encryption Chips Are Coming," *Electronics Week,* 20 May 1985, pp. 30–31.

841. P. Smith, "LUC Public-Key Encryption, *Dr. Dobbs Journal,* v. 18, n. 1, Jan 1993, pp. 44–49.

842. R. Solvay and V. Strassen, "A Fast Monte Carlo Test for Primality," *SIAM Journal on Computing,* v. 6, Mar 1977, pp. 84–85; erratum in ibid, v. 7, 1978, p. 118.

843. A. Sorkin, "Lucifer, a Cryptographic Algorithm," *Cryptologia,* v. 8, n. 1, Jan 1984, pp. 22–41.

844. O. Staffelbach and W. Meier, "Analysis of Pseudo-Random Sequences Generated by Cellular Automata," *Advances in Cryptology—EUROCRYPT '91 Proceedings,* Berlin: Springer-Verlag, 1991, pp. 186–199.

845. J. G. Steiner, B.C. Neuman, and J. I. Schiller, "Kerberos: An Authentication Service for Open Network Systems," *Usenix Conference Proceedings,* Feb 1988, pp. 191–202.

846. J. Stern, "Secret Linear Congruential Generators Are Not Cryptographically Secure," *Proceedings of the 28th Symposium on Foundations of Computer Science,* 1987, pp. 421–426.

847. A. Stevens, "Hacks, Spooks, and Data Encryption," *Dr. Dobbs Journal,* v. 15, n. 9, Sep 1990, pp. 127–134, 147–149.

848. R. Struik and J. van Tilburg, "The Rao-Nam Scheme Is Insecure Against a Chosen-Plaintext Attack," *Advances in Cryptology—CRYPTO '87 Proceedings,* Berlin: Springer-Verlag, 1988, pp. 445–457.

849. R. Sugarman, "On Foiling Computer Crime," *IEEE Spectrum,* v. 16, n. 7, Jul 79, pp. 31–32.

850. J. Tardo and K. Alagappan, "SPX: Global Authentication Using Public-Key Certificates," *Proceedings of the 1991 Symposium on Security and Privacy,* IEEE, Apr 1991, pp. 232–244.

851. J. Tardo, K. Alagappan, and R. Pitkin, "Public-Key Based Authentication Using Internet Certificates," *USENIX Security II Workshop Proceedings,* 1990, pp. 121–123.

852. A. Tardy-Corfdir and H. Gilbert, "A Known-Plaintext Attack of FEAL-4 and FEAL-6," *Advances in Cryptology—CRYPTO '91 Proceedings,* Berlin: Springer-Verlag, 1992, pp. 172–182.

853. M. Tompa and H. Woll, "Random Self-Reducibility and Zero-Knowledge Interactive Proofs of Possession of Information," *Proceedings of the 28th IEEE Symposium on the Foundations of Computer Science,* 1987, pp. 472–482.

854. M. Tompa and H. Woll, "How to Share a Secret with Cheaters," *Journal of Cryptology,* v. 1, n. 2, 1988, pp. 133–138.

855. G. Tsudik, "Message Authentication with One-Way Hash Functions," *IEEE INFOCOM 92,* Florence, Italy, May 1992.

856. S. Tsujii, K. Kurosawa, T. Itoh, A. Fujioka, and T. Matsumoto, "A Public-Key Cryptosystem Based on the Difficulty of Solving a System of Non-Linear Equations," TSUJII Laboratory Technical Memorandum, n. 1, 1986.

857. W. Tuchman, "Hellman Presents No Shortcut Solutions to DES," *IEEE Spectrum,* v. 16, n. 7, July 1979, pp. 40–41.

858. B. Vallée, M. Girault, and P. Toffin, "How to Break Okamoto's Cryptosystem by Reducing Lattice Values," *Advances in Cryptology—EUROCRYPYT '88 Proceedings,* Berlin: Springer-Verlag, 1988, pp. 281–291.

859. P. C. van Oorschot and M. J. Weiner, "A Known-Plaintext Attack on Two-Key Triple Encryption," *Advances in Cryptology—EUROCRYPT '90 Proceedings,* Berlin: Springer-Verlag, 1991, pp. 318–325.

860. J. Van Tilburg, "On the McEliece Cryptosystem," *Advances in Cryptology—CRYPTO '88 Proceedings,* Berlin: Springer-Verlag, 1990, pp. 119–131.

861. A. Vandemeulebroecke, E. Vanzieleghem, T. Denayer, and P. G. Jespers, "A Single Chip 1024 Bits RSA Processor," *Advances in Cryptology—EUROCRYPT '89 Proceedings,* Berlin: Springer-Verlag, 1990, pp. 219–236.

862. S. Vaudenay, "FFT-Hash-II is Not Yet Collision-Free," *Advances in Cryptology—CRYPTO '92 Proceedings,* Berlin: Springer-Verlag, forthcoming.

863. U. V. Vazirani and V. V. Vazirani, "Trapdoor Pseudo-Random Number Generators with Applications to Protocol Design," *Proceedings of the 24th IEEE Symposium on the Foundations of Computer Science,* 1983, pp. 23–30.

864. U. V. Vazirani and V. V. Vazirani, "Efficient and Secure Pseudo-Random Number Generation," *Proceedings of the 25th IEEE Symposium on the Foundations of Computer Science,* 1984, pp. 458–463.

865. U. V. Vazirani and V. V. Vazirani, "Efficient and Secure Pseudo-Random Number Generation," *Advances in Cryptology—Proceedings of CRYPTO '84,* Berlin: Springer-Verlag, 1985, pp. 193–202.

866. I. Verbauwhede, F. Hoornaert, J. Vaenderwalle, H. De Man, and R. Govaerts, "Security Considerations in the Design and Implementation of a New DES Chip," *Advances in Cryptology—EUROCRYPT '87 Proceedings,* Berlin: Springer-Verlag, 1988, pp. 287–300.

867. S. von Solms and D. Naccache, "On Blind Signatures and Perfect Crimes," *Computers & Security,* v. 11, 1992, pp. 581–583.

868. V. L. Voydock and S. T. Kent, "Security Mechanisms in High-Level Networks," *ACM Computing Surveys,* v. 15, n. 2, Jun 1983, pp. 135–171.

869. N. R. Wagner, P. S. Putter, and M. R. Cain, "Large-Scale Randomization Techniques," *Advances in Cryptology—CRYPTO '86 Proceedings,* Berlin: Springer-Verlag, 1987, pp. 393–404.

870. E. J. Watson, "Primitive Polynomials (mod 2)," *Mathematics of Computation,* v. 16, 1962, p. 368.

871. P. Wayner, "Mimic Functions," *Cryptologia,* v. 16, n. 3, Jul 1992, pp. 193–214.

872. P. Wayner, "Mimic Functions and Tractability," forthcoming.

873. G. Welchman, *The Hut Six Story: Breaking the Enigma Codes,* New York: McGraw-Hill, 1982.

874. A. L. Wells Jr., "A Polynomial Form for Logarithms Modulo a Prime," *IEEE Transactions on Information Theory,* Nov 1984, pp. 845–846.

875. S. R. White, "Covert Distributed Processing with Computer Viruses," *Advances in Cryptology—CRYPTO '89 Proceedings,* Berlin: Springer-Verlag, 1990, pp. 616–619.

876. White House, Office of the Press Secretary, "Statement by the Press Secretary," 16 Apr 1993.

877. B. A. Wichmann and I. D. Hill, "An Efficient and Portable Pseudo-Random Number Generator," *Applied Statistics,* v. 31, 1982, pp. 188–190.

878. M. J. Weiner, "Cryptanalysis of Short RSA Secret Exponents," *IEEE Transactions on Information Theory,* v. 36, n. 3, May 1990, pp. 553–558.

879. M. V. Wilkes, *Time-Sharing Computer Systems,* New York: American Elsevier, 1975.

880. H. C. Williams, "A Modification of the RSA Public-Key Encryption Procedure," *IEEE Transactions on Information Theory,* v. IT-26, n. 6, Nov 1980, pp. 726–729.

881. H. C. Williams, "An Overview of Factoring," *Advances in Cryptology: Proceedings of Crypto 83,* Plenum Press, 1984, pp. 71–80.

882. H. C. Williams, "Some Public-Key Crypto-Functions as Intractable as Factorization,"*Advances in Cryptology—CRYPTO '84 Proceedings,* Berlin: Springer-Verlag, 1985, pp. 66–70.

883. II. C. Williams, "An M^3 Public-Key Encryption Scheme,"*Advances in Cryptology—CRYPTO '85 Proceedings,* Berlin: Springer-Verlag, 1986, pp. 358–368.

884. R. S. Winternitz, "Producing One-Way Hash Functions from DES,"*Advances in Cryptology:*

Proceedings of Crypto 83, Plenum Press, 1984, pp. 203–207.

885. S. Wolfram, "Random Sequence Generation by Cellular Automata,"*Advances in Applied Mathematics,* v. 7, 1986, pp. 123–169.

886. S. Wolfram, "Cryptography with Cellular Automota,"*Advances in Cryptology—CRYPTO '85 Proceedings,* Berlin: Springer-Verlag, 1986, pp. 429–432.

887. M. C. Wood, technical report, Jamestown, N.Y.: Cryptech, Inc., Jul 1990.

888. M. C. Wood, "Method of Cryptographically Transforming Electronic Digital Data from One Form to Another," U.S. Patent 5,003,596, 26 Mar 1991.

889. M. C. Wood, personal communication.

890. M. C. Wunderlich, "Recent Advances in the Design and Implementation of Large Integer Factorization Algorithms," *Proceedings of The 1983 Symposium on Security and Privacy,* Piscataway, N.J.: IEEE Press, 1983, pp. 67–71.

891. Y. Y. Xian, "New Public-Key Distribution System," *Electronics Letters,* v. 23, n. 11, 1987, pp. 560–561.

892. M. Yagisawa, "A New Method for Realizing Public-Key Cryptosystem," *Cryptologia,* v. 9, n. 4, Oct 1985, pp. 360–380.

893. C. H. Yang, "Modular Arithmetic Algorithms for Smart Cards," IEICE Japan, Technical Report, ISEC92-16, 1992.

894. C. II. Yang and H. Morita, "An Efficient Modular-Multiplication Algorithm for Smart-Card Software Implementation," IEICE Japan, Technical Report, ISEC91-58, 1991.

895. A. C.-C. Yao, "Theory and Applications of Trapdoor Functions," *Proceedings of the 23rd IEEE Symposium on the Foundations of Computer Science,* 1982, pp. 160–164.

896. K. Yiu and K. Peterson, "A Single-Chip VLSI Implementation of the Discrete Exponential Public-Key Distribution System," *IBM Systems Journal,* v. 15, n. 1, 1982, pp. 102–116.

897. K. Yiu and K. Peterson, "A Single-Chip VLSI Implementation of the Discrete Exponential Public-Key Distribution System," *Proceedings of Government Microcircuit Applications Conference,* 1982, pp. 18–23.

898. M. Yung, "Cryptoprotocols: Subscriptions to a Public Key, the Secret Blocking, and the Multi-Player Mental Poker Game," *Advances in Cryptology—CRYPTO '84 Proceedings,* Berlin: Springer-Verlag, 1985, 439–453.

899. G. Yuval, "How to Swindle Rabin," *Cryptologia,* v. 3, n. 3, Jul 1979, pp. 187–190.

900. K. C. Zeng, C.-H. Yang, and T. R. N. Rao, "On the Linear Consistency Test (LCT) in Cryptanalysis with Applications," *Advances in Cryptology—CRYPTO '89 Proceedings,* Berlin: Springer-Verlag, 1990, pp. 164–174.

901. K. C. Zeng, C.-H. Yang, D.-Y. Wei, and T. R. N. Rao, "Pseudorandom Bit Generators in Stream-Cipher Cryptography," *IEEE Computer,* v. 24, n. 2, Feb 1991, pp. 8–17.

902. Y. Zheng, T. Matsumoto, and H. Imai, "Impossibility and Optimality Results in Constructing Pseudorandom Permutations," *Advances in Cryptology—EUROCRYPT '89 Proceedings,* Berlin: Springer-Verlag, 1990, pp. 412–422.

903. Y. Zheng, T. Matsumoto, and H. Imai, "On the Construction of Block Ciphers Provably Secure and Not Relying on Any Unproved Hypotheses," *Advances in Cryptology—CRYPTO '89 Proceedings,* Berlin: Springer-Verlag, 1990, pp. 461–480.

904. Y. Zheng, J. Pieprzyk, and J. Seberry, "HAVAL—One-Way Hashing Algorithm with Variable Length of Output," *Advances in Cryptology—AUSCRYPT '92 Proceedings,* Berlin: Springer-Verlag, forthcoming.

905. N. Zierler, "Primitive Trinomials Whose Degree Is a Mersenne Exponent," *Information and Control,* v. 15, 1969, pp. 67–69.

906. N. Zierler and J. Brillhart, "On Primitive Trinomials (mod 2)," *Information and Control,* v. 13, 1968, pp. 541–544.

907. C. Zimmer, "Perfect Gibberish," *Discover,* v. 13, n. 12, Dec 1992, pp. 92–99.

908. P. Zimmermann, *PGP User's Guide,* 4 Dec 1992.

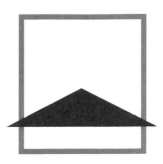

Index

THE APPLIED CRYPTOGRAPHY SOURCE CODE DISK SET

There is a source code disk set (two disks) associated with this book, available directly from the author. Included on these disks are:

Symmetric Algorithms:
Vigenère Cipher
Playfair Cipher
Hill Cipher
Crypt (1)
Enigma
DES (several versions)
Crypt (3)
Lucifer
NewDES
FEAL-N
FEAL-XN
REDOC II
REDOC III
LOKI89
LOKI91
IDEA
CA-1.1
MDC
SEOC
ZIP
NewDE
NSEA
Rcrypt

Public-Key Algorithms:
RSA
Diffie-Hellman
DSA
El Gamal
LUC

One-Way Hash Functions:
Snefru
N-Hash
MD4
MD5
MD2
SHA
HAVAL
RIPE-MD
MDC-4
RIPE-MAC

Complete Systems:
RIPEM
PGP

TIS-PEM
RSA-REF

Other:
LaGrange Threshold Scheme
Mimic Functions
Probabilistic Prime Number Generation
Random Number Generation Using Oscillators
Random Number Generation Using Keyboard Latency
Frequency Analysis
WordPerfect Password Cracker

Text:
Defense Trade Regulations
Privacy-Enhanced Mail RFCs
sci.crypt FAQ

And more!

This disk set also includes a file containing corrections for any mistakes found in the book, as well as any updated information on topics covered in the text: new algorithms, new protocols, new cryptanalytic results, etc.

The disk set is available from the author and will be updated twice a year. It is two high-density MS-DOS disks. The cost is $30 for the disk set and $90 for a two-year subscription. Please send check or money order to:

Bruce Schneier
Counterpane Systems
730 Fair Oaks Avenue
Oak Park, IL 60302

Please allow four weeks for delivery. Due to the export restrictions on many of the algorithms on this disk, it will only be mailed to addresses within the United States and Canada. My apologies to the readers of this book who reside in other countries.